Pro SharePoint 2013 Administration

Rob Garrett

T0239305

Apress·

Pro SharePoint 2013 Administration

Copyright © 2013 by Rob Garrett

This work is subject to copyright. All rights are reserved by the Publisher, whether the whole or part of the material is concerned, specifically the rights of translation, reprinting, reuse of illustrations, recitation, broadcasting, reproduction on microfilms or in any other physical way, and transmission or information storage and retrieval, electronic adaptation, computer software, or by similar or dissimilar methodology now known or hereafter developed. Exempted from this legal reservation are brief excerpts in connection with reviews or scholarly analysis or material supplied specifically for the purpose of being entered and executed on a computer system, for exclusive use by the purchaser of the work. Duplication of this publication or parts thereof is permitted only under the provisions of the Copyright Law of the Publisher's location, in its current version, and permission for use must always be obtained from Springer. Permissions for use may be obtained through RightsLink at the Copyright Clearance Center. Violations are liable to prosecution under the respective Copyright Law.

ISBN 978-1-4302-4941-2

ISBN 978-1-4302-4942-9 (eBook)

Trademarked names, logos, and images may appear in this book. Rather than use a trademark symbol with every occurrence of a trademarked name, logo, or image we use the names, logos, and images only in an editorial fashion and to the benefit of the trademark owner, with no intention of infringement of the trademark.

The use in this publication of trade names, trademarks, service marks, and similar terms, even if they are not identified as such, is not to be taken as an expression of opinion as to whether or not they are subject to proprietary rights.

While the advice and information in this book are believed to be true and accurate at the date of publication, neither the authors nor the editors nor the publisher can accept any legal responsibility for any errors or omissions that may be made. The publisher makes no warranty, express or implied, with respect to the material contained herein.

President and Publisher: Paul Manning
Lead Editor: Jonathan Hassell
Technical Reviewer: Pranav Sharma
Editorial Board: Steve Anglin, Ewan Buckingham, Gary Cornell, Louise Corrigan, Morgan Ertel, Jonathan Gennick, Jonathan Hassell, Robert Hutchinson, Michelle Lowman, James Markham, Matthew Moodie, Jeff Olson, Jeffrey Pepper, Douglas Pundick, Ben Renow-Clarke, Dominic Shakeshaft, Gwenan Spearing, Matt Wade, Tom Welsh
Coordinating Editor: Kevin Shea
Copy Editor: Robin Perlow
Compositor: SPi Global
Indexer: SPi Global
Artist: SPi Global
Cover Designer: Anna Ishchenko

Distributed to the book trade worldwide by Springer Science+Business Media New York, 233 Spring Street, 6th Floor, New York, NY 10013. Phone 1-800-SPRINGER, fax (201) 348-4505, e-mail orders ny@springer-sbm.com, or visit www.springeronline.com.

For information on translations, please e-mail rights@apress.com, or visit www.apress.com.

Apress and friends of ED books may be purchased in bulk for academic, corporate, or promotional use. E-Book versions and licenses are also available for most titles. For more information, reference our Special Bulk Sales–e-Book Licensing web page at www.apress.com/bulk-sales.

Any source code or other supplementary materials referenced by the author in this text are available to readers at www.apress.com. For detailed information about how to locate your book's source code, go to www.apress.com/source-code.

I dedicate this manuscript to my wife, Jessica. Without her support and encouragement for writing, this book would never have become a reality.

Contents at a Glance

Contents

Foreword

Thank you for taking the time to read this book. Whether you are interested in dipping in to find answers to your SharePoint questions, or are intending to read it from cover to cover, this book has plenty of information to quench your thirst for SharePoint 2013 administration knowledge.

Pro SharePoint 2013 Administration is intended for SharePoint administrators. However, this book will not be lost on readers who want an end-user SharePoint 2013 manual. It provides plenty of useful information about the new SharePoint 2013 platform and the changes since the previous version, and expert information for non-SharePoint administrators.

SharePoint, like any other web server–based product, requires a certain amount of care and feeding to keep it operational, so the underlying theme of this book is to help both end-users and administrators ensure that their SharePoint 2013 farm runs at its finest. The aim of this book is to provide you with consistent and reliable knowledge of the SharePoint 2013 platform, so that you have an arsenal of information to install SharePoint 2013, configure it, and maintain it.

Within these sixteen chapters, you will read about a variety of topics, including the installation and securing of a SharePoint 2013 farm; management of content, documents, and metadata; social networking features; business intelligence; Microsoft Office integration; and search.

Why should you buy this book? Reading *Pro SharePoint 2013 Administration* will help you by providing you with an all-around understanding of SharePoint 2013 administration and the features of the new SharePoint platform. This book is not a quick read nor a huge reference textbook for the occasional glance, but it is a nice comfortable read for anyone interested in SharePoint 2013.

Please Enjoy.

—Rob Garrett

About the Author

Robert Garrett ("Rob" for short) has worked in the field of SharePoint since 2006 and has grown his career as a SharePoint developer and now as an established SharePoint architect. Prior to 2006, Rob was an enthusiastic software developer, talented in many programming languages, including C++, C#, Visual Basic, and even Java.

Pro SharePoint 2013 Administration is the second SharePoint administration book Rob has written, following on his success with *Pro SharePoint 2010 Administration*.

Rob has designed, developed, and deployed various high-profile customer web sites, intranet, and extranet solutions using SharePoint Server 2007, 2010, and now 2013. These days Rob works exclusively as a SharePoint architect (when not writing or reviewing books) and continues to design and build custom SharePoint solutions with Planet Technologies for the United States Federal Government.

As Microsoft continues to invest in the SharePoint product, Rob plans to keep staying ahead of the SharePoint technology curve and to share new and interesting information with anyone who cares to read what he writes.

Rob is very active in the social community and likes to tweet fun SharePoint facts and solutions to problems, as well as follow other like-minded SharePoint experts on Twitter. You can follow Rob on Twitter using his handle: @rgarrettpro.

About the Technical Reviewer

Pranav Sharma is a co-founder at Almond Labs (@AlmondLabs). He possesses five years of deep SharePoint expertise, and he is also a Microsoft Certified SharePoint Solution Developer (MCTS) and SharePoint IT Professional (MCITP). Pranav has a diverse background that allows him to approach technology and business challenges and solutions from multiple perspectives. As a well-versed SharePoint consultant he has learned to tackle technology and business concerns from all angles, and he works to understand his clients' true business needs before proposing a technology solution. This business-first approach allows Pranav to become a trusted adviser and valued member of any team. Over the years, he has helped clients to understand and leverage the SharePoint platform to meet their long-term strategic goals. He specializes in the architecture and development of complex custom solutions, he is adept at project management, and he is a strong proponent of SCRUM (an agile software development methodology). Pranav has successfully worked for prestigious firms including Accenture Technology Consulting and Portal Solutions, a boutique SharePoint provider. Pranav is an alumnus of the University of Maryland with degrees in computer engineering and business management.

Acknowledgments

I would like to take this opportunity to thank the following people for their support and encouragement in my writing of this book:

Jessica Garrett—my wife, who tirelessly encouraged me to write this book, who waited patiently when I said "just one more paragraph," and who kept me nourished on long weeks and evenings. Thanks for being my anchor in this fast-paced world.

Pranav Sharma—a good friend and colleague, who is both the technical reviewer of this book and talented in the field of SharePoint development and administration.

Prashant Bhoyer—who dedicated his free time to helping review the technicalities in this book and was happy to do so in exchange for just the wealth of knowledge.

My Family (The Village) for all the support they provided, especially Dexter and Pam, who kept the Internet and power going during those stormy book-writing weekends and holidays in Richmond.

All my colleagues at Planet Technologies as well as others in the field of SharePoint development and administration whom I have had the pleasure of working with in some capacity.

Introduction

Hello, and welcome to *Pro SharePoint 2013 Administration*. In the next sixteen chapters of this book, you will discover administration of the latest version of SharePoint.

SharePoint administration can be intimidating to anyone looking at the platform for the first time, and so this book was written to cover all the major areas and demonstrate configuration in a systematic fashion. Chapter 1 kicks off with an overview of the new SharePoint 2013 platform, changes from the previous version, and what you can expect of the new features.

In this book, you will read about the installation of SharePoint Server 2013 on a new Windows Server. Chapter 1 highlights the prerequisites for the installation and minimal hardware and operating system software requirements. Even if you are a seasoned SharePoint administrator and have performed many installations of SharePoint before, you might gain additional insight from this chapter. Chapter 2 also serves as a great instruction set for anyone looking to install SharePoint 2013 for the first time.

With SharePoint installed, you will embark on a journey through the various areas of SharePoint 2013 covered in this book, which include security and policy; user profiles; social networking; documents, records, and metadata; business intelligence; Microsoft Office integration; health and disaster recovery; search; and user interface branding; among others.

Thank you—for your interest in this book and SharePoint 2013 administration.

Who This Book Is For

The title gives it away that this book is focused at SharePoint administrators (or want-to-be administrators), but this is not to say that *Pro SharePoint 2013 Administration* has no value for business experts or developer audiences. It should appeal to anyone with an interest in SharePoint 2013—installing it, configuring it, and using many of the best features the platform has to offer.

If you are new to SharePoint, congratulations on joining a large community of like-minded SharePoint enthusiasts. You will gain a wealth of information on grassroots installations, configuration, and administration of SharePoint 2013 from this book. For those audience members familiar with SharePoint 2013, this book serves as great reference material and best practice for what you may already know. For the casual reader in the bookstore, this book should, I hope, whet your palate regarding what SharePoint 2013 has to offer and provide you with an overview if you are curious about what SharePoint is or interested in finding out how the platform has changed since the 2010 version.

Contacting the Author

Should you have any questions or comments—or even spot a mistake that you think the author should know about—you can contact the Rob at feedback@robgarrett.com. Feel free to visit the author's blog at http://blog.robgarrett.com.

CHAPTER 1

■ ■ ■

SharePoint 2013 Overview and New Features

Hello, and welcome to SharePoint 2013. Microsoft has provided another great release of the SharePoint Server platform. Since the earliest version of SharePoint 2001, and Content Management Server prior to that, Microsoft has continued to expand and grow the SharePoint platform into the sophisticated information storage and retrieval system it is today.

Thank you for buying this book (or thinking about buying it, if you are browsing it in the store or online). In the next sixteen chapters, you will learn about the various new features and capabilities of SharePoint 2013 from an administration point of view, and how to use these capabilities to host your own SharePoint 2013 farm.

As with all good technical books, you can read this book cover to cover or dip into the chapters that interest you the most. I cannot make any assumptions about your previous experience with SharePoint, and so I wrote this book to appeal to a range of experience levels, starting with new administrators through to seasoned SharePoint experts. This book *is* an administration book, so if you are looking for development knowledge, then I recommend reading one of the development books in the SharePoint series from Apress. If you fall into the category that consists of new and upcoming SharePoint administrators, then I urge you to read all chapters in *Pro SharePoint Administration 2013*, starting with this chapter, where I offer an overview of SharePoint 2013. Those with extensive experience in SharePoint can also benefit from this chapter, because I cover the additions and enhancements in SharePoint 2013. Without further delay, it is time to start learning SharePoint 2013.

No More Doughnut

No, you are not seeing things, and yes, this is the topic of this section. In the previous version of SharePoint—SharePoint 2010—Microsoft liked to show off a circle diagram that described the various high-level modules in the platform. Magazine articles and books frequently included this diagram; my previous book (*Pro SharePoint 2010 Administration* [Apress, 2011]) was no exception. The circle diagram, or donut, as I liked to call it, described the six main areas of SharePoint 2010: Sites, Composites, Communities, Insights, Content, and Search. I could have included this diagram, except that Microsoft has now adopted a new way to describe the main modules of SharePoint 2013.

I always thought the classifications in the SharePoint 2010 donut were a little lofty, which is to say they resembled language you might expect to find in typical business literature or words used in meetings. With SharePoint 2013, Microsoft has adopted simple terms to describe better the aims of the high-level areas of the new SharePoint platform. The following summarizes each term that classifies the high-level capabilities of SharePoint 2013:

- *Share*—The term "sharing" has become ubiquitous with the explosion of social media. No longer do we grant access to our content, we share it instead. Throughout the various pages in SharePoint 2013, you will see share icons dotted around, which give owners of content the ability to share their content with other users. Sharing is also about empowering users to share their content across multiple devices and platforms while maintaining content in one place—SharePoint.

- *Organize*—Organization is about how you store your content in SharePoint. Whether you use lists or document libraries, it is about site hierarchy and structure to represent your content; it is about the metadata you assign your content to make it available to search; it is about synchronizing SharePoint content with your desktops so you can organize access to your content. Organizing is all about how you structure your data for optimum use in SharePoint 2013.

- *Discover*—Discovery focuses on the capability to search for content in SharePoint. Much of the functionality associated with content access in SharePoint 2013 utilizes search. Microsoft has included the search platform formerly known as FAST as the default Enterprise Search Platform in SharePoint 2013 (at no extra cost). Discovery also includes business intelligence capabilities and ability to discover information presented after applying business intelligence logic to related data.

- *Build*—Microsoft has made some significant changes in the way it builds applications for SharePoint 2013. The new App Model supports creation of portable and lightweight applications that host in SharePoint 2013 and other Office applications. The Microsoft App Marketplace promotes sharing of custom applications with other organizations and individuals, much like how the Marketplace for Windows Phone operates.

- *Manage*—SharePoint 2013 provides better capabilities to "manage" itself, whether as an on-premises SharePoint farm or as part of an Office 365 account (Microsoft's Office in the cloud). SharePoint 2013 integrates well with Exchange and Lync 2013, and the configuration of this integration is robust and not overcomplicated to achieve. Many of the sophisticated features of SharePoint, such as business intelligence, records management, search, etc., have greater flexibility in their management and configuration.

From the previous list, you should see that Microsoft has strived to describe the core capabilities of SharePoint 2013 with labels that make sense to everyone. I know I certainly appreciate the new labels when asked to provide a simple one- to two-sentence answer to the question "What is SharePoint?"

Foundation and Server

Similar to its predecessor, SharePoint 2013 comes in two different flavors: Foundation and Server. Foundation is the core platform for SharePoint Server and is free to install and use as long as you have proper Microsoft Windows licenses. SharePoint 2013 Server builds atop of Foundation and includes many more features. Unlike Foundation, Microsoft charges for SharePoint Server licenses (more on licensing shortly), and Server provides either Standard or Enterprise license types, each offering a different set of features.

Deciding on the version of SharePoint you want usually involves determining your purpose for SharePoint. Use of Foundation is certainly compelling at zero cost (having licensed Windows Server first), but it is very limited in functionality out of the box. If you simply need to provide team collaboration and a location to upload documents, with no frills, then Foundation might be enough. In my experience, organizations that are serious about implementing an information management solution in SharePoint tend to go with SharePoint Server because it provides many attractive features that easily justify the expense. However, I have seen some very nice working solutions running on Foundation.

When deciding to implement SharePoint Server, organizations must choose whether to purchase a Standard or Enterprise version. Both versions use the same installation. Which license you activate will determine the features available for use in your farm.

Table 1-1 lists the high-level features available in Foundation, Server Standard, and Server Enterprise. Server Enterprise provides the complete suite of features, whereas Foundation and Server Standard provide a subset. Do not worry if you have not heard of many of the features in Table 1-1; I cover the majority of them throughout this book.

Table 1-1. *Feature Comparison in SharePoint 2013*

Feature	Available in Foundation	Available in Server Standard	Available in Server Enterprise
Access Services (2010 and 2013)	No	No	Yes
Application Management	Yes	Yes	Yes
Business Connectivity Services	Yes	Yes	Yes
Business Intelligence	No	No	Yes
e-Discovery and Records Management	No	Yes	Yes
Excel Services	No	No	Yes
Health Analyzer	Yes	Yes	Yes
Managed Metadata Service	No	Yes	Yes
PerformancePoint	No	No	Yes
Search	No	Yes	Yes
Secure Store Service	No	Yes	Yes
Social Features	No	Yes	Yes
State Service	No	Yes	Yes
Usage and Health Data Collection	Yes	Yes	Yes
User Authentication and Authorization	Yes	Yes	Yes
User Profiles	No	Yes	Yes
Visio Graphics Service	No	No	Yes
Web Content Management	No	Yes	Yes
Windows PowerShell Cmdlets	Yes	Yes	Yes
Word Automation	No	Yes	Yes
Workflow	No	Yes	Yes

Of course, Table 1-1 is not exhaustive. SharePoint includes many features and to list them all would consume several pages. Table 1-1 covers the high-level features, some of which include different capabilities depending on the version and license. For example, not all capabilities of Business Connectivity Services are available in Foundation, such as use of the Secure Store Service.

Licensing

SharePoint licensing is confusing. Depending on which Microsoft representative or SharePoint vendor/provider you talk with, you may get a different answer on the cost of Standard and Enterprise licenses.

Like Windows, SharePoint requires a Client Access License (CAL) for every user or device accessing SharePoint. As I mentioned earlier, Foundation is free as long as you have Windows CALs for all your users and you are not exposing SharePoint to anonymous users on the Internet (more on this in a moment), so assume I am talking about SharePoint 2013 Server with regards to licensing, from here on. Depending on your desired functionality from SharePoint, you must buy either Standard CALs or Enterprise CALs, which have different prices. The cost per CAL differs depending on the license provider, how many CALs you buy in each purchase batch, and whether you qualify for Microsoft discounts (typically applicable only to government, not-for-profit, and charity organizations)—I did say licensing is complicated.

Prior to SharePoint 2013, you had to decide whether to purchase Enterprise CALs or Standard CALs for all users of your SharePoint farm. SharePoint Server 2013 introduces the ability to mix and match Standard and Enterprise CALs in the same farm. For example, you may have a small subset of users in your organization who require use of the Enterprise features, whereas the majority of users require only Standard features. Rather than buy all users Enterprise CALs, you can now save expense by buying Enterprise CALs for only those users who require them. By default, SharePoint Server 2013 operates in single license type mode. To enable per user license types, use the following PowerShell Cmdlets on the server running Central Administration:

1. Click the Start button.

2. Click All Programs and then click Microsoft SharePoint 2013 Products.

3. Click SharePoint 2013 Management Shell (this loads PowerShell).

4. Type in the Cmdlet: `Get-SPUserLicensing` at the prompt and press Enter.

5. If per user licensing is disabled the Cmdlet will return False.

6. To enable per user licensing, enter the following Cmdlet at the prompt and then press Enter: `Enable-SPUserLicensing`

7. You may now map different license types to users or groups.

8. Enter the following PowerShell Cmdlets to assign a license type to a set of users in an AD group (enter each Cmdlet on a new line, followed by Enter):

   ```
   $a = New-SPUserLicenseMapping -SecurityGroup "AD group" -License Type
   Add-SPUserLicenseMapping -Mapping $a
   ```

9. In the previous Cmdlets, you can provide the license type as Unlicensed, Standard, Enterprise, Project, and WACEdit.

■ **Note**   Discussion of the various license types available in per user licensing is outside the scope of this book, but Standard and Enterprise correlate to those license types listed in Table 1-1.

User and device CALs work for on-premise scenarios when you know exactly how many users to support, and all your users authenticate with your SharePoint 2013 farm, but what about scenarios involving anonymous users for public-facing solutions in SharePoint? The good news is that Microsoft has finally addressed this need in SharePoint 2013. In prior versions, you had to buy a different type of license called "SharePoint for Internet Sites," which came at a high premium because it assumed use of all Enterprise features. With SharePoint 2013, Microsoft requires you to buy only the SharePoint Server product. Of course, if you use your farm for both Internet-facing and internal-facing sites, you still need to provide CALs for users authenticating with SharePoint from within the office.

■ **Note**   To understand more on SharePoint Server 2013 licensing, consult a Microsoft representative or third-party vendor of SharePoint.

System Requirements

Like any other server platform, SharePoint 2013 has a number of hardware and software requirements. Hardware requirements are strongly recommended by Microsoft but open for deviation, depending on your deployment plan for SharePoint. Adherence to hardware requirements ensures optimal operation and good user experience and caters to most situations involving all features enabled in the platform. On the other hand, you must meet the minimal software requirements to install and operate SharePoint 2013 (both Foundation and Server).

Hardware Requirements

When Microsoft devises the hardware requirements for SharePoint, it assumes typical scenarios that account for average user load and availability of features. Of course, what may work for one organization may not work for another—the hardware requirements to support thousands of concurrent users, utilizing search and business intelligence, with redundant hardware is very different from those of a one- or two-server farm for a small back-office deployment (see Chapter 5 for server farm planning and redundancy). Fortunately, Microsoft published its hardware requirements for SharePoint 2013 to account for a variety of scenarios, as shown in Table 1-2.

Table 1-2. *SharePoint Web and Application Server Minimum Hardware Requirements*

Scenario	Deployment Type and Scale	RAM	Processor	Hard Drive Space
Single SharePoint Server with built-in database or separate SQL Server	Development deployment with minimum number of services installed.	8GB	64-bit, 4 cores	80GB for system drive
Single SharePoint Server with built-in database or separate SQL Server	Development deployment with minimum number of services installed and Visual Studio 2012.	10GB	64-bit, 4 cores	80GB for system drive
Single SharePoint Server with built-in database or separate SQL Server	Development deployment with all available services installed and Visual Studio 2012.	24GB	64-bit, 4 cores	80GB for system drive
SharePoint Server in a three-tier farm	Staging or production deployment with all services installed.	12GB	64-bit, 4 cores	80GB for system drive

I remember when Microsoft first released the beta version of SharePoint 2013 and published the hardware requirements for development farms. I was shocked to read that my development server would need 24GB of RAM, especially since I typically use close to this amount of RAM for complete virtual server host. However, with further clarification, you can see from Table 1-2 that 8GB of RAM could work for most development scenarios, but it assumes the absence of Visual Studio (an application that is heavy on RAM) and installation of a minimum number of services.

Notice the last line in Table 1-2, which caters to staging and production environments. These deployments host SQL Server separately and assume separate SharePoint application and web servers (three-tier). To cater to typical user load on a single web server, 12GB of RAM with a four-core CPU should provide enough horsepower. The beauty of SharePoint is that it scales, so if you overload one server with concurrent user requests, then you may add additional servers to the farm and load balance requests. Each new web or application server added to the farm requires the same minimum hardware specifications as listed in Table 1-2. Just as with SharePoint 2010, SharePoint 2013 requires 64-bit hardware and operating system to operate.

■ **Note** See the following information for SharePoint 2013 capacity planning:
`http://technet.microsoft.com/en-us/library/Cc261700.aspx`.

I covered the hardware requirements for SharePoint web and application servers in the previous paragraphs. SQL Server also requires minimum hardware requirements. The requirements shown in Table 1-3 assume that you dedicate SQL Server to one SharePoint 2013 farm instance. SQL Server supports multiple instances and can host databases for any number of other applications, which could exceed the capacity of your SQL Server hardware.

Table 1-3. *SQL Server Minimum Hardware Requirements for SharePoint 2013*

Component	Minimum Requirement
Processor	• 64-bit, 4 cores for small deployments (fewer than 1000 users) • 64-bit, 8 cores for large deployments (between 1000 and 10,000 users)
RAM	• 8GB for small deployments (fewer than 1000 users) • 16GB for large deployments (between 1000 and 10,000 users) Review Microsoft capacity planning guidelines for deployments consisting of more than 10,000 users.
Hard Disk	80GB for system drive Space for content and logs is dependent on your plan for SharePoint and what content your organization wishes to store in SharePoint. Allocate separate logical disks for content and logs for optimal performance.

Software Requirements

Unlike with hardware requirements, SharePoint 2013 is very strict on the minimum level of software it requires to install and operate. Since SharePoint 2010, servers and host operating systems must be 64-bit. SharePoint 2013 no longer supports SQL Server prior to 2008 R2. SharePoint requires at least Windows Server 2008, as shown in Table 1-4.

Table 1-4. *Minimum Software Requirements for SharePoint 2013*

Component	Minimum Requirements

Database server in a SharePoint 2013 farm	• One of the following:
	   • 64-bit edition of Microsoft SQL Server 2012
	   • 64-bit edition of Microsoft SQL Server 2008 R2 (SP1)
	• One of the following:
	   • 64-bit version of Windows Server 2008 R2 (Standard, Enterprise, or Datacenter)
	   • 64-bit edition of Windows 2012 (Standard or Datacenter)
	   • Microsoft .NET Framework 4.5
	   • All recent hotfixes

Single SharePoint 2013 Server with built-in database server	• One of the following:
	   • 64-bit version of Windows Server 2008 R2 (Standard, Enterprise, or Datacenter)
	   • 64-bit edition of Windows 2012 (Standard or Datacenter)
	• Microsoft .NET Framework 4.5
	• All recent hotfixes
	• SharePoint installs Microsoft SQL Server 2008 R2 Express

SharePoint 2013 web servers and application servers	• One of the following:
	   • 64-bit version of Windows Server 2008 R2 (Standard, Enterprise, or Datacenter)
	   • 64-bit edition of Windows 2012 (Standard or Datacenter)
	• Microsoft .NET Framework 4.5
	• All recent hotfixes

I cover SharePoint 2013 installation in Chapter 2. Installation consists of running a prerequisite installer, which installs any prerequisite software and configures server roles in Windows Server.

Development or Production?

Before jumping into the new and exciting changes that SharePoint 2013 brings, I wanted to mention environment type planning briefly. It is not my intent to dive deep into the topic of planning for development, staging, and production environments. Many good books exist on this topic that explore the differences among each environment type and considerations of each. However, before I turn you into an experienced SharePoint administrator (if you are not already) through your reading the pages in this book, I wanted to brief you on this topic before you start installing and configuring SharePoint.

Development and production SharePoint farms behave very differently. Typically, a development environment is looser with security constraints, has all or most features enabled, and is seldom optimized. Compare this to a production farm, which has limited administration access (SharePoint administrators only), has only those features enabled to provide a working solution, and undergoes rigorous performance testing and configuration tweaking.

In Chapter 2, I shall walk you through the process of installing SharePoint 2013 Server. I discuss use of the Farm Configuration Wizard (not to be confused with the Installation Configuration Wizard), which is a helpful automated process for provisioning services and service applications. Bear in mind that this wizard is strictly for development and non-production environments. The Farm Configuration Wizard makes assumptions about service databases, default service application configuration, allocation of application pools, and default configuration as a whole. The preferred approach to standing up a production environment is to use SharePoint PowerShell Cmdlets (see Chapter 3) to script a minimal footprint installation and configuration. This requires intricate working knowledge of SharePoint 2013 configuration and the use of many PowerShell Cmdlets. I touch on many of these Cmdlets throughout this book and guide you in configuration for best practice. However, after reading this book, do consider further research on best practices for advanced SharePoint 2013 deployment.

User Interface and User Experience Changes

The first thing you will notice when opening SharePoint 2013 is the new user interface and experience changes. Compare the screenshot from SharePoint 2010 (Figure 1-1) to that of SharePoint 2013 (Figure 1-2). The versions have similar page layouts and high-level functional areas, with links to various operations. SharePoint 2013 now adopts the "Windows 8" theme (formally known as "Metro"). I cover SharePoint 2013 branding in detail in Chapter 16, but as you read this book, you will begin to appreciate the new branding.

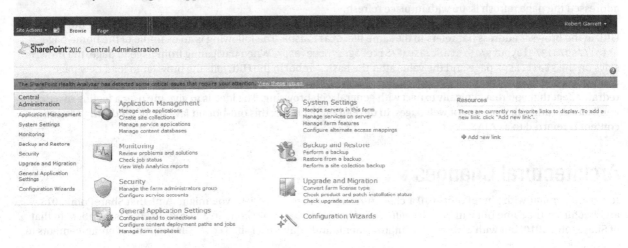

Figure 1-1. *Central Administration in SharePoint Server 2010*

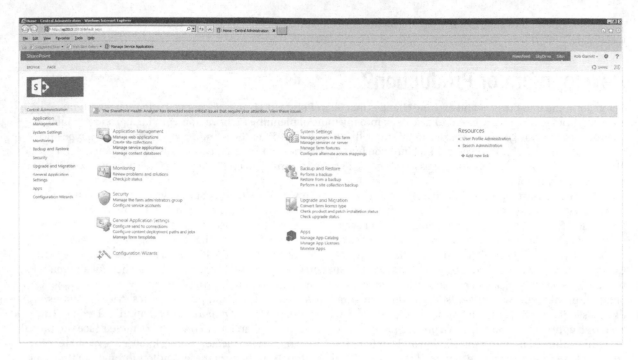

Figure 1-2. *Central Administration in SharePoint Server 2013*

Although not immediately obvious from the previous screenshots, one change apparent to anyone using SharePoint 2013 after SharePoint 2010 is the change to the Site Actions menu. In SharePoint 2010, the Site Actions menu resided in the top left corner and provided access to view all site content and settings for SharePoint sites. SharePoint 2013 replaces the Site Actions menu with a gear icon (or cog, if you prefer), which resides in the top right corner. SharePoint 2013 clusters the pervasive operations in the top right, as the go-to place for users to administer their site and access personal settings.

SharePoint 2010 introduced dialog boxes to limit the number of page refreshes inherent in SharePoint 2007. Dialogs certainly made working with SharePoint better, but they added to the complexity of the user interface. SharePoint 2013 minimizes dialog boxes—a number of the settings pages revert to regular pages. Microsoft has addressed the page refresh issue with in-place refresh.

Open a regular team site in SharePoint 2013. As you navigate around the site, you should notice that the page URL in the browser address bar refers to the same file: `start.aspx`. The following is an example of the home page: `http://sp2013/_layouts/15/start.aspx#/SitePages/Home.aspx`. When navigating from page to page, the browser stays on the `start.aspx` page and the value after the hash symbol in the URL tells the browser to load new page content via JavaScript. This effectively gives the user the impression that page refreshes occur snappily without the redraw effect that you may typically expect with general web browsing. The idea is to give the user a feeling of a rich application, rather than a view of web pages. In development circles, this out-bound JavaScript rendering of page content is referred to as AJAX.

Architectural Changes

If you are familiar with SharePoint 2010 architecture, from a high-level view, you might think that SharePoint 2013 architecture is the same but with a UI facelift. In fact, much of the architecture in SharePoint 2013 is identical to that of SharePoint 2010, but with a number of improvements and additions. I shall cover the majority of enhancements in this section, although the list is not exhaustive. I could write a chapter on each of these architectural enhancement areas, and I recommend further reading on these in addition to my synopsis in this chapter.

Database Enhancements

Microsoft SQL Server 2012 contains many new enhancements to support SharePoint 2013 business intelligence (BI) features. SQL Server 2012 is also cloud-ready. This is not to say that your experience of SharePoint 2013 is sub-par on SQL Server 2008 R2, just that some of the more advanced BI features require the latest version of SQL Server.

Part of the new enhancements to SharePoint databases includes support for Shredded Storage, which I shall discuss in the next section. In addition, Microsoft has optimized SharePoint database schema to optimize input/output (IO) for large lists and document libraries. All SharePoint databases comply with Windows Azure criteria, which I assume is to support SharePoint in the cloud as part of Office 365.

Shredded Storage

Shredded Storage is new to SharePoint 2013 and a regularly talked-about topic in the SharePoint community. Shredded Storage reduces the amount of data flowing to and from SQL Server from SharePoint servers by sending only deltas—that is, changed data only.

Shredded Storage really comes into its own when saving and loading large documents (BLOBs) to and from the database, because instead of transmitting large documents (megabytes in size) SharePoint 2013 now sends only the incremental changes. Think about how you collaborate with peers on document creation; most of the time you might make small changes that you regularly save back to SharePoint. Shredded Storage optimizes this process for faster and more responsive load and save times.

In an effort to use industry standards (or to at least publish standards for use by others), Microsoft built Shredded Storage using the MS-FSSHTTP standard protocol: Microsoft File Sync via SOAP over HTTP. This protocol handles synchronization of small file changes (delta) via SOAP (Simple Object Access Protocol) via HTTP (Hyper Text Transmission Protocol)—it is a bit of a mouthful!

With MS-FSSHTTP, users can see the benefit in working with files stored in SharePoint and work together with peers on the same document, because MS-FSSHTTP manages synchronization of independent changes to the same file by different users. Some of the benefits of Shredded Storage are

- Reduced network bandwidth

- Significantly reduced database size

- Faster read and save times

- Ability to read cached documents

- Ability to start work on a document before the entire file has downloaded

- Background saving of changes, giving the impression that documents save immediately

Shredded Storage is not limited to Office-type documents. SharePoint 2013 and Shredded Storage support any file type. SharePoint utilizes a feature of Windows called Remote Differential Compression (RDC) to ascertain deltas in binary files.

■ **Note**   When upgrading from SharePoint 2010 to SharePoint 2013, existing content does not use Shredded Storage; it is used only when modifying an existing file or adding a new file to SharePoint 2013. Thus upgrading from SharePoint 2010 does not reduce the size of content databases. For more information on Shredded Storage, read http://blogs. technet.com/b/wbaer/archive/2012/11/12/introduction-to-shredded-storage-in-sharepoint-2013.aspx.

Request Management

Request Management assists in directing incoming web requests from client web browsers to servers capable of servicing the requests. In essence, Request Management is a rules-based engine that directs incoming client requests to SharePoint servers in order to serve users quickly and appropriately.

Request Management exists in SharePoint 2013 as a service called SharePoint Foundation Web Application Service. The presence of the word "Foundation" should tip you off that Request Management operates in all versions of SharePoint 2013, including Foundation, as well as Server. Each web-front-end server in a SharePoint 2013 farm runs the service and can therefore play a part in Request Management.

Request Management relies on a series of rules to determine how to route incoming web requests. You can add new rules or change the provided rules to influence how different servers in your farm respond to different requests. Furthermore, you can configure Request Management rules to deny certain requests to your farm and manage load-intensive web requests with throttle rules.

Request Management assumes the existence of multiple servers to satisfy web requests (Request Management has little purpose in a single-server farm). I cover Request Management in detail in Chapter 5.

New Workflow Framework

"Workflow" is a common term given to any process flow that involves work. In business, we use workflow all day long—as part of company policy, in the way we do our jobs, and in the way we use information systems to handle data. Automated workflow is the delegation of certain business processes to computers and systems such that we can alleviate repetitive and mundane tasks normally assigned to humans.

Microsoft introduced Windows Workflow some time back before the release of SharePoint 2007. In fact, Windows Workflow is not a SharePoint-based technology; Microsoft released the Windows Workflow Framework with the early version of .NET 3.0. Since SharePoint 2007, Microsoft has embraced the use of automated workflow in the platform to handle document approval, language content translation, and task assignment, and as part of a number of other areas in SharePoint. Because Windows Workflow exists as a framework, SharePoint has always supported custom workflows, implemented in either SharePoint Designer or Visual Studio. As the workflow framework has evolved, SharePoint has continued to support it in SharePoint 2010 and now as part of SharePoint 2013.

Automated workflow can consume system resources. Each running workflow relies on the framework to track its status, interact with users with delegated tasks, integrate with e-mail and SharePoint, and utilize with data. As a result, some complicated workflows (there is no end to how complicated you can make custom workflows) consume RAM and processor resources in SharePoint. Microsoft has addressed this issue with a completely redesigned distributable workflow system, which Microsoft hosts in the cloud as part of its Azure Cloud Services.

Figure 1-3 shows the new workflow architecture integrated into SharePoint 2013. The new architecture supports both legacy workflow ("Workflow 2010") and the new distributed workflow infrastructure in Azure. The new architecture abstracts the workflow plumbing and allows you to create new custom workflows in SharePoint Designer and Visual Studio, as before. The SharePoint Object Model continues to provide access to the SharePoint infrastructure so you can design custom workflow around data and events with SharePoint sites. Within the SharePoint 2013 object model is the Workflow Services Manager, which handles the execution of custom workflow, either via the legacy Workflow 2010 engine, by making Representational State Transfer (REST) calls, or hosted Workflow in Azure (Windows Azure Workflow).

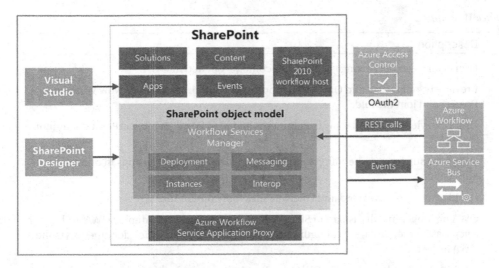

Figure 1-3. *New workflow architecture*

Windows Azure Workflow (WAW) does not integrate with SharePoint 2013 out of the box. In Chapter 12, I cover the steps to configure WAW and demonstrate distributed workflow.

■ **Note**   See http://msdn.microsoft.com/en-us/library/jj163177.aspx for more information on the new workflow model in SharePoint 2013.

Separation of Office Web Applications

Office Web Applications (OWA) complement the full suite of Office applications by allowing users to open Office documents in a web browser. Office Web Apps support opening Word documents, Excel documents, PowerPoint presentations, and OneNote notebooks, either from SharePoint document libraries or via SkyDrive. The purpose of OWA is to provide the basic editing capabilities of Word, Excel, PowerPoint, and OneNote without users having to install full Office applications.

Prior to SharePoint 2013, OWA consisted of an installable package (binaries), which hosted OWA services in SharePoint 2010. Installation was separate from the main SharePoint installation, and at times complicated to configure. With the release of SharePoint 2013, OWA now consists of a separate server application, which you must install on a separate server to that of SharePoint—OWA will not let you install it on a SharePoint server. Part of the reason to separate OWA from SharePoint is because OWA consumes a large amount of RAM and processor on the server, which affected operation of SharePoint when multiple users were editing documents in OWA applications. Another likely reason for the separation is that Microsoft now provides OWA services via Office 365, its Office in the cloud. To support the many users who might use OWA and SharePoint, it makes sense to provide OWA as a stand-alone product.

Like much of SharePoint 2013, Office Web Apps have a number of new features as part of the new release. Table 1-5 summarizes the enhancements and changes in OWA.

Table 1-5. *Changes in Office Web Apps*

Change/Enhancement	Description
Change Tracking	Users can view track changes in Word documents opened in OWA.
Co-authoring	Previously, only Excel and OneNote supported co-authoring in OWA. Now Word and PowerPoint join the fold.
Comments	Users can view, add, and reply to comments added to Word and PowerPoint documents in OWA.
Embedding	OWA now supports embedding Word, Excel, and PowerPoint web apps in other applications.
Ink Support	Enables users to view Word and OneNote files that contain Ink.
Installation	OWA no longer installs as part of SharePoint. Instead, install and deploy OWA and a separate server and then configure SharePoint 2013 to open Office documents via the OWA Server.
Licensing	Editing of Office documents in OWA requires that users have the appropriate license. If users have no license or you have not configured SharePoint user licensing, then users can only view and not edit Office via OWA.
Quick Preview	When integrated with SharePoint 2013, users can hover over search results and OWA will display previews of documents listed in the search results.
Share by Link	Users may send a URL to a document and allow other users to open the document in OWA.

■ **Note** I cover integration of an existing OWA Server with SharePoint 2013 in Chapter 14. For additional information, consult the following article: http://technet.microsoft.com/en-us/library/ff431685.aspx.

Distributed Cache

Prior to SharePoint 2013, SharePoint provided per-server caching. Each SharePoint server held items in its memory cache until either someone removed the item from the cache or the cache time expired and the cache infrastructure removed it. SharePoint itself would use its cache, and developers of custom solutions could make good use of the cache to speed up access to data. If an item exists in memory cache, SharePoint has no need to fetch the data item from a SQL database or other data repository.

The problem with per-server caching is that load balanced servers cannot take full advantage of caching to increase performance. Different web servers in a SharePoint farm may service two identical sequential web requests. If the first server queries the database for an item and then loads the item into cached memory, the cached item is good only as long as subsequent requests query the same server. SharePoint 2013 includes the Distributed Cache, which alleviates this problem with a common cache for all servers in the farm.

The SharePoint 2013 Distributed Cache Service (DCS) builds on the Microsoft App Fabric 1.1 caching model. A number of SharePoint components utilize DCS to maintain cached data across all servers in the farm; these components include elements of the user newsfeeds, search, and authentication.

■ **Note**   For more information on App Fabric Caching, consult the following article: http://msdn.microsoft.com/
en-us/library/ff383731%28v=azure.10%29.aspx.

When installing SharePoint 2013, the installation process installs a version of the App Fabric Caching model. This
is important to note, because SharePoint 2013 requires the precise version of App Fabric it installs, and not necessarily
a later or earlier version of App Fabric available from Microsoft. DCS relies on several open TCP ports to communicate
across server boundaries. If all SharePoint servers communicate on the same network, behind firewalls, then you have
no need to open these ports on your firewalls. However, if you have a distributed SharePoint farm, then make sure
you open the TCP ports 22233–22236. Table 1-6 lists the SharePoint 2013 components that rely on DCS, and in what
capacity.

Table 1-6. *SharePoint 2013 Use of the Distributed Cache Service*

Component	Details
Feeds	SharePoint stores activities and events in DCS for My Site newsfeeds. SharePoint leverages the cache mainly for activities you follow and for displaying the Everyone feed (see Chapter 6 for more information on My Site newsfeeds).
Logon Tokens	SharePoint 2013 federates authentication by using a Secure Token Service, which identifies authenticated users with signed SAML tokens (Security Assertion Markup Language). Each signed SAML token (which is an encrypted and signed XML file) represents a user identity that authenticated and has permitted access to SharePoint (see more information in Chapter 8). This token is the "Logon Token" for the user.
	SharePoint continuously performs security checks as users access parts of the platform, which is why SharePoint 2013 requires access to each user's logon token to ensure that the user is still authenticated (i.e., their session has not expired) and is authorized. SharePoint stores logon tokens in DCS, so every server in the farm can access the token without requiring the user to re-authenticate on each server.
Search	The Content Search Web Part stores queried data in DCS so that multiple SharePoint web-front-end servers can optimally render pages without repeated search queries. (See Chapter 15 for more information on search and the Content Search Web Part).

The App Fabric Cache operates as a Windows service on each SharePoint server. However, you should never
make configuration changes to App Fabric Caching directly, and instead use SharePoint 2013 Central Administration.
Later in this book, you shall see examples of how to start, stop, and configure services running within the SharePoint
2013 farm. The Distributed Cache Service is one of these services. Ideally, you should never have to play with the DCS
settings, but on occasion, if DCS should fail (authentication, My Site newsfeeds, and Content Search Web Parts will
break) you may have to look to the DCS settings to get to the root of the problem.

■ **Note**   For more details on the Distributed Cache Service, see
http://technet.microsoft.com/en-us/library/jj219613/8v=office.159.aspx.

Service Application Changes

SharePoint 2010 introduced the new Service Application Architecture, which replaced the legacy Shared Service Provider (SSP) in SharePoint 2007. SharePoint 2013 continues to use the Service Application Architecture, with some changes to existing service applications and some new service applications added. I shall now briefly recap the Service Application Architecture.

Service Application Architecture Overview

SharePoint is a highly scalable platform, which Microsoft made possible with its distributed architecture. A SharePoint farm (2010 and 2013) can contain any number of web-front-end servers to handle user web requests and any number of application servers to distribute back-end services, such as search, business intelligence, managed metadata, etc. Prior to SharePoint 2010, SharePoint 2007 only allowed scaling of web-front-end servers and limited services to a single server as part of the SSP. Since SharePoint 2010, the Service Application model implements a Software-As-A-Service (SAAS) design, such that the platform makes a variety of services available across a SharePoint farm, and each service may reside on any SharePoint server—this is known as distributed services. Furthermore, because of the distributed nature of the design, multiple SharePoint farms may share the use of services from other SharePoint farms.

Each service provided by SharePoint 2013 operates on one or more servers in the farm. I say one or more because a SharePoint farm may require only one instance of a running service to perform some work, but running the service on multiple servers ensures redundancy and allows for load balancing. Take PerformancePoint as an example. PerformancePoint runs as a physical SharePoint service on an application server in your farm. If you enable this service, you can take advantage of the business intelligence capabilities PerformancePoint has to offer. However, enabling the PerformancePoint Service on one or many application servers in your farm is not enough to distribute this service as available across the farm.

Each distributed SharePoint Service exposes a WCF (Windows Communication Foundation) end point, which is a fancy way of saying that the service exposes itself as a web service. The PerformancePoint Service exposes an end point, which any WCF client may connect to utilize PerformancePoint business intelligence. Management and configuration of the service require a Managed Application. Managed Applications are similar to regular web applications in SharePoint (see Chapter 2), but instead of hosting site collections, they associate with services on the server to allow configuration.

Continuing to use the PerformancePoint Service as an example, if you open SharePoint 2013 Central Administration, click the link to manage service applications and then click the PerformancePoint Service Application (assuming you have it installed), the PerformancePoint Service Application renders pages in your browser to configure the working parameters of the PerformancePoint Service.

Typically, each SharePoint service and service application has one or many associated databases to maintain configuration settings and working data. These three components represent the server side of a distributed service.

A proxy is required for servers in the SharePoint farm to communicate with SharePoint Services hosted on a different server. The proxy is a WCF client that communicates directly with the distributed WCF service end point and enables use of the remote functionality on the local server in which the proxy resides. Irrespective of where the service resides, each server looking to consume a service requires a locally installed proxy. In a single-application SharePoint farm, each service and associated service application also has a local proxy talking with the service on the same server.

In conclusion, SharePoint 2013 provides a number of service applications each performing a role. Examples include Business Connectivity Services, Search Service, PerformancePoint Services, Excel Services, Managed Metadata Service, etc. Each service application consists of the following components:

- Configuration databases

- The WCF service with exposed end point

- A Managed Service Application (IIS application) that provides management and configuration

- A proxy to communicate with the service end point.

New Service Applications

With the Service Application Architecture recap out of the way, I shall now discuss some of the service applications that Microsoft added to SharePoint 2013. SharePoint 2013 includes three new service applications, as follows:

- Machine Translation Service
- Work Management
- App Management

■ **Note**   The Machine Translation Service is the only one of the three service applications that you may distribute cross-farm. The Work Management and App Management services work only within their respective farms.

The Machine Translation Service provides language translation services for sites, pages, and managed term sets in SharePoint, by using Microsoft Bing to perform the translation work. This managed service relies on a handful of timer jobs to process requested translation tasks by sending content to Bing and replacing foreign-language content with translated data.

The Work Management Service aggregates user tasks to provide a centralized task list. This service aggregates tasks from Exchange, Project Server, and SharePoint 2013 and allows users to manage centrally all their tasks via their My Site.

■ **Note**   For more information on configuring synchronization with the Work Management Service, please consult the following article: http://technet.microsoft.com/en-us/library/jj554516.aspx.

The App Management Service is responsible for hosting new SharePoint apps, either custom-developed or installed from the App Marketplace. Everything is an app in SharePoint 2013; Microsoft refers to lists and libraries as apps—the task list is a particular type of list app that handles storage of tasks. When adding a new list or library in SharePoint 2013 you should see the Add an App menu item, under the Settings menu (gear icon); see Figure 1-4.

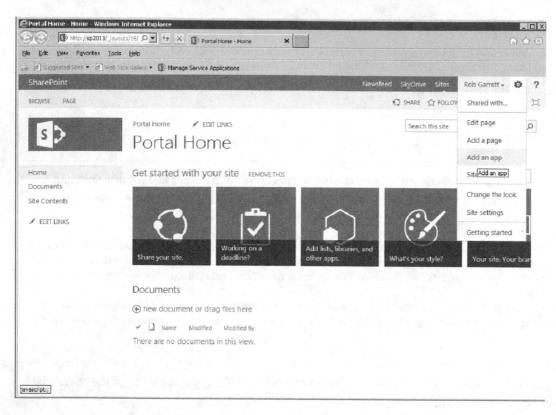

Figure 1-4. *Add an app in the Settings menu*

Apps are not just the new terminology for lists and libraries in SharePoint 2013. Apps are modules of functionality that you may host in SharePoint and/or other Office applications. With the mass adoption of Office 365 and hosting business SharePoint in the cloud, apps allow development of lightweight functionality, which you may deploy to O365, whereas full-blown farm features may deploy only to on-premise SharePoint.

Figure 1-5 shows a screenshot of the App Marketplace (App Store) within my SharePoint team site. The App Store itself resides with Microsoft, but SharePoint 2013 does a great job of integrating it with the platform as if it is part of your site. If you have permissions to install apps in your site, feel free to download some of the apps in the store and install them.

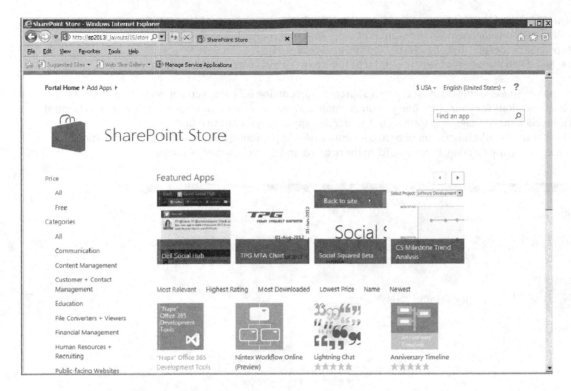

Figure 1-5. *The App Store for SharePoint apps*

To host apps inside your SharePoint sites, you must:

1. Enable the App Managed Service in SharePoint.

2. Enable the Microsoft SharePoint Foundation Subscription Settings Service.

3. Create a Managed Service Application for the App Managed Service.

4. Create a Managed Service Application for the Subscription Settings Service.

5. Create proxies for both of the previous Managed Application Services.

6. Create an Apps Catalog.

To start the App Management and Subscription Settings services, open Central Administration and click the link for "Services on Server"; from here you can start each service, if not already started. To create the managed service applications and proxies, first open a PowerShell window with the following steps:

1. Click the Start button.

2. Click All Programs and then click Microsoft SharePoint 2013 Products.

3. Click SharePoint 2013 Management Shell (this loads PowerShell).

Next, execute each of the following PowerShell Cmdlets (followed by Enter after each):

```
$appPool= Get-SPServiceApplicationPool -Identity "Name of Managed Service Account"
$app = New-SPSubscriptionSettingsServiceApplication -ApplicationPool $appPool '
  -Name SettingsServiceApp -DatabaseName SettingServiceDB
```

```
$proxy = New-SPSubscriptionSettingsServiceApplicationProxy -ServiceApplication $app
$appServ = New-SPAppManagementServiceApplication -ApplicationPool $appPool '
    -Name AppManServiceApp -DatabaseName AppManServiceDB
$appProxy = New-SPAppManagementServiceApplicationProxy -ServiceApplication $appServ
```

To host apps in SharePoint, you must create a Managed App Catalog for each web application. If you have multiple web applications for your sites then you must create a Managed App Catalog for each. Navigate to Central Admin and then click the Manage App Catalog link under the App Management heading.

Figure 1-6 shows the administration page to configure a new App Catalog for a selected web application. To manage an existing App Catalog, type the URL in the text box and then click the OK button.

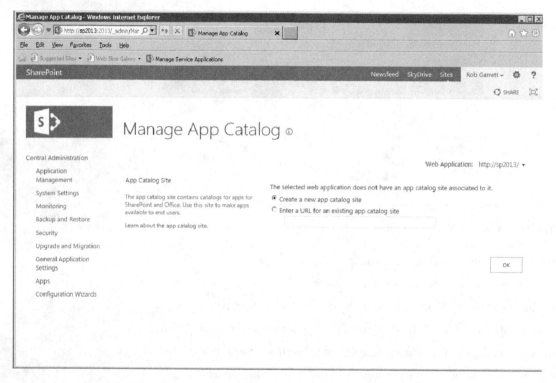

Figure 1-6. *Manage App Catalog in Central Administration*

■ **Note**   For more information on the SharePoint App Model and App development, please consult the following article: http://msdn.microsoft.com/en-us/library/jj164084.aspx.

Depreciated and Changed Service Applications

With any new version of SharePoint, you can expect Microsoft to depreciate or change certain features. This section discusses depreciated and changed Managed Service Applications.

Microsoft implemented a new version of the Search Service Application, from the ground up. SharePoint 2010 offered FAST as an alternative Enterprise Search Platform at additional cost while still providing SharePoint Enterprise

Search. SharePoint 2013 includes FAST as the default Enterprise Search offering, which meant redesigning the Search Service Application. I cover search in much detail in Chapter 15.

SharePoint 2013 offers a more robust version of the Managed Metadata Service (MMS) Application. MMS now supports term properties; you can provide site navigation using terms in the term store and pin terms to reduce the number of duplicate terms in the store. Microsoft has also improved how users can create terms and term sets. See Chapter 9 for details on the Managed Metadata Service.

Web Analytics no longer exists as its own Managed Service Application; Microsoft rolled this functionality into the SharePoint 2013 search platform.

As mentioned earlier in this chapter, Office Web Apps is no longer a service application. OWA now exists as a stand-alone server application.

SharePoint 2013 brings a new improved User Profile Service (UPS). If you have experience with UPS in SharePoint 2010, you may remember the vast number of configuration issues and errors associated with UPS provisioning and setting up directory synchronization. Each hotfix and service pack solved some issues with UPS and introduced others. Fortunately, the User Profile Service and synchronization capabilities of SharePoint 2013 are more robust. UPS synchronization still uses Forefront Identity Management (FIM) services as the core for user profile synchronization, but SharePoint 2013 also provides an additional synchronization feature that allows one-way synchronization with Active Directory, much like that provided in SharePoint 2007. This additional synchronization feature allows for the more common configuration of one-way synchronization with Active Directory without the overhead of FIM.

Microsoft built a new version of Access Services but kept the original version from SharePoint 2010, which it calls Access Services 2010. I would expect that the legacy version might disappear with the next release of SharePoint.

SharePoint 2013 includes a new PowerPoint Automation Service, which is similar to the Word Automation Service, for translating PowerPoint presentations into other formats, such as HTML and PDF. PowerPoint Automation Services is not strictly a Managed Application Service, because it consists of only the service, meaning there is no configuration aspect to this feature.

Finally, the Business Connectivity Services Managed Service Application has undergone some enhancements. Namely, BCS now supports Open Data (OData) and JavaScript Object Notation (JSON) protocols for communicating with external sources. BCS also adds the very much anticipated event receivers for external data, such that custom code can detect changes to external data. Other changes include support for the new SharePoint Apps Model and a number of performance enhancements for external lists and external content types.

Security Changes

Not much has changed in the security features of SharePoint 2013. Similar to SharePoint 2010, SharePoint 2013 supports Claims-Based-Authentication, using federated authentication (see Chapter 8 for more information on Claims-Based-Authentication). Earlier in this chapter, I touched on how the Distributed Cache Service maintains copies of logon tokens—signed and encrypted XML files representing authenticated user identities. One notable change is that SharePoint 2013 requires all web applications created from Central Administration to use Claims-Based-Authentication. It is still possible to create web applications that use Classic Mode Authentication, via PowerShell, but Microsoft no longer supports this method of authentication, and you can expect Microsoft to retire it completely in later releases of SharePoint.

With the inclusion of the new App Model, SharePoint now supports the OAUTH authorization protocol. OAUTH provides a method for clients to access server resources on behalf of a resource owner (such as a different client or an end user). It also provides a process for end users to authorize third-party access to their server resources without sharing their credentials (typically, a username and password pair).

OAUTH enables users to authorize SharePoint 2013 to provide tokens instead of credentials (for example, username and password) to their data hosted by SharePoint 2013. Each token grants access to a specific site (for example, a SharePoint document repository) for specific resources (for example, documents from a folder) and for a defined duration (for example, 30 minutes). This enables users to grant a third-party site access to information that is stored with SharePoint without sharing their username and password and without sharing all the data that they have on SharePoint. OAUTH makes it possible to run apps developed and hosted by other people inside the context of your SharePoint site, such that the app can only access certain resources for a definite length of time.

Summary

I hope that this chapter has given you a taste of what to expect in SharePoint 2013. I also hope that I have given you a sense of what to expect in the remaining fifteen chapters in this book. It was my goal to give you an overview of the SharePoint platform, from an administrative perspective, and to dive into many of the new features and changes with this new release. I deliberately stayed away from lengthy descriptions of SharePoint from a business standpoint and the sort of information that I would provide business users when asked of the end-user purpose of SharePoint 2013. Instead, I hope I provided you with enough insight into SharePoint 2013 as a technical person, and set the stage for the administration theme of this book.

In this chapter, I covered the different versions of SharePoint 2013—Foundation and Server—and spent some time detailing the license differences between SharePoint 2013 Server Standard and Enterprise.

I furnished you with the hardware and software prerequisites, so that you start on the right track with your installation and deployment.

I was excited to cover the new architecture changes that SharePoint 2013 brings over its predecessor and to cover additions and changes to the Managed Service Application infrastructure. I included details about the new App Model and a brief note on the use of the OAUTH authorization protocol for apps.

This chapter was a short one, and it was my intention to use it as a springboard for the rest of the book. Do not worry if some of the topics mentioned in this chapter caught you by surprise. I cover many of the topics in detail throughout this book. Where possible, I provide you with reference links to topics outside the scope of this book. With the introduction out of the way, now it is time to begin Chapter 2, where you will learn how to install SharePoint 2013.

CHAPTER 2

■ ■ ■

New Installation and Configuration

In this chapter, we shall follow a series of steps for the installation of SharePoint 2013. Some readers may have experience with installation of SharePoint 2013, or a previous version of SharePoint. The installation of SharePoint 2013 is similar to that of SharePoint 2010. Whether you are a SharePoint guru, or you are new to SharePoint, this chapter will guide you through the typical steps and best practices for standing up a small farm, for use in your organization, or for use as part of your development environment. The principles for standing up a large farm also follow those in this chapter and involve repeating many of the steps for additional web-front-end (WFE) or application servers in your farm.

SharePoint 2013 Prerequisites

SharePoint 2013 includes a prerequisites installer application, which ensures that SharePoint has all the necessary software components to operate. Such components include various hot fixes, SQL Server Reporting and Analysis components, .NET 4.5, Microsoft Sync Framework, Windows Server AppFabric, and Windows Identity Framework. . . to name a few.

The prerequisites installer is available in the root folder of the SharePoint 2013 installation media and named PrerequisiteInstaller.exe. Executing this application with no command-line argument parameters will present you with the dialog shown in Figure 2-1.

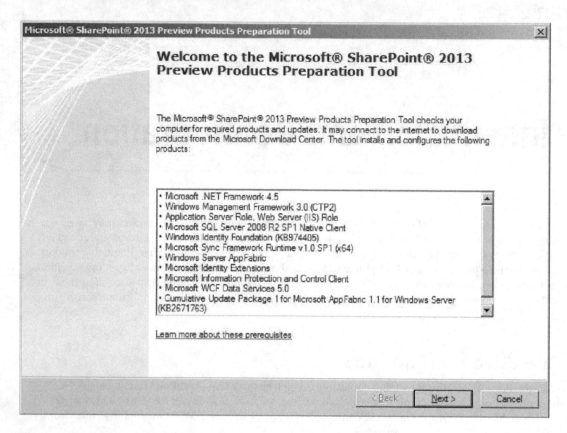

Figure 2-1. The prerequisites installer opening dialog

■ **Note** When executing any of the installation applications for SharePoint 2013, be sure to run as an elevated privilege administrator if you have Windows User Account Control enabled. See the following link on Windows UAC: http://windows.microsoft.com/en-US/windows-vista/What-is-User-Account-Control.

As you can see in Figure 2-1, the prerequisites installer also configures the server with the Application Server and Web Server (IIS) roles, which SharePoint 2013 requires to operate.

The prerequisites installer does not require all the packages to be available on the server before installing them and will attempt to download any package before installing. Of course, in certain scenarios, automatic download of software may violate company policy in a secure environment, so the prerequisites installer allows the administrator to choose which packages to install using the command line, by providing the path to previously downloaded packages. Running the prerequisites installer from the command line with the '/?' option will display the dialog shown in Figure 2-2.

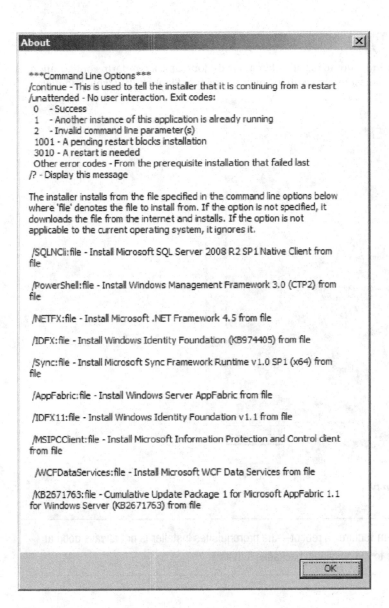

About [x]

```
***Command Line Options***
/continue - This is used to tell the installer that it is continuing from a restart
/unattended - No user interaction. Exit codes:
  0   - Success
  1   - Another instance of this application is already running
  2   - Invalid command line parameter(s)
  1001 - A pending restart blocks installation
  3010 - A restart is needed
  Other error codes - From the prerequisite installation that failed last
/? - Display this message

The installer installs from the file specified in the command line options below
where 'file' denotes the file to install from. If the option is not specified, it
downloads the file from the internet and installs. If the option is not
applicable to the current operating system, it ignores it.

/SQLNCli:file - Install Microsoft SQL Server 2008 R2 SP1 Native Client from
file

/PowerShell:file - Install Windows Management Framework 3.0 (CTP2) from
file

/NETFX:file - Install Microsoft .NET Framework 4.5 from file

/IDFX:file - Install Windows Identity Foundation (KB974405) from file

/Sync:file - Install Microsoft Sync Framework Runtime v1.0 SP1 (x64) from
file

/AppFabric:file - Install Windows Server AppFabric from file

/IDFX11:file - Install Windows Identity Foundation v1.1 from file

/MSIPCClient:file - Install Microsoft Information Protection and Control client
from file

/WCFDataServices:file - Install Microsoft WCF Data Services from file

/KB2671763:file - Cumulative Update Package 1 for Microsoft AppFabric 1.1
for Windows Server (KB2671763) from file
```

[OK]

Figure 2-2. Prerequisites installer options

■ **Note**   Paul Papanek wrote a great blog post that includes a PowerShell script to download all the prerequisites ahead of time, for cases when you are installing SharePoint 2013 without an Internet connection: www.dontpapanic.com/blog/?p=241.

Choosing the Installation Type

Like its predecessor, SharePoint allows an administrator to install either a stand-alone or a server farm configuration. Running setup.exe from the installation media presents you with the dialog shown in Figure 2-3, at which point you must make a choice.

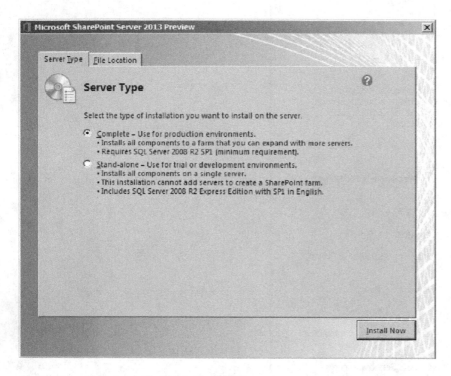

Figure 2-3. *Choosing a SharePoint installation type*

■ **Note**   Setup.exe will determine if the system requires a reboot—the prerequisites installer is not always good at ensuring a reboot and leaves this determination to the individual packages it installs.

Stand-Alone Installation

First and most important, be sure that the stand-alone installation is right for you. Too often, SharePoint administrators install a stand-alone configuration of SharePoint to try out the product and then find they have to support it in production, because end users have quickly loaded SharePoint with working content (documents and so on). **Therefore, I do not recommend stand-alone installations**, but understand that sometimes they serve a purpose.

If that scenario does not scare you away, or does not apply, then consider the following list of limitations specific to the stand-alone installation:

- **No Domain Controller**: The stand-alone installation will fail if you attempt to install it on a domain controller.

- **Installation of SQL Server 2008 R2 SP1 Express**: The installer will install a new instance of SQL Server 2008 R2 with Service Pack 1 Express Edition, regardless of whether you have an installation of full SQL Server on the same server. Express has a limit of 4GB storage, causing a major headache for the IT team later when the stand-alone install of SharePoint generates increased user adoption.

- **Inability to scale**: The stand-alone installation does *not* allow the integration of additional WFE servers or query/index servers to scale the farm. Essentially, a stand-alone installation tells SharePoint that the one single server *is* the farm in its entirety and that the administrator is fine with not scaling out later.

- **Use of Network Service and Local System accounts**: Microsoft designed the stand-alone install as a simple option, leaving the user with few complications in setup. The decisions simplified include those surrounding security and managed accounts (more on managed accounts later in this chapter). The stand-alone install will leverage the built-in Network Service and Local System accounts to configure SharePoint services—including the SharePoint timer service. These accounts share across the server, and service packs and other product installs may affect the volatility of their configuration and system-level passwords, rendering the SharePoint installation susceptible to problems.

- **Selective Services**: The stand-alone installation does not allow installation of all service applications, such as the User Profile Synchronization Service.

After considering these facts, if you still wish to continue with the stand-alone installation, click that option on the dialog as in Figure 2-3. From here on the install is very much hands-off and concludes with Internet Explorer opening to Central Administration having created default service applications, a default web application, and site collection.

Server Farm Installation

If you are reading this far, then you have probably decided to pass on the stand-alone install—the stand-alone install is fine for testing and development purposes but not recommended for scalable production uses of SharePoint. Click the server farm installation option on the dialog (shown in Figure 2-3) and we shall walk through the steps.

After choosing the server farm installation option, the setup application begins installation and shows progress as in Figure 2-4.

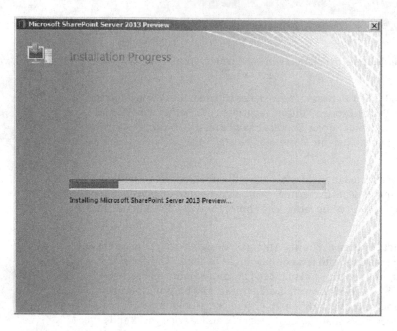

Figure 2-4. *Installation progress*

After a brief break to refresh your cup of coffee, while the installer installs SharePoint 2013 binaries, you should see the dialog shown in Figure 2-5 upon your return. Leaving the check box checked and closing this dialog will launch the SharePoint Products Configuration Wizard allowing you to configure your new SharePoint farm or join this server to an existing farm. If you uncheck the option to run the Configuration Wizard now (if you are installing binaries on multiple WFE servers first), you can execute the Configuration Wizard from the SharePoint Products group in Windows.

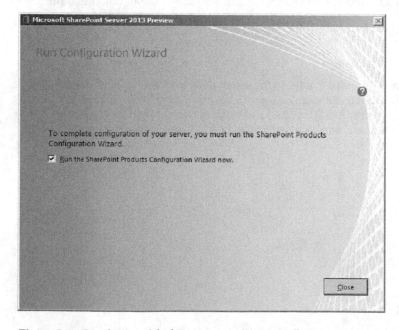

Figure 2-5. *Conclusion of the binary server farm installation*

SharePoint Products Configuration Wizard

We are now ready to proceed through the SharePoint Products Configuration Wizard—or Configuration Wizard for short. The Configuration Wizard performs the tasks necessary to join a server (with SharePoint binaries installed) to an existing farm, or to provision a new farm. In simple terms, a farm consists of one or more SharePoint servers associated with a central SQL Server instance, containing a main configuration database. When creating a new farm, the wizard provisions a new configuration database and content database for Central Administration in the designated SQL Server instance.

The Configuration Wizard is responsible for more than adding and removing servers from a farm. After applying service packs, the wizard also ensures that database schemas correlate with that of the latest installed binaries and ensures database integrity. At this stage, we are concerned only with provisioning a new farm, as part of our installation steps.

After a brief welcome message and a popup message about restarting some services, you will see a dialog like that of Figure 2-6.

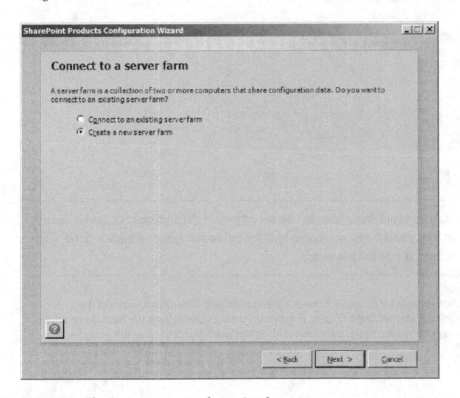

Figure 2-6. *The Connect to a server farm wizard page*

Assuming this is your first installation of SharePoint 2013 and you have no existing SharePoint farm to join, choose the option to create a new server farm, followed by a click of the Next button.

The dialog shown in Figure 2-7 asks you to specify a SQL Server name and default configuration database name for SharePoint 2013. This server is the location of the main farm configuration database and Central Administration web site content database. Provide the user credentials of the SharePoint farm account for connecting to the database (see the later section on Managed Accounts).

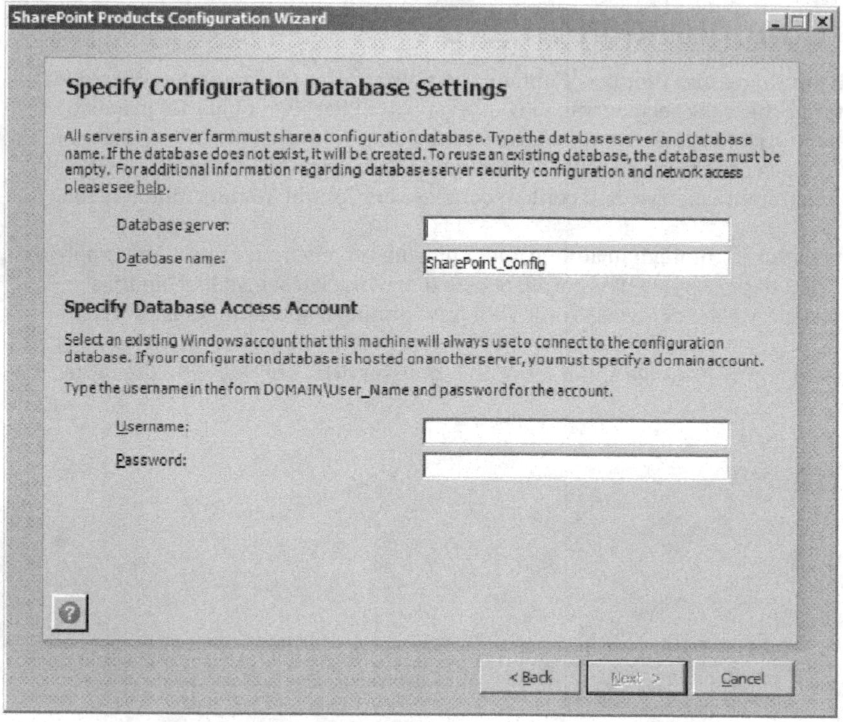

Figure 2-7. *SQL Server parameters*

■ **Note**   You must assign the "Setup user administrator account," the securityadmin and dbcreator SQL Server security roles, during setup and configuration. This account does *not* need to be in the local admin group on the SQL Server. This account is different from the farm account specified in this wizard.

The dialog that follows (Figure 2-8) asks for the passphrase for the installation. SharePoint requires the passphrase later when adding additional servers to the farm or removing existing servers from the farm, so be sure to keep the passphrase safe. You may change the passphrase later with PowerShell, but retrieving the passphrase is impossible—you may only reset it.

Figure 2-8. *Passphrase dialog*

Figure 2-9 asks you for the port number and authentication type for the Central Administration Web Application. Like any other web site running on SharePoint, Central Administration is a special web site running its own web application within IIS (Internet Information Server). The Configuration Wizard will suggest a port for the Central Administration web site, based on a random available port on the server. I typically like to override the chosen port with 2013 as an easy-to-remember port number.

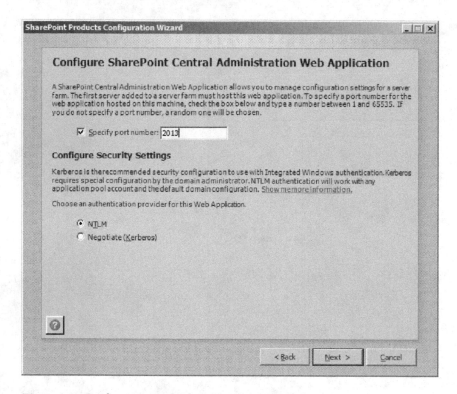

Figure 2-9. *Configure Central Administration Web Application*

Options for security include NTLM or Kerberos. NTLM (Windows Challenge-Response Authentication) is the typical choice in most installations as this is the default Windows authentication type for most applications. However, if you are familiar with Kerberos and have this authentication mechanism configured in your infrastructure, then feel free to use it here.

■ **Note** The Configuration Wizard creates a new IIS Web Application on the server at the following location: c:\InetPub\wwwroot\wss\VirtualDirectories\{PortNumber}. What is interesting is that the port number in the disk location is that originally chosen by the wizard, and not the value entered by the administrator.

Before proceeding with the configuration, the Configuration Wizard provides a summary of the configuration you entered (Figure 2-10). Double-check these values—changing them later potentially involves removing the server from the farm and going through the Configuration Wizard steps again.

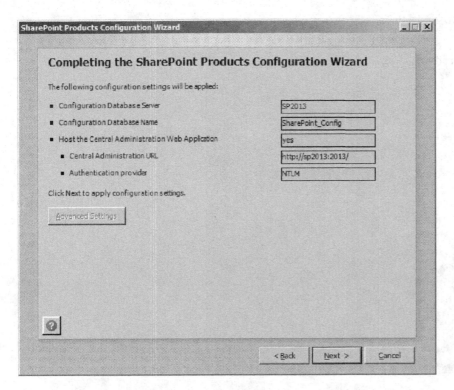

Figure 2-10. *Summary of farm settings before provisioning the farm*

Once the Configuration Wizard starts the provisioning process, you should not interrupt it, unless you need to cancel the operation and start again. A failed provision process leaves stale databases and configurations in SQL Server, which you should remove before attempting another run at configuration.

Figure 2-11 shows the provisioning process in operation. The Configuration Wizard completes several steps (approximately ten) in the process, which include creating databases, creating new IIS web applications, etc.

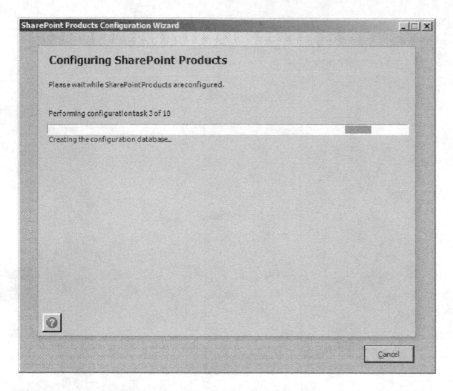

Figure 2-11. *Provisioning process by the Configuration Wizard*

Once complete, the Configuration Wizard should show a dialog like that in Figure 2-12. If, on the other hand, the wizard encounters a problem, it will show an error message and a link to the log file, so you may troubleshoot what caused the error.

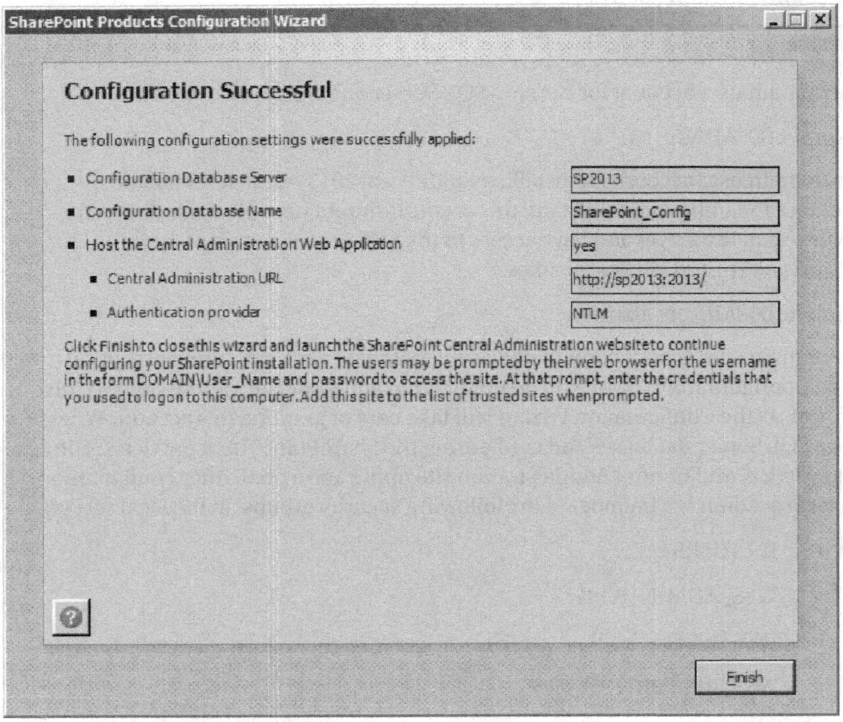

Figure 2-12. *Configuration Wizard completed*

Managed Accounts

SharePoint makes use of various domain-level accounts to operate securely. Even if your SharePoint installation operates on a single server and is part of a work group, all accounts used in SharePoint 2013 require the full domain name syntax: *DOMAIN\username* (domain is the machine name in a stand-alone installation). SharePoint 2010 had the same requirement.

As with its predecessor, SharePoint 2013 uses *managed accounts*. Managed accounts allow administrators to maintain Windows system accounts, in use by SharePoint, in a central location. Thus, if you need to change SharePoint to use a different service account, you have to change it in only one place in Central Administration, and not across various services and applications (except for a few rare circumstances). Managed accounts also allow SharePoint to manage password change, enforced by Domain Group Policy.

I will discuss managed accounts further, a little later in this chapter; for now I am focusing on the various accounts required in the domain and their purposes as managed accounts. Table 2-1 lists the accounts that Microsoft recommends for a maintainable and secure SharePoint farm (you can choose the account names, as long as you can assign the permissions as listed).

Table 2-1. *Recommended Domain Accounts for SharePoint 2013*

Account	Purpose
SQL Server Service Account	The domain user account for running SQL Server and SQL Server Agent. Example: DOMAIN\sp_sql
Setup User Account	The domain user account for installing SharePoint 2013 on each server and running the Configuration Wizard; this account should have local administrator privileges on the server and have access to the SQL Server as part of the securityadmin and dbcreator roles. Example: DOMAIN\sp_admin
Server Farm Account	The domain user account nominated as the database account during execution of the Configuration Wizard; you do not need to apply specific permissions to this account, as the Configuration Wizard will take care of granting this account access to the SQL Server databases and configuring the SharePoint Timer Service, Code Host Service, and Central Administration site application pool. After configuration, the farm account is a member of the following security groups on the local server: • IIS_IUSRS • WSS_ADMIN_WPG • WSS_WPG • WSS_RESTRICTED_WPG • Performance Log Users • Performance Monitor Users The farm account also has the following local security policy rights: • Adjust memory quotas for a process • Logon as a service • Replace a process-level token Example: DOMAIN\sp_farm
Application Pool Account	The domain user to run all SharePoint web site applications in the farm; do not grant any explicit privileges—you may have several managed accounts (one for each web application) in the farm, but only need one domain user account. Example: DOMAIN\sp_app_pool
SharePoint Service Account	The domain user account with no explicit privileges to run SharePoint service applications. Example: DOMAIN\sp_service

(*continued*)

Table 2-1. (*continued*)

Account	Purpose
Search Crawl Account	The domain user account with no explicit privileges to crawl content for indexed search.
	Example: `DOMAIN\sp_crawl`
User Profile Synchronization Account	This account must have domain replication rights for UPS to operate correctly.
	Example: `DOMAIN\sp_ups`
Business Intelligence Account	The domain user account and trusted account for Reporting Services and Performance Point when not using Kerberos; grant database access as appropriate to access external content.
	Example: `DOMAIN\sp_bi`

You need only the first three accounts in Table 2-1 to install SharePoint 2013, and in many test and development environments, you can live with just the first five accounts for all aspects of the farm configuration. However, in the spirit of good practice and in preparation for the day when you have to stand up a production SharePoint 2013 farm, I recommend getting in the habit of creating all of these accounts for configuration.

■ **Note**   To ensure smooth installation of the User Profile Synchronization Service, grant the farm account Replicating Directory Changes permission in the domain.

Configuring Your SharePoint Farm

The SharePoint Farm Configuration Wizard (called the "White Wizard" in some circles, as opposed to the "Gray Wizard," which is the Products Configuration Wizard) walks the administrator through configuration of the farm. As with any wizard, SharePoint makes certain assumptions to guide you. If you are looking for a more hands-on tailored configuration setup, then you must perform configuration manually. The wizard saves you most of the complications of manual configuration but makes default configuration decisions on your behalf.

■ **Note**   If you skip the Farm Configuration Wizard after completing the SharePoint Products Configuration Wizard, you may execute it at any time from the bottom-right link of the main Central Administration home page.

The first page of the Farm Configuration Wizard asks if you want to participate in a Customer Experience Improvement Program—a worthwhile exercise if you have not done this before. Skipping this dialog takes you to the page with a wizard summary and the chance to cancel the wizard or begin the process, as shown in Figure 2-13.

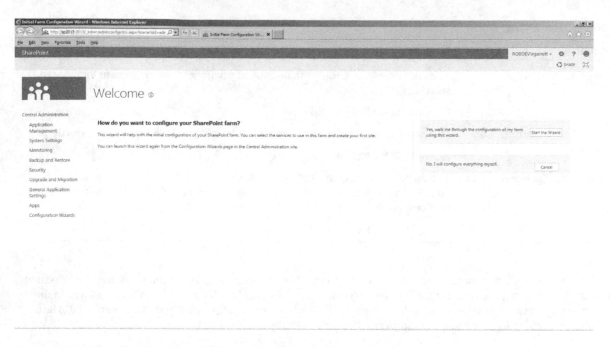

Figure 2-13. *Start of the SharePoint 2013 Farm Configuration Wizard*

Click the button to start the wizard, and you should see the page shown in Figure 2-14. The top section of the page allows you to specify the service account for all Managed Services, created by the wizard. Use the DOMAIN\sp_service account you read about earlier in this chapter. You may be tempted to use the SharePoint farm account to run your services. Microsoft recommends supplying a dedicated service account, with lesser privileges than the farm account.

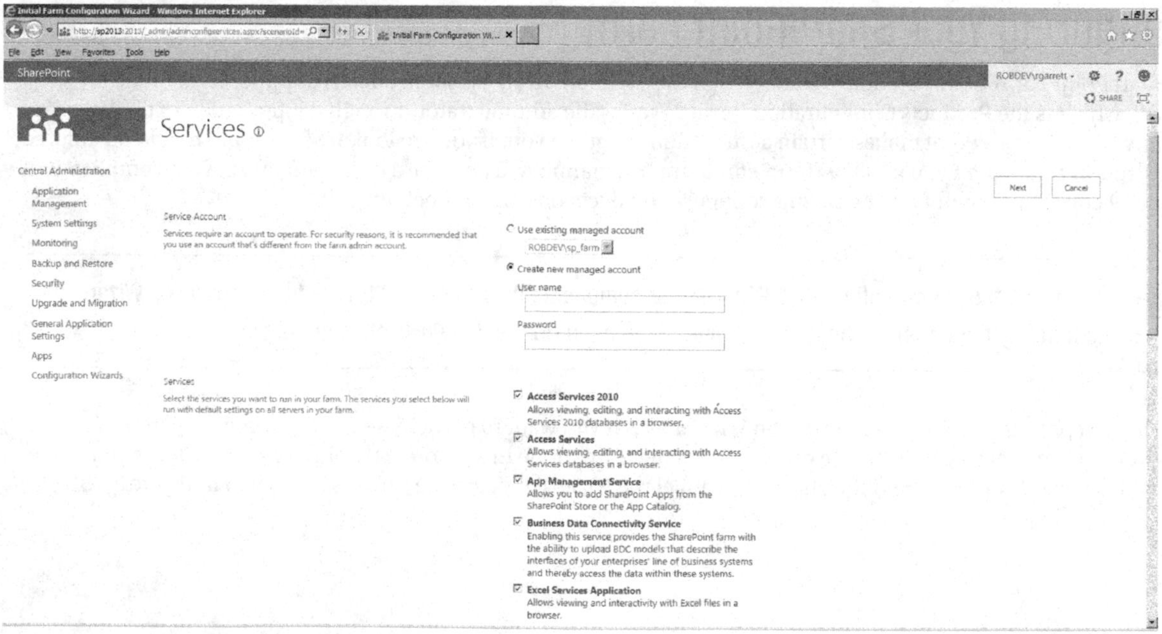

Figure 2-14. *Service configuration*

The remainder of the page, shown in Figure 2-14, allows you to configure the various Managed Services included in the default service group of the farm. Service groups allow you to define different groups of services for different purposes. For example, a publishing web site might need only a restricted set of services provisioned, whereas a corporate intranet might require many more services, such as the Office service applications. SharePoint 2013 insists on a default group of services, which SharePoint applies to any web application created where you have not specified a service application group (more on this in a later section on creating web applications).

Select your desired default service applications and then click the Next button. If you are unsure what service applications you need by default, it is always safe to err on the side of minimal. Typical service applications to include are (do not worry for now if you are unsure of the purpose of each of the listed service applications).

- Managed Metadata Service

- App Management Service

- Application Discovery and Load Balancer Service Application

- Search Service Application

- State Service

- Secure Store Service

- Secure Token Service Application

By now, you will have noticed that SharePoint 2013 has a similar look and feel to Microsoft Windows 8 User Interface (previously known as Metro). Microsoft has taken some tips from Google and made its applications friendlier, and SharePoint 2013 now gives you a nice friendly "Working on it . . . " message, as shown in Figure 2-15.

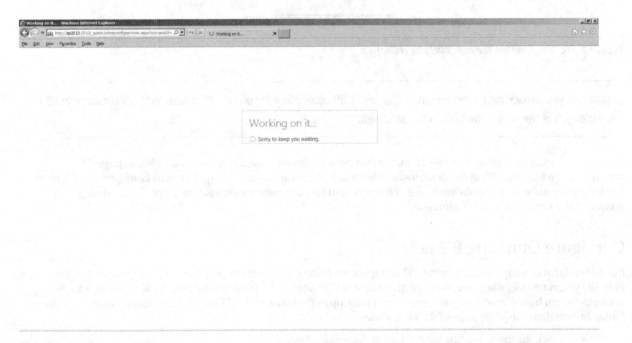

Figure 2-15. *Friendly progress message*

After completing the configuration of farm services, the farm wizard prompts you to configure the top-level root site collection, as shown in Figure 2-16. At this stage, SharePoint has already provisioned a new IIS Web Application—called SharePoint 80—on the default HTTP port (80) and presented the page shown in Figure 2-16 so the user may choose the site definition (template) for the new site collection at the root of this new application. Administrators of the previous SharePoint 2010 version may already be familiar with creating new site collections, and the following page is similar to that of the previous version.

Figure 2-16. *Configuring the top-level site collection*

■ **Note**   If you already have a working non-SharePoint IIS application/site on port 80, SharePoint will disable it in IIS to allow creation of the default application in SharePoint.

After creating the default site collection, the farm wizard should show a summary completion page. The summary page lists the URL of the default site collection and the various service applications configured in the farm. To change the default web application, site collection, and service applications, visit the Application Management section in the Central Administration site.

Configure Outgoing E-Mail

Before our farm is ready for use, you should configure outgoing e-mail settings. SharePoint is very social and likes to notify you via e-mail when events occur on sites, so it is important that you at least configure outgoing e-mail correctly. If you have closed your browser, open it back up to the home page of Central Administration (or click the Finish button if on summary page of the farm wizard).

- Click the main heading for the section System Settings.
- Click the Configure Outgoing E-Mail Settings link.
- Provide configuration for your outbound SMTP server. You can leave the code page as default (65001 – Unicode) for most purposes.

■ **Note**   Installation and configuration of a local SMTP server on the SharePoint server is outside the scope of this book and not recommended for production installs. The following URL references instructions for installing SMTP in IIS 7 for development and testing purposes: `http://technet.microsoft.com/en-us/library/cc772058%28v=ws.10%29.aspx`.

Welcome to the Central Administration Web Site

If you read the previous sections of this chapter, you will already have seen references to the SharePoint Central Administration web site (Central Administration for short). I previously glossed over the use of Central Administration, so now shall take you on a more extensive tour.

Simply put, the Central Administration web site is the graphical user interface to management of a SharePoint 2013 farm. Figure 2-17 shows the opening Central Administration home page, familiar to any administrator who has installed SharePoint 2013.

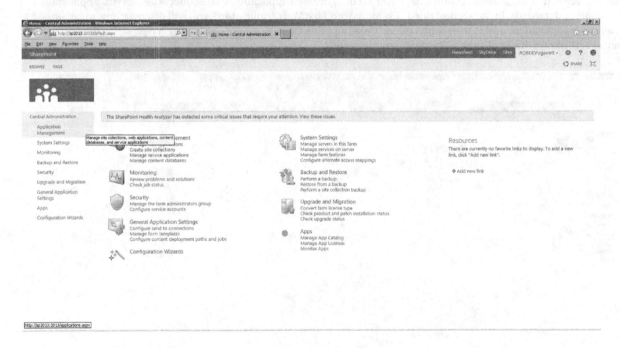

Figure 2-17.   *The Central Administration web site home page for SharePoint 2013*

The Central Administration interface is not the only means to administer SharePoint 2013. Microsoft provides a whole bunch of PowerShell Cmdlets to script SharePoint administration. I shall cover PowerShell in Chapter 3. Users who administered SharePoint 2007 may remember the STSADM tool, which Microsoft now considers legacy. SharePoint 2013 still includes STSADM in the C:\Program Files\Common Files\Microsoft Shared\Web Server Extensions\15\bin directory, but PowerShell is the new way of scripting SharePoint administration.

■ **Note**   All examples in this book will assume use of the SharePoint graphical user interface or PowerShell.

No doubt, you have already realized that the Central Administration site runs atop of SharePoint itself and consists of the typical navigation elements and ribbon that users of a SharePoint team site would expect. The Central Administration home page provides a plethora of links to various functional areas for configuration and administration of the farm, and SharePoint groups these links by functional area (also listed in the left navigation). Clicking on the heading name for any of these functional areas takes you to another sub-page with many more links to configure SharePoint in that functional category. The following sections describe the functional areas, at a high level, available in Central Administration. The majority of these functional areas will be covered in greater depth in later chapters.

Application Management

The Application Management section allows you to configure web applications, site collections, service applications, and content databases. In the section titled "Creating Your First Web Application," you will discover how to create a new web application, and in the section titled "Creating a Site Collection," you will create a new site collection. Figure 2-18 shows the Application Management operations.

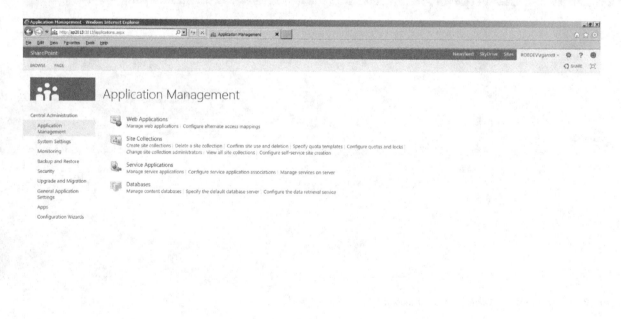

Figure 2-18. *Application Management in Central Administration*

A web application is a physical ASP.NET application that resides on disk within each WFE SharePoint server and registers within IIS to handle incoming requests on a given URL. Since a web application is an ASP.NET application, a web app has a web.config file that contains all application-relevant settings.

A site collection is the topmost content collection for sites in SharePoint. Sites, lists, documents, web parts, et al., must all belong to a site collection. SharePoint stores the site collection in a content database, and a web application renders a site collection on a URL. A site collection can only store in one content database, but a content database can store multiple site collections. A web application can render multiple site collections, if each site collection has a unique URL. A single web application renders a site collection, but multiple extended web applications may render the same site collection. (In SharePoint 2007, this was how you could achieve multiple authentication types for a given site collection. SharePoint 2010 and now 2013 provide Claims-Based-Authentication, avoiding the need for extended web applications.) Figure 2-19 shows the relationships between web applications, site collections, and content databases, at a high level.

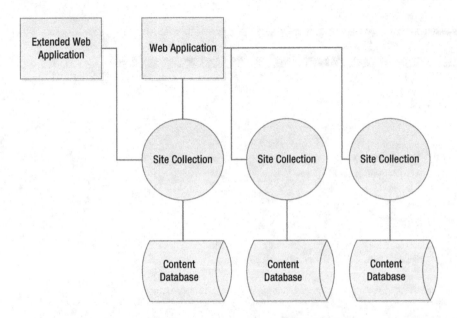

Figure 2-19. *Relationship between web applications, site collections, and content databases*

Anything and everything related to web applications is accessible via the Manage web applications link. I cover alternate access mappings in the section titled "Alternate Access Mappings," which deals with providing access to web applications on different URLs and mapping external URLs to internal URLs.

The Site Collections subsection within Application Management allows you to perform many operations. You may create and delete site collections, modify the settings of site collections (view all site collections), allow users to create their own site collections via self-service, impose quotas, and apply policy to site collections when dormant.

I provided an overview of Services and Service Applications in Chapter 1, as part of SharePoint Architecture. You can create new service applications, delete them, and configure existing service applications via the Manage service applications link. You may start and stop services on a given WFE/app server using the Manage services on server link.

The last subsection under Application Management deals with content databases. Content databases store (you guessed it): content from one or many site collections. You may create new content databases, delete them, or control storage limits for each content database (number of site collections, etc.) using the Manage content databases link. This subsection also allows you to specify the default SQL Server for content databases and configure retrieval protocols for access to the data, via the Configure data retrieval service link.

System Settings

The System Settings section contains settings for management of servers in the farm and services on a server, configuring outgoing and incoming e-mail, and managing farm settings for installed custom and third-party solution packages. Notice this Farm Management subsection also contains a link to configuring alternate access mappings, which is the same link as in the Application Management section. Figure 2-20 shows the System Settings in Central Administration.

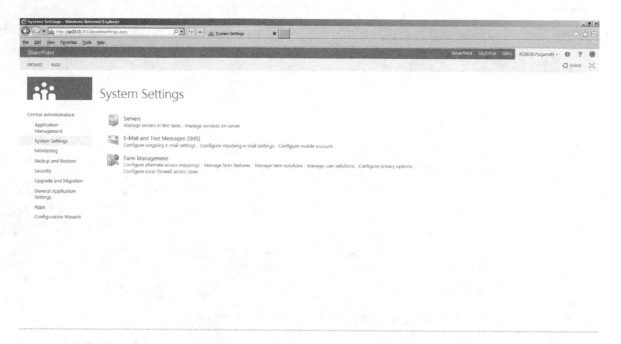

Figure 2-20. *System Settings in Central Administration*

Probably the most important link in this section, when setting up a new farm, is Configure outgoing e-mail settings, because SharePoint likes to use e-mail a lot for notifications.

Developers will likely frequent the Manage farm solutions and Manage user solutions settings. A farm solution consists of a WSP (SharePoint Solution Package) and might deploy DLLs to the GAC or web application BIN folder, or install files in the hive (c:\program files\common files\Microsoft Shared\Web Server Extensions\15). User solutions, on the other hand, may only install content to a site collection and not deploy any asset that may affect other site collections or web applications running in the farm. App model manifests can also deploy WSP files.

Features provide discrete functionality, such as a feature to install a list in a site collection, or a feature to add web.config settings to a web application. Features may have one of four scope levels: farm, web application, site, and web. The scope depends on the functionality that the feature provides. In the System Settings section of Central Administration you may activate and deactivate features at the farm scope.

Monitoring

The Monitoring section is very important for diagnosing problems in your farm. The Reporting subsection contains links to settings to configure administrative reports, diagnostic logging, health reports, and usage reports. Developers and administrators who install custom components that have failed are likely familiar with the diagnostic logging section, which allows you to throttle the severity of information, warning, and error messages reported in the ULS

(Unified Logging System) log. I shall cover logging in more depth in Chapter 5 when we discuss Monitoring, Health, and Disaster Recover. Figure 2-21 shows the Monitoring section in Central Administration.

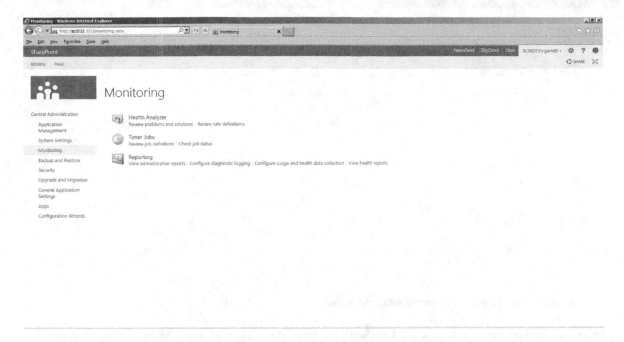

Figure 2-21. *Monitoring in Central Administration*

Timer jobs are an important part of SharePoint infrastructure. A centralized timer service (OWS Timer) runs on each SharePoint server and coordinates communication between different SharePoint servers, and also executes tasks at scheduled times. SharePoint maintains a number of scheduled tasks—jobs—to maintain the health of the farm and to background-task lengthy processes, which would otherwise delay users in real time. You may review scheduled timer jobs and change settings for jobs in the Timer Jobs subsection of Monitoring.

Backup and Restore

Backup and Restore is an important process in the operation of your farm. In the event of disaster, a previous backup and successful restore might be the difference between continued use of your farm with full data integrity and full/partial loss of services and data. I cover Backup and Restore in greater depth in Chapter 5. Figure 2-22 shows the Backup and Restore section in Central Administration.

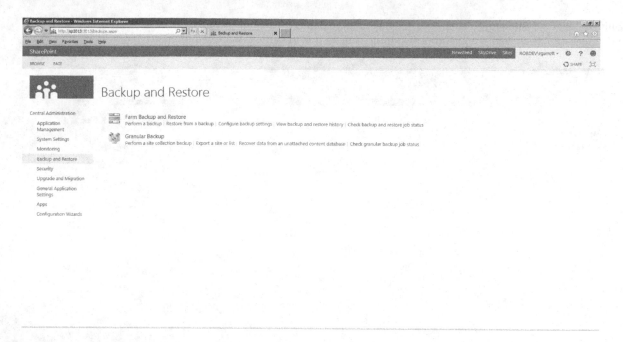

Figure 2-22. *Backup and Restore in Central Administration*

SharePoint backup comes in two flavors: farm and granular (and there is SQL backup for those diehard database admins). Farm backups allow you to select what parts of your farm you wish to back up and can consist of the entire farm or a particular service or content database. Granular backup is essentially site collection backup and export of sites and lists. SharePoint 2007 provided granular backups via STSADM; since SharePoint 2010, administrators can perform granular backups from this section of Central Administration. SharePoint 2013 provides "unattached database restore," which essentially means you can restore content to your farm if you have an offline database file; I discuss this method and other disaster recovery methods in Chapter 5.

Security

The Security section in Central Administration allows you to configure all aspects of security at the farm level. Typically, one of the most frequented settings in this section is the setting to manage the farm administrators group. A farm administrator is the highest level of security a user may obtain, and with this level of access, a user can perform all operations in the farm.

The setting to specify user policy for a web application allows you to grant or deny access (different permission levels) to users for a given web application. The same setting exists as an icon in the ribbon on the management page of a selected web application under Application Management.

User policy for a web application is ideal when granting user access without needing to add the user as a site collection administrator in all site collections under a web application. Figure 2-23 shows the Security section in Central Administration.

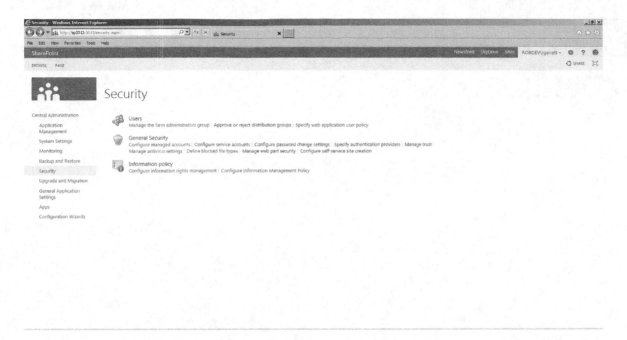

Figure 2-23. *Security in Central Administration*

General Security and Information Policy subsections provide you access to settings for Managed Accounts (see earlier in this chapter), managing trust, specifying authentication providers, anti-virus, web part security, and self-service site creation (same link as in Application Management). The setting to configure service accounts is worth an important mention because you may apply different service accounts to any or all of the service applications in your farm. When configuring your farm via the farm wizard, SharePoint uses the same service account for all services, which you might not desire if you want to secure service applications differently.

The settings in the subsection for Information Policy allow you to configure rights management with Active Directory or RIMS (Rights Information Management Service). The information management policies allow you to enable available policies throughout the farm, such as bar codes, retention, Office document labels, etc. I cover Information Management in greater depth in Chapter 11.

Upgrade and Migration

The Upgrade and Migration section has very few settings. This section allows you to upgrade the license type of the farm and take advantage of the enterprise features—you would provide an enterprise license key and enable the enterprise features if you had previously installed your farm with a standard license and wished to upgrade to the enterprise version.

This section also provides a link to determine the status of database attach upgrades from SharePoint 2010. I cover upgrading from SharePoint 2010 to SharePoint 2013 in greater depth in Chapter 4. Figure 2-24 shows the Upgrade and Migration section in Central Administration.

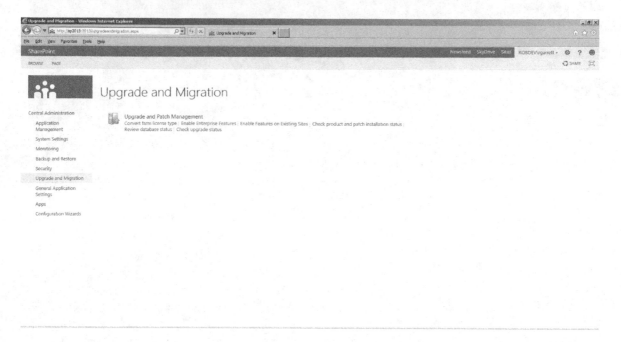

Figure 2-24. *Upgrade and Migration in Central Administration*

General Application Settings

The General Application Settings section provides configuration of InfoPath services, SharePoint Designer, Content Deployment, External Service Connections, and Search. Links to search administration and crawler impact rules are identical to those when managing the settings for a SharePoint Search Service Application in Application Management.

Microsoft introduced InfoPath services in SharePoint Server 2007 as an enterprise feature and allows SharePoint to host custom-developed InfoPath forms. InfoPath forms are Microsoft's answer to hosting dynamic forms, which business users otherwise would accomplish with third-party or custom-developed ASP.NET forms, PDF forms, or Word forms. Since SharePoint 2010, InfoPath fully integrates into the platform, rather than being an add-on service like that of SharePoint 2007. Using SharePoint Designer, developers can convert regular list edit forms into InfoPath forms for custom data input and form design for users. This subsection of the General Application Settings section allows you to upload form templates, for use across the farm, manage data connections—in the case where forms call out to SharePoint or external data sources to show data in forms—and configure InfoPath services to use web services. I cover more on InfoPath integration and InfoPath services in Chapter 14.

Figure 2-25 shows the section for General Application Settings in Central Administration.

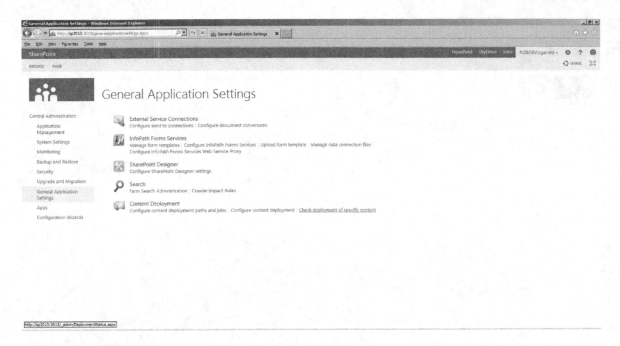

Figure 2-25. *General Application Settings in Central Administration*

Apps

The Apps section in Central Administration is new to SharePoint 2013. Microsoft has introduced the concept of the Apps, App Store, and Marketplace to Office and SharePoint. The idea is that developers will now develop small applications that integrate with any Office application and SharePoint, and authenticate users through a common OAUTH protocol.

This section in Central Administration provides configuration with a Microsoft App Store, integrated apps in the farm, and permission of apps. Monitoring of apps and configuration of app licenses is also possible from this section.

Figure 2-26 shows the Apps section in Central Administration.

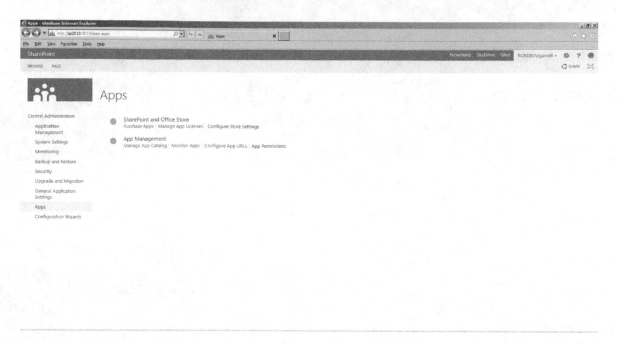

Figure 2-26. *Apps section in Central Administration*

■ **Note**   At the time of this writing, SharePoint 2013 is still in beta—notice the icons for the App settings are generic icons, used by Microsoft as placeholders in beta versions of SharePoint.

Other Noteworthy Areas of Central Administration

Before we move on to the next section in this document, I would like to highlight some other noteworthy areas in Central Administration that you should be aware but that do not warrant a section of their own in this chapter.

Navigation

SharePoint 2010 introduced the ribbon to users of SharePoint. Prior to SharePoint 2010, navigation consisted of page links, the site actions menu, and tabs. Introducing the ribbon into SharePoint followed Microsoft's strategy of enhancing navigation and control in Office applications. Anyone who has used SharePoint 2010 or Office 2010 applications is likely very familiar with how the ribbon works, with icons appearing on the ribbon bar, based on current context.

As you would expect, Microsoft continued the use of the ribbon in SharePoint 2013. Figure 2-27 shows an example of the ribbon in SharePoint 2013 within the Application Management section of Central Administration.

Figure 2-27. *The ribbon in SharePoint 2013*

A New Look

Since the release of Windows 8 tablets and upcoming release of Windows 8 for the desktop, Microsoft has adopted a new look for the development of the user interface in their applications. At present the name of this new look is being debated because Microsoft gave it the name "Metro," which has recently come under fire because of a copyright issue, so for now the new look goes by the name "Windows 8 UI."

The new look is crisp and clean. Personally, it took me a little while to get used to the plainness of the UI, but once I embraced the clean, no-cluttered, and rapid rendering user experience, I soon learned to appreciate it. SharePoint 2013 now includes the Windows 8 UI look. I shall not belabor this point, as you can see it for yourself by looking back at the various screenshots in this chapter and by installing SharePoint 2013 and immerse yourself in the experience.

Creating Your First Web Application

In Chapter 1, you read about SharePoint 2013 Architecture. As you have probably gathered, SharePoint maintains a collection of web applications, where each web application is synonymous with a typical ASP.NET application, hosted in IIS, complete with associated binaries and a location on disk under `c:\inetpub\wwwroot\WSS\VirtualDirectories\{Port}`. Think of a SharePoint web application as the bridge between incoming requests in IIS and dynamic content processing in SharePoint.

You may recall from an earlier section of this chapter that the Farm Configuration Wizard provisions a default SharePoint web application on port 80 (default HTTP web port). The wizard was helpful, but you are reading this book to know how to perform such operations yourself. Thus, this section demonstrates creating your first web application—manually. Like most configurations, you start from the home page of SharePoint 2013 Central Administration.

1. Click on the Manage Web Applications link.

2. The next page shows a list of already configured web applications, which includes Central Administration and possibly the My Sites host application.

3. Click the icon in the ribbon to create a new web application.

4. Next, SharePoint shows a dialog with a form for you to enter details about the new web application, as in Figure 2-28. Here we see a new feature, introduced in the previous version (SharePoint 2010), dialogs, reducing the amount of navigation between pages that users experienced in SharePoint 2007.

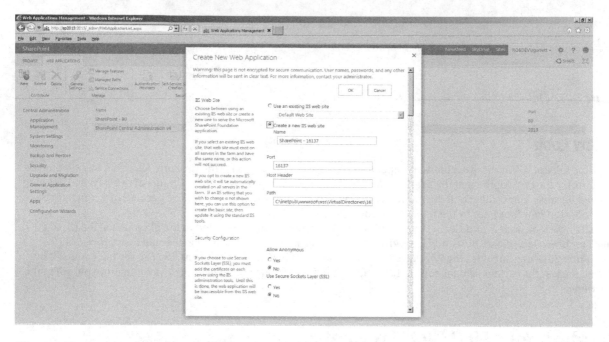

Figure 2-28. *Create a new web application*

5. Complete the details for IIS, the name of the web application, location on disk (I advise sticking with the default location), port number, and any host headers.

6. Configure anonymous access if you intend to expose your SharePoint sites to the Internet.

7. If you have preconfigured an SSL certificate for your web application and domain name, you may select to use SSL, otherwise leave this option set to: No.

8. If you plan to allow public access to your site, or parts of your site, click Yes to Allow Anonymous access (you will need to allow this in the site collection also).

9. SharePoint 2013 now insists on Claims-Based-Authentication for web applications, and no longer supports Classic Mode. Enable Windows Authentication and configure any ASP. NET membership providers and/or third-party trusted claims providers.

10. I recommend using the default sign-in page and changing this to a custom page later, once the application is up and running.

11. Leave the Public URL and Zone as default.

12. Create a new Application Pool, using an application pool managed account. If you have not defined an application pool managed account, you may do so by clicking the Register managed account link.

13. Provide the name of a new Content Database and database authentication as Windows.

14. Leave Failover database as empty (unless you have a failover in place).

15. Choose your service application group (or default if you have none defined).

16. Choose whether to enroll in the Customer Experience Improvement Program.

17. Click OK and wait a few seconds while SharePoint creates your new web application.

After SharePoint finishes creating the web application, you should see a page with a completion message, a link to create a site collection, and an OK button. Clicking OK will return you back to the manage web applications page in Central Administration.

Administering Your Web Application

Now that you have a new web application, you will most likely want to configure this application (if not now, later). In this section, I shall briefly show you some of the settings associated with your web application and how to configure your web application by changing these settings.

1. Open Central Administration.

2. Click Application Management.

3. Click the link to manage web applications.

4. Click one of the listed web applications—a good one to experiment with is the web app you just created in the previous section in this chapter, not the Central Administration app.

5. You should see the ribbon enabled, like that in Figure 2-29.

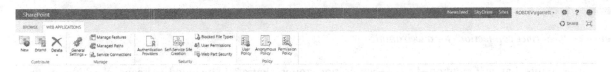

Figure 2-29. *Ribbon for managing a web application*

The tab section of the ribbon labeled "Contribute" provides operations to add a new web application (you read about this in the previous section), extend a web application, or delete a web application.

Extended web applications are similar to regular web applications except that they expose the same site collections as the parent web application. Think of an extended application as a mirror copy of the parent, only as far as IIS is concerned, the extended application has a separate location on disk, and separate entry in the web sites list of IIS. Why the need for such extended application? In the days of SharePoint 2007, the only possible way to configure multiple authentication types for a given web site was to host the web site (site collection) in different web applications, each with their own authentication settings in the web.config file. This approach had the drawback that each application must reside on a different domain or port. SharePoint 2010 introduced Claims-Based-Authentication (CBA) and the ability to federate authentication outside of SharePoint; thus you needed only one web application for multiple authentication types. Both SharePoint 2010 and now SharePoint 2013 provide extended web applications, because administrators still like to host separate applications in different zones with different authentication access. For example, a good practice is to extend an NTLM authenticated web application, hosting a public web site collection, and configure the extended app to disable all authentication methods. The administrator then exposes the extended application only outside the company firewall on a separate public IP address and domain name to that of the parent Windows authenticated site. This provides a layer of security—the internal employees can log into the site and make content changes (via the NTLM app), while anonymous users have no way to access secured areas of the web site.

The Manage tab allows you to configure general settings, managed paths, features, and service associations. Clicking the Service Connections link in this tab of the ribbon shows a dialog like in Figure 2-30.

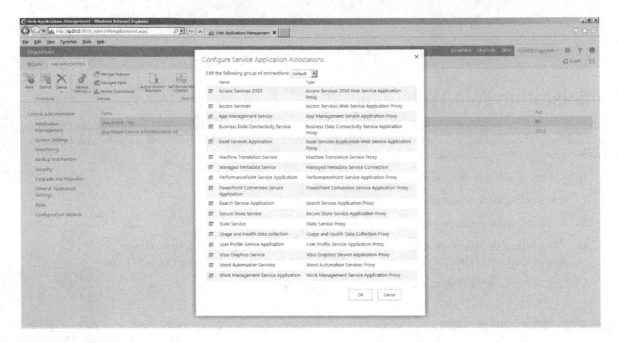

Figure 2-30. *Service connections for a web application*

Earlier in this chapter, I mentioned service application groups. Figure 2-14 included a screenshot asking you to choose the default service applications. These same service applications are those selected in the dialog in Figure 2-30. To change the service application associated with the current web application, change the group to another, or select Custom, and choose service applications from the list in the dialog. It is important to associate a web application with the correct service applications. For example, in a multi-tenant installation, where each client has a dedicated web application, you should associate each client web application with its own Search Service Application instance, so each client sees only search results for its sites, and not that of another client.

The General Settings icon in the Manage tab provides you access to general application settings, such as those listed in Figure 2-31.

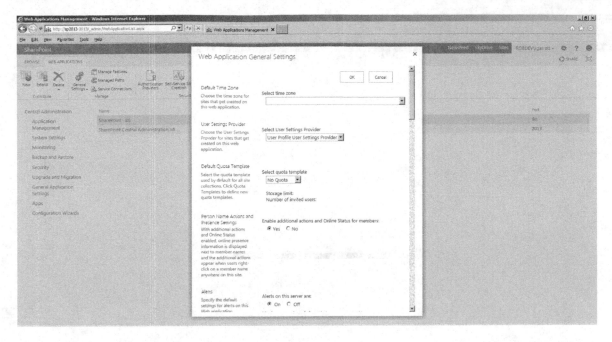

Figure 2-31. *General web application settings*

The security tab allows you to configure authentication providers, self-service sites, user permissions, web part permissions, etc. These settings are similar to those listed in the General Security section (under the main Security section) in Central Administration, only in this context they apply to the selected web application.

The last tab, labeled "Policy," allows you to apply user and anonymous permission policies to the selected web application. The permissions policy icon allows you to create a permission-set (permission level) to apply as policy to either users or anonymous users, using the other two icons in the tab.

Creating a Site Collection

With our web application created, it is now time to create a root site collection, so that we can host content and make use of our new web application as a SharePoint site. The following steps take you through the process of creating a new site collection for the web application created earlier:

1. Open Central Administration.

2. Click Application Management.

3. Click the Create Site Collection link.

4. Select the correct web application in the drop-down box at the top left of the page (Figure 2-32).

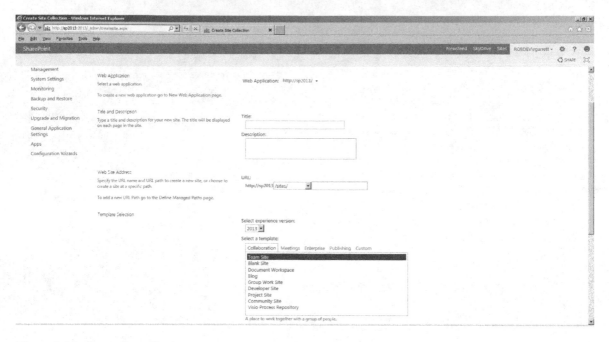

Figure 2-32. *Create site collection*

5. Give the site collection a name and description.

6. Choose the desired template. Various template types (site definitions) exist, each with its own set of features enabled and default sub-sites and lists. Choose Team as an example of an intranet collaboration work site.

7. Provide a DOMAIN\name username for the primary and secondary site collection administrators (you can add additional site collection administrators later) using the site collection administrator settings on the site collection.

8. Leave the quota option default.

9. Click OK to create the site collection.

SharePoint should complete the site collection provisioning process with a page containing the default link to the new site collection and a message indicating successful creation.

Alternate Access Mappings

Alternate access mappings allow mapping of multiple internal and public URLs to a given SharePoint web application. Think of them as a fancy way of informing SharePoint about requests on a given alternate URL domain.

For example, a company may access its intranet internally on http://intranet, but outside the organization, the same intranet is accessible at http://intranet.company.com. As far as SharePoint is concerned, requests coming in on either domain resolve to the same place. Without an alternate access mapping, SharePoint would resolve all URLs per the default application URL, which might be http://server-name:port. Even though IIS might have multiple host headers configured, and all requests reach SharePoint, without an AAM, SharePoint will convert all relative URLs to absolute with the internal application URL.

Typical uses of AAM include the creation of multiple public URLs to map to a single SharePoint application so that the application is accessible from different zones, each with its own different authentication scheme. The topic of AAM can get quite involved, so I have attempted to explain the configuration of AAM, at a high level, using the following scenarios.

Scenario 1: Extended Publishing Site

In this scenario, two web applications exist in SharePoint; the first is an internally based application on the URL `http://intranet`, which requires NTLM authentication for users on the internal network to access the company intranet. The site collection attached to the web application is a publishing site. The extended web application uses forms-based authentication with a SQL database as the user store and allows external users of the network to log into the company intranet across the Internet using the URL `http://intranet.company.com`.

Figure 2-33 shows the Alternate Access Mappings for the intranet application described in the scenario. Here we see two public URLs mapped to each internal URL. Depending on which URL a user contacts the site, SharePoint will infer absolute links to pages, documents, and other content on the site: `http://intranet/lists/mylist/blah.doc` or `http://intranet.company.com/list/mylist/blah.doc` as an example.

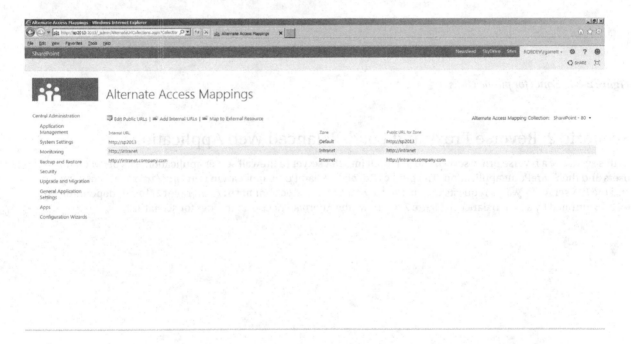

Figure 2-33. *Alternate Access Mappings for scenario 1*

Click Edit Public URLs to see the public URLs for a given application. Each public URL associated with a SharePoint application binds to one of five zones: Default, Intranet, Internet, Custom, or Extranet (shown in Figure 2-34). The names of these zones hold no functional meaning except to provide the administrator meaningful labels for each public access point to the web application.

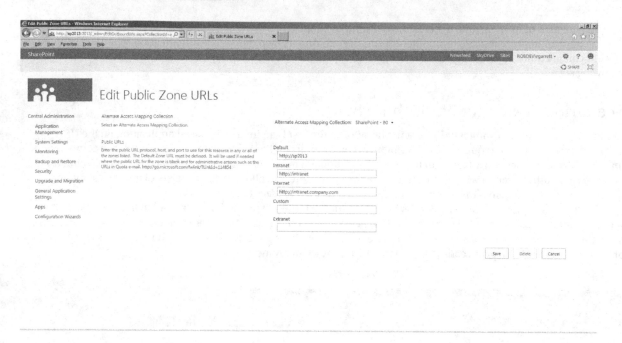

Figure 2-34. *Zones for public URLs*

Scenario 2: Reverse Proxy and Load-Balanced Web Application

In this scenario, a reverse proxy server, like that built into ISA server (a firewall server application) sits between the users and the SharePoint application. The public URL of the SharePoint application is `http://intranet.company.com`, and the ISA server forwards requests to either `http://intranet1.local` or `http://intranet2.local`, depending on load (controlled by a load balancer). Figure 2-35 shows the Alternate Access Mappings for scenario 2.

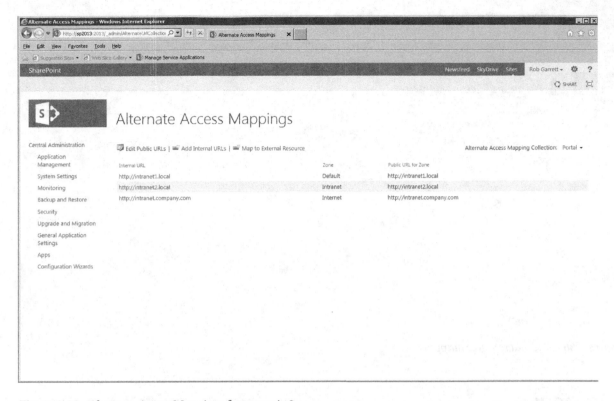

Figure 2-35. *Alternate Access Mappings for scenario 2*

Users access the site using the public URL http://intranet.company.com and the ISA server performs reverse proxy to authenticate the users before forwarding the request to SharePoint. Regardless of which load-balanced server ISA redirects the user, all links on returned pages start with http://intranet.company.com. This ensures that there are no broken links and that the user does not see links to an internal server application. To add additional internal URLs, click the link for adding internal URLs; in the resulting page, add the new internal URL and choose the zone to map to the public URL, in this case the intranet zone.

Mapping to an External Resource

Clicking the Map to External Resource link on the AAM page allows the administrator to map a URL, not hosted in SharePoint, to a web application. This feature is especially useful when configuring federated search to crawl an external resource. For example, let us assume that the administrator has configured search to crawl a separate HR site that is not in SharePoint—http://hrsite. This URL is not accessible to users coming into the SharePoint application on a public URL across the Internet but is available on http://hrsite.company.com.

In Figure 2-36, I created a new external resource called http://hrsite, by clicking the Map to External Resource link. I then clicked Edit Public URLs and added the URL http://hrsite.company.com to the intranet zone for the external resource I just created. SharePoint search will index the site http://hrsite, but the links in the search results show http://hrsite.compamy.com (you may need to provide a server name mapping in the search settings—see Chapter 15) if the user accessed the hosting SharePoint application from the Internet. This behavior is very much like that in scenario 1, but in this case, the resource is not a SharePoint application but an external HR site.

Figure 2-36. *External resource mapping*

Summary

This chapter covered installation of SharePoint 2013 from scratch on a new server infrastructure. We visited the infrastructure requirements, had a look at the SharePoint 2013 prerequisites installer, and walked though a server farm installation. I detailed Managed Accounts and which Active Directory Domain accounts Microsoft recommends for a best-practice setup of a SharePoint 2013 farm.

This chapter covered both the SharePoint Products Configuration Wizard, detailing the process of establishing a new SharePoint farm with SQL Server 2008 R2 SP1, and the SharePoint Farm Configuration Wizard in Central Administration, and we visited the various areas of the Central Administration web site.

This chapter is by no means exhaustive, and I could write many, many, more pages on the topic of installation and configuration alone. However, I wanted to provide you with a blend of useful insight on the installation and configuration process and the right amount of technical detail to enable you to stand up a typical SharePoint 2013 farm for development, QA, or production purposes.

CHAPTER 3

■ ■ ■

Working with PowerShell

Anyone familiar with SharePoint 2010 or Windows Server Administration is likely familiar with PowerShell—it is hard to escape it. Microsoft introduced PowerShell as a more advanced script language to replace legacy DOS batch files, which are clunky and difficult to work with. PowerShell includes a number of programming concepts that we are used to seeing in modern-day programming languages, like C# and VB.NET. Furthermore, Microsoft built PowerShell atop of the .NET platform, so scriptwriters can take advantage of the .NET Framework to manipulate objects, instead of strings.

SharePoint 2010 embraced PowerShell with Cmdlets (units of functionality accessible in PowerShell scripts) and allowed users to script SharePoint via the API. With the release of SharePoint 2013, PowerShell is now the accepted standard for configuring SharePoint, via script, as opposed to via the graphical user interface (GUI).

Windows 7 and Server 2008 R2 include PowerShell out of the box, which is good, because SharePoint 2013 requires, at a minimum, Windows Server 2008 R2. All the same, installing SharePoint 2013 gets you a PowerShell instance, called the SharePoint 2013 Management Shell. In this chapter, I shall introduce you to the basics of PowerShell. You will also learn how to write scripts that interface with your SharePoint 2013 farm.

Like many topics in SharePoint, PowerShell is a vast one, and many good books exist on the topic. I included this chapter on PowerShell so you may appreciate the script functionality available to you as a SharePoint administrator. This chapter focuses on the basics of PowerShell and specifics relating to SharePoint Administration. If you are familiar with PowerShell, feel free to skip some of the sections in this chapter, or the complete chapter.

What About STSADM?

The web user interface to SharePoint is powerful, but as good as Central Administration is you cannot escape the need to script commands in batch via a command line. SharePoint 2007 included a nifty command-line application, called STSADM. STSADM is a versatile and very powerful tool for administering SharePoint and operates, like many command-line tools, with string parameters and switches.

As SharePoint evolved, from the early beta version of MOSS 2007/WSS 3.0, through SharePoint 2010, and now SharePoint 2013, STSADM also evolved. The problem was that STSADM became bloated with many operations, and yet the tool remains limited by command-line string parameters. Microsoft released PowerShell so we could administer Windows, so it made sense to add support for PowerShell in SharePoint. STSADM still exists as a tool, and some SharePoint administrators will continue to use it until the tool is snatched from their tight clutches. However, Microsoft has deemed PowerShell the new standard for command-line interaction with SharePoint, and we can expect STSADM to depreciate over time.

Many of the operations you can perform in STSADM, you can also perform in PowerShell, but with better control, since PowerShell works with objects instead of string parameters. SharePoint 2013 includes the same operations via STSADM as it always has, but any new functionality is now part of PowerShell. Thus, STSADM commands are a subset of those available in PowerShell.

PowerShell Basics

If you have read the introduction in this chapter, I hope I have convinced you that PowerShell is the way forward for scripting command-line operations in SharePoint 2013. Without further delay, I will now dive into the basics of PowerShell. You begin by opening a PowerShell window.

1. Log in to your SharePoint Application server (the same server hosting SharePoint Central Administration).

2. Search for the application named SharePoint 2013 Management Shell and execute it.

3. You should see a new shell window, like that in Figure 3-1.

Figure 3-1. SharePoint 2013 Management Shell

That was easy! Opening a PowerShell window is as easy as opening a command prompt window. If you are familiar with the PowerShell window available via Windows, you might be tempted to use this entry into PowerShell, rather than the SharePoint Management Shell. If you take this route, I shall make you aware of the required plug-in to enable SharePoint Cmdlets.

Loading the SharePoint Cmdlets

Microsoft has provided a number of SharePoint-specific Cmdlets, so you can easily manipulate SharePoint objects (applications, site collections, sites, lists, etc.) via PowerShell. These Cmdlets are available to you via a DLL plug-in, which you must enable in a regular Windows PowerShell window. If you launch the SharePoint Management Shell, the shell preloads the SharePoint Cmdlets for you. Type the following commands into your PowerShell window to see if you have the SharePoint Cmdlets loaded:

```
Get-PSSnapin -Registered | Where-Object { $_.Name -eq "Microsoft.SharePoint.PowerShell" }
```

The preceding command executes a PowerShell Cmdlet to get all registered snap-in objects, which you then pipe to another built-in Cmdlet, called Where-Object, to filter the list to a specific snap-in for SharePoint. If the SharePoint snap-in is loaded, you should see details about the registered snap-in object. If the preceding command produces no output, you can register the snap-in with the following:

```
Add-PSSnapin "Microsoft.SharePoint.PowerShell"
```

After adding the snap-in, re-run the script to check for the registered snap-in, and you should see details of the snap-in.

■ **Note**   It is a good idea to use the SharePoint Management Shell for all SharePoint scripts, since all Cmdlets and functions run within the same thread. Scripts that run in the standard Windows PowerShell use separate threads for Cmdlets and functions, which can cause memory leaks when using SharePoint objects.

PowerShell Syntax

Once you start using PowerShell frequently, you will understand the terminology and syntax for PowerShell Cmdlets and script notation. PowerShell Cmdlets assume the syntax *verb-prefix noun*. The verb always indicates the action on the Cmdlet, and PowerShell supports the verb standards, listed in Table 3-1.

Table 3-1. *PowerShell Verbs*

Verb	Action
Add	Adds an object to a container or attaches an item to another item
Clear	Removes all objects from a container
Close	Changes the state of an object to closed
Copy	Copies an object from one container to another
Enter	Specifies an action that allows the user to enter a resource
Exit	Specifies an action that allows the user to exit out of a resource
Find	Looks for an object in a container
Format	Formats an object to a specific form or layout
Get	Retrieves a specific object; paired with the Set verb
Hide	Makes an object undetectable; paired with the Show verb
Join	Combines objects to one single object
Lock	Secures an object; paired with the Unlock verb
Move	Moves an object from one container to another
New	Creates a new object instance; the Set verb may often be used
Open	Opens an existing object
Pop	Removes an object from the top of a stack container
Push	Pushes an object to the top of a stack container
Redo	Resets an object to a state that was undone; pairs with the Undo verb
Remove	Removes an object from a container
Rename	Renames the name of an object
Reset	Sets an object to its default state

(continued)

Table 3-1. (*continued*)

Verb	Action
Search	Creates a reference to an object in a container; do not use Find or Locate verbs
Select	Locates an object in a container
Set	Creates an object that contains data, or replaces data on an object; paired with the Get verb
Show	Makes an object detectable; paired with the Hide verb
Skip	Bypasses an object in a sequence
Split	Separates parts of an object, such as a string
Step	Moves to the next object in a sequence
Switch	Specifies an action that alternates between two objects, such as to change between two locations, responsibilities, or states
Undo	Set an object to its previous state; paired with the Redo verb
Unlock	Releases a locked object; paired with the Lock verb
Watch	Continually monitors an object for changes

The prefix in a Cmdlet is usually a two-letter qualifier that identifies the technology; for example, PS identifies PowerShell, AD identifies Active Directory, and SP identifies SharePoint. Finally, the noun is the affected object or resource; for example, Get-SPSite calls the SharePoint Cmdlet to "get" a new SharePoint "site" object.

Exploring SharePoint Cmdlets

As I mentioned in the earlier sections, SharePoint provides a number of Cmdlets, enabling you to interface with SharePoint and configure your farm. What do you do if you want to see a list of these Cmdlets? In using STSADM, you could provide the –o parameter to see a list of operations. Fortunately, PowerShell has a nice built-in Cmdlet called Get-Command.

Executing the Get-Command Cmdlet with no parameters will list every single available Cmdlet in PowerShell—yes, all of them! Passing the –Noun parameter to the Get-Command Cmdlet allows you to filter the list by a given noun name. If you cast your memory back to the previous section, you may remember that I mentioned standard syntax includes a noun prefix to identify the technology. SharePoint prefixes all nouns with "SP," so you can easily get a list of all SharePoint Cmdlets as follows:

```
Get-Command –Noun SP*
```

The previous command uses a wildcard character, which tells the Get-Command Cmdlet to return any Cmdlets that start with "SP" and end with any other string of characters. There is still a large number of Cmdlets listed just for SharePoint operations; the following command tells us exactly how many (my install lists over 770):

```
(Get-Command –Noun SP*).Count
```

I think you need to narrow down the list; the Get-Command Cmdlet allows you to search for specific words in the noun. For example, if you wanted to list all the Cmdlets that deal with subsites (SPWeb) objects, you would use the following syntax:

```
Get-Command -Noun SPWeb
```

Figure 3-2 shows a much smaller (and manageable) list of Cmdlets. You can use the same trick to find all Cmdlets for site collection control—using the SPSite noun, rather than SPWeb.

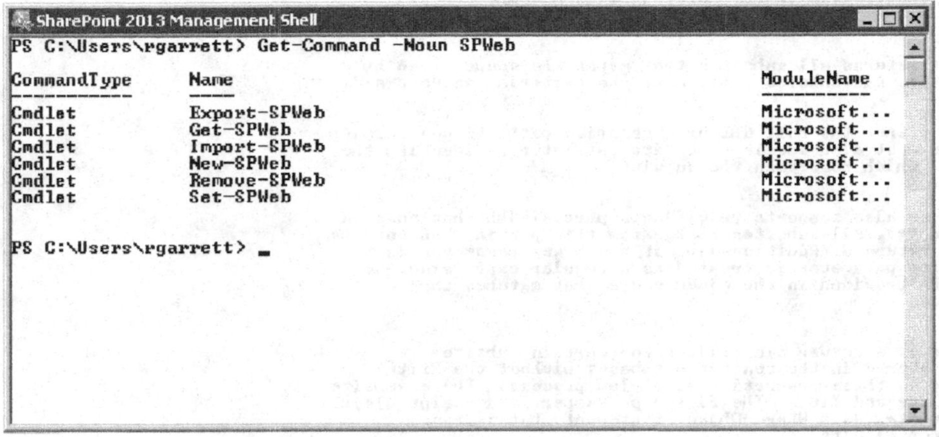

Figure 3-2. *SPWeb Cmdlets*

Getting Help

Getting a list of PowerShell Cmdlets is good, but knowing more about a specific Cmdlet is better. PowerShell includes another built-in Cmdlet to get help for a specific Cmdlet: Get-Help. The Get-Help Cmdlet provides details about Cmdlets, providers, aliases, functions, and scripts. The following line demonstrates how to execute the Get-Help Cmdlet to get help about the Get-SPWeb Cmdlet:

```
Get-Help Get-SPWeb
```

Figure 3-3 shows a screenshot of the Get-Help Cmdlet used with the Get-SPWeb Cmdlet as a parameter. As you can see, the Get-Help Cmdlet displays the name, a synopsis, syntax, and description of the Cmdlet passed as argument. The syntax information is probably most important because it details the various arguments for the Cmdlet.

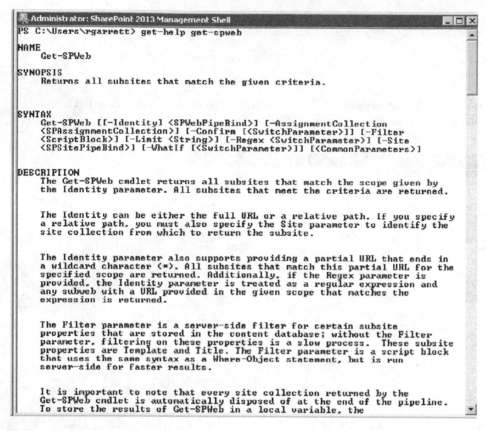

Figure 3-3. *Using Get-Help Cmdlet*

■ **Note** PowerShell incorporates auto-complete with the Tab key. Typing a '-', followed by Tab will cycle through the various arguments of a Cmdlet.

The Get-Help Cmdlet includes parameters to get information that is more detailed on a Cmdlet. Passing the –Examples parameter will return various examples to demonstrate the use of the Cmdlet. Passing the –Detailed parameter will give more detail beyond the basic information, and passing the –Full parameter will provide the complete help file for a Cmdlet. Try out the Get-Help Cmdlet on a number of well-known Cmdlets as well as some you have not encountered to get a good understanding of available help information.

The –Parameter argument is helpful in conjunction with the Get-Help Cmdlet because it provides details about a given parameter. Typically, when introduced to a new Cmdlet, you would use the Get-Help Cmdlet to get the syntax of available parameters and then provide the –Parameter argument to get details on a specific parameter for a Cmdlet. You can pass a * as the name to the –Parameter argument to get detailed information on all parameters supported by a Cmdlet.

Aliases

An alias is a shortcut for lengthy Cmdlets. For example, typing the lengthy Cmdlet named Get-SPBrowserCustomerExperienceImprovementProgram might get annoying quickly. By creating an alias for the

Cmdlet, you can then use the alias in place of the full-length Cmdlet. Of course, I deliberately chose a Cmdlet name that stood out as long, but the likelihood of needing to get the browser customer experience program too often is small. However, this example does demonstrate that some PowerShell Cmdlets can get quite long.

The following example demonstrates how to create an alias, called web, for the Get-SPWeb Cmdlet:

```
Set-Alias –Name web –Value Get-SPWeb
```

You can then get the alias value with the following line:

```
Get-Alias web
```

To use the alias, simply replace the full name of the Cmdlet with the alias, complete with required parameters, as follows:

```
web http://sp2013
```

■ **Note** Aliases exist only in the current PowerShell session. If you close and reopen the PowerShell window, any previous aliases are gone.

Pipelines

Pipelines, in my opinion, really set PowerShell apart from standard command-line operations in Windows. Pipelines allow passing of output information from one PowerShell script or Cmdlet to another. Earlier in the chapter, I mentioned that PowerShell deals with objects rather than strings, and this becomes apparent when using pipelines.

The following Cmdlet lists all SPList objects within the root web of a site collection:

```
(Get-SPSite http://sp2013).RootWeb.Lists
```

Looking at the preceding command, you see that I use parentheses around the Get-SPSite Cmdlet and then access the RootWeb property and Lists collection. This further illustrates the fact that PowerShell uses objects—the Get-SPSite Cmdlet returns a SPSite object, which has a property called RootWeb. Now, back to our discussion about pipelines.

If you execute the preceding command, you will get back pages of unhelpful information as PowerShell displays every SPList object returned from the Lists collection. By default, PowerShell displays all information about an object if you do not specify the property or method associated with the object.

The following modified example shows the same command piping the output to the ForEach Cmdlet. The ForEach Cmdlet iterates a collection and allows you to control fine-grained operation on each object in the collection.

```
(Get-SPSite http://sp2013).RootWeb.Lists | ForEach-Object { $_.Title }
```

The preceding command pipes the results to the ForEach Cmdlet, which iterates the collection and executes the commands in the curly braces. When working with Cmdlets that iterate over collections or filter collections, the special syntax $_ denotes the current object in the iteration. The preceding command outputs the title of each list in the collection.

PowerShell and SharePoint

In the previous section and subsections of this chapter, I introduced you to the beginning concepts in PowerShell. As mentioned in the introduction, whole books exist on the subject, and my goal was to get you started on PowerShell, such that you can administer SharePoint 2013. With the basics out of the way, I shall now dive into specifics about managing SharePoint via PowerShell.

If you followed the examples in the previous section about the `Get-Command` and used this Cmdlet to get a list of SharePoint Cmdlets, you will know that SharePoint 2013 has many, many, many Cmdlets. My goal in this chapter is not to bore you by reviewing every Cmdlet laboriously, but to cover the mainstream of Cmdlets required to perform typical administration of your SharePoint 2013 farm.

Administration Permissions

If you have used STSADM in any capacity, you might understand the frustration that comes from failure to execute operations because the current user does not have enough permissions in SharePoint content and configuration databases. The typical response from IT is to provide you the credentials of the SharePoint farm account and have you run the SharePoint Management Shell as the farm user—not ideal.

SharePoint requires the current user (running the PowerShell session) to be a member of the SharePoint Shell Access role, and be a member of the local Windows security group WSS_ADMIN_WPG. Assuming you have administrator rights on the SQL Server hosting SharePoint, and the local SharePoint server, you could assign users to the SQL role for a SharePoint database and assign the same users to the local security group via server management. However, this is a chapter on PowerShell, so you should learn how to accomplish the same result using the SharePoint Management Shell.

To grant administration rights for a user, you first have to possess administration rights—a chicken and egg situation. In all likelihood, because you are reading this book, you have already established farm administration rights and have SQL administration rights on the SQL Server. All the same, it is good to try out the following commands and assign an otherwise-non-admin user permissions to execute shell commands against SharePoint.

In this example, I am going to grant my user permissions on my default WSS content database, by providing the database parameter. If you do not include the database parameter in the following command, then SharePoint will assign the permission in the main SharePoint configuration database—this is fine if you plan to perform PowerShell commands that configure the farm. If you plan to use PowerShell to administer site collections, subsites, lists, etc. belonging to a specific content database, then I recommend using the database parameter with a specific content database.

```
$db = Get-SPContentDatabase -Identity WSS_Content
Add-SPShellAdmin -database $db -UserName ROBDEV\sp_admin
```

Follow up the preceding command with the following one to get a list of shell administrators for the default content database:

```
$db = Get-SPContentDatabase -Identity WSS_Content
Get-SPShellAdmin -database $db
```

It probably goes without saying (but I will say it regardless) that you can revoke shell administration rights with the following commands:

```
$db = Get-SPContentDatabase -Identity WSS_Content
Remove-SPShellAdmin -database $db -UserName ROBDEV\sp_admin
```

Content Databases

In the previous section, "Administration Permissions," I included the Cmdlet `Get-SPContentDatabase`. This Cmdlet is one of a small list that deals with content databases. A content database, as you may already know, stores all content for one or many site collections. The following command lists the content database Cmdlets, explained in Table 3-2. Of course, you can leverage the `Get-Help` Cmdlet to get more information on any of the listed Cmdlets.

```
Get-Command *SPContentDatabase*
```

Table 3-2. *Content Database Cmdlets*

Cmdlet	Description
Dismount-SPContentDatabase	Detaches a currently mounted content database from its associated web application—use this command if you are planning to take a content database out of service. The database remains attached to SQL Server.
Get-SPContentDatabase	Gets an instance of a content database; an example of this Cmdlet is in the previous section on administration permissions when you assigned shell permissions to a content database.
Mount-SPContentDatabase	Attaches an existing content database to an existing web application. If the content database requires upgrade to a newer version, SharePoint will perform the upgrade before mounting. I demonstrate use of this Cmdlet as part of SharePoint 2010 to 2013 upgrade in Chapter 4. SharePoint requires you to have attached the content database to SQL Server already.
New-SPContentDatabase	Creates a new content database and attaches it to a specified web application. This Cmdlet assumes you do not already have a content database by the designated name in SQL Server.
Remove-SPContentDatabase	Similar to the `Dismount-SPContentDatabase` Cmdlet, but this Cmdlet will detach the content database from SQL Server and delete it. *Do not use* this Cmdlet if you wish to retain the database (and data within) for later attach to another SharePoint farm.
Set-SPContentDatabase	Sets global properties of an existing content database, such as the maximum number of site collections, status, etc.
Test-SPContentDatabase	Tests a content database against an existing web application to verify that all customizations referenced within the content database also reside in the web application. You can issue this Cmdlet against a content database currently attached to the farm, or a content database not connected to the farm, and it is useful for testing SharePoint 2010 content database pre-upgrade.
Upgrade-SPContentDatabase	Initiates upgrade of an existing content database that otherwise failed to upgrade in a previous operation. This Cmdlet assumes the content database attached to SQL Server.

Of the Cmdlets listed in Table 3-2, the Cmdlet Mount-SPContentDatabase plays an important part in database-attach upgrades from SharePoint 2010 to SharePoint 2013. We use the Get-SPContentDatabase Cmdlet most often because it returns an object instance representing the content database, which we may then pass to other Cmdlets. This Cmdlet returns a SPContentDatabase object, which has many properties. To see a list of them, execute the following command:

```
Get-SPContentDatabase | Format-List *
```

The Format-List Cmdlet displays the properties of a piped object in list format (Figure 3-4).

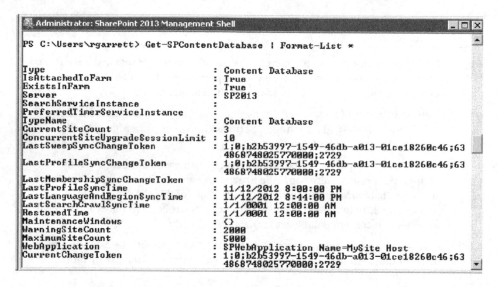

Figure 3-4. *List properties for the Get-SPContentDatabase Cmdlet*

The Get-SPContentDatabase Cmdlet lists all content database–associated web applications; using the -WebApplication parameter, provide the name of the web application.

```
Get-SPContentDatabase -WebApplication "SharePoint -80"
```

Every site collection resides in at least and no more than one content database, which you can establish using the -Site parameter, as follows:

```
Get-SPContentDatabase -Site "http://hostname/sitecollection"
```

Web Applications

PowerShell includes a selection of Cmdlets to manipulate web applications. A web application is the hosting application that resides in Internet Information Server and hosts one or many site collections. Execute the following PowerShell command to obtain a list of web application Cmdlets:

```
Get-Command -Noun SPWebApplication
```

Table 3-3 provides a description of each of the web application–related Cmdlets.

Table 3-3. *List of Web Application Cmdlets*

Cmdlet	Description
Convert-SPWebApplication	Converts the authentication mode of an existing web application from Classic to Claims-Based Authentication (CBA). SharePoint 2010 used to allow you to create Classic Mode web applications via Central Administration, and this Cmdlet provided conversion to CBA after creation. Since the default authentication mode in SharePoint 2013 is CBA, this Cmdlet comes into play only if you create a Classic Mode web application via PowerShell and then decide to convert to CBA later.
Get-SPWebApplication	Gets an instance of a SPWebApplication object. Pipe the result of this command to the Format-List Cmdlet to see the properties belonging to the object. Use this Cmdlet with other Cmdlets to make changes to or operate on an existing web application in your farm.
New-SPWebApplication	Creates a new web application in the farm. This Cmdlet takes a number of parameters, including the content database, application pool managed account, URL, port, etc. Cast back to Chapter 2 when I demonstrated creating a new web application via Central Administration—the dialog for creating a new web application contained many options, all of which are also available to this PowerShell Cmdlet.
Remove-SPWebApplication	Deletes an existing web application for all zones or a particular zone. Using this command preserves content databases and, depending on the –DeleteIISSite parameter, will delete the IIS site entry.
Set-SPWebApplication	Takes in a SPWebApplication object and allows you to set properties on the web application. This Cmdlet provides behavior in PowerShell similar to how you can edit an existing web application's settings via Central Administration.

Now that I have covered web applications in PowerShell, I shall examine site collections next, followed by sites and subsites.

Site Collections (SPSite)

A site collection represents the taxonomy of a web site, and hosts a hierarchy of sites. In Central Administration, you create, edit, and delete site collections under the Application Management section. Table 3-4 lists the available Cmdlets; you can see a list of these Cmdlets by executing the following command:

```
Get-Command –Noun SPSite
```

Table 3-4. *List of Site Collection Cmdlets*

Cmdlet	Description
Backup-SPSite	Performs a backup of a site collection to a file on disk. This Cmdlet locks the site collection while the backup process completes. The –UseSqlSnapshot parameter ensures integrity when backing up the site collection while allowing users to read and write to the active site collection.
Copy-SPSite	Copies a site collection to a new URL and content database. This Cmdlet assumes the ability to create SQL snapshots and effectively provides the same operation as using the Backup and Restore Cmdlets with SQL snapshot and content database parameters. When copying the site collection, the new site collection has a new unique identifier.

(continued)

Table 3-4. (*continued*)

Cmdlet	Description
Get-SPSite	Gets a new instance of a SPSite object from a provided URL.
Move-SPSite	Moves a site collection to a new URL and content database. During the move, SharePoint applies a no-access lock on the site collection so users cannot read or write to the site collection.
	Similar to the Copy Cmdlet, the new site collection has a new unique ID and resides in a new content database.
New-SPSite	Creates a new site collection. This Cmdlet accepts parameters for site owners, target URL, and template for the new site collection.
Remove-SPSite	Removes an existing site collection, including all contained sites and subsites.
Repair-SPSite	Performs a health check on the site collection and automatically repairs any encountered issues (when possible). Run the Test-SPSite Cmdlet to get a report on repairs required.
Restore-SPSite	Restores a site collection from a backup file on disk. This Cmdlet will not allow you to overwrite an existing site collection at the destination URL, unless you provide the –Force parameter.
	A content database may not host multiple site collections with the same unique identifier, which the backup operation preserves. Therefore, to restore a site collection to a different URL in the same farm as the backup, create a new content database and pass an object instance of this database to the Restore Cmdlet.
Set-SPSite	Provides ability to set property values on a provided SPSite object and the site collection. To obtain a list of available properties, use the Format-List * Cmdlet with the SPSite object.
Test-SPSite	Runs the same set of rules as the Repair-SPSite Cmdlet without repairs, and produces a report of issues.
Upgrade-SPSite	Performs an upgrade on site collection as either build-to-build (default) or version-to-version. Execute this Cmdlet after patching for build-to-build. When executing in version-to-version mode the Cmdlet performs a health check before performing an upgrade.

The more common of the SPSite Cmdlets are the Backup and Restore Cmdlets. As administrators, we are familiar with the STSADM backup and restore commands, which provide granular backup of complete site collections (often used when deploying a version of a web solution from development to staging and production). The new PowerShell Backup and Restore Cmdlets support the use of SQL snapshots, which ensures integrity of the backup, while allowing users to continue reading and writing to the active site collection. STSADM backup places a read-only lock on the site collection, prohibiting backup of a busy SharePoint site collection during business hours.

Sites (SPWeb)

Consider a modern intranet or public web site, which consists of multiple levels, accessible via navigation elements. A site represents a single level in a site hierarchy. In SharePoint, a single site contains document libraries, lists, and subsites. It does not matter if the site is a publishing site, team site, meeting site, etc. The site represents one node in the overall site taxonomy.

The SharePoint object model, and hence PowerShell, represents a site as a SPWeb object. Similar to other objects in PowerShell, you can get an idea of the number of properties associated with the SPWeb object by using the following command:

```
Get-SPWeb http://web-url | Format-List *
```

Table 3-5 lists the available Cmdlets, using the following command:

```
Get-Command –Noun SPWeb
```

Table 3-5. *List of Site Cmdlets*

Cmdlet	Description
Export-SPWeb	Exports a subsite hierarchy, starting at a particular site node in the site collection, to a file on disk (if using compression, or files in a directory otherwise).
	Unlike backing up a site collection, exporting a subsite hierarchy allows you to attach the sub-tree to another site collection or another subsite in a different location. Export assigns new IDs to objects.
	This Cmdlet provides export of the entire site (and subsites), or a single document library, or single list in the site.
Get-SPWeb	Returns a series of SPWeb objects representing sites that match the scope in the identity parameter –URL or site collection SPSite object.
Import-SPWeb	Imports a previously exported site hierarchy, list, or library to an existing site, whether the root site in the site collection or another subsite.
New-SPWeb	Creates a new subsite under an existing site, whether the parent is the root site in the collection or an existing subsite in the hierarchy. This Cmdlet expects the URL of the new site, which resides under an existing site in the site collection. You may provide a template for the new site or assume the default template associated with the site collection.
Remove-SPWeb	Removes a site from the site collection and any subsites belonging to the site specified. Deleting the root (top-level) site in a site collection causes deletion of the site collection, since every site collection must include at least one site.
Set-SPWeb	Provides ability to set the value of a property on an existing SPWeb object. Use the Format-List * Cmdlet to get a list of available properties.

Typically, the most common of the preceding SPWeb Cmdlets is the Get-SPWeb Cmdlet, with which you might perform multiple operations via different SP Cmdlets. The SPSite site collection maintains a list of all SPWeb objects available in the site collection, which you can iterate as follows:

```
(Get-SPSite http://sp2013).AllWebs | Foreach-Object { $_.Title }
```

The preceding command gets SPWeb objects via the AllWebs collection on the SPSite object returned by the Get-SPSite Cmdlet. In my example, I am simply displaying the title of each site in the site collection, but I could just as easily pass the SPWeb object to a Cmdlet that performs an operation on the SPWeb object.

Memory and Disposal

Developers of SharePoint applications understand the need for memory disposal practice. SharePoint objects, such as SPSite, SPWeb, etc., consume resources, and it is the developer's responsibility to release these resources by calling the Dispose method on these types of objects when done using them. Do you have to concern yourself with memory disposal when using these objects in PowerShell? Fortunately, PowerShell, in conjunction with the SharePoint object model, assists in the disposal of expensive SharePoint objects.

Earlier in this chapter, I mentioned using the SharePoint Management Shell, rather than the standard Windows PowerShell, because each command or single-line pipeline runs in a single thread. This is important when using objects like SPSite and SPWeb, because we often like to pipe these objects and Cmdlets that return these objects together, which would ordinarily leak memory in a multi-threaded Windows PowerShell window.

So, how does PowerShell manage memory disposal? I shall provide an example.

```
Get-SPWebApplication | Get-SPSite -limit all | Foreach-Object { $._Url }
```

The preceding command iterates over every site collection for every web application in the farm. For each site collection, the command displays the URL. The issue with this command is that the call to Get-SPSite for each web application uses space in memory for the new SPSite object. In a standard Windows PowerShell, not disposing of the SPSite object after each iteration would cause a memory leak. The SharePoint Management Shell caters to these scenarios and ensures disposal of all objects allocated in the preceding pipeline sequence.

Now, consider the following scenario, where SPSite and SPWeb objects are used over several lines of a PowerShell script:

```
$site = Get-SPSite "http://sp2013"
Foreach ($web in $site.AllWebs) {
    Write-Host $web.Title
}
```

The preceding script gets a new instance of a SPSite object for a site collection URL, then iterates every site in the site collection (represented by SPWeb objects) displaying the title. In this example, PowerShell cannot help you because it has no way of knowing whether to dispose of the SPSite object nor each SPWeb object in the iteration, since the operations span several lines in the script. In this case, disposal is the responsibility of the script developer.

As a rule, I like to dispose of all SharePoint objects that implement the IDisposable interface. The following modified script ensures disposal:

```
$site = Get-SPSite "http://sp2013"
try {
  Foreach ($web in $site.AllWebs) {
    try {
      Write-Host $web.Title
    } finally {
      $web.Dispose();
    }
  }
} finally {
  $site.Dispose();
}
```

Although the second version of the script ensures disposal of memory, the script is messy. Developers writing code in C# have a shortcut to clean up disposable objects with the *using* keyword. In PowerShell, we also have a shortcut, shown as follows:

```
Start-SPAssignment -Global
$site = Get-SPSite "http://sp2013"
Foreach ($web in $site.AllWebs) {
     Write-Host $web.Title
}
Stop-SPAssignment -Global
```

Wrapping our script between the Start-SPAssignment -Global and Stop-SPAssignment -Global statements ensures that PowerShell disposes of any object allocated and assigned to the global space. Objects in the global space are those that the script has not scoped to a particular named space. The following example shows the script using two scoped name spaces:

```
$siteScope = Start-SPAssignment
$site = Get-SPSite "http://sp2013"
for ($i=0;$i -lt $site.AllWebs.Count; $i++) {
  $webScope = Start-SPAssignment
  Write-Host $site.AllWebs[$i].Title
  Stop-SPAssignment $webScope
}
Stop-SPAssignment $siteScope
```

As you have discovered, memory management of SharePoint objects in PowerShell is important. If you are writing small scripts that have a short execution time—as in they complete within a few seconds—then memory-management is probably not one of your major concerns. However, if you have a script that iterates a large site collection and performs significant processing, then you can easily find yourself eating memory until your PowerShell instance crashes.

Before I conclude this section on memory and disposal, there is one more important point to be aware of—PowerShell does not clean up leaked objects at the end of scripts. In other words, if you have a leaky script, which you execute several times (perhaps because you are debugging), PowerShell is unable to claim the leaked memory until you terminate the PowerShell process. Again, this is not a big consideration if you are executing your scripts in a short window of time, but if you have a PowerShell script running for a lengthy duration, pay close attention to the amount of memory the PowerShell process consumes.

Summary

In this chapter, I introduced you to the basic concepts of PowerShell, including how to establish available Cmdlets, get help on Cmdlet syntax, and learn about pipelines. You then jumped into administration of your SharePoint 2013 farm with the common SharePoint objects: SPWebApplication, SPSite, and SPWeb.

Throughout this chapter, I provided examples on how to use some of the Cmdlets for manipulating site collections, sites, and web applications. You read about permissions required to execute PowerShell scripts against SharePoint. Finally, I provided you some best practices for memory disposal of expensive objects.

In Chapter 4, I will show you how to use some of your knowledge of PowerShell to perform an upgrade of content in a working SharePoint 2010 farm to a new empty instance of a SharePoint 2013 farm.

CHAPTER 4

■ ■ ■

Upgrading from SharePoint 2010

It seems like only yesterday that Microsoft released SharePoint 2010. But almost as soon as the previous book I authored, *Pro SharePoint 2010 Administration* (Apress 2011), hit the shelves, I was working on this book for the new version: SharePoint 2013. Many organizations are still using SharePoint 2010 because it remains a solid platform for information collaboration and sharing.

As with previous versions of SharePoint, Microsoft has addressed the need to upgrade from SharePoint 2010 to SharePoint 2013. Those who have traveled the upgrade path in the past for previous incarnations of SharePoint will likely have some concerns about the upgrade process, since upgrade of past versions of SharePoint were rife with problems. The good news is that Microsoft has addressed many of the upgrade ills of the past and you can now look forward to an upgrade process that takes you from SharePoint 2010 to SharePoint 2013 with less frustration.

In this chapter, I shall walk you through the planning exercise—because you should always plan your approach when upgrading SharePoint—the upgrade process itself, and considerations along the way, such as how to deal with customizations in your SharePoint farm. Without further delay, I will discuss the planning process.

Planning

Before entering into the process of a SharePoint upgrade, it is important to understand what is involved. If you are reading this chapter, then in all likelihood, you have a production version of SharePoint 2010, hosting data for users in your organization, and you have plans to upgrade your SharePoint farm to SharePoint 2013. Although Microsoft has made the upgrade process better (over time), there is still much to consider, which is why you need to plan.

Undoubtedly, upgrade of your SharePoint 2010 farm, which I will call the "legacy farm," will involve some downtime for users and at the very least impact users if the legacy farm is read-only for the duration of upgrade. The planning process takes into account impact on your data and users of your SharePoint farm, and if executed correctly, planning will provide data integrity and peace of mind that you are minimizing downtime and disruption to your users.

■ **Note**   Similar to previous upgrade versions, you can upgrade to SharePoint 2013 only from SharePoint 2010. There exists no direct upgrade path from earlier versions of SharePoint.

What Is New?

You might be familiar with the SharePoint upgrade process already. Perhaps you upgraded SharePoint 2007 to SharePoint 2010 and are now about to embark on a similar process for upgrade to SharePoint 2013. Do not worry if you are new to SharePoint upgrade. If you are staring at your SharePoint 2010 production farm and wondering where to start in upgrading to SharePoint 2013, this chapter applies to you as much as to a seasoned SharePoint administrator.

Those of you familiar with the upgrade process of SharePoint 2007 to SharePoint 2010 may remember the various flavors of upgrade: in-place, database attach, and hybrid. As the names suggest, in-place consisted of upgrading the legacy farm by installing the new version on top of the old. Database attach was, and remains today, the process of attaching legacy databases to a new SharePoint farm. The hybrid approach consisted of parts of both in-place and database attach methods to minimize downtime to users of the legacy farm.

SharePoint 2010 to 2013 upgrade does not support in-place upgrade. This makes a whole lot of sense because an in-place upgrade was volatile; if something went wrong in the upgrade process, then the legacy farm was lost! Those with virtual farms could roll back to an earlier snapshot, prior to upgrade, but that meant rolling back SQL and SharePoint servers, and this was often a thankless exercise. In-place upgrade allowed organizations with limited hardware to upgrade to the latest version of SharePoint, whereas database attach and hybrid required additional hardware. In my experience, most organizations took my recommendation for using the database attach route, so that they could maintain their legacy SharePoint farm in the event of upgrade failure.

■ **Note**   Microsoft no longer supports in-place upgrade from SharePoint 2010 to 2013.

SharePoint 2013 uses a similar service architecture to that of SharePoint 2010. This makes the process of upgrading some of the shared service applications easier. The upgrade process now supports database attach of some of the service applications. Table 4-1 shows the service applications in SharePoint 2010 that SharePoint 2013 will support as a database attach upgrade.

Table 4-1. *Services Supporting Database Attach Upgrade*

Service Application	Details
Business Data Connectivity	SharePoint 2013 Server and SharePoint 2013 Foundation support this service application.
Managed Metadata	SharePoint 2013 Server only supports this service application.
PerformancePoint	SharePoint 2013 Server only supports this service application.
Secure Store	SharePoint 2013 Server only supports this service application.
User Profile (Profile, Social, and Sync)	SharePoint 2013 Server only supports this service application.
Search Administration	SharePoint 2013 Server only supports this service application. SharePoint 2013 now includes what was previously called FAST—a complete Enterprise Search Platform—thus, SharePoint 2013 only supports upgrade of the Search Administration site. You must reconfigure your search topology anew in SharePoint 2013.

SharePoint 2010 required administrators to upgrade all site collections immediately as part of an in-place upgrade or either immediately or individually using PowerShell. SharePoint 2013 provides "deferred site collection upgrade" via site collection settings. This allows administrators of site collections to choose when they wish to upgrade from the legacy SharePoint 2010 user interface to the new SharePoint 2013 user interface. Because SharePoint 2013 supports side-by-side binaries, layouts, and control templates, administrators can continue to use the legacy look and feel while other site collection owners in the farm use the new SharePoint 2013 interface. Both reside on the new SharePoint 2013 platform. Additionally, site collection owners and administrators can request an "evaluation" site collection, so they can see what their content looks like in the new branding without losing their production site collection. The evaluation site is essentially referencing the site collection data from the legacy version but leveraging the new branding and binaries to host the content in SharePoint 2013 look and feel. I shall discuss evaluation site collections and deferred upgrade later in this chapter.

■ **Note**   Site collection owners and administrators can now defer upgrade of their site collection user interface to SharePoint 2013 look and feel.

The entire upgrade process now flows through the Health Checker. Similar to how the Health Checker service provides feedback to farm administrators on the health of and potential issues with the SharePoint farm, the Health Checker provides site collection owners and administrators with information on the health of their upgrade process. SharePoint 2013 also includes throttling to ensure that multiple requests for site collection owners and administrators do not take down a server or farm.

Database Attach Process

Figure 4-1 shows a high-level view of the database attach upgrade process. The process consists of five main parts, described as follows:

1. Database attach requires a working SharePoint 2013 farm, ready for you to attach legacy databases from a SharePoint 2010 farm.

2. You copy databases from the legacy farm to your new SharePoint 2013 farm database server. This process typically involves using backups or detaching the databases from the legacy farm first (which incurs downtime).

3. First, you upgrade service applications in the new SharePoint 2013 farm by attaching service application databases. See earlier in this chapter, and Table 4-1, for a list of applicable services you may upgrade.

4. Next, you upgrade content databases in the new SharePoint 2013 farm.

5. Finally, site collection owners and administrators may decide when to upgrade their site collections to the new user interface and branding (this replaces the visual upgrade process in SharePoint 2010).

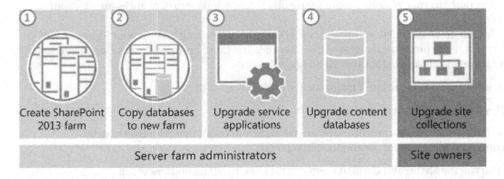

Figure 4-1. The SharePoint 2013 Upgrade Process

In Chapter 2, I detailed the process for installing and configuring a new SharePoint 2013 farm. This described process begins the upgrade process, as shown in Figure 4-1. There are some slight differences in the configuration of the new SharePoint 2013 farm. If you are upgrading service applications (described in Table 4-1), you have no need to provision these services in the new farm. The farm wizard normally creates new web applications and service application databases for each desired service application, so you should not run the configuration wizard after provisioning a new SharePoint 2013 farm instance. Instead, you will create new application instances for each service application and attach the legacy service database. I cover the upgrade process in detail later in this chapter.

Minimizing Downtime

When upgrading an existing SharePoint 2010 system, minimizing downtime and maintaining data integrity are very important. You might not impress users of your current legacy system if the SharePoint site goes down. Furthermore, an offline SharePoint system, used for business, could cost your organization serious revenue if offline for a long length of time. Fortunately, SharePoint provides capability to allow you to maintain your legacy system online while you work on the upgrade to SharePoint 2013 in parallel.

Setting the legacy SharePoint content and system databases to read-only allows users continuous use of your legacy system as a read-only resource. SharePoint 2010 is smart enough not to throw errors when encountering read-only SQL databases, and instead allows a read-only view of the data. This means users can continue to read documents and information in the legacy site and continue business as long as they do not need to write data back to SharePoint. Read-only use of data in the legacy system also ensures that users do not update data, which would render any copy in use for upgrade stale.

Setting SharePoint as read-only only buys you a small amount of time (relative to the size of your legacy system and number of users accessing it). You might have some angry users knocking on your door if you leave the legacy site read-only for a number of days without providing a new system to store new content. What you need is a fast way to upgrade content in the new SharePoint 2013 system.

SharePoint 2013 supports parallel upgrade of service application and content databases. Since the new farm is not yet operational, there is no real downside to pushing the resource limits of the system with parallel upgrades, if doing so allows a faster upgrade path. Since SharePoint 2013 also supports deferred site collection upgrade and side-by-side customizations (with side-by-side 14 and 15 hive directories), you can roll out the new SharePoint 2013 farm as soon as you have completed content and service application upgrades. The idea is to move users over to using the new SharePoint 2013 platform as quickly as possible, without causing discomfort to your users with a new user interface and changes in customizations.

I shall demonstrate read-only databases and parallel upgrade in the section on upgrading, later in this chapter.

Pre-Upgrade Maintenance

Generally, SharePoint upgrades go much smoother when sourced from a well-maintained legacy SharePoint farm. If your legacy farm is several versions behind on service packs and fixes, your legacy farm reports critical issues in your health monitoring service, or perhaps your Windows event log reports some serious errors, chances are that your upgrade will not go well.

As part of any upgrade plan, it is essential that you take care of some housekeeping tasks in your legacy system first. I mentioned a few of them in the previous paragraph. The following lists those I previously mentioned and some more maintenance tasks for you to consider before starting an upgrade:

- Patch all SharePoint servers to the latest major service pack.

- Patch all SQL servers to the latest major service pack.

- Consider patching to the latest Cumulative Update (taking into account that Microsoft usually does not recommend these updates on production servers).

- Ensure that you run the SharePoint Configuration Wizard after installing updates on all servers.

- Check the SharePoint version number of each server in your farm to ensure that each server is fully patched. I have witnessed a number of upgrades go wrong because one server was not at the same patch level as other servers in the farm.

- Review all Windows event log errors and warnings and fix as many of these as possible.

- Take care of any critical errors reported in the Health Monitor service (Health Checker).

- Delete any unused subsites and site collections. You can obtain a report containing last accessed date of sites—consult with your users on whether a site is no longer required.

- Carefully review large lists (containing more than 2000 items). SharePoint 2010 supports large lists, as does SharePoint 2013. However, large lists can make the upgrade process more complex and so consider the implications of their upgrade in the overall process.

- Review the size of your content databases. Typically, a database of 10GB will upgrade quicker than a database of 1TB. Plan for upgrade of large databases by avoiding parallel upgrades, since parallel upgrading of large databases might overtax your new SharePoint 2013 farm.

- Consider splitting multiple site collections in large databases to smaller and more manageable databases.

- Look for wide-lists—lists with a large number of columns and metadata. You can use the PowerShell Cmdlet `Test-SPContentDatabase` to search for wide-lists.

- Consider reducing the number of document versions maintained in document libraries, as these can significantly increase the time it takes to complete an upgrade. Use PowerShell and code against the SharePoint API to reduce stored versions.

- Uninstall any unused customizations as customizations can add complexity to the upgrade process (more on customization in the next subsection of this chapter).

- Remove any PowerPoint broadcast sites because SharePoint 2013 does not support these site templates. The new Office Web Apps server provides PowerPoint broadcast support.

- Remove any FAST Search Center sites because these sites do not upgrade in SharePoint 2013. SharePoint 2013 supports standard Enterprise Search Administration upgrade. If you use FAST in SharePoint 2010 you must provision a new SharePoint 2013 Enterprise Search Application.

- Make sure that all site collections and sites use the SharePoint 2010 experience, which you can check using the PowerShell Cmdlet:

```
Get-SPSite | ForEach-Object{$_.GetVisualReport()}
```

- Ensure that you repair any issues in content databases, prior to upgrade, using STSADM to check for corruption.

- Check for any issues with Variation Publishing sites (multilingual sites).

Managing Customizations

Although not unheard of, seldom have I seen a SharePoint system without any customization. Customization of a SharePoint farm, site collection, or subsite may consist of the installation of a third-party module, in-house developed components, and/or branding. Since SharePoint builds on top of ASP.NET, and Microsoft promotes extending SharePoint capabilities with an extensive API, any manner of customizations can be conceived of in a SharePoint 2010 farm, prior to upgrade.

If something is to go wrong with an upgrade, the first place I usually look (having combed the log files) is at any customizations. Even when an upgrade appears to complete without issue, I am expecting something in the new SharePoint 2013 farm to fail if the legacy farm included customizations. If you think about it, this is inevitable: Microsoft cannot account for every possible scenario in the development of the upgrade process and can really account only for situations occurring from its own technology. So, if a third party extends SharePoint (especially if it does not maintain Microsoft SharePoint development guidelines), it is entirely possible that a third-party customization will break the upgrade process. This is not to say you should avoid installing third-party SharePoint components, or shy away from SharePoint custom development; the key is isolating these customizations during the upgrade process.

The first task in managing customizations is to itemize them. If you have only ever installed customizations using SharePoint deployment packages (Microsoft best practice), then you are in a good place. However, if your SharePoint site has evolved over time with various manual edits to files in the hive (the file location where SharePoint maintains static files), manual changes to configuration files, and manual placement of custom assemblies in the GAC or web application, then you have a greater task to manage.

SharePoint 2007 to 2010 upgrade used to include a pre-upgrade check tool, which would list all potential issues prior to an upgrade. This tool included a report of all installed features and customizations in the farm. Microsoft has since retired this tool. Although the process of identifying customizations is not as straightforward as with the pre-upgrade checker, the good news is that SharePoint 2013 supports parallel hives, so you can maintain your customizations in a "14" hive directory structure without breaking your customizations.

■ **Note**   SharePoint 2013 no longer supports the pre-upgrade checker.

I recommend that you upgrade all customizations to SharePoint 2013, which might involve installing the latest version of a third-party product, or may involve some in-house development of custom components. However, this process need not hold up the upgrade process and prevent users using the post-upgraded site on the new platform while your development team undertakes this effort.

Once you have itemized your customizations, you should next evaluate the impact of each customization on the upgrade. Customizations typically fall into one of three categories, as described in Table 4-2.

Table 4-2. *Customization Categories*

Category of Customization	Types of Customization	Potential Effects on Upgrade
Visual	Master pages Themes Custom controls Web pages Web Parts Custom JavaScript Custom CSS files	No impact on database attach upgrades; should work in SharePoint 2010 user interface mode; likely requires change to work in SharePoint 2013 user interface
Data Structure	Content types List types Web templates Site definitions	May affect database upgrade if content or list types conflict with new SharePoint 2013 list or content types; missing list definitions or templates may also cause the upgrade to fail
Non-Visual	Web services Windows services HTTP handlers HTTP modules Custom classes	Might not work with SharePoint 2013; test thoroughly in the new platform and consider updating to a new version (third-party) or developing against the latest version of SharePoint 2013 API (in-house development)

After evaluating every customization and assessing the impact of the customization on the upgrade to the new SharePoint system, you can decide the outcome of each customization as follows:

- *Keep the customization but do not upgrade site collections*—In cases where a customization depends on the SharePoint 2010 platform, e.g., a particular branding married to the SharePoint 2010 branding style, you can continue to use the customization in the legacy visual mode. Users are unable to use some of the newer features of SharePoint 2013 (especially some of the visual capabilities) until you convert the customization to use SharePoint 2013.

- *Replace the customization*—Perhaps you are taking this upgrade opportunity to redesign your site or redevelop existing customizations. In this case, redeveloping customizations or deploying the latest SharePoint 2013–supported version of a third-party component will allow your users to take full advantage of the SharePoint 2013 capabilities.

- *Discard the customization*—Sometimes a customization is no longer relevant. Perhaps SharePoint 2013 now provides capabilities that SharePoint 2010 lacked and the customization fulfilled. Perhaps the upgrade is part of a larger strategy to redesign and there is no place for a particular customization. In these cases, retire the customization from service and remove references of the customizations prior to upgrade (as part of pre-maintenance). The extent of the customization in the database (e.g., a content type) will determine how easy it is to remove the customization prior to upgrade, and therefore determine if you should remove the customization from a production copy of your SharePoint 2010 farm, rather than production itself—I never said dealing with customizations is easy.

Different types of customization require different consideration in their upgrade to work in SharePoint 2013. Let me assume you have a customization that you intend to upgrade to SharePoint 2013 and fully integrate into the new visual style of SharePoint 2013. The implementation type of the customization will determine the best course of action to upgrade, as shown in Table 4-3.

Table 4-3. Customization Types and Upgrade Approach

Customization	Upgrade Approach
Site definition	Apply the main components of your site definition to an existing definition in SharePoint 2013—apply features, files, etc. In cases where you no longer wish to create new sites based on the custom site definition in SharePoint 2013, you can move over the custom site definition as is and run legacy sites in SharePoint 2010 mode.
Feature	Evaluate your feature and redesign as necessary. The feature-packaging model in SharePoint 2013 is identical to that of SharePoint 2010—it is the capabilities contained in the feature itself that usually require redevelopment.
Workflow and server controls	Upgrade of workflow and server components depends on the implementation and typically aligns closely to a business need. Consult the users of said workflow or component to determine the need of such functionality in the new SharePoint 2013 system.
Event handler	Event handlers should continue to operate in SharePoint 2013 after upgrading content. However, any API calls that event handlers make, or assumptions about the environment, may affect the continual successful operation of these event handlers.
Themes	You should re-create themes, based on best practices for creating themes for SharePoint 2013.
Master pages and CSS files	Rework visual customizations into SharePoint 2013 master pages and CSS files so your brand works with the latest SharePoint 2013 user interface.
JavaScript	Validate that your JavaScript works with the new SharePoint 2013 page mode, and redevelop as appropriate.
Web Parts	Similar to event handlers, Web Parts may make API calls, which require changes to support SharePoint 2013 API. Additionally, visual Web Parts should comply with XHTML and support the user interface of SharePoint 2013 if not operating in legacy SharePoint 2010 compatibility mode.

(continued)

Table 4-3. (*continued*)

Customization	Upgrade Approach
Services	Services should remain unaffected by an upgrade to SharePoint 2013, if you host the service outside of SharePoint. Services hosted inside SharePoint infrastructure follow the same rules as any other code customization that leverages the SharePoint API and should adhere to the new version of API.
Authentication providers	SharePoint 2013 implements Claims-Based-Authentication (CBA), which Microsoft introduced in SharePoint 2010. SharePoint 2013 has dropped support for Classic Mode Authentication, so you should redevelop any custom authentication provider that supported Classic Mode and not CBA. Redeploy and provide to the new SharePoint 2013 farm as part of the upgrade process.
Custom search solutions using SQL syntax	SharePoint now uses FQL (FAST Query Language) and KQL (Keyword Query Language) instead of SQL-based search query. Redevelop any component that uses the legacy SQL syntax.

Having itemized, evaluated, and reworked (when necessary) your customizations, the final step is to determine the packaging type of your customization. Table 4-4 details the various packaging and deployment types for customizations to a SharePoint farm.

Table 4-4. *Packing Consideration of Customizations*

Package Type	Details
MSI files	Vendors sometimes like to package their customizations into MSI files. In this situation, contact the vendor for the latest version of the package with customizations that support SharePoint 2013.
Manually deployed–dropped files on the server	As with the previous version, you can deploy these customizations the same way in SharePoint 2013. As a best practice, I recommend that you use this opportunity to package all manual configurations into SharePoint solution packages and features for easy deployment and retraction.
Sandbox solutions	Sandbox solutions (user solutions) deploy to a site collection and live in the content database. These solutions operate within a restricted environment, which SharePoint 2013 supports. You need not make any changes to these types of deployed customizations, since they upgrade with the content database.
Solution packages (WSP)	Solution packages are the Microsoft-recommended way to deploy customizations. Redeploy these solution packages to the new farm and validate correct operation of your customizations in the new SharePoint 2013 farm.
Administrator-deployed form templates	These templates live in the SharePoint farm and therefore do not upgrade as part of service application and content database upgrade. Extract these form templates as XSN files and redeploy them to the new SharePoint 2013 farm.

Upgrade

Now that you have completed the planning stage for your SharePoint 2010 to SharePoint 2013 upgrade, it is time to get down to the business of the actual upgrade.

The journey to upgrade SharePoint is seldom uneventful. In my experience, no two SharePoint system upgrades are the same. Therefore, I strongly recommend that you execute a few test upgrade runs before rolling out a final upgrade of SharePoint 2010 to 2013 to production. The theory is that you can perform as many test upgrades as you need to feel comfortable that you may predict the outcome of the final production upgrade—the upgrade, which typically occurs over a weekend or late night outside core business hours. The beauty of database attach upgrades is that you can perform them over and over again on test SharePoint 2013 farms without ever affecting users of your current production legacy farm.

■ **Note**   Perform a number of test upgrades before settling on the final upgrade for production.

In the following subsections of this chapter, I shall walk you through the process of upgrading a SharePoint 2010 farm to an already provisioned SharePoint 2013 farm. If you are unsure how to stand up a new SharePoint 2013 farm, flip back to Chapter 2, where I detail the installation and configuration steps.

Before diving into the upgrade process, I shall discuss version compatibility first. Similar to SharePoint 2013, SharePoint 2010 shipped in various editions. Editions of SharePoint 2010 must match editions of SharePoint 2013 for a successful upgrade. Table 4-5 lists the various product editions of SharePoint before upgrade with those editions supported and unsupported post upgrade.

Table 4-5. *Upgrade Edition Compatibility*

Pre-Upgrade SharePoint	Supported SharePoint 2013	Unsupported SharePoint 2013
SharePoint Foundation 2010	SharePoint Foundation 2013	
	SharePoint Server 2013	
SharePoint Foundation 2013	SharePoint Server 2013	
SharePoint Server 2010	SharePoint Server 2013	SharePoint Foundation 2013
SharePoint Server 2013	SharePoint Server 2013	SharePoint Foundation 2013
Search Server 2010	SharePoint Server 2013	SharePoint Foundation 2013
	Search Server 2013	
Project Server 2010 with SharePoint Server 2010, Enterprise Edition	Project Server 2013 with SharePoint 2013, Enterprise Edition	SharePoint Foundation 2013

Looking at Table 4-5 it is easy to see that Foundation editions of SharePoint upgrade to SharePoint Server 2013. Foundation 2010 also upgrades to the newer Foundation 2013. However, downgrading from SharePoint Server to a Foundation version of SharePoint 2013 is unsupported.

Additionally, the license version of SharePoint plays a part in the upgrade to SharePoint 2013. Table 4-6 shows the license compatibility matrix when upgrading to SharePoint 2013.

Table 4-6. *License Compatibility for SharePoint 2013 Upgrade*

Starting Edition	Supported SharePoint 2013 Edition	Unsupported SharePoint 2013 Edition
SharePoint Server 2010, Standard Edition	SharePoint 2013, Standard Edition	SharePoint Server 2013, Enterprise Edition—you can convert to Enterprise after upgrade
SharePoint Server 2010, Enterprise Edition	SharePoint Server 2013, Enterprise Edition	SharePoint Server 2013, Standard Edition
SharePoint Server 2010, Trial Edition	SharePoint Server 2013, Trial Edition	SharePoint Server 2013, Full Product Edition— you can convert to the full product version after upgrade

It might appear obvious that you cannot downgrade the license version of SharePoint as part of the upgrade to SharePoint 2013 process. I have seen cases where an organization wishes to drop its Enterprise License to Standard and expects to perform this operation as part of the upgrade. Furthermore, the same is true for the opposite direction—if you plan to upgrade to SharePoint Server 2013 Enterprise, install the Enterprise License after the product upgrade.

Copying Legacy Databases

At this stage, I shall assume that you have a working SharePoint 2010 farm and a new installation of SharePoint 2013 on different hardware (virtual or physical). In this section, I shall demonstrate the process of setting the legacy databases to read-only, backing them up, and copying them to the new SharePoint 2013 farm—ready for upgrade.

For my examples, I have a working SharePoint 2010 farm with the following configuration:

- Two web applications, one on port 80 and another on port 5000

- A team site collection at the root of the port 80 application—"The Intranet"

- A publishing site collection at the root of the port 5000 application—"The Web Site"

- The publishing site collection contains custom branding

- The team site includes an external content type to a SQL Adventure Works database

- The team site includes an external list based on the external content type

- The farm includes a Managed Metadata Store with a default group, term set, and terms, associated with both applications

- I configured a search service for each of the Intranet and Web Site applications

- I configured the User Profile Service and associated it with the Intranet application

Figure 4-2 shows a screenshot of an example publishing site with some branding (thanks to Andrew Connell and Andy Drisgill). This site includes a custom master page, custom page layout, some custom CSS, and image files.

Figure 4-2. *Sample publishing site with branding*

Figure 4-3 shows a screenshot from SQL Management Studio for my SharePoint 2010 farm. I created the databases with prefix ROBDEMO with script when I established my farm, and the Search Service Application databases via Central Administration for the purpose of this demonstration.

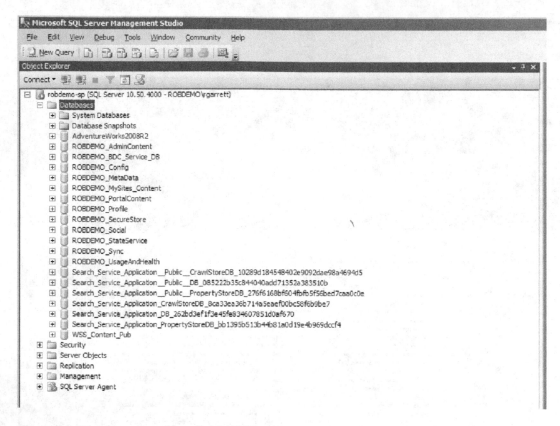

Figure 4-3. *Databases in my SharePoint 2010 farm*

Recall, from earlier in the chapter, that SharePoint 2013 supports some service application upgrades via database attach. You can upgrade the business data, managed metadata, and search administration, as well as your content databases. Using SQL Management Studio, I shall set each of the following databases (listed previously in Figure 4-3) to read-only and then create a backup of each:

- ROBDEMO_BDC_SERVICE_DB

- ROBDEMO_METADATA

- ROBDEMO_PROFILE

- ROBDEMO_SOCIAL

- ROBDEMO_SYNC

- ROBDEMO_SECURESTORE

- SEARCH_SERVICE_APPLICATION__PUBLIC__DB_*GUID*

- SEARCH_SERVICE_APPLICATION_DB_*GUID*

- ROBDEMO_PORTALCONTENT

- ROBDEMO_MYSITES_CONTENT

- WSS_CONTENT_PUB

- ADVENTUREWORKS2003R2

This list includes databases for the content of my Intranet and public Web Site, My Sites content, the BDC database, managed metadata database, User Profile Service databases, and the administration sites for search. Notice that I did not back up the other search databases because SharePoint 2013 does not support upgrade of the property database and crawl store.

For those of you unfamiliar with SQL Management Studio, the following steps detail how to set a database as read-only:

1. Right-click the database in SQL Management Studio.

2. Select the Properties menu item.

3. Choose the Options category on the right of the dialog (Figure 4-4).

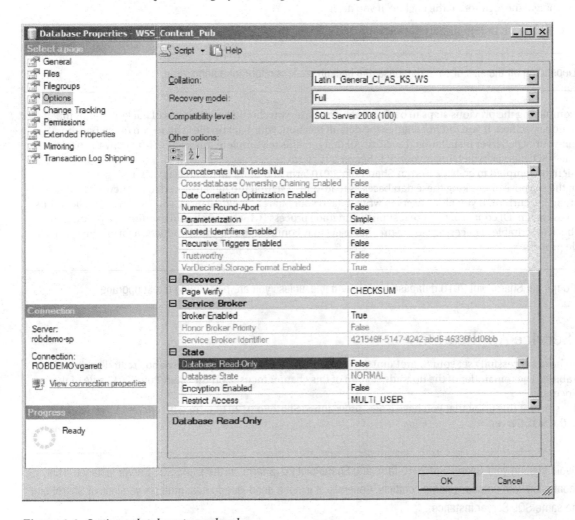

Figure 4-4. *Setting a database to read-only*

4. Scroll down to the option for Database Read-Only.

5. Set the option to True and then click the OK button.

Repeat the preceding steps for all of the databases you wish to set as read-only. I recommend that you perform this operation outside peak usage hours, so that you lessen the impact on your users.

With the databases set to read-only, verify that you can continue to use your SharePoint sites in a read-only state. Follow these steps to create a backup of each of the aforementioned databases.

1. Right-click the database in SQL Management Studio.

2. Click the Tasks menu item.

3. Click the Backup Sub-task menu item.

4. Make sure the backup type is Full.

5. Change the location of the backup, if you desire.

6. Click the OK button to start the backup.

■ **Note**   Depending on the size of each database, the backup process might take some time.

After completing the previous steps to backup each database, you should have a series of backup files in the backup location specified. If you did not change the default location, your backup files will reside in the Backups folder within your SQL Server installation directory. All that remains to complete this section is to copy the backup files to the new SQL Server, which hosts your SQL Server 2013 farm.

You might be tempted to go back to your SharePoint 2010 farm and mark all databases writable again. Remember, the purpose of marking these databases as read-only is so that the data restored to the new SharePoint 2013 farm remains current. If you allow users to write data to your SharePoint 2010 farm, you will have to repeat the backup process again. Of course, if you are testing the upgrade process (which you should), setting the production databases back to writable is necessary to ensure that users may continue to use your production farm while you test the upgrade process.

■ **Note**   Do not set SharePoint 2010 database back to writable, unless you are performing a test upgrade.

Attach Service Applications

By now, you have successfully set your SharePoint 2010 production databases to read-only and created backups of each database. The remainder of the upgrade section of this chapter focuses on the SharePoint 2013 side of the upgrade process.

I shall assume at this point that you have a new provisioned SharePoint 2013 farm with copies of the database backups on the SQL Server.

■ **Note**   Avoid hosting your SharePoint 2010 farm and SharePoint 2013 farm on the same SQL Server instance. This can cause confusion with database name conflicts. Generally, it is not a good idea to host multiple versions of SharePoint farms on the same SQL Server instance.

I recommend that you take a quick look at the service applications provisioned in your SharePoint 2013 farm. SharePoint will not prohibit you from upgrading a legacy service application while a new SharePoint 2013 version of the same service application exists in the farm. However, for demonstrating a clean upgrade process, ensure that you have only the bare minimum farm provisioned.

You are now ready to begin the process of attaching your service application database. Cast back to the previous subsection and review the list of databases—you should have a backup file for each database listed. The following steps detail how to restore these databases using SQL Management Studio:

1. Open SQL Management Studio.

2. Right-click the Databases node in the Object Explorer.

3. Click the Restore Database menu item.

4. Change the source location as From device.

5. Click the ellipses and then the Add button on the next dialog.

6. Browse for the database backup file.

7. Click the OK button.

8. Check the check box to restore the selected database (Figure 4-5).

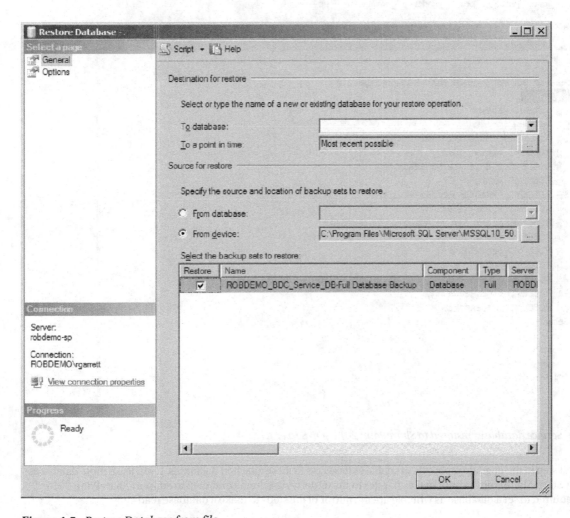

Figure 4-5. Restore Database from file

9. Click the drop-down for the destination database.

10. Select the database to restore.

■ **Note**   Do not restore to an existing database; you should see the new name of the database found in the backup. If you have a name conflict, provide a new database name in the database drop-down box.

Repeat the previous steps to restore databases from backup for all of the application service databases you created a backup for in the previous section of this chapter. Figure 4-6 shows a screenshot of my SQL Management Studio with databases restored.

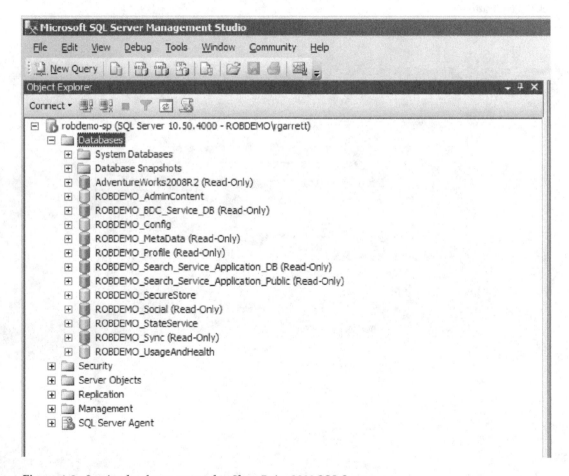

Figure 4-6. *Service databases restored to SharePoint 2013 SQL Server*

The next step in the upgrade process is to enable write access to these attached databases. If you leave these databases in read-only state, SharePoint cannot make changes to the underlying schema and data to support SharePoint 2013. The steps required to set a database as writable are the mirror of the steps to make a database read-only.

1. Right-click the database in SQL Management Studio.

2. Select the Properties menu item.

3. Choose the Options category on the right of the dialog.

4. Scroll down to the option for Database Read-Only.

5. Set the option to False and then click the OK button.

Up until now, life has been peachy. Now is the part where you marry your legacy service configuration with your new SharePoint 2013 farm. If you have any database issues, or did not configure the destination correctly, now is the time when you will run into issues (hopefully not). This highlights the need for good planning and pre-upgrade maintenance.

Before embarking on the process of upgrade, this is a good time to review each of the restored databases, making sure that you can query each, and that security is intact. If you share a common Active Directory between environments, and use Windows accounts for all SQL databases, chances are that security and permissions remain intact.

The process to upgrade service application databases into working service applications requires four major steps, described as follows:

1. Start the service instances.

2. Create service applications and attach the databases.

3. Create proxies for each service application.

4. Verify that proxies reside in the default group.

Using the Business Connectivity Services (BCS) as an example, I shall now review the major steps and provision a new service application from the legacy backup data and demonstrate BCS working in my new SharePoint 2013 farm. I shall begin by ensuring that I have started the BCS service in the farm.

1. Open Central Administration.

2. Click the link for Manage Services on Server.

3. Scroll to the Business Connectivity Services service.

4. Click the link to start the service (if not started).

5. Feel free to start other service for service applications you intend to upgrade later.

STARTING THE SEARCH SERVICE

Unfortunately, you cannot start the search service instance from Central Administration, but you can accomplish this task using PowerShell, demonstrated as follows:

1. Open a SharePoint 2013 Management Shell (see Chapter 3) with elevated permissions

2. Enter the following PowerShell Cmdlets:

```
$SearchInst = Get-SPEnterpriseSearchServiceInstance
Start-SPServiceInstance $SearchInst
```

You have now successfully started the services in the SharePoint 2013 farm. SharePoint services typically translate to Windows services on the SharePoint servers and provide a specific set of operations. SharePoint provides access to these service operations via hosted service applications. A service application consists of a WCF service, hosted in Internet Information Services (IIS) server, which exposes an endpoint so application proxies can connect to the service application and leverage the functionality of the underlying service. The following steps demonstrate how to provision a new Business Connectivity Service application and proxy, using PowerShell:

1. Open a SharePoint 2013 Management Shell (see Chapter 3).

2. Obtain the identity of the service application pool with the following Cmdlet:

   ```
   $applicationPool = Get-SPServiceApplicationPool -Identity 'App Pool Identity'
   ```

3. The name of my application pool is "SharePoint Hosted Services." You can obtain a list by executing the previous Cmdlet with no assignment or parameters.

4. Create a new BCS service application with the following Cmdlet, replacing the name of the database with that attached to SQL Server, mentioned earlier.

   ```
   New-SPBusinessDataCatalogServiceApplication -Name 'BCS Service' -ApplicationPool
   $applicationPool -DatabaseName 'BDC_Service_DB'
   ```

5. Open Central Administration.

6. Click the link to check the upgrade status, under the Upgrade and Migration heading.

7. You should see a page like that in Figure 4-7.

■ **Note**   Each service application uses different PowerShell Cmdlets to provision a new service application instance and proxy. I demonstrate creating a service application and proxy for BCS. Refer to the following MSDN article for creating a service application and proxy for the other upgrading services:
http://technet.microsoft.com/en-us/library/jj839719.aspx.

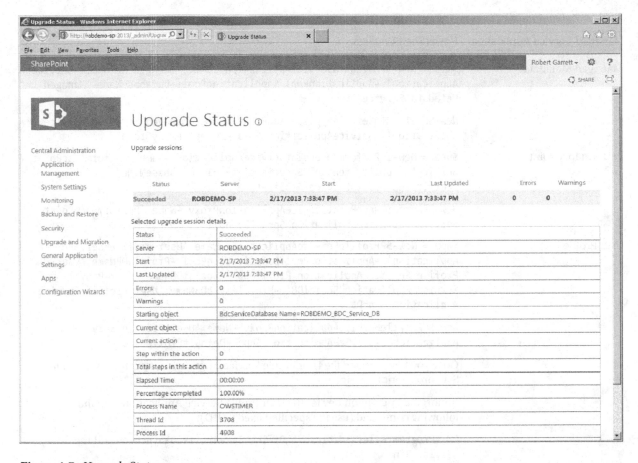

Figure 4-7. *Upgrade Status*

The preceding example should provide you with the necessary steps to upgrade the Managed Metadata Service, Secure Store, PerformancePoint, User Profile, and Search, as well. To assist you further, refer to Table 4-7 for the specific PowerShell Cmdlets to perform the database and service upgrades.

Table 4-7. *PowerShell Cmdlets for Service Application Upgrades*

Managed Service Application	PowerShell Cmdlets

Secure Store	`$sss = New-SPSecureStoreServiceApplication -Name 'Secure Store' -ApplicationPool $applicationPool -DatabaseName 'SecureStore_Upgrade_DB' –AuditingEnabled`
	
	`$sssp = New-SPSecureStoreServiceApplicationProxy -Name ProxyName -ServiceApplication $sss -DefaultProxyGroup`

Business Data	`New-SPBusinessDataCatalogServiceApplication -Name 'BCS Service' -ApplicationPool $applicationPool -DatabaseName 'BDC_Service_DB'`

(continued)

Table 4-7. (*continued*)

Managed Service Application	PowerShell Cmdlets

Managed Metadata	`$mms = New-SPMetadataServiceApplication -Name 'Managed Metadata Service Application' -ApplicationPool $applicationPool -DatabaseName 'Managed Metadata Service_DB'`
	
	`New-SPMetadataServiceApplicationProxy -Name 'Managed Metadata Service Application' -ServiceApplication $mms –DefaultProxyGroup`

PerformancePoint	`$pps = New-SPPerformancePointServiceApplication -Name 'PerformancePoint Service' -ApplicationPool $applicationPool -DatabaseName 'PerformancePoint Service Application_DB'`
	
	`New-SPPerformancePointServiceApplicationProxy -Name 'PerformancePoint Service' -ServiceApplication $pps -Default`

User Profile	`$upa = New-SPProfileServiceApplication -Name 'User Profile Service Application' -ApplicationPool $applicationPool -ProfileDBName 'User Profile Service Application_ProfileDB' -SocialDBName 'User Profile Service Application_SocialDB' -ProfileSyncDBName 'User Profile Service Application_SyncDB'`
	
	`New-SPProfileServiceApplicationProxy -Name 'User Profile Service Application' -ServiceApplication $upa –DefaultProxyGroup`
	
	Once you have created the User Profile Service Application, start the User Profile Synchronization Service.
	
	Import the Encryption Key for the User Profile Service Application with the following command (use the specified fixed GUID):
	
	`Cd %Program Files%\Microsoft Office Servers\15.0\Synchronization Service\Bin\`
	
	`miiskmu.exe /i Path {0E19E162-827E-4077-82D4-E6ABD531636E}`

Search Administration	`$searchInst = Get-SPEnterpriseSearchServiceInstance -local`
	
	`Restore-SPEnterpriseSearchServiceApplication -Name '<SearchServiceApplicationName>' -applicationpool $applicationPool -databasename '<SearchServiceApplicationDBName>' -databaseserver <ServerName> -AdminSearchServiceInstance $searchInst`
	
	`$ssa = Get-SPEnterpriseSearchServiceApplication –Identity '<SearchServiceApplicationName>'`
	
	`New-SPEnterpriseSearchServiceApplicationProxy -Name '<SearchServiceApplicationName>' -SearchApplication $ssa`
	
	`$ssap = Get-SPEnterpriseSearchServiceApplicationProxy –Identity '<SearchServiceApplicationName>'`
	
	`Add-SPServiceApplicationProxyGroupMember –member $ssap -identity " "`

Now that you have completed upgrade of all of the managed service applications, you must check that each proxy resides in the default group. Open a SharePoint 2013 Management Shell and execute the following PowerShell Cmdlets:

```
$pg = Get-SPServiceApplicationProxyGroup -Identity " "
$pg.Proxies
```

Specifying a blank name for the proxy group tells the preceding Cmdlet that you want the "default" proxy group.

Attach Content Databases

If you have followed the previous section about attaching service application databases, then the process for attaching content databases should not phase you. The process to attach content databases to the SharePoint 2013 SQL Server instance is identical to that of the service applications, as follows:

1. Open SQL Management Studio.

2. Right-click the Databases node in the Object Explorer.

3. Click the Restore Database menu item.

4. Change the source location as From device.

5. Click the ellipses, then the Add button on the next dialog.

6. Browse for the database backup file.

7. Click the OK button.

8. Check the check box to restore the selected database.

9. Click the drop-down for the destination database.

10. Select the database to restore.

Once you have attached the content databases, you will notice that the databases are read-only (if you followed the earlier detachment process). The following steps demonstrate setting the content databases as writable, which SharePoint 2013 requires to perform an upgrade:

1. Right-click the database in SQL Management Studio.

2. Select the Properties menu item.

3. Choose the Options category on the right of the dialog.

4. Scroll down to the option for Database Read-Only.

5. Set the option to False and then click the OK button.

With the content databases attached to SQL Server and set as writable, you are now ready to begin the upgrade process. Each web application hosts a single content database, so you must create your web applications first, before attaching the content databases for upgrade.

Before creating your web applications, consider the following points, which will make the process of upgrading to SharePoint 2013 smoother:

- Create your web applications on the same URLs and ports, to keep compatibility with bookmarks and Office applications

- Configure alternate access mappings and managed paths so site collections upgrade correctly

- Use the same authentication configuration—if you wish to upgrade from Classic to Claims-Based-Authentication, upgrade the web application post database upgrade

- Configure e-mail settings for the application

- Configure self-service settings for the application

- Re-create any web application security policies

You can create new web applications within Central Administration. However, CA will create a default content database, and CA will not allow you to create Classic Authentication Mode applications. As is often the case, PowerShell provides granular control and is what I shall use in my demonstration.

Remember from earlier in this chapter that I had two applications provisioned in my legacy SharePoint 2010 farm: one for my Intranet and one for my public-facing Web Site. I shall re-create both these applications in my new SharePoint 2013 farm. I adopted best practice and used Claims-Based-Authentication prior and so provision the new web applications the same. The following Cmdlet creates a new web application for my Intranet:

```
New-SPWebApplication -Name 'Intranet' -ApplicationPool 'Intranet App Pool' -ApplicationPoolAccount
'ROBDEMO\sp_app_pool' -URL 'http://robdemo-sp/' -Port 80 -AuthenticationProvider
(New-SPAuthenticationProvider)
```

The following Cmdlet creates a similar web application for my public facing Web Site:

```
New-SPWebApplication -Name 'Public Web Site' -ApplicationPool 'Public Site App Pool'
-ApplicationPoolAccount 'ROBDEMO\sp_app_pool' -URL 'http://robdemo-sp/' -Port 5000
-AuthenticationProvider (New-SPAuthenticationProvider) –AllowAnonymousAccess
```

Notice that in the previous Cmdlet I specified a different port allow anonymous access, because my public site does not require authentication for most users.

INSTALL CUSTOMIZATIONS

Now that you have your web applications created, it is a good time to install any customizations that apply to the applications. You can ignore any visual customizations and metadata customizations that reside in the database because the database attach upgrade will take care of these. However, you must install any Global Assembly assemblies, assemblies installed in the web application BIN, and files deployed to the hive.

If you have any "globally deployed" solution packages, you can deploy them to the farm and activate any web application scoped features. Make sure you also deploy any site collection and site scoped features; even though the site collection or sites in the database reference the feature, you still need to ensure that you deploy any dependencies (such as hive files).

If you have made manual configuration changes to your configuration files in the legacy farm, and not packaged these as solution packages (tsk, tsk), now is also the time to apply these changes to the newly created web applications.

My demonstration sites do not depend on any visual files in the hive (they live in the Style Gallery and Master Page Gallery), so I have no need to perform any additional customizations to my SharePoint 2013 farm.

■ **Note** SharePoint 2013 supports legacy hive customizations. Deploy any legacy customizations to the `Web Server Extensions\14` directory if you plan to operate sites in SharePoint 2010 legacy mode. New customizations deploy to the `Web Server Extensions\15` directory.

Before you upgrade your content databases and attach them to your web applications, you should test them first. Content databases can reach large sizes, and the last thing you want is to wait hours for an upgrade only to have it fail part way. The following PowerShell Cmdlet allows users to test a content database. If you have multiple content databases for a web application, test them all:

```
Test-SPContentDatabase -Name DatabaseName -WebApplication URL
```

Now, finally, the moment you have been waiting for—it is time to mount your legacy content databases and let SharePoint 2013 upgrade them. Issue the following PowerShell Cmdlet for each of your content databases:

```
Mount-SPContentDatabase -Name DatabaseName -DatabaseServer ServerName -WebApplication URL
```

Earlier in the chapter, I mentioned parallel upgrades as an aid to reduce the upgrade time, and thus time the production SharePoint remains in read-only state. You can execute as many mount Cmdlets as you wish to upgrade multiple databases in parallel.

■ **Note** Use separate PowerShell windows to upgrade multiple content databases in parallel.

I executed the following PowerShell Cmdlets in my environment to upgrade my two web application content databases:

```
Mount-SPContentDatabase -Name 'WSS_Content_Pub' -DatabaseServer ROBDEMO-SP -WebApplication
http://robdemo-sp:5000
Mount-SPContentDatabase -Name 'ROBDEMO_PortalContent' -DatabaseServer ROBDEMO-SP -WebApplication
http://robdemo-sp
```

Similar to upgrading the service application database, you can check on the status of your content database upgrades from Central Administration, under the Upgrade and Migration heading (Figure 4-8).

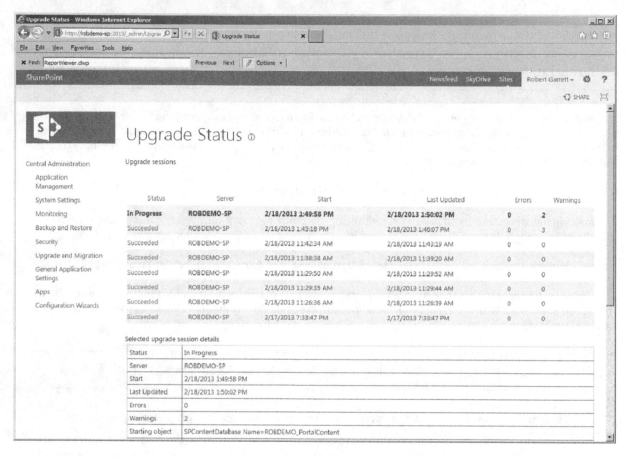

Figure 4-8. *Upgrade Status of content databases*

■ **Note**   Upgrading the My Sites database is a similar process to upgrading content databases. However, make sure that you have a working My Site Host web application and that you upgrade the database containing the My Site Host root site collection first.

Upgrading Site Collections

The visual upgrade approach that existed in SharePoint 2010 for upgrades from SharePoint 2007 has changed. SharePoint 2013 now uses "deferred site collection upgrade." Essentially, SharePoint 2013 puts visual upgrade of site collections in the hands of the site collection owners.

In the previous sections of this chapter, I demonstrated upgrading managed service application databases and content databases. My example used a team site (my Intranet) and a publishing site (my Web Site). Figure 4-9 shows a screenshot of my team site running in SharePoint 2013 after upgrade. Notice the pink banner at the top of the page, prompting the site collection administrator to upgrade the site collection to the new SharePoint 2013 (aka SharePoint 15) look and feel. If you look at the publishing site, you will see the same banner when you log into the site as a site collection owner or site collection administrator.

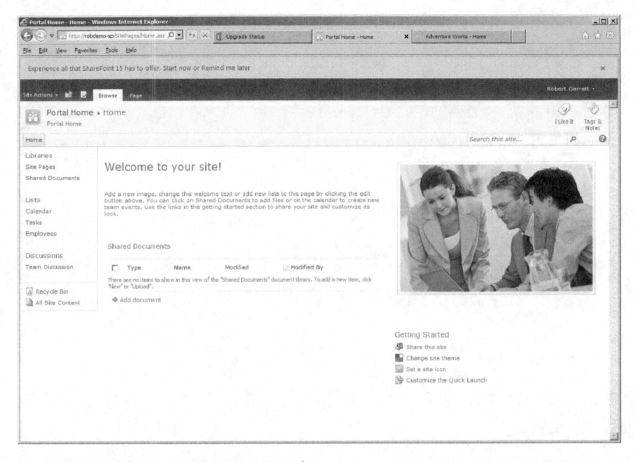

Figure 4-9. *Upgraded team site in SharePoint 2010 mode*

If you click the *X* to close the red banner, or opt for SharePoint to remind you later, you can always return to site collection upgrade from the Site Collections Settings page. If you are not a site collection owner or site collection administrator you probably will not see the red banner, but owners and administrators might find SharePoint nagging, because the banner appears frequently until you proceed with the upgrade.

If you do not see the red banner, have site collection administration permissions, and want to perform an upgrade, you can perform the upgrade as follows:

1. Open the Site Collection.

2. Click the Site Actions menu (remember you are still using SharePoint 2010 look and feel).

3. Select Site Settings from the menu.

4. Click the link for site collection upgrade from the Site Collection Administration section.

5. You should see a page like that in Figure 4-10.

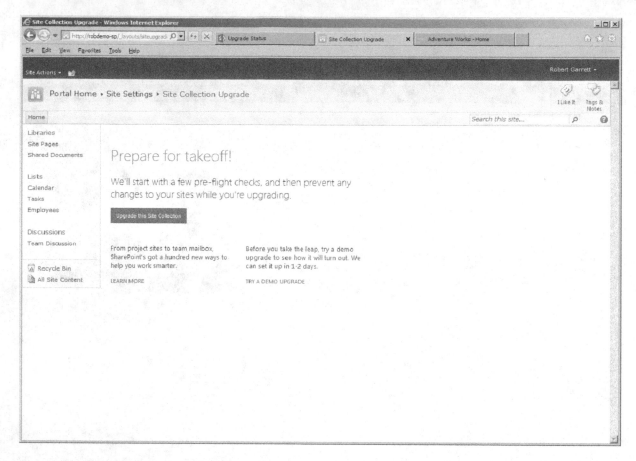

Figure 4-10. *Site Collection Upgrade page*

■ **Note** You might notice the Visual Upgrade link in the Site Settings page. Ignore this option—Visual Upgrade is an option in SharePoint 2010.

Notice the link on the Site Collection Upgrade page (Figure 4-10) to try a demo upgrade. This is the "Evaluation Site Collection" feature and is new to SharePoint 2013. You can stand up a test site collection, containing the same content as your upgraded site, but using the new SharePoint 2013 user interface. You can decide to let selected users loose on the evaluation site to validate that the site operates correctly in the new style.

1. Click the link to try a demo upgrade.

2. Click the button to create an evaluation site.

3. SharePoint lets you know that it might be a day or two before the evaluation site is available.

4. You do not need to wait so long.

5. Open Central Administration.

6. Click the Monitoring heading.

7. Click the link to review job definitions.

8. Scroll to the job called Create Upgrade Evaluation Site Collections job for the specific web application.

9. Run this job to complete evaluation site creation for the web application.

If you have e-mail configured correctly, the site collection administrator should receive an e-mail when SharePoint completes the process of creating an evaluation site. You can easily find the URL of evaluation sites from Central Administration.

1. Open Central Administration.

2. Click the Application Management heading.

3. Click the link to view all site collections.

4. Change the drop-down to the desired web application.

5. Open the evaluation site collection.

6. You should see a page similar to Figure 4-11.

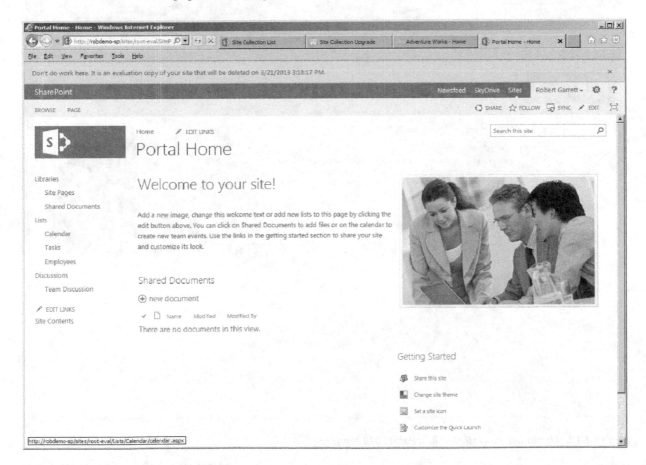

Figure 4-11. *Evaluation site collection*

Figure 4-11 shows that SharePoint has provided an evaluation site for 30 days (implied by the date). SharePoint also lets you know that you should not do any work in the evaluation site collection—evaluation site collections are copies, and you lose any changes made to them when they expire.

If you are happy with your evaluation site and get the thumbs-up from your test group of users (let your users decided when an upgrade is working), you can now complete the site collection upgrade.

1. Return to the upgraded site collection.

2. Either click the link on the red banner to Start now, or click the link to upgrade the site collection from the Site Collection Settings page.

3. On the Upgrade page (Figure 4-10), click the button to upgrade the site collection.

4. Click the button to confirm that you wish to continue.

5. SharePoint displays a temporary page, showing progress of the upgrade.

6. When complete, click the link to see the new site.

7. Your site should look something like that in Figure 4-12.

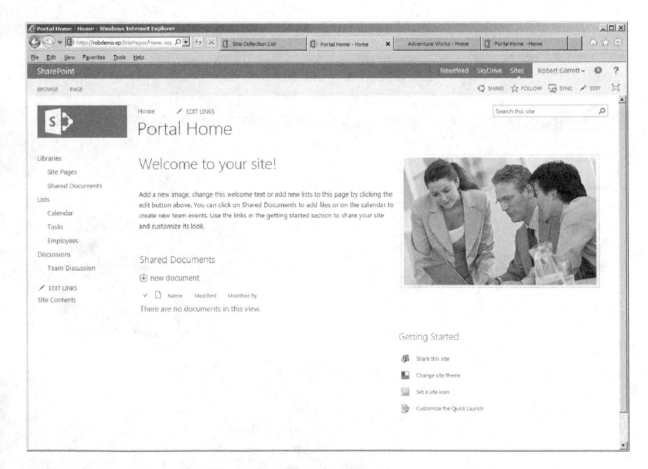

Figure 4-12. *Upgraded team site in SharePoint 2013 branding*

Summary

In this chapter, I demonstrated the overarching process to upgrade SharePoint 2010 to SharePoint 2013. The upgrade process is often a daunting one, and many SharePoint engineers groan at the prospect. However, if you undertake the necessary planning and go into the upgrade process aware of all the potential pitfalls, the process need not be so scary.

I devoted half of this chapter to planning, where I discussed the changes to the SharePoint upgrade process. I covered pre-upgrade maintenance tips and shared some suggestions on handling customizations, the typical sticking point in many SharePoint upgrades.

In the second half of this chapter, I walked you through the upgrade process itself, using a demonstration SharePoint 2010 farm in my development environment. All of the examples in this chapter (and this book) use real examples running within my SharePoint development farm, so you can have peace of mind that my examples work.

As part of the upgrade section, you read about upgrading the managed service application services that SharePoint 2013 supports: Secure Store, Managed Metadata, PerformancePoint, User Profile, Search Administration, and Business Data. I then showed you how to upgrade content databases and attach them to working SharePoint 2013 web applications.

In the last section of this chapter (not including this summary), I covered the site collection upgrade changes in SharePoint 2013 and how they replace the legacy visual upgrade process in SharePoint 2010. Site collection owners and administrators now have the power to roll out visual changes in their own time, having viewed new user interface changes in evaluation site collections.

In Chapter 5, you shall read about health monitoring and disaster recovery.

CHAPTER 5

■ ■ ■

Health Monitoring and Disaster Recovery

As more and more organizations deploy SharePoint within an enterprise, and user adoption of the SharePoint solutions snowballs with each deployment, disaster recovery becomes very important. SharePoint 2013 has the capability to host terabytes of important data, so backup of this data is likely to be high on the agenda for any IT group that maintains SharePoint in an organization.

SharePoint includes capabilities to make backup and restoration easier than in the past, and SharePoint continues to provide good backup and restore functionality to maintain the integrity of important data. I devote a large chunk of this chapter to the administration of disaster recovery features in SharePoint 2013, but, as the title suggestions, this chapter also contains details on health and monitoring of a SharePoint 2013 infrastructure.

SharePoint provides extensive logging, but previous versions before SharePoint 2010 lacked some key monitoring functionality that administrators require to ensure that their SharePoint solution is operating at peak performance. Administrators of SharePoint 2007 could consult the ULS logs and the Windows event log, but these features require a certain amount of proactive behavior from the SharePoint administrator. SharePoint 2010 and 2013 include sophisticated health and monitoring features to alert the administrator when SharePoint is feeling a little under the weather.

After reading this chapter, any SharePoint administrator will, I am confident, be able to provide his or her organization with the peace of mind that its data integrity is intact and that the organization can count on bounce back of its SharePoint service in the event of downtime or disaster.

Planning for Disaster Recovery

It is never a happy day for the IT group when an online service goes down, and this includes SharePoint. As fantastic as SharePoint is, it is inevitable that at some point in the life cycle, your SharePoint solution will suffer from downtime. Of course, downtime may occur for any number of reasons: human error, underlying hardware failure, power outage, faulty customizations, and so on. Since failure cannot be entirely averted, your role as a SharePoint administrator is to account for such downtime and restore service to the users of the platform in a timely manner. Planning for and recovering from loss of service is what I refer as to as planning for disaster recovery.

Minimizing downtime and averting loss in a disaster involves proactive processes and planning. Those unfortunate readers who have experienced loss of data are likely all too familiar with data backup, which is one aspect of disaster recovery—I will discuss managing content and data integrity shortly in this chapter. Another important aspect of disaster recovery includes techniques to minimize service downtime.

Minimizing downtime of a service factors both the *total time* to recover the service and the *point in time* from which recovery resumes. In short, if recovery consists of restoring data in a SharePoint site collection because of database corruption, then the time to restore the database from backup and the time when the last backup took place are both important factors for the success of restoration of the SharePoint site collection. A speedy restore is one thing, but if the data is already three months old then, depending on the frequency of change of the live data, the restoration is not necessarily successful.

Data/content recovery is one piece of a good disaster recovery plan—restoration of system hardware, the underlying operating system, system software, and configuration are all part of the plan. Since this book is about SharePoint administration, the topics concerning hardware and operating system recovery are outside its scope, but I will say that virtualized platforms and snapshots now play a major part in alleviating many of the ills associated with hardware failure and/or operating system failure. At a conceptual (and practical) level, consider the techniques in the following sections to minimize downtime and provide warm recovery of service.

Warm recovery is the quickest form of recovery in the event of a disaster and typically involves a level of hardware and software redundancy. Conversely, cold recovery refers to the restoration of service from scratch in a completely inoperable state. Cold recovery typically involves restoration of data from an offline backup store. A good disaster recovery strategy involves both warm and cold recovery methods.

Load-Balanced Service

Load balancing involves either a hardware or a software load balancer, which intercepts all incoming web traffic on a specific IP address and redirects it to one of at least two web servers to service the request. The load balancer directs traffic either to the server with the least load (intelligent load balancing) or in turn, based on which server served the previous request (round-robin).

Load balancing serves two purposes: distributing user requests load and warm redundancy in the event of a server failure that was serving requests. SharePoint 2013 includes a new request manager service to manage intelligently which servers in a multiple server farm handle which requests. I shall discuss the request manager later in this chapter.

Load balancing SharePoint consists of pointing a configured load balancer to multiple front-end SharePoint servers in the farm that serve pages. A SharePoint farm may include as many front-end web and application servers as the infrastructure can provide; thus, scaling out to handle more traffic is simply a case of adding a new web server to the farm and registering the IP with the load balancer.

As well as providing for distributed load, most load balancers can detect if one of the servers in the pool is not responding and then redirect all traffic to the other responding servers. Large enterprise organizations that have the capability to host different servers in multiple geographic locations may redirect traffic to passive SharePoint servers, or completely mirrored SharePoint farms, to achieve redundancy and rapid recovery if a primary site hosting the main SharePoint infrastructure fails.

SQL Server Failover Clustering

SQL Server clustering consists of multiple SQL Server nodes, managed by a root cluster that provides redundancy at the SQL Server application level.

A cluster typically consists of an active node and at least one passive node, although you can have multiple nodes. The cluster maintains all nodes so that any database write operations update both the active and passive nodes, but the active node is handling all of the incoming requests. In the event that the active node fails, then the Windows Failover Cluster Service switches over to use one of the passive nodes (running on different hardware). I should highlight some important points about SQL clustering:

- SQL clustering does not help performance, since only one node of the cluster is active at any one time

- Recovery in the event of failure of the active node is dependent on the time it takes to bring a passive node online—this is not always an immediate process and dependent on when the Windows Failover Cluster Service detects a down node

- SQL clustering uses shared storage to ensure timely and accurate copies of data from the active node to the passive nodes

The specifics of Microsoft SQL Server 2008 and 2012 clustering are outside the scope of this book, but I will note that clustering abstracts redundancy away from SharePoint and provides data integrity without SharePoint ever needing to switch database servers. This is the beauty of it. SharePoint talks to a SQL cluster in the same way it talks to a single SQL Server and never gets involved when the cluster fails over to a passive node.

■ **Note** You can read more about setting up clustering on SQL Server 2008 R2 at the following location:
http://msdn.microsoft.com/en-us/library/ms189134.aspx.

I recommend the use of SQL clustering in any large organization or enterprise where SharePoint data is critical and exceeds 100GB, and the organization must limit the downtime in the event of failure. Traditionally, large-scale organizations using SharePoint with SQL clustering would host the actual data on a Storage Area Network, attached to the cluster, to provide an extra level of data redundancy and hot swap capability with inexpensive disk storage.

SQL Server Database Mirroring

SQL Server mirroring also provides data redundancy at the SQL Server, but unlike clustering, where the cluster is the data repository in entirety, mirroring consists of a warm backup SQL Server, separate from the main live server.

Clustering involves multiple storage nodes, connected by network links to a root SQL instance. Mirroring consists of two completely independent SQL Servers with either *synchronous* or *asynchronous* copy, managed by each SQL Server instance. Synchronous mode provides hot standby because SQL Server ensures no data discrepancy between the principal and the mirror, whereas asynchronous provides warm backup and operates in a more passive copy mode.

■ **Note** You can read more about SQL Server 2008 mirroring at the following link:
http://msdn.microsoft.com/en-us/library/ms189852.aspx.

Administrators may provide high availability for SharePoint when using SQL Server mirroring in synchronous mode and using the database failover capabilities built into the SharePoint platform. SharePoint requires a SQL Server witness to manage the failover, in the event that the principal fails. The details surrounding SQL Server mirroring fall outside the scope of this book, but I will show you how to configure SharePoint for it, assuming you have SQL Server 2008 or 2012 mirroring established in your infrastructure.

The following steps consist of PowerShell commands. Launch the SharePoint Management Shell to begin, where you will enter the following commands:

1. Enter the following command into the PowerShell console to configure mirroring for the SharePoint configuration database:

```
$database = Get-SPDatabase | where {$_.Name -match "SharePoint_Config"}
$database.AddFailoverServiceInstance("mirror server name")
$databse.Update()
```

2. Enter the following command into the PowerShell console to configure mirroring for your content database:

```
$database = Get-SPDatabase | where {$_.Name -match "WSS_Content"}
$database.AddFailoverServiceInstance("mirror server name")
$databse.Update()
```

■ **Note** Both of the preceding commands assume your configuration database has the name SharePoint_Config and you have named your content database as WSS_Content. Change the names in the script to match your database names.

If you prefer to configure database mirroring via Central Administration, follow these steps:

1. Open Central Administration.

2. Click the Application Management heading link.

3. Click the Manage Content Databases link.

4. Choose the relevant web application from the drop-down list.

5. Select the relevant content database.

6. On the settings page for the selected database, populate the Failover Database Server field with the mirrored server.

7. Click the OK button.

SharePoint Farm Design

The design of your SharePoint farm has a large impact on the level of disaster recovery. At the lower end of the scale, a simple farm with minimal redundant hardware provides little to no recovery in the event of failure, whereas a multiple server farm with multiple redundant servers provides rapid recovery. Microsoft designed SharePoint 2013 to scale, to allow reuse of common services across multiple infrastructure hardware, and to embrace virtualization. In this section, I shall discuss some of the high-level considerations when planning an Enterprise SharePoint infrastructure for maximum uptime.

Looking at a SharePoint farm from a 50,000-foot view, we see the farm essentially consists of a data storage component, some service middleware, and web-front-end to render pages to end users. Consider Figure 5-1 as the bare minimum components of a SharePoint farm, which consists of

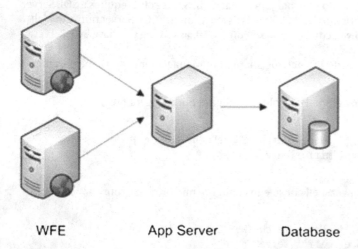

WFE   App Server   Database

Figure 5-1. *Minimal SharePoint infrastructure for an enterprise*

- A SQL data store

- An application server for middleware services

- Two web-front-end servers

The diagram in Figure 5-1 provides very little redundancy—should the SQL Server fail, the farm goes offline. SharePoint can partially operate without a working application server, but services like search, user profiles, Business Connectivity Services, business intelligence, managed metadata, etc. that rely on the application server will fail, rendering SharePoint to basic collaboration. There is minimal redundancy with two web-front-end servers and the ability to distribute user request load to these servers. This is important because the WFE servers are the entry to the SharePoint farm for users, and without them, the farm might as well be inoperable.

Now consider the diagrams in Figure 5-2 and Figure 5-3—this infrastructure is vastly larger than the example presented in Figure 5-1. This design separates the farm into six tiers, consisting of the web server tier, application server tier, search index and query tier, other search components tier, database search tier, and database content tier. One immediate observation in this larger design is the separation of search services and search data from other tiers in the farm. SharePoint 2013 relies heavily on the Search platform (FAST) to allow users' to search and discover content. Unlike previous versions of SharePoint, SharePoint also leverages the search platform for content rollup and rendering of dynamic content, which constantly changes. As you can imagine, with the search platform playing such an important role in the SharePoint farm, it deserves big consideration in the overall farm design. The search platform itself consists of multiple components, which, like the rest of the farm, require redundancy to combat anticipated failure.

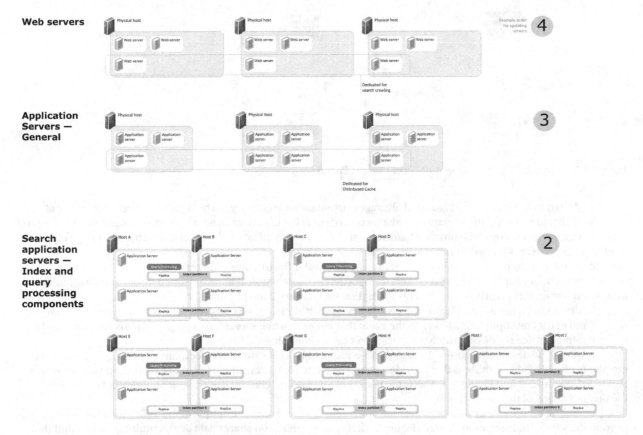

Figure 5-2. *Large Enterprise SharePoint Farm Design (Part A)*

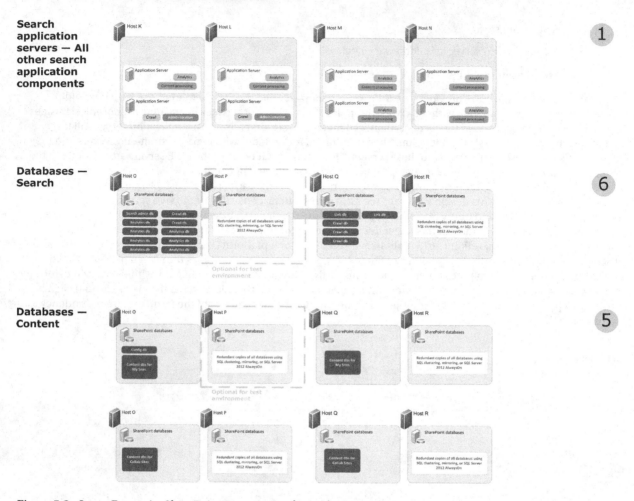

Figure 5-3. *Large Enterprise SharePoint Farm Design (Part B)*

The design in Figure 5-2 and Figure 5-3 leverages virtual server technology, which provides greater number of redundant virtual servers. Infrastructure consisting of large number of servers benefit from virtual servers, running on multiple virtual host servers (the physical hardware) and save the organization the cost for procurement of physical hardware and costs associated with maintaining physical hardware.

Notice the design provides redundancy across the physical infrastructure – multiple virtual hosts – as well as redundancy with multiple virtual servers. This is important because physical hardware often fails. Operating multiple redundant virtual servers on one physical host fails disaster recovery if the physical server dies.

The design in Figure 5-2 and Figure 5-3 also caters for distribution of services and data across multiple virtual servers and across multiple host servers. In the event that either a virtual server fails, or a physical server fails, the data and operating service resides on another virtual server on another physical host.

Of course, the design in Figure 5-2 and Figure 5-3 is quite elaborate and caters for many disaster scenarios. There are plenty of scaled-down designs that provide a good level of redundancy, which fall in between the design shown in Figure 5-1, Figure 5-2 and Figure 5-3. This is the beauty of SharePoint; you can design your SharePoint farm around the business need of the organization.

Depending on the size of your organization, you might have to consider multiple global office locations across in your SharePoint infrastructure design (Figure 5-4). If your organization shares data across multiple offices and that data resides in SharePoint, it may not make sense to host one copy of the data in a single SharePoint farm at one office location. SharePoint 2013 scales globally and allows cross-pollination of data between multiple offices. This design provides location redundancy—if an entire office goes dark (perhaps because of power failure or natural disaster), the business can continue using one of the other office locations.

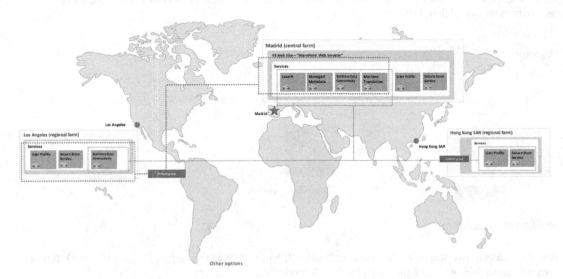

Figure 5-4. *Global SharePoint*

Design of globalized SharePoint farms is nontrivial and impacts network connectivity design. Globalized scenarios require considerable planning for how to replicate data and must consider peak usage of data for multiple offices in multiple time zones. This design is outside the scope of this book, but the diagram in Figure 5-4 illustrates the vast capabilities of SharePoint 2013 for almost any deployment scenario.

Maintaining Content Integrity

When I discuss disaster recovery, I am really talking about minimizing loss of user data and access to that user data. Loss of actual data (documents, files, web page content, data in a database or line of business system, and so on) is a disaster, and we strive to avoid it in any trustworthy data management system, but loss of access to data because of downtime of the management system is almost as bad. In today's connected world, users rely on the uptime of data management systems—like SharePoint—and trust that these systems maintain the integrity of their content. Fortunately, SharePoint provides a number of approaches to maintaining content/data integrity.

SharePoint stores all content of your site in a content database. SharePoint content databases may contain one or many site collections, associated with a web application. One site collection *may not* span multiple content databases, which is important to note because backing up your content databases ensures complete recovery of your site collection. I discuss backup and restore of content and configuration databases a little later in this chapter.

Database backup is good in a disaster scenario. What if a user loses a single document from a document library and wants to recover it? A complete database restore would be overkill, not to mention considerable work in restoring the database to a separate location to retrieve the file. As administrators, we know users tend to lose files all the time. Fortunately, SharePoint includes features to retain content and data integrity without the need for complete database restore after small losses.

The Recycle Bin

Since SharePoint 2007 (WSS 3), the Recycle Bin has provided a mechanism for users to retrieve deleted lists and list items—this includes documents and document libraries. Users can find the Recycle Bin on the top right of the Site Contents page (see Figure 5-5). In addition to lists and libraries, since SharePoint 2010 Service Pack 1, SharePoint allows administrators to recover deleted sites.

Figure 5-5. *Location of Recycle Bin*

The Recycle Bin works in two stages, as described in Table 5-1, and scopes to the web application level. Different web applications may have different configurations for their Recycle Bin.

Table 5-1. *Recycle Bin Stages*

Stage	Location	Details
Stage one	Site	The stage one Recycle Bin is available to users with Contribute, Design, or Full Control permissions. Items and lists deleted at the site level reside in the stage one Recycle Bin until a time (defined by the administrator in Central Administration—typically 30 days) when the content moves to the stage two Recycle Bin. Content in the stage one Recycle Bin counts toward user storage quota.
Stage two	Site Collection	The stage two Recycle Bin lives at the site collection level and is populated from stage one Recycle Bin content by a timer service. Only a site collection administrator may restore content from a stage two Recycle Bin, and content resides in this Recycle Bin for a time or until the Recycle Bin reaches a size, both specified by an administrator in Central Administration, before SharePoint deletes the oldest items. In addition to lists and list items, populated from the stage one Recycle Bin, the stage two Recycle Bin contains deleted sites.
		The size of the stage two Recycle Bin is a percentage of the quota allocated to the entire site collection. Items in the stage two Recycle Bin do not count toward user storage quota, but they do eat up space in the overall site collection quota.

The following steps demonstrate how administrators may configure the Recycle Bin from Central Administration, to allow different item expiration times.

1. Open Central Administration.

2. Click the Manage Web Applications link under the Application Management heading.

3. Select the desired web application.

4.   Click the General Settings icon on the ribbon.

5.   Scroll to the Recycle Bin section (see Figure 5-6).

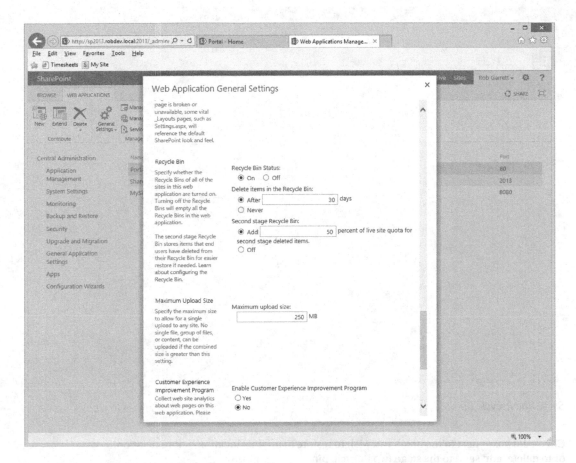

Figure 5-6. *Recycle Bin settings for the web application*

The following steps demonstrate working with the stage one and stage two Recycle Bins:

1.   Navigate to a SharePoint site with at least contributor permissions.

2.   Navigate to the All Site Contents page.

3.   Click the Recycle Bin link.

4.   Figure 5-7 shows my stage one Recycle Bin for my root site.

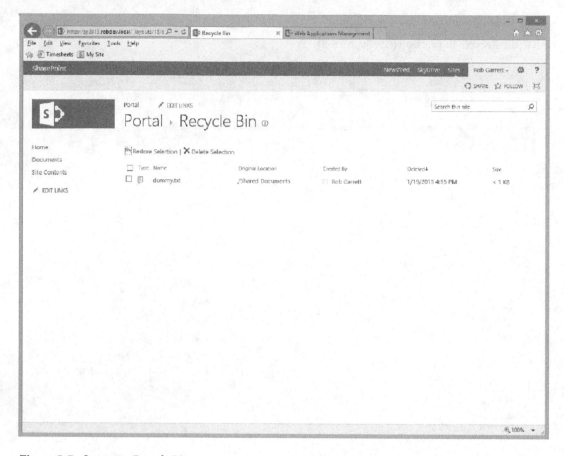

Figure 5-7. *Stage one Recycle Bin*

5. Check the boxes next to the items you wish to restore to original location before deletion, or to delete, and send to the stage two Recycle Bin.

■ **Note** The root site collection Recycle Bin is not the stage two Recycle Bin; the root site also has a stage one Recycle Bin.

Items in the stage one Recycle Bin remain there until you either delete them or the time elapses (see Figure 5-6) and SharePoint moves the items to the stage two recycle bin. Once they are in the stage two Recycle Bin, you can view these deleted items, as follows:

1. Navigate to the root site of the site collection.

2. Clear the gear icon and select the Site Settings menu option.

3. Click the Recycle Bin link under the Site Collection Administration heading.

4. Click the link in the left navigation to show items deleted from the end user Recycle Bin.

5. Figure 5-8 shows the site collection stage two Recycle Bin page.

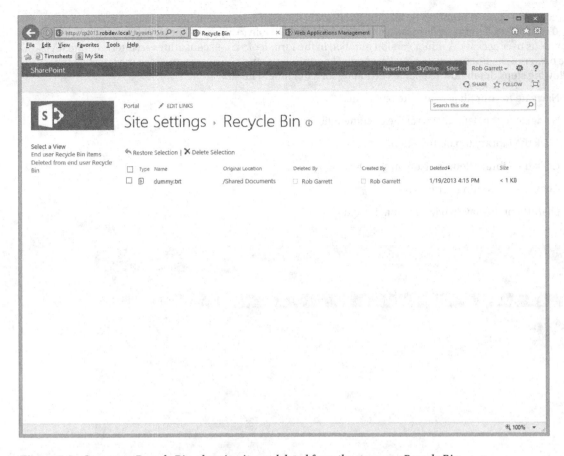

Figure 5-8. *Stage two Recycle Bin, showing items deleted from the stage one Recycle Bin*

You might be wondering about the difference between the views for the End User Recycle Bin items and Deleted from End User Recycle Bin. As I demonstrated previously, the link for Deleted from End User Recycle Bin shows all items moved from stage one Recycle Bins in subsites to the stage two Recycle Bin in the site collection. The link for End User Recycle Bin shows all items that currently reside in stage one Recycle Bins across the site collection hierarchy.

In similar fashion to the stage one Recycle Bin, you can delete items from the stage two Recycle Bin by selecting items in the Deleted from End User Recycle Bin page and clicking the link to delete selection.

■ **Note** You cannot recover any item deleted from the stage two Recycle Bin.

Versioning

Document and page versioning is another way in which users may self-maintain integrity of their content in SharePoint. Library owners may enable versioning on a list or library so that when users with collaborative permissions upload changes, SharePoint keeps track of the version history. SharePoint library versioning is not new to SharePoint 2013; Microsoft introduced it with WSS 2.0, and it comes in two flavors:

- Major version numbers
- Major and minor version numbers

Major and minor version numbers tie into the *publication status* of a document item. A major version in the format of xx.0 constitutes a published version, meaning that it is available to all users (including anonymous if the site allows anonymous user access). A minor version number, in the format of xx.1-9, constitutes an intermediate revision, and only the owner of the document, users with approval permissions, and site owners may see the latest changes.

The following steps detail how to enable versioning for a document library:

1. Navigate to your SharePoint site or subsite.

2. Navigate to the default view of the document library.

3. Click the Library tab on the ribbon.

4. Click the Library Settings icon on the ribbon.

5. Click the Versioning Settings link.

6. SharePoint displays a page like that in Figure 5-9.

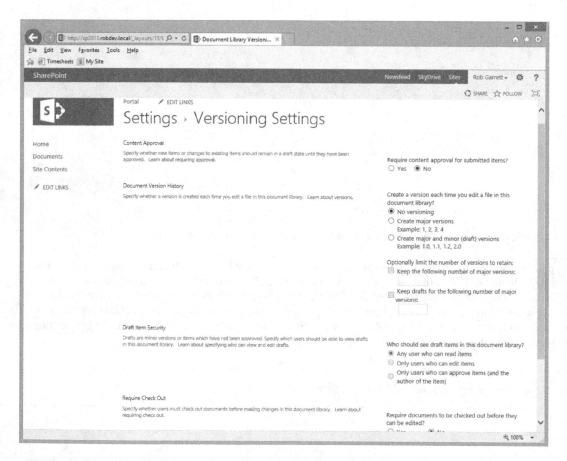

Figure 5-9. *Enable versioning in a document library*

7. Under Document Version History, select the desired versioning type.

8. Select the maximum number of draft and major versions to keep.

■ **Note** Lists allow major versioning but do not provide minor (draft) versioning capability.

On the Version Settings page (Figure 5-9), you may have noticed the other options, to enable content approval and require check out before editing. These options also allow you to maintain the integrity of your content.

Enabling content approval turns on the parallel approval workflow, which requires one or several approvers (in the approvers security group) to approve changes to content before SharePoint publishes the content to a major version. I discuss the parallel approval workflow in Chapter 10 as part of Publishing.

Requiring users to check out content before editing ensures no two users can overwrite each other's changes. Of course, this limits work to a single thread, and only one user can make changes to a document at a time. Furthermore, there is nothing preventing one user from checking out a document indefinitely. Microsoft introduced co-authoring to address the need for multiple users to edit a document at the same time. I discuss co-authoring in Chapter 14.

Backup and Restore

Backup and restoration of user data and system configuration is an intricate part of disaster recovery planning. After all, the user data is most precious and typically tantamount to the running of the organization's business. SharePoint 2013 includes a number of backup and restoration methods, from complete farm backup/restore to granular backup/restore, such as site import and export and site collection backup. In this section, I will visit each method and discuss the specific benefits and shortcomings of each, enabling you as the SharePoint administrator to make effective decisions in your disaster recovery plan.

As a general rule of thumb, I recommend that you employ various backup methods to ensure that you are able to recover your SharePoint farm in the event of a disaster. The following list summarizes, from a high level, what you should back up:

- All content databases

- All configuration and service application databases

- The SharePoint 2013 hive on each web server
  (c:\program files\common files\Microsoft shared\web server extensions\14\)

- All virtual application directories on each web server
  (c:\Inetpub\wwwroot\wss\VirtualDirectories)

- Any custom databases or additional files that do not live in the hive or virtual application directories on each web server

- Site collection backups for faster restore, in the event of isolated data corruption or data loss in a particular site collection

When it comes to backup, more is better. If space for backup is not as plentiful, then backup of all databases and custom "changes" to the hive and virtual application directories should allow you to recover your farm after a new installation.

With the high-level stuff out of the way, I shall now detail the various backup methods available in SharePoint 2013.

Site Collection Backups

Site collection backups are compelling in that they enable administrators to save a complete site collection to a file on disk. Administrators may back up a site collection using the STSADM command, PowerShell, or Central Administration—I shall demonstrate each.

> ■ **Note** Site collection backup puts stress on SharePoint and consumes resources to complete the process. Microsoft does not recommend backing up site collections of more than 15GB, because of the drain on the live site collection, hosting web application, and the time to complete the backup. Site collection backup works well when moving data from one farm to another, or in conjunction with another backup scheme to ensure data integrity.

Site Collection Backup and Restore Using PowerShell

The following steps demonstrate backing up a site collection to a disk file, using PowerShell:

1. From the Start menu, choose All Programs.

2. Click Microsoft SharePoint 2013 Products.

3. Click SharePoint 2013 Management Shell to launch the console.

4. Type the following text into the console, replacing the appropriate placeholders:

   ```
   Backup-SPSite <site collection URL> -Path <backup file> [-Force]
   [-NoSiteLock] [-UseSQLSnapshot] [-Verbose]
   ```

Include the [Force] parameter to overwrite an existing backup file. I recommend *not* using the [NoSiteLock] option, as this prevents SharePoint from putting the site collection in read-only state, meaning that users can write to the site collection during backup and potentially corrupt the database. Use the [UseSQLSnapshot] option if you have SQL Server Enterprise edition, for more consistent backup. The [Verbose] option provides additional output.

Now that I have shown you how to back up your site collection, restoring it is just as easy. The following command demonstrates restoring a site collection from a backup file, using PowerShell:

5. Type the following text into the console, replacing the appropriate placeholders:

   ```
   Restore-SPSite <site collection URL> -Path <backup file> [-DatabaseServer
   <database server name>] [-DatabaseName <database name>] [-HostHeader
   <host header>] [-Force] [-GradualDelete] [-Verbose]
   ```

Include the [Force] parameter to overwrite an existing backup file. Use the [-DatabaseServer] option if the server is not part of your farm. Include the [-GradualDelete] option to minimize locks on the database and provide for better restore performance for backups over 1GB when replacing an existing site collection, which SharePoint marks as deleted; the timer service deletes the legacy site collection later. Use the [-HostHeader] option if restoring a site collection to a web application that requires a unique host header.

Site Collection Backup and Restore Using STSADM

Use the following STSADM command, inside a command shell, to back up a site collection to a disk file, replacing the appropriate placeholders:

```
STSADM -o backup -url <site collection url> -filename <filename>
```

Similar to the PowerShell command for backing up a site collection, you may provide the -overwrite option to overwrite an existing backup file, -nositelock to prevent site collection lock, and -usesqlsnapshot to use SQL Server Enterprise snapshot. Use the following STSADM command to restore a site collection from a backup file, replacing the appropriate placeholders:

```
STSADM -o restore -url <site collection url> -filename <filename>
```

Similar to the PowerShell command for restoring a site collection, you may provide the -overwrite option to overwrite an existing site collection, -hostheaderwebapplicationurl to provide a host header URL, and -gradualdelete to provide better performance in overwriting an existing site collection (marks the overwritten site collection as deleted and the timer service deletes it later).

Site Collection Backup and Restore Using Central Administration

The following steps demonstrate backing up a site collection to a disk file, using Central Administration:

1. Open Central Administration.

2. Click the Backup and Restore heading.

3. Click the Perform a Site Collection Backup link. You will see a page like that in Figure 5-10.

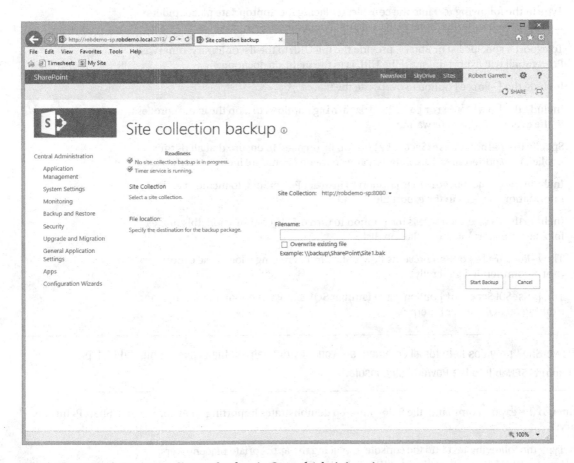

Figure 5-10. *Perform a site collection backup in Central Administration*

4. Click the drop-down control to change the site collection.

5. In the resulting dialog box, select the web application containing the site collection.

6. Provide the UNC path of the file name to save the backup.

7. Click the Start Backup button.

Export and Import

SharePoint supports granular export and import of sites, lists, and libraries. In this section, I shall demonstrate exporting and importing using the three tools of choice—PowerShell, STSADM, and Central Administration.

Export and Import Using PowerShell

The following steps demonstrate using PowerShell commands from the PowerShell console to export a site to a file:

1. From the Start menu, choose All Programs.

2. Click Microsoft SharePoint 2013 Products.

3. Click SharePoint 2013 Management Shell to launch the console.

4. Type in the following text into the console, replacing the appropriate placeholders:
   Export-SPWeb <site/list/library URL> -Path <filename>

5. To export a specific list or library, provide the full URL to the list or library, otherwise PowerShell will export the site if the URL is to the main site location.

6. Include the [-Force] option to overwrite the file.

7. Include the [-HaltonError] or [-HaltOnWarning] options to stop the export process in the event of an error or warning.

8. Specify the [-IncludeUserSecurity] option if you need to ensure that all permissions applied to exported sites, lists, libraries, and contained items are included in the export file.

9. Include the [-IncludeVersions] option to instruct PowerShell to include version information of items in the export file.

10. Include the [-NoFileCompression] option to turn off file compression; this makes for a faster export but larger files on disk.

11. The [-NoLogFile] option prevents PowerShell from creating a log of the export (not recommended generally).

12. The [-UseSQLSnapshot] option is the familiar SQL snapshot option for deployments running on SQL Server Enterprise.

■ **Note** PowerShell provides help for all commands—you may get help on the export command by typing Get-help Export-SPWeb into the PowerShell console.

In partner to the export command, the following step demonstrates importing an export file to a SharePoint site, list, or library:

13. Type the following text into the console, replacing the appropriate placeholders:
    Import-SPWeb <site/list/library URL> -Path <filename>

To import a specific list or library, provide the full URL to the list or library, otherwise PowerShell will import the site if the URL is to the main site location. For brevity, most of the options specified in the previous export steps exist for the import command. Use the Get-help feature of PowerShell to see all options.

Exporting of lists and libraries was new to SharePoint 2010. In SharePoint 2007, administrators could export and import sites only, using STSADM. SharePoint 2010, and now 2013, supports STSADM export/import, but adds the capability of list and library export by providing the full URL to the list or library.

Export and Import Using STSADM

The following steps demonstrate export of a site, list, or library using the STSADM command from a regular Windows command prompt:

1. Type the following text into the console, replacing the appropriate placeholders:

   ```
   STSADM -o export -url <site/list/library url> -filename <filename>
   ```

2. To export a specific list or library, provide the full URL to the list or library. Otherwise, PowerShell will export the site if the URL is to the main site location.

3. Include the -overwrite option to overwrite the file.

4. Include the -haltonfatalerror or -haltonwarning options to stop the export process in the event of an error or warning.

5. Specifying the -includeusersecurity option will ensure that all permissions applied to exported sites, lists, libraries, and contained items are included in the export file.

6. The -versions option instructs PowerShell to include version information of items in the export file.

7. Include the -nofilecompression option to turn off file compression; this makes for a faster export but larger files on disk.

8. The -nologfile option prevents PowerShell from creating a log of the export (not recommended generally).

9. The -usesqlsnapshot option is the familiar SQL snapshot option for deployments running on SQL Server Enterprise.

The following steps demonstrate using STSADM to import a site, list, or library. Look back through the command options previously listed for the export, as some also apply to the import command.

10. Type the following text into the console, replacing the appropriate placeholders:

    ```
    STSADM -o import -url <site/list/library url> -filename <filename>
    ```

11. To import a specific list or library, provide the full URL to the list or library.

Export Using Central Administration

In this section, I demonstrate how to use Central Administration to export a site, list, or library. You may have noticed that this section does not cover import via the Central Administration web browser interface—this is because Central Administration does not provide a mechanism for site, list, or library import from a file. To import, use either STSADM or PowerShell options, previously discussed.

1. Open Central Administration.

2. Click on the Backup and Restore heading link.

3. Click the Export a Site or List link under the Granular Backup heading.

4. Select the site collection and then the site and/or list (see Figure 5-11).

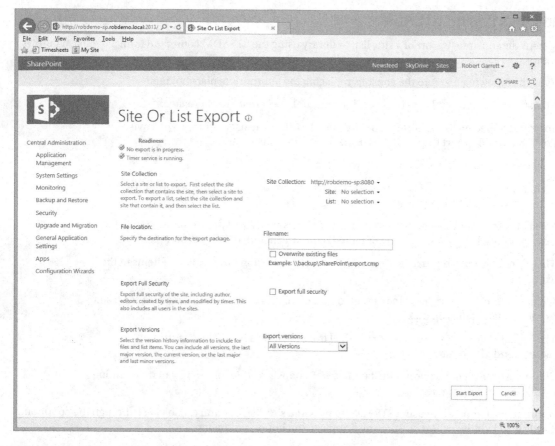

***Figure 5-11.** Exporting a site, list, or library from Central Administration*

5. Provide the file location and toggle options for security and versions.

6. Click the Start Export button to begin the export.

Unattached Content Database Data Recovery

IT staff and database admins like to back up SQL databases—and there is nothing wrong with that! SQL Server provides options to administrators to run nightly backups, and many good backup applications include a SQL agent to back up live SQL database data to backup storage. What is not to like? The problem is that full SQL Server database backups only provide all-or-nothing restore of data. Restoring a single piece of data, such as a document, requires standing up content backup in a new SharePoint web application and site collection to access the required data.

Rewind the clock a couple of years to the days of SharePoint 2007. In the event that an administrator wanted to restore selected data (such as a site, list, or library) from an offline database, the process went something like the following:

1. Restore the SQL database backup from cold storage to a disk location, seen by SQL Server.

2. Attach the offline database data file and log file to SQL Server, using a different name from the current live SQL Server, now becoming the backup database.

3. Associate the backup database with a fresh web application in SharePoint 2007, or another SharePoint 2007 farm.

4. Export the selected content from the backup, using STSADM (the minimum granularity was a subsite).

5. Import the exported content to the current live site collection.

6. Restore the site, list, or library to the correct place in the live site collection using SharePoint content tools, such as the Content Management UI.

The steps above seem like a lot of work to me. Further complications arose for the administrator in that SharePoint 2007 required installation of any feature customizations to the backup web application before the administrator could access the backup site collection. If using a separate farm to host backup content data, the administrator would have to ensure that the version of the production farm was equal to or exceeded that of the backup farm for the data import to work. Yuk!

You no longer need to worry. SharePoint now allows you to drill into a SQL content database without ever having to attach it to the farm, as the following steps demonstrate:

1. Open Central Administration.

2. Click the Backup and Restore heading link.

3. Click the Recover Data from an Unattached Content Database link.

4. Provide the SQL Server name and database name for the warm unattached database backup (you still need to host the offline database in SQL Server somewhere).

5. SharePoint displays a page like that in Figure 5-12.

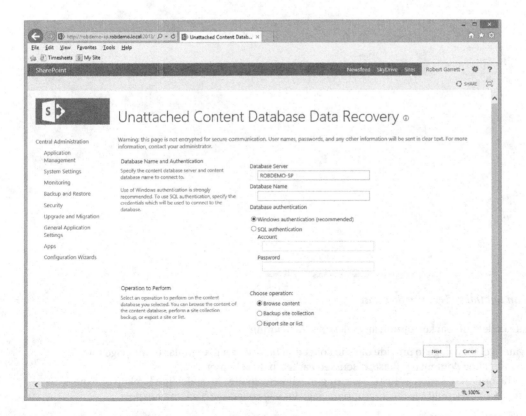

Figure 5-12. *Unattached Content Database Recovery*

6. In the Operation to Perform section, you have three choices:

    a. Browse content in the backup database.

    b. Backup a site collection contained in the database.

    c. Export a site or list from the database.

7. Select the Browse content option.

8. Click the Next button.

9. On the next page (Figure 5-13), you may browse a site collection, site, and list and then either back up the site collection or export the selected site and list.

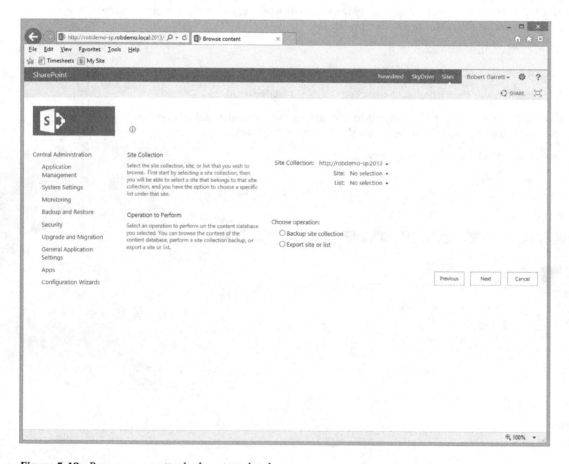

Figure 5-13. *Browse an unattached content database*

10. Try the site collection backup option and click the Next button.

SharePoint navigates you to a page to provide the site collection backup details, similar to the page for site collection backup of an attached content database, discussed earlier in this chapter.

Had you selected the option to export a site or a list, or gone directly to the site collection backup or export operation on the main page, you would see the appropriate page for site collection backup or export.

11. Click the Start Backup button.

So far, I have covered the granular backup methods. Next, I will visit complete farm backup and restore capabilities for SharePoint 2013. Before leaving granular backup, navigate back to the Backup and Restore page in Central Administration and click the Check Granular Backup Job Status link. Figure 5-14 shows the Job Status page for all granular backups, which provides for easy review of the health of your backup operations.

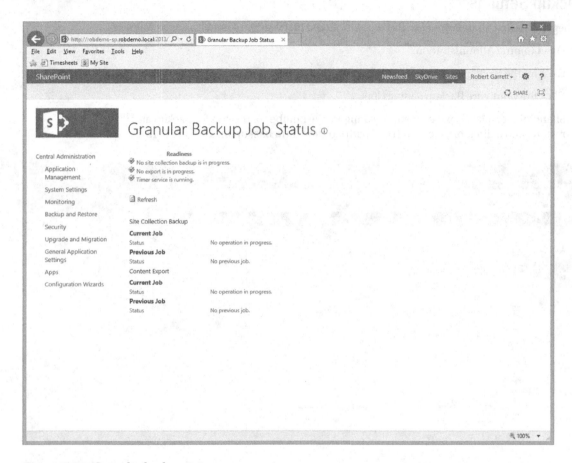

Figure 5-14. *Granular backup status*

Farm Backup and Restore

SharePoint provides complete SharePoint farm backup, using Central Administration. SharePoint also allows for complete backup and restore of the farm using PowerShell, and I will present steps for both procedures in this section of the chapter.

Up to now, I have discussed backup of content. Of course, content is vitally important because it is the user data of a system that gives the system its value, and contributes to the running of the business for which the organization employs the system. But now that I am discussing farm backup, more than just content has to be considered—for example, system configuration settings. When faced with a total disaster and system loss, the IT team and administrators want to get a new system online as quickly as possible. Unfortunately, SharePoint, like most other enterprise systems today, has a considerable number of configuration options, and no administrator wants to reconfigure a virgin SharePoint farm installation, from the ground up, under the pressure of disaster recovery. Fortunately, the features in SharePoint 2013 that provide for complete farm backup allow for configuration backup. I shall discuss configuration backup and restore as part of farm backup.

In the following sections, I shall walk you through backup via the Central Administration browser interface, and then I shall cover PowerShell backup and restore commands.

Farm Backup Settings

Before you begin your first SharePoint farm backup, you should first visit the settings page, as follows:

1. Open Central Administration.

2. Click on the Backup and Restore heading link.

3. Click the Configure Backup Settings link.

4. SharePoint displays a page for you to configure the number of threads for backup and restore, and a directory location (UNC path) to store farm backup files (Figure 5-15).

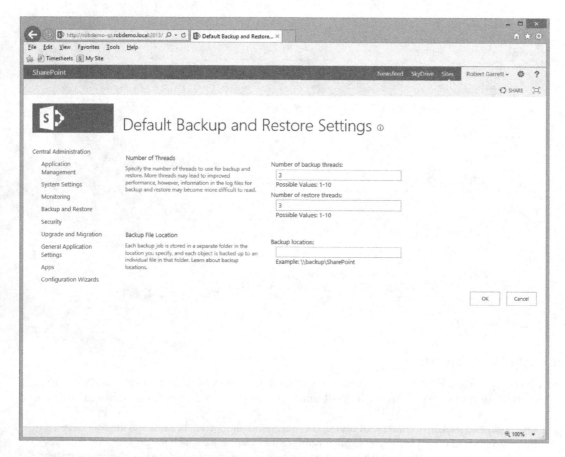

Figure 5-15. *Backup and Restore Settings*

5. The default of three threads is fine for most purposes.

6. Provide a UNC path for the backup directory because the timer service (which performs the backups) may not have the same drive mappings as your current user context.

"Threads," in computer terms, much like the threads in clothing, consist of granular processing in the overall application process life cycle. The CPU in the server slices time given to threads in a process to give the illusion of multi-threading or multiple things happening at once. Modern CPUs consist of multiple cores, which can process separate threads of a process at the same time (true multi-threading). Backup and restore operations work well with multi-threading because each thread dedicated to a CPU core may run independent backup and restore operations, thus providing for a more efficient backup and restore, which by its very nature is a timely process.

Performing a Backup

With the overall farm backup settings configured, you are now ready to perform your first backup. Follow the steps below:

1. Navigate to the Backup and Restore page in Central Administration.

2. Click the Perform a Backup link.

3. SharePoint displays a page like that in Figure 5-16.

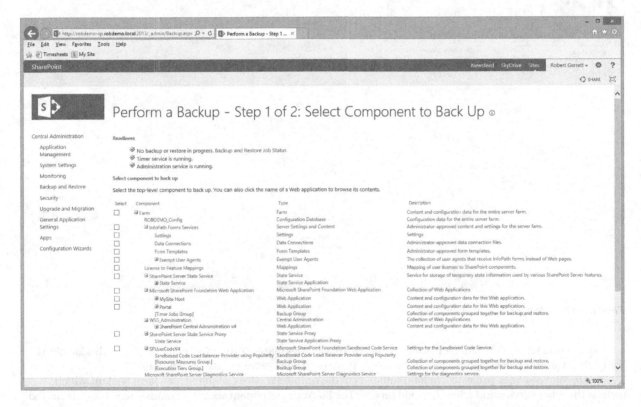

Figure 5-16. *Back up the farm from Central Administration*

This page is where it is all happening! Looking at Figure 5-16, which shows a summary of my farm, you can see several selection options to include in the farm backup.

Checking the check box at the top Farm level will enable all the options below it, which include backup of the content databases, web application settings, and service application configuration. At this point you may choose what to back up à la carte style, but for demonstration purposes, I shall assume backup of the entire farm. This will also give you an idea of how long the process for complete farm backup usually takes (which changes by order of magnitude based on the content in your farm and services installed).

■ **Note** When backing up content, backup files typically consume 1.5 times as much space as the original content databases.

4. Check the check box next to the Farm level, and then click the Next button.

5. Figure 5-17 shows the next page, where you specify the backup type.

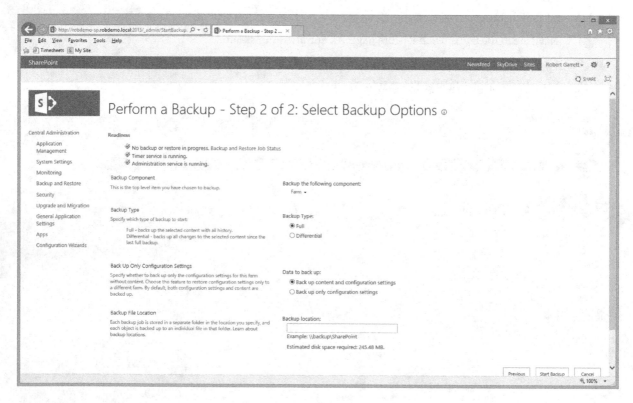

Figure 5-17. *Select farm backup options*

If you provided a UNC path for backups in the backup settings (earlier), then SharePoint suggests this location in the Backup Options page (Figure 5-17). If you didn't, there is no need to worry; just provide it now.

SharePoint provides you with a helpful summary of the running services, required for a farm backup, which include the timer service and administration service. The Backup Component section reminds you what you selected in the previous screen.

1. Select the backup type as either Full or Differential.

A full backup is exactly that—SharePoint backs up everything. Differential backups run much smaller and faster, but they only back up changes since the last full backup. Consider the restore process when choosing the backup types. Full backup restores are easier but take longer than differential, which require multiple restores of the various differential backups to get the system current after a disaster.

■ **Note** As a good practice, I recommend a weekly full backup and daily differential backups.

---

2. For demonstration purposes, and since this is your first backup, choose Full.

The next section of the Backup page allows you to specify backup of both content and configuration, or just configuration. The latter option comes in handy if you already have a content redundancy or backup process in place and now just want to save the farm configuration.

3. Click the option to back up both content and configuration.

4. Click the Start Backup button to begin the process.

5. SharePoint shows the status of the backup (Figure 5-18).

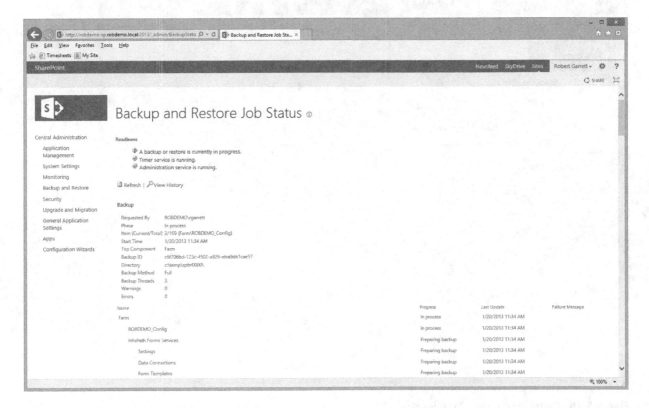

Figure 5-18. *Farm backup status*

6. Navigate back to the Central Administration main Backup and Restore page.

7. Click the View Backup and Restore History link to see a history of past backups.

8. If the backup is still running, then SharePoint will inform you with a link to the Status page at the top of the History page—Backup and Restore Job Status.

9. You may also get to the Backup and Restore Status page by clicking the Check Backup and Restore Job Status link in the Backup and Restore page.

Performing a Restore

Performing a SharePoint farm restore is much the inverse of the backup process. Assuming you have performed a successful farm backup, the following steps demonstrate the farm restore process:

1. Navigate to the Backup and Restore main page in Central Administration.

2. Click the Restore from a Backup link.

3. SharePoint displays a page like that in Figure 5-19.

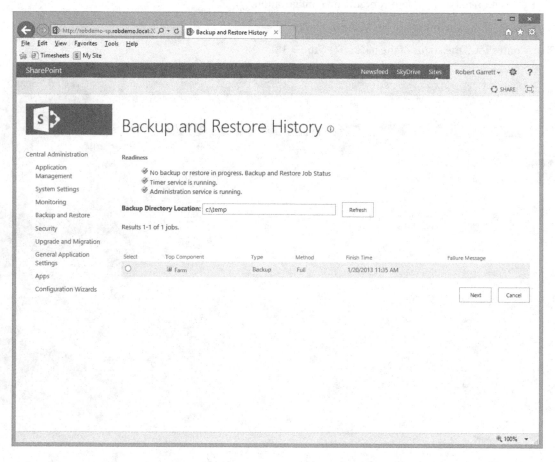

Figure 5-19. *Restoring the farm from backup*

4. Provide the backup directory location.

5. Choose the backup instance from the history list, and then click the Next button.

6. SharePoint shows a page like that in Figure 5-20.

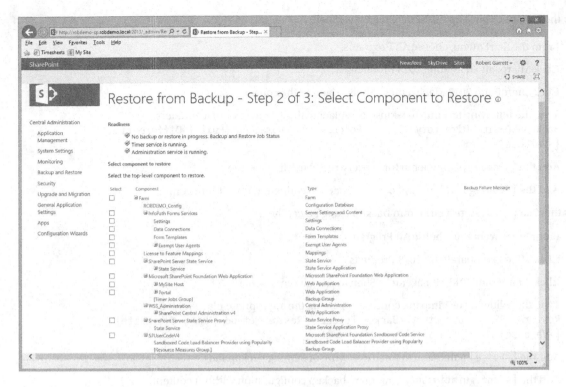

Figure 5-20. *Farm restore selection*

Similar to the backup process, this selection screen allows you to choose what configuration and content in the farm to restore.

7. Make your selection and then click the Next button.

8. The next page (too large to illustrate here) shows various options for the selected service and content configuration.

9. Choose whether you wish to overwrite configuration or create new.

10. The option to create new services from backup is useful when restoring a new farm from scratch after a disaster.

11. Use Overwrite when replacing the existing configuration.

12. Click the Start Restore button to begin the restore process.

Using PowerShell

As one might expect, SharePoint allows administrators to perform farm backup with PowerShell.

■ **Note** Before embarking on this route of backup/restore, ensure that the user running the script is a member of the SharePoint_Shell_Access role in the main SharePoint configuration database and is a member of the Windows security group WSS_ADMIN_WPG.

Follow these steps to back up the farm using PowerShell.

1. From the Start menu, choose All Programs.

2. Click Microsoft SharePoint 2013 Products.

3. Click SharePoint 2013 Management Shell to launch the console.

4. Type the following text into the console, replacing the appropriate placeholders:
   `Backup-SPFarm –Directory <Backup Folder> -BackupMethod {Full | Differential}`
   `[-Verbose]`

5. Add the [-Force] parameter to force overwrite of existing backup files.

6. Add the [-ConfigurationOnly] option to backup configuration without content.

Follow these steps to restore a farm from backup using PowerShell.

1. From the Start menu, choose All Programs.

2. Click Microsoft SharePoint 2013 Products.

3. Click SharePoint 2013 Management Shell to launch the console.

4. Type the following text into the console, replacing the appropriate placeholders:
   `Restore-SPFarm –Directory <Backup Folder> -RestoreMethod {New | Overwrite}`
   `[-Verbose]`

5. Add the [-Force] parameter to force overwrite of existing backup files.

6. Add the [-ConfigurationOnly] option to backup configuration without content.

SharePoint 2013 Request Management

Request Management is a new feature of SharePoint 2013. Although the topic of Request Management does not directly relate to disaster recovery and health, I wanted to include mention of this new service in this chapter because Request Management maintains load on a SharePoint farm, and therefore correlates to the overall health of your SharePoint 2013 farm.

Request Management allows SharePoint to understand more about, and control the handling of, incoming requests for pages, documents, and any other content that SharePoint may deliver to end users. The Request Management service encompasses a rules engine to make decisions on delegation of server requests to different servers in a multi-server SharePoint 2013 farm.

A new SharePoint service called "Microsoft SharePoint Foundation Web Application" handles Request Management for the SharePoint farm. The following steps show the location of this service in Central Administration:

1. Navigate to Central Administration.

2. Click the link for Manage Services on Server, under the System Settings heading.

3. Scroll down the list of services.

4. The Microsoft SharePoint Foundation Web Application should have a state of *Started*.

As the service name suggests, Request Management is part of the core SharePoint platform and available to all versions of SharePoint 2013, including Foundation.

Wait a minute! Request Management sounds like the job of a load balancer, outside the responsibility of SharePoint. Yes and no. Any administrator responsible for a multi-server and multiple web-front-end SharePoint farm is probably aware of the role of a hardware or software load balancer. A load balancer sits in front of all incoming requests and redirects traffic to one of a pool of web servers, depending on availability of these servers. Typically, load balancers make determinations on what server they forward requests to based on DNS settings and servers that respond to IP requests. Some more intelligent load balancers can monitor server utilization and route traffic based on available load. However, SharePoint is a dynamic platform, which might consist of many different servers, providing different services. Some servers in a SharePoint farm may provide multiple functions. Request Management provides better granular control over which servers receive which requests, based on data in each request. For example, by looking at the user agent, content type, etc. within a request, the Request Management service can direct traffic to a SharePoint server that is best equipped to service a response.

The Request Management Process

Request Management consists of the Web Application service, running on every SharePoint server in the farm. This is important to note—Request Management requires knowledge of the performance and characteristics of each SharePoint server available to service requests, and this is the job of this service.

The Request Manager (the service running on each SharePoint server) provides three levels of operation:

- Load balancing
- Prioritization
- Throttling and routing

Figure 5-21 illustrates rule flow of Request Management in SharePoint 2013. Based on a set of routing rules, Request Management makes decisions on where to route server requests.

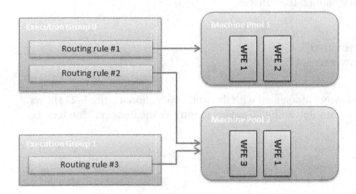

Figure 5-21. *Request Management flow*

Each potential target server to respond to a request resides within a machine pool. Each server in a machine pool has a static weighting and health weighting, which the routing rules use to determine the eligibility of servers to service requests. Static weights are numeric values assigned by administrators to weight particular servers in the farm, whereas SharePoint changes health weights as the performance and health of servers changes over time.

Routing rules group into execution groups, of which there are three: Execution Group 0, 1, and 2 (Execution Group 2 not shown in Figure 5-21). Any rule not explicitly assigned to an execution group assumes Execution Group 0. Execution groups denote precedence; rules in Group 0 are evaluated before those in Group 1, which are evaluated before those in Group 2. It is the job of routing rules to determine which machine pool will service an incoming request.

Throttling rules (not shown in Figure 5-21) refuse incoming requests that match these rules, and act as a gatekeeper for all requests. For example, requests that have inappropriate parameters or request data might trigger a throttling rule.

The Request Manager evaluates which server shall service an incoming request as follows:

1. Compare the request with a set of throttling rules; if the request matches any of these rules then refuse the request.

2. Evaluate the request by matching it against all routing rules in Execution Group 0, followed by Execution Group 1, and then Execution Group 2.

3. Depending on matching to routing rules in a specific execution group, route the request to the machine pool associated with the routing rule satisfied by the request.

Any routing rule can route requests to any machine pool. The presence of the routing rule in one of the execution groups ascertains priority. Thus, rules in Execution Group 0 will evaluate first and target machine pools determined best equipped to satisfy the requests.

Request Management Administration

There is no browser user interface for Request Management in SharePoint 2013. Instead, administration of Request Management is via PowerShell Cmdlets.

The following example demonstrates how to get access to the Request Management settings for a particular web application:

1. From the Start menu, choose All Programs.

2. Click Microsoft SharePoint 2013 Products.

3. Click SharePoint 2013 Management Shell to launch the console.

4. Type the following text into the console:

```
$app = Get-WebApplication "http://webappUrl"
$rmSettings = $app | Get-SPRequestManagementSettings
$rmSettings
```

You should see a list of settings for the Request Manager associated with the web application. Figure 5-22 shows a screenshot from my console when I executed the previous PowerShell Cmdlets to retrieve the Request Management settings for my default web application.

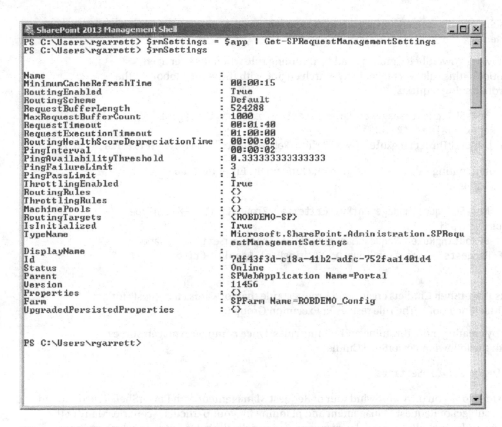

Figure 5-22. *Request Management settings for web application*

The following set of steps demonstrates how to create a couple of machine pools:

5. Type the following PowerShell Cmdlets into the console:

   ```
   $pool1 = Add-SPRoutingMachinePool –RequestManagementSettings $rmSettings
   -Name "Machine Pool 1" –MachineTargets @("Server1", "Server2")
   ```

6. The previous PowerShell assumes Server 1 and Server 2 belong to a new machine pool, called Machine Pool 1.

7. Add another machine pool, as follows:

   ```
   $pool2 = Add-SPRoutingMachinePool –RequestManagementSettings $rmSettings
   -Name "Machine Pool 2" –MachineTargets @("Server3")
   ```

8. The previous PowerShell assumes Server 3 belongs to a new machine pool, called Machine Pool 2.

9. Now to add some static weightings for servers in the pools.

10. Enter the following PowerShell Cmdlets:

    ```
    $rmServerInfo = $rmSettings | Get-SPRoutingMachineInfo –Name "Server1"
    Set-SPRoutingMachineInfo –Identity $rmServerInfo –StaticWeight 8
    ```

11. Repeat step 10 for each server in both pools.

12. With the machine pools created and servers in those pools, I will demonstrate adding a throttling rule.

13. Type the following PowerShell Cmdlets to add a throttling rule when the user agent includes "Robot"—this rule will prevent any search engine with the word "Robot" in the user agent from issuing requests.

```
$criteria = New-SPRequestManagementRuleCriteria -Property UserAgent
-MatchType Regex -Value ".*Robot.*"
$rmSettings | Add-SPThrottlingRule -Name "Refuse Robot Agents" -Criteria $criteria
```

14. Now to add some routing rules, which bind to machine pools. Enter the following PowerShell Cmdlets:

```
$criteria = New-SPRequestManagementRuleCriteria -Property Url -MatchType
Regex -Value ".*\.pdf"
$rule = Add-SPRoutingRule -RequestManagementSettings $rmSettings -Name
"Handle PDF Requests" -ExecutionGroup 0 -MachinePool $pool1 -Criteria
$criteria
```

15. The previous PowerShell Cmdlets create a new request rule that forwards all requests for PDF files to Machine Pool 1. The rule resides in Execution Group 0.

16. Experiment by creating more throttling and routing rules. Once complete, you can survey the rules with the following PowerShell Cmdlet:

```
Get-SPRoutingRule | $rmSettings
```

The previous set of steps took you on a whirlwind tour of Request Management with PowerShell. I recommend that you read more on the subject of Request Management and planning for your particular scenario. Many of the Cmdlets in the previous examples include additional parameters—especially the rules Cmdlets, which support multiple property and matching types.

Health and Monitoring

The health of your new SharePoint 2013 deployment is very important. Your organization, you, and your administration team have likely spent considerable time installing, configuring, and deploying SharePoint to accommodate the needs of the enterprise. In my time as a SharePoint architect, I have seen a number of organizations stop here, but the fact of the matter is that SharePoint requires a certain amount of care and feeding, just like any enterprise computer system. This is not to say that SharePoint left alone will fall over in time, but as more users pump data into the system, eating up storage space, and the system grows a larger user base, administrators should expect to monitor SharePoint and the underlying server infrastructure for stress areas and efficiency optimization.

Organizations understand that it is costly to stand up large-scale enterprise systems, and they rely on them as an integral part of their daily business. Spending more money ensuring that such systems remain healthy and sustain significant uptime is just as important as the upfront investment in the creation of the system. Consider how much money an organization might lose if its core information system falls over and suffers downtime.

Earlier in this chapter, I covered disaster recovery. I demonstrated several planning techniques to recover in the event that your SharePoint infrastructure fails. Disaster recovery is akin to planning for what to do when a hurricane hits your town, but it would sure be nice to factor in some notice before the storm hits—this analogy is what health and monitoring is all about.

In the previous versions of SharePoint, administrators tended to work in reactive mode—typically, users of the system would report performance issues or loss of access to their data in SharePoint, and the IT department would then jump on the case to rectify the issue. SharePoint now provides health and monitoring features to give the IT group a heads-up of potential issues in the platform, long before users ever see an issue. In the remainder of this chapter, I shall describe these new features. I will discuss how to configure these features to give you advanced warning of problems brewing in the platform, so that you may remedy issues and users may never know there was a problem in the first place.

Logging

Logging is an important part of health monitoring because it is via various log files that SharePoint may alert administrators to issues in the system. The Unified Logging Service (ULS provides administrators with an extensive dump of information, warnings, and errors occurring in the platform. When something goes wrong, the user typically sees either a custom-developed "oops" message in his or her browser, or a default SharePoint error message. It is the job of SharePoint administrators to find out what went wrong, and the ULS logs will likely give an indication of the problem—especially if it is recurring.

■ **Note** By default, the ULS logs live on each SharePoint 2013 server in the Logs folder of the hive, typically `c:\program files\common files\Microsoft shared\web server extensions\15\logs`.

Figure 5-23 shows the explorer view of the ULS log folder on my SharePoint 2013 development server. The log folder consists of a number of files, both log and usage files (all text files), that have a file name in the format of year, month, day, and time. If you crack open any of the log files you can see lots of detail, reported by the various functional areas of the SharePoint platform—notice that the Timer Service reports lots of information events.

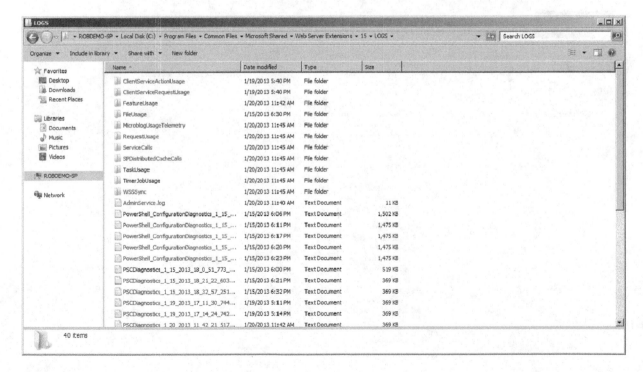

Figure 5-23. *The ULS log folder on a SharePoint 2013 server*

Viewing the ULS log files in the raw is not always helpful. Fortunately, you can download a ULS viewer application to browse ULS. Explicit details of the ULS viewer application are outside the scope of this book, but the tool provides filtering capabilities and continued monitoring of the log entries in real time. I strongly recommend this tool to anyone looking to scrutinize the ULS log for SharePoint issues.

■ **Note** Download the ULS viewer tool from `http://archive.msdn.microsoft.com/ULSViewer`.

SharePoint allows you to fine-tune the ULS log files to contain information most important to you. The Trace Log Windows Service, which controls output of the ULS log files, also operates in a variety of verbosity modes, ranging from error reporting to very detailed information for every action in the platform. As you might expect, Central Administration is the place to configure the ULS settings, as demonstrated in the following steps:

1. Open Central Administration.

2. Click on the Monitoring link.

3. Click the Configure Diagnostic Logging link.

4. SharePoint shows a page like that in Figure 5-24.

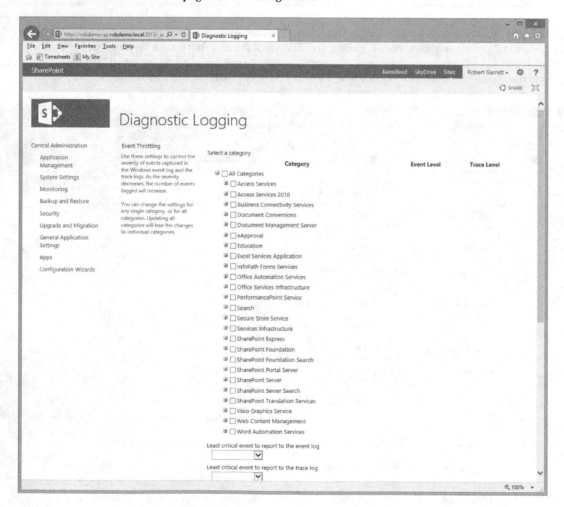

Figure 5-24. *ULS logging configuration*

5. Expand the Categories node.

6. Specify the types of events you wish SharePoint to log in the ULS logs.

7. When an error occurs in the platform, SharePoint reports events to both the ULS and Windows event log; you may control the severity (verbosity level) of events logged to both in the Throttling section of the page.

■ **Note** This page does not show you the current configuration for throttling; it defaults to empty drop-down controls and no categories selected.

---

8. Flood protection consists of preventing SharePoint logging the same repeated event to the Windows event log when a consistent problem arises. For example, if a timer service job runs every five minutes and fails, you really do not want hundreds of event log errors of the same message because an administrator did not get to the issue for a few hours.

9. Finally, the Trace Log section defines the location of ULS log files, the number of days of history to store, and the maximum size of log files.

■ **Note** When changing settings for diagnostic logging, I recommend you restart the SharePoint 2013 Tracing Service in Windows Services. Also, stop this service if you need to delete any of the ULS log files.

Correlation IDs

Since the previous version of SharePoint, Microsoft has introduced Correlation IDs GUIDs (Global Unique Identifiers) that map an event in SharePoint with the error or warning in the ULS log (see Figure 5-25). Prior to SharePoint 2013, the administrator had to hunt and peck through the log files looking for the event that caused the error. Correlation IDs now allow a user experiencing a problem and an error page to send the ID to the administrator to find more details about the issue.

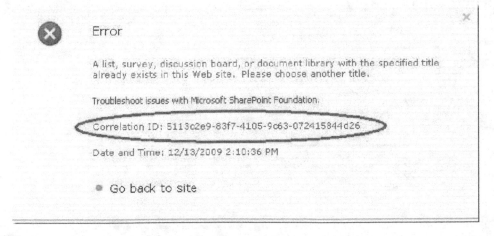

Figure 5-25. Correlation ID in a SharePoint error page

As well as using a text-editor-find action to find errors in the ULS log files, SharePoint includes a very nice PowerShell command to simplify finding the messages with a given Correlation ID:

```
Get-SPLogEvent | ?{$_.Correlation -eq "<ID>"}
```

The Logging Database

The logging database in SharePoint provides developers with a central data store to capture all events occurring in the platform. Microsoft introduced the logging database both to provide a transactional database of all events for easy query and to herd developers away from executing custom queries directly against content and configuration databases in the farm.

The logging database provides a central location to query all events occurring in the farm, whereas ULS logs only report information per the verbosity settings (see previous sections of this chapter) and spread across servers in the farm. The following steps demonstrate how to configure the logging database for your farm:

1. Open Central Administration.

2. Click the Monitoring heading link.

3. Click the Configure Usage and Health Data Collection link.

4. Figure 5-26 shows a page for configuring the health data collection events.

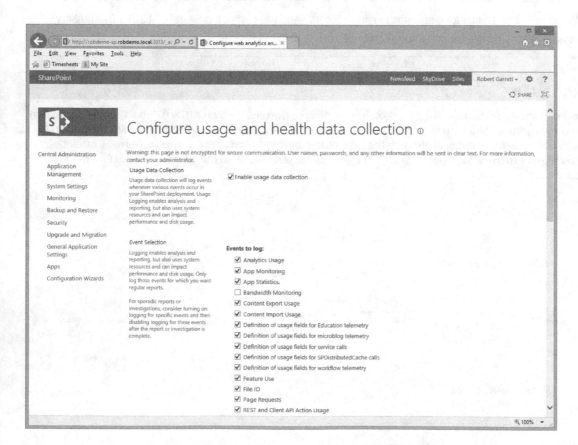

Figure 5-26. *Configure Health Data Collection*

5.   Ensure that the topmost check box is checked to enable usage data collection.

6.   Select the events you wish SharePoint to capture.

■ **Note**   In the Usage Data Collection Settings section, notice that the location defaults to the same folder as ULS logs; if you look into this folder you should see usage files as well as the familiar log files.

---

7.   Check the box for the Health Data Collection setting to monitor SharePoint farm health, which is in addition to usage.

8.   Click the Health Logging Schedule link if you wish to change the schedules that the health logging timer services run (several of them).

9.   SharePoint populates the logging database using the various usage files on each SharePoint server.

10. A timer service collects data from these files and populates the database configured in the Logging Database Server section.

11. Click the link to configure the schedule of the log collection timer service.

Allow the usage collection to run for a day or two and interact with your farm to generate usage events. Next, I shall show you the logging database, which in my farm is the ROBDEMO_UsageandHealth database.

1.   Open SQL Server Management Studio.

2.   Navigate to the logging database.

3.   If you expand the Tables node, you should see a large number of partitioned tables, which is not too helpful.

4.   Expand the Views node instead.

5.   You may execute SQL queries against the views.

6.   In Figure 5-27, I ran a select T-SQL statement over the dbo.FeatureUsage view.

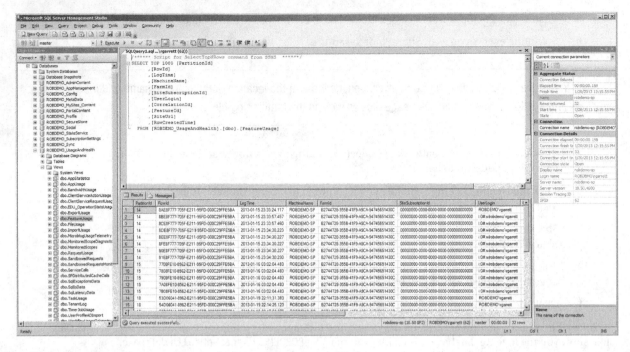

Figure 5-27. *SQL Server Management Studio and the logging database*

The logging database also contains a number of stored procedures that return tabular usage data. As you can see, the logging database provides a nice collection of usage event data that developers may query in custom controls, without having to dip into the main farm content and configuration databases. The premise here is that Microsoft optimizes the configuration and content databases for SharePoint and does not guarantee consistency in the schema between versions. The logging database is isolated from the other farm databases and offers consistency, allowing developers the confidence that their queries remain working with future upgrades of the platform.

Analytics

In the previous version of SharePoint—SharePoint Server 2010—the Web Analytics Service Application maintained usage and analytics data for the SharePoint farm. With the new SharePoint 2013 platform, Microsoft redesigned the analytics components and integrated analytics with SharePoint search.

■ **Note**   SharePoint 2013 replaces the Web Analytics Service Application of SharePoint 2010 with the new analytics engine that is part of search.

From a high level, the new analytics features of SharePoint 2013 provide the following advantages:

- User recommendations based on usage data tracking

- Promoted search results based on usage and visit tracking of content

- More sophisticated usage tracking with the SharePoint search engine platform

- Search is ubiquitous across the SharePoint platform and, therefore, better equipped to manage usage and analytics

I cover search configuration and usage reports in Chapter 15.

The Health Analyzer

The previous few sections of this chapter were concerned with reviewing the health of SharePoint proactively. When I first mentioned health and monitoring in this chapter, I said that SharePoint has the capability to monitor and report itself and give administrators a heads-up when potential problems in the platform are brewing. This is the job of the Health Analyzer. The following steps demonstrate how to access the Health Analyzer settings and reports from Central Administration:

1. Open Central Administration.

2. Click the Monitoring heading link.

3. Review the links under the Health Analyzer heading.

Because the job of the Health Analyzer and reporting issues is important, you may notice that the Health Analyzer displays a banner on the Central Administration home page when it detects errors or warnings. If you do not see this banner on your Central Administration home page then all is good with your farm. Do not be alarmed if you just installed SharePoint 2013 and now see a red or yellow banner (see Figure 5-28). The Health Analyzer has a number of extensive rules, which it uses to report anything that might pertain to a configuration, security, or operational issue. Sometimes, these rules trigger to warn users, but the issue is not always serious—such as the rule that warns users of the potential to run out of disk space, which occurs if the amount of memory in the system is more than half the available disk space on the system drive (for core dump purposes). This being said, you should pay attention to every warning and error, just in case SharePoint reports a serious issue.

■ **Note**   You should pay close attention to every warning and error reported by the Health Analyzer.

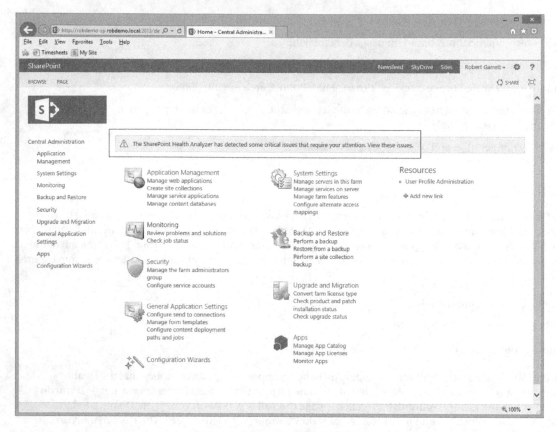

***Figure 5-28.** Health Analyzer alerts in Central Administration*

Click the View these issues link, which navigates you to the same page as the Review problems and solutions link under the Monitoring heading. If the Health Analyzer has picked up issues to address in your farm, the Review Problems and Solutions page should list those issues. See Figure 5-29 for an example from my development farm. In my case, I was expecting a number of warnings in my development environment because I had not completed a full farm configuration at the time I wrote this chapter, such as configuration of search and outgoing e-mail. If I were configuring a farm for production, I would want to address all the issues reported.

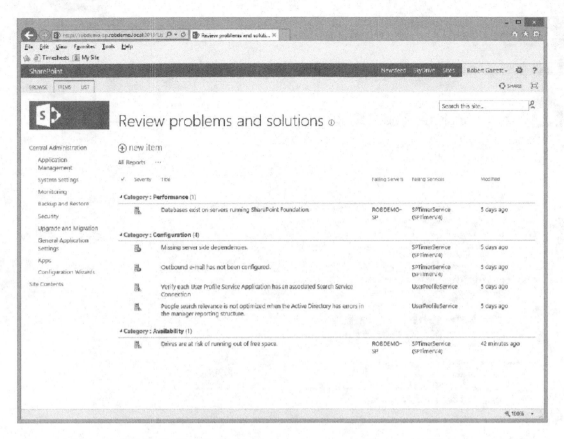

Figure 5-29. *Issues reported by the Health Analyzer*

1. Click any of the issues, and SharePoint will open a page with more specifics about the issue.

2. In some cases, SharePoint can help you fix issues, with the Repair Automatically icon on the dialog ribbon.

3. If SharePoint cannot automatically fix an issue, fix the issue manually and then come back to the issue and click the Reanalyze Now icon to request that the Health Analyzer determine if you remedied the issue.

The Health Analyzer uses a series of rules to determine if a particular area of the SharePoint platform needs attention.

1. Navigate back to the Monitoring page in Central Administration.

2. Click the Review Rule Definitions link.

3. SharePoint shows a page consisting of a standard list of rules (Figure 5-30).

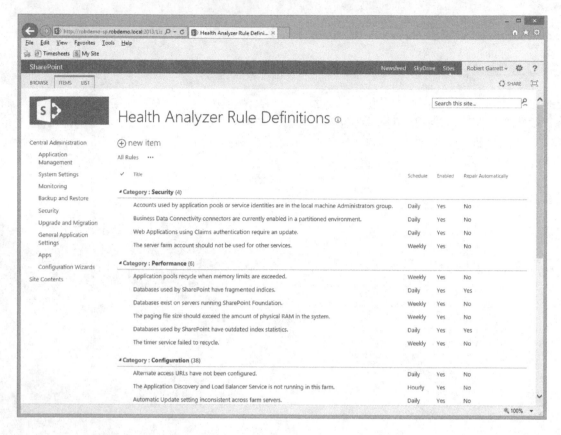

Figure 5-30. *Rule definitions for the Health Analyzer*

4. Click the name of any list item in the appropriate category to view the rule definition.

5. You may click the Edit icon to edit the rule list item—you may change the name, scope, schedule, and whether SharePoint can configure the issue automatically.

Timer Jobs

Timer jobs work at the heart of a SharePoint farm. Each SharePoint server (web-front-end or application server) hosts a SharePoint timer service, which is a Windows service. This service is responsible for running SharePoint jobs—designated units of functionality to execute a designated time and perhaps recurring.

SharePoint relies on a vast number of timer service jobs to maintain operation of the farm. The following steps demonstrate how to view the available timer job definitions in the farm:

1. Open Central Administration.

2. Click the Monitoring heading link.

3. Click the Review Job Definitions link, under the Timer Jobs heading.

4. SharePoint displays a page like that in Figure 5-31.

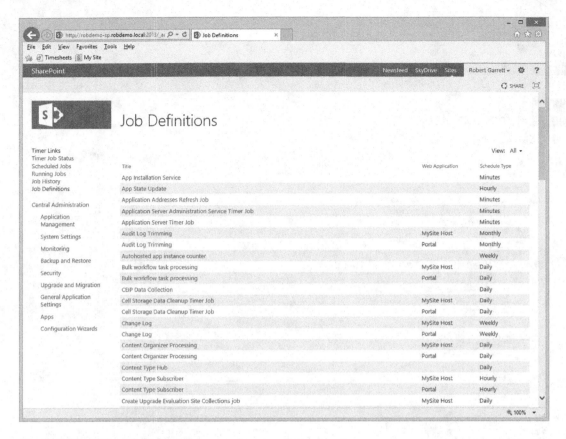

Figure 5-31. *Timer Job Definitions*

Timer job definitions are SharePoint Foundation Timer services, or associated with other SharePoint services, such as the Access or Excel services.

5. Click the View drop-down box in the top right to list timer services by web application, services, or list all jobs.

6. Click the name of any of the timer job definitions to see the details of the job.

Administrators may change the schedule of most jobs. They may also disable and enable jobs. SharePoint allows creation of new jobs only via code and feature deployment, so seek a developer if you need a special job created. Some of the functional features of SharePoint create timer jobs to perform their tasks; for example, Content Deployment creates a new timer job to deploy content to another farm.

7. Navigate back to the Monitoring page of Central Administration.

8. Click the Check Job Status link.

9. SharePoint shows you a page of upcoming scheduled jobs, running jobs, and a history of jobs executed, with their completion status (Figure 5-32).

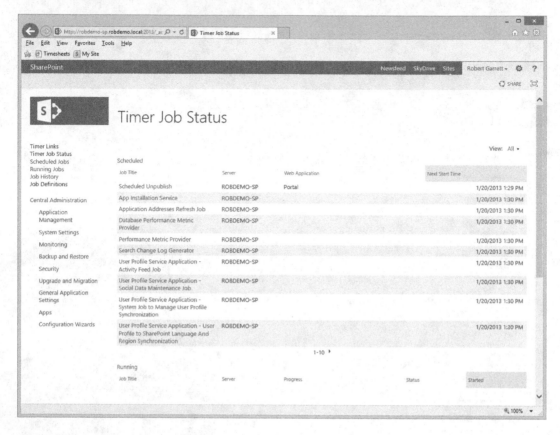

Figure 5-32. *Timer Job Statuses*

The Developer Dashboard

As much as this book is about administration and not development, I need to say a few words about the SharePoint Developer Dashboard. Microsoft introduced this feature with SharePoint 2010, and it provides performance and tracing information within SharePoint rendered pages. Developers (and administrators) may diagnose slow-rendering pages using the Developer Dashboard. Figure 5-33 is an example of the Developer Dashboard output.

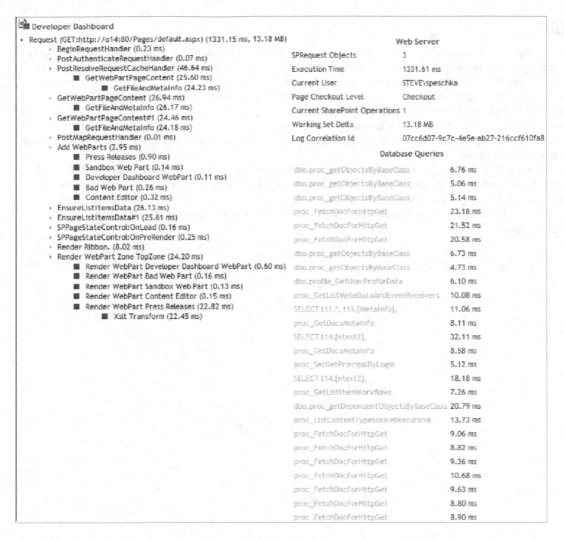

Figure 5-33. *Example output from the Developer Dashboard*

The following STSADM command demonstrates enabling the Developer Dashboard:

```
STSADM-o setproperty -pn developer-dashboard -pv ondemand on
```

The following command disables it:

```
STSADM-o setproperty -pn developer-dashboard -pv ondemand off
```

Summary

In this chapter, I discussed planning for disaster, and you read about how to recover in the event of service downtime. Good planning of your infrastructure enables you to take advantage of warm standby scenarios, and I covered how SharePoint may leverage SQL clustering, SQL mirroring, and failover.

SharePoint provides users of the platform with a degree of control over content integrity, via document versioning and the Recycle Bin to recover deleted lists and list items.

No disaster recovery plan is complete without a mention of backup and restore of content and configuration. I walked you through backup and restore of both content and SharePoint configuration, using Central Administration, PowerShell, and STSADM tools.

Toward the end of this chapter, you explored the Health Analyzer, usage, and health monitoring capabilities of SharePoint 2013 to alert administrators of potential problems in their SharePoint farm. As a nice treat for developers, I introduced you to the Developer Dashboard, so that you may troubleshoot slow-rendering pages in SharePoint.

In Chapter 6, I will change topics and discuss user profiles and the social capabilities of SharePoint 2013. See you on the next page.

CHAPTER 6

■■■

Users, Profiles, and Social Networking

SharePoint revolves around user collaboration. User collaboration thrives with user adoption of a SharePoint system, and for a SharePoint solution to engage users requires integration of user identity in the system. In Chapter 7, I shall cover security, which has an identity component and focuses on authentication in SharePoint 2013. In this chapter, I will discuss user profiles, which map user identity to the details about users.

Each user profile in SharePoint retains metadata about a person using the SharePoint platform, such as their role in the organization, photo, summary of skills, office demographics, and so on. After reading this chapter, you will know what constitutes a user profile and how you can configure the User Profile Service (UPS) application in a SharePoint 2013 farm, establishing two-way synchronization between user profiles in SharePoint and those of the organization Active Directory. You will also learn about configuring people search.

Later in this chapter, I shall dive into social networking. Thanks to the proliferation of social networking sites such as Facebook, Google+, and others in most people's personal lives, social networking has crept into the business world. Microsoft has addressed the need for social networking components, such as newsfeeds, event tracking, and likes, within the SharePoint platform, and I shall highlight some of the new features within SharePoint 2013.

A User's Profile

A user profile is a collection of data about a person. SharePoint synonymizes the term "people" with "users"; therefore, user profiles in SharePoint consist of data about users of the SharePoint platform. When you think about the profile of a user, you typically think about demographic information—name, address, phone, e-mail, and so on. SharePoint stores this demographic data, and more, as fields in the user profile associated with a user in a SharePoint farm. SharePoint terms these fields "profile properties."

Users of a SharePoint site may view their profile at any time by clicking their name either on the top right of the ribbon (followed by the About Me link), or next to any document or list item when shown. SharePoint will display a page with main demographic information, a picture (if you have one in your profile), and other information about you—such as the About Me description, and skills. Your profile page also includes an Edit My Profile link, allowing you to edit your own profile. Later on in this chapter, I will demonstrate how to add profile properties, in addition to the default properties included with SharePoint, so that users may add more data about themselves. Figure 6-1 shows the default profile for my user identity in my SharePoint 2013 development farm. Notice that I added a picture to my profile to make it appealing to those viewing it.

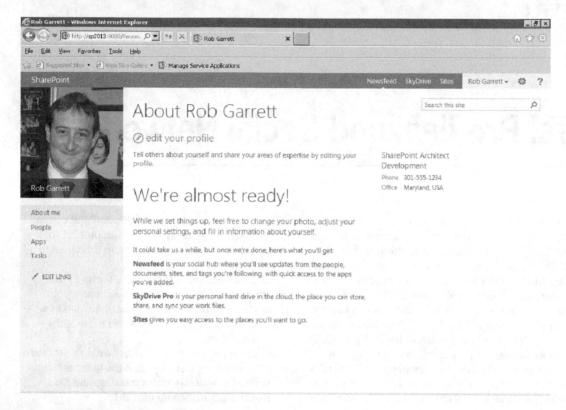

Figure 6-1. *Default Profile page in SharePoint 2013*

Similar to the way you view your own profile; other users of SharePoint may see your public profile information by clicking your name where it appears next to list items and documents in the site. Your association with a user governs how you see his or her profile. For example, users can set the visibility of their profile properties to Everyone, Manager, Team, Colleagues, or just themselves.

If you are thinking that user profiles in SharePoint are very much like user records in Active Directory (or any other directory system), you are right. Keeping user profile information in both places may seem like unnecessary work, which is why Microsoft provided the User Synchronization Service in SharePoint, so you can populate user profiles in SharePoint with those in your directory system. User Profile Synchronization now also allows you to establish bidirectional sync, so that users may update their profiles in SharePoint and see the changes reflected in the directory store. I will cover User Profile Synchronization in the next section of this chapter.

The User Profile Infrastructure

In this section, my aim is to give you some context for various architectural components that combine to make the user profile and User Profile Synchronization infrastructure. Figure 6-2 offers a pictorial overview of the components and provides a logical view of the services and service applications involved. Following this infrastructure overview, you will configure a new User Profile Service and Synchronization in a virgin SharePoint 2013 farm.

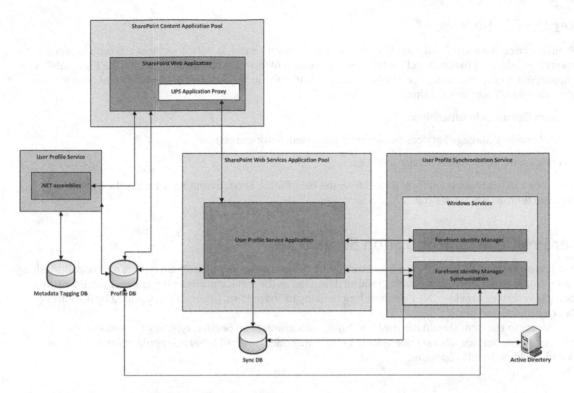

Figure 6-2. *The user profile infrastructure architecture*

■ **Note**   Although most deployments of User Profile Synchronization use Active Directory, there is no reason why you cannot configure User Profile Synchronization to another directory store, such as an LDAP service.

The User Profile Service Application

A SharePoint service application exists in a context similar to that of a SharePoint web application—it resides in Internet Information Services (IIS) and offers application presence to other SharePoint and non-SharePoint services on the network. Within Internet Information Services Manager 7.0 (INETMGR), expand the SharePoint Web Services application to see a list of IIS applications, some with GUID names—these are the service applications hosted on the current server of your farm.

The User Profile Service application is actually a WCF (Windows Communication Foundation) service, which exposes service end-points. Other servers in the farm may leverage the User Profile Service application to access user profile data. Discussion of WCF is beyond the scope of this book, but I will say that all SharePoint service applications operate as WCF services and expose functionality via the standard WCF service patterns. The User Profile Service application uses three SharePoint databases to host user profile–related data, which I will discuss in the section on configuration, later in this chapter.

Administrators may configure multiple User Profile Service applications in the farm, but only one User Profile Service application associates with a User Profile Synchronization SharePoint Service.

The User Profile Service

The User Profile Service is a *SharePoint* service. Note that a SharePoint service is *not* the same as a *Windows* service. SharePoint services exist only in the SharePoint context and consist of functionality abstracted into .NET assemblies within the SharePoint platform and exposed to the administrator in the list of services in the SharePoint farm in Central Administration. Take the following steps to view this list:

1. Open Central Administration.

2. Click the link Manage Services on Server in the System Settings section.

3. Look for the User Profile Service in the list.

Only one server in the SharePoint farm should have the User Profile Service running, which is the service machine instance for the User Profile role.

The User Profile Synchronization Service

Like the User Profile Service, the User Profile Synchronization Service exists as a SharePoint service and lists alongside its sibling User Profile Service on the server in the farm, delegated as the service machine instance for the User Profile role. This particular service provides .NET wrapper functionality to SharePoint, beyond that provided by the Forefront Identity Manager (discussed next).

Only one server in the farm should run the User Profile Synchronization Service, typically the same server running the User Profile Service. This service associates with only one User Profile Service application and accepts credentials under which the FIM operates.

The Forefront Identity Manager (FIM)

SharePoint bundles a lightweight version of the Forefront Identity Manager application, which has the primary job of managing user and server identity. The FIM consists of two Windows services—configured by the User Profile Synchronization Service SharePoint Service.

■ **Note**   The FIM client tool, part of Windows, does not support customizing the FIM services that bundle in SharePoint 2010 and 2013 but supports monitoring and troubleshooting.

The topic of Forefront Identity Management is outside the scope of this book, but it is worth understanding its role in the User Profile Synchronization infrastructure as managing identity as it pertains to users in SharePoint.

You can find the FIM client tool for SharePoint at the following location on the service machine instance: `C:\Program Files\Microsoft Office Servers\14.0\Synchronization Service\UIShell\miisclient.exe`.

Configuring User Profile Synchronization

Configuration of User Profile Synchronization in SharePoint is a task that seems to give administrators more trouble than any other area of SharePoint installation and configuration. User Profile Synchronization in SharePoint is complicated and therefore gives administrators the most trouble when it does not work. Do not worry, though—I shall guide you through the configuration of User Profile Sync on a virgin SharePoint 2013 environment.

■ **Note** The steps in this chapter assume no prior configuration of User Profile Service and no User Profile Service application existing in the farm. They also assume the use of Active Directory (AD) as the source of user profiles, although you may use another directory service.

Establishing Managed Accounts

Establishing the correct credentials and configuring the necessary services and service applications under the correct set of credentials is essential to ensuring smooth installation and operation of User Profile Service and Synchronization. Most of the time, when User Profile Service and User Profile Synchronization fails, it is because of incorrect credentials, or credentials with insufficient privileges.

Chapter 2 introduced the notion of managed service accounts in SharePoint—rather than specifying Active Directory account credentials everywhere, you can map these credentials to a managed account name in SharePoint in one central location. Assuming that you have installed SharePoint 2013 and have access to the Central Administration site, the following steps allow you to view a list of managed service accounts in the farm:

1. Open Central Administration.

2. Click the Security section heading.

3. Click the link Configure Managed Accounts in the General Security subsection.

You should see a page similar to Figure 6-3, although you will likely see a different list of managed accounts from that in my environment.

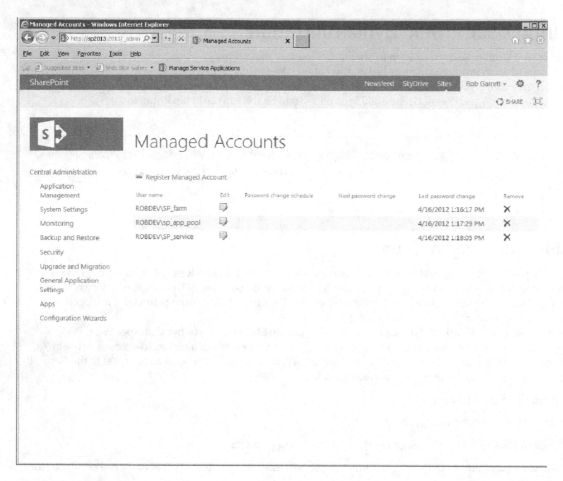

Figure 6-3. *Managed Accounts*

Before you begin configuring the User Profile Service infrastructure, make sure the following statements are true:

- SharePoint is installed and configured without a User Profile Service application (you can delete the application and proxy from the managed service applications list).

- You have configured a farm account, e.g. `DOMAIN\spfarm` as a managed account.

- You have *not* logged into the server or Central Administration as the farm account.

- The farm account is *not* a local administrator on the server running User Profile Service.

- Your farm *does not* use a Fully Qualified Domain Name or IP address to connect SharePoint 2013 with SQL Server—use a SQL alias or NetBIOS name to avoid issues with provisioning services later.

- Your environment has the latest Cumulative Update applied.

With the above provisions met, you are ready to begin configuring User Profile Synchronization in your SharePoint 2013 farm.

■ **Note**   Follow all steps, from this point on, in sequence. Do not be tempted to skip or attempt steps in a different order, or you will risk failure in the setup.

The first step, and pertinent to this section, is to create some service accounts in your organization's Active Directory forest. In a typical SharePoint 2013 configuration, you will need at least the following three domain accounts:

- `DOMAIN\spcontent`
- `DOMAIN\spservices`
- `DOMAIN\spups`

Ensure that these accounts exist as normal users with no password expiration. The `DOMAIN\spups` account must have Replicating Directory Changes permission in the Active Directory. This account does not run any Windows or SharePoint services nor does it run any application pools.

■ **Note**   Not granting Replicating Directory Changes to the User Profile Service account is typically the first mistake administrators make when configuring User Profile Synchronization, and this may lead to issues later.

The following steps detail how to grant Replicating Directory Changes from within the Active Directory Users and Computers configuration snap-in (please note that these steps require AD Security Account Operators rights):

1. Log on to your server hosting Active Directory.
2. Right-click the domain name in Active Directory Users and Computers.
3. Choose Delegate Control and then click the Next button.
4. Add the DOMAIN\spups account and click the Next button.
5. Select Create Custom Task to Delegate and click the Next button.
6. Click the Next button again.
7. Select the Replicating Directory Changes permission and click the Next button.
8. Click the Finish button.

Next, you configure Replicating Directory Changes on the Configuration Naming Context for the domain:

1. Run `ADSIEDIT.msc`.
2. Connect to the Configuration partition.
3. Select Configuration in the Select a Well-Known Naming Context drop-down list.
4. Right-click the Configuration partition and choose Properties.
5. Select the Security tab.
6. Add the DOMAIN\spups user to the list and give it Replicating Directory Changes permission.

> ■ **Note** When running the Domain Controller on Windows 2003 or earlier, add the DOMAIN\spups user to the Pre Windows 2000 Compatible Access built-in group.

The SharePoint farm account must have Log on Locally rights on the server performing User Profile Sync. The following steps detail how to configure this:

1. Log on to the server running SharePoint and host for User Profile Synchronization.

2. Open Administration Tools.

3. Open either Group Policy editor or the Local Security Policy editor.

4. Navigate to Security Settings, Local Policies, User Rights and Assignments.

5. Click Allow Logon Locally.

6. Make sure the farm account is either in one of the groups listed or explicitly listed.

7. If running SharePoint on a domain controller (this is a bad practice), use GPMC.msc to edit the default domain policy.

8. Execute GPUPDATE.exe from an elevated command line to refresh the policy.

> ■ **Note** At this stage, I recommend a server reboot to ensure that the DOMAIN\spups account picks up all permission and policy changes—this will help avoid issues with the service provisioning process hanging later.

Next, register managed accounts for the DOMAIN\spcontent and DOMAIN\spservices accounts:

1. Open Central Administration.

2. Click the Security section heading.

3. Click the link Configure Managed Accounts, in the General Security subsection.

4. Click Register Managed Account.

5. Provide details for the two domain accounts to register.

6. You can register the DOMAIN\spups account if you like, but User Profile Service does not use managed accounts and expects a Windows domain account, so there is little point.

With Windows domain accounts and managed accounts configured, now create two web applications—one to host your site collection and another to act as the My Site Host. Use the content account as the application pool account for both web applications. Create a new site collection in the My Site Host, using the My Site Host Template. Flip back to Chapter 2 if you need a refresher on how to create web applications and site collections.

■ **Note**   As a best practice for large deployment (more than 5000 users), consider hosting a My Site Host in a separate web application.

After creating a new host application for My Sites, and provisioning service accounts, you can now configure the User Profile Service application.

Creating the User Profile Service Application

The following steps assume that you have completed the steps in the previous section to establish managed service accounts. This is very important; failure to establish correct accounts and permissions affects the steps in this and following subsections. Assuming that you have completed the prior steps with no errors, or issues, follow these steps to provision the User Profile Service application:

1. Open Central Administration.

2. Click the Application Management link.

3. Click the Manage Service Applications link.

4. Make sure no other User Profile Service application or proxy exists in the list. If there are any, delete them.

5. From the ribbon, click the New icon and then select User Profile Service Application from the list.

6. Give the new service application a name, such as User Profile Service Application.

7. Create a new application pool for the application and use the DOMAIN\spservices account.

8. Check the names of the three databases—Profile, Sync, and Social. Either leave the default names, or change them to your desired names.

9. Enter the My Site Host application (the form will validate this entry).

10. Select the managed path and site name scheme.

11. Leave the proxy setting as is.

12. Click the Create button and wait while SharePoint creates the User Profile Service application.

13. If the NetBIOS name is different from the Fully Qualified Domain Name, configure the service application with the following PowerShell script:

    $upssa = Get-SpServiceAplication -Id <Guid of the User Profile Service Application>
    $upssa.NetBIOSDomainNamesEnabled = 1
    $upssa.Update()

You should now have a working User Profile Service application and proxy in your farm (you may need to refresh the Managed Services List page). The next section details the steps for starting the necessary SharePoint services for User Profile Synchronization.

Starting the Services

At this point, you should have completed the steps in the previous sections and have a working User Profile Service application and proxy. Take the following steps to start the User Profile Service and User Profile Sync Service SharePoint Services:

1. Add the DOMAIN\spfarm account to the Administrators group on the server running FIM/UPS (you can remove this account from the group later).

2. Perform an IISRESET and reset the SharePoint timer service.

3. Open Central Administration.

4. Click the System Settings section title link.

5. Click the Manage Services on Server link.

6. If not already started, start the User Profile Service, which requires no options.

7. Start the User Profile Sync Service (see Figure 6-4).

Figure 6-4. *Starting the User Profile Synchronization Service*

8. Select the User Profile Service Application in the drop-down.

9. Enter the farm password and click OK (Yes, the account is hard coded to the farm account, which is less than ideal.).

10. Wait. The status of the service will appear as Starting. Do not be alarmed if the status remains in the Starting state for 10 minutes or longer, as SharePoint is doing a lot of work to configure FIM.

11. While you wait, open the services control panel (`SERVICES.msc`).

12. You should see two Forefront Identity services in the list. The User Profile Sync Service starts these services. *Do not be tempted to start these services yourself—this will break User Profile Synchronization in SharePoint.*

13. Once the User Profile Sync Service has started, remove the DOMAIN\`spfarm` account from the administrators group on the FIM/UPS server.

14. Perform an IISRESET and reset the SharePoint timer service.

15. If you have a named instance of SQL, you may need to allow inbound connections to MSDTC on the server running FIM.

If all has gone according to plan and you have a green Started status next to both your User Profile Service and User Profile Sync Service in your Services list, give yourself a pat on the back—if something goes wrong, it typically happens before now.

Importing User Profiles from Active Directory

This procedure assumes you have completed the steps in the previous section—and thus have a working User Profile Service application, and the User Profile Service and User Profile Sync Service started in SharePoint. The following steps demonstrate setting up a connection to Active Directory to perform a profile import for the users in the domain:

1. Open Central Administration.

2. Click the Application Management link.

3. Click the link for Manage Service Applications.

4. Find the User Profile Service application, which you created earlier in this chapter.

5. Click to the right of the name to highlight the row; then click Manage from the ribbon.

6. If all is well, you should see a page like that in Figure 6-5.

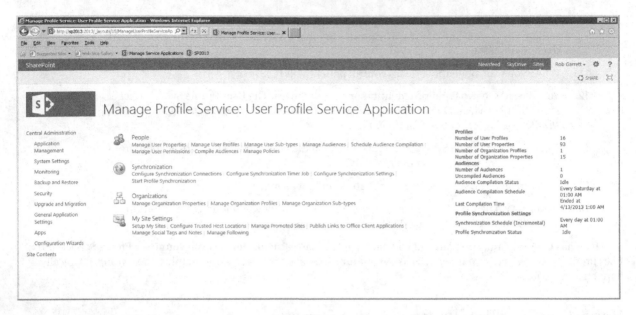

Figure 6-5. *User Profile Service Administration page*

7. In the Synchronization section, click the Configure Synchronization Connections link.

8. Click the Create New Connection button.

9. Give the connection a name and set the type as Active Directory.

10. Enter the forest name (you can use the domain name for purposes of demonstration).

11. Select the authentication type as Windows.

12. Enter the credentials as DOMAIN\spups and its password; you must use this account as it is the account used by FIM to establish sync with AD.

13. Click the Populate Containers button to get a list of containers, as shown in Figure 6-6.

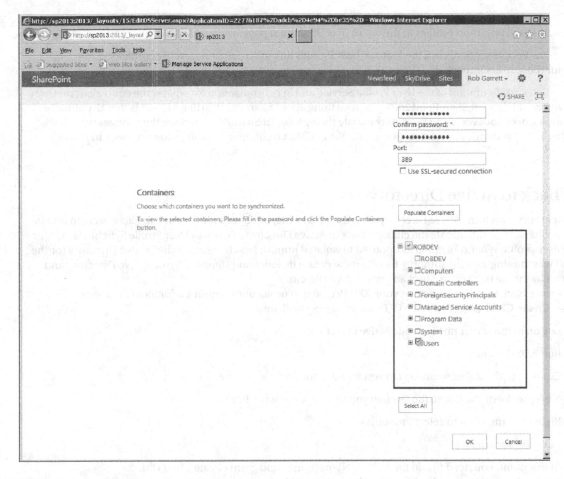

Figure 6-6. Populated containers for AD connection—import

14. You might be tempted to click the check box for the entire domain, or hit that Select All button. *Avoid this*; instead, expand the hierarchy and select the OU that contains the users.

15. Click the OK button, and SharePoint will configure the import connection.

16. Navigate back to the User Profiles Admin page.

17. Click the Start Profile Synchronization link.

18. On the next page, change the radio button to Full Synchronization and click OK.

19. Refresh the User Profile Service Administration page, and you should see the synchronization status on the right of the page change from Idle to Synchronizing.

20. The synchronization process is very slow! So be prepared to wait a while.

21. To see the status of the import, you can click the Synchronizing link. For a more verbose view of the import status, run the FIM client tool, available from C:\Program Files\ Microsoft Office Servers\15.0\Synchronization Service\UIShell\miisclient.exe.

22. Assuming there were no errors, once the synchronization job completes, you can see the number of imported profiles in the top right of the Admin page.

23. In the People section, click the Manage User Profiles link to search and view user profiles for those users imported.

This completes configuration of the User Profile Service and Synchronization for what is the equivalent one-way import that you could do with SharePoint 2007. The nice thing about SharePoint 2010 and 2013 is that User Profile Synchronization works both ways—so users may update their profile in SharePoint and see the changes push back to AD (or other LDAP system). The next section covers the additional configuration steps to write back to Active Directory.

Writing Back to Active Directory

One-way synchronization from Active Directory to SharePoint is fine, but better is the ability to allow users to update their profile in SharePoint and update the changes back to Active Directory. Two-way User Profile Synchronization defines true user-profile synchronization as opposed to isolated import, which assumed that Active Directory (or the LDAP server) was the single-point authority for all profile data. The following steps configure Active Directory and SharePoint to allow write back of profile changes to Active Directory.

To allow write back to Active Directory, your `DOMAIN\spups` sync account requires additional directory permissions—Create Child Objects (for the OU you are writing back into).

1. Log on to the server hosting your Active Directory.

2. Run ADSIEdit.msc.

3. Connect to the default-naming context for the domain.

4. Navigate down the tree to the OU that you wish to allow write back.

5. Right click the OU and select Properties.

6. Click the Security tab.

7. At this point, you need to add the DOMAIN\spups user and grant Create Child Objects permission and read and write permissions—but wait!

8. The `DOMAIN\spups` user already exists in this list because you delegated Directory Replicating Changes permission. If you are tempted to add the additional permissions to this user, do not. This will result in breaking the profile import.

9. From the dialog shown in Figure 6-7, click the Add button, to add the user again.

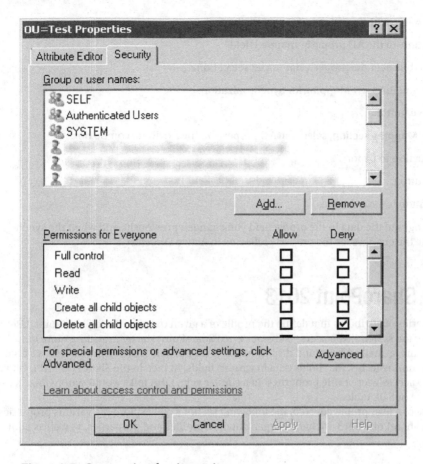

Figure 6-7. *Organzational unit security*

10. Do not click OK just yet.

11. Click the Advanced button, and in the dialog that appears, scroll down to the instance of DOMAIN\spups account that has <not inherited>.

12. Click the Edit button.

13. Ensure that the Apply To combo box value is This Object and All Descendent Objects.

14. Click the check box in the Allow column for the permissions: Write All Properties and Create Child Objects.

15. Click OK several times to get back to the main ADSIEdit.msc window.

At this stage, the profile import connection, which you established in an earlier configuration stage, imports only! If you think about it, this makes sense—could you imagine how upset HR might be if SharePoint were to overwrite its profile data with user changes, without management control?

The following steps configure the User Profile Synchronization Service for more granular control of properties written back to AD:

1. Return to the User Profile Service Administration page.

2. Click the Manage User Properties link.

3. Choose the property, with mapping to AD, to write back.

4. Make a mental note of the AD property-mapped field.

5. Click the combo box over the property name and select Edit.

6. Scroll to the section Property Mapping for Synchronization.

7. Click the Remove button.

8. In the Add New Mapping section, select the AD property in the Attribute combo box.

9. Change the direction to Export.

10. Click the Add button.

11. Click the OK button to save changes.

You can now make changes to the data in the profile field you changed previously, and when the synchronization process runs, you should see the changes for the property reflected in Active Directory.

User Profiles in SharePoint 2013

A user profile consists of a series of attributes that define the profile of a given user known to SharePoint. User profiles effectively give individuals of the system—the users—substance in a SharePoint site by providing more details about a user than his or her username, e-mail address, and display name. A user profile is synonymous with a struct, or method-less class, in programming terms, that holds data in various fields. In fact, in the SharePoint API/Object Model, there exists a class to access user profile properties. In a similar vein, DBA folks would synonymize a user profile with a database record or SQL table.

With the basic principle of a user profile covered, the following sections will explore the various properties and subtypes of a user profile in SharePoint 2013, including organizational profiles and properties, as well as audiences and policy for user profiles.

User Profile Properties and Subtypes

SharePoint 2013 looks after user profile management via a dedicated managed service application. I will revisit the User Profile Service and User Profile Service application later in this chapter, but at this stage, I can demonstrate view of the user profile properties via the managed service in Central Administration, as follows:

1. Open Central Administration.

2. Click the Application Management link.

3. Click Manage Service Applications in the Service Applications section.

4. Scroll to the User Profile Service application—do not worry if you do not see one in the list; I discussed configuring User Profile Service earlier in this chapter.

5. SharePoint shows the User Profile Service Admin page (see Figure 6-5 earlier in this chapter).

6. Click the Manage User Properties link.

7. You should see a page like that in Figure 6-8.

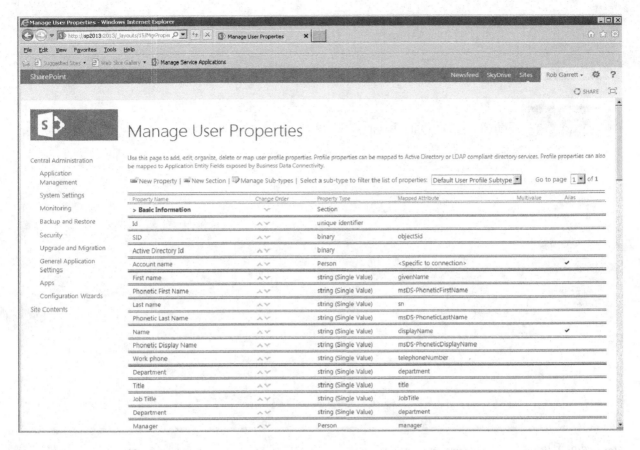

Figure 6-8. *User profile properties*

In Figure 6-8, notice the Mapped Attribute column, which shows how a profile property maps to an attribute in Active Directory, or other LDAP directory service, configured as part of User Profile Synchronization. Out of the box, SharePoint provides a default set of user profiles to describe an individual in an organization. Not all profile properties map nicely to Active Directory user attributes, which is why not all properties have a mapping.

Each profile property consists of a type, shown in the Property Type column in Figure 6-8. The property type indicates the type of value data a user profile instance might contain for the property. For example, the First Name property is a single String type, because first names typically contain alphanumeric characters and most names have a length less than 255 characters (the SharePoint limit for strings). Other property types used by SharePoint include integers, Booleans, date/time, unique identifiers, person, and binary.

Now to explore a user profile property—I will start with an easy one: the last name.

1. Scroll down the page shown in Figure 6-8 and find the Last Name property.

2. Hover over the name of the property.

3. In the drop-down combo box, select Edit.

4. You should see a page like that in Figure 6-9.

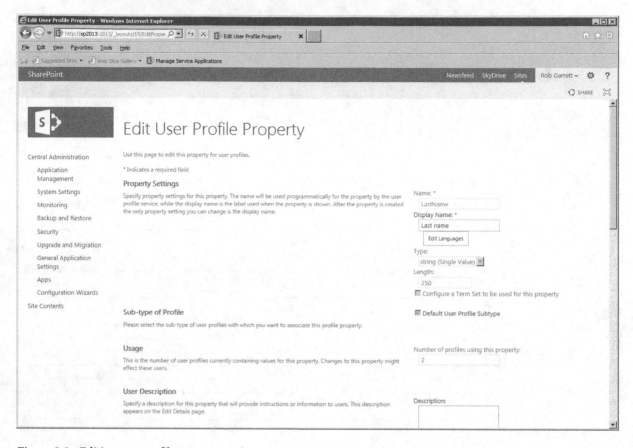

Figure 6-9. Editing user profile property settings

The Property Settings page displays a number of sections for editing specific details about the property. Table 6-1 details the various sections.

Table 6-1. User Profile Property Settings Page Sections

Section Name	Details
Property Settings	Defines the name, display name, property type, length, and whether the property maps to a term set in the term store
Subtype of Profile	The subtype that this property associates (more on subtypes in a moment)
Usage	The number of active profiles in the user profile store that have data values in this property—this is important information because SharePoint search only indexes user profile properties that have data; if this value is 0, then this property will not show up in search mapping later
User Description	Description of the property, displayed when users are asked to enter data for the property when editing their profile

(continued)

Table 6-1. (*continued*)

Section Name	Details
Policy	Policy for the profile property; you will learn more about policy for user profiles later in this chapter
Edit Settings	These determine whether users can edit the data in this property or not
Display Settings	The context of where this property displays
Search Settings	Alias and Index settings for user profile search (more on user profile search later in the chapter)
Property Mapping for Synchronization	I briefly discussed use of this section and the next section in configuring two-way profile synchronization—this section defines the property mappings to Active Directory and LDAP stores
Add New Mapping	Section to establish a new mapping to an existing Active Directory or LDAP store connection (configured in User Profile Synchronization)

User Profile Subtypes

User profile subtypes provide a more granular grouping of property types for a user profile. They allow the creation of different kinds of user profiles, each with its own unique fields, for different purposes. For example, suppose an organization wants a special user profile type for contractors to complete, which has all the attributes of a default user profile but with additional properties. The following steps demonstrate creating the Contractor subtype.

1. Open Central Administration.

2. Click the Manage Applications link.

3. Click the Manage Service Applications link under Service Applications.

4. Scroll down to the User Profile Service application.

5. Click to the right of the name and then click Manage from the ribbon.

6. From the User Profile Service Administration page shown, click the link Manage User Subtypes.

7. Figure 6-10 shows the page for managing user profile subtypes.

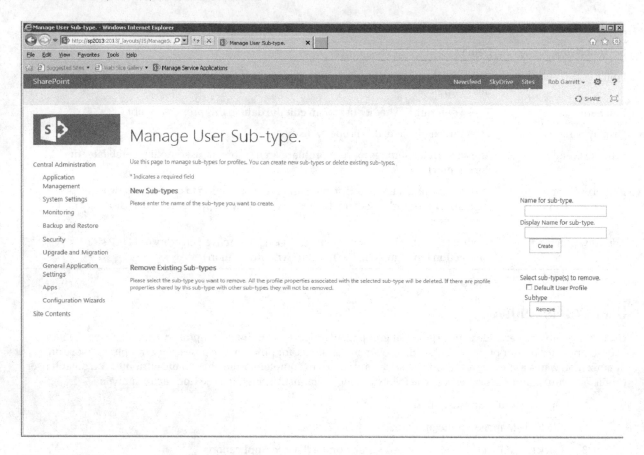

Figure 6-10. *Managing user profile subtypes*

8. Enter a name in the Name field for the new subtype, such as Contractor.

9. Enter a display name.

10. Click the Create button.

11. You should now see a new subtype listed in the section below this button.

12. Navigate back to the User Profile Service Administration page.

Next, you can create a new custom property to include in the Contractor subtype—one that regular profile users need not populate.

Adding Custom User Profile Properties

The SharePoint User Profile Service allows the addition of custom profile properties, in addition to those provided by SharePoint. The set of user properties that SharePoint provides is quite extensive, but an organization may require its own custom properties for capturing very specific details about people in the organization. Just like the out-of-box user profile properties, custom profile properties surface in user profile pages, indexes for search, and groups in user profile subtypes. The following steps show how to create a new user profile property and add this property to the subtype created in the previous subsection:

1. From the User Profile Service Administration page, click the Manage User Properties link.

2. Click the New Property button at the top of the page.

3. SharePoint shows a new Profile Property Settings page with blank form fields to configure the property (see Figure 6-11).

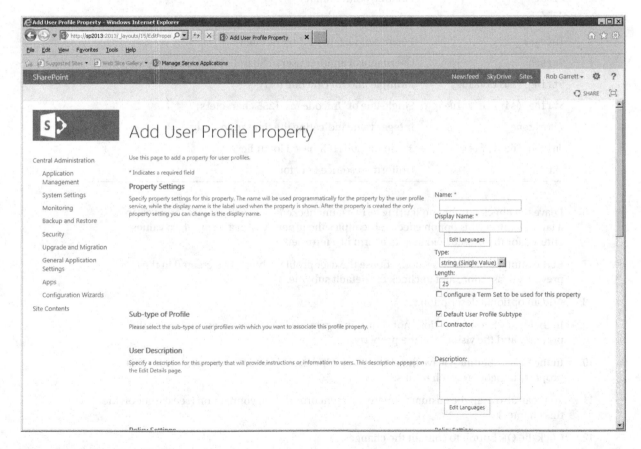

Figure 6-11. *New User Profile Property page*

4. Give the property a name and a display name.

5. Set the property type and max character length of the field—see Table 6-2 for a list of available user profile property data types.

Table 6-2. *User Profile Property Data Types*

Data Type	Description
Big integer	Large positive or negative 64-bit number
Binary	Binary blog data (usually populated programmatically)
Boolean	True or False
Date	Date
Date no year	Date without the year (ideal for birthday)
Date time	Date and time
E-mail	E-mail address
Float	Floating point number
HTML	Text with Hypertext Markup
Integer	Positive or negative 32-bit number
Person	Username of another user in SharePoint or directory system
String (multivalue)	Multiple lines of Unicode text
String (single value)	Single line of Unicode text (255 characters)
Time zone	Integer value indicating the time zone offset
Unique identifier	32-bit unique HEX based identifier
URL	Uniform Resource Locator

6. Leave the check box for configuring term set unchecked—you will explore term sets in a later chapter—this option effectively couples the property with a term set, so values entered for the profile field map to a term in a term set.

7. In the Subtype of Profile section, choose the user profile subtype you created in the previous subsection, and uncheck the default subtype.

8. Add an optional description.

9. In the Policy Settings section (not shown in Figure 6-11), set the privacy policy for the property and the visibility of the property.

10. In the Search Settings, leave the check box for Indexed checked to surface data for this property in people search results.

11. You may also map the custom property to a synchronization connection (see earlier on in this chapter).

12. Click the OK button to commit the changes.

13. Assuming there are no errors on the form, SharePoint takes you back to the profile properties list—notice the absence of the new property in the list; this is because you created the property for the Contractor subtype, and by default the Properties page shows those properties for the default subtype.

14. At the top of the page, change the subtype to Contractor.

15. Scroll to the bottom of the page and you should see the new property in the Custom Properties section.

A Custom Profile Property and Subtype in Action

Having completed the steps in the previous two sections, you should now have a new custom user profile property added, and you have contained this custom property in a new Contractor subtype. The following steps show the subtype and custom property in action:

1. Navigate back to the User Profile Service Administration page.

2. Click the Manage User Profiles link.

3. For the sake of demonstration, I will create a new user profile by hand.

4. Click the New Profile button.

5. Figure 6-12 shows the new user profile form.

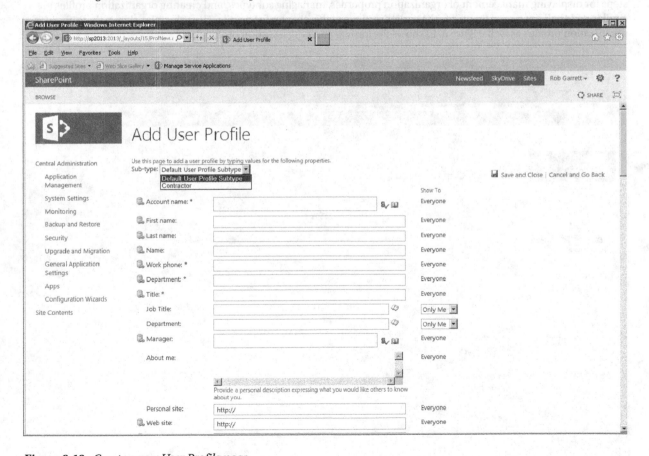

Figure 6-12. *Create a new User Profile page*

6. Notice the combo box at the top of the page that allows you to change the subtype—select the new Contractor subtype.

7. Changing the subtype to Contractor exposes the new property you added a few subsections back, and thus defines this user profile as type Contractor.

8. Scroll to the bottom of the page to see the new custom property.

Organization Profiles

SharePoint 2007 managed organization staff hierarchy via the Manager property of the profile, which was a property of type Person. The main limitation of this approach is that it does not provide much flexibility to arrange an organization chart. For example, if you reported to multiple managers, or you were not the manager of your direct report, or if you had managers with multiple roles, then the organization chart became unmanageable in SharePoint 2007. The Organization Profile feature of SharePoint 2010 and 2013 User Profile Service aim to remedy this issue with better control over the organization structure.

Organization profiles work in a similar vein to user profiles. Within the User Profile Service Admin page, you should see three links: Manage Organization Properties, Manage Organization Profiles, and Manage Organization Subtypes. The steps for displaying management of organization properties, managing subtypes, and creating organization profiles are similar, so I shall not repeat them; see the earlier sections of this chapter for details. The principles shown there apply to organization profiles as well. Figure 6-13 shows the form to enter organization profile data.

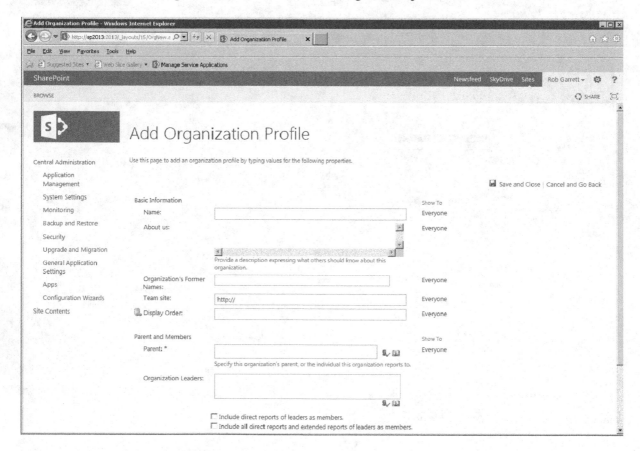

Figure 6-13. *Create a new Organization Profile page*

Following are some points worth noting about organization profiles:

- Every organization profile may define one or many leaders

- Every organization profile may include one or many members

- All direct reports of a leader may be members automatically

- Every organization profile has a mandatory parent person or group

- Correct management of your organization chart in SharePoint allows users of your sites to see a graphical org chart

Audiences

An audience defines a set of people who see *targeted content*. Do not confuse audiences with SharePoint security groups—although both combine a set of users, audiences define only those users who see specific content in lists and list items, and you define membership of an audience by rule criteria, not explicit inclusion.

For example, a publishing page on a SharePoint site may include a specific content area that only certain users see. Users who are not in the audience get to see all other content areas on the page, and the page itself. Only members of the audience can view the specific content area with designated audience assigned. To accomplish this same behavior without audiences would involve multiple page instances with different security permissions and duplicate content across these pages.

You must compile audiences before use, and they can allow targeting of content at the list or list item level. The following steps demonstrate how to create a new audience from the User Profile Service application and use the audience in targeted areas. Start configuration in Central Administration.

1. Open Central Administration.

2. Click the Manage Applications link.

3. Click the Manage Service Applications link, under Service Applications.

4. Scroll down to the User Profile Service application.

5. Click to the right of the name and then click Manage from the ribbon.

6. From the User Profile Service Admin page, click the link Manage Audiences.

7. The page shown in Figure 6-14 displays the total existing audiences and any non-compiled audiences.

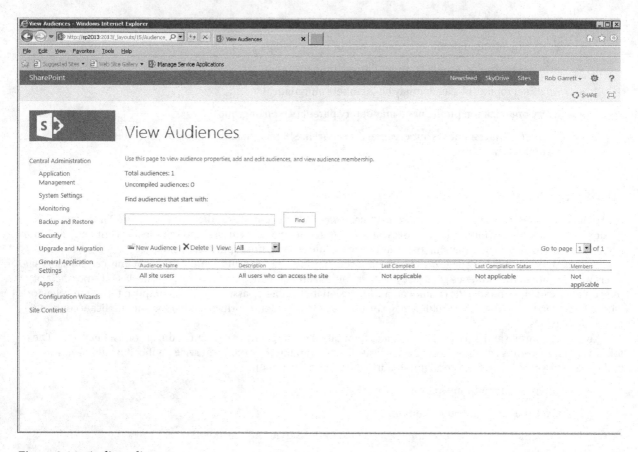

Figure 6-14. *Audience list*

8. Click the New Audience button.

9. Give the audience a name, description, and owner.

10. Decide whether members must satisfy all criteria or some criteria of the rules.

11. Click the OK button.

12. In the next screen, shown in Figure 6-15, Create a rule based on the value of a user/group property or user association.

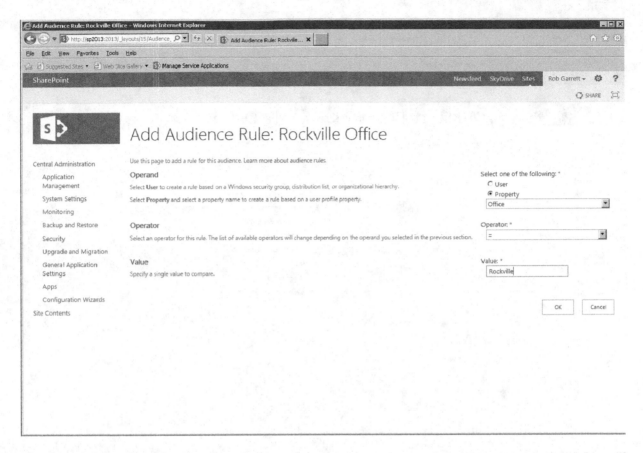

Figure 6-15. *Rule creation for an audience*

13. In my example, I created a rule that all users of my audience must have the profile property Office set as Rockville.

14. Click the OK button when ready to save your rule.

The Audience Properties page, shown in Figure 6-16, details the audience you just created and the rule(s) you applied for inclusion of users in the audience. Notice that the status of the audience shows as not compiled. I mentioned earlier that any audience requires compilation. This compilation process allows SharePoint to process the rules and process existing user accounts, such that SharePoint can deliver audience targeted content efficiently for any member of the audience who views a page with targeted content based on this audience. Compilation is an important process; without it, SharePoint would have to process rules for every audience definition applied to targeted content. Compilation provides efficiency because SharePoint has processed rules ahead of time. Of course, this means SharePoint must continually compile audiences as new users join the farm and audience criteria change.

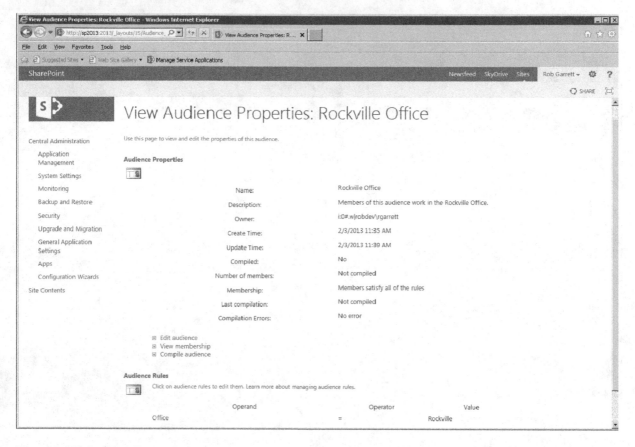

Figure 6-16. *Audience Properties page*

In the prior steps, I demonstrated creating an audience with a single criteria rule—based on a user profile property. Feel free to experiment by adding additional rules for more complex inclusion criteria. With the audience defined, I shall now demonstrate how to compile your audience.

1. Click the Compile Audience link.

2. SharePoint will now include members in the audience that satisfy the audience inclusion criteria.

3. Once compilation completes (without error), click the View Membership link to see all those members in the audience.

■ **Note** SharePoint updates audience membership based on a schedule, which you may change from the Schedule Audience Compilation link in the main User Profile Service Admin page.

Once you complete the compilation of an audience, you may then use this audience to target content to those members for list items and Web Parts. The following steps configure audience targeting for a list:

1. For a list in your site collection, click the List Settings from the ribbon.

2. Click the Audience Targeting Settings link in the General Settings section.

3. Check the check box to enable audience targeting for the list.

4. Click the OK button.

To apply audience targeting for a specific list item, follow these steps:

1. View the properties of the list item.

2. Find the item field named Target Audiences.

3. Choose a compiled target audience and save the item.

Web Parts provide a location in their Web Part properties to assign targeted audiences.

Social Networking

"Social networking," also referred to as "social computing," is the practice of many people collaborating and sharing information about their lives, preferences, thoughts, and feelings online. The IT industry and personal computing space have seen a prolific increase in the adoption of social networking, through community-based web sites like Facebook.com and Twitter.com, and collaboration via blogs and wikis. SharePoint has always been about collaboration in the workspace, and with the large drive in social networking from the home and personal computing space, corporations and non-corporate organizations are waking up to the benefits that social networking provides.

If you ask any person familiar with social networking to define it, he or she will most likely mention Facebook. In recent years, Facebook has become a household name in the social networking space because it provides an intuitive means for those who can use a computer and the Internet to share information about themselves and collaborate on this information with others. Prior to Facebook, those with writing skills, and something to write about, hosted blogs on sites like blogger.com and livejournal.com. In fact, the livejournal.com site today is very different from what it was a few years ago; it embraces collaboration and user adoption through information sharing and is no longer a space to write a monolithic stream of thought.

SharePoint has always provided a level of personal space in the platform, from as far back as SharePoint Portal Server 2003, with My Sites, which allow users in an organization to store documents and lists and disseminate their own content to others in the organization. SharePoint 2007 went the next step and introduced wiki and blog site definitions, and with the addition of public-facing web site capability via the publishing infrastructure, SharePoint could participate in the public blogosphere world. SharePoint included many of the information-sharing and content-tagging features that users have come to expect from other social networking platforms. SharePoint 2010 also introduced the Managed Metadata Service, which allows organizations to build managed taxonomy of tags and allow user self-expression tagging—folksonomy—with custom tagging capabilities. Blogs and wikis still exist in SharePoint, only better—they now include the ability to host rich media in the form of video and audio content in their pages.

How has SharePoint 2013 enhanced the social networking scene? SharePoint 2013 includes all of the aforementioned social networking features of SharePoint 2007 and 2010, with a fresh branding and new layout. SharePoint 2013 also centralizes users' social networking around their newsfeed—the core of any good social networking platform. Users of SharePoint 2010 had use of the newsfeed. SharePoint 2013 makes the newsfeed easier to use and more intuitive, and organizations no longer need to look to third-party tools to provide the rich immersive experience they have come to expect from social networking.

A feature new to SharePoint 2013 is integration of SkyDrive Pro, which allows organizations to treat SharePoint like their professional version of the public SkyDrive offering from Microsoft. Users in the organization can synchronize folders on their workstations with SharePoint, just as they do with the cloud at home. I discuss SkyDrive Pro integration in detail in Chapter 14.

You will visit the social networking features of SharePoint 2013 in the upcoming sections in this chapter. Those of you familiar with SharePoint 2010 will see how Microsoft has enhanced the look and feel and capabilities in the platform.

My Sites

Each My Site in SharePoint exists as a personal site collection for individuals in the organization. My Sites provide a space for users to store documents, host custom and out-of-the-box lists, access their profile information, show their news, and contribute thru a blog, feed, and so on. The My Site is the central hub for identity in a SharePoint infrastructure and is the place that each user can call his or her own. Just as a Facebook or Twitter account is the identity of a user in these social network platforms, the My Site is the main area for users in their working social space.

■ **Note** SharePoint 2013 does not require users to have a My Site to view their user profile information. However, My Sites tie together many of the social networking features and are a requirement for many of the social components.

Creating the My Site Host Site Collection

Each My Site exists as a separate site collection. Site collections provide a level of independence in that each defines its own security model and each may reside in different databases from other site collections. Think of each site collection as its own contained ecosystem for data, which makes them ideal for hosting each My Site—an ecosystem for one particular user in the organization (flip back to Chapter 2 for more details on site collections). Since each My Site is its own site collection, each My Site has at least one site collection administrator, who is typically the owner of the My Site and person with whom a user profile associates.

SharePoint maintains many site collections for My Sites in a single web application, called the My Site Host application. If you utilized the Farm Configuration Wizard to configure your SharePoint farm, then you likely have a My Site Host application instantiated. Since this is an administration book, I shall assume that you want to know how to create your own My Site infrastructure without the aid of the wizard. To start, I shall demonstrate the steps to create a new My Site Host application and root site collection using the My Site Host template. As you so often do, start by opening Central Administration.

1. Open Central Administration.

2. Click the Manage Web Applications link from the home page.

3. On the next page, if you see an application with a name that looks like it might be a My Site Host, then the My Site Host application may already exist.

4. Click the New icon from the ribbon.

5. Complete the form for the new web application (see Chapter 2).

■ **Note** Typically, I like to create a My Site Host on port 8080 and then create an alternate access mapping on port 80 with a fully qualified domain name, such as http://my.domain.com.

---

6. Return to the Central Administration home page.

7. Click the Application Management link.

8. Click the Create Site Collections link.

9. In the next page, select the correct web application in the drop-down box.

10. Give the site collection a name and description.

11. Choose the My Site Host template.

12. Provide a DOMAIN\name username for the primary and secondary site collection administrators.

13. Leave the quota option default.

14. Click the OK button to create the site collection.

If you completed all of the previous steps without error, you should now have a new My Site Host root site collection residing in a dedicated My Site Host web application. The root My Site Host collection is the administration site for all My Sites. I previously mentioned that each My Site is a site collection that resides in the My Site Host application. The root My Site Host administration site collection allows you to provide settings that pertain to all user My Sites in the application.

■ **Note**   It is a good practice to create a dedicated web application as a My Site Host and only store the root My Site Host site collection and user My Sites in this application.

Configuring Managed Paths

Before you are ready to create site collections for user My Sites, you must define a managed path. Managed paths tell SharePoint the location for hosting site collections within a host web application.

By default for each web application, SharePoint creates an explicit managed path for the root ("/") and a wildcard managed path for offspring site collections ("/sites/"). I shall assume you created a My Site Host application and a My Site Host root site collection in the previous sections.

In my environment, I have a web application at `http://myserver:8080/`. When users provision their My Site collections, I would like these site collections to reside at `http://myserver:8080/personal/name-of-person/`. To accomplish my goal, I need to define a wildcard managed path for "/personal/" as follows:

1. Open Central Administration.

2. Click the Manage Web Applications link from the home page.

3. Click to the right of the name of the new My Sites Host application.

4. From the ribbon, click the Managed Paths icon.

5. Add a wildcard managed path for "personal."

Great! Now you have a My Site Host, My Site administration root site collection, and a wildcard managed path to store all user My Site collections. However, you are not quite done with the configuration. You need to configure the User Profile Service, such that User Profile Service knows where to create new site collections for user My Sites. You will do this now.

At this stage, you should have a working My Site Host application and root site collection; you also have a managed path to host all user site collections (personal) and the host application path (my). The next set of steps assumes a working User Profile Service.

1. From the Central Admin home page, click the Application Management link.

2. Click the Manage Service Applications link.

3. Click to the right of the existing User Profile Service application name listed.

4. Click the Manage icon on the ribbon.

5. Scroll to the My Site Settings section.

6. Click the link to Setup My Sites.

7. You should see a page like that in Figure 6-17.

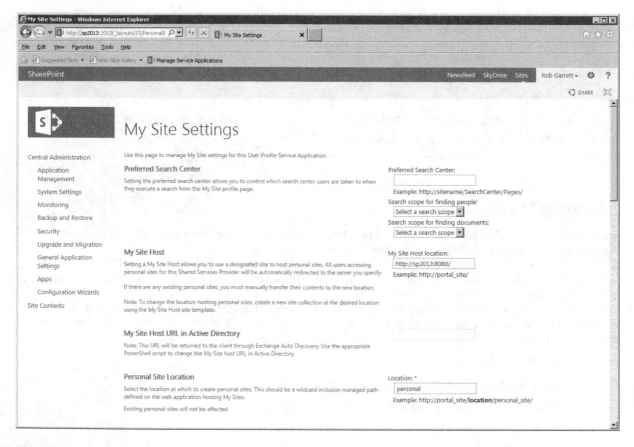

Figure 6-17. *My Site Setup page*

8. Set the My Site Host location as the location of the root site collection in your My Site Host application (or site collection location if not at the root).

9. Set the personal site location as the managed path you created earlier for the location of user My Site collections.

10. Optionally, click the Configure Trusted Host Locations link to configure other trusted host locations. Trusted host locations are other My Site Host locations in which users of a specific audience host their My Site collection. For example, if you have an audience for all contractors in your organization and want their My Sites to host in a separate location from all other users, then Trusted My Site Locations are what you need.

■ **Note** If you created an alternate access mapping for your My Site Host application (perhaps on port 80), change the location in the User Profile Service application so users can access their My Sites on this address.

The My Site Settings section in the User Profile Service application provides a few other options that administrators may deem useful in the organization—personalization site links and publish links to Office applications.

Personalization site links are additional links added to each user My Site, based on audience membership. For example, say your organization has a series of committees, and each user belongs to zero, one, or many committees, stipulated by a profile property. When users visit their My Site, they should see links to their committee sites in the organization. The following steps assume the existence of committee audiences and demonstrate configuration of personalization site links:

1. Navigate to the My Sites Settings section in the User Profile Service Application page.

2. Click the Configure Personalization Site link.

3. Click the New link.

4. Provide the URL to the landing page of the committee, the committee name in the description field, the owner, and the target audience.

Published links to Office applications are a feature that SharePoint provides to expose known locations in your portal that users may access in Microsoft Office applications. For example, if a user wishes to save his or her Microsoft Word document to a common location in SharePoint, and the location is available as a published link, the user may select Save to SharePoint from Microsoft Word and use this link location. Users may similarly save to SharePoint published links in other Office applications. The following steps demonstrate configuration of published links in SharePoint:

1. Navigate to the My Sites Settings section in the User Profile Service Application page.

2. Click the Publish Links to Office Client Applications link.

3. Click the New link.

4. Provide the URL for the published link and description.

5. Select the publication end-point type in the drop-down.

Capacity Planning for My Sites

My Sites are individual site collections, supporting document libraries, lists, and subsites. By default, the owner of a My Site has full control over the collection, and carte blanche on what he or she may store in the collection. This suggests that the size of the default content database for the My Site Host application may grow quite large, as the number of users in an organization (with a My Site) grows. Furthermore, SharePoint provides incentive for users to store content and track events in their My Site, thus increasing user adoption and the need for better capacity planning.

It is good practice to ensure portability of the content databases and dispersal of My Sites across many content databases in the host application. You may recall from Chapter 2 that each site collection may occupy at most one content database, but a content database may host multiple site collections. Since each user's My Site is a site collection, you need to make sure that as more users sign up for My Site space, SharePoint ensures creation of new content databases as the number of site collections grow.

How many content databases do you need, and what limit should you set for the number of My Site collections per database? This depends on the expected amount of content in each My Site (site collection). Microsoft now allows database sizes up to four terabytes, and this limit will grow in the future. Depending on your need for portability and desire for smaller database sizes, the number of site collections in a given database and the expected size of these site collections will roughly define the size of your database. Quota management (see the settings of the My Site Host web application, in the web application list) will allow administrators to restrict the amount of content that users upload to their personal My Sites. If you have the luxury of multiple SQL Servers, you may decide to host My Site content databases on a different server from other areas in your SharePoint farm. The following steps demonstrate restricting My Site collections in a content database to 50 instances:

1. Open Central Administration.

2. Click the Application Management link.

3. Click the Manage Content Databases link.

4. Select the content database for the My Site Host application.

5. In the Database Capacity Settings section, change the maximum number of sites to 50, and set the warning 10% less (45). This ensures that the administrators receive a warning when the number of sites in the current content database grows to 45 and when at 50 SharePoint will create a new content database.

A Tour of SharePoint 2013 My Sites

My Sites in SharePoint 2013 have a new look and feel compared to those of the previous version. Like the rest of the user interface of SharePoint 2013, Microsoft redesigned the look and feel of user profile information and My Sites for a more social immersive experience. In previous versions of SharePoint, the My Site was clunky and often perceived as an afterthought, and interrupted the flow of the user interface. Even SharePoint 2010 had issues with the clear delineation of My Content and My Profile in the top My Site navigation.

With My Site capability enabled in the farm, users now see a pervasive set of links at the top right of the page; these links link to the current user's newsfeed, favorite sites, and SkyDrive location in My Site. Figure 6-18 shows an image of the standard team site in my development environment. Because I have My Sites enabled, I see the Newsfeed, SkyDrive, and Sites links at the top right. No matter what page I visit in the site, I always see these links.

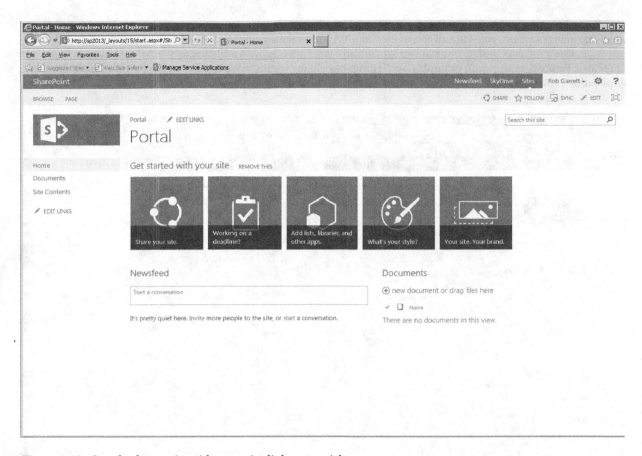

Figure 6-18. *Standard team site with pervasive links at top right*

The familiar display name of the current user also displays in the top right, and irrespective of whether you have enabled My Sites, clicking the name and selecting the "About Me" menu option will display a profile page of the current logged on user. This is an important distinction—in the past I have witnessed confusion among users of SharePoint who believed you had to enable My Sites to take advantage of user profiles and user profile management in a SharePoint farm.

■ **Note**   User profiles and profile editing operate independent of My Sites, but inclusion of My Site enhances the social experience for users.

My User Profile Page

SharePoint 2013 continues to support user profiles as it always has done since SharePoint 2007. The way in which SharePoint manages profile organization under the hood has changed over time, but users have always been able to see some demographic details about themselves and their peers, irrespective of My Sites. Even WSS 3.0 and Foundation provided some rudimentary user profile management, albeit a series of user properties and not a complete implementation of the user profile infrastructure offered by the full SharePoint version of the time.

If you have not configured the User Profile Service application and, by extension, not configured the My Site Host application in your farm, you can still access user settings. These settings are the very basic settings of a user and do not constitute a full user profile, nor can you synchronize these settings with any directory service, such as Active Directory. Figure 6-19 shows an example User Settings page in my team site when I do not have a User Profile Service application provisioned.

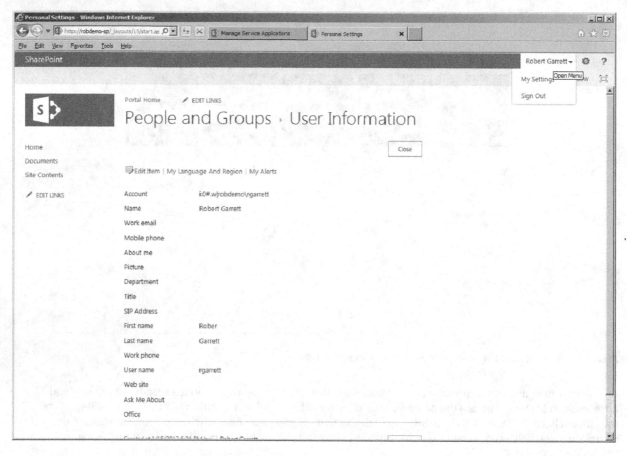

Figure 6-19. *Basic user setting with absence of User Profile Service*

Contrast the basic User Settings page (Figure 6-19) with that of the User Profile page from the User Profile Service application. When clicking the name of the logged on user, instead of seeing the "My Settings" link, you should see an "About Me" link, which, when clicked, shows a page like that in Figure 6-20. Also, notice the absence of the Newsfeed, SkyDrive, and Sites links, which require User Profile Service and a working My Site. I do have to admit that my User Profile page in my development farm is a little bland, so I at least uploaded a picture to make it more appealing.

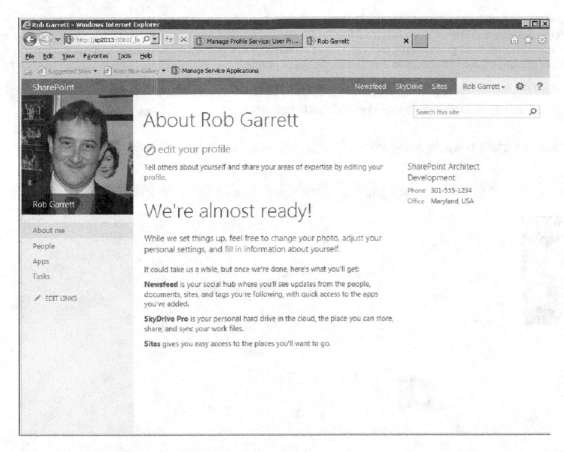

Figure 6-20. *User Profile page from User Profile Service*

Even with the User Profile Service application provisioned and a My Site Host application and root site collection, I want to make a clear distinction between user profiles and user profiles with My Sites. Some organizations want to take advantage of social networking in SharePoint but have concerns about providing a space for users to upload documents and content. Up to now, I have not actually provisioned a My Site. I am using features of the My Site Host root site collection to display profile information. By default, the User Profile Service will provision user My Sites in the background. You can disable user access to My Sites, leaving the rest of the user profile and social networking pieces intact, with the following steps:

1. Open Central Administration.

2. Click the Manage Service Applications link.

3. Click to the right of the existing User Profile Service application name listed.

4. Click the Manage icon on the ribbon.

5. Click the link to manage user permissions.

6. Disable Create Personal Site option for authenticated users.

■ **Note** Disabling creation of personal sites will disable newsfeed and personal content storage, such as documents.

Looking at Figure 6-20, you see that SharePoint is in the process of provisioning My Site and that you should see content and your newsfeed shortly. A timer service (User Profile Service Application—Activity Feed Job), which runs every 10 minutes, completes the provisioning process. I could switch over to Central Administration and run the job now but will use this opportunity to show you how to edit the user's profile.

1. From the About Me page, click the Edit link to edit the profile.

2. SharePoint displays the Edit Profile page, like that in Figure 6-21.

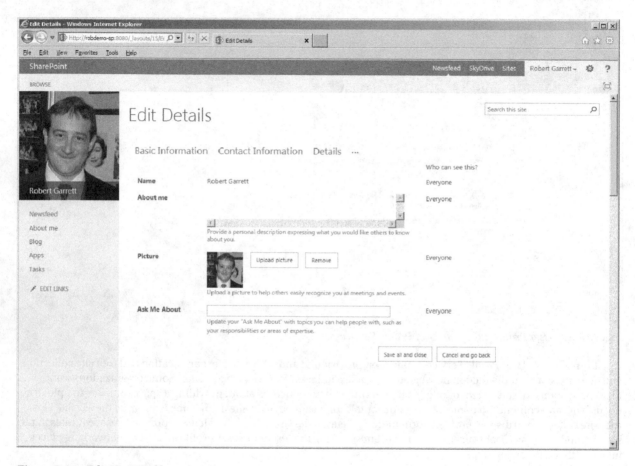

Figure 6-21. *Edit User Profile page*

The Edit User Profile page is much simpler than in previous versions of SharePoint. For instance, you do not have to scroll through lots of profile properties; all the common properties reside on one page, under the Basic Information tab. Try clicking the Contact Information tab, Details, and ellipses to see other profile property values you can change. To demonstrate, I uploaded my profile picture.

You might see that some of the profile properties do not allow you to edit the value. Typically, these profile properties link to Active Directory, or perhaps some other directory service, with the synchronization direction set as import only. In these cases, you cannot edit the profile property value because the value comes from the imported profile of the directory service.

My Newsfeed

The newsfeed is akin to those seen on Facebook and Twitter and shows a feed of current activity of my colleagues and me. Activities on the newsfeed consist of a list of SharePoint tracked events, configured in each personal profile. Clicking the name of any of my colleagues in the newsfeed takes me to that colleague's Profile page, which includes a newsfeed filtered to that person's activities.

After SharePoint finished completing provisioning of My Site, the About Me page for my profile shows my newsfeed, as in Figure 6-22. Since I have not yet interacted with SharePoint socially, you do not see any activities in my feed. As I begin interacting with other users and adding content to My Site, my newsfeed will start to show activities.

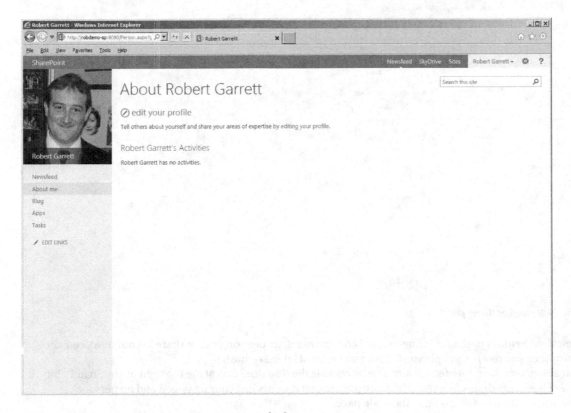

Figure 6-22. *User Profile page with empty newsfeed*

SharePoint tracks many social networking activities across the farm. By default, your newsfeed will show everything you do, but you might want to change the sorts of events that appear on your newsfeed. You can change which activities and events show in your newsfeed from your Edit User Profile page, as follows:

1. From your About Me page, click the Edit link to edit your user profile.

2. Click the ellipses.

3. Click the Newsfeed Settings tab.

4. SharePoint displays a page like that in Figure 6-23.

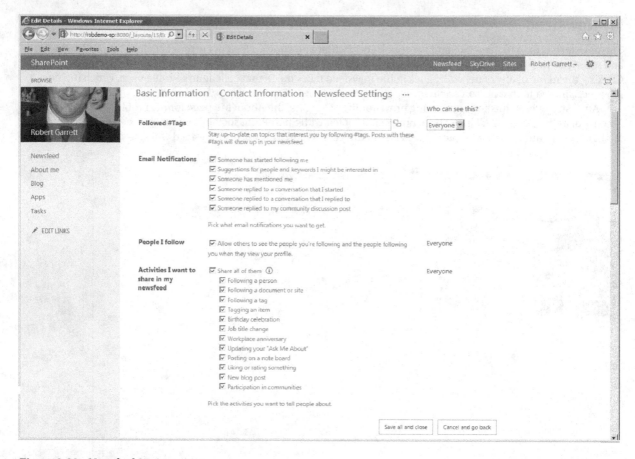

Figure 6-23. *Newsfeed Settings page*

The Newsfeed Settings page allows fine-grained control over activities you wish to share in your newsfeed, the e-mail notifications you receive, people you follow, and topics of interest—hash tags.

You can also access your newsfeed at any time by clicking the Newsfeed link at the top right of any SharePoint page. The Newsfeed page differs from the About Me page in that it shows just your newsfeed and no personal demographic information like that on the About Me page.

My Content

SharePoint 2010 used the concept of "My Content" and provided a link on the top menu of your My Site that linked the user to stored content. SharePoint 2013 also allows stored content and is one of the main reasons to provision a My Site (in addition to newsfeeds, etc.). Unlike SharePoint 2010, SharePoint 2013 integrates your My Site content in with your User Profile page and newsfeed, as part of the social space that belongs to you in the SharePoint farm. SharePoint no longer views personal storage as a separate entity from a user's profile, even though from a technical perspective they are. When you view your profile, or someone else views your profile, in SharePoint 2013, the expectation is to see everything about you, which includes any personal stored content, assuming you have shared it.

Notice the absence of a "My Content" link anywhere on your My Site or profile pages. This is because your content combines in with your profile information. To see what I mean, click the Blog link in the left navigation. You should see a page like that in Figure 6-24. Look carefully at the URL and you should see that your blog hosts under your My Site location, which indicates that you have personal content in your My Site.

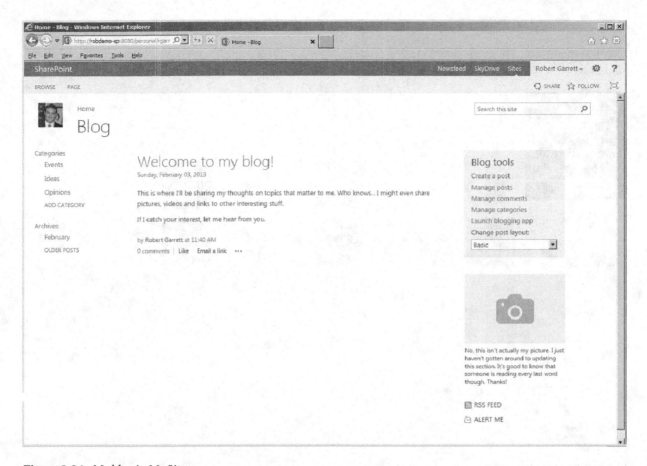

Figure 6-24. *My blog in My Site*

Just like any other site collection for which you have owner or site collection administration rights, you can click the gear icon in the top right corner and see all site content and site settings for your My Site. Since your My Site is just another site collection, the settings behave similarly to those of any other site collection settings you have seen in this book.

As a simple example to demonstrate further hosting your own personal content in your My Site, I shall demonstrate creating a new document library in your My Site (there already exists document libraries and lists, which you can access from the gear icon and site content).

1. Click the gear icon in the top right of any of your profile pages.

2. Click the Site Contents menu item.

3. You should see a familiar page, like that in Figure 6-25.

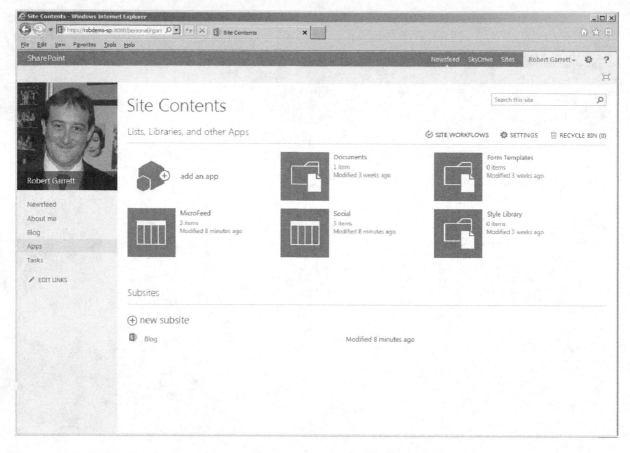

Figure 6-25. *My Site Contents*

4. Click the Add an App tile (remember lists and libraries are apps).

5. Click the Document Library tab.

6. Give the document library a name and click the OK button.

7. Notice that a new link to the document library appears in the left navigation, under Recent.

SharePoint tracks recent activity and maintains links to recently created apps in the left navigation. I can of course make my new document library a permanent fixture in the left navigation by changing the library settings to display in quick links.

Notes and Tagging

"Tagging" is the flavor of the Internet these days. With the explosion of social networking, and sites like Facebook, everyone is in the mode to tag and "like" content. SharePoint 2013 is on the tagging bandwagon and offers users the ability to perform extensive tagging using the Managed Metadata Service application.

When discussing SharePoint tagging, notes, and social networking capabilities, the topic of metadata will invariably come into play. Metadata is "data about data." For example, a database schema defines the structure and properties of SQL tables—this is metadata for the actual row data in the table. In the world of SharePoint, tags are metadata, because they give the reader of certain content some level of categorization and thus context. SharePoint bakes metadata into the platform and surfaces it in basic lists, document libraries, document and records management, publishing, and social networking. The topic of metadata is vast enough that I cover it in Chapter 9.

Tagging in SharePoint 2013

Tagging is ubiquitous throughout the site collection. At the top right of any standard SharePoint page, you will see the Share and Follow icons. (I say "standard SharePoint page" because publishing pages follow templates defined by site designers and may not include these icons, except as part of the ribbon when editing the page.) See Figure 6-26 for an example of these icons.

Figure 6-26. *Share and Follow icons*

The SharePoint Follow icon is synonymous with "Like." When clicking the Follow icon, SharePoint tags the site and it appears under favorite sites, which you may access at any time from the Sites link in the top right. SharePoint allows following of various objects in the platform, including

- Sites
- Lists
- Libraries
- List Items
- Documents and Images
- Pages

I clicked Follow on a few sites and a document in my development environment. As you can see from Figure 6-27, activities are starting to show up in my newsfeed. Just like with Facebook, the more interaction you have with SharePoint, the more populated your newsfeed becomes.

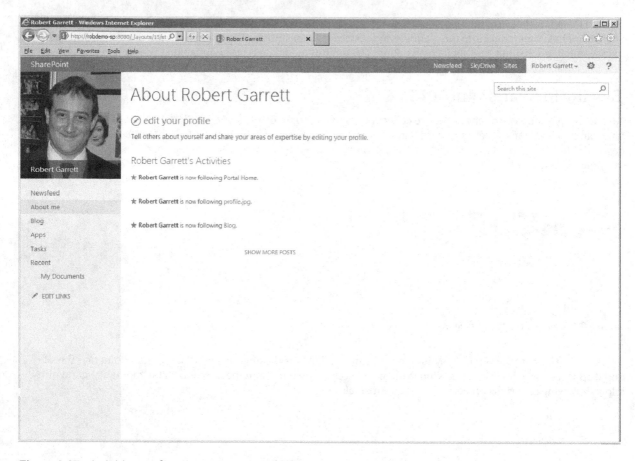

Figure 6-27. *Activities are showing up in my newsfeed*

■ **Note**　New content tagged or new notes added to your SharePoint MySite do not show up in your newsfeed immediately. The Activity Feed Job in Central Administration updates newsfeeds on a schedule.

Document libraries do not enable the tagging capability on contained documents by default. The following set of steps details how to enable tagging for a document library:

1. From any Document Library View page, click the Library tab from the ribbon.

2. Click the Library Settings icon from the ribbon.

3. Click the Enterprise Metadata and Keywords Settings link.

4. Check the Add Enterprise Keywords check box to add the Enterprise Keywords Metadata column to the document library. SharePoint will not allow you to opt out of this option once it is checked and the Settings page saved. The Enterprise Keywords Metadata column allows folksonomy behavior for documents in the library.

5. Check the Metadata Publishing check box to allow any folksonomy tags entered for a document to appear in your newsfeed, profile pages, tag cloud, and so on, as a social tag.

■ **Note** When saving a document from Microsoft Word to a SharePoint 2010/2013 document library with an Enterprise Keywords column, the Save As dialog displays a Tags text box to save entered tags to the Enterprise Keywords column in the library list item associated with the document.

Ratings

Like its predecessor, SharePoint 2013 includes ratings. Ratings collect user feedback with star ratings—similar to ratings seen in iTunes and Windows Media Player. When you enable the feature for a list or library, users can apply their rating for the list item or document and SharePoint keeps track of all user ratings to display a collective ranking. Figure 6-28 shows an example of ratings in action.

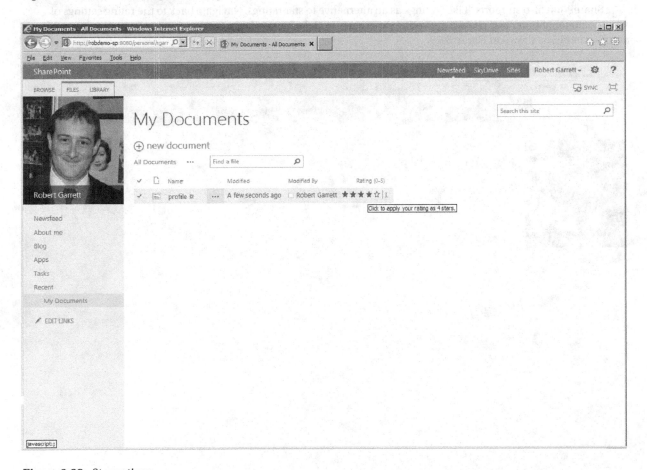

Figure 6-28. *Star ratings*

SharePoint does not enable ratings on lists or document libraries by default. The following steps demonstrate how to enable rating functionality for a document library:

1. From any Document Library View page, click the Library tab from the ribbon.

2. Click the Library Settings icon from the ribbon.

3. Click the Rating Settings link.

4. Set the radio button option for Allow Items in This List to Be Rated as Yes.

■ **Note**   If you are trying to find the Rating Settings and not seeing it (perhaps you are attempting the preceding steps for a document library on your My Site), then ensure that you have enabled the Site Collection Publishing feature.

In Figure 6-28, I am hovering the mouse over the rating for a document in one of my document libraries. SharePoint indicates that I have rated the document with four stars. SharePoint keeps current track of my rating but collates all user ratings for the document. Notice the numeric counter next to the rating that shows how many ratings this document has received.

SharePoint also supports "Like" ratings as an alternative to star ratings. Navigate back to the rating settings of your document library and change the voting experience to "Like." Instead of star ratings, users can now elect to like your list items, as shown in Figure 6-29.

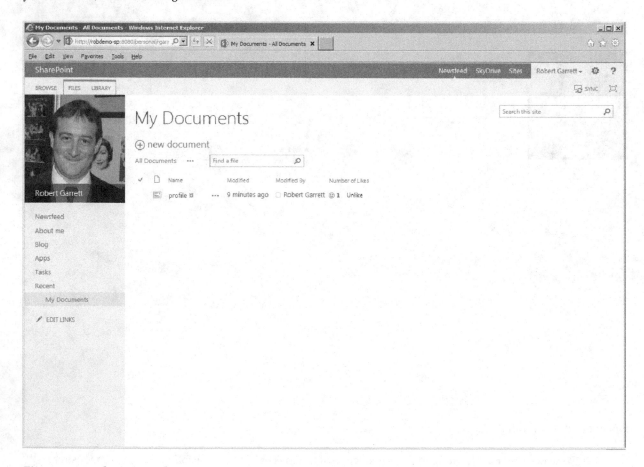

Figure 6-29. *Like voting style*

Blogs

Long before sites like Facebook and Twitter, blogs (short for weblogs) existed for those people who had something to share with the Internet. Initially, techie and literary folks had blogs and wrote articles for select pockets of readership. Around the year 2000, the blogosphere evolved and people woke up to the fact that they could easily host a blog and say whatever they wanted to the world via the Internet. It seemed that everyone had a blog, ranging from intellectual ideas to ramblings of one's personal life and social sharing. Sites such as Live Journal promoted personal blogging and were part of the beginnings of social networking.

Microsoft acknowledged the demand for blog engines and incorporated the blog site definition in SharePoint 2007. SharePoint 2010, and now 2013, continues to offer blogging capabilities and offers more integration with My Sites and social sharing of self-authored content in the enterprise. I'll begin with blogs in My Sites.

1. Click the name of your logged on user in the upper right corner of the page.

2. Select the menu option "About Me."

3. Click the Blog link in the left navigation of your My Site.

4. If you do not have a blog, SharePoint will create you one.

5. Your My Site blogs exists at the following location, by default:
    `/mysite-managed-path/<username>/Blog/default.aspx`

6. See Figure 6-24 for a typical newly created blog in My Site.

Blogs are not just limited to My Sites; administrators and site owners may add them into the site collection anywhere as subsites. Follow these steps to create a new blog underneath a site of your choice in your site collection:

1. Click the gear icon in the parent site or root site collection.

2. Click the Site Contents menu item.

3. Scroll to the bottom of the page and click the New Subsite link.

4. SharePoint shows a new Subsite Creation page, like that in Figure 6-30.

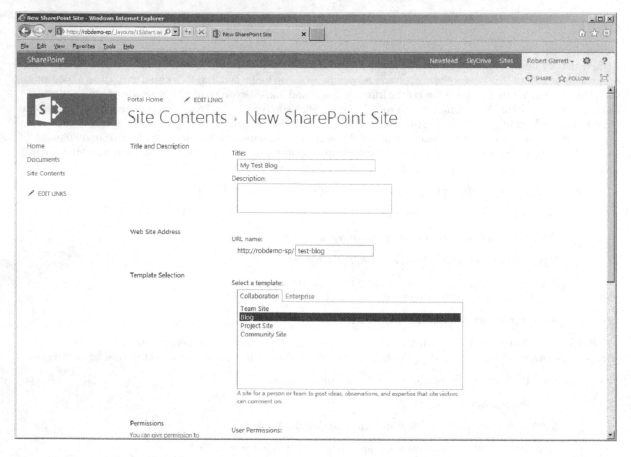

Figure 6-30. *New SharePoint Site*

5. Provide a name and description for the blog site.

6. Provide the URL of the blog subsite.

7. Select the Blog template.

8. Change any of the navigation and permissions settings, if you desire.

9. Click the Create button.

Blog posts are effectively a collection of list items in a dedicated list, called Posts, in the blog site. From the Blog landing page, click the gear icon, followed by the Site Contents menu item. You should see the Posts list. Also, notice the Comments and Categories lists, which store—you guessed it—the comments and categories of blog posts.

Wikis

A wiki is a web site that allows users to create and edit any number of interlinked pages. Wiki pages typically render as HTML, and users edit text and image content on wiki pages using WYSIWYG (What-you-see-is-what-you-get). The purpose of wiki sites is to foster collaboration of content creation and editing by allowing any user to edit the content, regardless of his or her security access. Wiki sites, like Wikipedia.com, have become trusted sources for information on the Internet because readers constantly vet and update the content.

Microsoft designed wiki sites in SharePoint for ease of use for the content owners and contributors. Like most other content containers in SharePoint, a wiki exists as a list in a site, and the pages of a wiki exist as the list items in the wiki library.

In SharePoint 2007, wiki lists were more of an afterthought, whereas wikis integrate better into the SharePoint 2010 and 2013 platform. For example, the new Team and Blank site definitions now default to use wiki libraries and pages for all content pages. This replaces the legacy Web Part pages of SP 2007, in which content owners would have to drop content Web Parts into specific zones of the page to host content. Content contributors now have free rein to place text content anywhere on the page and still use Web Part zones—determined by site designers in the page layout—thus wrapping text and image content around typical functional Web Parts.

Users create wiki sites in SharePoint 2013 much like any other site, and I shall demonstrate the steps in just a moment. Before doing so, I must distinguish between SharePoint Enterprise wiki sites and Blank or Team sites.

SharePoint 2007 Blank and Team sites used Web Part pages, which are ASPX pages containing HTML markup and Web Part zones for users to drop Web Parts. Site designers would need to use the publishing features and site templates if they wanted to provide page customization and web content management capabilities in SharePoint 2007. Sites created from the Enterprise wiki template in SharePoint 2010 and 2013 include a special library and publishing features typically associated with publishing sites—page ratings, managed metadata, customization capabilities, and so on. Sites created from Team and Blank site templates consist of the standard collaboration features, offered in the Foundation platform, and a Site Pages library, to contain wiki pages. SharePoint Blank and Team sites allow wiki-style editing of content and the placement of Web Parts without the need for Web Part zones, and rudimentary customization of the page, because of the free flow of content editing that wiki pages provide.

Enterprise wiki sites, in SharePoint, provide users with greater control of content, using the publishing features, and adhere more to web content management. Wiki pages in an Enterprise wiki site use page layouts and master pages, so designers may customize metadata on wiki pages, much like on publishing pages.

You may create wiki libraries by creating a new wiki site or by adding a wiki library to an existing site. The following steps demonstrate both approaches:

New wiki site:

1. Click the gear icon and click the Site Contents menu item.

2. Scroll to the bottom of the page and click the New Subsite link.

3. Give the wiki site a name and description.

4. Provide a subsite URL.

5. Click the Publishing tab in the templates section.

6. Your page should look something like that in Figure 6-31.

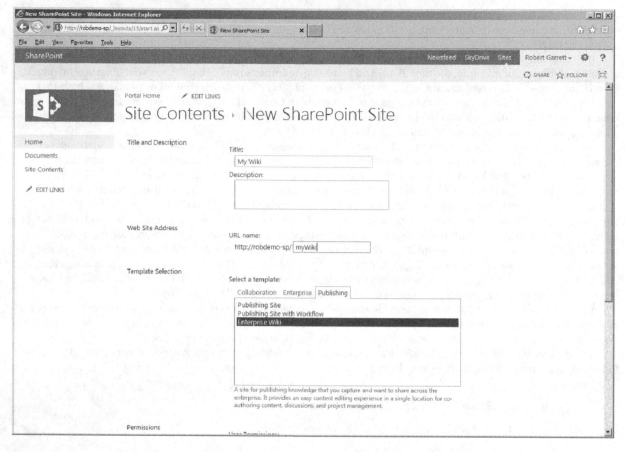

Figure 6-31. *Create an Enterprise wiki site*

7. Click the Enterprise wiki site.

8. Click the Create button when ready to create the wiki site.

New wiki library:

1. Click the gear icon and click the Site Contents menu item.

2. Click the Add an App tile.

3. Find the Wiki Page Library app and click its tile.

4. Give the library a title and click the Advanced Options link if you wish to apply more options before SharePoint creates the library.

5. Click the Create button.

A wiki site is really just a team site with a default wiki library, with the Site Welcome page pointing to the main landing page in the wiki library.

Since both blogs and wikis consist of list/library containers to store content, site owners and collaborators may make use of all the tagging, notes, and rating social networking tools in the platform in conjunction with blog and wiki content.

Summary

In this chapter, you took an in-depth look at configuring the User Profile Service in SharePoint 2013—one of the most troublesome areas to configure. You read about user profiles, along with their properties and user subtypes and looked at organization profiles in brief. Another key concept is audiences—administrators can generate groups of people based on inclusion rules and then apply those audiences to targeted content areas.

In the second half of this chapter, you read about social networking and some of the features that SharePoint 2013 provides as part of the My Site infrastructure. I demonstrated the newsfeed, tagging, rating, and the use of blogs and wikis as part of social networking.

In Chapter 7, I will switch topics and look at the security aspects of SharePoint 2013.

CHAPTER 7

■ ■ ■

Security and Policy

Asking users to upload important documents and information content to SharePoint without providing a level of security to protect their data is like driving without a seatbelt. Users like to know that their data is secure when they are asked to move it from their work machines to shared servers and collaborative platforms, like SharePoint. Therefore, Microsoft has ensured that SharePoint, since the early days, has had security measures baked into the platform. The security model in SharePoint 2013 itself has not changed a lot since the previous versions, SharePoint 2007 and 2010, which benefits users of the legacy versions, since they do not have to learn a new model for securing user content.

Security in SharePoint has similarities to typical file system security—as in Windows' New Technology File System (NTFS), for example. The implementation of security in SharePoint is very different from that of file system security, but the model and security configuration are similar. The model consists of Access Control Lists (ACLs) to secure sites, lists, files, and folders; permissions to perform actions on the secured objects; and users or groups with collections of permissions for the secured objects.

At the heart of any good security model is a set of permissions, allowing users of the model to perform certain actions in a specific context. The context might pertain to a location in a hierarchical structure and the set of permissions established for sets of users to a particular securable object. For example, in SharePoint terminology, the security model grants users, or groups of users, access to secured objects—such as sites, lists, and list items. This chapter walks you through the various concepts that constitute the security model in SharePoint 2013.

Security Administration

The IT department typically played a large role in web site security administration in days of old. For its SharePoint collaboration tool, Microsoft wanted to break this dependency on IT and empower end users—content owners—to have control of the content they create and disseminate to their audience. However, Microsoft also recognized that no large enterprise content management system operates completely without involvement from IT. So it structured the security model in hierarchical fashion so that IT can manage high-level access and overall control, while allowing content owners to manage their own content islands with SharePoint sites and site collections.

In Chapter 2, we visited the Central Administration web site, which allows the IT folks and SharePoint administrators to configure SharePoint 2013—and security configuration is no exception. From Central Administration, administrators may configure web application permission policies, grant users site collection rights to new and existing site collections, and configure the farm with farm administration rights.

You should have noticed by now that I throw around the term "SharePoint administrator" loosely. In fact, a well-organized SharePoint farm consists of various types of administrators for different configuration areas. So before getting knee-deep in security terminology, I will visit the different types of SharePoint administrators.

SharePoint Administrators

Have you seen a SharePoint farm configured where the farm administrator account has rights to perform every SharePoint task under the sun? I am willing to bet that the farm administrator account has local server administration rights on the web-front-end servers and database cluster, too. Convenient as this scenario is, it leaves a large attack surface open for hackers; once a hacker gains access to the farm account, he or she has access to the entire farm configuration. The alternative SharePoint provides is to assign administrators specific roles. Read on through this section for the various administration roles in SharePoint.

- *Local Server Administrators*—Contrary to common belief, the main SharePoint Farm account does not have to be a local server admin—Microsoft recommends quite the opposite. One exception is when installing SharePoint 2013 (see Chapter 2), where making the farm account user a local admin ensures access to configure IIS, access to SQL, and installation of SharePoint binaries. After installation, ensure that the farm account is not a local administrator by accessing the Administrators Security Group under Server Management in Windows.

■ **Note**   All members of the local server administrators group are automatically SharePoint farm administrators.

- *SharePoint Farm Administrators*—They have full control of the entire SharePoint farm. Ensure that the main SharePoint farm account is a member of this group (the default post-installation) for SharePoint 2013 to function correctly. Members of the local server administrators group already have farm access. An existing farm administrator may add another user, not part of the local server administrators group, via Central Administration, as follows:

    1. Click the Manage the Farm Administrators Group link, under the Security heading.

    2. SharePoint shows you the list of users already in the farm administrators group.

    3. From the horizontal sub-menu, click the New button and select Add Users from the drop-down box.

    4. A people picker dialog should appear and allow you to select users from any of the user credential stores (the default is typically Active Directory).

    5. To remove one or more users from the farm administrators group, click the Actions menu after selecting existing users from the list (check the check box next to each user to delete) and then Remove Selected Users from Group.

- *PowerShell Administrators*—PowerShell administrators require additional permissions to provide administration operations via the SharePoint Management Shell (PowerShell). The following PowerShell Cmdlet provides shell administration permissions. Supply the usernames to receive shell administration permissions and the content database instance in which they can perform operations.

    ```
    Add-SPShellAdmin -UserName <user name> -Database <database name>
    ```

- *Service Administrators*—Service administrators control specific service applications and cannot administer service applications other than those they are granted access to by farm administrators. For example, a farm administrator may delegate administration of the Managed Metadata Service Application to one set of administrators and the Search Service Application to another set. To grant administration access to a service application, visit Central Admin ➤ Application Management ➤ Manage Service Applications ➤ Highlight the service application item, and then click the Administrators icon on the ribbon for the selected managed service application.

- *Feature Administrators*—Feature administrators manage administration of particular features as part of existing managed service applications. Not all managed service applications permit such granular control with permissions, but for those that do—such as the User Profile Service Application—you can highlight the Manage Service Applications item in Central Administration (see the previous bullet) and then click the Permissions icon on the ribbon to access the settings.

- *Site Collection Administrators*—Site collection administrators have rights to configure and change settings across a particular site collection. Farm administrators by default do not belong to all site collection administration groups, but they do have the power to add themselves to any site collection administration group via Central Administration. Regardless of how users secure content within a site, within a list, or at the list item, site collection administrators have exclusive full control access to all content in the site collection. *Thus, assign users to the site collection administrators group with care.* A farm administrator may add a user as a site collection administrator from Central Administration as follows:

1. Click the Application Management heading.

2. Under Site Collection, click the link to change site collection administrators.

3. You should see a page like Figure 7-1.

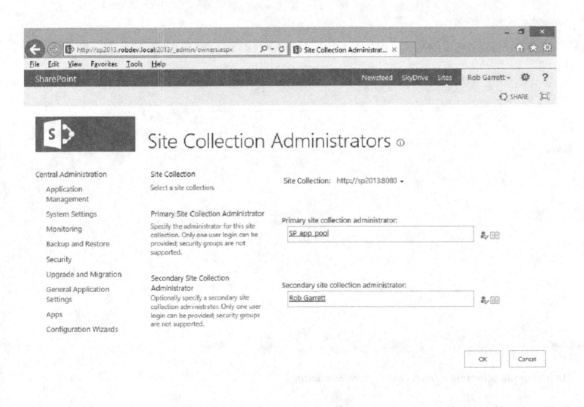

Figure 7-1. Assigning site collection administrators from Central Administration

4. Ensure that the correct site collection is in the drop-down.

5. Central Administration enables assignment of one primary and one secondary site collection administrator; use the people picker boxes on this page to assign them.

- Existing site collection administrators may add other users to the site collection administrators group from the site collection, using the following steps:

1. Click the gear icon.

2. Click the Site Settings menu option from the menu.

3. Click the Site Collection Administrators link from the Users and Permissions heading.

4. Add users in the page shown in Figure 7-2.

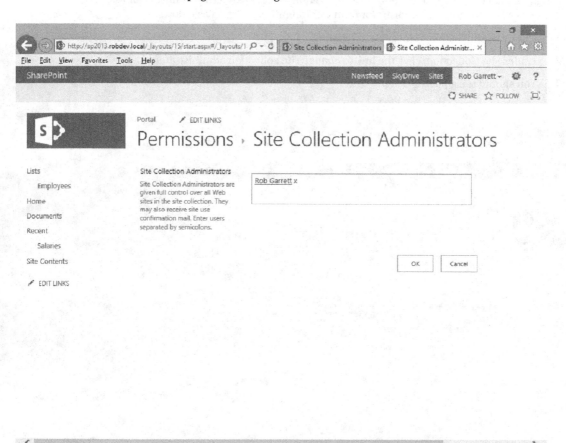

Figure 7-2. *Assigning site collection administrators from Site Settings*

5. You should see existing site collection administrators, already assigned by a farm administrator—SharePoint will not allow you to remove all site administrators.

Permissions and Permission Levels

A single permission in SharePoint is a specific action that a user may take on a securable object. For example—reading the value of a SharePoint list item is a specific permission, often granted to groups of users who need to read lists and their contained items. SharePoint maintains many permissions in the platform, and the different permissions available to users depend on what an administrator (or owner of content) wishes to secure. Documents in document libraries offer a different set of permissions from those of a site in a site collection. Table 7-1 shows a sample subset of permissions available for lists; other permissions exist for sites and personalization.

Table 7-1. *Subset List Permissions in SharePoint*

Permission	Description
Add Items	Add new items to lists and add new documents to document libraries.
Edit Items	Edit items in lists and edit documents in document libraries.
Delete Items	Delete items from lists and documents from document libraries.
View Items	View items in lists and documents in document libraries.
Open Items	View the content within documents of a document library, not just the metadata of the associated list item.
View Versions	View previous versions of a list or document library.
Delete Versions	Delete previous versions of a list or document library.
Create Alerts	Create e-mail alerts for lists whenever something changes (configured when the user creates the alert).
View Application Pages	View forms, views, and application pages. The view lockdown feature turns off this permission on pages and document libraries in publishing sites so anonymous users may not view back-end list content.
Approve Items	Approve a minor version of a list item in a list or document in a document library.
Override Checkout	Override checkout by another user on a list item in a list or document in a document library.
Manage Lists	Create and delete lists, add and remove columns in a list, and add and remove public views of the list.

With the vast number of permissions available in the SharePoint platform, managing them and assigning the correct permissions to users or groups of users is no trivial task, which is where *permission levels* come in. A permission level is analogous to a permission set—a set of permissions that group together and when applied to a securable object provide the user or user group with related operations on the securable object. For example, the Read permission level consists of various read permissions for most read-like operations of a securable object and the Contribute permission level provides a number of write permissions to securable objects.

Microsoft labels permission levels with role-like titles, which new users sometimes confuse with those of SharePoint security groups. If you think about it, using role names makes sense, as a set of permissions often defines the role of the user or groups of users applied. Table 7-2 defines the standard set of permission levels available in SharePoint.

Table 7-2. Standard Permission Levels

Permission Level	Description
Full Control	Users with this permission level have full access to all operations on the secured object, including that of administrative operations. This is not the same as the distinct set of permissions granted to site collection administrators, who have a greater set of administration capabilities.
Design	Users at this permission level have contributor rights and certain permissions to effect change of a securable object, but not administrative rights. Designers typically have permission to change the content in containers (lists and sites) and configure containers, whereas contributors can only write and delete content within containers. Users with Design permission level may also approve content in lists with content approval enabled.
Contribute	This is a standard permission level to grant users or groups of users add, edit, and delete rights to lists and list items. Typically, users asked to join a SharePoint site to collaborate on content have contribute rights to make edits to existing content, add new content, or delete old content.
Read	Users with the Read permission level can access all content in containers in read-only mode. Readers may download documents in document libraries and view lists and list items but not change anything.
Limited Access	This permission level is special in that SharePoint grants it to users or groups of users for a specific secured object that has custom permissions. For example, if the owner of a list applies specific permissions, not as part of a specific permission set, then SharePoint shows the permission set as Limited Access. Limited Access permissions typically apply only to one item at a time in the container, not to all other items.
View Only	Users or groups of users with View Only permissions cannot download content. This level has similar permissions to the Read permission level but does not allow users to download documents from document libraries.
Restricted Read	This permission level is similar to the Read permission level but has only four of the eleven permissions that Read contains. This permission is available only in publishing sites. It provides users with this permission level access to read content without the ability to create alerts, browse user information, or use client integration (interact with Microsoft Office).
Approve	This permission level is available in publishing sites only and grants users or groups the capability to edit list items and documents as well as approve items in lists with content approval enabled.
Manage Hierarchy	This permission level is available in publishing sites only and is similar to the Design permission level. It enables users or groups of users to create sites and edit list items and documents. The major difference between the Design permission level and the Manage Hierarchy level is that this permission level does not grant approval rights on list items or documents in lists that have content approval enabled.

Figure 7-3 shows an example list of permission levels applied to a site. To get to this page, select Site Permissions under the Users and Permissions section within Site Settings, and then click Permission Levels on the ribbon.

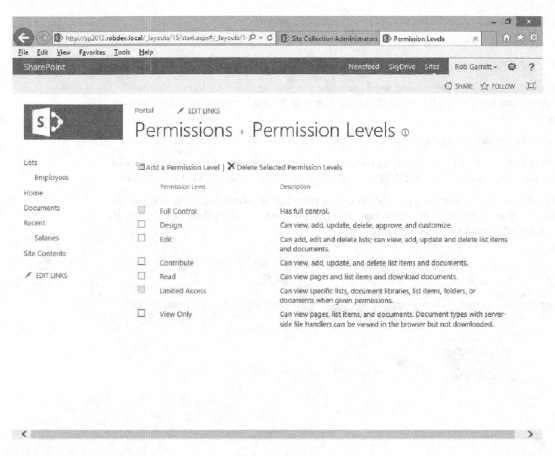

Figure 7-3. *Site Permission Levels*

Creating Custom Permission Levels

SharePoint allows site administrators to create their own unique permission levels. For example, perhaps the content owner would like to allow contributor access to items in a list, but prevent deletion of any list item. The standard permission levels provide only Contributor or Read levels, but not a mix of the two, so a custom permission level can solve this requirement.

The easiest method for creating a permission level in SharePoint is to create the new level based on an existing permission level—in this case use the Contribute permission level. Permission levels reside at the site level and inherit through subsites in the hierarchy. Choosing to add a new site permission level at the top of the site collection enables use of the permission level across the entire site collection.

■ **Note**   Permission levels reside within sites.

---

1. Click the gear icon and select the Site Settings menu option.

2. Click the link for Site Permissions.

3. Click the Permission Levels icon on the ribbon.

4. Click the link for the permission level you want to copy—in this case, the Contribute permission level. SharePoint will show you a page of the permissions contained in the selected permission level.

5. Scroll to the bottom of the page and click the Copy Permission Level button.

6. Provide a name and description for the new permission level and change the contained permissions. In this case, find the Delete Items permission and uncheck the check box.

7. Scroll to the bottom of the page and click the Create button. SharePoint will navigate you back to the site Permission Levels page with the new permission level shown along with the default permission levels (Figure 7-4).

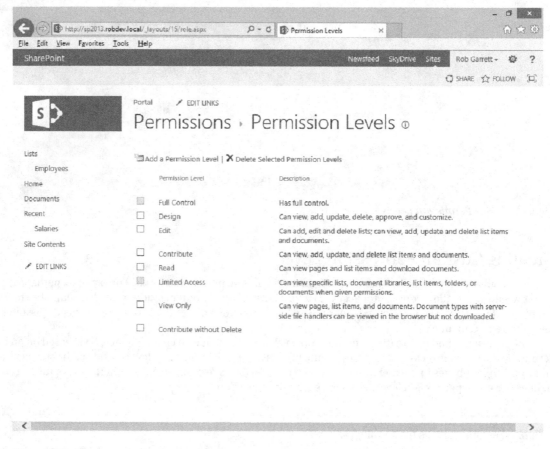

Figure 7-4. *New permission level created*

How do you create a new permission level without starting from an existing one?

1. Follow steps 1 and 2 in the previous procedure.

2. Click the Add a Permission Level button at the top of the list in the Permission Levels page.

3. Provide a name and description and select the desired permissions in the permission level.

■ **Note**   Some permission items depend on others, so you may see SharePoint automatically select permissions based on the permissions you choose to include in the permission level.

---

4. Click the Create button to create the new permission level.

Editing an existing permission is also an easy process, although *not recommended*. Microsoft best practices stipulate that it is better to create a new permission level based on an existing one. Users familiar with SharePoint expect that the stock permission levels behave as installed, and changing these permission levels may affect the stability of user permissions in the site hierarchy. If you wish to proceed, follow these steps:

1. Follow steps 1 and 2 of the first procedure in this section.

2. Click the Permission Level Name to edit. SharePoint will show the name, description, and contained permissions in the permission level.

3. Edit the permission level and then click the Submit button at the bottom of the page.

Deleting permission levels is also an easy process.

1. Follow steps 1 and 2 at the beginning of this section.

2. Check the check box next to the permission levels you desire to delete.

3. Click the Delete Selected Permission Levels button at the top of the page.

4. SharePoint will display a confirmation dialog, like that in Figure 7-5; click OK to proceed with the delete or Cancel to revert.

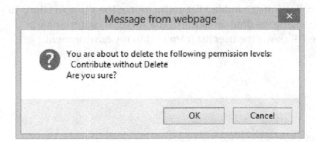

Figure 7-5. Confirmation dialog to delete permission levels

> ■ **Note** Deletion of a permission level that is in use by a user or group for a particular context (site, list, or whatever level) causes SharePoint to lose the permissions for the deleted level. Take care in deleting permission levels, especially the standard permission levels, which Microsoft *does not recommend*.

SharePoint Users

Most security models assume the existence of users and groups of users. Different users require different sets of permissions to perform their work, depending on the level of access to data in the system. In a previous section of this chapter, I covered the topic of SharePoint administrators—an administrator is a specific type of user with elevated permissions within the SharePoint farm or site collection.

At the basic level, a user of SharePoint is an "identity." User identity typically consists of various attributes that describe the user with access to the SharePoint site collection. SharePoint retains minimal information about a user to distinguish one user from another, which typically involves the username, password, and display name from the credential store that the user authenticates (Active Directory). SharePoint 2007 classified users using either the Active Directory username DOMAIN\username or a username with membership provider prefix (more on membership providers later in this chapter). SharePoint 2010, and now SharePoint 2013, uses Claims-Based-Authentication (CBA), which tracks user identity via abstract token (more on CBA in Chapter 8).

> ■ **Note** With the exception of administrators, SharePoint maintains topmost user security at the site collection level. Farm administrators must grant relevant access to users for each site collection in a web application.

Most users of SharePoint identify other users by the friendly display name, and, by default, Active Directory uses the first name and last name. Any object that I modify or own in SharePoint shows my name as "Rob Garrett," but under the hood, SharePoint uses the username or unique token to identify my user identity.

Users have more than just username, password, and display name attributes in SharePoint. In Chapter 6, I discussed user profiles, which consist of collections of attributes for each user known to SharePoint. Each user profile associates with a user identity by the unique user identity token or username.

SharePoint tracks each user added to a site collection in a hidden list at the root of the site collection. To view this list, type the following URL into your browser (replacing the domain name of the server, as appropriate): http://domain_name/_catalogs/users/. Figure 7-6 shows the user list from within my environment.

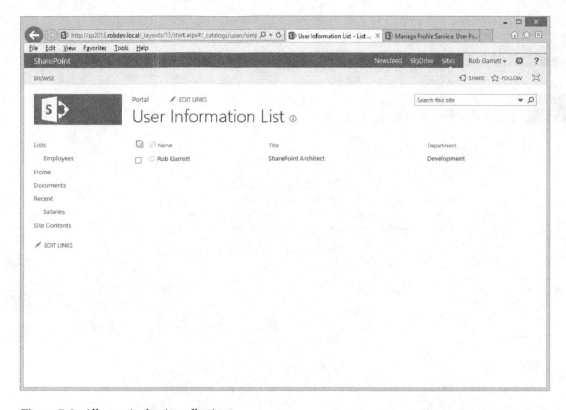

Figure 7-6. *All users in the site collection*

SharePoint Security Groups

SharePoint security groups are groups of users, defined within a site collection, and assigned permissions to secured objects. Security groups work to make administration of security easier by collecting users in groups according to their access role. For example, the default Visitors, Members, and Owners groups of a site collection establish separation of users that have permissions to view secured objects (visitors), write and change secured objects (members), and enjoy full access to secured objects (owners). Follow these steps to view the current groups in the site collection:

1. Click the gear icon (from the top right of the home page of the site collection).

2. Click Site Settings from the menu.

3. Under the Users and Permissions heading, click the People and Groups link.

4. By default, SharePoint will open a page of the Members group.

5. From the quick launch left navigation, click the Groups heading.

6. You should see a page like Figure 7-7.

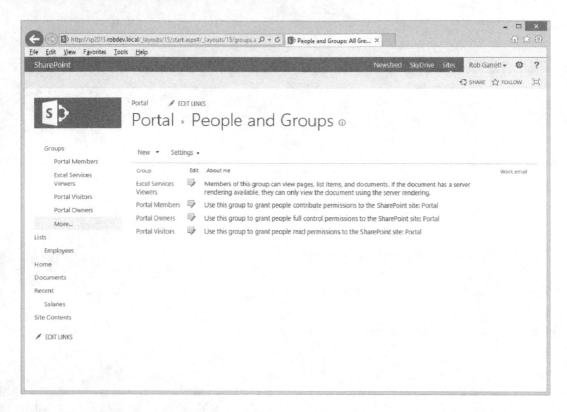

Figure 7-7. *Default groups in a team site collection*

Notice, in Figure 7-7, that SharePoint created default groups, described as follows:

- *[Site Name] Members*—This group has Contribute permission level access to the site; thus, any users in this group have contribute access to the site and subsites that inherit permissions from this site. Add those users to this group whom you wish to allow contributor access, so those users may add, edit, or delete content in lists and containers, and edit pages and other content.

- *[Site Name] Owners*—This group has Full Control permission level access to the site; thus, any users in this group have full control access to the site and subsites that inherit permissions from this site. Add those users to this group who have ownership rights, so those users may add, edit, or delete content and change, add, edit, or delete lists, subsites, and so on.

- *[Site Name] Visitors*—This group has Read permission level access to the site; thus, any users in this group have read access to the site and subsites that inherit permissions from this site. Add those users to this group who have read-only access to see content in lists and subsites, but who may not change anything.

- *Excel Services Viewers*—This group allows rendered view only of pages, list items, and documents using server rendering. For example, users in this group only cannot download documents to open in Microsoft Word. This group primarily provides access to users for Excel Services–rendered sheets.

Publishing and Enterprise site collections have the following additional default groups:

- *Approvers*—Users added to this group have approval rights for any lists that have content approval enabled.

- *Designers*—Users added to this group have design rights (see the previous section in this chapter on permission levels for a description of the Design permission level).

- *Hierarchy Managers*—Users in this group have hierarchical change rights (see the previous section in this chapter on permission levels for a description of the Hierarchy Management permission level).

- *Restricted Readers*—Users in this group have restricted read rights (see the previous section in this chapter on permission levels for a description of the Restricted Read permission level).

All security groups in SharePoint work the same way via the SharePoint user interface. For the sake of brevity, the sets of steps in the following subsections discuss adding and removing users from the Members group, via the page in Figure 7-7, but the same steps apply to any other group in SharePoint.

Adding Users to a Group

The following steps detail how to add a new user to an existing group:

1. Click the gear icon (from the top right of the home page of the site collection).

2. Click Site Settings from the menu.

3. Under the Users and Permissions heading, click the People and Groups link.

4. By default, SharePoint will open a page of the Members group.

5. From the sub-menu (New, Actions, and Settings), click New (or the arrow next to New and select Add Users).

6. SharePoint will show a dialog like that in Figure 7-8. Add users to the dialog by typing in their usernames, names, or e-mail addresses.

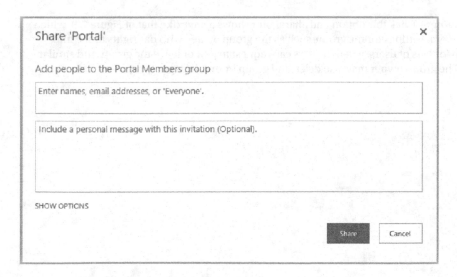

Figure 7-8. New share dialog in SharePoint 2013

The new share dialog in SharePoint 2013, shown in Figure 7-8, replaces the people picker dialog. When you grant users access to a site, list, or list item in SharePoint 2013 you are effectively "sharing" the content with them, hence the name of the new dialog. You might be wondering how you can search users. The new share dialog automatically searches for users in SharePoint (or other sources available via membership and claims providers); just start typing to see suggestions.

Removing Users from a Group

The following steps detail how to remove a user from the Members group:

1. Click the gear icon (from the top right of the home page of the site collection).

2. Click Site Settings from the menu.

3. Under the Users and Permissions heading, click the People and Groups link.

4. By default, SharePoint will open a page of the Members group.

5. Check the check box next to each user you wish to remove from the group.

6. From the sub-menu (New, Actions, and Settings), click Actions, and then click Remove Users from Group.

7. Click OK in the warning dialog that appears.

■ **Note**   Removing a user from a SharePoint security group does not remove the user from the site collection.

Group Settings and Permissions

From within any of the Group pages (see the previous subsections), click the Settings menu item from the sub-menu (New, Actions, and Settings). The following list describes the various settings options available for the group in context:

- *Group Settings*—Click this option and SharePoint shows a page like that of Figure 7-9, which details general settings for the group, such as the group owner, who has rights to see into the group for lists of users, whether users can request to join or leave the group, and similar actions. The group owner may also delete the group from this page.

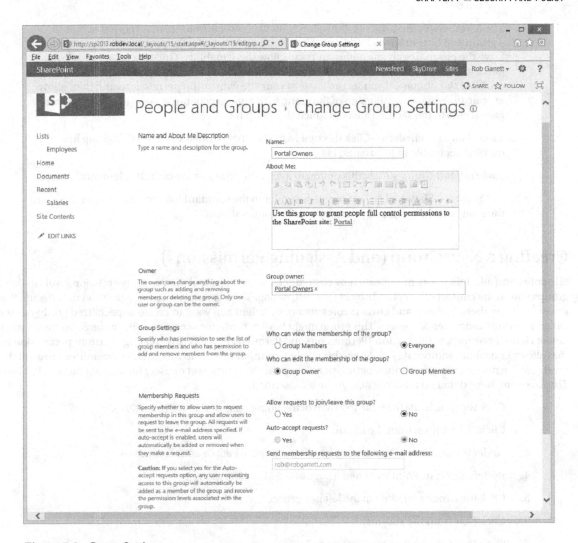

Figure 7-9. *Group Settings*

The Name and About Me sections of this page contain the name and description of the group. The Group Owner field is a people field that contains the name of the person who created the group and is therefore the owner.

The Group Settings section allows you to specify who has access to view the members in the group and who may edit members of the group. Either all group members have access to see other members of the group or everyone with access to the site collection has this access. You may choose either the group owner or members of the group (thus delegating responsibility of group membership to other members of the group) to allow editing of membership of the group.

The Membership Requests section allows you to control how users may request access to a group and how to leave. By default, SharePoint does not allow requests from users to join or leave the group. Toggle the option to Yes to allow this capability. Once users may request to join a group, the second option tells SharePoint whether to auto-accept all requests. *Be careful enabling this option*—if you secure areas of your site with group permissions and then allow anyone to request membership of the group with auto-accept turned on, then any user can gain access to the secured areas to which the group has access.

- *View Group Permissions*—Click this option to see what permission levels this group has and for what securable objects (sites, lists, pages).

- *Make Default Group*—Click this option to assign the group as the default "Members" group.

- *List Settings*—Shows a List Settings page similar to the standard list settings page; in this case the group owner can modify the views and columns shown.

Creating a New Group (and Assigning Permissions)

Site collection administrators may create new custom security groups, and then apply permission levels to these groups within the context of a secured object (site, list, or page). For example, your organization may decide that the default Members, Visitors, and Owners roles are not sufficient and want to create a specialized group of users, called Steering Committee Members. This group might have contributor access to a site in the collection but not delete rights. Look back at the section "Permissions and Permission Levels" for creating a custom permission level that allows contribute without delete. Apply this custom permission level to this custom committee group at the site level (see the next section on granting permissions) to grant this unique set of users the custom permission level. The following steps detail creating the new group as described:

1. Click the gear icon (from the top right of the home page of the site collection).

2. Click Site Settings from the menu.

3. Under the Users and Permissions heading , click the People and Groups link.

4. By default, SharePoint will open a page of the Members group.

5. Click the Groups heading in the left navigation.

6. Click New from the sub-menu.

7. SharePoint displays a page like Figure 7-10.

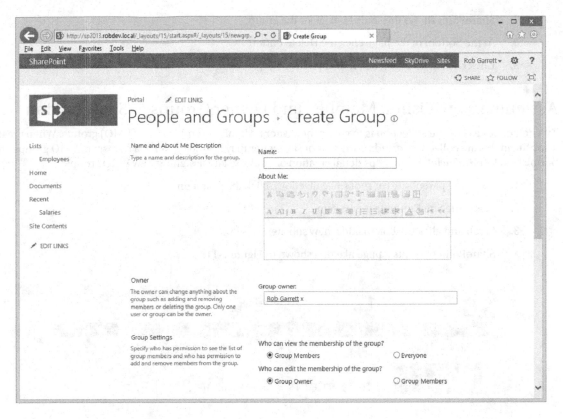

Figure 7-10. *Create a new group*

8. Give the group a new name and description.

9. Configure the group settings and assign the default permission levels.

10. You do not have to assign default permission levels at this stage; you can do so later when applying permissions to a secured object for users contained in this group.

11. Click the Create button to create the group.

Deleting a Group

Deleting a SharePoint Security Group is a straightforward process, summarized in the following steps:

1. Click the gear icon (from the top right of the home page of the site collection).

2. Click Site Settings from the menu.

3. Under the Users and Permissions heading, click the People and Groups link.

4. By default, SharePoint will open a page of the Members group.

5. Click the Groups heading in the left navigation.

6. Click the Edit icon next to the group you wish to delete.

7. SharePoint shows the settings page for the group.

8. At the bottom of the page click the Delete button.

9. Click OK on the dialog box that appears.

Assigning New Visitor, Member, and Owner Groups at Site Creation

The default for a new site collection is to create the Visitors, Members, and Owners (VMO) groups. When creating a subsite in the site collection, an administrator or site owner may decide to create a new set of VMO groups and assign permission levels. The following steps detail creation of a subsite and assigning new VMO groups:

1. From the parent site (or root site collection), click the gear icon.

2. Select the Site Contents menu item.

3. Scroll and click the link to add a new subsite.

4. SharePoint presents a page like that shown in Figure 7-11.

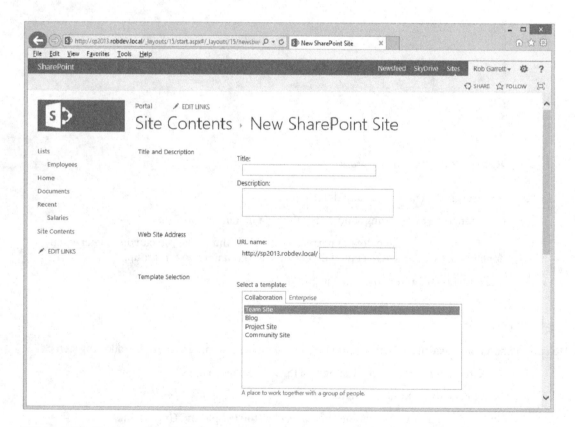

Figure 7-11. *Create a new subsite*

■ **Note** SharePoint 2013 presents a page for creating new subsites, which differs from the Silverlight dialog that SharePoint 2010 provided as part of the new subsite creation process.

1. Fill in the title and URL name fields and choose a template for the new subsite.

2. Scroll to the Permissions section.

3. By default, SharePoint assumes you want to inherit the same site permission level assignments as that of the parent site; change this option to use unique permissions (for this demonstration).

4. Leave all the other options as default and click the Create button.

5. After a brief moment, SharePoint navigates you to a page like that shown in Figure 7-12.

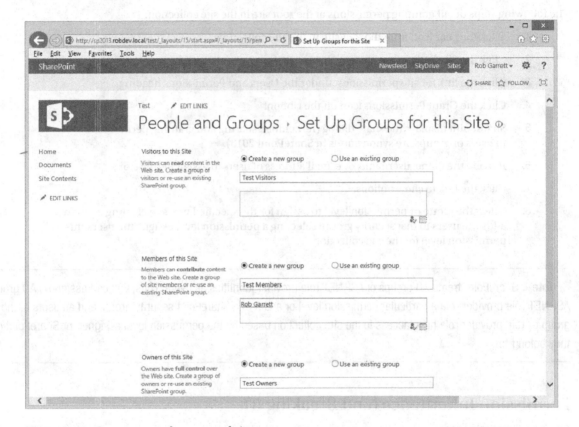

Figure 7-12. *Set up groups for a new subsite*

6. On this page, you can specify creation of new groups for the new site created. SharePoint helps you out with the naming by prefixing the site title to the group type, but you may change the groups to anything you like.

7. Click the OK button, and SharePoint creates the new subsite and new default groups. Navigate back to the Groups page and you should see the three new groups created and stored at the site collection level.

Granting Permissions

At this stage of the chapter, I have established how SharePoint handles groups of related permissions within permission levels, reviewed basic user identity, and discussed security groups and best practices in using them. In this section I discuss granting of permissions (via permission levels) to groups of users for specific securable objects (sites, lists, pages, list items, and so on) in a site collection.

Granting Permissions at the Root Site Collection

The following steps detail granting permissions at the root site in the site collection:

1. Click the gear icon from the root site in the site collection.

2. Click the Site Settings menu item.

3. Click the link for site permissions, under the Users and Permissions heading.

4. Click the Grant Permissions icon on the ribbon.

5. SharePoint displays the share dialog (remember, sharing and granting permissions to users or groups are synonymous in SharePoint 2013).

6. Provide the name, username, or e-mail address of users to assign permission.

7. Click the link to show options.

8. Select the group or permission level to assign for the specified users—selecting a group adds the users to that security group; selecting a permission level assigns the users this permission level for the site collection.

■ **Note**　SharePoint treats AD groups or ASP.NET role provider identities as users. Thus, you can assign an AD group or ASP.NET role provider role a particular permission level or add it to a SharePoint security group, and all users of the AD group or role provider role have access to the site collection based on the permission level assigned or SharePoint group they belong to.

Permission Inheritance (and Breaking It)

Granting permissions to users or AD groups for a subsite is identical to the procedure shown in the previous section, "Granting Permissions at the Root Site Collection"—*as long as the subsite breaks inheritance*. Permission inheritance is an important topic and worthy of a mention here.

Every subsite belongs to one parent site, and the root site of the site collection is special because it has no parent site. Every list or document library resides within a site or subsite. You can quickly see that nested subsites chained together create a tree hierarchy: your site hierarchy. Your site hierarchy is analogous to that of a folder structure in a file system, where sites are synonymous with folders. Similar to file and folder structures, you can assign default permissions for users or groups of users to the top-level site (the root site) and all subsites in the tree inherit the permissions from the parent site. For example, if all subsites inherit from their parent, and I assign my user identity collaboration access via the collaboration permission level, then I have collaboration permissions across the entire site collection hierarchy.

Permission inheritance does not stop at the site level—lists and libraries also inherit permissions from their container site (by default). Thus, in the previous example, I have collaboration access to all lists and libraries in each subsite.

If you can simply grant permissions at the top of a site collection, why bother with permissions for subsites, lists, and libraries? The situation may arise in which the default permissions do not work at a particular level in the hierarchy. For example, you might grant collaboration access across the site collection, but the accounting subsite requires special consideration and only members of the accounting SharePoint group have access. In this case, you would "break" inheritance at the accounting subsite and then assign discrete permissions for the accounting security group.

As a general rule of thumb, it is a good practice to assign permissions at the site collection level that reflect the general populous, and then break inheritance for specific circumstances. For example, if your site is an intranet then perhaps you want generalized read-only access for all users across the site collection (except site collection administrators who have full control) and then will grant specific Write or Collaboration permissions for certain subsites. Contrary, if your site collection represents a collection of project sites, to which everyone has collaboration rights, then it makes sense to grant collaboration rights to the site collection and then restrict rights to particular subsites that do not fit the generalized rule.

The following steps demonstrate how to break inheritance for a subsite:

1. Navigate to the subsite where you wish to assign unique permissions (break inheritance).

2. Click the gear icon and then choose the Site Settings menu item.

3. Click the link for Site Permissions under the Users and Permissions heading.

4. SharePoint displays a page like that in Figure 7-13.

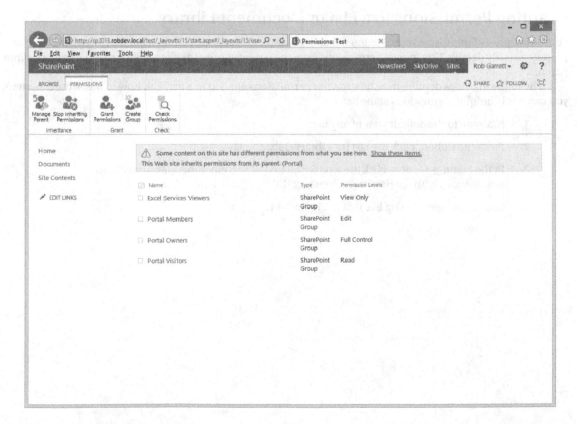

Figure 7-13. *Site permissions*

5. Notice the helpful information panel in yellow—SharePoint 2013 tells you if you have any lists, libraries, or list items that have unique permissions (i.e., broken permission inheritance further down the chain).

6. In my example, my subsite inherits permissions from the parent, but I have a micro-feed list in the site that has its own unique permissions. (Click the link in the yellow information box to see content with unique permissions.)

7. Click the icon on the ribbon to stop inheriting permissions.

8. SharePoint now copies all the permissions of the parents and assigns them as copies to the current subsite.

9. You may now change the existing permissions of the subsite and/or grant new permissions.

10. To revert back to inheriting permissions, click the icon to Delete Unique Permissions.

■ **Note**   If you find yourself breaking permission inheritance often, to prevent user access, then this suggests that you have too many permission rights applied further up the hierarchy. The best practice is to apply restrictive permissions higher up the chain and less restrictive permissions in specialist sites deeper down the chain.

Granting Permissions to a List or Document Library

For the purpose of this discussion, documents and lists work the same way when it comes to applying unique permissions. By default, lists inherit permissions from the parent site, just as sites inherit their permissions from their parent.

The following steps demonstrate how to view permissions applied to a list, and how to break the inheritance so you can apply unique permissions at the list level:

1. Navigate to the default view of any list.

2. From the ribbon, click the List (or Library) tab.

3. In the Settings section, click the icon for Shared With (remember permissions are synonymous with sharing in SharePoint 2013).

4. You should see a dialog like that in Figure 7-14.

Figure 7-14. *Shared With dialog*

5. Click the link to invite people, which shows a dialog similar to that in Figure 7-8.

6. Click the link for advanced settings to see a page with the assigned permissions for the list (similar to the page for site permissions—Figure 7-13).

Clicking the Advanced link on the Shared With dialog (Figure 7-14) shows the Permissions page for the list. This Permissions page works exactly like the Permissions page for a site. To grant unique permissions, break the permission inheritance and assign specific permission levels to new or existing users or groups of users.

Granting Permissions to a List Item or Document

Granting unique permissions to list items or documents in a document library is a process similar to granting permissions at the site and list levels. The difference is in how you navigate to the Permissions page.

1. From a List View page, select the List item.

2. Click the ellipses and choose the Shared With menu item (Figure 7-15).

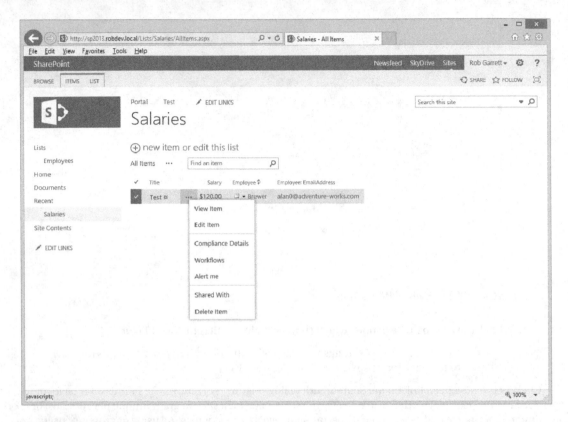

Figure 7-15. *Shared With for a list item*

3. SharePoint shows a dialog, similar to that shown for list permissions (Figure 7-14).

4. Click the link for advanced options.

5. As you did with sites and lists, you must break the permission inheritance to apply unique permissions to the list item.

■ **Note**   Try to avoid granting unique permissions to list items and documents in a document library. Doing so is bad practice and may lead to security management difficulties later.

Anonymous Access

By default, SharePoint requires users to authenticate before gaining access to a site collection. In some cases, the organization may have a desire to open a site to anonymous users. Anonymous users are those users who visit a SharePoint site without ever authenticating—as far as SharePoint is concerned, there is no user information or user context for the user accessing the site collection anonymously. Typically, anonymous user access does not make a whole lot of sense for team sites and intranet-like site collections, but it makes perfect sense when used in conjunction with publishing web sites in SharePoint.

■ **Note**   A publishing site is a site based on the Publishing Site Collection template, which provides content management services for owners of an organization's public web site (see Chapter 10 for more information on publishing and public-facing web sites in SharePoint 2013).

Anonymous access begins with the web application, which ties configuration to the application in Internet Information Server (IIS). If an administrator does not enable anonymous access at the creation of the web application, or later in the web application settings, then SharePoint does not allow anonymous access at the site collection level. See Chapter 2 for the details of creating a web application and enabling anonymous access. The following steps detail how to enable anonymous access for an existing web application:

1. Open Central Administration.

2. Click the Manage Web Applications option under the Application Management heading.

3. Select the desired web application from the list.

4. Click the Authentication Providers icon on the ribbon.

5. SharePoint shows a dialog containing configured zones for the web application (Figure 7-16).

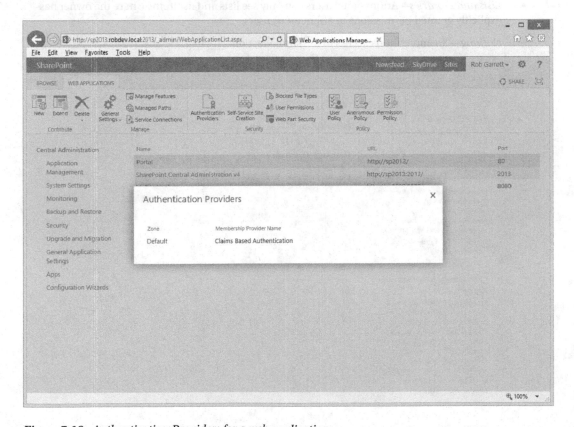

Figure 7-16. Authentication Providers for a web application

6. Click the title of the zone to change the authorization and enable anonymous access (typically Default).

7. In the dialog that appears, check the check box in the Anonymous Access section.

8. Scroll to the bottom of the dialog and click the Save button. (Note: you may notice a slight delay before the dialog closes.)

You should now have enabled anonymous access for the web application. However, you must now also enable anonymous access at the site collection. The following steps demonstrate how to achieve this:

1. Open the site collection of the site to enable anonymous access.

2. Click the gear icon and then select the Site Settings menu option.

3. Click the link for site permissions, under the Users and Permissions heading.

4. Click the Anonymous Access icon on the ribbon (this icon grayed out if anonymous access not enabled at the web application level).

Figure 7-17 shows the options for anonymous access:

- *Entire Web Site*—Anonymous users see everything in read mode.

- *Lists and Libraries*—Anonymous users can only see lists and list items where the owner has explicitly granted permissions to anonymous users.

- *Nothing*—No anonymous access to the site collection.

Figure 7-17. *Anonymous Access permissions*

The Client Object Permission Requirement ensures that anonymous users cannot interact with your site collection without the Remote Interfaces permission. *This is important*—without this option checked, anonymous users can write script via the Client Object Model to interact with your site collection. This is not to say that secure content in the site collection is available to anonymous users—the Client Object Model respects security—but leaving this option checked provides another layer of protection.

Web Application Policies

Site collection security, discussed in the previous sections of this chapter, provides nice granular control of user access to the site collection, sites, lists, and even list items. However, sometimes an administrator needs to grant access to users for an entire web application. SharePoint provides this capability via the Central Administration web site.

■ **Note** Granting users access to the entire web application via Web Application policy bypasses all security settings applied at the site collection, subsite, list, and list item levels. I strongly recommend you use this capability under only special or rare circumstances, such as troubleshooting or granting access to very important administrators.

---

1. Open Central Administration.

2. Click the Security heading from the home page.

3. From the Users section, click Specify Web Application User Policy.

4. SharePoint shows a page like that in Figure 7-18.

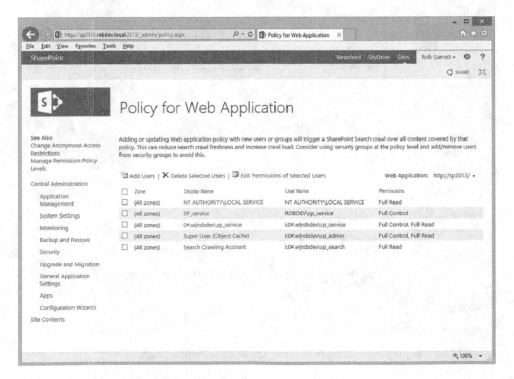

Figure 7-18. *Web application security policies*

The page, shown in Figure 7-18, displays a list of current user policies for the selected web application in the drop-down on the far right. Notice the strange user names, like `i:0#.w|robdev\sp_admin`, which is how SharePoint stores user identity as part of the Claims-Based-Authentication model (see Chapter 8).

1. Ensure that you select the correct web application (top right).

2. Click Add Users from the sub-menu.

3. From the next page, choose the desired zone or all zones if you want the new policy to apply to all security zones for the application.

■ **Note** SharePoint maintains four zones for each web application: Default, Custom, Intranet, and Internet. The labels are not important but help administrators assign policy for typical purposes. The drop-down that appears in step 3 shows only those zones in which the administrator has configured an authentication scheme (Windows, Kerberos, or Claims-Based).

---

4. Click the Next button.

5. Enter the users or AD groups in the Users box; then click the tick icon to validate the entered text, or click the book icon to choose users via the people picker dialog (Figure 7-19) .

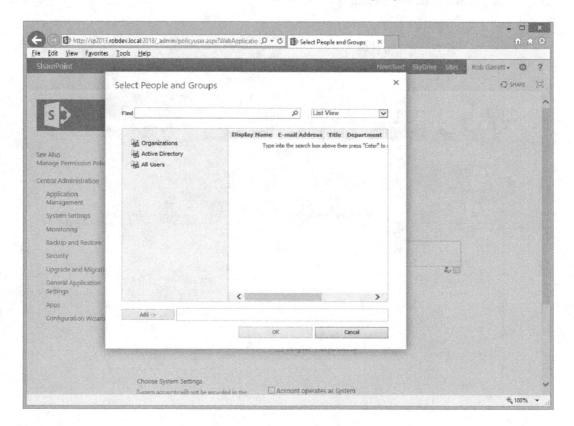

Figure 7-19. *People picker dialog in the Web Application Policies page*

6. Select the appropriate permissions—this is the only place in the SharePoint security model where an administrator may deny access rights. This feature comes in handy if an administrator needs to revoke access for users in the web application, without editing the permissions in site collections.

7. You may choose to operate the account policy as System, meaning the account does not show up in user information lists (it's effectively hidden).

8. Click the Finish button to enact the policy.

Returning to the web application security policies, shown in Figure 7-18, you see a big bold message at the top of the page about search crawling. Changing the security policy for a web application instructs SharePoint to execute a full search crawl (see Chapter 15)—this is to ensure security trimming of content per the policy and permissions assigned to all users. For example, if you create a new security policy to deny a user access to content in all site collections hosted by the web application, then that user should not see this content in search results. Making multiple changes to the web application security policy might add strain on your environment if these changes cause a search crawl during busy usage periods. The information message recommends applying web application policies to security groups; thus, adding users to and removing users from the group avoids a full search crawl.

Also on the Web Application Security Policies page are some links (top left) to change policy for anonymous users and to change the permission levels for policy. Similar to how you grant or deny access to specific users for the entire web application, you can perform these actions for anonymous users. Thus, if you want to deny access to all anonymous users without turning off anonymous access, you can add a policy to deny access at the web application level.

The link to manage permission policy levels takes you to a page that lists all permission levels for web application security policy (Figure 7-20). Similar to permission levels for site and site collections, the available permission levels for web application security policies reflect typical groupings of permissions for a specific role. You can add your own permission levels to apply as policy to the web application, and change the existing permission policy levels, but this is not recommended; it is always best to create your own permission levels.

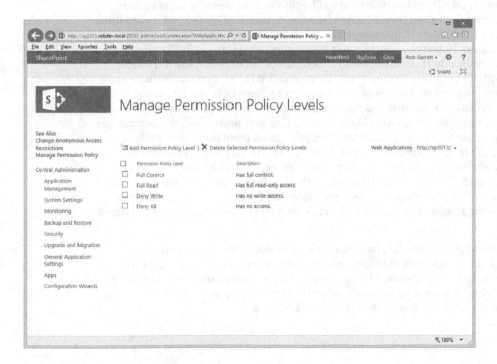

Figure 7-20. Permission Policy Levels

Best Practices

When working with clients, I often receive questions about the Microsoft best practices for applying security permissions to sites, lists, and pages in SharePoint. Although there is no hard-and-fast right or wrong answer to configuring SharePoint security, there are some good best-practice rules to follow, which involve the use of security groups.

- *Avoid granting permissions (permission levels) to individual users.* I am sure we have all been there—someone calls the help desk and asks that "Bob" have access to a SharePoint site, list, or document. The quick-and-dirty solution is to find the securable object and grant contributor permission rights to Bob. The problem is what happens when Bob no longer works for the organization and someone else needs to follow up on his work. Magnify this issue across multiple users in the organization and in different areas of the site collection hierarchy, and you will have a security management nightmare growing. Adding Bob into a security group and applying permissions to the group is more effective, because you as the administrator can add more users into the group, and/or remove Bob from the group without having to go hunting for areas where Bob has specific permissions.

- *Avoid too much security group specialization.* The default Visitors, Members, and Owners group should suffice in most scenarios, but on occasion you may need to create a group for users who have a specific set of permissions in a given security context. This approach is fine in rare circumstances, but if you find yourself managing more than a handful of specialized security groups and needing to remember complicated permission assignments, then I recommend rethinking your security model and clumping your users into more abstract groups.

- *Employ Active Directory groups as users in SharePoint.* SharePoint does not really distinguish between AD users and AD groups; both have an identity from the user store, and both may receive permissions for a given secured object (site, list, or page). AD groups are a good thing in general because they allow IT to manage user access to Windows-based services (for example, file shares). However, applying direct permissions to AD groups in SharePoint tightly couples your site collection permissions with IT operations. For example, say you assign permissions within your site collection to an AD group called Developers. Somewhere along the line, you want to grant access to your new developer recruit—Bob—to the site collection. Now you have to call IT to ensure that Bob is in the correct AD group. In theory, if IT is religious about putting new employees in the correct AD groups and removing ex-employees from AD groups, then all is peachy, but if not, then you cannot grant Bob access to the site collection until IT commits. Instead, if you add the Developers AD group to a SharePoint security group, and then assign permissions to the SP group, you can add Bob temporarily to the SP group until IT adds him to the AD group. With the introduction of continuous search crawling in SharePoint 2013, changing user permissions on a site, list, or list item triggers a crawl. Leveraging groups allows you to add and remove users from groups without triggering search crawl.

- *Apply permission levels to collections only.* Anyone who manages file system permissions will tell you that it is a nightmare managing permissions applied to individual files, simply because there are too many of them. The same theory applies to SharePoint list/library items. SharePoint administrators will have a much easier time applying permissions to collections (lists, sites, and so on) rather than individual list/library items.

- *Break permission inheritance only when necessary.* SharePoint leverages inheritance of security permission levels from the root of the site collection, through sites and subsites, into lists and list items. When applying permissions to users (via SP groups) at the top of a virgin SharePoint site collection, the same permissions apply to the user for all subsites, lists, and list items—that is, until someone breaks the permission inheritance. Breaking the security inheritance chain in a subsite, list, or list item means that any change to the permissions at a level above will not affect the permissions configured below the break point. This is often done deliberately when separating sections of the site collection hierarchy from the main site trunk access, but when it happens too often, administrators have a hard time applying new permissions from the top level to all sites and lists below.

Summary

In this chapter, I took you on a brief tour of SharePoint security. SharePoint uses role-based security, which requires an understanding of the permissions model. I covered the existence of permission levels, how to use them, and the creation of custom levels. I visited best practices and discussed how to leverage SharePoint security groups to apply permissions to a particular securable object (sites, lists, pages, list items, and so on). In the next chapter, Chapter 8, I shall continue discussion about security as it relates to Claims-Based-Authentication and Identity Management.

CHAPTER 8

■ ■ ■

Claims-Based and Federated Authentication

SharePoint 2010 introduced a new Claims-Based-Authentication (CBA) method for authenticating users. SharePoint 2013 continues use of CBA as the now only mechanism for authenticating users.

CBA addresses the need of the industry to identify users of a system via claims, rather than via username and password. In this chapter, I shall detail Digital Identity and open standards for identifying users in electronic systems, such as SharePoint. SharePoint and CBA support federated authentication, meaning abstraction of the authentication process from the SharePoint platform. I shall cover integration of Active Directory Federated Services for providing abstraction.

Digital Identity

Have you ever stopped to consider the number of systems you access with a username and password? I have a wonderful password management system to take the headache out of remembering multiple passwords, and it tells me that I have accounts on at least 93 different web sites. Imagine if every one of these systems used a different username and password set . . . many of them do! The OpenID Foundation saw this as an issue in 2005, when it produced a new standard—the OpenID standard—for identifying users by more than a username and password.

OpenID is a standard that describes how users may authenticate with a system in a decentralized manner, eliminating the need for systems to maintain their own credentials and authentication mechanisms. OpenID also describes user identities as consisting of sets of attributes, or claims, rather than a username specific to an authentication scenario.

As OpenID gained rapid adoption from 2005, Microsoft, and other system implementation vendors, adopted OpenID standards in its products and systems. Microsoft first introduced Windows Card Space as the solution to avoiding usernames and passwords, and instead managing a set of *claims* about a person with a given card. SharePoint 2010 includes Claims-Based-Authentication to fully abstract authentication from the SharePoint platform and identifies authenticated users via a set of augmented claims. The remainder of this section of this chapter discusses the principles of OpenID and Digital Identity. In the sections that follow, I shall demonstrate how these principles apply to SharePoint 2013, which also adopts Claims-Based-Authentication.

Identity Management

The principal idea of Identity Management is that identities consist of a set of attributes in a given context space. In simple terms, an identity for a given individual might consist of several attributes, such as first name, last name, e-mail address, social security number, etc. On its own, each attribute means very little, but combined with other attributes constitutes the identity. For example, my name is Rob Garrett; several other people in the world have the same first name, and likely the same last name. My first name, last name, or even both together do not uniquely identify me as a person, so how is a system, like SharePoint, to know I am who I claim to be? Add my e-mail into the mix and we begin to define my identity, and not that of another Rob Garrett, since my e-mail is unique to me. As we continue to add more attributes to my identity, there is no doubt that the identity refers to me specifically, and not some other fortunate person to share the name Rob Garrett.

Although I am one individual with one physical presence, I can have multiple identities in the electronic world. My bank might require my identity to have a large collection of attributes, to ensure I am really who I claim to be, whereas a social site might not need so many attributes because security is more relaxed. Of course, when I refer to the attributes of my identity, what I am really describing are "claims"—I claim my last name is Garrett, I claim my first name is Robert, and I claim my twitter ID as @RGarrettPro. Figure 8-1 shows a graphical view of identities and attributes (claims) and how they map to entities (people and objects) in the real world.

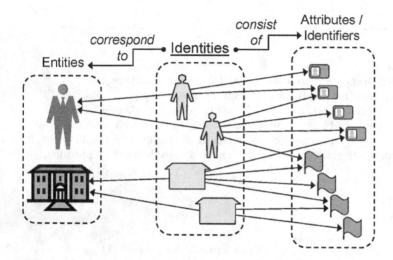

Figure 8-1. *Relationship of identities to entities*

Identity Authentication

With an understanding of how identity works, how does an entity (person) authenticate with a system that supports digital identifiers? There is lots of information about this subject on the Web, so I shall cover the process at a high level. To begin, the following are the main components in an abstracted authentication process:

- *Identity*: a set of attributes describing the user or other form of entity with secured access to a system.

- *Relying Party*: the system that requires authentication of an entity—the system itself, in our case—SharePoint.

- *Claim*: a piece of information (attribute) of a given identity. A set of claims constitutes an identity. We use the term "claim" rather than attribute because the delivery of claims is such that an entity asserts a set of claims about him/her, rather than looking up an attribute in a directory by the Relying Party.

- *Security Token*: an encrypted piece of information, consisting of a set of claims and request of a given Relying Party. An Issuing Authority might encrypt a Security Token and always signs it. The signature is very important because this ensures that only the Issuing Authority created the token and not anyone else.

- *Issuing Authority*: the party responsible for providing a set of claims about an entity. The Relying Party passes the responsibility of authentication of an entity to one or more Issuing Authorities, who provide a Security Token for an authenticated entity. The Issuing Authority makes use of X509 certificates to sign Secure Tokens so that the Relying Party can validate secured tokens as authentic.

- *Secure Token Service (STS)*: a service that issues Secure Tokens according to WS-Trust and WS-Federation protocols. Examples of STS include Active Directory Federated Services (ADFS) and the STS built into SharePoint 2010 and 2013.

- *Client*: typically a web browser and user looking to authenticate with a web application (Relying Party).

Figure 8-2 shows a basic authentication scenario, described as follows:

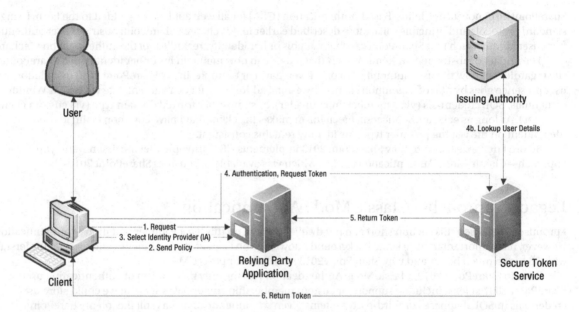

Figure 8-2. *Basic authentication scenario*

1. Client sends a request to the Relying Party (RP) to access secured content.

2. RP sends back policy for authentication—RP may send a selection of identity providers for user to choose.

3. User selects an identity provider (if multiple providers)—the Secure Token Service (STS) of an Issuing Authority (IA).

4. Client sends an authentication request to the STS of an IA.

5. Assuming successful authentication with the IA, the STS sends an encrypted and signed token back to the RP.

6. The STS sends the same token back to the client. The RP and client now have a common trust via a shared secure token.

Secure Tokens

Secure Tokens consist of an XML file (typically encrypted) that includes a list of claims about an identity. This XML file goes by the common name of Security Assertion Markup Language (SAML) token.

The number of claims within a SAML token and provided by a Secure Token Service depends on the policy of an Issuing Authority and the policy of a Relying Party discovering a set of claims about an entity. The SAML token is encrypted using the public key of an RP (if encrypted) and signed using the private key of an IA—this ensures that the RP can check that the token originated from the IA and that only the RP can decrypt the secure token. Should someone intercept a secure token in transit, the signature and encryption ensure that a third party cannot read or modify the contents of the token.

SharePoint Authentication

SharePoint 2013 now uses Claims-Based-Authentication (CBA) for all web applications added to the farm. Using standard protocols and principles, like those described earlier in this chapter, SharePoint abstracts user authentication from user identity such that SharePoint can maintain his or her identity, regardless of the authentication mechanism.

The impact of abstracted authentication is that a user can now maintain his or her identity in a SharePoint site regardless of how the user authenticated on a given day. For example, in my SharePoint 2013 installation, my user presence goes by that of a common claim—my e-mail address—but I can authenticate via NTLM Windows credentials, SQL credentials (via a membership provider), or some other trusted domain type (via custom claims provider). As long as each authentication mechanism makes the claim that I have common claim identifier (dependent on the issuing provider type) my identity remains consistent.

Before I delve deeper into how SharePoint 2013 implements CBA principles, let me first remind you of the legacy approach—Classic Mode Authentication (CMA), which was available to you as of SharePoint 2010.

Legacy Approach—Classic Mode Authentication

I promise I shall keep this section short and not dwell too much on this legacy implementation of authentication. However, it is important to have some background knowledge on Classic Mode Authentication so you understand why CBA is so much better and why SharePoint 2013 no longer supports CMA.

Prior to SharePoint 2010, Classic Mode Authentication was the only mechanism of authenticating users. SharePoint 2007 at least included support for custom membership credentials such that we could store user credentials in SQL databases or third-party systems. Even so, authentication was still the job of SharePoint.

Let us consider a common scenario, implemented for many SharePoint 2007 solutions. Users can authenticate with their Active Directory credentials: when in the office they access the company intranet using their workstation credentials and when at home they access the intranet via a forms-based login. In both cases, the username and password is the same, just the authentication mechanism differs. In the office, users authenticate using NTLM—standard Windows challenge response protocol synonymous with workstation login. When accessing the Internet from home, users enter their credentials into an SSL-hosted form, and SharePoint authenticates these users against Active Directory using a Microsoft Membership Provider component.

Everything seems peachy, but there are a couple of major drawbacks with this implementation:

1. SharePoint 2007 allows only one authentication mechanism per web application (a restriction because SharePoint builds on ASP.NET). Therefore, the implementation consists of a primary web application, using NTLM, and an extended web application, configured for forms authentication.

2. The identity of the user ties to the username of the user—if accessing the site from the office the user has the username DOMAIN\username, whereas accessing the intranet via forms gives a username of Membership-Provider:username.

Perhaps we can overcome the first issue, although it does mean accessing the intranet from a URL in the office different from that outside the office because each SharePoint application requires a unique domain name or port number. I have seen some clever DNS tricks to redirect users to a different domain based on location in the network. This aside, bookmarks become a problem with different URLs because the links you saved in the office differ from those used when accessing the same document or pages at home.

The second issue is more of a deal-breaker—consider how identity mapped to username and authentication method affects services like User Profile Import. User Profile Import maps users with a given username to records in a directory, such as Active Directory or an LDAP system. If we have multiple usernames then the profile import has no way of knowing that each username is that of the same person: we effectively have multiple identities and thus multiple profiles. The problem also surfaces when tracking version history and changes to a document, since this also assumes unique username.

Fortunately for us, SharePoint 2010 introduced Claims-Based-Authentication, and made the world a better place. SharePoint 2010 still supported CMA and we had a choice when provisioning a new web application of which mode of authentication to use. With the release of SharePoint 2013, Microsoft depreciated CMA, and CBA is now the only mechanism for authentication.

Claims-Based-Authentication Approach

Claims-Based-Authentication is a new flexible and abstract approach to user authentication. CBA supports a variety of credential systems, including Active Directory, Live ID, LDAP directories, and any credential store that adopts CBA and federated authentication standards (via SAML).

CBA is composed of a number of components, akin to those described in the earlier part of this chapter. These components operate in unison to authenticate users per the following high-level process:

1. A non-authenticated user (anonymous user) attempts to access secured content in SharePoint.

2. SharePoint determines available identity providers—CBA supports Windows (NTLM), Membership Provider, and Trusted Claims Provider types. If the application allows for multiple providers, then SharePoint presents the user with a choice to select the desired provider, otherwise SharePoint uses the only selected provider.

3. For Windows and Membership authentication, SharePoint forwards the request to the Secure Token Service, which integrates with SharePoint 2013 on the same server. The request to STS uses the industry standard web service protocol WS-Trust. Requests destined to trusted providers route to the STS of each provider.

4. STS looks up the username in a credential store and verifies the given password with that in the store. In the case of Windows NTLM or Membership Provider, SharePoint uses the built-in STS; in the case of Trusted Claims Provider, the STS might exist elsewhere.

5. If successfully authenticated, the STS returns a SAML token, containing claims about the user's identity. In the case of built-in STS, the claims returned are limited to details provided by the directory or membership provider.

SharePoint CBA uses the Windows Identity Foundation (WIF), a collection of APIs that provides for creation of claims-aware applications and federated identity.

With the theory part of CBA covered, I will now run through a series of steps for creating a new CBA web application and configuring it for multiple authentication types.

Configuring a Claims Web Application

In Chapter 2, I demonstrated how to create a new web application in SharePoint 2013. Since all user web applications are CBA applications in SharePoint 2013, I shall summarize the same steps, but provide additional details for the configuration of different authentication methods (NTLM, Membership Provider, etc.). Further, in this section, I shall demonstrate how to make changes to the authentication methods for an existing web application.

Creating a New CBA Application

The following set of steps demonstrates how to create a new Claims-Based-Authentication aware web application in SharePoint 2013. The steps below demonstrate creating our application via Central Administration.

1. Open Central Administration.

2. Click the Manage web application link.

3. Click the New button in the ribbon.

4. Under the IIS Web Site section, give the web application a name, port number, host header (optional), and path (default is fine).

5. Under the Security Configuration, check Allow Anonymous if you intend to make your application available to anonymous users.

6. Click User Secure Sockets Layer (SSL) if you have a certificate ready for your application.

7. Skip the Claims Authentication Types and Sign In Page URL sections (we'll come back to these in a moment).

8. Leave the public URL as default, unless you need to change it.

9. Create a new application pool (unless you wish to reuse one of the existing ones). It is generally good practice to give each web application its own application pool, so you can recycle it without affecting other applications.

10. In the Database Name and Authentication section, provide a name for the database, and credentials for application to access the content database—I usually leave the credentials blank and SharePoint uses the farm account.

11. If you have a mirrored failover database server, you may specify it in the Failover Server section.

12. Select the associated service applications in the Service Application Connections section.

13. Finally, choose to opt in or out for the Customer Experience Improvement Program.

14. At this point, we are ready to look closer at the Claims Authentication Types and Sign In URL sections—scroll back up until you see the dialog like in Figure 8-3.

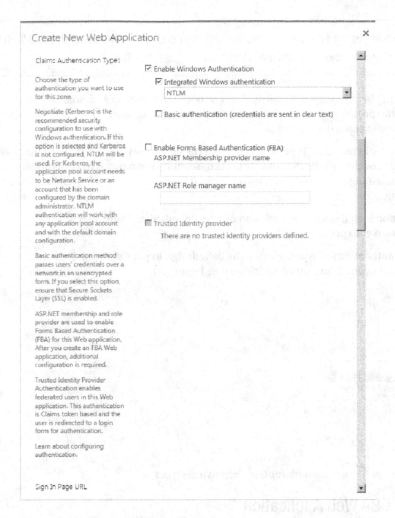

Figure 8-3. *Claims authentication types*

15. Out of the box, SharePoint supports Windows and Membership Provider authentication types.

16. Windows Authentication comes in two flavors: NTLM and Kerberos, with NTLM being most typical. Kerberos is a ticket-based authentication system and recommended by SharePoint. However, using Kerberos requires that you configure the application pool account as NETWORK SERVICE or a domain account configured for Kerberos. In most all scenarios I have come across, administrators use NTLM.

17. You should not allow Basic Windows Authentication unless you have a good reason to do so—this option passes passwords in plain text and was the only way to allow Netscape and early non-Microsoft browsers to authenticate with SharePoint. Most modern browsers, including Firefox, support NTLM.

18. Forms-Based-Authentication (FBA) uses the traditional Membership and Role Provider model to incorporate custom, SQL, or AD authentication with a forms login page.

■ **Note** Developers should note that custom Membership and Role Provider code now runs under the STS Web Service Application Pool, so `SPContext` and `HttpContext` objects may return null.

19. Check Enable ASP.NET membership and specify either or both Membership and Role providers. Membership providers concern themselves with authentication and users, whereas Role providers expose custom groups.

The last option in the Claims Authentication Types section is for Trusted Identity Providers. SharePoint allows you to specify an IPSTS as trusted provider. An IPSTS forwards users to separate login pages to authenticate users, before returning SAML tokens containing claims. I discuss use of Trusted Identity Providers (specifically ADFS) in the section titled "Federated Authentication."

20. The Sign In URL section includes a toggle option to use the default SharePoint sign in page or a custom sign in page you specify.

21. If you have multiple authentication types selected the default sign in page shows a drop-down option when you attempt to authenticate (see Figure 8-4).

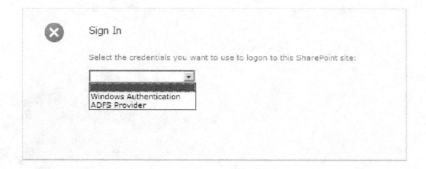

Figure 8-4. Default Sign In Page, with multiple authentication types

Configuring an Existing CBA Web Application

In this section, we shall configure an existing CBA web application to use claims-aware providers.

1. Open Central Administration.

2. Click the Manage web application link.

3. Select an existing web application in the list shown.

4. Click the Authentication Providers icon in the ribbon, and SharePoint will display a dialog like that in Figure 8-5.

Figure 8-5. Authentication providers for a web application

5. The dialog in Figure 8-5 shows the authentication type assigned to each web application zone in use. In my case I only have one—the default zone. In SharePoint 2010, you had the option of using classic mode or CBA. SharePoint 2013 now insists on CBA, so this is all you should ever see in this dialog.

6. Click the zone you wish to configure CBA.

7. SharePoint shows a dialog, similar to that which we saw when creating an application (Figure 8-3), only now with sections to configure the Claims Authentication Types, Anonymous Access, Sign In Page URL, Client Integration, and an option specific to this dialog for Client Object Model Permissions Requirement.

Configuring SSL for SharePoint

When dealing in any kind of web-based security, we must rely on the industry standard use of Secure Socket Layer, which operates via the use of X509 Public/Private key certificates. In-depth discussion on X509 and SSL is outside the scope of this book, but you can read more about it at the following links:

- http://en.wikipedia.org/wiki/Transport_Layer_Security

- http://en.wikipedia.org/wiki/X.509

SharePoint 2013 supports use of SSL, and it is a requirement when integrating federated authentication. To establish a certificate for SSL, the process typically goes something like this:

1. An administrator exports a Certificate Server Request (CSR) from IIS for a given application and domain name.

2. The administrator sends the CSR to a trusted authority, such as VeriSign.

3. The trusted authority validates the authenticity of the purchaser via a series of security protocols.

4. With trust established, the trusted authority generates a new SSL certificate for the purchaser's domain name and signs it as trusted.

5. The administrator installs the certificate in IIS.

6. Users who request secure pages from the organization's application can trust returned data because the encryption certificate is trusted from a well-known source—VeriSign or other root certificate provider.

■ **Note**   For more information on purchasing an SSL certificate, visit http://verisign.com.

For development purposes and demonstration, purchasing of an SSL certificate might seem overkill. Fortunately, we can generate self-signed certificates, via IIS. These self-signed certificates are untrusted, because a trust source has not signed them, but they provide a suitable free alternative for demonstration and development. The following steps detail how to create a self-signed certificate for SharePoint 2013, via IIS:

1. Open Internet Information Service Manager 7.

2. Click the server name in the left navigation tree and then double-click the Server Certificates icon on the right, under IIS section (Figure 8-6).

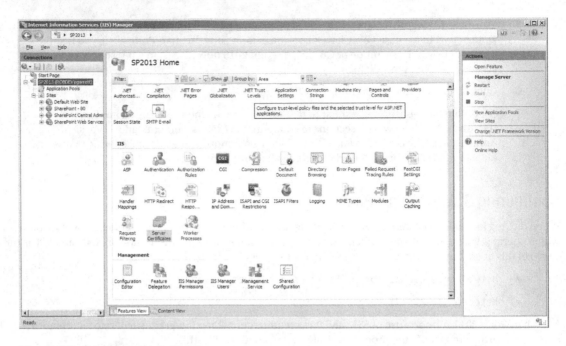

Figure 8-6. *Server certificates in IIS*

3. Click the link to create a self-signed certificate.

4. Give the certificate a friendly name, and then click the OK button.

5. Double-click the Self-signed certificate to see the details.

6. Click the Details tab and then click the button to copy the certificate to a file.

7. Click the Next button.

8. Select the option to *not* export the private key, then click the Next button.

9. Choose the export format (I chose the default DER format) and then the Next button.

10. Give the certificate a file name and browse to a location on disk.

11. Click the Next button, then Finish button to export the certificate to the file.

12. Open the Microsoft Management Console (MMC.exe).

13. Add the certificates snap-in for the computer account and local machine.

14. Import the certificate into the Trusted Root Certificate Authorities node.

15. Import the certificate into the SharePoint node.

In the preceding steps, we have created a new certificate and allowed the local server to trust the certificate by adding it to the Trusted Root Certificate Authorities store. This avoids annoying messages in Internet Explorer about untrusted certificates. Even though we trust the certificate, we have to inform SharePoint it may trust the certificate also, via the steps that follow:

■ **Note** Never use self-signed certificates in production or non-development environments.

16. Open Central Administration.

17. Click the Security header.

18. Click the link to manage trust.

19. Click the new icon from the ribbon.

20. Provide a friendly name and browse for the certificate (CER) file in the dialog shown in Figure 8-7.

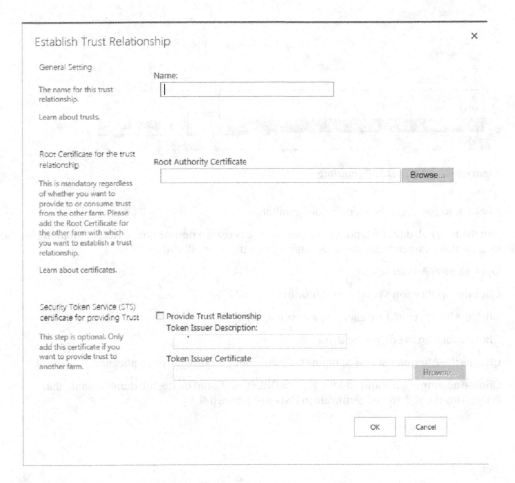

Figure 8-7. *New certificate in Manage Trust*

21. Click OK.

Now, we need to associate our new self-signed certificate with our web application in IIS, as follows:

22. Return to IIS Management.

23. Click the SharePoint application in the left navigation, under Sites.

24. Click the Bindings link (on the far right).

25. Click the Add button.

26. Choose HTTPS, and select the certificate to use (Figure 8-8).

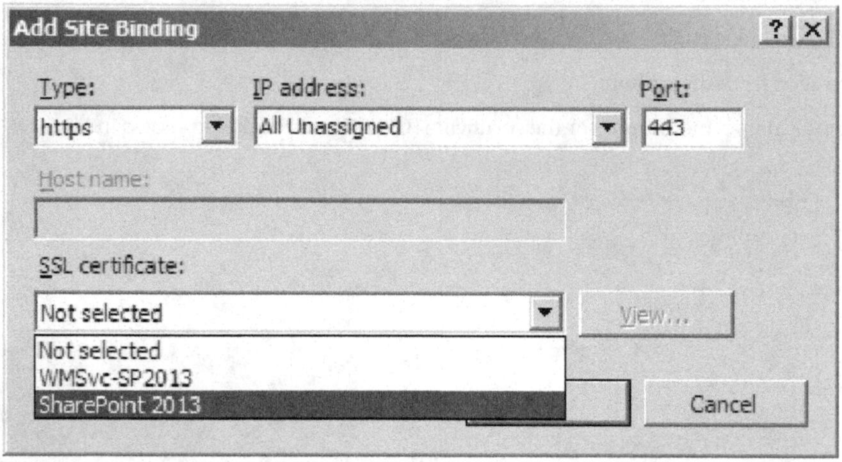

Figure 8-8. *Add an HTTPS binding*

27. Click OK to complete the binding configuration.

Lastly, with the new SSL domain binding in place, we must create a new Alternate Access Mapping for the application so SharePoint understands requests coming in on the new SSL URL:

28. Open Central Administration.

29. Click the Application Management heading.

30. Click the link to configure alternate access mappings.

31. Click the button to edit public URLs.

32. Change the Alternate Access Mapping Collection for the correct web application.

33. Choose an empty zone and add the HTTPS URL (this should be the full domain name that is listed for the self-signed certificate in IIS)—see Figure 8-9.

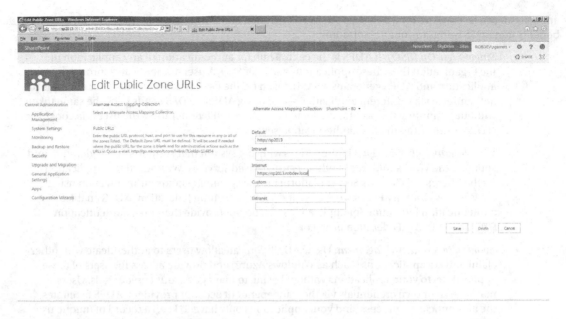

Figure 8-9. Configure AAM for HTTPS

34. You can now access your web application on the new HTTPS/SSL URL.

■ **Note** If you access your SharePoint Web Application from another machine, the certificate is untrusted, unless you repeat the preceding steps 12 to 14 for the machine you are using.

Federated Authentication

In the section titled "Configuring a Claims Web Application" I briefly touched on federated authentication within SharePoint via Trusted Identity Providers. In this section, we shall explore the use of federated authentication, using Active Directory Federated Services.

Active Directory Federated Services

Active Directory Federated Services is a service provided by Microsoft to provide federated claims authentication. ADFS uses the WS-Federation standard protocol and returns secure tokens in Security Assertion Markup Language format. The current version is 2.0, which is the version I refer to in this chapter when I discuss ADFS.

Administrators may download ADFS from the following link, install it, and configure it via a Microsoft Management Console (MMC): www.microsoft.com/en-us/download/details.aspx?id=10909.

Why would you be interested in federated authentication and why ADFS? Although SharePoint is not strictly federating authentication, since the platform is still authenticating users, it has abstracted authentication via its own Secure Token Service. ADFS brings true federated authentication because ADFS is a separate service that any application can leverage, as long as it supports WS-Federation and SAML. The following is a list of some of the benefits that ADFS brings to your organization:

- *Single-Sign-On (SSO)*: If ADFS is the central hub for authentication of any application in the organization then these applications can offer SSO. A user authenticates through one application and ADFS generates a SAML token for the user. When the same user attempts to authenticate via a different application—also using ADFS—ADFS sends back the same token without prompting the user for credentials because ADFS remembers the user (via cookie or NTLM token) from the first authentication success.

- *WS-* Interoperability*: ADFS interoperates with any system that supports WS-Federation and supports the WS-* standards of other security-based services. Without ADFS, applications on the Microsoft Windows Server platform must implement claims authentication using the Windows Identity Framework to support authentication federation. ADFS enables authentication federation for applications that do not provide their own authentication federation via WS-Federation protocols.

- *Avoids Credential Management*: Using ADFS, you can allow users to authenticate with other claims-aware applications (such as Windows Azure) and provide access for users of these applications to your applications without having to manage account credentials. Users maintain their own credentials via these independent account providers, ADFS facilitates the authentication process, and your applications only have to keep a record of unique user identity (based on claims in SAML tokens) to identify an authenticated user.

- *Claims Mapping*: ADFS understands claims provided by federated providers and can map them into different claim types in use in your organization.

- *Extensible Architecture*: ADFS supports custom claims augmentation (associating claims with a user's identity), via custom extensions implemented by developers and third parties.

ADFS System Requirements

ADFS will install on all of the following Windows Server platforms:

- Windows Server 2008 Datacenter
- Windows Server 2008 Enterprise
- Windows Server 2008 R2
- Windows Server 2008 R2 Datacenter
- Windows Server 2008 R2 Enterprise
- Windows Server 2008 R2 Foundation
- Windows Server 2008 R2 Standard
- Windows Server 2008 Service Pack 2
- Windows Server 2008 Standard
- Windows Small Business Server 2008 Premium
- Windows Small Business Server 2008 Standard

ADFS requires the following software components installed to operate correctly:

- Internet Information Server (IIS) 7 or above

- .NET Framework 3.5 with Service Pack 1

- SQL Server 2005 (Express, Standard, or Enterprise) or SQL Server 2008 (Express, Standard, or Enterprise)

Install Certificate Authority

ADFS requires certificates to encrypt and sign SAML tokens. In a production deployment, you would install purchased certificates, signed by a trusted root certificate authority such as VeriSign. However, for development and demonstration purposes, we shall install Active Directory Certificate Services and create our own Certification Authority for issuing ADFS certificates.

1. Open the Windows control panel.

2. Double-click the Program and Features icon.

3. Click the link to turn Windows features on or off.

4. Click Roles in the left navigation.

5. If Active Directory Certificate Services is not installed, click the link to add a new role.

6. Select the Active Directory Certificate Services role from the list (Figure 8-10), then click the Next button.

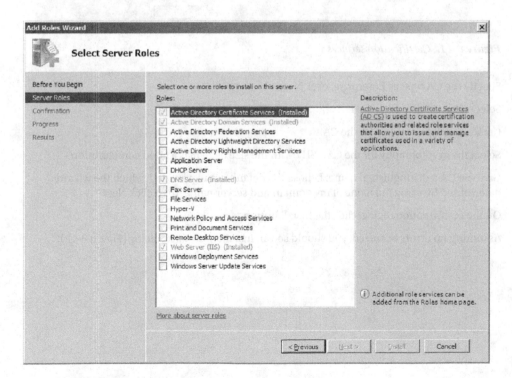

Figure 8-10. *Select the Active Directory Certificate Services role*

7. Select Certification Authority and Certification Authority Web Enrollment services (Figure 8-11).

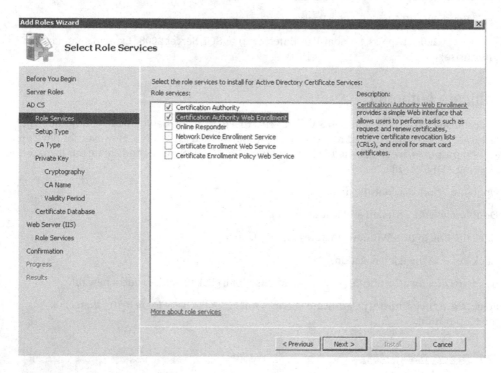

Figure 8-11. *Certification services*

8. Specify the CA type as Enterprise, click Next.

9. Select Root CA and click Next.

10. Create a new private key for the CA.

11. Select the cryptography for the CA—SH1 with the size of 2048 is a good configuration.

12. Give the CA a distinguished name. I chose the default name provided, which the wizard determined by using the name of my domain and server name, then click Next.

13. On the confirmation dialog, click the Install button.

14. Assuming no errors occurred, you should see an installation status dialog (Figure 8-12).

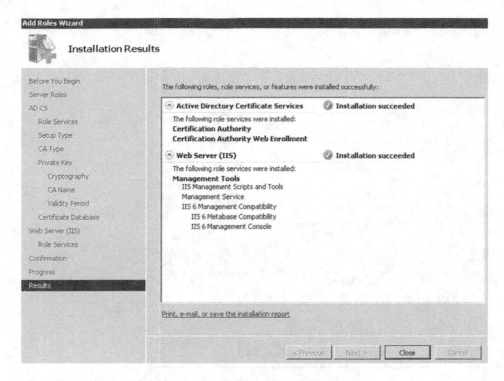

Figure 8-12. *Successful configuration of Certification Authority*

Preparing for ADFS Installation

Before we install ADFS, it is important that we complete a series of pre-installation steps, to establish a new DNS name and certificate with which we shall access ADFS. The following steps assume you completed the steps in the earlier section "Install Certificate Authority."

1. Create a new ADFS user account in the domain; do not add the account to any groups. ADFS will assign privileges (Figure 8-13).

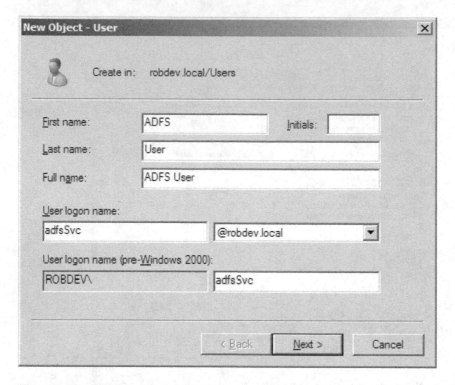

Figure 8-13. Create an account for ADFS

2. Run the Microsoft Management Console (MMC.exe).

3. Add the following snap-ins:

   a. Certificate Templates

   b. Certificates (Local Computer)

   c. Certification Authority (Local Computer)

   d. ADFS 2.0

4. Expand the Certificate Templates node.

5. Right-click the Web Server template and select the option to duplicate the template (Figure 8-14).

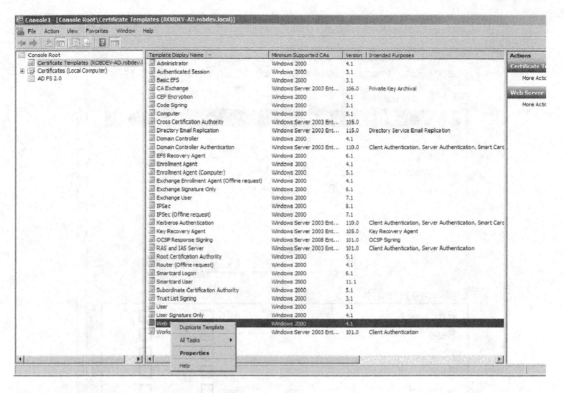

Figure 8-14. *Duplicate the Web Server certificate template*

6. Select the version of template for Windows Server 2008 Enterprise.

7. Give the template a name and display name of ADFS.

8. Click the security tab to assign the new ADFS service account, Read and Enroll permissions (Figure 8-15).

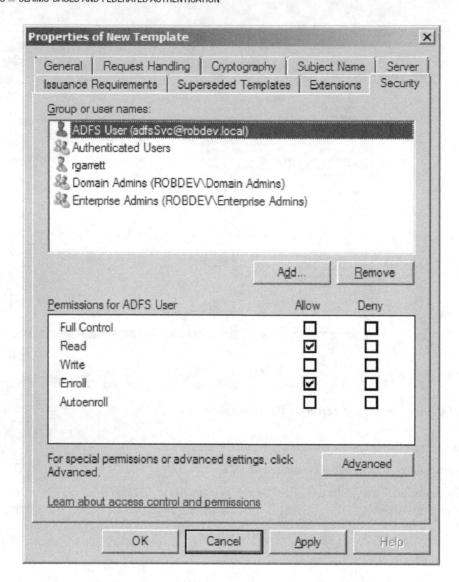

Figure 8-15. *Read and Enroll permissions for the ADFS service account*

9. Assign authenticated users the Read and Enroll permissions (I had to do this to allow me to create a new certificate later).

10. Click the Request Handling tab and then check the option to allow the private key to be exported.

11. Click the OK button on the dialog.

12. Expand the Certification Authority node.

13. Expand the Server Name node.

14. Right-click Certificate Templates.

15. Select Certificate Template to Issue (Figure 8-16).

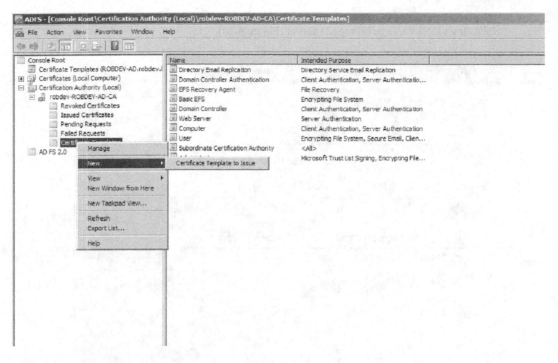

Figure 8-16. *Create new certificate template for ADFS*

16.   Choose the ADFS certificate template (Figure 8-17), then click the OK button.

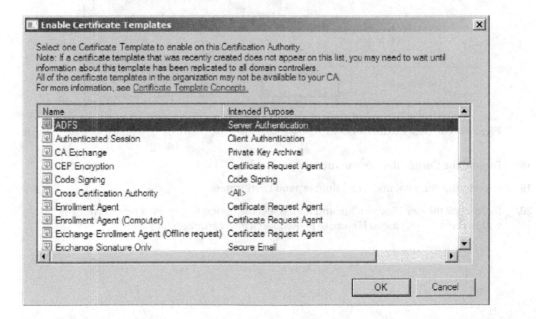

Figure 8-17. *ADFS Certificate Template for new ADFS certificate*

17. Create a new CNAME in your DNS, which resolves the IP of the ADFS server—I use the Windows DNS services on my AD server (Figure 8-18).

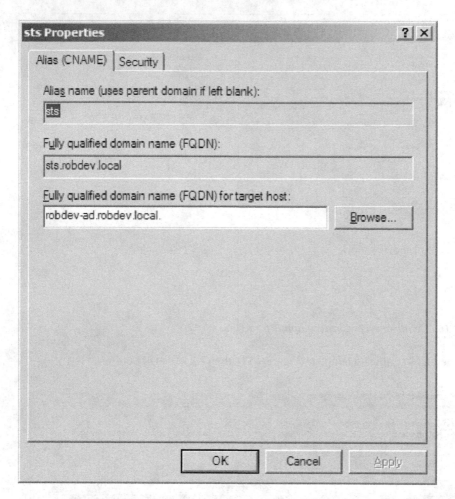

Figure 8-18. New CNAME in DNS

18. Expand the Certificates node in the MMC.

19. Expand the Personal node, and then expand Certificates.

20. Right-click the Certificates node and then select the option to request a new certificate, within the All Tasks menu (Figure 8-19. Request a new certificate for ADFS).

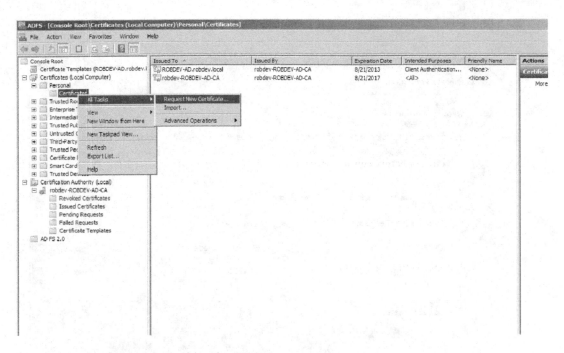

Figure 8-19. *Request a new certificate for ADFS*

21. Click the Next button on the certificate enrollment dialog.

22. Choose the Active Directory Enrollment Policy (Figure 8-20) and click the Next button.

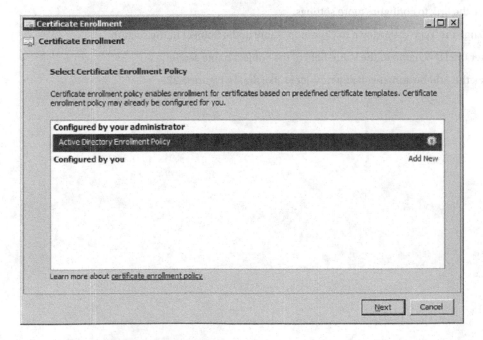

Figure 8-20. *Active Directory Enrollment Policy*

23. Check the ADFS certificate, shown in Figure 8-21.

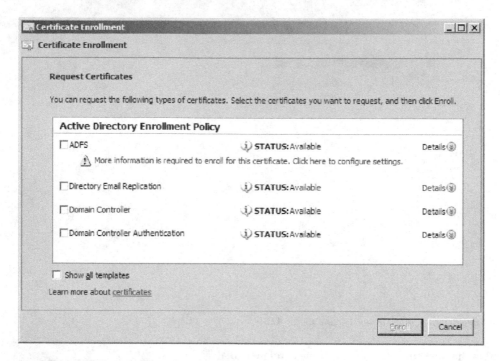

Figure 8-21. *Select ADFS certificate template*

24. Click the link to configure more settings.

25. Change the Type drop-down to Common Name in the Subject name section.

26. Enter the DNS name in the Value field of the Subject name section.

27. Click the Add button; my dialog now looks like that in Figure 8-22.

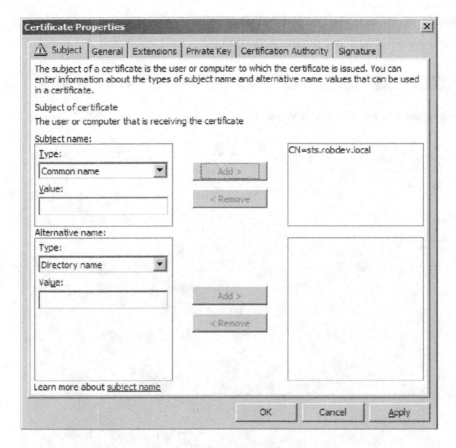

Figure 8-22. *Configuration settings for ADFS certificate*

28. Click OK to close the configuration settings dialog, then the Enroll button on the enrollment dialog.

29. Click the Finish button once the enrollment process completes.

30. Right-click the new certificate you just created.

31. Select All Tasks, then click the option to manage private keys.

32. Grant the ADFS service account Full Control and Read permissions.

With the pre-installation configuration steps complete, you are now ready to begin the installation of ADFS.

Installing ADFS

In this section, I shall walk you through the process of installing ADFS. If you do not have the installation downloaded already, you may download ADFS from the following URL: www.microsoft.com/en-us/download/details.aspx?id=10909. Please ensure you have completed the pre-installation steps in the section titled "Preparing for ADFS Installation."

1. Execute ADFSSETUP.EXE as an elevated administrator.

2. Click the Next button on the dialog show in Figure 8-23.

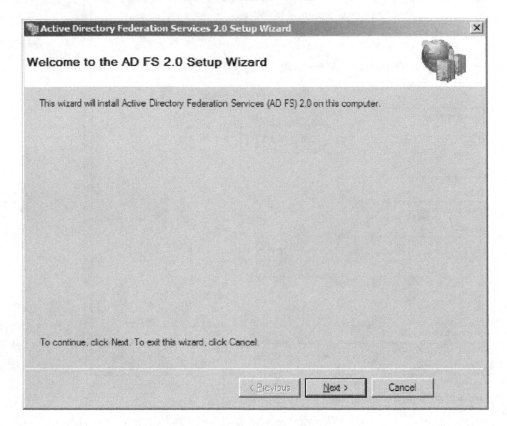

Figure 8-23. *First dialog for installation of ADFS 2.0*

3. Accept the license terms on the next dialog and then click the Next button.

4. In the dialog show in Figure 8-24, choose the Federation server role.

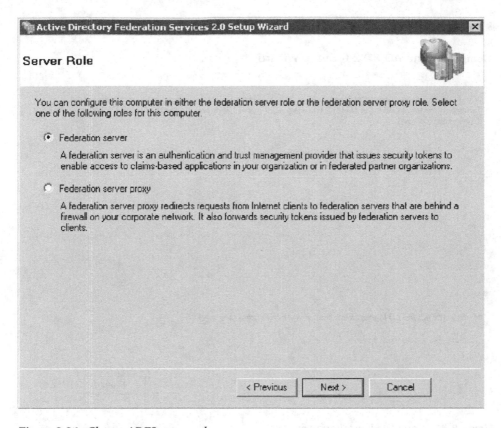

Figure 8-24. *Choose ADFS server role*

5. ADFS might show a dialog to install prerequisite software; click the Next button to proceed.

6. When you see the dialog in Figure 8-25, you have completed the installation. Next we move on to the configuration—check the check box to start the Management Console, and then click the Finish button.

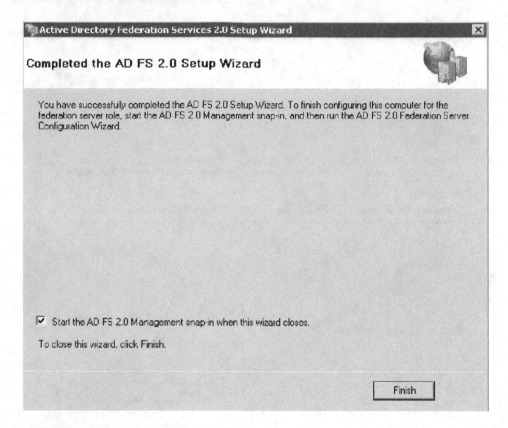

Figure 8-25. *Completed installation of ADFS*

7. When the Management Console launches, you should see something similar to Figure 8-26.

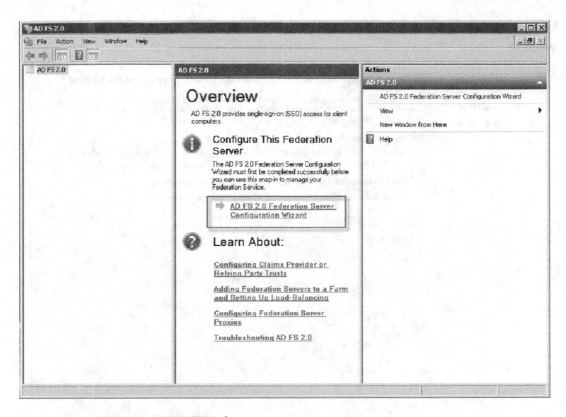

Figure 8-26. *ADFS Management Console*

8. Click the link to launch the ADFS Configuration Wizard, shown in Figure 8-26.

9. On the next dialog, shown in Figure 8-27, select the option to create a new federation
service.

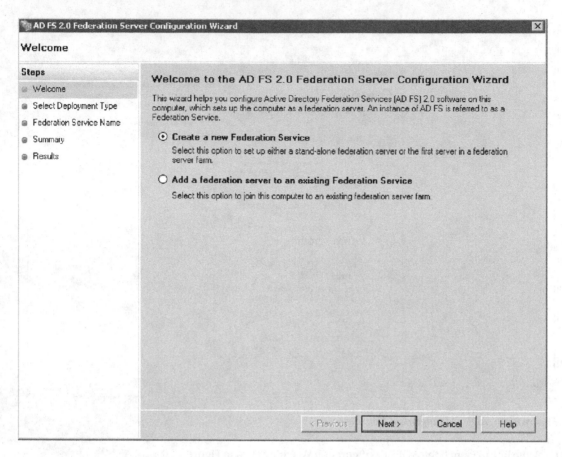

Figure 8-27. *Create a new Federation Service*

10. The next dialog provides you the option to install a federation farm or stand-alone farm.

Creating a new farm requires a SQL Server connection and is suited to production environments, or systems requiring multiple ADFS instances in a farm. The stand-alone option, much like SharePoint, will configure a local SQL Server instance and perform the configuration for you but will not allow you to add additional ADFS instances alongside the present instance of ADFS.

11. Choosing the farm installation type will prompt the installer to require SQL Server connection settings and credentials.

12. I chose the stand-alone option, and after clicking the Next button, I see a dialog like that in Figure 8-28.

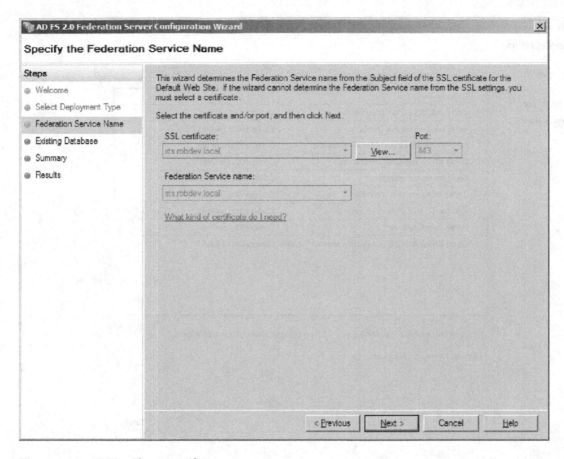

Figure 8-28. *ADFS—Choose certificate*

13. Click the Next button.

14. Provide the ADFS service account to use, and when prompted, click the Next button.

15. On the summary screen, click the Next button to begin the configuration.

■ **Note** The certificate used by ADFS, and shown in the wizard, is that of the SSL certificate configured for the ADFS default web site in Internet Information Services Manager. If you only have one SSL certificate configured, ADFS wizard fills out the certificate choice for you.

---

16. After a few dialogs showing installation progress, you should see a status dialog like that in Figure 8-29, showing the completed installation.

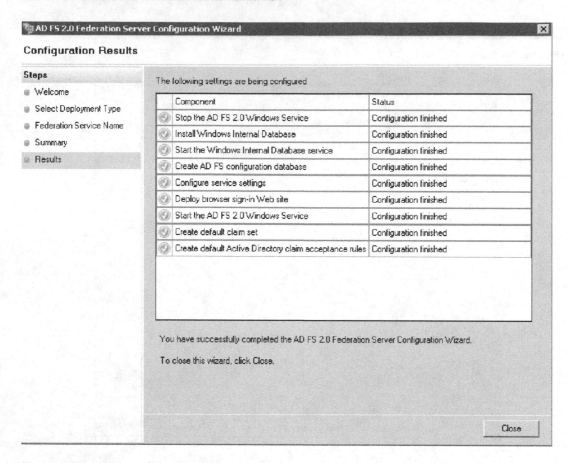

Figure 8-29. *ADFS installation status*

Configuring a Relying Party in ADFS

We have now installed and configured ADFS, and we are ready to create a Relying Party. We established in the beginning of this chapter that a Relying Party is a system or application that permits authenticated user access, but relies on an Issuing Authority (via Secure Token Service) to perform the actual authentication. In this case, SharePoint is our Relying Party, ADFS is our STS, and Active Directory is our Issuing Authority.

1. Open the ADFS 2.0 Management Console and click the link to create trusted relying party.

2. A wizard starts and shows a welcome message; after reading the dialog, click the Start button.

3. ADFS next asks for our data source, from which we can import configuration from a network resource or file, or configure manually (Figure 8-30).

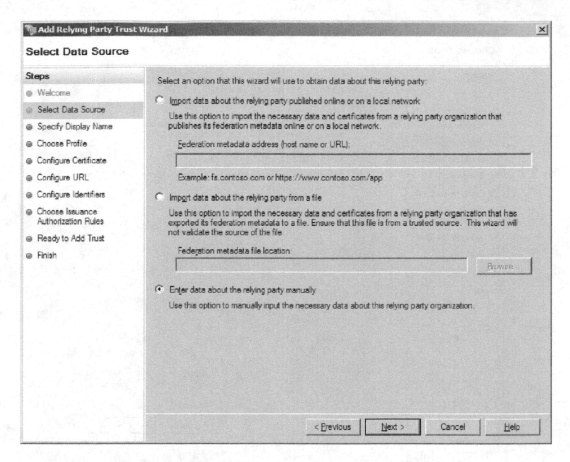

Figure 8-30. *Configure Relying Party data source*

4. For our SharePoint Relying Party, choose the manual option and click the Next button.

5. Enter a display name for the Relying Party and description (optional) on the next dialog.

6. ADFS supports legacy 1.0, 1.1, and the new 2.0 profile formats. We need the 2.0 format, which supports SAML via STS (Figure 8-31).

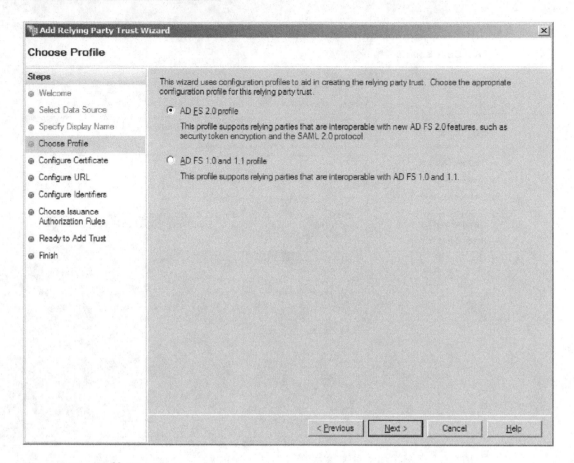

Figure 8-31. *Profile Type*

7. The next dialog gives you the option to encrypt SAML tokens with selected certificate, which we would normally do, but since SharePoint requires an SSL address to communicate with the ADFS STS, this is unnecessary, so click the Next button.

8. ADFS requires us to configure a URL for WS-Federation at the Relying Party (Figure 8-32)—this is the URL with which ADFS will return SAML tokens. At this point, we can also configure Web SSO for SAML Single-Sign-On, but this is outside scope of these instructions.

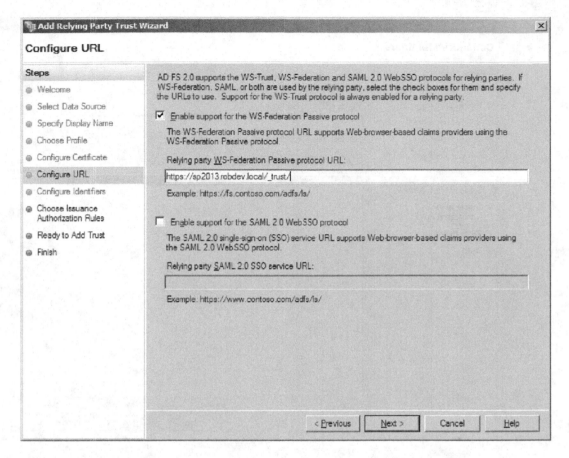

Figure 8-32. *Configure URL*

9. In the dialog shown in Figure 8-32, check the Passive option, and provide an SSL-based URL for your SharePoint site. SharePoint 2013 includes a special URL end point for acceptance of SAML tokens: `https://domain-name/_trust/`.

___

■ **Note** Before configuring SharePoint as a Relying Party, remember to set up SSL for the site—ADFS requires a secure connection to pass back SAML tokens.

___

10. In the next dialog (Figure 8-33), add an additional identifier for the realm—the realm is the identifier that SharePoint will pass to ADFS to identify itself as the Relying Party. Typically, the realm is in the format `urn:domain:server`.

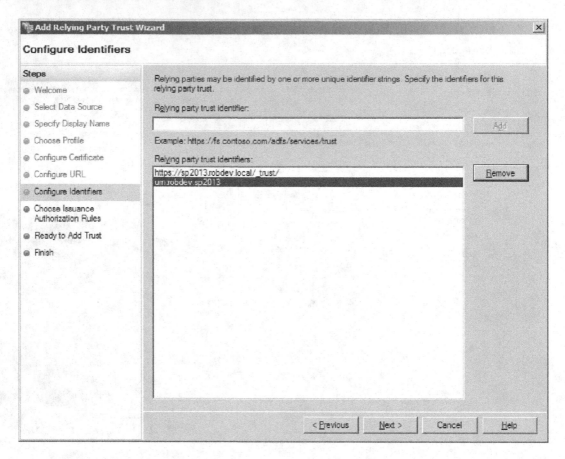

Figure 8-33. *Configure realm as an identifier*

11. Click the Next button, and then check the Radio button to permit all users to access the Relying Party, followed by the Next button.

12. Click the Next button on the summary dialog to finish creation of Relying Party configuration.

13. The last dialog (Figure 8-34) should show a successful message and include a check box to add claims rules, which we shall do next, after clicking the Close button.

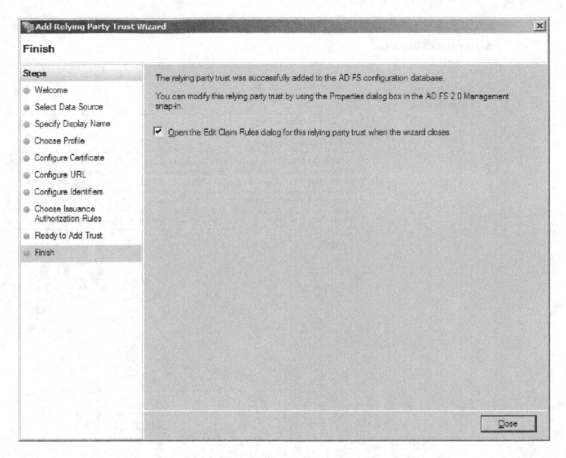

Figure 8-34. *Successful configuration of the Relying Party*

14. A dialog should appear to add claims rules.

15. Click the Add Rule button.

16. In the dialog that appears (Figure 8-35), select the option to send LDAP attributes as claims. Our Issuing Authority—Active Directory—provides user profile attributes via LDAP.

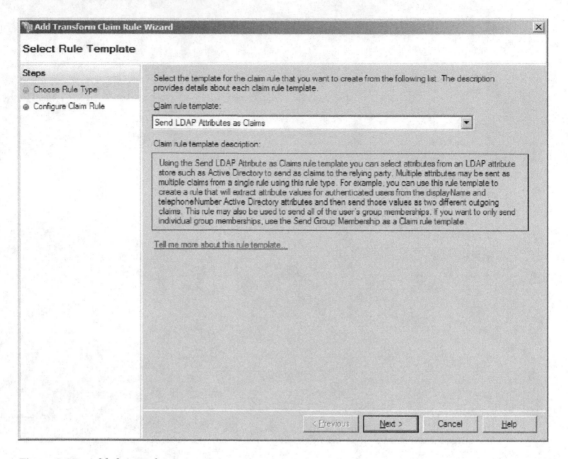

Figure 8-35. *Add claim rule*

17.   Give the rule name.

18.   Select Active Directory as the attribute store.

19.   Map E-Mail-Addresses to the E-Mail Address claim.

20.   Map Token Groups (unqualified names) to the Role claim.

21.   Map the User-Principal-Name to the UPN claim.

■ **Note**   Ensure that you populate the e-mail address in Active Directory user properties for the user.

---

22.   Click the Finish button on the dialog (Figure 8-36).

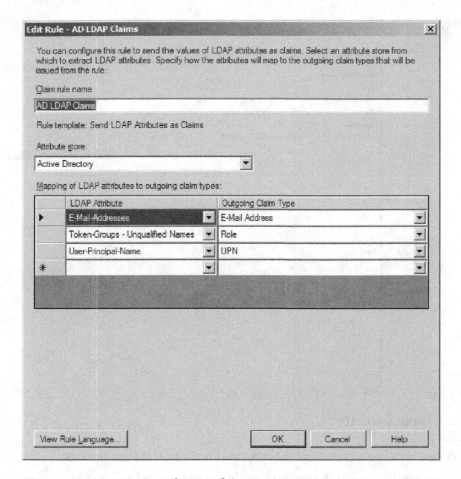

Figure 8-36. *Map LDAP attributes to claims*

23. Click the Add Rule button.

24. Select the option Pass Through or Filter an Incoming Claim.

25. Click the Next button.

26. Enter the name "Primary SID" and select the type as Primary SID.

27. Click the OK button on the rules dialog.

We have now successfully configured SharePoint 2013 as our Relying Party in ADFS. Earlier in the chapter you may have configured your SharePoint 2013 web application for HTTPS requests; if not, you must enable SSL for your application, since ADFS expects all relying parties to communicate on secure transport channels. Flip back to the section "Configuring SSL for SharePoint" to find out how to enable SSL for your SharePoint web application.

The final part of our configuration for ADFS Authentication Federation involves configuration of SharePoint 2013 with a trusted provider to use ADFS. First, we need to export the signing certificate from ADFS and add it to SharePoint as a trusted certificate.

1. Open the ADFS Management Console.

2. Expand the Service node and click Certificates (Figure 8-37).

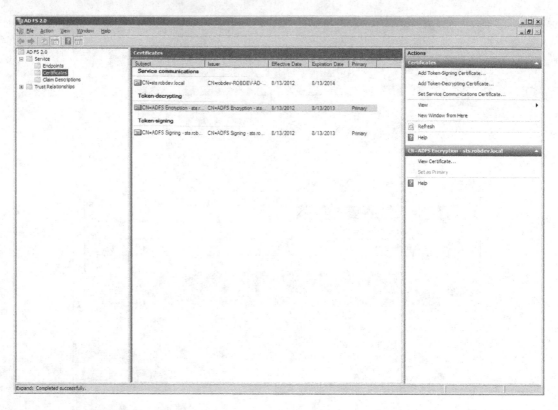

Figure 8-37. *Certificates in ADFS*

3. Right-click the Token-signing certificate and click View Certificate in the pop-up menu.

4. You should see a dialog showing the certificate, like that in Figure 8-38.

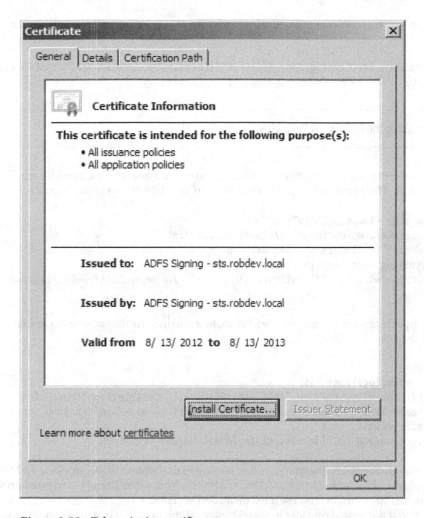

Figure 8-38. *Token-signing certificate*

5. Click the Details tab, then click the Copy to file button.

6. Click the Next button.

7. Select the option to *not* export the private key, then click the Next button.

8. Choose the export format (I chose the default DER format) and then click the Next button.

9. Give the certificate a file name and browse to a location on disk.

10. Click the Next button, then the Finish button to export the certificate to the file.

11. Open the Microsoft Management Console (MMC.exe) on the SharePoint server.

12. Add the Certificates snap-in for the computer account and local machine.

13. Import the certificate into the Trusted Root Certificate Authorities node.

14. Import the certificate into the SharePoint node.

After exporting the token-signing certificate, we shall now import the certificate into SharePoint, using a PowerShell script:

```
$cert = New-Object System.Security.Cryptography.X509Certificates.X509Certificate2("c:\ADFS.cer ")
New-SPTrustedRootAuthority -Name "ADFS Token Signing Cert" -Certificate $cert
```

■ **Note**   The above script requires the full path to the certificate file.

The final set of steps consists of running some PowerShell scripts to create a new Trusted Provider entry and allow SharePoint to federate with ADFS for authentication. First, we map the ADFS claims to those in SharePoint.

```
$map = New-SPClaimTypeMapping -IncomingClaimType
"http://schemas.xmlsoap.org/ws/2005/05/identity/claims/emailaddress" -
IncomingClaimTypeDisplayName "EmailAddress" -SameAsIncoming
$map2 = New-SPClaimTypeMapping -IncomingClaimType
"http://schemas.microsoft.com/ws/2008/06/identity/claims/role" -IncomingClaimTypeDisplayName
"Role" -SameAsIncoming
```

Finally, the following script creates the trusted provider. Do not forget to include the same realm as that of the Relying Party configuration in ADFS.

```
$realm = "urn:robdev:sp2013"
$signin = "https://sts.robdev.local/adfs/ls"
$ap = New-SPTrustedIdentityTokenIssuer -Name "ADFS SAML Provider" -Description "SharePoint
secured by ADFS SAML" -realm $realm -ImportTrustCertificate $cert -ClaimsMappings $map,$map2 -
SignInUrl $signin -IdentifierClaim
"http://schemas.xmlsoap.org/ws/2005/05/identity/claims/emailaddress"
```

The above commands include the claims mappings; realm; name and description of the provider; and HTTPS of the ADFS server, which is typically of the format `https://domain/adfs/ls`. Notice that SharePoint trusted providers require a designated claim to identify users, in this case the e-mail address claim.

Now that we have configured the trusted provider in SharePoint, it is time to enable it on one of our applications, as follows:

1.   Open Central Administration.

2.   Click the Manage web applications link.

3.   Click the web application to add the trusted provider.

4.   Scroll down to the Claims Authentication Types section, and you should see the new provider (Figure 8-39).

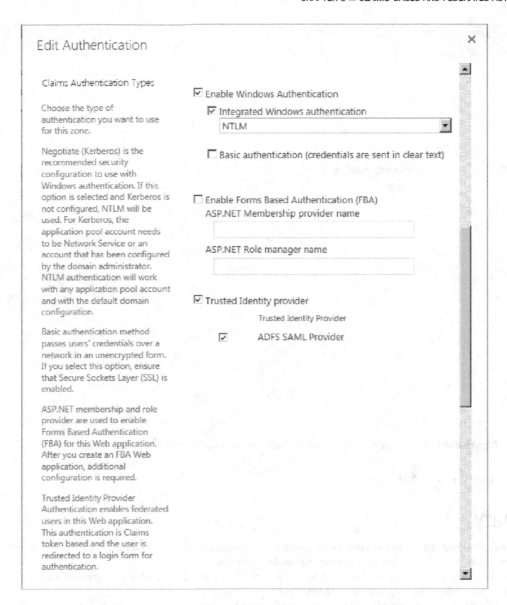

Figure 8-39. *Claims authentication types with trusted provider*

5. Check the check box to enable Trusted Identity Provider.

6. Check the check box for the SAML identity provider we just installed.

7. Click the Save button at the bottom of the dialog.

8. Open the web application in a new browser window.

9. If everything works properly, you see a page like that in Figure 8-40.

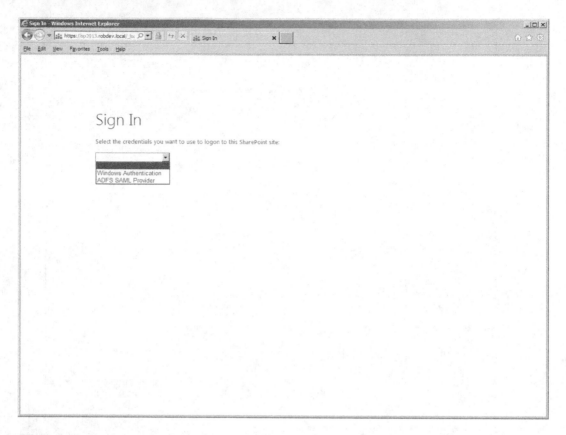

Figure 8-40. Sign in page with Windows Authentication and trusted ADFS provider

10. Select the ADFS SAML provider.

Summary

In this chapter, the concept of Digital Identities was explored. You read about how OpenID has created standards to support users with identities, rather than usernames and passwords.

I introduced Claims-Based-Authentication in SharePoint 2013. I briefly provided background on the legacy Classic Mode Authentication, so you could see why CBA is much better.

Finally, I devoted a large part of this chapter to configuring a secure CBA application with Secure Sockets Layer (SSL), establishing self-signed certificates and certificates via a local Certification Authority, and integrating federated authentication via Active Directory Federated Service.

I could write much more on the topic of secure federated authentication, and with enough research time, I would love to journey with you on integrating some third-party systems, such as Facebook and Google, with ADFS, for real-world example federation. However, I hope that the steps provided in this chapter, to install and configure ADFS, give you a sense of federated authentication and a zest to research further.

In Chapter 9, we switch gears to a new topic, and you shall learn about Content Models and Managed Metadata in SharePoint 2013.

CHAPTER 9

■ ■ ■

Content Model and Managed Metadata

"Metadata" is data about data and is essentially the categorization of the content within a content management system. A good example of metadata is in the classification of documents in a content management system (CMS) or document management system (DMS). A proposal document might have some essential attributes associated, aside from the actual content in the proposal document, such as Proposal Number, Client, Date, and so on. These attributes are the metadata associated with the document.

Why is metadata important? Simply, metadata allows rapid search of content in a system and grouping of content when browsing. Sophisticated search engines—such as the one included in SharePoint 2013—allow searching inside the content of documents, but sometimes a user wants to navigate quickly to a document without dealing with the search result noise typically associated with keyword searching. Metadata and categorization help users to *retrieve* content without a lot of hunting and pecking into document or file content.

Metadata also assists a search engine. Search engine optimization (SEO) algorithms assign more relevance to data stored in metadata, because content owners typically provide metadata explicitly.

In this chapter I examine metadata in SharePoint 2013, the Content Type Model, and the Managed Metadata Service—the central hub that manages metadata in SharePoint.

The SharePoint Content Type Model

If metadata is data about data, then a metadata model is a system that allows the creation, editing, and management of metadata. SharePoint has a metadata model—called the Content Type Model.

The SharePoint Content Type Model consists of metadata types: content types, which themselves consist of metadata fields; columns; and the management of these types in the core of the SharePoint platform. I cover SharePoint metadata types in the next section of this chapter, but first I shall present the SharePoint Content Type Model at a high level.

What are Content Types and Site Columns?

A SharePoint content type is a grouping of fields that describe a data entity in the SharePoint site collection or site, such as a document, calendar event, task, or any other list item. Each content type consists of one or multiple fields, better known as columns.

Content types exist at either the root site collection or subsite level. Lower sites in the hierarchy may use content types from parent sites to define data elements. In both cases, content types reside in the Content Type Gallery of the site or site collection.

The fields of content types exist as centrally managed site columns, at the same level as the containing content type or at parent levels to it. For example, a content type defined at a subsite level may contain site columns that reside in the root site collection or parent site in the hierarchy. Sites may not leverage content types and site columns at lower subsite levels than the current site—just up the hierarchy chain.

There is a difference between centrally managed site columns and list columns. When creating a custom list, the user may define columns specifically for the new list, meaning the columns bind only to that list. By contrast, site columns reside in the Site Column Gallery, and users may reuse these columns in lists (add an existing column) and content types.

Content types may inherit from other content types at the same level in the site hierarchy or a parent level. Even the most basic content types at least inherit from the stock Item content type, which contains the Title site column. Through inheritance, users may customize content types by defining new types that have the same columns as the parent, with additional columns to complete the specialization. For example, if you want to customize task list items with new columns, rather than creating a new content type, you can inherit the existing Task content type and add the new custom columns. Inheritance provides the added benefit that any changes to a parent content type apply to content subtypes.

■ **Note** Never change stock content types and site columns; always inherit from content types, and then specialize.

New Content Type Model Functionality

SharePoint has included lists, libraries, content types, site columns, and list columns since SharePoint 2007. However, each version of SharePoint has brought change to content types. Following are some of the more noteworthy features, beyond the basic content type behavior (described previously). Microsoft introduced many of the following features in SharePoint 2010, which of course also exist in SharePoint 2013.

- Content types and lists that use lookup site columns may specify additional columns of the lookup list to include, in addition to the primary lookup column.

- SharePoint includes referential integrity in lookup columns. For example, when you delete a list item from a list, referenced by a lookup column, SharePoint will delete the dependent list item, prevent the deletion of the parent, or do nothing, depending on a referential integrity setting.

- Document sets (a special content type) allow collection of documents in one list item. They are ideal for collecting multiple documents that combine to a single finished entity, such as a proposal.

- A Managed Metadata column type that maps to term sets in the Managed Metadata Service Term Store exists.

- An Enterprise Keywords column allows users to add their own tags (folksonomy) as part of the Managed Metadata Service.

- Since SharePoint 2010, users can now share content types across site collections via a centralized content type hub.

- SharePoint includes columns and content types to access external data via the Business Connectivity Service.

- SharePoint includes a Rating site column.

- Since SharePoint 2010, SharePoint includes advanced routing of documents via Content Organizer and policy rules.

SharePoint Metadata Types

Microsoft embraced metadata in SharePoint 2007; SharePoint 2003 incorporated "categories" for list data, but this was very different from deserving the title of metadata. SharePoint 2007 introduced the concept of the content type, which is a grouping of related attributes that describe a piece of content. Using the example in the preface of this chapter, a content type for a "proposal" document would typically contain all the attributes that content owners may assign to a proposal document.

SharePoint 2007 managed content types at the site collection level and enabled site collection administrators to create new content types in the Content Type Gallery, for use in the site collection hierarchy. Site owners of subsites in the hierarchy could elect to use content types defined at parent sites or the top-level site collection, or they could define new ones for their site and subsites. Content types also make inheritance possible, so site owners could inherit from a site collection content type and add additional attributes for the specific site instance.

The Managed Metadata Service—introduced with SharePoint 2010—provides a central hub in a SharePoint farm for management of metadata across site collections and web applications in the farm. Centralizing metadata in this fashion releases content owners from the shackles of the site collection, and it allows for content types shared across multiple site collections—very useful if the enterprise site consists of multiple site collections, as it should according to best practices for content distribution.

Before I dig into the specific details of the Managed Metadata Service, I will review the principal metadata components in SharePoint: site columns and content types.

Site Columns

SharePoint maintains a list of site columns, which represent attributes for metadata. If you have created a custom list, or looked at an existing list defined in SharePoint, then you will have seen the site columns in action as the "columns or fields" of the list.

For example, a list of contacts in a site maintains names and addresses of project members. The list retains the first name, last name, street address, city, state, ZIP code, and DOB of the contact. Each of these attributes exists as site columns in SharePoint, and when applied to a list definition they constitute the columns or fields of the list.

Site columns have attributes of their own: title, description, and type. Table 9-1 lists the various types of site columns in SharePoint.

Table 9-1. *Column Types in SharePoint*

Site Column Type	Description
Single line of text	String of text up to a maximum of 255 characters.
Multiple lines of text	Multiple lines of text; content owners specify how many lines to show in edit forms.
Choice	Single choice of fixed values; choices are defined with the site column and displayed as radio buttons or drop-down list.
Number	Floating-point number.
Currency	Two-decimal place number with currency symbol.
Date and Time	Date, Time, or both.
Lookup	Single or multiple-choice lookup of value from another list in the collection (at or below the location of the site column in the hierarchy).
Yes/No	Boolean value, shown as a check box in edit forms.

(continued)

Table 9-1. (*continued*)

Site Column Type	Description
Person or Group	Selection of people or groups from user credential store (Active Directory or other user store, such as LDAP).
Hyperlink or Picture	Either a link to another location or link to an image to display; the content owner chooses at site column creation.
Calculated	Site column value calculated from formula (Excel-like) from other columns in the list row.
Full HTML (Publishing)	HTML field available with the Publishing feature. Allows rich text or full HTML markup.
Image (Publishing)	Image-only field available with the Publishing feature.
Hyperlink (Publishing)	Hyperlink-only field available with the Publishing feature.
Summary Links (Publishing)	Allows collection of hyperlinks by the end user. When this column is added to a page layout and publishing page content type, page editors may add links to show as a collection on the page.
Rich Media (Publishing)	Inclusion of movie, audio, and image media on Publishing pages.
External Data	Single or multiple-choice lookup of value from an external list or content type.
Managed Metadata	These columns surface terms from a term set in the Managed Metadata Service Term Store and are further discussed later in this chapter.

The following steps show how to access the Site Column Gallery in a site collection, and how to add a new column for use in the site collection:

1. Click the gear icon.

2. Click the Site Settings menu item.

3. From the Site Settings page, in the Galleries section, click the Site Columns link.

4. SharePoint displays the Site Column Gallery, like that in Figure 9-1.

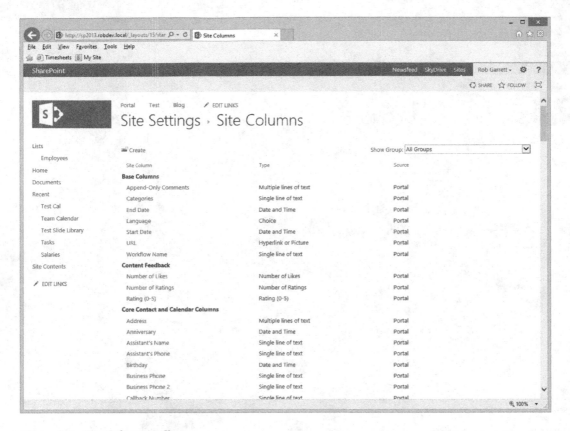

Figure 9-1. *Site Column Gallery*

The page in Figure 9-1 shows a list of the site column names, the type, and the location. If you access the Site Column Gallery from a subsite, the location values show where the site column resides in the hierarchy.

1. Click the Birthday column.

2. SharePoint displays the edit screen as in Figure 9-2.

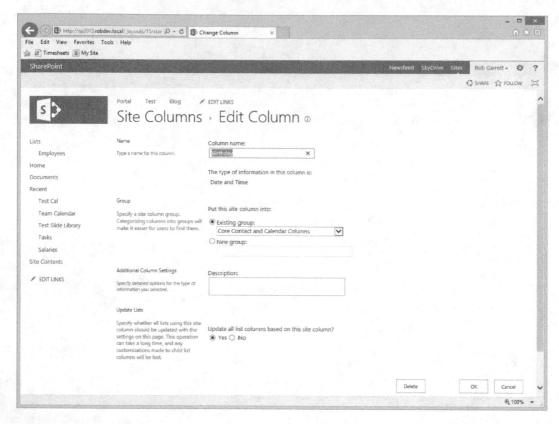

Figure 9-2. Edit site column properties

Here you may change the column name, contained group, description, and whether existing list columns based on this column will update with changes. To change the column type you have no choice but to create a new column, as follows:

1. Navigate back to the Site Column Gallery, showing the list of site columns.

2. Click the Create link.

3. SharePoint shows a new edit form to populate with site column properties.

4. Change the type to Person or Group.

5. Wait for the page to post back and then scroll to the bottom.

6. See the options to allow selection of people only, people and groups or a SharePoint Security Group to limit choice of person.

7. Complete all mandatory properties on this page and then click OK to create the new site column.

■ **Note**   The page posts back automatically when you select different site column types, because different types warrant additional properties.

Content Types

Content types provide content owners with the powerful capability to manage metadata content in SharePoint. The basic anatomy of a content type is that of a group of site columns (fields) that represents a content object in the content management system. For example, a content type may include several site columns that constitute a person's contact details—name, address, telephone, and so on.

Understanding the use of content types is important when discussing content and metadata management in SharePoint, because SharePoint uses content types practically everywhere there is categorization or definition of content schema. The following are some of the areas in which SharePoint employs the use of content types:

- Column definitions in lists and list items

- Document metadata (document properties) in document libraries

- Content fields in publishing pages

- External data definition via Business Connectivity Services

- Search filtering and scopes

Content types incorporate inheritance in the SharePoint Metadata System, which provides for greater levels of flexibility in metadata modeling and abstraction of content definition. Content owners may define basic content types and then subclass these content types to define new content types with greater refinement of metadata.

As an example, Table 9-2 defines a Bio-Page content type for a publishing page, containing biographic information for staff members on an organization's public web site.

Table 9-2. *Site Columns for a Bio-Page Content Type*

Site Column Name	Column Type	Description
First Name	Single line of text	First name of staff member
Last Name	Single line of text	Last name of staff member
Abstract	Multiple lines of text	Small blurb about the staff member
Biographic Text	Full HTML	Complete bio of the staff member
Biographic Image	Publishing image	Headshot image of the staff member

When coupling this content type with a page layout, SharePoint allows content owners to define new page instances, with the defined site columns, to contain data about a staff member. The page layout defines HTML markup, which tells SharePoint how to render the page content. The actual content of the page resides in a list item that is the page instance in a Pages document library.

The organization hosting the web site decides one day to provide a new advanced biographic page type that not only shows the standard details on a staff member, but also includes education information. To achieve this new advanced Bio-Page implementation, the site designers provide a new page layout, based on the standard Bio-Page layout, with placeholders for the new education fields. Rather than create a completely new content type to associate with the page layout, SharePoint allows the content owners to subclass the standard Bio-Page content type and add the additional fields.

Using content type inheritance, users may create elaborate metadata models with basic content types at the root of the model, and more specification of content types throughout the branches of the model. Figure 9-3 illustrates the concept of content type inheritance. Both the MSA and SOW content types exist as separate document content types, which inherit from the common Contract content type parent. The Contract content type inherits from the stock Document content type, which itself inherits from the stock Item content type. All the columns in each content type of the chain exist in the leaf content type, so the SOW content type includes the following columns: Project, Contact, Customer, Size, and File name.

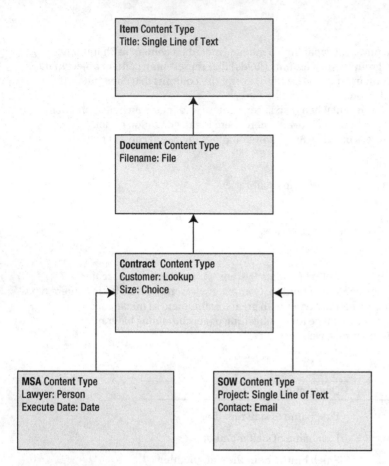

Figure 9-3. *Content type inheritance*

SharePoint defines a basic content type, called Item, which contains the site column Title. Examples of content types that subclass the Item content type include Document, which adds the Name column for the file name, and Announcement, which includes columns for the Body of an announcement and a date field for Expiration. SharePoint ships with many stock content types in Basic and Team site definitions, and even more in Publishing site definitions.

As it does with site columns, SharePoint maintains a list of content types in a site. The following steps demonstrate how to create a new content type for our Bio-Page (Table 9-2):

■ **Note**   Even though SharePoint will allow you to create content types and site columns at any subsite level in the site collection, as a general best practice, define all content types and site columns at the root of the site collection so you may use them throughout the entire hierarchy.

---

1. From the root of the site collection, click the gear icon.

2. Click the Site Settings menu item.

3. On the Site Settings page, under Galleries, click the Site Content Types link.

SharePoint shows all the content types defined in the site collection, as in Figure 9-4. There you can see that each content type belongs to a group and specifies both a parent and the source location in the site collection hierarchy.

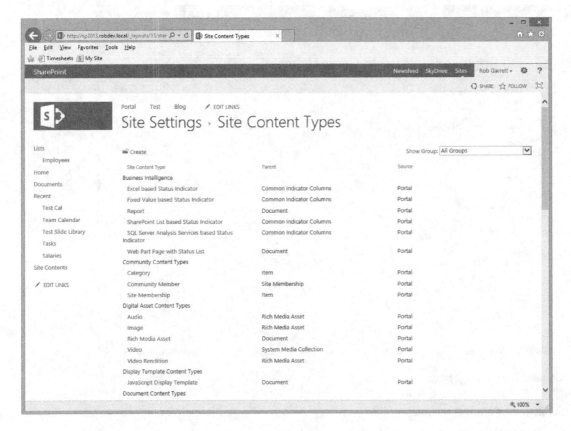

Figure 9-4. *Site Content Types*

■ **Note** Every content type inherits from a parent, even if it is just the base Item content type.

---

1. Click the Create link at the top of the page.

2. Give the new content type a name and a description.

3. Specify the parent content type. SharePoint helps you out here by providing a drop-down to restrict the choices by group.

4. Provide either an existing group or a new group name to file the new content type.

5. Click the OK button.

SharePoint should now show you the Settings page (Figure 9-5) for the content type created. SharePoint allows you to attach workflow and information management policy, change general settings for the content type in the Settings section of this page, and much more.

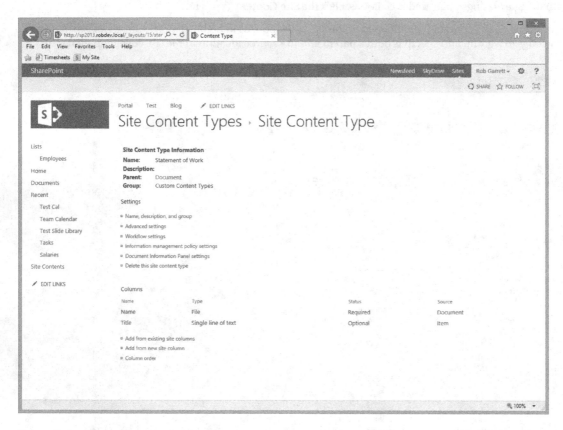

Figure 9-5. *Content Type Settings page*

1. Scroll to the Columns section.

2. You should see those columns present from the parent content type. In my case, I inherited from the Item content type, and so I see the Title column only.

3. SharePoint indicates the parent content type under the Source heading (linked). You may click this link to visit the settings of the parent content type.

4. Click the Add from existing site columns link to navigate to a page to choose from existing site columns at the current site and above (if not at the root of the site collection).

5. Click the Add from new site column link to create a new site column for the content type—any new site column created resides in the Site Columns Gallery of the current site.

Content types provide for powerful, yet flexible definition of the metadata. Like most things in life, this power and flexibility comes with caveats, as follows:

- You cannot delete a content type once it is in use by a container, list item, or page, or inherited by another content type.

- Once you create a content type, you may not change its inheritance relationship with the parent. You must delete the content type and re-create it to inherit from a different content type. This restriction, coupled with the first caveat, can make for difficulty in restructuring an existing metadata model in use by content. Design your model with flexibility at the onset.

- Deleting an inherited column from a content type is ill advised. Instead, make the column hidden.

- Avoid modifying stock content types. Instead, create a new content type and add customization to your new type—content owners expect standard behavior when using stock content types.

- You may not delete any content type deployed via a custom-developed feature.

Content types not only define metadata for documents in libraries and list items in lists, they also provide additional functionality, outlined in Table 9-3.

Table 9-3. *Functionality Associated with Content Types*

Content Type Functionality	Description
Templates	You may associate a document template with a document content type, such as a Contract content type that associates with a Word document, containing the skeleton of a contract document. When users create a new list item, using the content type, SharePoint will open the template so the user may begin editing the document.
	You may also specify an ASPX page in the SharePoint site collection as the template, so SharePoint opens a web page when a user creates a new content type.
Document Information Panel (DIP)	This panel appears in Office applications to show users the metadata associated with a document they opened from SharePoint. I cover the DIP and templates in Chapter 14.
Workflow	You may associate a workflow with a content type, so when users create a new list item based on the content type, SharePoint starts the workflow.
Management Policy	Management policy applies to content types. You may audit events on list items that use a content type, apply retention rules, and do similar tasks. I cover records management and auditing in Chapter 11.

Of course, Table 9-3 is not exhaustive. Content types play a major role in SharePoint and provide the central core for many data-associated functions. Content types provide data portability in that each content type describes data—the schema—such that you can use these content types anywhere you wish to apply specific functionality to certain data types.

Metadata in Lists

Lists and content types marry together nicely—if a content type describes some data, and lists contain instances of data, then the content type effectively describes the schema of a list. For example, if a list is to contain contact addresses, you could imagine the list having columns for the person's name, street address, city, state, ZIP, etc. If you create a content type, which includes these aforementioned columns, your content type defines the schema for hosting contact information in the list.

By default, new custom lists do not maintain columns with content types. You simply create a new list instance and begin adding columns to the list. In this case, SharePoint implies a local list content type from the list definition. Changing a list to allow the management of content types provides for greater control of content in the list—for one, a list may associate with multiple content types, and thus have list items with different columns. This is a very powerful concept, which separates SharePoint lists from tables found in relational databases (which limit rows to a single set schema). Using the previous example, picture the ability to add different classifications of contacts to the list, some US contacts and some European, where the US addresses contain City, State, and ZIP, and the European addresses contain City, Province, and Postcode.

The following steps demonstrate adding content types to a document library or list:

1. Navigate to a list or document library.

2. From the ribbon, click the Library tab, or List tab if a list.

3. From the ribbon, click the Library Settings (or List Settings) icon.

4. Under General Settings on the Settings page, click the Advanced Settings link.

5. Toggle the option to Allow Management of Content Types to Yes.

6. Scroll to the bottom of the page and click the OK button.

7. The List/Library Settings page should now show a Content Types section, as shown in Figure 9-6.

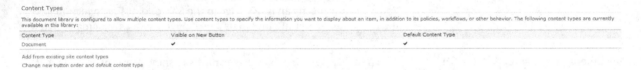

Figure 9-6. *Content types section in the List/Library Settings page*

In my example (using a document library), you see that my document library has one content type—Document—and this content type is the default for all new items added to the list. Farther down the page (not shown in the figure), in the Columns section, is the Title column, sourced from the Document content type. SharePoint adds the special Modified By, Create By, and Checked Out columns to each list, which are not associated with any content type. Add an additional content type to your library (assuming you are following at home using a document library; the steps work similarly for lists).

1. From the List/Library Settings page, click the Add from Existing Site Content Types link.

2. In the Content Type Section page, change the drop-down to display Document Content Types group.

3. Select the content type Picture, and click the Add button.

4. Click the OK button.

5. In the Library Settings page, within the Content Types section, you should see the addition of a Picture content type.

6. Scroll to the Columns section and notice the presence of new columns, as used in the Picture content type.

7. Navigate back to the default view of the Shared Documents library (hint: you can use the breadcrumb at the top of the page).

8. Click the Files tab on the ribbon.

9. From the ribbon, click the New Document (lower part of the icon), as shown in Figure 9-7.

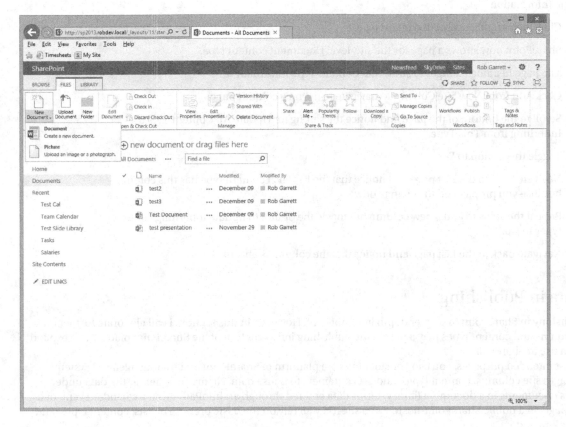

Figure 9-7. *Creating a new document of a specific content type*

You may apply the preceding series of steps to regular lists so that content owners and contributors may add list items to a list with different column data. This practice greatly comes into play when creating multiple content types for different publishing pages within a single Pages document library of a publishing site.

One area of confusion I have seen with lists and content types is in the inheritance chain. When adding a content type to a list, SharePoint makes a new content type at the list level, which inherits from the site content type of the same name. The purpose of this action is to provide a degree of abstraction from changes applied to content types at the site level that differ from specific changes at the list level.

■ **Note**   List-level content types inherit from site-level content types. This provides a level of abstraction, and provides data integrity at the list level if you delete columns from the site content type.

The following series of steps demonstrates this thinking:

1. Navigate to your Library Settings page.

2. Scroll to the Content Types section.

3. Click the Document content type.

SharePoint shows the Content Type Settings page for the Document content type. At the top of the page, notice that the parent of this selected content type is Document also. The heading at the top of the page shows as List Content Type Information.

4. Click the parent Document content type.

5. SharePoint now shows a page for the site-level Document content type.

6. The page heading changes to show Site Content Type Information.

7. Click Add from New Site Column to navigate to the new column page.

8. Scroll to the bottom of the page and notice the setting for Update All Content Types Inheriting from This Type.

9. Toggle this option to Yes.

10. Navigate back to the List page and notice that the list-level content type has this column because you propagated the change down.

11. Repeat the steps to add a new column but toggle the option to update inheriting content types to No.

12. Navigate back to the List page and notice that the column is absent.

Metadata in Publishing

I cover publishing in SharePoint in greater depth in Chapter 10. However, in this section, I will elaborate further on how site columns and content types play a part in the publishing infrastructure of the SharePoint platform, to expand on metadata use in SharePoint.

For most intended purposes, you can consider the core platform of SharePoint as a list management system, which leverages site columns, content types, and list containers to house data. No matter whether the data under discussion is documents in a document library, forms data entered through an InfoPath form, a calendar event, or a publishing page on a public SharePoint-hosted web site, they all rely on the basic premise of lists, content types, and site columns—metadata.

Publishing pages in SharePoint consist of the ASPX files that live in a document library—called *pages*. Unlike regular Web Part pages and wiki pages in non-publishing sites, publishing pages contain no data or markup, just references to a page layout in the Master Page Gallery, and metadata associated with the page file. Next time you open the Pages library in SharePoint for a publishing site, try downloading one of the page files to your local computer and opening the file with Notepad. You should see that the file consists mainly of XML references for the page layout and other publishing infrastructure data—the page will not contain any layout markup or content.

In Figure 9-8, the content type defines the columns that content owners of the page may edit (either in WYSIWYG mode or as page instance properties in the list item). The content type is associated with the Pages library—a list—and the page instance file resides in the library with applied metadata property values. The page layout resides in the Master Page Gallery, as another ASPX file, and contains HTML markup for the presentation of the page. Embedded in the markup are field controls that map metadata fields in the content type to the layout. When SharePoint renders the page instance, the platform replaces these field controls in the layout with the content stored as metadata and associated with the page instance file in the Pages library.

Without going too far into the specifics of Web Content Management and the publishing infrastructure in SharePoint (I shall leave that for the next chapter), the diagram in Figure 9-8 and the previous discussion give a high-level overview of how metadata works with publishing pages. The purpose of the model is to abstract content from presentation, so that content owners may influence content without concern for presentation (editing the metadata properties of a page list item), and page designers may work on one or multiple flavors of page design without requirement to embed content in their templates. Use of the publishing infrastructure and metadata model promotes not only content abstraction but also reuse of page design—using the same template for multiple pages—and the ability to change the visual design of the site without having to change the content.

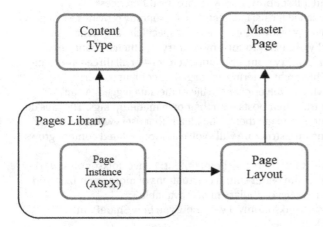

Figure 9-8. *Components of a publishing page*

Before I leave the topic of metadata in the publishing infrastructure, it is worth mentioning that the publishing feature includes a number of new site column types and content types. The following list describes some of the available site columns for publishing:

- Full HTML

- Image

- Hyperlink

- Summary Links

- Rich Media

These additional site column types provide for richer content on publishing pages, aside from the typical single/multiple lines of text, image, and hyperlink columns in the core platform. The Full HTML column type is interesting in that it allows content owners to embed full HTML in content areas on the page. A word of caution: don't break best practices here—try not to embed layout or branding elements with content in full HTML fields, as this tightly couples content with formatting, which is exactly what page layouts and content abstraction try to avoid.

The Managed Metadata Service

In this section, I shall discuss the Managed Metadata Service, which many associate with tagging and taxonomy, but it is essentially the central hub for managing metadata across site collections and applications in a SharePoint 2010/2013 farm (and potentially across farms, using the service and service proxy components).

The Managed Metadata Service exists as a managed service application in a SharePoint farm and acts as a central hub for the management of metadata. Content types and site columns (general metadata) are great but very much tied to a particular site collection (unless you use shared content types—more on this topic later). The Managed Metadata Service allows content owners to create sets of terms, forming a taxonomy, in a central location for use across any SharePoint web application connected to the service.

Taxonomy and Folksonomy

"Taxonomy" and "folksonomy" are now very prevalent terms in business. Thanks to the invasion of social networking, people have become more aware of the benefits of tagging and categorization of information, which require taxonomies and folksonomies. What exactly is taxonomy and folksonomy, and what are the differences?

Taxonomy describes a hierarchy of classification nodes, called terms. Each term in a taxonomy provides a category or classification of other data. The purpose of the hierarchy is to provide a greater level of specificity as you navigate down the hierarchy. For example, you could define a hierarchy of cities, grouped by country and then by continent. You might then tag a person's contact record with a city term, country term, or continent term—or all three—from the hierarchy. Taxonomies are typically defined as an organized hierarchy of terms, managed by content owners.

Folksonomy describes a user self-tagging vocabulary, which evolves over the life of the data tagged. As an example, users may submit articles to a newsfeed and categorize their posts with their own made-up tags. The tags do not belong to an overarching taxonomy, nor do content owners manage them. The idea is that users will gravitate to using the same tag names for related content, and the tagging infrastructure will evolve as more related content grows in the system.

Folksonomy provide a greater level of categorization growth as users tag their content; hence, folksonomy works best in scenarios where users self-publish content. Taxonomies are better suited to situations of more organized and restricted publication of content, where content owners restrict the vocabulary of tags available.

Now that you have a basic understanding of taxonomy and folksonomy, I will show you how SharePoint implements them via the Managed Metadata Service.

Initial Setup

Typically, the Managed Metadata Service already exists in a working SharePoint 2010/2013 farm. Since the majority of readers of this book are administrators, it would be a disservice on my part not to present the steps for provisioning the Managed Metadata Service. The following steps demonstrate how to create a new Managed Metadata Service from Central Administration:

1. Open Central Administration.

2. Click the Manage Service Application link under the Application Management heading.

3. In the list of service applications, if you see the Managed Service Application (or something like it), leave it alone—for the purpose of this demonstration you will just create another.

4. Click the New icon from the ribbon and select Managed Metadata Service from the drop-down list. SharePoint opens a dialog for the service provisioning properties, as shown in Figure 9-9.

Figure 9-9. New Managed Metadata Service dialog

5. Give the application a name.

6. Provide database details for storing the metadata service configuration and data.

7. The Managed Metadata Service is an application, hosted in SharePoint via IIS, and therefore requires an application pool account, so provide the credentials.

8. The content type hub is an existing site collection that acts as the central store for all shared content types, so provide the site collection URL for a new hub for this Managed Metadata Service application; you will use this later.

9. Check Report Syndication Report Errors if you want the service to report synchronization errors.

10. Check Add This Service Application to the Farm's Default List if you want all sites to use this service by default (recommended).

11. Click the OK button to provision the new Managed Metadata Service.

12. From the Managed Service Applications list, click the name of the new Managed Metadata Service application, or select it and then click the Manage icon on the ribbon.

13. SharePoint displays the Term Store Management Tool, shown in Figure 9-10.

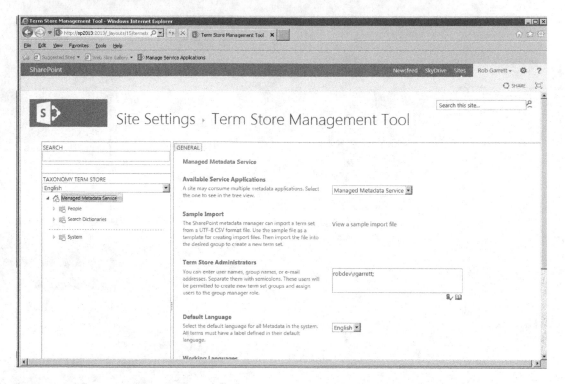

Figure 9-10. *The Term Store Management Tool*

What is a term store? Each Managed Metadata Service contains at least one term store, which consists of a hierarchy of term sets, or groups of term sets. I cover this terminology in more depth shortly, so for now you only need to know that a new provisioned Managed Metadata Service contains a default term store, which is the beginning of your tagging taxonomy.

The Term Store Management Tool enables administrators (and users with access rights to the service) to manipulate settings for the Managed Metadata Service. Table 9-4 identifies the various settings in Figure 9-10.

Table 9-4. *Settings on the Landing Page of Term Store Management Tool*

Setting	Description
Available Service Applications	Drop-down list of provisioned Managed Metadata Service Applications in the farm.
Sample Import	Click the sample link to see a sample CSV file so that you may create your own to import tags into the term store.
Term Store Administrators	Users who have full control over the term store.
Default Language	The Managed Metadata Service supports multilingual terms; this setting stipulates the default language.
Working Languages	Specifies the languages available for terms in the term store.

Associating with a Web Application

One of the options when provisioning a new web application is to opt into the default farm list of managed service applications, or allow the administrator to choose from available services.

Recall from the procedure for provisioning a new Managed Metadata Service the check box option "Add this service application to the farm's default list," which, when checked, adds the new Managed Metadata Service to the default farm list of available services. This is important to note, because if administrators choose to accept the farm defaults for service applications, they will include the new Managed Metadata Service you provisioned earlier in this chapter.

■ **Note**   To remove a managed service from the default farm list, use the Central Administration Farm Association Page under Application Management.

Worth mentioning is the Managed Metadata Service Properties page, which differs from the settings discussed in the previous section. From the list of managed service applications, click to the right of the name of the Managed Metadata Service Proxy and then click the Properties icon on the ribbon. SharePoint displays a dialog like that in Figure 9-11.

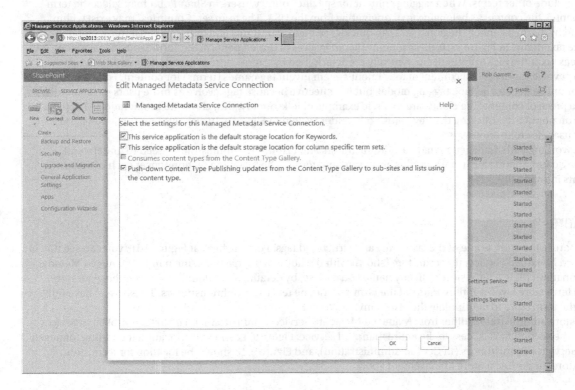

Figure 9-11. *Managed Metadata Service properties*

The first two check boxes tell SharePoint whether this Managed Metadata Service will be the default for Enterprise Keywords (folksonomy) and for term sets (taxonomy). Only one Managed Metadata Service may act as default storage location for tags of either type. The other two properties involve the use of content types and a hub, which I cover later in this chapter.

Access to the Term Store Management Tool from a Site

You might be wondering how to grant access to the Term Store Management Tool to your content owners, without providing them access to Central Administration. The good news is that this tool is also available via sites in a site collection, as follows:

1. Open the site collection.

2. Click the gear icon.

3. Select the menu option for Site Settings.

4. Click the Term Store Management link under the Site Administration heading.

Taxonomy—Managed Metadata

Earlier in this chapter, I discussed the differences between taxonomy and folksonomy. Here is a quick recap, since both principles apply to tagging in the Managed Metadata Service.

Taxonomy is the hierarchical structure of terms and terms sets, where a term is what SharePoint calls the definition of "tag." For example, "USA" might be a term identified in a term set called "Countries." This term set may likely include other terms. When tagging content for specific country, users in SharePoint may select the term "USA" to identify the content as belonging to or originating from the USA. The term set "Countries" may exist within a sub-hierarchy, perhaps under "Regions." You can quickly see how easily terms and term sets constitute a hierarchy, which is the taxonomy. In Figure 9-10, the taxonomy hierarchy lives in the left panel of the Term Store Management Tool.

Whereas taxonomy is structured, and typically predetermined by a term store or taxonomy administrator, folksonomy evolves as users of a content management system invent tag names (terms) for content. Folksonomy provides for only a flat and ad-hoc tagging model, but it is effective because tags evolve as more users participate in tagging of a piece of content. Tag clouds are a classic example of folksonomy; they show the proliferation of certain tags based on popularity. Clicking the Keywords node under System in Figure 9-10 displays Enterprise Keywords entered by users for folksonomy.

When working with managed metadata, administrators and taxonomy administrators need to understand the following components: term store, groups, term sets, and terms. The following sections cover each of these components individually.

Term Store

The term store is the entry home of the taxonomy and structured tags. Looking back at Figure 9-10, you can see that in our Managed Metadata Service, the term store (shown with the house icon) has the same name, "Managed Metadata Service." You may create a term store with any name you choose; by default, SharePoint has named the term store.

At the term store level, administrators of the farm may define term store administrators. These users have full control of the term store to manipulate the taxonomy.

Term store administrators differ from Managed Metadata Service administrators. The first control changes to a term store; the second have access to the entire managed service. Figure 9-12 shows the location for adding Managed Metadata Service administrators (in Central Administration), and Figure 9-13 shows the location for term store administrators (in the Term Store Management Tool).

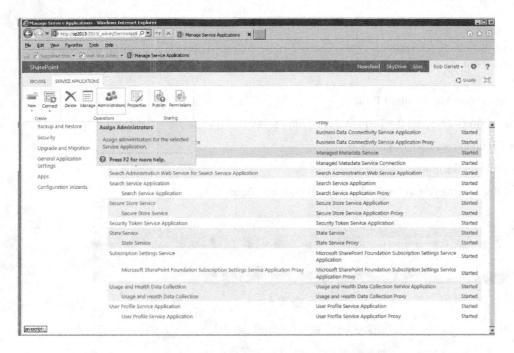

Figure 9-12. *The location for adding administrators for the Managed Metadata Service*

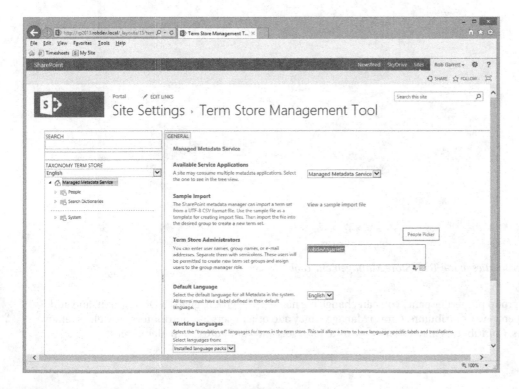

Figure 9-13. *The location for adding term store administrators*

Groups

Groups provide an important role in maintaining a collection of term sets. Groups provide security for the term sets they contain, as both group managers and contributors to the group. The following steps demonstrate how to create a new term set group:

1. Open the Term Store Management Tool.

2. Click the drop-down arrow on the Term Store node in the taxonomy tree.

3. Click New Group to create a new group.

4. Provide a name for the group.

5. SharePoint displays the Group Properties page, as shown in Figure 9-14.

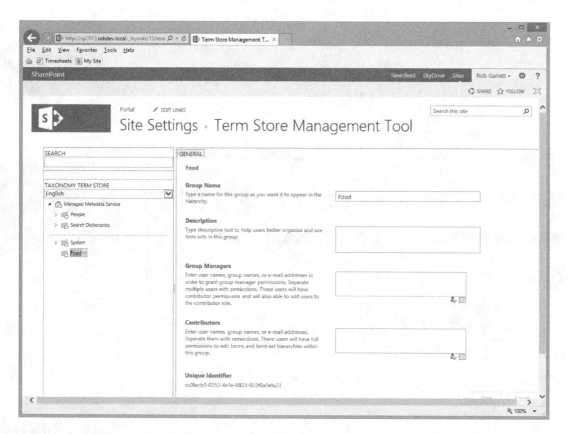

Figure 9-14. *Group properties in the Term Store Management Tool*

From within the group properties pane, you can change the name of the group, give it a Description, and add users to Group Managers and Contributors. Group Managers may add other users as contributors, as well as remove and add new term sets. Contributors may add new terms to term sets and configure group hierarchies.

Term Sets

A term set provides the container for terms. Later in this chapter, you will see how term sets bind to managed metadata columns in content types and lists so that users may choose from a set of term values in a given term set for the data of a column.

1. Create a new term group, per the previous section, if you have not already done so.

2. Click the drop-down arrow on the Group node to contain a new Term Set.

3. Click the New Term Set menu item.

4. SharePoint displays the term set properties pane, like that of Figure 9-15.

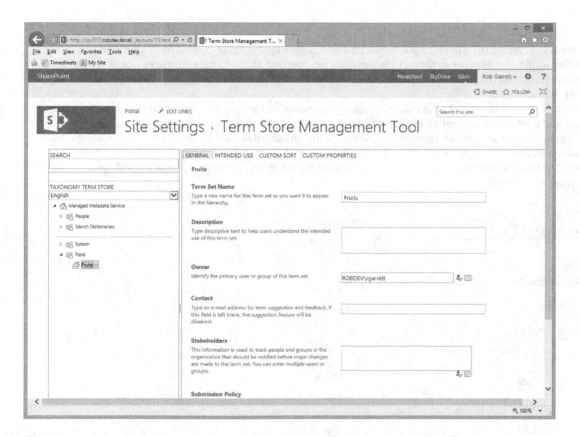

Figure 9-15. *Term Store Management Tool—term set properties*

Notice, when you clicked the arrow on the group to create a term set, you had the option to import term set data from a Comma-Separated Values (CSV) file. The Term Store Management Tool also allows you to import a whole set of groups, term sets, and terms at the top level of the term store. Importing data for your term store is very powerful and a must-have feature when deploying SharePoint—it makes for happier content owners if they do not have to type in lots of term store data whenever you deploy a new SharePoint farm.

On the properties pane of the term set, you may change the name of the term set and the description. The owner (typically the person who created the term set) is the person with full control of the life cycle of the term set. The term set owner and term store administrators may make significant structural changes to the terms in the term set.

Stakeholders are those users who receive e-mail notification when the term set owner or term store administrator makes changes to the term set. Imagine you have a body of people who want to monitor the evolution of terms for a given term set—these people would be the stakeholders.

The submission policy governs whether the term set allows users to add new terms to the set from managed metadata site columns. By default, SharePoint creates the term set as closed and assumes the term set owner and stakeholders wish tight management of the terms in the taxonomy term set. Toggling the policy to open allows users' and programmatic addition of terms in the set—edging more toward folksonomy than taxonomy behavior.

The property to set the term set as "Available for Tagging" tells SharePoint whether to show the term values in the managed metadata site column UI when a user starts typing a term value. The "Custom Sort" property allows the term set owner to custom sort the order of the terms contained in the set—alphabetical order may not always make sense to users for certain term sets.

Terms

Terms are the actual values used in managed metadata site columns for the value chosen from a defined set—the term set. For example, the term set might include terms for food such as fruits. In the site, a user would see the list of fruits to choose from, and the SharePoint user interface will limit the list of available terms as the user types the first few letters of a known term.

SharePoint supports nesting of term values, enabling the creation of a complete taxonomy of terms. For most, the grouping and term sets, constituting the first two levels of the taxonomy, followed by a list of terms in each term set, is enough for a rudimentary taxonomy. However, with additional nested terms you can create some quite elaborate taxonomies.

Figure 9-16 shows some term values I created by clicking the arrow on the right of a term set and selecting the option to create a new term.

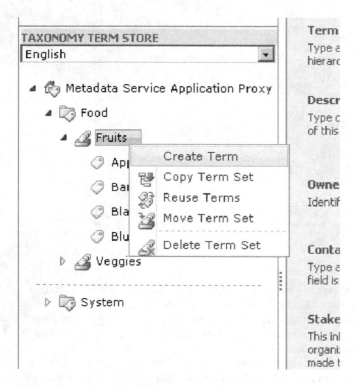

Figure 9-16. *Creating a new term*

A term has an expected name and description property, designated language, option for tagging, and other labels or properties. The language property is important—term set owners may designate certain term values for specific languages. For example, when viewing the site in French, users would see a different set of term values from users viewing the site in English.

The option to make a term available for tagging allows the owner to determine whether a particular term value shows up in the UI of choices for managed metadata site columns.

The Other Labels property provides synonym capability for the term. For example, *SPS* is a synonym for SharePoint Server. If a user selects the term value as *SPS* in a managed metadata site column, SharePoint understands that the value *SPS* corresponds to the SharePoint Server term.

Managed Metadata in SharePoint Sites

Terms within a Managed Metadata Service Term Store surface in a site collection via special site column types. Assuming the administrator has associated a SharePoint site with the term store contained in the Managed Metadata Service, content owners may add the new metadata columns to lists, content types, and the Site Column Gallery. Table 9-5 details the different Managed Metadata site column types.

■ **Note**   New to SharePoint 2013 is the ability to drive site navigation from term store metadata within a publishing site collection. I cover this topic in Chapter 10.

Table 9-5. *Managed Metadata Column Types*

Managed Metadata Column Type	Description
Managed Metadata	Provides a column mapping to a term set in the site-associated term store; depending on the configuration of the term set, this type will depict whether users see all available term sets when selecting a term, have the ability to submit feedback to the term set owner, or are able to add new terms. Use the Managed Metadata column type when you wish to provide users with a choice of tags from a given term set in the term store.
Enterprise Keywords	A special column type added to a list when users enable Enterprise Keywords in the Enterprise Keywords and Metadata Settings section of the List Settings page. Terms entered by users in Enterprise Keywords columns appear under the System/Keywords node in the term store. Use the Enterprise Keywords column type when you want to allow users to tag with their own tag values.

Earlier in this chapter, I demonstrated how to create a new site column. Follow the same steps to create a new site column in your site collection, except choose the Managed Metadata column type this time as the column type. After your browser posts back to display available properties for the selected column type, scroll to the section on Term Set Settings, as shown in Figure 9-17.

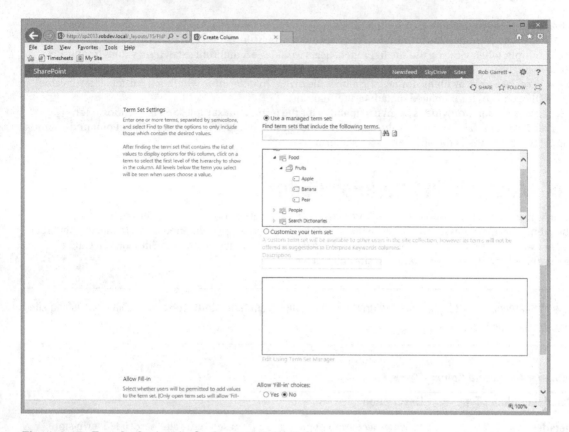

Figure 9-17. *Term Set Settings in the Create New Site Column page*

The Term Set Settings section includes the option to bind the new Managed Metadata column to a particular term set in the term store. In Figure 9-17, I created a simple group called *Food* and a term set called *Fruits*. In the next section of this chapter, I will show how SharePoint presents the available terms under this term set to the user via the user interface.

If the term set has an *open* policy, users can add new terms to the set from the column user interface. If the administrator specified the feedback e-mail address, then users also have the option to suggest terms via a feedback e-mail, which appears at the top of term selection dialogs.

Owners of a site column can choose to create a customized term set rather than use an existing term set in the term store, which then creates a term set in the Managed Metadata Service Term Store.

■ **Note**   If SharePoint displays an error message that there is no default term store associated with the site, ensure that you check the check box for default term store, as in Figure 9-11 earlier.

The Enterprise Keywords column type is a special SharePoint column type. The following steps demonstrate how to enable Enterprise Keywords on a list:

1. From a list page, click the List/Library tab on the ribbon.

2. Click the List/Library Settings icon.

3. Click the Enterprise Keywords and Metadata Settings link.

4. Enable the Enterprise Keywords option.

5. Return to the List/Library Settings page; you should see a new Enterprise Keywords column added to the list columns definition (Figure 9-18).

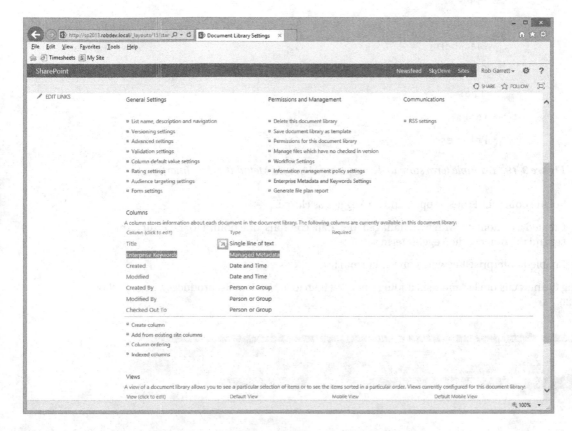

Figure 9-18. *Enterprise Keywords enabled on a list or document library*

■ **Note** You cannot create a new site column of Enterprise Keyword type. They apply only at the list/library level.

In the next section, you will see how both Enterprise Keywords and Managed Metadata columns appear to end users in the SharePoint site user interface.

Tagging User Interface

To demonstrate the user interface for Managed Metadata columns and Enterprise Keywords, I performed the following steps as a precursor, using the Term Store Management Tool:

1. Created two term sets—Fruits and Veggies (Figure 9-19).

305

Figure 9-19. *Example term store to demonstrate Managed Metadata User Interface*

2. Set the policy for Fruits as open and for Veggies as closed.

3. Created a custom list with two Managed Metadata columns, one bound to the Fruit term set and the other to the Veggies term set.

4. Enabled Enterprise Keywords on the custom list.

Creating the new custom list and then adding a new list item to my custom list produces a page as shown in Figure 9-20.

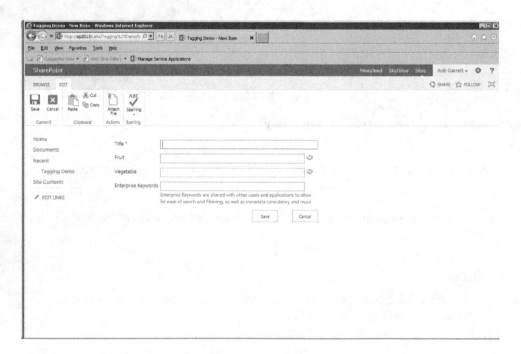

Figure 9-20. *New list item dialog with metadata columns*

With the page displayed, as in Figure 9-20, start typing the name of a fruit in the Fruit field. Start with the letter *B* (hint, hint), and SharePoint will show suggestions of all fruits beginning with the letter *B*. You can try the same test on the Veggies field, although, if you use the letter *B* you should notice that SharePoint has no suggestions because I did not create any vegetable terms starting with the letter *B*.

Switch to the Enterprise Keywords field and begin typing the name of a fruit that exists in the Fruit term set. Even though the term is part of another term set, SharePoint allows the Enterprise Keywords column to query terms in term sets of the same term store. Before leaving this field, type the name of another food that is neither a fruit nor a vegetable, save the list item, and then come back to this dialog to enter another item. Back in the Enterprise Keywords field, you can now start typing the name of the new food item (I chose donut) and see that SharePoint saved the new term.

■ **Note**   To prevent Enterprise Keyword fields from offering suggestions from a term set, uncheck the setting Available for Tagging in the term set settings.

Before leaving the New Item dialog, click the small tag icon to the right of the Fruit field. This icon links the user to the dialog for browsing terms, as shown in Figure 9-21. From this dialog, users may visualize all terms in a term set and select the appropriate term. Notice in the top of the dialog a link to Add New Item (term). Remember that I configured the Fruit term set as open, meaning that users can add new terms. Compare this dialog to that of the browse term dialog for the Vegetable field—the Add New Item link is missing in the Veggies dialog because the Veggies term set has a closed policy.

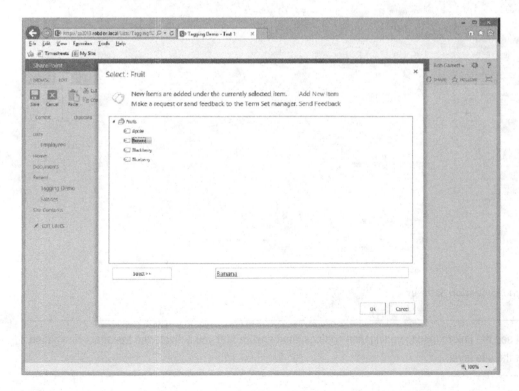

Figure 9-21. *Browsing for a term*

The Send Feedback link is a standard mail-to link that will open your mail application with the e-mail address configured in the Feedback setting for the term set.

Filtering

SharePoint allows you to filter data in lists using Managed Metadata values (similar to using facets in Search). In the previous section in this chapter, I set up a new demo list and add a couple of Managed Metadata site columns to the list. In this section, I will demonstrate how to add taxonomy browsing and keyword filtering to a list or document library.

1. Navigate to the list you created in the previous section.

2. Click the List tab on the ribbon and then click the List Settings icon on the ribbon.

3. From the List Settings page, click the Metadata Navigation Settings link.

4. SharePoint shows a page like that in Figure 9-22.

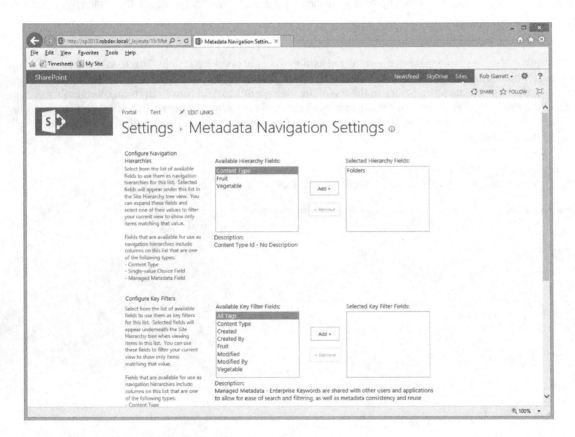

Figure 9-22. *Metadata Navigation Settings*

■ **Note** If you do not see the link to manage navigation settings, then ensure that you activate the Metadata Navigation and Filtering feature at the site level.

---

5. Choose one or multiple Managed Metadata fields from the list for the navigation hierarchy.

6. Choose one or multiple Managed Metadata fields from the list for the key filters.

7. Scroll to the bottom of the page and click the OK button.

8. Navigate back to the List page and add some list items.

9. From any of the List View pages, glance to the left under the quick navigation links, and you should see a tag browser and keyword filter (Figure 9-23).

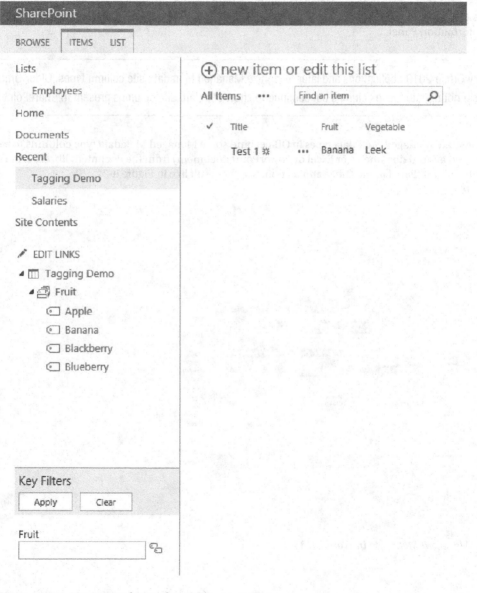

Figure 9-23. *Navigation hierarchy and keyword filters*

Here you can see that SharePoint has added a hierarchy tree for the Fruit field (I only added the Fruit column in my example, but you could just as easily add Vegetables or both) in my list. Selecting one of the terms in the tree filters the list of items, similar to filtering lists the traditional way from the list column in the view. The Key Filters feature also provides filtering, but it does so via typed keyword, with a UI similar to that of adding values to Managed Metadata fields.

Tagging in Office Applications

Office applications understand managed metadata (2010 and upwards) when applied to documents opened from a SharePoint source that have Managed Metadata columns. With the introduction of Managed Metadata site column types and the Managed Metadata Service in SharePoint, Office can now access term sets and term data from the Document Information Panel.

■ **Note**   Only Office 2010 applications and later recognize Managed Metadata site column types. Older Office applications cannot update these columns but continue to show standard site columns present in SharePoint 2007.

To demonstrate Managed Metadata types in Office, bind some Managed Metadata type columns to a document library, then open a Word document (or Excel or PowerPoint document) from the document library and view the Document Information Panel in the Office application. See the result like in Figure 9-24.

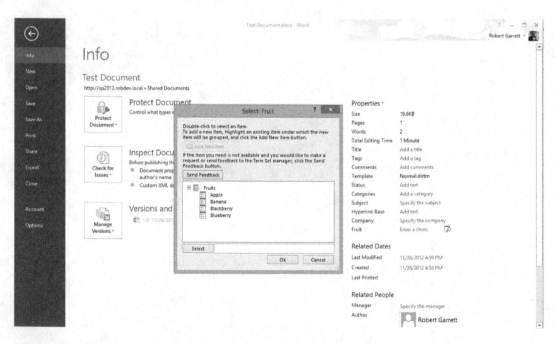

Figure 9-24. *Managed Metadata in Word 2013*

Content Type Hubs

Content types provide a powerful classification of content in SharePoint, whether it is a document, list item, publishing page, or external data. Most SharePoint content involves content types somewhere. SharePoint 2007 introduced content types, and users of SharePoint have never looked back since. However, in SharePoint 2007, content types had a major limitation—the scope of a content type went no higher than a site collection. SharePoint best practice is to use multiple site collections in large content systems to distribute content across content databases. This made for a major headache in managing content types in a large enterprise content management system. SharePoint 2010 and 2013 solve this issue with content type hubs.

Earlier in this chapter, I described the steps for creating a new Managed Metadata Service application. During the creation process, SharePoint allows the administrator to specify the site collection as a content type hub. As long as the Managed Metadata Service administrator has Site Collection Administration rights to a site collection, he or she can specify this site collection as the hub for all new content types. The content type hub is effectively the authoritative site collection for the management of content types, and all other content types that subscribe to the same Managed Metadata Service may share content types from the hub.

■ **Note** When delegating a site collection as a new content type hub, I recommend leaving the option to Report Syndication Errors so that the log contains important errors if content types fail to synchronize across site collections.

The following steps confirm the existence of a content type hub for an existing Managed Metadata Service Application, or the option to delegate a site collection as a content type hub:

1. Open Central Administration.

2. Click the Manage Service Applications link.

3. Scroll down to the Managed Metadata Service (or name you gave it).

4. Select the service (do not click it) and then click the Properties icon from the ribbon.

5. Scroll to the bottom of the dialog that appears in the content type hub section (Figure 9-25).

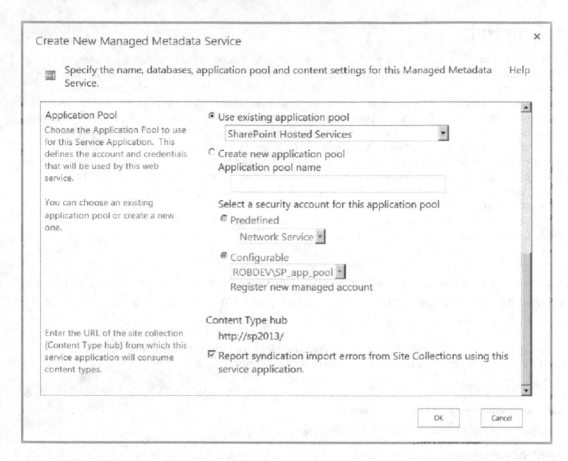

Figure 9-25. *Configure the content type hub in the Managed Metadata Service*

6. Ensure that a URL of a site collection exists in the field.

7. Ensure that the check box for Report Syndication Errors is checked.

■ **Note**   Ensure that you enable the Content Type Hub Syndication feature for the site collection that is to act as a content type hub.

With the hub established, head over to the site collection content type hub and see the introduction of new site collection settings.

1. Navigate to the Content Type Hub Site Collection URL in your browser.

2. Access the Site Settings page and scroll to the Site Collection Administration section.

3. You should notice two links: Content Type Publishing and Content Type Service Application Error Log.

SharePoint manages publication of content types from the hub and subscription to published content types from consumers of the hub via two timer jobs. The content type hub job publishes all new content types from the hub where the site collection administrator has marked a content type for publishing. This job also manages the syndication error log. The content type subscriber job exists for all applications where a contained site collection subscribes to the hub for a published content type. In the next subsection of this chapter, I discuss publishing a content type from the hub and consuming the content type in another site collection—the consumer.

Publishing, Un-publishing, and Republishing

The creation of a content type for publication in the content type hub is identical to that of creating a content type in a non-hub site collection. However, when a site collection administrator creates a content type in the hub, SharePoint displays additional configuration options in the Content Type Settings page. Once you have completed the steps in the previous section to designate a content type hub, the following steps demonstrate creating a new content type for publication to another subscriber site collection.

1. Open the Content Type Hub Site Collection.

2. Navigate to the Content Type Gallery from the Site Collections Settings page.

3. Click the Create link at the top of the page to create a new content type.

4. Give the new content type a name, description, and parent and save it.

5. I created a simple content type and inherited from the standard Item content type.

6. Navigate to the Content Type Settings page, like that in Figure 9-26.

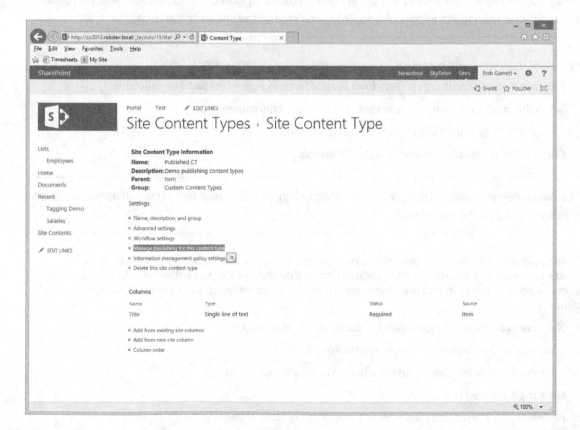

Figure 9-26. *Content Type Settings page with publishing options*

7. Click the link to Manage publishing for this content type.

8. The next page shows three options: Publish, Un-publish, and Re-publish (update).

9. Choose Publish and click the OK button.

■ **Note** If you receive an error about an incorrect proxy at this stage, then either your site collection hub in the Managed Metadata Service is incorrect (if it is a root site collection, use the / on the end of the URL), or you need to change the URL using the following PowerShell command:

```
Set-SPMetadataServiceApplication "Managed Metadata Service" –HubUri http://site_collection_hub
```

---

10. From the consumer site collection, navigate to the Site Settings page.

11. In the Site Collection Administration section, click the Content Type Publishing link.

12. If you do not see your published content type in the Hubs section, check the error log by clicking the link shown.

■ **Note** By default, the consumer timer job runs every hour and the hub timer job every 15 minutes. The consumer timer job looks after creating and updating shared content types in consumer site collections; the hub timer job notifies consumers of changes to existing shared content types or the existence of new shared content types.

To stop publishing the content type at the hub, continue with the following steps:

1. Navigate to the Content Type Gallery from the Site Settings page of the hub site collection.

2. Select the published content type to view the settings for the content type.

3. Click the Manage Publishing for This Content Type link.

4. Click the Un-publish option and then the OK button.

■ **Note** You cannot delete a published content type. In addition, changes to a content type in the hub do not update the consumers until you republish the content type.

Once a site collection administrator publishes a content type, the timer jobs complete and the content type is available to consumers, who may use the content type as if defined locally. Site collection administrators of the consumer site collection may inherit from the content type or use the content type in the sites and lists of the site collection.

1. Navigate to the Content Type Gallery in the consumer site collection.

2. Scroll to find the Consumed content type in the gallery.

3. Click the name of the Consumed content type to view the Settings page.

4. Click the Advanced Settings link.

5. By default, the Consumed content type is read-only; to allow changes to the Consumed content type, change the read-only setting.

The Error Log

When either the content type syndication consumer or publisher timer job encounters an error, it reports an error in the syndication error log—a list available under the Site Administration section of the Site Collection Site Settings page. Administrators may also access the error log from the link on the Manage Publishing for This Content Type page.

Assuming the administrator did not disable the setting to report syndication errors in the Managed Metadata Service, SharePoint tries to be as verbose as possible in the syndication log. Table 9-6 depicts the columns in the error log.

Table 9-6. *Columns in the Content Type Syndication Error Log*

Column Name	Description
Title	Error title
Taxonomy Service Store ID	GUID of the term store in the Managed Metadata Service
Taxonomy Service Name	Name of the Managed Metadata Service
Content Type Subscriber Site	Link to the consumer site with syndication error
Syndication Item	Content type that failed to synchronize
Syndication Failure Stage	Stage at which the syndication failed
Syndication Failure Message	Specific details about the error
Syndication Failure Time	Timestamp that the error occurred

Sometimes the error log may report no errors and after successful execution of syndication timer jobs, the consumer site collection has no content types from the hub. The following list identifies a few reasons for this that I have encountered during my research:

- The document ID feature is enabled on either hub or consumer but not on the other—this feature must be enabled or disabled on both.

- The Managed Metadata Service proxy is not configured to consume content type publications—enable it from the properties of the Managed Metadata Service.

- I came across one instance in which the consumer failed with an error in the log about unknown site ID. This occurred when I checked the option to consume content types in the properties of the Managed Metadata Service proxy, post creation of the consumer site collection. I remedied the issue by re-creating the site collection, once the Consumer Web Application MMS proxy allowed the content type consuming option.

Summary

In this chapter, I introduced the reader to basic metadata—site columns and content types. This chapter included details on how site columns and content types operate in sites and lists, and how content owners can build a metadata model via content type inheritance.

With the basics understood, you dove into the specifics of the Managed Metadata Service, which handles taxonomy, folksonomy, and use of both for content tagging. The Managed Metadata Service provides content type synchronization capabilities across site collections in the farm (and across farms), using the service and service proxy model of the Managed Service Architecture. I demonstrated how to designate a site collection as the content type hub, for published content types. I then demonstrated how other consuming site collections (within a consumer web application) consume published content types from the hub. I briefly covered the syndication error log that SharePoint utilizes when a failure occurs in synchronizing published content types.

Metadata and the Managed Metadata Service are important topics in the land of SharePoint. Of all the chapters in this book, this chapter is one I recommend revisiting, especially if you are deploying a content management system in SharePoint across the enterprise.

In Chapter 10, I cover publishing and Web Content Management, which requires a good understanding of metadata, described in this chapter.

CHAPTER 10

■■■

Publishing and Web Content Management

Web Content Management (WCM) is the management of web content. In the days of old, we used to place some static HTML pages on a web server and call it a day for the development of web sites. Although this served a purpose at the time, the sort of information we could display on the World Wide Web was really limited. Then, we matured some and added dynamic rendering with technologies like PHP, ASP, VBS, Java, etc. and could render content from databases and other data sources. The problem was that we still relied on IT to put anything on the web server and required developers to design and implement web sites, often a very costly endeavor. Meanwhile, content management systems were springing up to address the need for document management and centralized content management in the organization. What we needed was this same CMS technology for the Web—a Web Content Management system.

To put it succinctly, Web Content Management is about the tools and processes for managing web-based content, without the need for complex development and IT control. By web content, I refer to text content, streaming video and audio, interactive applications built in Silverlight, Flash applications, and now HTML5 content. No matter the technology, content is content—it is data someone wants to share with someone else, and a WCM system empowers content owners to manage and render their information for an audience without requiring the complex knowledge of the underlying technology.

This book is all about SharePoint 2013, so I shall focus on Web Content Management functionality in SharePoint. Microsoft builds diverse products, and most of its software solutions provide middle-of-the-road capability. This is not to say that SharePoint is an inferior product—far from it—just that SharePoint is everything to some, in comparison to some very expensive high-end dedicated CMS and WCM systems. In the following sections of this chapter, I will describe the WCM and publishing functionality that SharePoint 2013 has to offer.

SharePoint Publishing Infrastructure

If Web Content Management is the management of web site content, the SharePoint publishing infrastructure is the implementation of such WCM functionality. At the very basic level, the publishing infrastructure consists of a series of features and site templates. In this section of the chapter, I take a closer look at the main site collection and site-level features, master page, and page layouts that provide the core of WCM capabilities.

A Publishing Site

Before delving into the specific publishing features of SharePoint 2013, you will create a new publishing site collection, so that you may see the various features and functionality available as part of this site definition. Whether you plan to host a public-facing web site, an extranet, intranet (with WCM capabilities), or some other WCM-based site, you will likely want to start with the Publishing Site template (there are others, but the Publishing Site is most common).

1. Open Central Administration.

2. Click the link to create site collections.

3. Choose the hosting web application.

4. Provide a title, description, and URL.

5. Under the template selection section, click the Publishing tab.

6. Choose the Publishing Portal.

7. Provide the primary and secondary administrators.

8. Choose the quota profile.

9. Click the OK button to create.

10. Once SharePoint completes creation of the new site collection, navigate to the new site, which should look something like that in Figure 10-1.

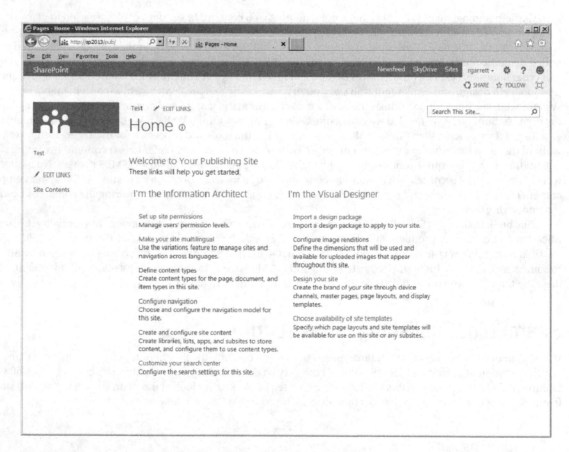

Figure 10-1. *Home page of a SharePoint 2013 publishing site*

The home page shown in Figure 10-1 provides some helpful links to get you started with the configuration of your new publishing site. All of these links point to admin pages, which you may also access through the site collection settings page. However, having a series of links in one place is helpful to more quickly configure the publishing site. I will now examine them in more detail.

Table 10-1 lists the jump links on the publishing home page, as shown in Figure 10-1. Configuring a publishing site is typically a two-team operation, consisting of the administration team and the designer team. Administrators follow the links on the left side of the page, and designers the links on the right side. The great thing about SharePoint is that each team may work in parallel, without relying on the other to complete its work. This is an important capability of SharePoint publishing sites: content owners and site administrators need not concern themselves with the visual design of the publishing site, and the designers need not concern themselves with the content of the site. This principle is one of the major pillars of a Web Content Management system: content people manage content, and design people manage look and feel.

Table 10-1. *Jump Links on the Publishing Site Home Page*

Link	Role	Description
Set up site permissions	Administration	Link to the site permissions page; assign site permissions to groups; SharePoint has a default set of permissions configured for the root site and any subsites inheriting the permissions; administrators may enable anonymous access for public-facing web sites
Make your site multilingual	Administration	Create variation labels for set up of site structure variants for each content language supported
Define content types	Administration	Link to the site content type gallery; define content types, which inherit from publishing content types (such as Page) to facilitate granular content storage
Configure navigation	Administration	Link to the navigation settings for the site; configure strategy for top navigation bar and quick launch navigation, as well as taxonomy-based navigation
Create and configure site content	Administration	Link to the view site content page; look to the pages document library to host publishing pages for the site
Customize your search center	Administration	Link to configure search settings; define a search center (either as a subsite or a separate site collection)—it is good practice to centralize search results with a search center
Import a design package	Designer	New capability in SharePoint 2013: import a design package for look and feel of the site
Configure image renditions	Designer	Link to the image renditions settings page; configure different image renditions for renditions (display) of image sizes
Design your site		New in SharePoint 2013: link to the new Design Manager pages
Choose availability of site templates		Link to the site templates and page layout settings; configure availability of page layouts and site templates for users creating subsites in the publishing site hierarchy

Table 10-1 includes a description of each link and the capability provided at each link destination; I shall cover more on each capability throughout this chapter.

Publishing Features

The publishing infrastructure consists of a number of features. Each feature is a unit of discrete functionality and exists within SharePoint as a collection of files in the hive and (most often) assembly files in the Global Assembly Cache.

The SharePoint User Interface exposes two publishing-based features—one at the site collection scope and another at each publishing subsite scope in the site collection. Of course, if you created a site collection using the Publishing Portal template, then SharePoint has already activated these features for you.

1. Navigate to the publishing site (or any other site collection if activating publishing).

2. Click the gear icon.

3. Select the Site settings menu item.

4. Click the link for site collection features, under the Site Collection Administration heading.

5. Scroll down the list of the features and ensure that the SharePoint Server Publishing Infrastructure feature is activated (Figure 10-2).

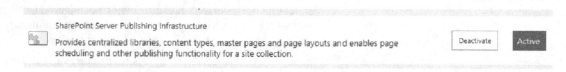

Figure 10-2. SharePoint Server Publishing Infrastructure site collection feature

6. Navigate to any subsite in the publishing site collection (you can also use the root site).

7. Navigate to the site settings (as previously).

8. Click the link to manage site features, under the Site Actions heading.

9. Ensure that the SharePoint Server Publishing feature is activated (Figure 10-3).

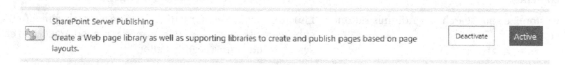

Figure 10-3. SharePoint Server publishing site feature

The SharePoint User Interface shows two features for publishing, but these two features rely on a number of other feature dependencies. When you activate the SharePoint Server Publishing Infrastructure feature and the SharePoint Server Publishing features, SharePoint requires activation of the dependent features. Ordinarily, you need not concern yourself about the details of the features, shown in Table 10-2, unless you are interested or one of these features failed to activate. You will not find any of the features listed in Table 10-2 via the SharePoint UI; instead, you must use PowerShell or STSADM to activate and deactivate these features. I provide the Global Unique Identifier (GUID) for each feature for this purpose.

Table 10-2. Publishing Feature Dependencies

GUID	Name	Description
A392DA98-270B-4e85-9769-04C0FDE267AA	Publishing Prerequisites	Calls an event handler to install prerequisites
AEBC918D-B20F-4a11-A1DB-9ED84D79C87E	Publishing Resources	Installs Web Parts, XSL, Silverlight
89E0306D-453B-4ec5-8D68-42067CDBF98E	Navigation	Installs custom actions and handlers for navigation
D3F51BE2-38A8-4e44-BA84-940D35BE1566	Publishing Layouts	Installs master pages, page layouts, and styles
EAF6A128-0482-4F71-9A2F-B1C650680E77	Search Server Web Parts	Installs search Web Parts
8B2C6BCB-C47F-4F17-8127-F8EAE47A44DD	Search Templates and Resources	Installs search templates and resources
A4C654E4-A8DA-4db3-897C-A386048F7157	HTML Design	Enables HTML Design
4BCCCD62-DCAF-46dc-A7D4-E38277EF33F4	Asset Library	Installs asset libraries
068BC832-4951-11DC-8314-0800200C9A66	Enhanced Theming	Installs theming controls
A942A218-FA43-4d11-9D85-C01E3E3A37CB	Enterprise Wiki Layouts	Installs content types, page layouts, and handlers for wikis
57CC6207-AEBF-426E-9ECE-45946EA82E4A	Mobile Publishing	Installs support for mobile browsing
915c240e-a6cc-49b8-8b2c-0bff8b553ed3	Ratings	Installs rating controls
0C8A9A47-22A9-4798-82F1-00E62A96006E	Document Routing Resources	Installs content types, fields, and handler for document routing
5BCCB9A4-B903-4fd1-8620-B795FA33C9BA	Record Resources	Installs policy fields and custom actions
5B79B49A-2DA6-4161-95BD-7375C1995EF9	Media Web Parts	Installs media Web Parts
4E7276BC-E7AB-4951-9C4B-A74D44205C32	Translation	Installs handlers for language translation
67AE7D04-6731-42dd-ABE1-BA2A5EAA3B48	Search Taxonomy Refinement Web Parts	Installs search refinement Web Parts, using taxonomy
8C34F59F-8DFB-4a39-9A08-7497237E3DC4	Search Taxonomy Refinement HTML Web Parts	Installs search refinement Web Parts, using taxonomy for HTML content
94C94CA6-B32F-4da9-A9E3-1F3D343D7ECB	Publishing Web	Main publishing feature for the web scope—visible in the UI
F6924D36-2FA8-4f0b-B16D-06B7250180FA	Publishing Site	Main publishing feature for the site scope—visible in the UI
22A9EF51-737B-4ff2-9346-694633FE4416	Publishing	Installs handlers and prerequisites for publishing
DFFAAE84-60EE-413A-9600-1CF431CF0560	Rollup pages	Installs rollup capability

Content Management

A primary reason for using SharePoint publishing is to make use of content management. The whole point of content management—Web Content Management to be precise—is to allow content owners to create and edit content without needing IT, or worrying about how their content impacts site design.

SharePoint publishing abstracts content management from user interface design and web site development by providing rich features for content orchestration, allowing content owners to do what they do best—worry about just content. Even though the end result is a web page consisting of content merged with HTML, JavaScript, and perhaps Silverlight, the content owners should never have to worry about these UI concepts. SharePoint performs the heavy lifting in providing content abstraction from presentation. At the core, SharePoint consists of lists, libraries, content types, and site columns (fields), and it is these core elements that provide the base content management capabilities. Of course, the assertions made in the preceding paragraph predicate good content model design. A page that consists of one page body field of HTML type is not good design, because content owners have only one place to insert their page content, and this model assumes the content marked up with HTML. A better model consists of pages and page templates with a variety of fields for more granular control of the content.

Site Columns

In Chapter 9, I covered the basics of content models and managed metadata, and I introduced site columns and discussed how they apply to lists and content types. The publishing infrastructure introduces some additional site column types, specifically for the purpose of publishing content.

SharePoint includes all site column types as part of the installation of the product. Although there is nothing stopping site owners from using them in any situation, Table 10-3 lists those site column types specific for use in publishing situations. Worth noting is that the site column types in Table 10-3 appear when creating new site column instances, but not all types listed appear when creating list columns.

■ **Note** SharePoint defines the publishing site column types in `C:\Program Files\Common Files\Microsoft Shared\Web Server Extensions\15\TEMPLATE\XML\FLDTYPES_Publishing.xml`. This file includes some non–user creatable site column types, not listed in Table 10-3, but required for publishing.

Table 10-3. *Site Columns for Publishing*

Site Column Type	Description
Full HTML content with formatting and constraints for publishing	This column type provides a richer text editing experience by using the Rich Text Editor. You use this column type to enable users to apply styles, apply table formatting, and work with reusable content. The column type stores HTML, and the editor provides these authoring and styling capabilities. This column type also helps you control or limit the options users have when creating new content by placing content field controls within SharePoint page layouts. Users may apply content and formatting constraints to the column to ensure that new content appears according to pre-established styles and themes.
Image with formatting and constraints for publishing	This column type stores links to images defined in the item properties. Each column displays a thumbnail preview in list views, and users may apply optional formatting. Use this column type to provide users with an easier way to add images rather than having to manually input the URL of the image or web reference. Control over images can be set when placing content field controls within SharePoint page layouts.

(continued)

Table 10-3. (*continued*)

Site Column Type	Description
Hyperlink with formatting and constraints for publishing	This column type stores hyperlinks and displays the hyperlink names defined in the item properties. Use the column type to provide a browsing interface that allows users to browse to an object to link to instead of typing a URL. Link formatting and other options can be set when placing content field controls within SharePoint page layouts.
Summary links data	This column type enables users to create bulleted content without the need for a dedicated list to populate the data. Use this column type on publishing pages to present grouped links that use a set of shared styles. Summary links include a title, description, image, and URL. Summary links control and behavior can be set when placing a Summary Links field in SharePoint page layouts.
Rich media data for publishing	This column type enables users to add video to a publishing page. Using this column type, you may link to a media file (audio or video) the same way you link to an image. You can insert this column type in a page layout to show the specified videos on pages using that layout.

Enabling the site and web publishing features, SharePoint creates a number of new site column instances. These site columns facilitate content management as suggested columns for typical content. However, content owners may create their own site columns, based on the site column types listed in Table 10-3 and in Chapter 9.

Content Types

Similar to how I covered site columns, I also covered content types in Chapter 9, so I shall not burden you with details about them, except to detail those content types available when activating the publishing features. Content types represent an entity in a SharePoint site collection or subsite and consist of a number of site columns. Content types are the schema of list items, where each contained field defines the columns of a list item row in a list or document library. In similar vein, page content types define the schema of a publishing page, where each field represents a content placeholder for a page instance, where each page instance is in fact a list item in a special document library—called Pages.

Having either activated the publishing features in your site collection or created a publishing site, follow these steps to access the publishing site content types:

1. Click the gear icon.

2. Select the Site settings menu item.

3. Click the link for site content types under the Web Designer Galleries heading.

4. Scroll down to Page Layout Content Types and Publishing Content Types (Figure 10-4).

Page Layout Content Types

Article Page	Page
Catalog-Item Reuse	Page
Enterprise Wiki Page	Page
Error Page	Page
Project Page	Enterprise Wiki Page
Redirect Page	Page
Welcome Page	Page

Publishing Content Types

ASP NET Master Page	System Master Page
Html Master Page	ASP NET Master Page
Html Page Layout	Page Layout
Page	System Page
Page Layout	System Page Layout

Figure 10-4. *Publishing and page layout content types*

The publishing content types include content types that represent base publishing objects, such as master pages, page layouts, and HTML page types. The page layout content types define specific page metadata types from which page instances are created. To illustrate these two sets of content types, I shall provide an example.

Imagine you have created a publishing site for a product company. The web site contains various page instances, each with details about a product that is part of the company's product line. On each product page, the company wishes to include a high-res image of the product, a brief description, and date the product went into production. One approach to representing products in the publishing site is to create a new content type, called Product, which inherits from the page content type because products display as pages. The page content type includes site columns for the image, production date, and description. You would then associate this product content type with the pages libraries in the publishing site to allow content owners to create page instances based on this new product content type. As you read further in this section, I shall explain how page layouts and master pages control the presentation of content by mapping content types. To continue my example, each page layout infers how SharePoint should render page content with HTML markup. Master pages define the general look and feel of the site, also including HTML markup, and define the common areas included on all pages in the site. Just like the page instances, page layouts and master pages also consist of properties, which SharePoint defines with the publishing content types.

If the page layout content types represent the metadata types for our page instances, why does SharePoint provide content types for the base publishing types? Master pages and page layouts live in the Master Page Gallery in your publishing site collection. The Master Page Gallery is a special document library that contains the master page and page layout files. Similar to other document libraries, and the documents contained in them, master pages and page layouts in the Master Page Gallery may have metadata associated with them. For example, the base page content type includes site columns to define start and end publishing date/time values for time-restricted content.

Master Pages

Typical modern day User Interface design of web sites calls for a consistent look and feel throughout all pages in the web site. Before SharePoint and WCM, creation and management of UI consistency across multiple pages was a painful experience—each page included the same cut and pasted markup for the design, and the only difference between one page and another was the main body content of each page. As the number of pages in the site grew, the tasks to maintain a consistent look and feel across them became increasingly more difficult. Then came the frightful day on which management requested a new UI design for the site; this involved editing every single page on the site and making the same design changes—a nontrivial task. Fortunately, ASP.NET 2.0, and SharePoint 2007 provided us with master pages.

Think of a master page as the skeleton of any page in a web site, containing HTML markup for common areas of all pages and placeholders for the areas that change from page to page. Common areas of a master page might include the page header and footer, top navigation, and left navigation, because these areas do not change (not much anyway) from one page instance to another. Using a master page, a site UI designer has to define the HTML and CSS markup for common page areas in only one place. Should the UI design change, then only the master page requires change.

To use a real-world example, a master page is like the framework of your house—the framework defines the structure of your house, where the rooms reside and the window and door locations, and includes fixed structure elements defined by the builder. The framework for every house in your neighborhood might be identical, but the interior decor, color, and style of doors and windows may differ with each property.

SharePoint 2013 includes several Master Page files, each serving a different purpose. SharePoint stores all Master Page files in the Master Page Gallery, a special document library that resides at the root of every site collection. Master Page files consist of HTML markup, with embedded ASP.NET controls, CSS styling, and placeholders for what will be actual content markup later—provided by page layouts (more on these in a moment). The main master page for user pages of a SharePoint site is the v5.master Master Page. All SharePoint master pages have the .master extension, and if you edit one, either by using SharePoint Designer or by downloading the file and opening it in Notepad, you will see familiar markup like that of a typical ASP.NET (ASPX) page.

By default, the out-of-the-box SharePoint 2013 Publishing Site uses two master pages (for most pages): v5.master and Application.master. The former defines the common elements for viewable publishing pages and the latter defines the common elements for administration pages. Typically, when designing a brand for a SharePoint publishing site, you would create a custom master page for publishing pages, with the v5.master file as a starting template.

■ **Note** It is generally not a good idea to edit the v5.master and other stock master pages directly—always make a copy with a different name and assign your site the new custom master page.

With the theory on master pages covered, I shall now walk you through the steps involved in customizing a publishing site, using a renamed copy of the v5.master page file.

To illustrate the common areas typically defined in a SharePoint master page, Figure 10-5 shows the header and left navigation areas in color and the page content—provided by a page layout—in black and white and blurred.

Figure 10-5. Master page colored elements

Page Layouts

Page layouts are template files, which map page instance content into HTML markup for rendered pages. ASP.NET 2.0 provided pages (ASPX files) and master pages (master files), and combined they rendered a complete HTML page, including content. SharePoint publishing, in addition to the same model as ASP.NET, abstracts the content from the ASPX page and stores this information as metadata in a pages library list item.

So, if the master page is the presentation of common page elements, and SharePoint abstracts page content data into list metadata columns, then what is the page layout? Simply put, a page layout is an ASPX file that lives in the Master Page Gallery and maps content column data to HTML markup.

Similar to how I illustrated master page elements in Figure 10-5, Figure 10-6 shows the page layout presentation areas in color and the common master page elements blurred out and in black and white.

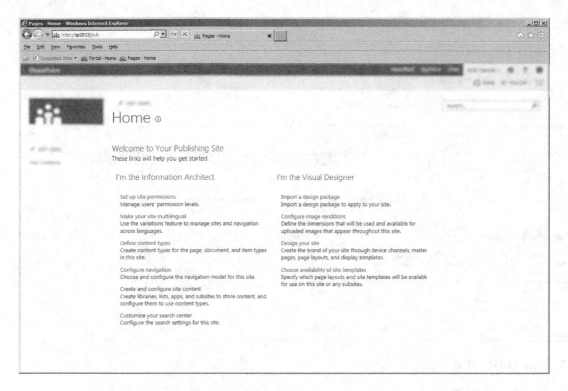

Figure 10-6. *Page layout colored elements*

Page layouts contain HTML markup, CSS, JavaScript, etc., similar to master pages, but in addition a SharePoint page layout associates with a publishing page content type and includes mapping of site columns in the markup. For example, a press release page might be represented with a content type, which consists of publication data, abstract text, header image, and main press release article text. To render press release pages in a SharePoint publishing site, you would create a page layout for all press releases and associate the press release content type with the page layout. The page layout will contain ASP.NET control references for each site column (field) in the associated content type that you wish to display as part of the rendered page.

Like master pages, page layouts reside in the Master Page Gallery at the root of the publishing site collection. Figure 10-7 shows some example HTML/ASP.NET markup from a page layout. Notice the presence of field value controls, which map specific site columns from the associated content type to the presentation within the page layout.

```
<asp:Content ContentPlaceholderID="PlaceHolderAdditionalPageHead" runat="server">
    <SharePointWebControls:UIVersionedContent UIVersion="3" runat="server">
        <ContentTemplate>
            <SharePointWebControls:CssRegistration name="<% $SPUrl:~sitecollection/Style Library/~language/Core Styles/pageLayouts.cs
            <PublishingWebControls:editmodepanel runat="server" id="editmodestyles">
                <!-- Styles for edit mode only-->
                <SharePointWebControls:CssRegistration name="<% $SPUrl:~sitecollection/Style Library/~language/Core Styles/zz2_editMo
            </PublishingWebControls:editmodepanel>
        </ContentTemplate>
    </SharePointWebControls:UIVersionedContent>
    <SharePointWebControls:UIVersionedContent UIVersion="4" runat="server">
        <ContentTemplate>
            <SharePointWebControls:CssRegistration name="<% $SPUrl:~sitecollection/Style Library/~language/Core Styles/page-layouts-2
            <PublishingWebControls:EditModePanel runat="server">
                <!-- Styles for edit mode only-->
                <SharePointWebControls:CssRegistration name="<% $SPUrl:~sitecollection/Style Library/~language/Core Styles/edit-mode-
                    After="<% $SPUrl:~sitecollection/Style Library/~language/Core Styles/page-layouts-21.css %>" runat="server"/>
            </PublishingWebControls:EditModePanel>
        </ContentTemplate>
    </SharePointWebControls:UIVersionedContent>
    <SharePointWebControls:CssRegistration name="<% $SPUrl:~sitecollection/Style Library/~language/Core Styles/rca.css %>" runat="ser
    <SharePointWebControls:FieldValue id="PageStylesField" FieldName="HeaderStyleDefinitions" runat="server"/>
</asp:Content>
<asp:Content ContentPlaceholderID="PlaceHolderPageTitle" runat="server">
    <SharePointWebControls:FieldValue id="PageTitle" FieldName="Title" runat="server"/>
</asp:Content>
<asp:Content ContentPlaceholderID="PlaceHolderPageTitleInTitleArea" runat="server">
    <SharePointWebControls:UIVersionedContent UIVersion="3" runat="server">
        <ContentTemplate>
            <SharePointWebControls:TextField runat="server" id="TitleField" FieldName="Title"/>
        </ContentTemplate>
    </SharePointWebControls:UIVersionedContent>
    <SharePointWebControls:UIVersionedContent UIVersion="4" runat="server">
        <ContentTemplate>
            <SharePointWebControls:FieldValue FieldName="Title" runat="server"/>
        </ContentTemplate>
```

***Figure 10-7.** Page layout markup*

Putting It All Together

Now that you have a general idea of how publishing content types, master pages, and page layouts work. I will demonstrate how they all work together. For the sake of my demonstration I shall use out-of-the-box content types, page layouts, and master pages.

In Chapter 16, I cover SharePoint Designer and branding. SharePoint Designer is a tool for editing page layouts within SharePoint sites. The alternative method of downloading page layouts, making edits, and uploading the file again is less palatable. Feel free to flip ahead and read Chapter 16 (I wrote this book with the intention that readers can choose chapters of interest) if you feel inclined to implement your own page layouts and master pages.

1. Open the SharePoint publishing site (created earlier in this chapter).

2. Click the gear icon.

3. Select the menu item to view all site content.

4. Click the Pages document library ellipses.

5. Navigate to the Pages document library settings.

6. Scroll to the section for content types.

Figure 10-8 shows the content types listed in my publishing site pages library, which tells me I can create Welcome Pages, Article Pages, Error Pages, and base Publishing Pages.

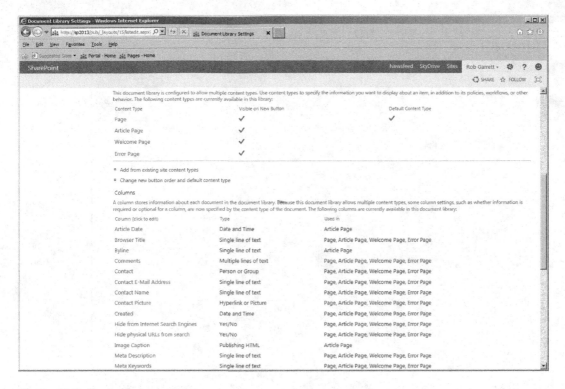

Figure 10-8. *Pages library settings*

■ **Note**   Error Pages are new to SharePoint 2013.

7.   Return to the Site contents page.

8.   Click the Pages document library to access the pages in the current site.

9.   You should see a page similar to that in Figure 10-9.

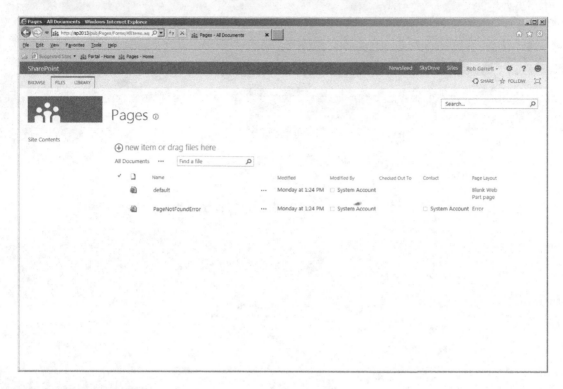

Figure 10-9. *Pages library*

As you can see by looking at Figure 10-9, the pages library is similar to any other document library, in that it contains a file and associated metadata—page instances. Each page instance is a list item with attached ASPX file. You might assume that the attached ASPX file is the page layout, but it is not. If you download the ASPX file and open the file in Notepad, the file contains references to the page layout in the Master Page Gallery and other publishing-related data.

10. Click the ellipses for the page instance.

11. From the settings popup ellipses, click the menu item to view properties.

12. Figure 10-10 shows a list of site columns and associated values.

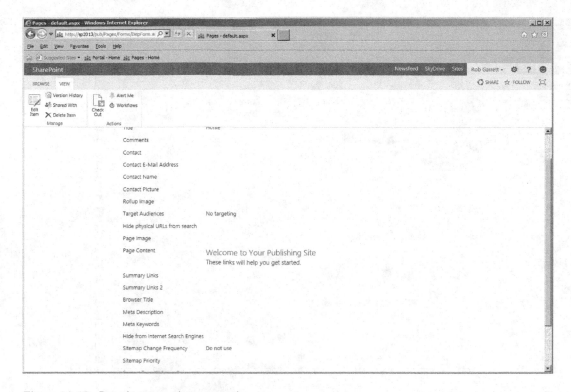

Figure 10-10. *Page instance view properties*

The page shown in Figure 10-10 is the "list view" of a publishing page. Just like any other list or document library, a content owner may edit the values (properties) for each column of the list item. Next, I shall show you how the property data renders on publishing pages, using a page layout.

13. Click the gear icon.

14. Select the menu item for creating a new page.

15. In the dialog that appears, give the page a name.

16. Click the OK button.

17. You should see a page like that in Figure 10-11.

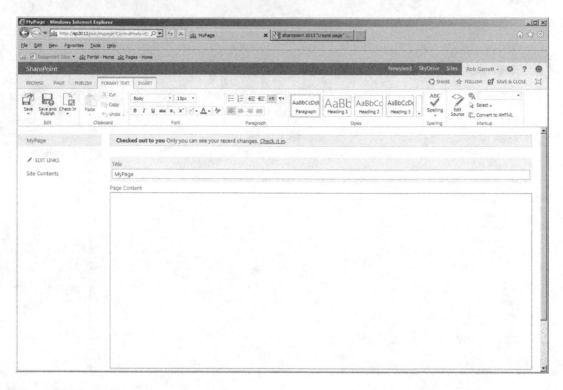

Figure 10-11. *New page instance created*

What just happened? In response to you requesting a new page, SharePoint created a new page instance in the Pages document library, using the default content type for the library and default page layout. You might be wondering how SharePoint decided which content type and page layout it chose. I shall enlighten you in the following steps:

18. Click the gear icon.

19. Select the Site settings menu item.

20. On the site settings page, click the link for page layouts and site templates.

21. Scroll to the section New Page Default Settings (Figure 10-12).

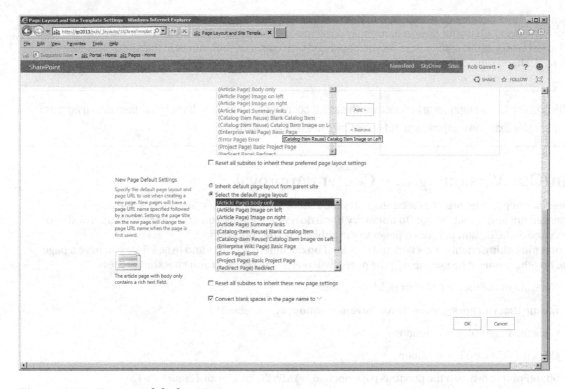

Figure 10-12. *New page default settings*

You remember from my description of page layouts, in an earlier section of this chapter, that page layouts associate with a content type; read Chapter 16 for details on creating new page layouts and associating them with content types. Page layouts must associate with a content type because they map the site columns of a content type to HTML markup.

As shown in Figure 10-12, SharePoint has provided a list of all available page layouts from the Master Page Gallery and their associated content types (in parentheses). You might have noticed that different page layouts associate with the same content type as others. Content owners create page instances using the content type, and the site designer can choose from a number of presentation formats, based on the chosen page layout. For example, the Article content type associates with the page layouts "Image on left" and "Image on right." The content owner does not care where the page image appears—this is the job of the site designer, and the reason for multiple layouts. The site designer can change the page layout of any given page as long as the content type of the page associates with the chosen page layout.

Getting back to the example, you created a new page instance, which defaulted to the Article content type and Body only page layout. I will show you how to change these for the page you just created if you did not want this content type or page layout.

22. Navigate back to the page view of the page you just created (Figure 10-11).

23. If you are not already in edit mode, click the gear icon and select the edit page menu item.

24. Click the Page tab on the ribbon.

25. Click the page layout icon, and SharePoint shows you a list of available of page layouts, grouped by content type.

26. Choose one by clicking on it (I chose one with a different content type).

27. SharePoint now shows you the page in the new layout.

What is nice about changing page layouts is that SharePoint will also change the associated content type of the page instance. The new effect is that your page instance may now have additional site columns and may have lost some you had before. Do not worry about content loss—if you populated with data a site column field that is not present in the new content type, SharePoint will retain the data, should you decide to switch back the content type and page layout.

■ **Note**   The process for creating page instances with default content type and page layout, and then changing page layout later, is simpler than the method required by SharePoint 2007 and 2010.

Check In/Out, Versioning, and Content Approval

If you followed the steps in the previous sections, you should have a publishing site and a new page instance—currently checked out and unpublished. Do not worry if you do not; I will walk you through content approval and versioning via one of the default published pages in the publishing site collection.

SharePoint publishing enables check-in and checkout on document libraries and lists. While you have a page checked out, no other content owner can edit the page. I will review the check-in and checkout process.

1.   Navigate to the root site of your publishing site.

2.   Ensure that you are signed in, if you have anonymous access enabled.

3.   Click the Page tab in the ribbon.

4.   Click the edit icon in the ribbon.

5.   SharePoint shows you the previous page open in WYSIWYG edit mode (Figure 10-13).

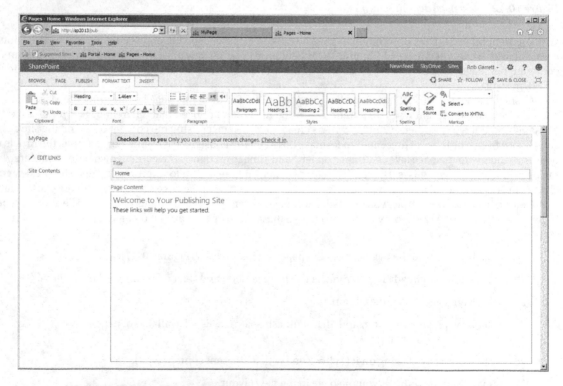

Figure 10-13. Publishing page edit mode

6. Make an edit to the page, such as adding content to one of the page areas.

7. Click the Page tab on the ribbon.

8. Click the save icon to save your changes.

9. SharePoint shows you the rendered page, but with a yellow banner, indicating you have the page checked out.

10. Either click the check-in link on the yellow bar or,

11. Click the Page tab in the ribbon.

12. Click the Check-in button.

13. Provide a comment in the dialog and then click the Continue button.

14. The page is now checked in.

Versioning

By default, document libraries in publishing sites have major and minor versioning enabled. SharePoint includes three options for tracking the versions of documents and list items in document libraries and lists, as follows:

- No versioning

- Major only

- Major and minor

No versioning is self-explanatory. Major version only tells SharePoint to keep a running count of integer value for the version number—each time you change and check in a document or list item, SharePoint increments the version number by one. Major and minor version works a little differently: this type of versioning consists of a numbering scheme as X.Y, where X is the major version number and Y is the minor version number. With each check-in, SharePoint increments the minor version number. Major version number increments have significance over minor version number increments in that major versions represent published content and minor versions represent draft-unpublished content.

Before I delve into an example of versioning, this is how to change the versioning method for any document library or list.

1. Navigate to a document library or list.

2. Click the Library or List tab in the ribbon.

3. Click the icon for Library or List settings.

4. Click the link for Versioning Settings.

5. Figure 10-14 shows a screenshot of the versioning settings.

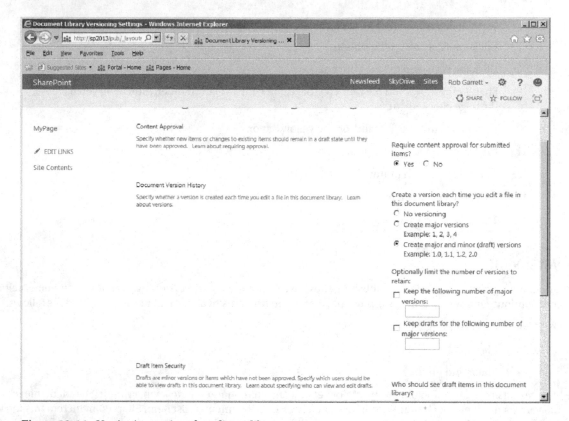

Figure 10-14. Versioning settings for a list or library

6. Ensure that major and minor versions are enabled.

7. For now, turn off content approval.

■ **Note**   Notice in Figure 10-14 there is the option to toggle content approval, which I shall demonstrate shortly.

If you followed all the steps in this section of the chapter, you should have checked out the default page, made a content change, and then checked in the file again. Since you have major and minor versions enabled (by default), SharePoint has incremented the version of the page from 1.0 to 1.1. Complete the following steps to view the version history of the site home page:

8. Navigate to the site home page (navigate to the site with no page specified).

9. Click the Page tab on the ribbon.

10. Click the icon for Page History.

11. SharePoint displays a page like that in Figure 10-15.

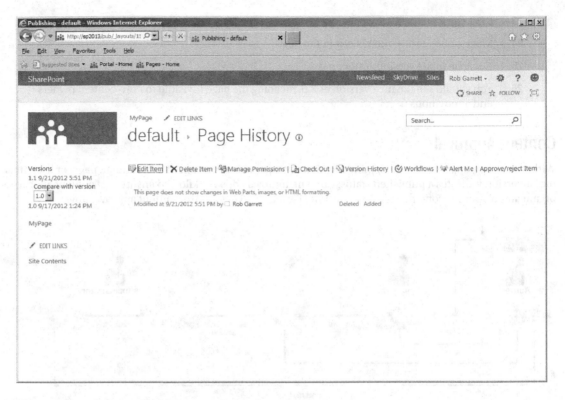

Figure 10-15. *Page version history*

12. Depending on what you changed in the page, the version history page shows the content changes from each version (not Web Part change).

Since you are currently using major and minor versions and you last checked in the page as a minor version, the status of the page is unpublished. The following steps demonstrate how to publish the page to the next major version number—anonymous users and non-content owners see changes once you publish the page.

13. Navigate back to the page.

14. Click the Publish tab in the ribbon.

15. Click the Publish icon.

16. Navigate back to the version history page.

17. You should see that the version now shows version 2.0.

What happens if you use major versioning only? You shall find out in the following steps:

18. Navigate to the list/library settings page.

19. Click the link for Versioning Settings.

20. Change versioning to Major Only.

21. Return to the content page.

22. Click the Page tab.

23.   Click the icon to edit the page.

24.   Make a change and then check in the page.

25.   Navigate to the version history page.

26.   You should see the next version as 3.0, meaning the page is visible to non–content owners and anonymous users.

Content Approval

Without content approval enabled, minor version indicates a draft version of a document, page, or list item, and major version indicates a published status. Content approval adds workflow to ensure that content approvers in the organization approve content before publication. Figure 10-16 depicts the content approval flow.

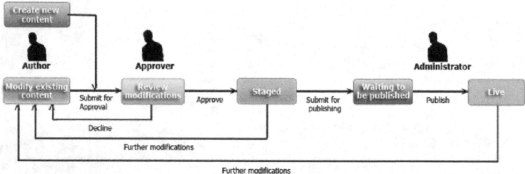

Figure 10-16. *Content approval process*

The flow in Figure 10-16 is straightforward and includes three actors: the Author, Approver, and Administrator. You are probably already familiar with the author and administrator roles by now. I have not previously mentioned approvers—these are users with a specific set of permissions to approve content in the content approval workflow. SharePoint classifies a user as a content approver by the assignment of approval permissions or by membership in the site approvers group. The approvers group is a default SharePoint group with approval permissions assigned.

When you created the publishing site, earlier in this chapter, SharePoint had already created the approvers group and assigned the group approval permissions. Out of the box, publishing content approval workflow uses the approvers group to determine which users may approve a document. I will now return to the example and demonstrate content approval in action.

1.   Navigate to the home page of your publishing site.

2.   Click the Library tab in the ribbon.

3.   Click the icon for Library Settings.

4.   Click the link for Versioning Settings.

5.   Enable content approval for the Pages document library.

6.   Make sure to enable major/minor versioning.

7.   Return to the home page.

8.   Click the Page tab in the ribbon.

9.   Click the edit icon in the ribbon and make an edit to the page.

10. Check in the page.

11. Click the Publish tab in the ribbon.

12. You should see an icon to submit the changes for approval; click it.

13. Log in as a user with approval permissions (site owner, administrator, member of the approvers group).

14. Click the Publish tab in the ribbon.

15. You should see options to approve or reject changes.

16. Click the Approve icon to approve the content and complete the publish step.

Content approval requires major and minor versioning enabled to work correctly. If you enable major versioning only, then pages, documents, or list items are either checked out for edit or published—there is no concept of checked in and draft.

■ **Note** The content approval process, illustrated in Figure 10-16, requires both content approval and major/minor versioning enabled.

Sometimes the content owner has approval rights—perhaps he or she is an administrator or the site owner—in which case he or she can skip the step to submit changes for approval and jump directly to published by clicking the Approve button in the Publish tab of the ribbon.

New in SharePoint 2013

Microsoft dazzled us with the introduction of publishing features in SharePoint 2007—organizations could now use SharePoint to host their public web sites, brand them, and manage content with WCM. SharePoint 2010 added robustness with better content deployment, richer UI (with AJAX), and managed metadata integration (tagging) and continued to offer the same functionality we grew to appreciate in the 2007 publishing offering. SharePoint 2013 continues to provide enhancements to the WCM and publishing features of SharePoint.

Content Authoring Improvements

SharePoint 2013 provides a better experience for content authors. The emphasis is on facilitating content upload and editing with greater ease. For example, content owners may cut and copy text from Microsoft Word, and SharePoint ensures that the content respects the style and markup, as intended by the site designer. This capability may seem trivial to techie types, but it is a big deal for content owners because they can lift content directly from company documents and host the same information on the organization's web site, without including irregular HTML formatting, which Word likes to include for preserving formatting.

Inclusion of video and media is now much simpler, with the help of Silverlight rendering and video content types for management of metadata. Furthermore, SharePoint will create thumbnail images for any uploaded video, which was often a task left to the marketing team or some third-party/custom component.

■ **Note** Video thumbnail creation requires Desktop Experience installed on the server—see http://technet.microsoft.com/en-us/library/cc772567.aspx.

Content owners can now insert IFRAME content into HTML fields to allow rich content from other existing web sites. SharePoint allows control of the sites sourced from IFRAME via the HTML Field Security option under Site Collection Administration in site settings.

Figure 10-17 shows a screenshot for default HTML Field Security, which includes references from a collection of well-known media sites.

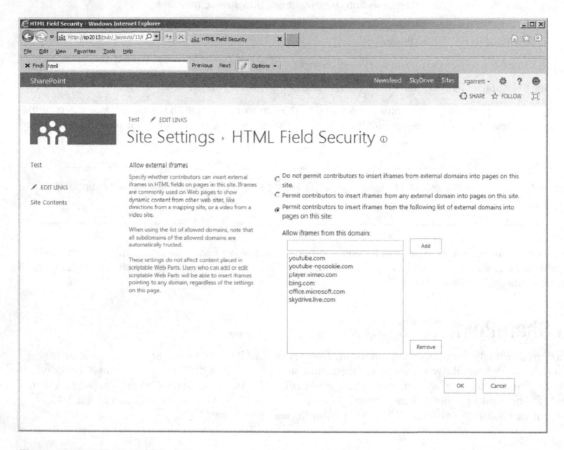

Figure 10-17. *HTML Field Security*

Image Rendition

Image Rendition controls the rendering of images, across a site collection, in different sizes. Previously, content owners had to upload different versions of image files—full size, low bandwidth sizes, thumbnails, etc.—for different views of a single image. SharePoint 2013 now provides content owners control over rendition of a single image file in different sizes.

Image Rendition is extremely important for minimizing space on the server and the amount of data downloaded to the client browser. For example, a content owner might upload several high-resolution images for display on a web site but want to provide a page of thumbnails for user selection. In previous versions of SharePoint, content owners accomplished this in one of three ways:

1. Upload the high-res images and thumbnail versions.

2. Upload the high-res image only and scale the image at the client.

3. Integrate third-party software to dynamically resize the high-res image.

Of the options above, the optimal solution is option three. Storing alternate versions (option one) quickly becomes unmanageable when images require multiple different size versions and content owners need to update a particular image. Option one is not especially optimal for storage space—it is fine for small numbers of images but quickly eats storage space as the number of images in the site grows. Option two is simply bad practice! Scaling images at the client requires the browser to download the full-size image and then reduce the size. Rendering a page of thumbnails with client scaling increases the payload of the page data downloaded.

Image Rendition is effectively option three, provided by SharePoint 2013.

■ **Note** Image Rendition requires configuration of Blob Cache.

Image Rendition requires configuration of Blob Cache. Blob Cache is a disk cache for storing rendered versions of images. With Blob Cache, the server does not have the overhead of converting images (often an expensive operation) when the image rendition is requested multiple times by client browsers. The following steps demonstrate configuring Blob Cache:

1. Ensure that you are a member of the administrators group on each SharePoint web-front-end server.

2. Open Internet Information Services (IIS) Management Console (see Figure 10-18).

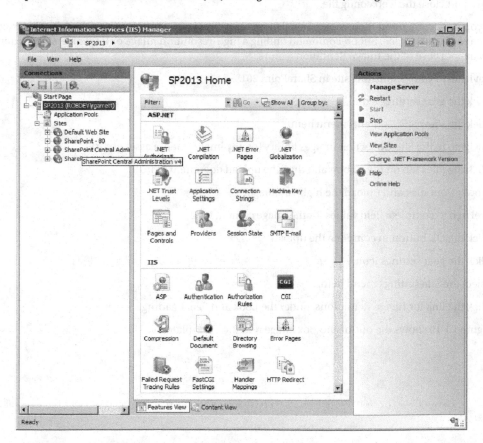

Figure 10-18. *Internet Information Server Management Console*

3. Expand the Local Server and Sites node in the left panel.

4. Right-click the web application to configure Blob Caching.

5. Click Explore from the menu to open the location of the web application on disk.

6. Edit the web.config file.

7. Look for the following line in the web.config file:

```
<BlobCache location="" path="\.(gif|jpg|jpeg|jpe|jfif|bmp|dib|tif|tiff|ico|png|
wdp|hdp|css|js|asf|avi|flv|m4v|mov|mp3|mp4|mpeg|mpg|rm|rmvb|wma|wmv)$" maxSize="10"
enabled="false" />
```

8. Provide a full path to a folder on disk, in the location attribute.

■ **Note** I recommend a Blob Cache location that is on a separate drive from system swap files.

---

9. Toggle the enabled attribute to True.

10. Save and close the web.config file.

Now that you have configured Blob Cache, I shall illustrate using image renditions. For the following exercise, you may use any image of your choice, but I recommend finding a high-resolution image or large size, since scaling these sized images is the purpose of the Image Rendition feature.

1. Navigate to your publishing site in SharePoint 2013.

2. Click the gear settings icon.

3. Click the View Site Contents menu item.

4. Navigate to the Site Collection Images library (or any image/media asset library).

5. Click the Files tab on the ribbon and then the upload document icon.

6. Browse your disk and upload the high-res image.

7. Feel free to complete field values for the image content type.

8. Click the OK button to complete the upload.

9. Click the gear settings icon.

10. Select the Site settings menu item.

11. Click the link for Image Renditions, under the Look and Feel heading.

12. Figure 10-19 shows the out-of-the-box image rendition templates.

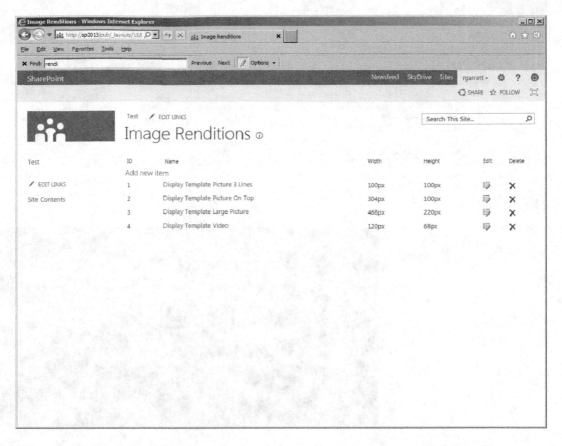

Figure 10-19. *Image Renditions*

13. Create the link to add a new item.

14. Give the new rendition a name, width, and height for image.

15. I created a rendition of 200 x 200px.

16. Navigate to a publishing page.

17. Edit the page and insert an image from the ribbon.

18. Click the ribbon icon to pick a rendition (Figure 10-20).

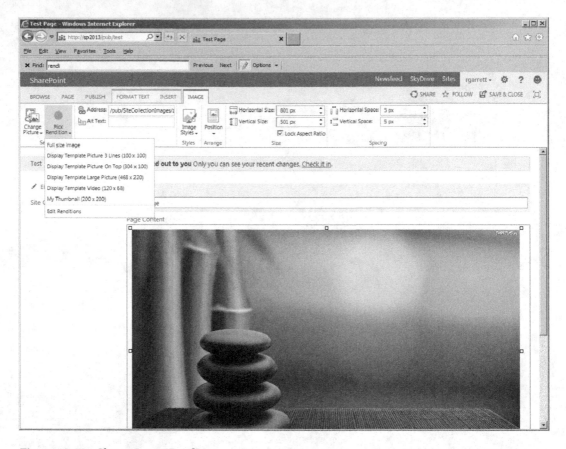

Figure 10-20. *Choose Image Rendition*

19. After choosing my rendition I see a newly rendered image of 200 x 200px.

■ **Note** To maintain aspect ratios, you may create image rendition templates with either width or height only.

SharePoint provides dynamic image renditions by providing a rendition ID in the URL of a SharePoint image. Using the image rendition in the previous steps, right-click the image when in page browse mode and check out the URL of the image. SharePoint will render any image in any rendition by providing the rendition ID parameter, as follows:

`http://sp2013/pub/SiteCollectionImages/zen.jpg?RenditionID=5`

To determine the ID of a specific rendition, follow these steps.

1. Click the gear icon.

2. Select Site settings from the menu.

3. Click the link for Image Renditions, under the Look and Feel heading.

4. The item ID in the list (Figure 10-19) is the rendition ID.

Cross-Site Publishing and Catalog Enabled Lists and Libraries

Cross-site publishing is a new feature in SharePoint 2013 that enables content owners to create content in one site collection and publish the same content in another site collection. If a content owner updates the content in the source collection then the update shows in the dependent collections. Cross-site publishing requires catalog enabled lists and libraries, as well as search configuration to work.

Figure 10-21 shows the infrastructure for cross-site publishing. Lists and libraries within the source site collection must enable cross-site publication and a search must crawl over these lists and libraries before the content is available in destination site collections.

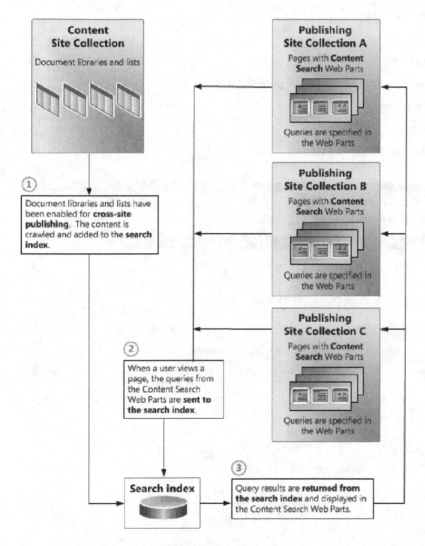

Figure 10-21. *Cross-site publishing infrastructure*

Destination site collections use cross-site published content via Content Search Web Parts. These Content Search Web Parts use the search index to retrieve the content from the source collection.

Catalog Enable List/Library

I shall now demonstrate this configuration, as follows:

1. Navigate to your publishing site collection.

2. Click the gear icon.

3. Select Site settings from the menu.

4. Click the link to access the site collection features, under Site Collection Administration.

5. Enable the Cross-Site Publishing feature.

6. Click the gear icon.

7. Click the link to view site contents.

8. Choose a list or library to catalog content for cross-site publishing.

9. View the list or library settings page.

10. Click the Catalog settings link.

11. SharePoint shows a page like that in Figure 10-22.

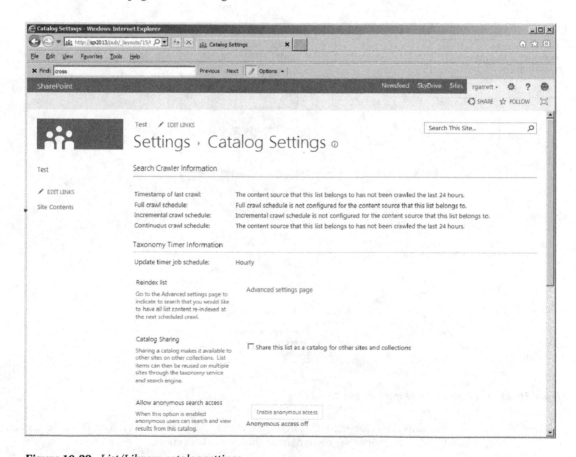

Figure 10-22. List/Library catalog settings

12. Check the check box under the Catalog Sharing section—this enables the list as a catalog.

13. If the content of this list/library is to show on anonymous-accessible pages, click the button to enable anonymous access.

14. Choose fields that represent the primary key for items (I used ID and Title).

15. If you wish to allow catalog navigation, select the tagging field from your list to bind to a term set.

16. Click the OK button.

Configure Search

In the previous subsections, I demonstrated how to enable cross-site publishing and how to enable cataloging in a list/library. Feel free to catalog several lists and libraries before completing the following steps to configure search crawling of these libraries.

■ **Note**   See Chapter 15 for more in-depth details on search configuration. The steps in this section assume that you have a provisioned Search Service Application—if not, use the farm wizard to create one for the purpose of this exercise.

---

1. Open Central Administration.

2. Click the General Application Settings header.

3. Click the Farm Search Administration link.

4. Choose a Search Service Application from the list.

5. Click the Content Sources link in the left navigation.

6. Edit the Local SharePoint Sites content source.

7. Ensure that this source includes the site collection (or root site collection if under a managed path) for your publishing site.

8. Return to the content sources page.

9. Start a full crawl of the content source.

10. Click the link for the Crawl log.

11. Monitor for errors and ensure that the crawler indexes content from your publishing site collection.

Using the Content Search Web Part

All being well, you have designated one or several lists/libraries as catalog enabled, and run a successful full search crawl over these lists. It is now time to demonstrate exposing the cross-published content in other site collections using the Content Search Web Part.

1. Navigate to a different site collection in your farm. For simplicity I created another site collection under a managed path of the same web application.

2. Navigate to a page on your site where you wish to include cross-published content.

3. Edit the page, and insert a Web Part from the ribbon.

4. Choose the Content Search Web Part, under Content Rollup (Figure 10-23).

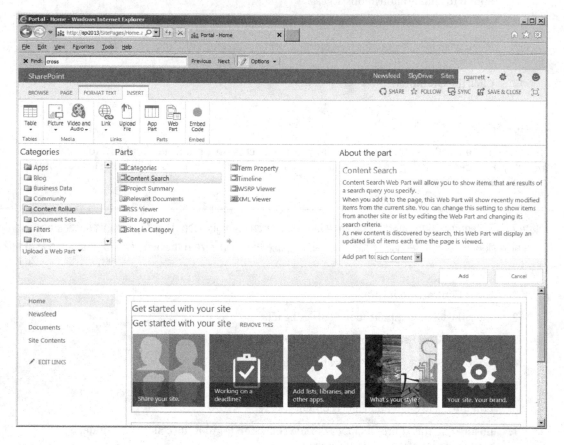

Figure 10-23. *Inserting a Content Search Web Part*

5. Edit the Web Part properties.

6. Click the Change Query button to edit the search query (using a query builder) and set result sources to refine the content shown in the Web Part.

■ **Note** See Chapter 15 for more information on query builder and result sources.

---

7. Choose a desired list template. If you want to see all available content exposed by the search results, select the diagnostic template.

8. You may change the presentation of search results by creating custom search templates from within site settings.

Managed Navigation

SharePoint 2013 now offers much-awaited custom navigation of sites via the Managed Metadata Term Store. I covered use of the Managed Metadata Service (MMS) in Chapter 9. SharePoint 2010 introduced managed metadata for tagging purposes, with hierarchical terms. This same hierarchical infrastructure bodes well for site navigation, which is also hierarchical. I often hear the word "taxonomy," pertaining to both tagging taxonomy and site structure, which just speaks to the fact that the Managed Metadata Term Store is great for managing custom navigation.

Prior to SharePoint 2013, custom navigation typically involved some custom component, to read navigation structure from a list, XML file, or some other hierarchical node store. The out-of-the-box offering provided very little in the way of custom navigation—just the ability to include headers and links at each site level. The main issue with the out-of-the-box offering is that it was limited in the number of nested navigation nodes, without adhering to the actual structure of sites and subsites in the collection. Despite typical site navigation following site structure, content owners should have the ability to store their content (sites and pages) in any structure and have the navigation look completely different. Content storage and structure suits how content owners maintain content, and navigation is about how end users access content, and the two may look very different. Managed metadata navigation finally allows content owners to create a navigation structure independent of that of their content model.

To demonstrate managed navigation, I shall first create a hierarchy in the default term store for our application:

1. Open Central Administration.

2. Click the link for manage service applications.

3. Scroll down the list and click Managed Metadata Service.

4. Click the Manage icon in the ribbon to open the term store editor (Figure 10-24).

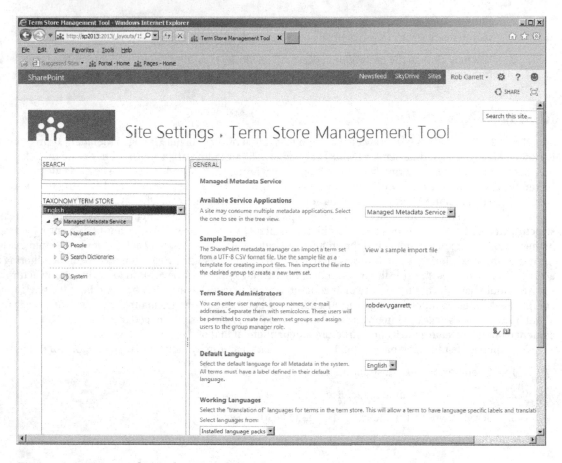

Figure 10-24. *Managed Metadata Term Store editor*

5. Ensure that you have permissions to edit the term store—add your username to the term store administrators field.

6. Managed navigation binds to term sets, so I created a new group for navigation and then a term set for site navigation.

■ **Note**   SharePoint creates a default term set in the Managed Metadata Term Store for your site collection; I created my own for demonstration purposes.

Figure 10-25 shows a sample managed navigation term set, which I defined for demonstrating custom managed navigation in my publishing site. Before you proceed to configuring your publishing site to use this structure, I must point out the steps to ensure that term sets behave as navigation nodes.

Figure 10-25. Sample managed navigation term set

1.   Create a term set structure, similar to that in Figure 10-25.

2.   Click the Site Navigation term set.

3.   In the right panel, click the Intended Use tab.

4.   Check the check box to enable the term set for navigation—you can also use the term set for tagging if you wish by toggling the other check box option.

5.   Click the Save button to save the changes.

6.   Click the tab for term driven pages—this page shows the settings for friendly URLs for the term set (more on friendly URLs shortly).

7.   Now you are ready to configure your publishing site to use the managed navigation.

8.   Open your publishing site (assuming the hosting web application uses the Managed Metadata Service you just configured).

9.   Click the gear icon, then select the menu item for site settings.

10. Click the link for Navigation, under the Look and Feel header.

11. SharePoint displays the navigation settings page like that in Figure 10-26.

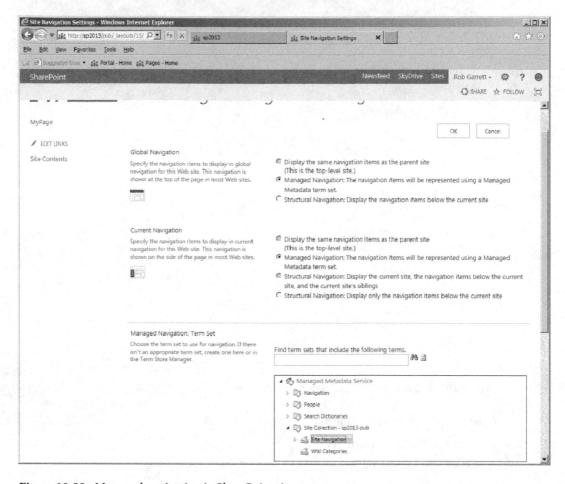

Figure 10-26. *Managed navigation in SharePoint site*

12. Choose the radio button option for Managed Navigation for either or both the left and global (top) navigation.

13. Scroll to the bottom of the page to the Managed Navigation Term Set section.

14. Select the term set to use for managed navigation.

15. The check boxes below the term set browser tell SharePoint whether to populate your term set with nodes when you create new pages in the site and whether to generate friendly URLs for new pages.

16. Click the OK button at the bottom of the page to save your changes.

Figure 10-27 shows the managed navigation nodes in the working site. If you compare the left navigation with the global (top) navigation, you should see that they show the same structure, except the global navigation renders navigation pop-out menus for levels greater than the two deep of the current node. This is typical behavior: left navigation usually shows two levels below the current site node and global navigation all, depending on the site design.

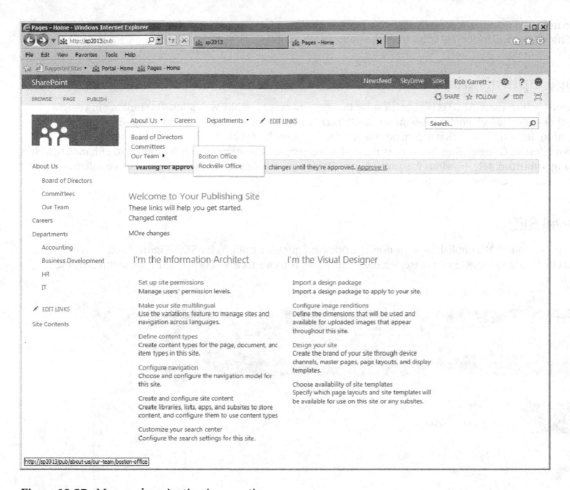

Figure 10-27. *Managed navigation in operation*

Friendly URLs

Try clicking one of the navigation nodes in the managed navigation structure you just created in the last section. You might see an unexpected Page Not Found error page. Firstly, the page is a nice 404-error page and rendered via the PageNotFoundError.aspx page in the pages library at the root of the site collection. Why could SharePoint not find the page? In my case, I created a managed navigation structure but did not back the structure with real content.

Notice that the URLs for the managed navigation nodes point to friendly URLs. You should understand friendly URLs as virtual URLs that do not point to a specific location. Instead, SharePoint maps these friendly virtual URLs to real pages. Friendly URLs are part of the managed navigation capabilities of SharePoint 2013.

1. Navigate to the Managed Metadata Term Store editor.

2. Find one of your navigation terms in the hierarchy and click it.

3. Click the Term Driven Pages tab in the right pane.

4. Scroll to the target page settings section.

5. Assign the actual URL for the friendly URL in the Managed Navigation node.

You do not need to map the friendly URL to a real page location for every node in the managed navigation structure. SharePoint will imfer real URLs from the parent node settings.

SEO Page Optimization

Search engine optimization (SEO) is big business for business owners of public web sites. Top ranking in Google, Bing, and other major search engines can mean the difference between thriving business and business going to the competition. It is no wonder that organizations want to improve their visibility on search engine results for popular search terms. Google, Bing, and others publish search engine optimization configuration to enhance search result ranking. Unfortunately, previous versions of SharePoint were a little thin in offering good SEO configuration capabilities—that has changed with SharePoint 2013.

Page-Level SEO

All pages in SharePoint 2013 publishing sites now include configuration options for SEO. Figure 10-28 shows a typical SEO configuration page, in this case, for my home page. You can access SEO optimization settings by the following steps:

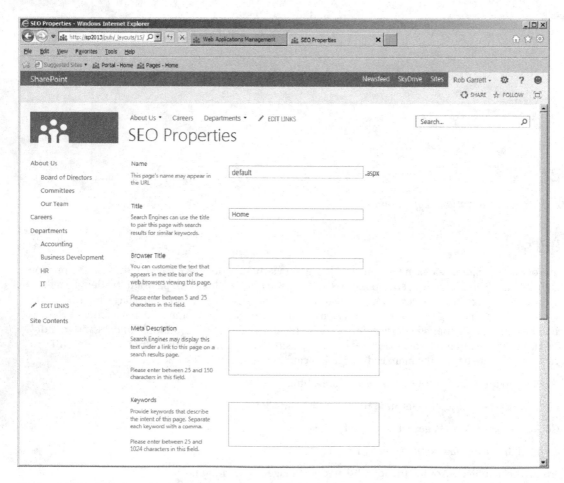

Figure 10-28. *Search engine optimizations for a publishing page*

1. Navigate to a publishing page.

2. Click the Page tab in the ribbon.

3. Click the down arrow at the bottom of the edit properties icon.

4. Select the menu item to edit SEO properties.

The SEO properties, shown in Figure 10-28, exist as site columns for pages derived from the publishing page content type. This means you can query SEO property values in code, use them as refiners in search, and query as part of cross-site query.

Table 10-4 lists the various properties for SEO optimization.

Table 10-4. *SEO Settings for Publishing Pages*

SEO Property	Description
Title	Page title and in navigation
Browser Title	Title shown in the browser title bar and also used in search engine search results
Meta Description	Description sometimes shown in search engine search results
Keywords	Keywords to categorize the page contents, rarely used by search engines
Sitemap Priority	Priority when generating a sitemap XML—special jump links in search results
Sitemap Change Frequency	Frequency with which the XML sitemap changes
Exclude from Internet Search Engines	Renders a NOINDEX field in the robots.txt file for the page

Site Collection SEO

Of course, editing SEO properties for every page on the site is somewhat tedious. Fortunately, SharePoint allows content owners to modify SEO properties at the site collection level, as follows:

1. Navigate to the root of the site collection.

2. Click the gear icon.

3. Click the menu item for the site settings page.

4. Click the link for Search Engine Optimization Settings, under Site Collection Administration header.

5. SharePoint shows a page like that in Figure 10-29.

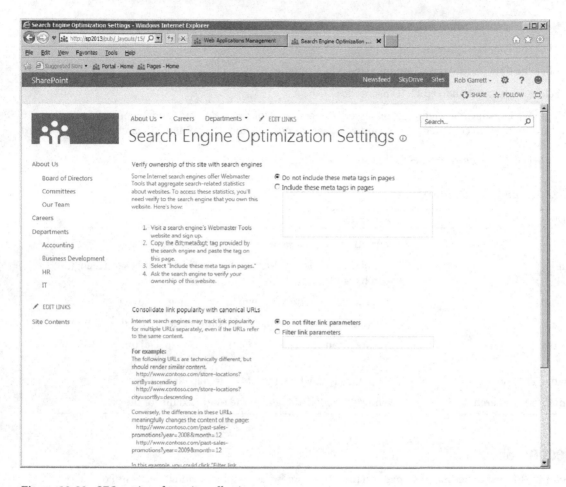

Figure 10-29. SEO settings for a site collection

XML Site Map

Have you ever seen search results from Google or Bing that include a series of jump links, like that in Figure 10-30? Search engines determine these useful jump links from sitemap XML. SharePoint 2010 had very little support for sitemap XML for SEO. SharePoint 2013 provides greater support, with the addition of a site collection feature.

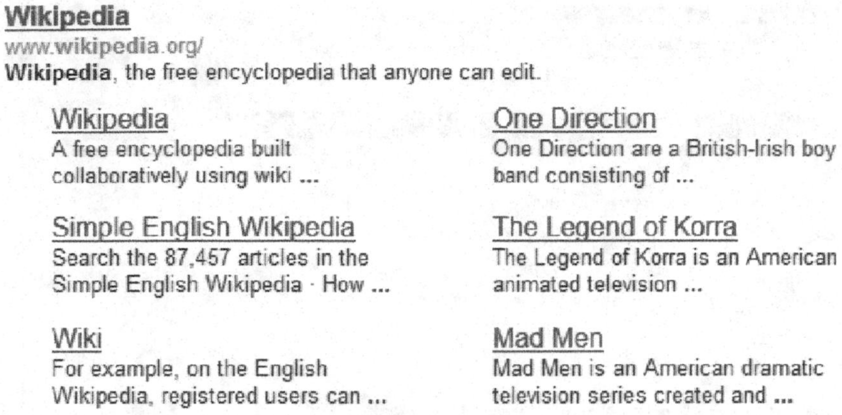

Wikipedia
www.wikipedia.org/
Wikipedia, the free encyclopedia that anyone can edit.

Wikipedia
A free encyclopedia built
collaboratively using wiki ...

One Direction
One Direction are a British-Irish boy
band consisting of ...

Simple English Wikipedia
Search the 87,457 articles in the
Simple English Wikipedia · How ...

The Legend of Korra
The Legend of Korra is an American
animated television ...

Wiki
For example, on the English
Wikipedia, registered users can ...

Mad Men
Mad Men is an American dramatic
television series created and ...

Figure 10-30. *Search engine search results with jump links*

1. Navigate to the root of your publishing site collection.

2. Click the gear icon.

3. Select the menu item for site settings.

4. Click the link for site collection features, under Site Collection Administration header.

5. Scroll down the page and activate the Search Engine Sitemap feature.

After activating the feature in the preceding steps, SharePoint adds a link into the robots.txt file to the sitemap XML file. SharePoint generates the sitemap XML from the site structure file using a timer job.

■ **Note**   You must enable anonymous access on your site collection to use the search engine sitemap.

Site Design Manager

SharePoint 2013 introduces the Design Manager (DM) to assist site designers in branding publishing sites. The Design Manager incorporates uploading and application of design packages, editing of page layouts and master pages, and managing device channels—specific rendering for different devices. In this section, I shall provide just an overview of the Design Manager capabilities and leave the specifics to Chapter 16.

1. Open your publishing site.

2. Click the gear icon.

3. Select the Design Manager menu item.

4. SharePoint displays the Design Manager welcome page (Figure 10-31).

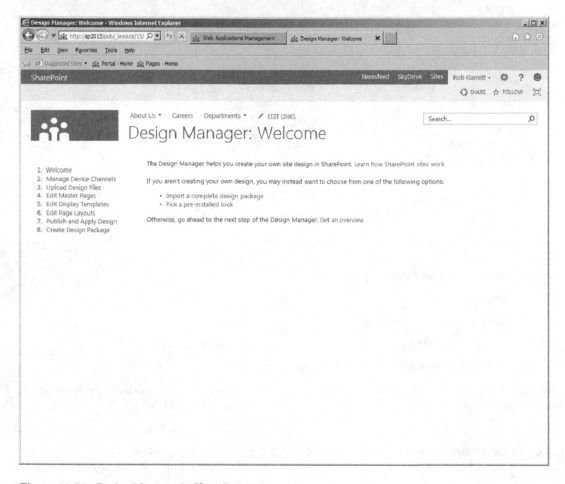

Figure 10-31. *Design Manager in SharePoint 2013*

From the DM home page, you should see two links: one to import a design package and another to pick a predefined look. Both of these options essentially deal with themes. Changing the look with a predefined look is pretty much like changing themes in Windows—SharePoint will provide you a series of themes to choose, and then you can try out the look on your site before committing to it.

Device Channels

Device channels allow SharePoint to render different content design for different devices. Each device channel uses criteria in the user agent string as part of every HTTP web request to SharePoint.

Imagine you can define different content based on the functionality of the device accessing SharePoint. For example, Apple iPad will not render Flash content. Using device channels, you can define a channel for Apple devices where SharePoint renders different content in place of any Flash content.

Defining a device channel is as easy as following these steps.

1. Open your publishing site.

2. Click the gear icon.

3. Select the Design Manager menu item.

4. Click the left navigation link to manage device channels.

5. On the next page, click the link to create a device channel.

6. Provide name, description, alias, etc.

7. Provide substrings of a user agent string to identify the device.

8. Click the Save button.

Leveraging device channels in publishing pages requires the mobile browsing support feature activated. The publishing features in SharePoint enable mobile support automatically.

SharePoint associates different master pages with different device channels. After you have created a device channel, follow these steps to associate a master page with the channel.

1. Open your publishing site.

2. Click the gear icon.

3. Select the Design Manager menu item.

4. Click the link for Master Page under the Look and Feel heading.

5. Select the device channel and associated master page.

6. Click the OK button to save your changes.

Upload Design Files

Clicking the link to upload design files from the Design Manager provides you with a page to configure a mapped drive to the Master Page Gallery. SharePoint has essentially exposed the Master Page Gallery via WEBDAV. Mapping a drive to the Master Page Gallery makes life easier for designers looking to upload files, without needing the SharePoint UI or SharePoint Designer.

1. Open your publishing site.

2. Click the gear icon.

3. Select the Design Manager menu item.

4. Click the link to upload design files.

5. SharePoint shows a page like that in Figure 10-32.

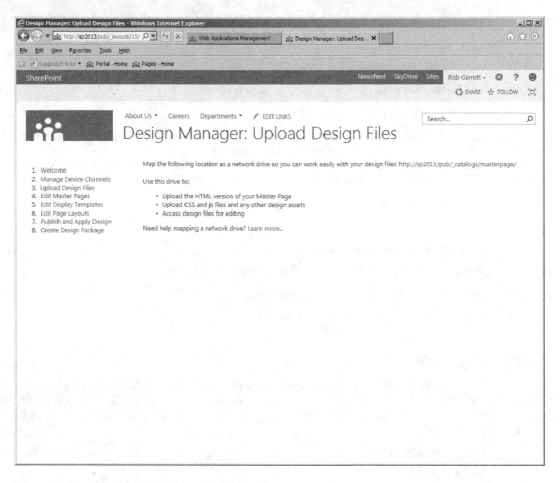

Figure 10-32. *Upload design files in the Design Manager*

6. Copy the location specified in the top left of the page.

7. Open file explorer on your Windows client.

8. Find and click the option to map a network drive.

9. In the dialog that appears (Figure 10-33), choose a drive letter.

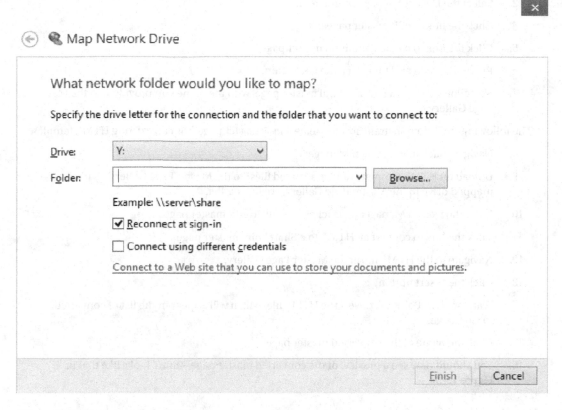

Figure 10-33. *Map a network drive*

10. Paste the WEBDAV location, specified in the Design Manager (Figure 10-32).

11. Click the Finish button.

12. You can now upload files to the Master Page Gallery using the new mapped drive letter.

■ **Note** You must enable the Desktop Experience feature in Windows Server if you wish to use WEBDAV on the server.

Edit Master Pages

SharePoint 2013 now makes the task of creating new master pages and uploading custom branding for master pages easier. The Design Manager contains capability to convert HTML into master pages for your site and to create new starter master pages, without the need for SharePoint Designer.

1. Open your publishing site.

2. Click the gear icon.

3. Select the Design Manager menu item.

4. Click the link to edit master pages.

5. Click the link to create a minimal master page.

6. Provide a name and then click the OK button.

7. SharePoint creates a new minimal master page, with the name you provided, in the Master Page Gallery.

The following steps demonstrate how to create a new master page from an existing HTML template:

8. Navigate back to the Design Manager.

9. Upload an HTML template (and associated files) to the Master Page Gallery—I used a mapped drive to the Master Page Gallery, created earlier.

10. From the Design Manager page, click the link to edit master pages.

11. Click the link to convert an HTML to a SharePoint master page.

12. Navigate to the HTML file in the Master Page Gallery.

13. Click the Insert button.

14. Wait for SharePoint to convert the HTML file, which will appear in the list of converted master pages.

15. Click the name of the converted master page.

16. You should now see a preview of the converted master page—mine looks like that in Figure 10-34.

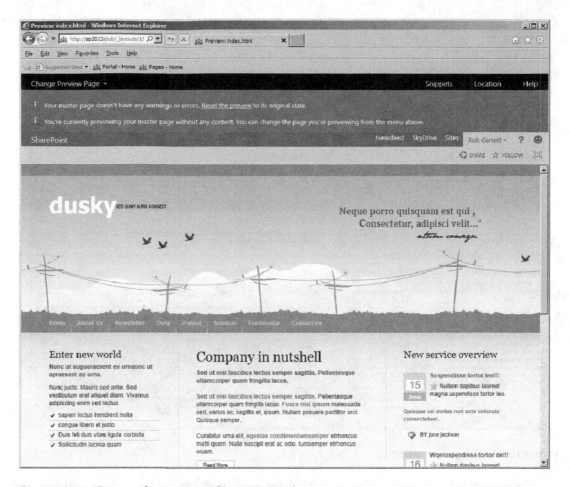

Figure 10-34. Converted master page from HTML

17. Click the Snippets link at the top of the page.

18. You should now see the snippets manager (Figure 10-35).

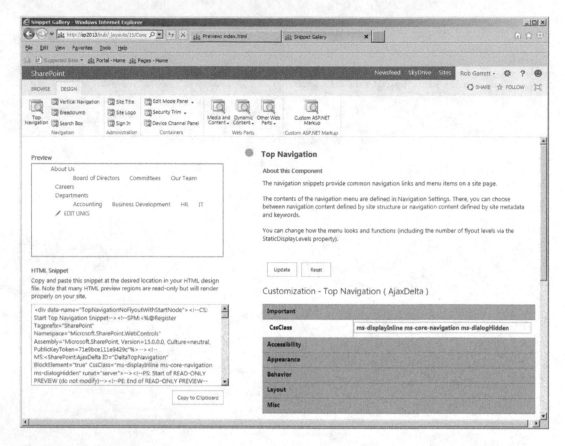

Figure 10-35. *Snippets manager*

The snippets manager, shown in Figure 10-35, allows you to insert common SharePoint markup into your converted master page file. Typical snippets include those for navigation, breadcrumbs, site logo, etc. We shall revisit the snippet manager in Chapter 16.

Edit Display Templates

Display templates provide markup for search results and search-related Web Parts in SharePoint 2013. Previous versions of SharePoint rendered all search results the same, unless you customized the output with XSL and custom code. Design templates are small pieces of HTML that search components use to render specific output by injecting content into the specified templates before rendering the output.

Consider the page of search results in Figure 10-36; the search results use three different display templates:

- Template for the person result
- Template for documents by the person
- Template for the standard search results

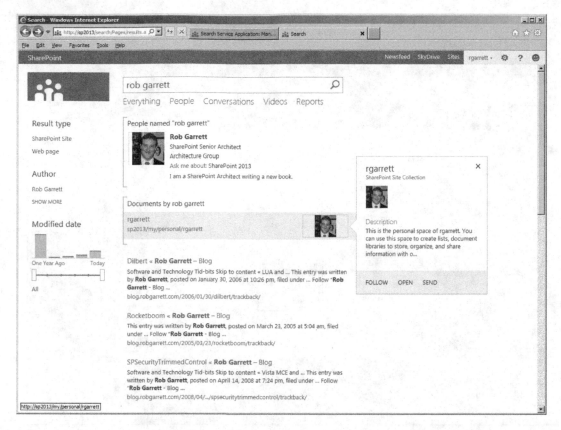

Figure 10-36. *Search results using display templates*

The easiest way to create display templates is to copy an existing template, by navigating to the display templates page in the Design Manager and then copying a display template list item and attachment. Each display template list item has an attached HTML file, which contains the markup of the template. You may use display templates by configuring their use via search settings and search-related Web Parts (such as the site search box).

Edit Page Layouts

I covered the premise of page layouts earlier in this chapter. Like master pages, SharePoint 2013 supports creation of new page layouts via the Design Manager. The following steps demonstrate creating a new page layout that has an associated content type and uses an existing master page:

1. Open your publishing site.

2. Click the gear icon.

3. Select the Design Manager menu item.

4. Click the link to edit page layouts.

5. Click the link to create a new page layout.

6. You should see a dialog, like that in Figure 10-37.

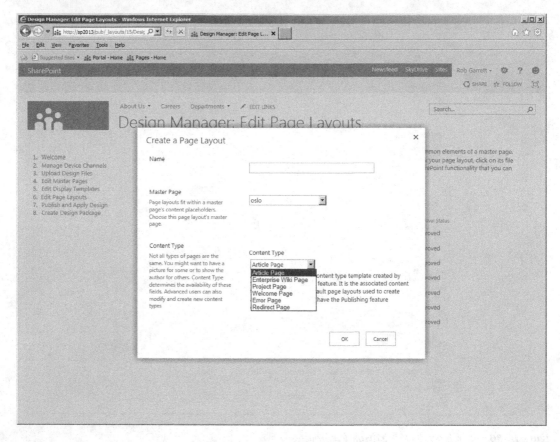

Figure 10-37. Create a page layout from Design Manager

7. Give the page layout a name.

8. Associate the page layout with a content type and existing master page.

9. Once created, you can access the page layout by clicking the name of the page layout in the list.

Similar to master page conversion, you can preview your new page layout and access the snippets manager. Snippets for page layouts differ from those in master page creation in that you may apply page fields, media content, zones, dynamic content, etc.

■ **Note** I shall cover end-to-end creation of branding, via the Design Manager, in Chapter 16.

Publish and Apply Design

The link to publish and apply a design, from the Design Manager, essentially provides links to the master page settings page for the current site collection. From this page, you can apply the master page and assign a specific design channel.

Create Design Package

The last link on the left side of the Design Manager enables you to complete the last task and package the branding design for reuse, as described below:

1. Open your publishing site.

2. Click the gear icon.

3. Select the Design Manager menu item.

4. Click the link to create a design package.

5. Provide the name for your package.

6. Check whether you wish to include search configuration (display templates, etc.).

7. SharePoint will provide a link to a WSP file.

Once you have completed the generation of the design package, SharePoint will provide a link to the WSP. The WSP file is also available in the user solutions gallery for the site collection.

Content Deployment

In most organizations, the public web site is of significant importance. The web site presents an organization's public image, along with the products and services it offers, to a public audience and is susceptible to criticism if the site breaks or is offline for any duration. Therefore, when it comes to the infrastructure that hosts a web site, typically the organization will maintain a production, staging, and perhaps a development copy of the site. Open any good book on best practice web site deployment, and you will most likely find reference to staging and production environments.

Microsoft developed the web publishing aspects of SharePoint with content integrity in mind. Content owners may edit and add new content to the web site, free from worry that the public audience will see their changes before new and changed content undergoes an approval and publish process. The content approval process and versioning/publish features in SharePoint allow complete confidence that the public may view an approved version of content and design while editors and designers work on the same infrastructure without jeopardizing the public view. Even so, management and the IT group often balk at the idea of making changes to the production web site. This is where content deployment comes in.

Content deployment allows content owners to work on one SharePoint farm—completely independent from the production farm—and then deploy published changes to the production environment on a schedule. The instructions in the following section provide high-level configuration of content deployment from Farm A to Farm B.

■ **Note** Content deployment deploys only user content from one SharePoint farm to another—sites, list, list items, documents, metadata, and so on. It will not deploy customizations (such as code deployed via features and package solutions).

Configuring the Destination Farm

Take the following steps to configure a destination farm for content deployment:

1. Open Central Administration on the destination farm.

2. Click the General Application Settings link in the left navigation.

3. Scroll to the section for Content Deployment.

4. Click the Configure Content Deployment link to allow the destination farm to accept incoming content deployment.

5. Set the import server in the destination farm to accept the import content (Figure 10-38).

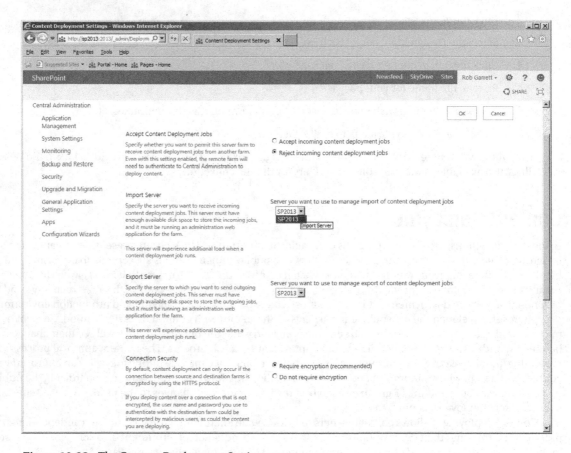

Figure 10-38. *The Content Deployment Settings page*

Configuring the Source Farm

Take the following steps to configure a source farm for content deployment:

1. Open Central Administration on the source farm.

2. Click the General Application Settings link in the left navigation.

3. Scroll to the section for Content Deployment.

4. Click the Configure Content Deployment link.

5. Configure the export server for this farm, by providing a path for the export files and specifying whether you want to use encryption (in case you are deploying across network security boundaries).

6. Navigate back to the General Application Settings page.

7. Click the Configure Content Deployment Paths and Jobs link.

8. Click the icon to create a new path (Figure 10-39).

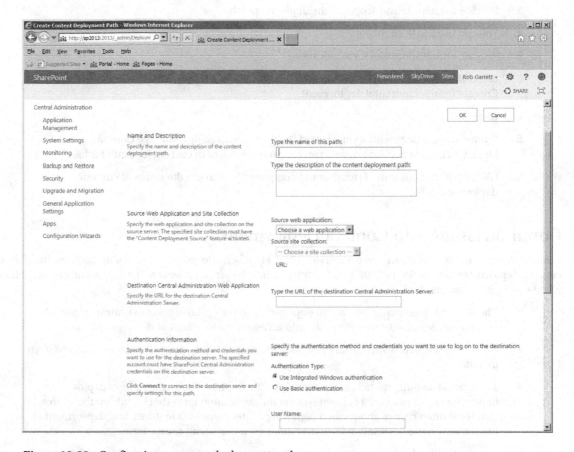

Figure 10-39. *Configuring a content deployment path*

9. Give the path a name and description, and specify the source web application and source site collection.

10. Provide the URL of the destination Central Administration site.

11. Provide the authentication (I recommend using the Farm account on the destination farm), click the Connect button, and make sure you see the "Connection succeeded" message.

12. Select the destination web application and site collection.

13. Check the check box to deploy user names (typically a good idea if you want the users to persist in the site collection, unless your production farm allows new user login).

14. Set the security information for the content deployment and click OK.

With the path defined, you now need to configure a job to deploy on a schedule.

1. Click the icon to create a new content deployment job.

2. Provide a name for the job.

3. Provide a schedule and scope for the deployment job.

4. You can use a SQL snapshot.

5. Provide e-mail addresses for notification.

6. Select the deployment type—Deploy All Content is a full deployment, New or Changed Content is an incremental deployment.

7. Click OK.

8. From the same page where you created the deployment path—Manage Content Deployment Path and Jobs page—you can view the status of current jobs and paths.

9. Click the Status column of running and completed jobs to see the status of content deployment jobs.

Common Issues with Content Deployment

Content deployment is complicated to get working right. Microsoft addressed a number of the bugs, since introducing content deployment in SharePoint 2007, that frustrated administrators. However, there are some known points to note when configuring content deployment:

- The first time you configure content deployment to your production environment, provide a new blank site collection as the destination. Then run a full content deployment job.

- Once you complete a successful full content deployment job, run only incremental jobs from then on.

- Try to avoid deleting metadata elements from the destination farm—content deployment balks when it cannot find a content type on the destination farm that it finds on the source. This issue often comes about when deploying content types via features, and deployment of the feature on the destination farm may differ from that of the source farm.

- Ensure that the destination farm has all the same features deployed as the source farm.

Summary

Publishing is an important part of SharePoint functionality, and in this chapter, you read about the fundamentals of publishing. I covered the basics of creating a new publishing site collection in SharePoint 2013 and the features that the publishing infrastructure brings to content owners and site designers.

In the first half of the chapter, you read about Web Content Management, which includes the use of site columns, content types, lists, and workflow to provide WCM capability. You also read about master pages and page layouts, from the designer's perspective, and how content maps to presentation for SharePoint publishing pages.

SharePoint 2013 brings about some exciting new features, such as friendly URLs, managed navigation (via the Managed Metadata Service), SEO optimization, image renditions, cross-site publishing, and better branding with the Design Manager. I wrote about each of the aforementioned new features in turn and provided examples to wet your publishing taste buds.

Finally, at the end of this chapter, I covered content deployment—often underused and a very powerful capability of SharePoint to publish content across SharePoint farms—development to staging to production.

CHAPTER 11

■ ■ ■

Documents and Records Management

Walk into any enterprise organization and ask someone in a department to describe his or her document storage and processing operations, and the person will likely give you a story about how management of documents and data is far from ideal.

In the time that I have been working with SharePoint and various clients looking to implement an information management system in SharePoint, the situation has been typical—documents and files scattered on a shared drive or file share, no categorization, multiple copies of the same document floating around in e-mails. Even the more organized groups have issues with multiple document and information silos.

Documents Management Systems and Records Management Systems are about the "management" of documents and data at an enterprise level. This chapter focuses on documents and records management features in SharePoint.

Before diving into the topics of document management and records management, I should mention that both of these fall under the umbrella of Enterprise Content Management (ECM) in SharePoint.

What Is a Documents Management System?

Even though the name implies management of documents in an organization, document management is really about empowering users who create and collaborate around documents to do so with more structure and control. Consider asking users of your organization the following questions:

- How many documents does your organization produce in a year?

- Are these documents stored on a central file-share with any form of structure?

- How do users search and browse for particular documents?

- Does your organization suffer from multiple versions of the same document in your document store?

- Are users' e-mail copies of documents, or links to documents, stored in a central location?

- Are any documents in your organization security-sensitive? If so, how does your organization secure them?

- Does your organization have a business policy or practices for the location of documents, movement of documents, and archiving?

- How does your IT department back up the organization document silo?

- Does your organization use non–Microsoft Office type documents?

- Do you know of any approval or manual workflow for documents, such as proposal management?

The preceding questions are a small subset of those that I send new clients who are looking to move from a file-share document silo to a Documents Management System. A Documents Management System aims to provide a secure, central location for storage of all documents in an organization. Typical features of a Documents Management System include the following capabilities:

- Apply metadata to categorize documents

- Promote browsing and searching of documents based on document content or metadata

- Manage versions and change control of documents

- Secure sensitive documents to groups of users without intervention of the IT department

- Provide a consistent reference link to a document, so that despite the location of the document in the Documents Management System, users can still access the document from a shared link

- Scale to handle growth of document and metadata content

Any good Documents Management System provides features/functionality to address some or all of the questions raised previously. The next section introduces the features of SharePoint 2013 document management.

Document Management in SharePoint 2013

At the core platform, SharePoint provides document libraries for storage of documents. This feature addresses an immediate need to prevent e-mailing of multiple copies of a document under construction. Instead, users can e-mail a link to the most recent document in a SharePoint site. This is collaboration in basic form.

SharePoint offers many more features in the document management suite. The best way to get started exploring these features is to create a new site collection with the Document Center features installed, as in the following steps:

1. Open Central Administration.

2. If you need to create a new IIS web application, see Chapter 2 for instructions.

3. Click the Application Management heading on the Central Administration home page.

4. Under Site Collections, click the Create Site Collection link.

5. SharePoint displays the Create Site Collection page.

6. Change the web application to the application you want to host the new site collection.

7. Give the site a name, and a URL suffix if it is not a root site collection.

8. In the Site Templates section, click the Enterprise tab and then select Document Center as the template type.

9. Provide the primary and secondary (optional) site administrators.

10. Click the OK button and wait for SharePoint to finish creating the Document Center, which is our Documents Management System.

■ **Note** You may install/activate all the features available in the Document Center in another site template, but for the purpose of this chapter, it is easier to create a Document Center site collection. The Document Center site template is an easy way to create a new site collection with all the document management features included. Some document management features default to document libraries, so users may make use of these features in any site that uses document libraries.

---

11. Navigate to the new Document Center site, and you should see a page like that in Figure 11-1.

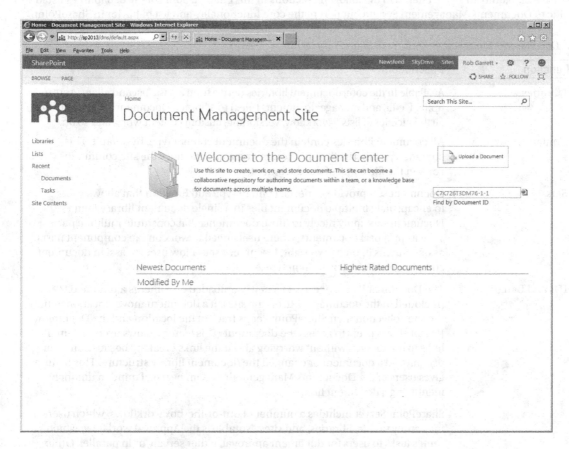

Figure 11-1. *Document Management Site*

The home page of the SharePoint 2013 Document Center consists of various content Web Parts, some content query Web Parts, to display recent documents, and the Find by Document ID Web Part. You may arrange these Web Parts differently by editing the page, and you may place these Web Parts on any other page in the site collection that includes Web Part zones.

Overview of Documents Management System Features

With the Document Center, created in the previous section, you are now ready to explore the document management features in SharePoint. The first place I would like you to look is in the Site Collection Features page:

1. Click the settings gear icon.

2. Select Site Settings from the menu.

3. In the Site Collection Administration section, click the Site Collection Features link.

4. Notice the activated Document ID Service and Document Sets features.

Table 11-1 describes the Documents Management System capabilities in SharePoint 2013 at a high level, and I will discuss each capability in greater depth in the following sections in this chapter. Some of the capabilities listed are not specific to Documents Management System but part of the core functionality and list behavior in SharePoint.

Table 11-1. *Documents Management Features in SharePoint 2013*

Capability/Function	Description
Document Libraries	Available in the core, document libraries derive from a basic list and allow users to upload, edit, and manage documents (files) to a library. Document libraries provide all the niceties of lists—workflow, versioning, custom content types, and so on.
Document Content Types	All document libraries contain the document content type, by default. This content type inherits the item content type and includes the site column to contain the file name of the document.
Document Sets	Document sets provide a special content type and function that allows users to encapsulate multiple document files in a single document library item. Document sets apply nicely to those documents that constitute multiple parts, such as proposal documents, where users need to work on the component parts as documents in their own right. Document sets allow users to assign document components their own content type.
Document IDs and Barcodes	The Document ID Service assigns newly uploaded documents a unique ID (included in the document URL on the site). If a document moves location within the site collection then SharePoint keeps track of the location and the Document ID still allows users to access the document. This feature allows users to e-mail links to documents without worrying about the links breaking because another user moved a document or changed the document library structure. This feature gives users of the Documents Management System peace of mind in uniquely identifying a document link.
Workflows	SharePoint Server includes a number of out-of-the-box workflows, which users may apply to lists, libraries, and sites. Notable is the Approval workflow, which routes tasks to users for document approval, either serially or in parallel. Other workflows, including Collect Signatures, Collect Feedback, and Disposition Approval, execute on document library items.
Document Versions	Document libraries and lists maintain versions and change (when enabled) so users may roll back to prior versions of a list item in time. SharePoint supports Major Version numbers, in which each major version constitutes publication of the list item for non-approver users, and Major/Minor Versions, in which a minor version denotes draft version, and users need to publish the item as a major version to make the changes available to non-approvers. In addition to versioning, SharePoint lists and libraries also support check in/out, so any one user may ensure another does not change a document while he or she has it checked out for edit.
Document Workspaces	Document workspaces provide user collaboration for a document. At any time, a user with collaboration rights to a document, and site creation rights, may elect to create a new document workspace site, which contains lists and libraries to collaborate on the document. For example, a proposal document may require a team of people to complete, who meet regularly and keep detailed notes and managed tasks for their work on the document.

(continued)

Table 11-1. (*continued*)

Capability/Function	Description
Drop off Libraries	Rather than leaving users the arduous task of deciding or knowing where to upload/save documents to a library in a site collection hierarchy, a drop off library provides a single upload point for all documents. Based on metadata and document content, administrators of the drop off libraries may then apply rules to uploaded documents to move them to correct locations automatically.
Search within Documents	SharePoint indexes the content of typical Microsoft Office documents (Word, Excel, PowerPoint, Access, Visio, and so on). SharePoint 2013 can access other non-MS document types as long as an IFILTER exists. New in SharePoint 2013 is the ability to search within PDF documents out-of-the-box. When users search for documents by keyword, SharePoint will use the data found in documents, as well as the metadata applied to each document list item, to provide search results.
Document Conversion Service	The Document Conversion Service is a SharePoint Managed Service Application, which handles the load balancing and conversion of documents converted from one format to another.

■ **Note** The capabilities/functions listed in Table 11-1 may belong to specific SharePoint site or site collection features or be part of the core platform.

Document Library Settings Page

The typical approach to navigating to the Document Library Settings page is to click the Library tab on the ribbon and then click the Library Settings button in the settings section. However, you may also access the same library settings as follows. Throughout this chapter, when I reference navigating to the Library Settings page, I assume that you will either follow the steps below or click the Library Settings icon on the ribbon within the Library tab.

1. Click the settings gear icon.

2. Click the View Site Contents menu item.

3. SharePoint shows you a page that looks like Figure 11-2.

Figure 11-2. Site Contents

4.   Hover over the document library.

5.   Click the ellipses.

6.   Click the settings link on the details box that appears.

Document Content Types and Document Sets

In Chapter 9, I discussed content types at length. I showed you how to create new custom content types and how to use them in lists and libraries. If you are new to content types, I recommend taking a quick look back at this chapter to familiarize yourself with creation of content types.

Document Content Types

Why are content types important in a Documents Management System? Any good Documents Management System must allow users to distinguish one document type from another, without expecting users to open documents. Metadata, and thus content types, provide the baseline functionality to allow content owners to categorize their content with properties—the fields of content types.

The action of creating a content type and applying a content type to a document constitutes basic categorization—without even adding fields/properties to the aforementioned content type. For example, in my project management system I may need documents for Project Plans, Statement of Work, Client Presentation, Invoice, and so on. Creating custom content types, which derive from the stock document content type, and then adding these content types to a document library allows users to upload Office documents of the designated aforementioned types.

■ **Note** A good practice is to remove the stock Document and Item content types from the document library, which forces users to choose a content type that classifies the document.

The following lists some best practices to consider when creating new content types for documents in your Documents Management System:

- *Avoid ambiguous content type names.* Ironically, "Document" itself is a bad example of a content type name because it is too generic, but it suffices as a base type.

- *Try not to create content types too specific to context.* For example, "*Customer Name* Weekly Meeting Notes" restricts the content type to a particular client and meeting context. A better example (in this case) is "Meeting Notes."

- *Create content types at the root site collection.,* This way you may repurpose them throughout the Documents Management System site collection.

- *Avoid adding too many properties/fields to any one content type.* This suggests that the content type is too specific to context. Abstracting properties to a base content type is more effective and manageable.

- *Use Choice, Lookup, and Manage Metadata fields when possible.* This will ease the population of metadata for the end user. If you insist on too many string or text fields, users will likely skip filling them in when uploading or saving a document, thus defeating the point of metadata. Best practice with SharePoint is to use the Managed Metadata fields because the Managed Metadata Service gives the greatest flexibility to manage taxonomy and tagging.

- *Use just the right blend of required and optional fields in your content types.* SharePoint will insist that users provide values for all required fields before allowing them to upload/save a document. If you specify too many required fields, users will become frustrated; if there are no required fields, some users might not populate any metadata.

- *Limit the choice of content types for your document library to a finite amount.* A good rule of thumb is ten or fewer. Too many content types, especially when they are similar, will cause your users confusion.

Once a user adds a document to a document library in SharePoint, and then applies metadata via content type, subsequent editing of the document from SharePoint integrates the field/properties in Microsoft Office applications (I cover this in Chapter 14). Say I create a content type for a Statement of Work (SOW) document, including properties for client, contract type, and cost estimate, and then upload an SOW document to a library and then classify the document as an SOW. When I open the same document from SharePoint, I can see and edit the properties directly from the Office application. The following series of steps demonstrates this example:

1. Navigate to the Document Center site we created earlier.

2. Click the settings gear icon.

3. Click the Site Settings menu item.

4. From the Site Settings page, click the Site Content Types link under Web Designer Galleries.

5. Click the Create link.

6. Give the new content type the name Statement of Work.

7. Inherit from the parent Document content type in Document Content Types.

8. Choose an existing or custom group in which to place your content type.

■ **Note** It is usually a good idea to put all custom content types in a separate group from the stock content types.

---

9. Click OK to create the content type.

10. Click the Add from New Site Column link.

11. Add a new Choice column to the content type, called Estimate Range. Assign the Choice column the values: Less than $50k, $50k to $100k, More than $100k.

12. Choose an existing group or custom group in which to place the site column.

13. Leave all other options as default and click the OK button.

14. Add a Single Line of Text column, called Client Name, using similar steps to that of the Choice column you created.

15. This concludes the creation of your content type.

16. Navigate to the Documents Library Settings page.

17. Scroll to the Content Types section, notice the presence of the link to Document and Document Set content types—I will discuss these later.

18. Click the Add from Existing Site Content Types link.

19. Add the Statement of Work content type (this is where groups come in handy).

20. Navigate back to the All Documents view of the document library.

21. Click the Files tab on the ribbon; then click the *lower portion* of the New Document icon; see Figure 11-3.

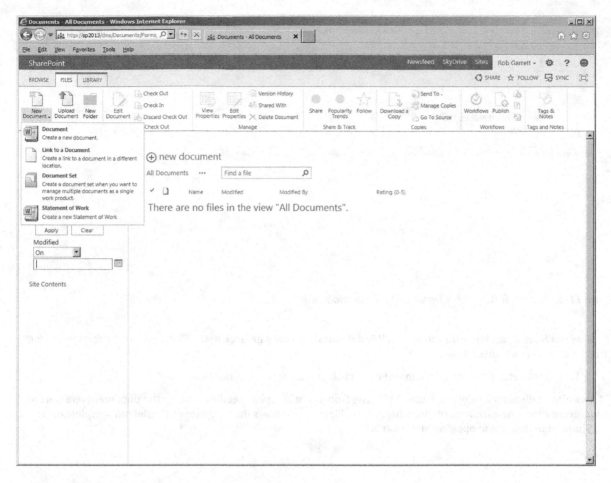

Figure 11-3. *Create a new document with content type*

22. You might be tempted to click the Add Document link. However, this assumes the default content type and does not demonstrate use of our Statement of Work content type.

23. Click the Statement of Work menu item.

24. If you have Microsoft Word installed, it will open with a new document.

25. Notice the Document Information Panel in Word, as shown Figure 11-4 (Office 2007, 2010, and 2013 versions only).

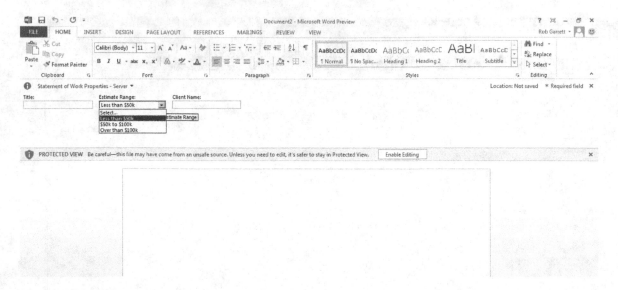

Figure 11-4. *Microsoft Word with Document Information Panel*

How did SharePoint know how to open a Word document? Navigate back to the Statement of Work content type in the Content Types Gallery to see.

1. In the settings page of the content type, click the Advanced Settings link.

SharePoint displays a page like Figure 11-5. The Document Template section governs the document template to use when creating a new list item of this content type. Figure 11-5 shows the template as the default template.dotx; thus, SharePoint defaults to opening Microsoft Word.

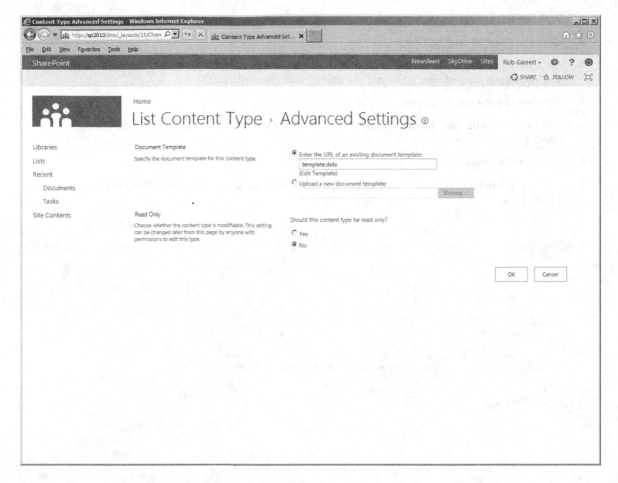

Figure 11-5. *Advanced Settings page for our custom content type*

2. Compare this setting with that of other stock content types to see how this setting influences the default document.

3. Before leaving the content type settings page, click the Document Information Panel settings link.

4. In this settings page, SharePoint allows you to specify the XSN of a custom InfoPath form, or the URL location of a custom page to render from the Office application.

■ **Note**   Document Information Panel requires at least Office 2007, 2010, or 2013.

Uploading a Document

Perhaps you have a document on disk and want to upload it to a SharePoint document library. How does SharePoint know which content type to assign? It asks you.

1. Navigate back to the All Documents view of the document library.

2. Click the Files tab on the ribbon.

3. Click the Upload Document icon (if your browser supports it and your SharePoint site is in the Intranet or Trusted Sites zone, you can upload multiple documents).

4. Navigate to a document on disk.

5. You can upload the document as a new version, if the file already exists, by checking the check box.

6. Click the OK button.

7. After a brief moment during the document upload, SharePoint displays a dialog like that in Figure 11-6.

Figure 11-6. *Select document content type after upload*

8. Change the drop-down to the desired content type and fill in the fields.

9. Click the Save button to commit the metadata to the document and complete the upload process.

Using the Save As feature in an Office application and then specifying the location as a SharePoint document library renders a similar dialog to choose the content type (Figure 11-7).

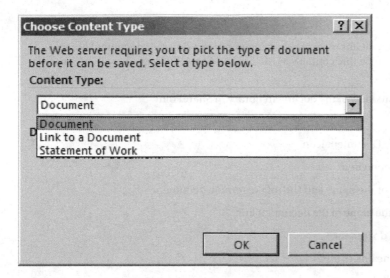

Figure 11-7. Choose Content Type from Microsoft Word

■ **Note**   SharePoint will assume the library default content type and field values when uploading multiple documents.

Saving a Document to SharePoint from Office

Office 2007, 2010, and 2013 applications allow you to save directly to a SharePoint location from within the application. The following steps demonstrate how to save an open Word 2013 document to an existing document library in SharePoint 2013:

1. From inside Microsoft Word 2013, click the File tab in the top left corner.

2. Click the Save As link from the left navigation.

3. Click the Browse button.

4. In the Save As dialog, provide the URL of the document library in the file name field.

5. Click the OK button to save the file.

6. Choose the content type in the dialog that appears (Figure 11-7).

7. Click the OK button to complete the save.

■ **Note**   The easiest way to get the URL of a document library is to navigate to the library page in your browser and then strip off the `/Forms/AllItems.aspx` part from the URL. For example, `http://server/site/ DocumentLibName/`.

Linking to Other Documents

SharePoint allows users to add links in a document library to another document in a different document library. SharePoint achieves this with a simple content type that contains a URL field and an ASPX page that allows a user to enter the name and URL of the linked document.

1. Navigate back to the All Documents view of the document library in SharePoint.

2. Click the Files tab on the ribbon.

3. Click the lower portion of the New Document icon.

4. Choose the Link to a Document menu item.

5. SharePoint shows a page, asking for the name and URL of the remote document.

6. Provide any name you desire for the name of the document link.

7. Provide the full URL to the linked document.

8. You can test the URL by clicking the link to test.

9. Click the OK button to create the link.

10. When you click the link in the document library, SharePoint will open the document at the end of the link.

Document Sets

A document set consists of several documents in a single list item of a document library. The purpose of document sets is to group related documents and manage the set as a single item, just like a regular document list item.

A good example of the use of a document sets is for a proposal document. Typically, in business, a proposal is a large document and requires contributions from many authors to complete. One way to accomplish the creation of the proposal is to have authors write independent documents for the various sections and then combine these documents into a finished proposal document at the end. I have seen this approach in action on earlier versions of SharePoint (pre-2010), and the authors maintained the document pieces in a folder of a larger project document library. Document sets now allow users to continue to work on document pieces but manage them together in a document set of a document library. Since a document set is a special content type, each document set has its own metadata, in addition to the metadata specified by the content types of the documents contained inside the document set.

The following steps demonstrate how document sets operate using Document Center and default document library:

1. Navigate back to the All Documents view of the document library in SharePoint.

2. Click the Files tab on the ribbon.

3. Click the lower portion of the New Document icon.

4. Choose the Document Set menu item.

■ **Note**   If you do not see the Document Set menu item, follow the steps at the bottom of this section for adding document sets to existing document libraries.

---

5. SharePoint asks for the name and description of the document set.

6. Give the document set the name Proposal and click the OK button.

7. SharePoint displays a Document Set page, like that in Figure 11-8.

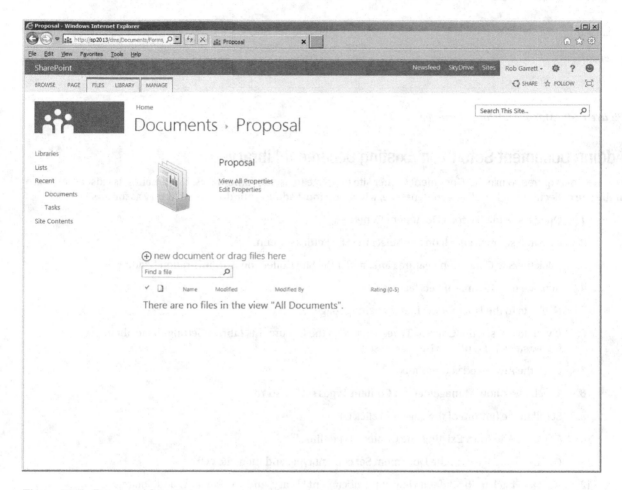

Figure 11-8. *Document Set page*

The Document Set page provides a similar interface to that of a regular document library. Click the Manage tab on the ribbon (Document Set). The ribbon shows various options for the document set (Figure 11-9), such as

- *Edit Properties:* Populate the fields, defined in the Document Set content type

- *Permissions*: Permissions for the document set

- *Delete:* Delete the document set

- *E-mail a Link:* Send a link of this document set to a colleague

- *Capture Version*: Create a version label of documents in the set

- *Version History*: See the history of changes

- *Workflows:* Apply workflow to the document set

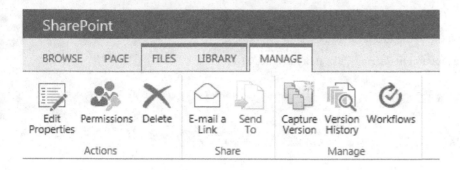

Figure 11-9. *Manage tab for a document set*

Adding Document Sets to an Existing Document Library

You are not required to use the Document Center site template to use document sets. Document sets exist as a feature at the site collection level, and as a content type, which you must add to your document library as follows:

1. Open a site that is *not* a Document Center.

2. Click the settings gear icon and select the Site Settings menu.

3. Click the Site Collection Features link, under the Site Collection Administration heading.

4. Activate the Document Sets feature.

5. Navigate to the Documents Library Settings page.

6. If you do not see the Content Types section on the Documents Library Settings page, then follow steps 7-11; otherwise, skip to step 12.

7. Click the Advanced settings link.

8. Toggle the Allow Management of Content Types setting to Yes.

9. Scroll to the bottom of the page and click OK.

10. Click the Add from Existing Site Content Types link.

11. On the next page, add the Document Set content type, and then click OK.

12. Navigate back to the default view of the document library, and you can now add document sets, per the information preceding this subsection.

Document Workflows

Like many of the topics in SharePoint, *workflow* is the subject of whole books. A workflow is a process, either automated by computer or manual with human intervention. Workflow may consist of both human and automated elements, but the premise is the same—a workflow management system keeps track of the steps in a process (the *activities*) and alerts different actors in the process of tasks to complete an activity/step in the process chain. Microsoft workflows come in two flavors: sequential, meaning that each step succeeds the next; and state machine, in which the workflow system tracks overall state at any time and transition from state to state via activities.

SharePoint uses Microsoft Workflow Foundation (WF) to provide business process on documents, web pages, forms, and list items. SharePoint allows attachment of workflow to sites, lists, libraries, and content types. Since workflow in SharePoint uses WF, developers may create custom workflows to automate the process of documents and list items, or process data in a site. SharePoint Designer allows developers to create sequential workflows, with drag-and-drop ease, and Visual Studio provides for creating more elaborate coded workflow. Even though SharePoint allows for the adoption of custom workflow, the platform provides out-of-the-box workflow for use of document approval, signature collection, disposition approval, and so on. Table 11-2 describes the out-of-the-box workflows available.

Table 11-2. *SharePoint 2013 Workflows*

Workflow Name	Description	Available in SharePoint Foundation
Three-State	Tracks the business state of a document through three defined phases	Yes
Publishing Approval	Sends a document for approval, typically before publishing	No
Disposition	Handles document expiration and disposition	No

■ **Note**   SharePoint 2010 included the Collect Feedback, Collect Signatures, and Approval workflows. These workflows are still available by activating the site collection workflows feature.

In the days of SharePoint 2007, users could only apply workflow activation to lists. Since SharePoint 2010, users are able to apply workflows to sites and content types. Because content types provide portability of metadata in a site collection, applying workflow to content types now means that users can provide business process with reusable workflows. If a content type exists for a proposal document in an organization site collection, the organization can attach the workflow process whenever someone creates a new proposal document—anywhere in the site collection, not just in a particular list instance.

Adding a Workflow to a Library or List

Take the following steps to add a workflow to a library or list:

1. Browse to the list or library.

2. Click the List or Library tab on the ribbon.

3. Click the Workflow Settings icon on the ribbon.

4 On the Workflow Settings page (Figure 11-10), click the Add a Workflow link.

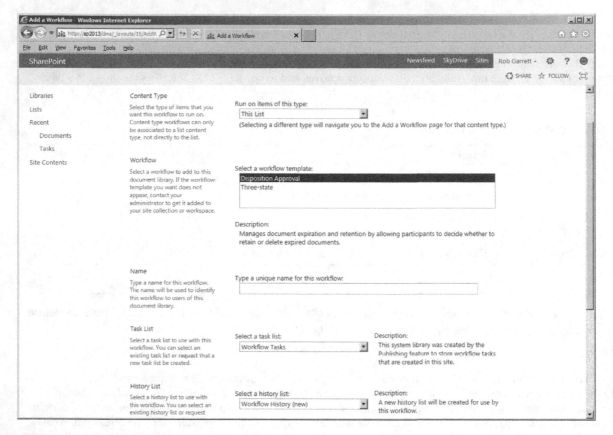

Figure 11-10. *Add a workflow to a list*

5. Select the workflow.

6. Assign the tasks and history lists.

7. Apply the appropriate options.

Adding a Workflow to a Library or List Content Type

Take the following steps to add a workflow to a library or list content type:

1. Navigate to the List or Libraries Settings page.

2. Scroll to the Content Types section (if it is missing, enable Content Types under Advanced Settings).

3. Click the name of the content type to associate with the workflow.

4. Click the Workflow Settings link.

5. On the Workflow Settings page, click the Add a Workflow link.

6. Select the workflow.

7. Assign the tasks and history lists.

8. Apply the appropriate options.

Adding a Workflow to a Site Content Type

Adding a workflow to a site content type is a similar process to that of adding to a list content type, only you access the content type via the Content Type Gallery instead of the list.

Take the following steps to add a workflow to a site content type:

1. Click the settings gear icon.

2. Choose the Site Settings menu item.

3. Click the Site Content Types link under Galleries.

4. Click the name of the content type to associate the workflow.

5. Click the Workflow Settings link.

6. On the Workflow Settings page, click the Add a Workflow link.

7. Select the workflow.

8. Assign the tasks and history lists.

9. Apply the appropriate options.

Editing and Developing Custom Workflow

With a whole workflow platform and plenty of ideas to automate business process, it is natural that users will want to create their own custom workflows. Creation of custom workflow falls under development and is out of the scope of this administration book. However, I do wish to mention some of the new enhancements that SharePoint brings to workflow in the platform.

- SharePoint Designer 2013 allows editing of out-of-the-box workflow.

- SharePoint Designer 2013 deploys custom workflow as WSP (SharePoint Package) files, which developers may then open and edit in Visual Studio.

- SharePoint 2013 brings many more SharePoint-based activities, for inclusion as workflow steps.

- SharePoint 2013 provides more events to subscribe workflow.

Document Tracking

Any good Documents Management System allows users to reference documents from the system, without concern about other users changing the location of such documents in the Documents Management System. The blog sphere addressed this very topic with permalinks—links that do not directly link to blog articles but provide virtual links, which the blog engine translates into the physical link. SharePoint 2007 pretty much ignored the issue of document link tracking, but fortunately, SharePoint 2010 and now SharePoint 2013 provide this functionality. I shall describe the various methods for document tracking in the following sections.

The Document ID Service

SharePoint incorporates a Document ID Service feature for keeping track of the location of documents and providing users with virtual URLs for documents with unique ID. The platform does not enable the Document ID Service feature by default, although the Document Center template does enable it. To confirm the existence of Document ID tracking, follow these steps:

1. From the root of the site collection, click the settings gear icon.

2. Click the Site Settings menu item.

3. Click the Site Collection Features link in the Site Collection Administration section.

4. Scroll down the list and see if the Document ID Service feature is activated.

5. Navigate back to the Site Settings page for the site collection.

6. Click the Document ID Settings link in the Site Collection Administration section.

7. SharePoint displays a page like that in Figure 11-11.

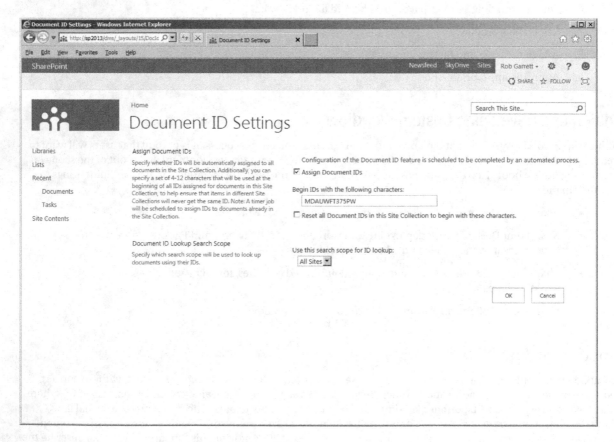

Figure 11-11. *Document ID Settings for the site collection*

8. Ensure that the box for Assign Document IDs is checked.

9. You may optionally change the prefix for all document IDs and change the search scope for lookup search.

10. Upload a new document to one of the document libraries in the site.

11. From the All Documents view, select the name of the document you just uploaded.

12. Click the ellipses to show the document summary.

13. Click the ellipses on the summary popup (Figure 11-12).

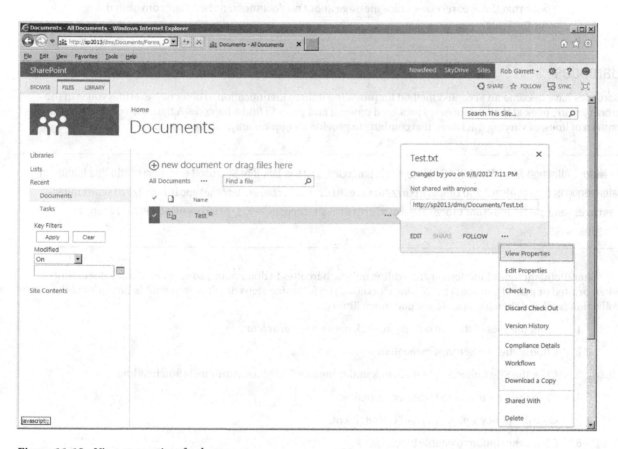

Figure 11-12. *View properties of a document*

14. Click the View Properties link in the menu.

15. Look for the Document ID field and assigned Document ID on the displayed page.

16. Hover over the Document ID and get the properties of the hyperlink from your browser. It should look something like this:
`http://site-collection/_layouts/15/DocIdRedir.aspx?ID=MDAUWFT375PW-1-3.`

■ **Note**   The document ID link does not reference any particular document library, just a common redirection page, and the document ID.

---

17. Move the document to another document library and repeat the steps to get the Document ID—notice that the link remains the same. Users may e-mail this link around the organization without fear of the link breaking because the document has moved.

18. Try deleting the document and then accessing the Document ID link from the earlier step. Notice that the user receives a nice message about no document, not a 404 or convoluted error message.

Barcodes

Barcodes have become an accepted method for providing unique identification to objects. Next time you visit the grocery store, peek at the back of every packaged product and you will find a barcode. A barcode consists of a unique pattern of lines, of varying thickness, that combine to provide a unique stamp for the object.

■ **Note**   Although SharePoint 2013 still supports barcodes, there is talk that Microsoft may depreciate this feature in later versions of SharePoint and Office: http://office.microsoft.com/en-us/sharepoint-help/discontinued-features-and-modified-functionality-in-microsoft-sharepoint-2013-preview-HA102892827.aspx#_Toc330374495.

SharePoint includes functionality for adding unique barcodes to documents, so users may track documents when printed or part of a manual processing workflow. The following steps detail how to enable barcodes at the site collection level and then for a particular document library:

1. From the root of the site collection, click the settings gear icon.

2. Choose the Site Settings menu item.

3. Click the Site Collection Policies link under the Site Collection Administration heading.

4. Click the Create link to create a new policy.

5. Give the policy a name and policy statement.

6. Check the option to enable barcodes.

7. Click OK.

8. Navigate to the list to apply the new policy.

9. Navigate to the Library Settings page.

10. Click the content type to apply the policy (ensure that content types are applied to the library under Advanced Settings).

11. Click the Information Management Policy Settings link.

12. Change the radio button option to Use a Site Collection Policy, and select the new policy you created.

13. Click OK.

14. From the desired view for the document library, add the Barcode and Barcode Value columns (modify this view from the ellipses).

15. Upload a document and select the correct content type, and see that SharePoint assigns barcodes (Figure 11-13).

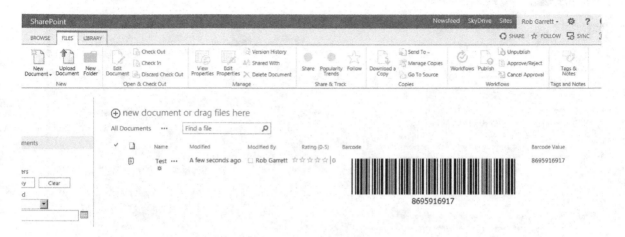

Figure 11-13. *Barcodes added to a document library*

Document Conversion

SharePoint includes a Document Conversion Service for converting documents of one type to another, such as Word document to PDF. Document conversion is important in any Documents Management System because it allows users to upload documents of a type and allow other users to read and edit these documents in another type, typically a common type that most users can access. Office 2010 and upward uses an XML format for document data, and the Document Conversion Service converts documents of these types to viewable web pages for those users who do not have Microsoft Office 2010 or 2013 installed on their desktop.

The Document Conversion Service consists of two parts: a Load Balancer Service and a Launcher Service. SharePoint requires both services configured and running to enable the Documents Conversion Service. The following steps detail how to configure document conversion in your SharePoint farm.

■ **Note**   You must start the Load Balancer Service before the Launcher Service for document conversion to work. The Launcher Service stops if the Load Balancer Service is not started or is stopped.

---

1. Open Central Administration.

2. Click the Manage Services on Server link, under System Settings (Figure 11-14).

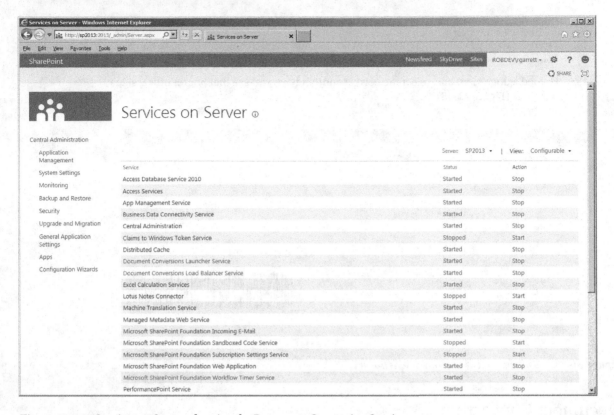

Figure 11-14. *Services on Server, showing the Document Conversion Services*

3. Click the Start link for the Document Conversions Load Balancer Service.

4. Click the Start link for the Document Conversions Launcher Service.

5. Select the server for the launcher, load balance server, and port number.

6. Click OK.

7. You may change the settings of either service by clicking the name of the service; options include choosing the server on which the service is running and port numbers.

The next set of steps demonstrates how to enable document conversion in a web application.

1. Open Central Administration.

2. Click the General Application Settings section title.

3. Click the Configure Document Conversions link under External Service Connections.

4. Select the web application in the drop-down control.

5. Flip the setting to enable document conversion.

6. Specify the load balancer server.

7. Configure schedule for blocks of conversion.

8. SharePoint lists the current installed converters at the bottom of the page as a series of links (Figure 11-15). Click the link to configure the converter.

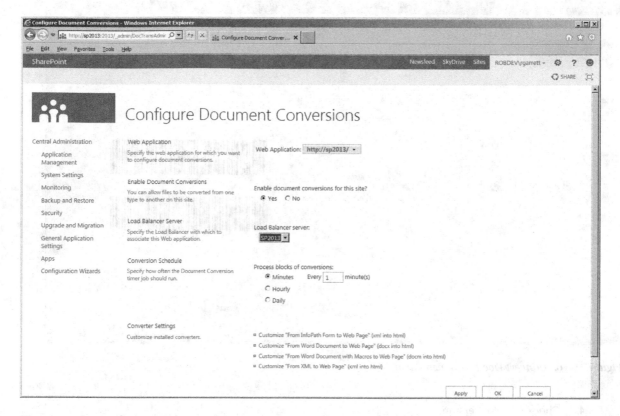

Figure 11-15. *Configure Document Conversions*

9. Click the OK button when done configuring.

With the conversion services started, and the web application configured for document conversion, navigate to any document library in a site/site collection hosted by the web application. Upload a Word DOCX document, and then follow these steps to convert the document:

1. Click the ellipses for the document in the list.

2. In the popup properties box, click the ellipses.

3. Select the Convert Document menu item (Figure 11-16).

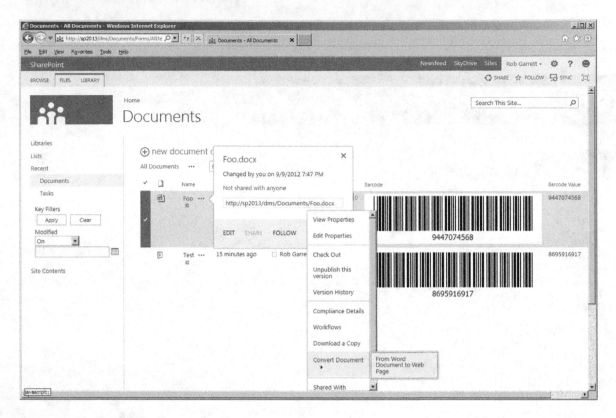

Figure 11-16. *Convert Document menu item*

4. Choose the conversion.

5. SharePoint will display a page for obtaining settings for the conversion process (e.g., Figure 11-17).

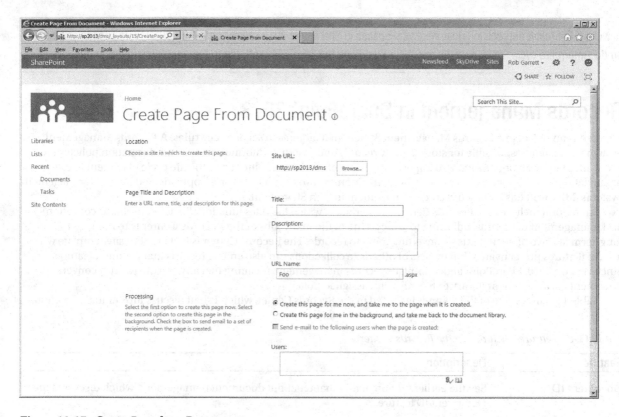

Figure 11-17. *Create Page from Document*

If you are not seeing the menu option to convert a document, ensure the following:

- The document is in an Office XML (DOCX, XLSX, PPTX) format

- The Document Conversions Load Balancer Service is started

- The Document Conversions Launcher Service is started (after the load balancer)

- The web application has document conversion enabled

- The site content type (as opposed to the list content type) allows document conversion

Document Workspaces

SharePoint has always been great at providing space for users to collaborate. At the core of the platform, Foundation offers basic and team sites, which include task lists, calendars, document libraries, and so on for users of the space to share and collaborate on a topic of interest.

SharePoint 2007 and 2010 included document workspace site templates for users to collaborate on a specific document. Microsoft depreciated the document workspace in SharePoint 2013, and users should now utilize team sites for document collaboration.

■ **Note**   Microsoft depreciated document workspaces in SharePoint 2013—use SharePoint 2013 team sites to collaborate on document life cycle. You can re-enable them by editing the WEBTEMP.XML file in the templates folder on the hive.

Records Management in SharePoint 2013

A record is an object in a Records Management System that adheres to set of policy rules. A Records Management System is a system responsible for storing many records and asserting information policy. Information policies are rules, adopted by an organization, to impose restriction on the use of content and the life cycle of content in the organization. Just like document management, the industry provides a number of sophisticated Records Management Systems. Microsoft has included records management in with SharePoint.

SharePoint includes the Records Center site template, which includes functionality for centralized collection and management of records, adhering to policy. One of the many jobs of the Records Center is to manage the long-term archive of documents—converting them to records. The Records Center is just another site template with a set of features pre-activated, but owners of other site collections can also enable records management features. Since version 2010, SharePoint allows in-place records management, meaning that any site owner may convert documents of a document library to records, with assigned policy.

Table 11-3 lists some of the features included in the Records Center, which I shall discuss further in this section.

Table 11-3. *Features Included in the Records Center*

Feature	Description
Document ID	See the earlier section of this chapter about document management, which discusses the Document ID feature.
Content Organizer	Routes documents and records in the Records Center based on defined policy.
Drop Off Libraries	Let the user drop documents in the drop off library and have the Content Organizer route dropped documents, based on policy.
Records Retention	Determines when documents and records expire and how SharePoint handles deposition.
Hold and e-Discovery	Provides auditing and tracking of external actions that might interrupt normal document life cycle (for example, because of litigation).

To start, the following steps demonstrate how to create a new instance of a Records Center. I created a managed path (see Chapter 2) to host my Records Center in my default web application.

1. Open Central Administration.

2. Ensure that you have a web application provisioned to host your Records Center (see Chapter 2).

3. Click the Create Site Collections link (under Application Management).

4. Select the web application to host the new Records Center site collection.

5. Give the site collection a name (such as Records Center).

6. Select the desired URL to host the site collection.

7. In the Template Selection, click the Enterprise tab, and then select Records Center.

8. Provide user names for the administrators.

9. Click OK.

10. Once it is complete, navigate to the new Records Center site collection (Figure 11-18).

Figure 11-18. *Records Center in SharePoint 2013*

The Records Center home page includes a handful of helpful Web Parts to assist you with management of records in the Records Center. Remember, a record is an object (typically a document) in Records Management System with policy applied. The SharePoint Records Center deals primarily in list item and document records. Click the Submit a Record button and SharePoint will prompt you for a file to upload (Figure 11-19) and convert to a record. SharePoint leverages the Content Organizer to route the file to a correct location, based on policy rules. I shall discuss the Content Organizer in the next section.

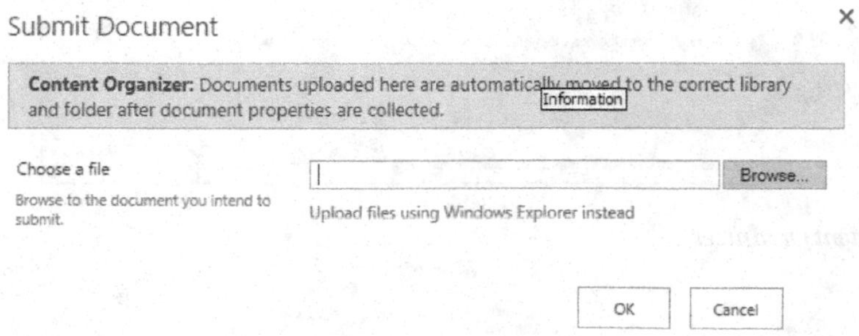

Figure 11-19. *Submit a document as a record*

Setting Up the Content Organizer

The Content Organizer feature is responsible for routing documents to other areas in SharePoint. In the next section, I take a closer look at the Content Organizer in the context of the Records Center, which you created in the previous section. First, look at the Content Organizer settings in the Records Center site settings, as follows:

1. Navigate to the Records Center.

2. Click the settings gear icon.

3. Click the Site Settings menu item.

4. Click the Content Organizer Settings link, under the Site Administration heading.

5. SharePoint shows a page like that in Figure 11-20.

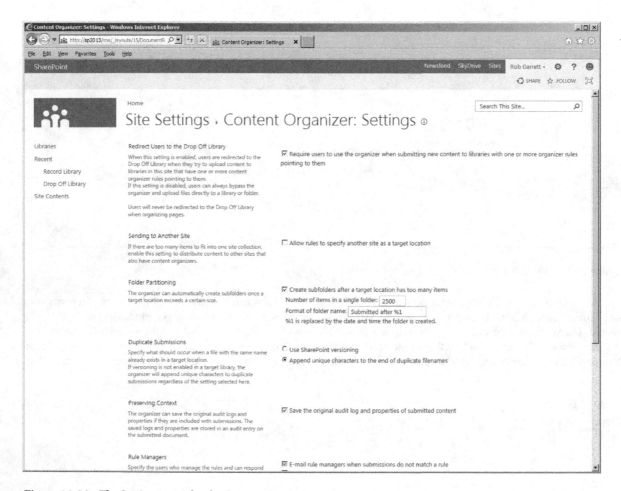

Figure 11-20. *The Settings page for the Content Organizer*

The Content Organizer Settings page provides the following settings:

- *Redirect Users to the Drop Off Library:* Ensures that users cannot upload documents to document libraries that have content organizer rules assigned. This forces the user to comply with using the drop off library to route content to final location in SharePoint, rather than decide manually.

- *Sending to Another Site:* Check this option if you would like to submit documents to another location. Check it for this exercise so you can try this capability later.

- *Folder Partitioning:* Ensures that target document libraries do not become too large by partitioning them into several folders of a maximum number of documents per folder.

- *Duplicate Submissions:* Tells the Content Organizer how to handle repeat submissions of the same document.

- *Preserving Context:* When checked, SharePoint will preserve audit and document properties with the submitted document.

- *Rule Managers:* Specifies the users who can execute rules for incoming content and who receive notification for rules mismatch.

- *Submission Points:* URLs for other sites to submit documents to this site collection Content Organizer.

■ **Note**   Content Organizer settings and rules apply to sites and subsites. Each discrete subsite may have Content Organizer rules different from another subsite.

Ordinarily, when configuring Content Organizer rules in a Records Center, you would likely want documents routed to a document or record library. For the purpose of demonstration, I am going to show you how to specify the Documents Center site collection as a destination location. Once configured, users can submit a record (document) and have the document routed to the Document Center.

1. Open Central Administration.

2. Click the General Application Settings link from the left navigation.

3. Click the Configure Send To Connections link, under External Service Connections.

4. Add a new connection to a documents library in the Document Center, such as http://server/sites/dms/_vti_bin/officialfile.asmx.

5. You may need to enable the Content Organizer feature for the destination site. I did, because it was not enabled in my Documents Center.

6. You may configure the connection properties with action to copy, move, or move and leave a link to the new destination.

7. To establish the destination URL for the connection, visit the Content Organizer settings for a site in the destination site collection—in my case, my Documents Center.

8. See Figure 11-21 for how I configured a Send To link for my Documents Center.

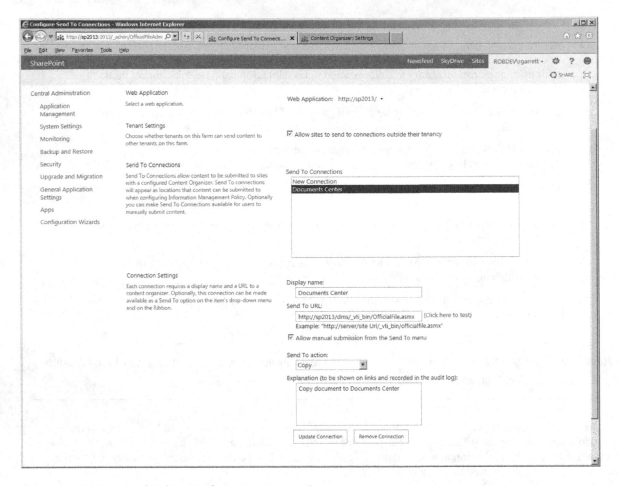

Figure 11-21. *New Send To location for my Documents Center*

■ **Note** The URL `http://server/sites/dms/_vti_bin/officialfile.asmx` is specific to the structure of the target site.

---

9. Navigate to the Document Center site collection.

10. Navigate to the site that has the target location to route documents, in my case the root of the site collection.

11. Click the settings gear icon, and then click the Site Settings menu item.

12. Click the Manage Site Features link.

13. Activate the Content Organizer feature (if not already activated).

Setting Up the Records Center

Assuming you followed the steps in the earlier section, you now have a new Records Center site collection. The following steps detail setting up the Records Center to accept documents as records.

1. Navigate to the Records Center.

2. Click the settings gear icon.

3. Notice the new menu item Manage Records Center; click it.

4. The Manage Records Center page provides high-level steps for establishing tasks and file plans so the new Records Center may accept documents as records (Figure 11-22).

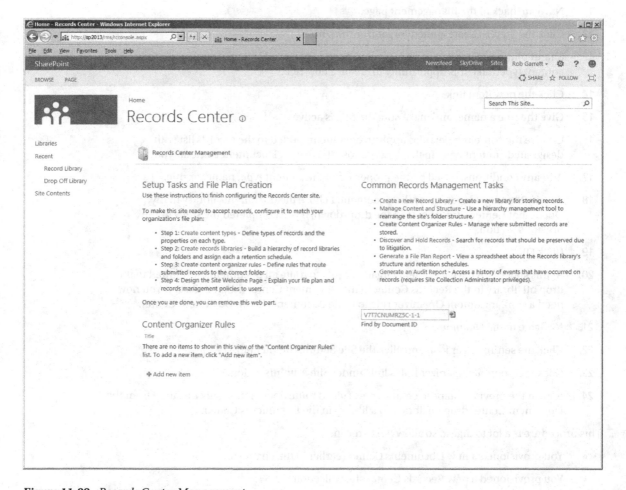

Figure 11-22. *Records Center Management*

5. Click the Step1: Create content types link, and SharePoint navigates you to the site collection Content Type Gallery.

6. Create content types for all documents you wish to store as records in the Records Center. Please review Chapter 9, on metadata, for steps for creating content types.

7. Navigate back to the management page.

8. Click the Step2: Create records libraries link. SharePoint navigates you to a page to create new libraries.

9. Under Libraries, click Record Library.

10. In the resulting page, give the new library a name and click the Create button.

■ **Note** The Records Center has a default record library and drop off library.

---

11. Navigate back to the management page.

12. Click the Step3: Create content organizer rules link.

13. SharePoint navigates you to a list of rules. Each contains a list item based on the rule content type. Take this opportunity to create a new rule.

14. Click the new item link.

15. Give the rule a name, and make sure the rule is active.

16. Choose the content type; rules apply to documents added to the records list with designated content type. In this case, choose the default Document content type.

17. Add any conditions, based on the properties of the content type, name, or title.

18. Specify the target location for the document. I chose the documents library in my Document Center site—shown in the drop-down, if you completed the steps in the previous section.

19. Click OK.

20. At this stage, you have a Content Organizer rule to route all documents submitted to the drop off library in the Records Center to the Document Center drop off library. You now need a similar Content Organizer rule to route documents in the Document Center.

21. Navigate to the Document Center.

22. Click the settings gear icon and click the Site Settings menu item.

23. Click the Content Organizer Rules link, under Site Administration.

24. Repeat the previous steps to create a new rule to route documents, only this time from the Document Center drop off library to a library in the Documents Center.

This procedure is a lot to digest, so allow me to recap.

- You provisioned a new Documents Center (earlier in the chapter).

- You provisioned a new Records Center site collection.

- You created Send To rules for the Documents Center in Central Administration.

- You set up the Content Organizer to route documents from the Records Center drop off library to the Documents Center drop off library.

- You set up the Content Organizer to route documents from the Documents Center drop off library to a document library in the Documents Center.

Assuming all is well, you can now click the Submit a Record button, on the home page of the Records Center, specify a document, and see the document route to the Document Center.

1. Click the Submit a Record button on the home page of the Records Center. This effectively is the same process as dropping a document in the drop off library in the Records Center.

2. Choose a document from your computer.

3. Click OK.

4. SharePoint shows a dialog to provide a title and confirm the file name.

5. Click the Submit button.

6. SharePoint pauses to think and then shows a dialog with status. If all worked, then the status indicates that the Content Organizer routed your document to the drop off library in the Document Center.

7. Head over to the Document Center drop off library, and notice that it is empty; this is because the Content Organizer rule in the Document Center routed the document to the documents library. The net effect here is that the document passed from Record Center drop off library, to Document Center drop off library, and then to a final document library in the Document Center.

Hold and e-Discovery

Any organization that maintains a large enough collection of documents, and defines policy that warrants the use of Records Management, may need to locate documents and put policy on hold. One common example in US business is that of litigation—when a court wants to review an organization's documents, the organization may want to isolate documents from typical routing and retention polices. This is where the Hold and e-Discovery feature of SharePoint comes in handy.

SharePoint 2013 includes a new site template for e-Discovery, called the e-Discovery Center. The e-Discovery Center allows management of discovery cases and holds placed on content, such that an organization may analyze and collaborate around the content for a given case. Each new e-Discovery subsite represents a case and consists of a document library to store documents relating to the case, lists of queries and exports for the case, and various sources of content (Exchange mailboxes, SharePoint sites, and file shares).

Follow these steps to create a new e-Discovery site collection for an already provisioned web application or managed path.

1. Open Central Administration.

2. Ensure that you have a web application provisioned to host your e-Discovery Center (see Chapter 2).

3. Click the Create Site Collections link (under Application Management).

4. Select the web application to host the new e-Discovery Center site collection.

5. Give the site collection a name (such as Discovery Center).

6. Select the desired URL to host the site collection.

7. In the Template Selection, click the Enterprise tab, and then select Discovery Center.

8. Provide usernames for the administrators.

9. Click OK.

10. Once it is complete, navigate to the new e-Discovery Center site collection (see Figure 11-23).

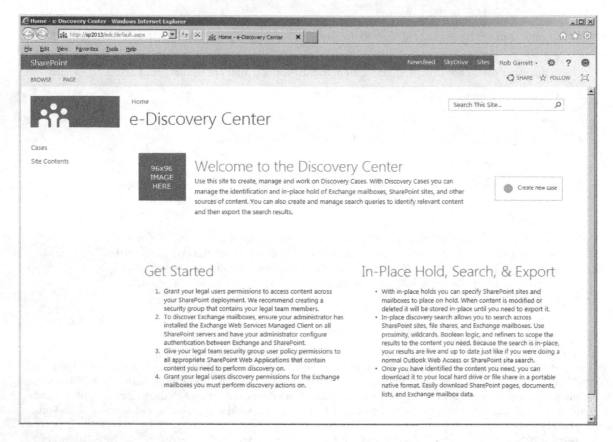

Figure 11-23. *e-Discovery Center*

The home page of the e-Discovery Center provides helpful information to set up security and permissions for your legal team, working on discovery cases. A good practice is to create a new group for all members of your legal team (in Active Directory) and then grant rights to this group to review content in SharePoint sites, file shares, and Exchange mailboxes (specific steps outside the scope of this chapter).

Creating a Case

Imagine that the legal team has taken on a big case to audit all content across the organization. I will now demonstrate the functionality of the e-Discovery Center, using a fictitious case. Exchange and file share discovery is outside the scope of this book, so I shall concentrate on discovery of SharePoint sites. Start by creating a new case.

1. Open the e-Discovery Center.

2. On the home page, click the button to create a new case.

3. SharePoint displays a page to create a new e-Discovery subsite for the new case (Figure 11-24).

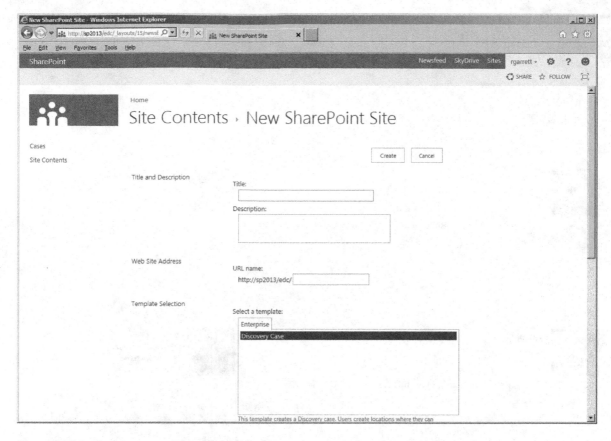

Figure 11-24. *Create a new e-Discovery subsite for a case*

4. The page to create a new e-Discovery subsite is not too different from that of creating any other subsite.

5. Give the case site a name, description, and URL.

6. Decide if the site should inherit permissions from the parent e-Discovery Center.

7. Decide on navigation options for left and top bar.

8. Click the OK button to create the case subsite.

9. SharePoint displays the home page of the new case subsite (Figure 11-25).

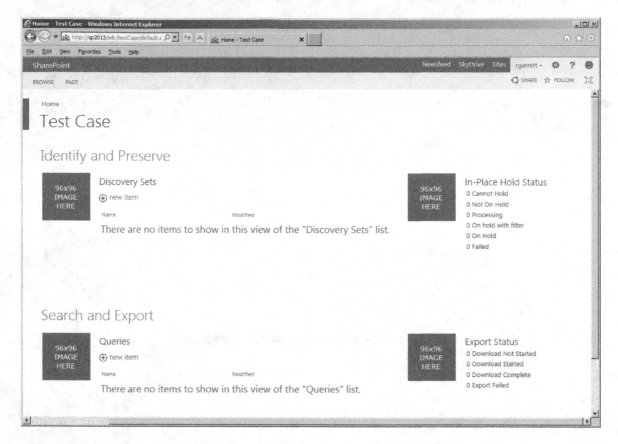

Figure 11-25. Home page of an e-Discovery case subsite

___

■ **Note** The look and feel of the e-Discovery Center and case subsites is subject to change once SharePoint 2013 releases to market.

___

Now that you have a new case collaboration site, the next task is to start collecting content to review, which is where Discovery Sets come in.

1. Click the new item link, next to the tile for Discovery Sets.

2. I created a new Discovery Set for the Documents Center and Records Center sites, created earlier in this chapter.

3. Provide a name for the Discovery Set.

4. Click the link to add and manage sources.

5. SharePoint displays a dialog to add new sources and manage existing sources (Figure 11-26).

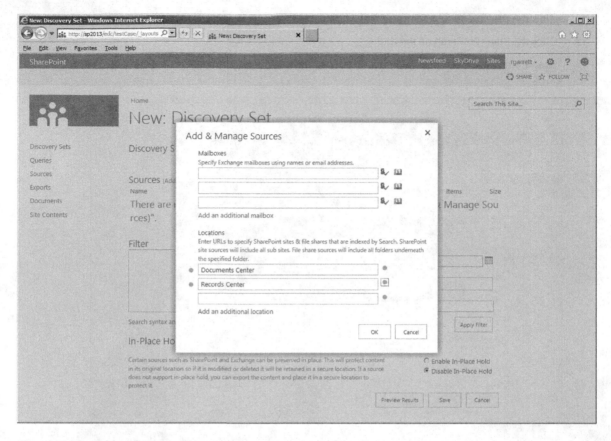

Figure 11-26. *Add and manage Discovery Set sources*

■ **Note**   Discovery of SharePoint content requires the content to be indexed by search and permissions to view the content. I cover search in Chapter 15.

---

6.   Make sure that you have crawled the SharePoint sites with search.

7.   Add the sources and click the icon on the right to validate each source.

8.   Click the OK button.

9.   Apply any filters, such as content by a particular author or for a date range.

10.   Select to enable/disable in-place holds.

■ **Note**   Enabling in-place hold means the content stays in the source location until someone modifies or deletes it, in which case the held content moves to a secured location.

---

11. Click the Preview Results button.

12. Click the SharePoint tab on the dialog.

13. SharePoint shows a summary of sites, lists, libraries, list/document items (Figure 11-27).

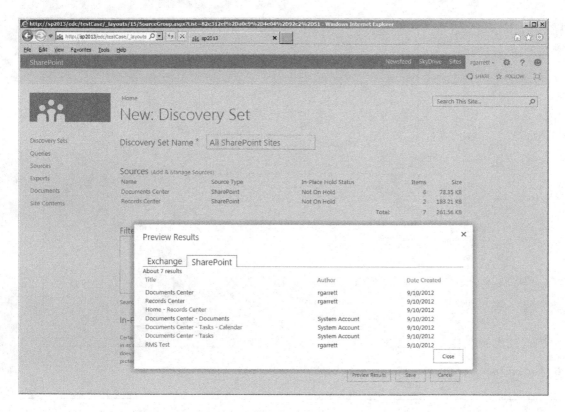

Figure 11-27. *Summary of the discovered content*

14. Click the Close button on the dialog.

15. Click the Save button on the Discovery Set page.

16. SharePoint is now busy discovering content, using the sources you provided.

17. Click the In-place Holds link (top-right tile) to see a summary of the holds status.

18. While the status shows "processing" SharePoint is applying holds to the content.

19. Once the discovery and holds process completes, the status of the in-place holds shows like that in Figure 11-28 (at least for my configuration).

In-Place Hold Status

0 Cannot Hold

0 Not On Hold

0 Processing

0 On hold with filter

2 On Hold

0 Failed

Figure 11-28. *In-place holds summary*

■ **Note** A timer job, called *Discovery In-Place Hold Processing*, runs hourly to process holds.

In my example, I have created discovery of two SharePoint site collections and applied holds to them. I enabled in-place hold so that any changes to content do not affect the original discovered content. If I were to change content in either of the site collections, defined in Discovery Sets, SharePoint would move the original content to a secured location in the site collection. Now that there is some held content, I shall demonstrate how to query this content, which is typically the role of the legal team, as part of their content reviewing tasks.

Querying Held Content

In the previous section, you created a new Discovery Case, defined a Discovery Set within the case, and successfully held SharePoint sources (defined within the Discovery Set). As part of their job, the legal team must present reports of discovered content and export the content for review. The following steps demonstrate how to accomplish these tasks:

1. Navigate to the e-Discovery Center Case subsite.

2. Click the new item link next to the Queries tile.

3. SharePoint displays a page to create a query (Figure 11-29).

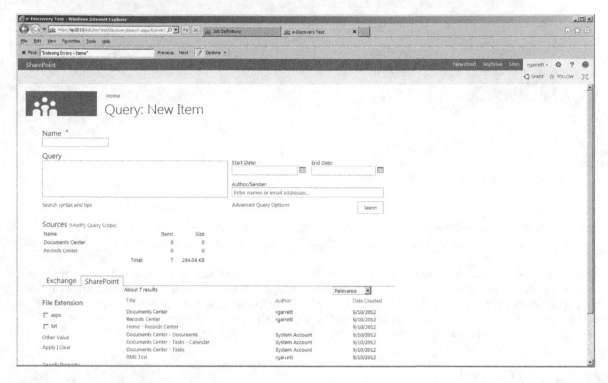

Figure 11-29. *Create a new query of held content*

4. Provide a name for the query.

5. Enter the search query syntax in the query box.

6. Provide optional filters for date range and author.

7. Click the Search button, and SharePoint will indicate found data.

8. Click the SharePoint tab.

9. You may restrict results by file extension and additional properties.

10. When done, click the Save button to save the query.

11. At this point you may close the Query page, or begin the export process.

12. Click the Export button to create an export job.

13. SharePoint displays a page for the creation of a new export (Figure 11-30).

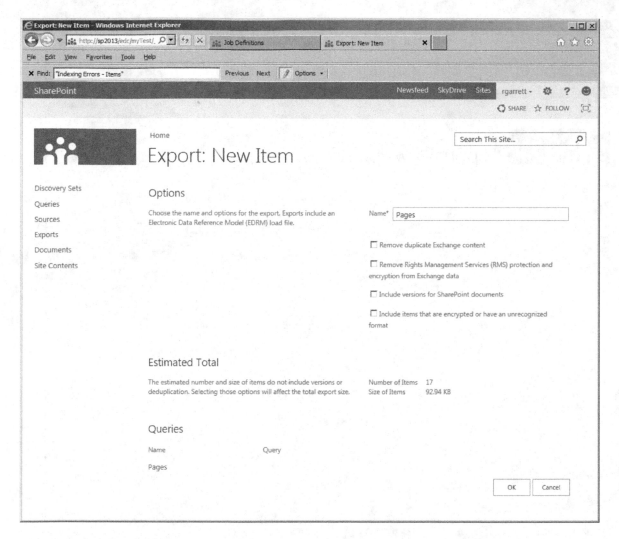

Figure 11-30. *Export held content*

14. Decide on any of the options to include version information, remove rights management protection, include encrypted content, and remove duplicates, etc.

15. Click the OK button.

16. SharePoint displays a page, where you may download the content (Results) and a report of the queried content (Report). (Figure 11-31).

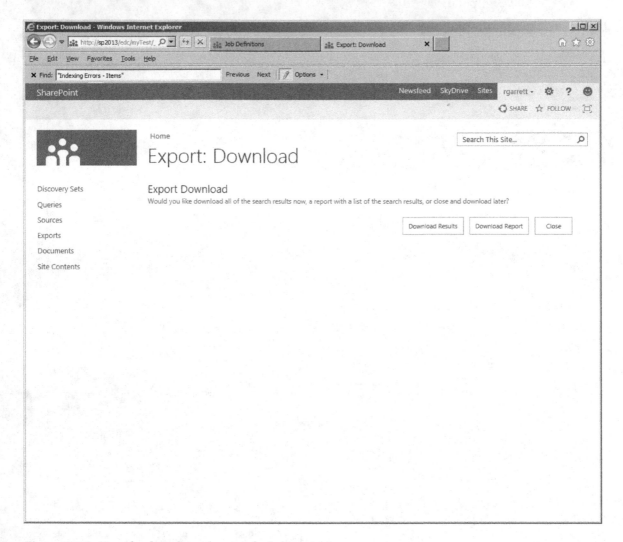

Figure 11-31. *Download results and reports for held content*

17.   Click the button to Download Results.

18.   Specify a folder on disk to save the exported content.

19.   Click the button to Download Report.

20.   Specify a folder on disk to save Excel reports of the exportable content.

21.   When finished, click the Close button.

22.   The discovered, held, and exported content is now on your disk—in a folder you
      designated.

23.   You also have a report of discovered, held, and exported content.

Closing a Case

When the legal team has completed their work, it is time to close the case. Case closure releases any holds on content and marks the case subsite as closed. The following steps allow you to close the case:

1. Navigate to the e-Discovery Center Case subsite.

2. Click the gear icon for the site.

3. Click the Case Closure menu item.

4. SharePoint will display a brief message about undoing holds.

5. Click the Close This Case button.

Records Retention

Records retention and deposition is the process of managing the life cycle of a document, from inception to depreciation. Records retention is vitally important in some organizations that deal with sensitive information, which they must ensure is current and that older versions are depreciated over a finite time.

The good news is that SharePoint provides records retention and deposition functionality at the very core of its records management features. SharePoint considers every list item or document a record, once it has undergone adoption of policy—policy that defines retention and deposition. In this section, my aim is to show you the core functionality inherent in SharePoint for records management.

In an earlier section, we created a Records Center site collection. For the purpose of this section, I shall continue use of this Records Center in my demonstration steps. To begin, I will review records retention for SharePoint sites, which is new in SharePoint 2013.

Sites Records Retention

New in SharePoint 2013 is records retention for site. SharePoint 2010 supported records retention at the list/library and content type level. Now, site owners may apply similar policies to the life cycle of their sites within SharePoint. I shall demonstrate this functionality with a new subsite within the Records Center, which you can create now by following these steps.

1. Navigate to the Records Center site collection.

2. Click the Site Contents link in the left navigation.

3. Scroll to the bottom of the page.

4. Click the New Subsite link.

5. Give the subsite a name, description, and URL.

6. Choose a site template; for demonstration, I chose the blank site template.

7. Click the Create button to create the subsite.

With your new subsite created, you can now define a retention policy, which you configure at the site collection level. You may define multiple different retention policies for different sites, but they all reside at the site collection level.

1. Navigate to the Records Center top level site (root of the site collection).

2. Click the gear icons.

3. Select the Site Settings menu item.

4. Click the link for Site Policies, under the Site Collection Administration heading.

5.   Click the Create button to create a new site policy.

6.   SharePoint shows a page like that in Figure 11-32.

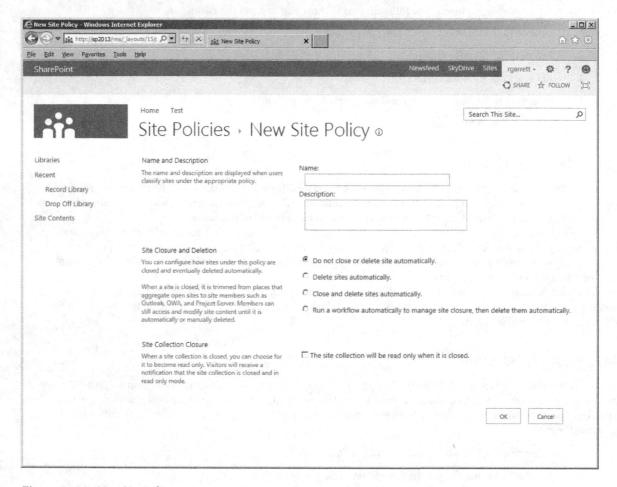

Figure 11-32. *New Site Policy*

7.   Give the policy a name and description.

8.   Choose the site closure policy type (see Table 11-4).

Table 11-4. *Site Deletion Policies*

Policy	Description
Do not close or delete site automatically	Default option—the policy ensures that a site is never deleted automatically and only site owners and administrators may delete the site manually.
Delete site automatically	Provide a time after site created or closed that SharePoint deletes a site, define times when site owners receive notifications and how many times they may postpone deletion.
Close and delete sites automatically	Provide a time when SharePoint should close a site, and when SharePoint should delete a site, define times when site owners receive notifications and how many times they may postpone deletion.
Run a workflow automatically to manage site closure	Run a workflow at a time after site creation and optionally repeat the workflow until the site closes. Provide a time after closure that SharePoint deletes the site, and define times when site owners receive notifications and how many times they may postpone deletion.

■ **Note**   You may optionally make a site collection read-only when closed via site policy, by checking the check box on the Site Policy creation page.

9. Once you have defined site policies for sites, navigate to the subsite you created earlier.

10. Click the gear icon, then select site settings from the menu.

11. Click the link for site closure and deletion, under the Site Administration heading.

12. Choose the site policy for this subsite (Figure 11-33).

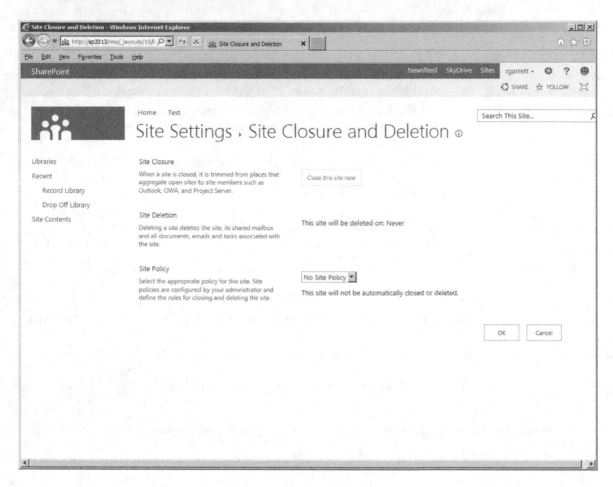

Figure 11-33. *Apply site policy to a site*

13. You may use this page to close the site now, assuming you assign a policy.

■ **Note**   Users may continue to access closed sites in read-only mode.

Content Type Retention Policy

Content types provide good portability in a site collection. A site content type defines an entity—list item or document—in a site collection to which the content type belongs. Applying retention policy to a content type instructs SharePoint to apply the policy to all list items or documents that use the content type. In the same way that content types provide abstraction of metadata (site columns), they also provide abstraction and portability of policy. This is because the policy is not restricted to one specific list item, document, or containing list.

In this section, I shall demonstrate the steps involved in creating a new retention policy and applying it to a document content type. As previously, start by using the Records Center.

1. Navigate to the Records Center site collection.

2. Click the settings gear icon.

3. Select the Site Settings menu item.

4. Click the Site Content Types link under Galleries.

5. Click the content type name to add a retention schedule; I chose the Document content type.

6. Click the Information Management Policy Settings link.

7. Check the Enable Retention check box (wait for the page to post back). (See Figure 11-34.)

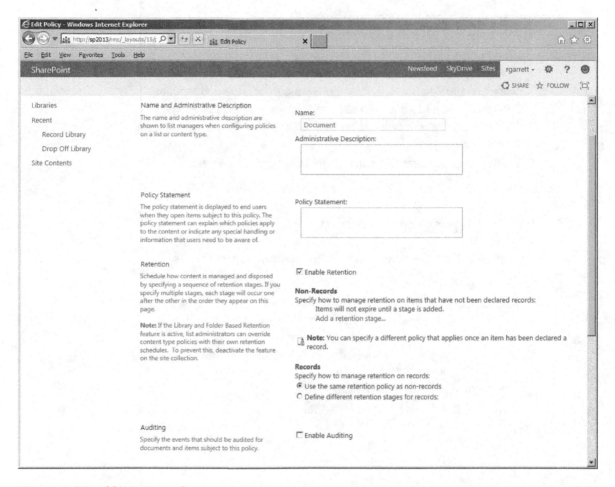

Figure 11-34. *Add retention policy to a content type*

I am sure that you have already gathered that content type retention policies apply to records and non-records. Non-records are essentially list items or documents that a user has not converted to a record. Why allow different retention policies for non-records and records? Content owners may wish to treat non-records differently from records. For example, a content owner may decide that records undergo more stringent retention policy than that of non-records, and content owners define documents as records when they require special consideration. In my example, I shall define different retention policies for records and non-records, as follows:

8. Click the link to add a retention stage for non-records.

9. SharePoint displays a dialog, like that in Figure 11-35.

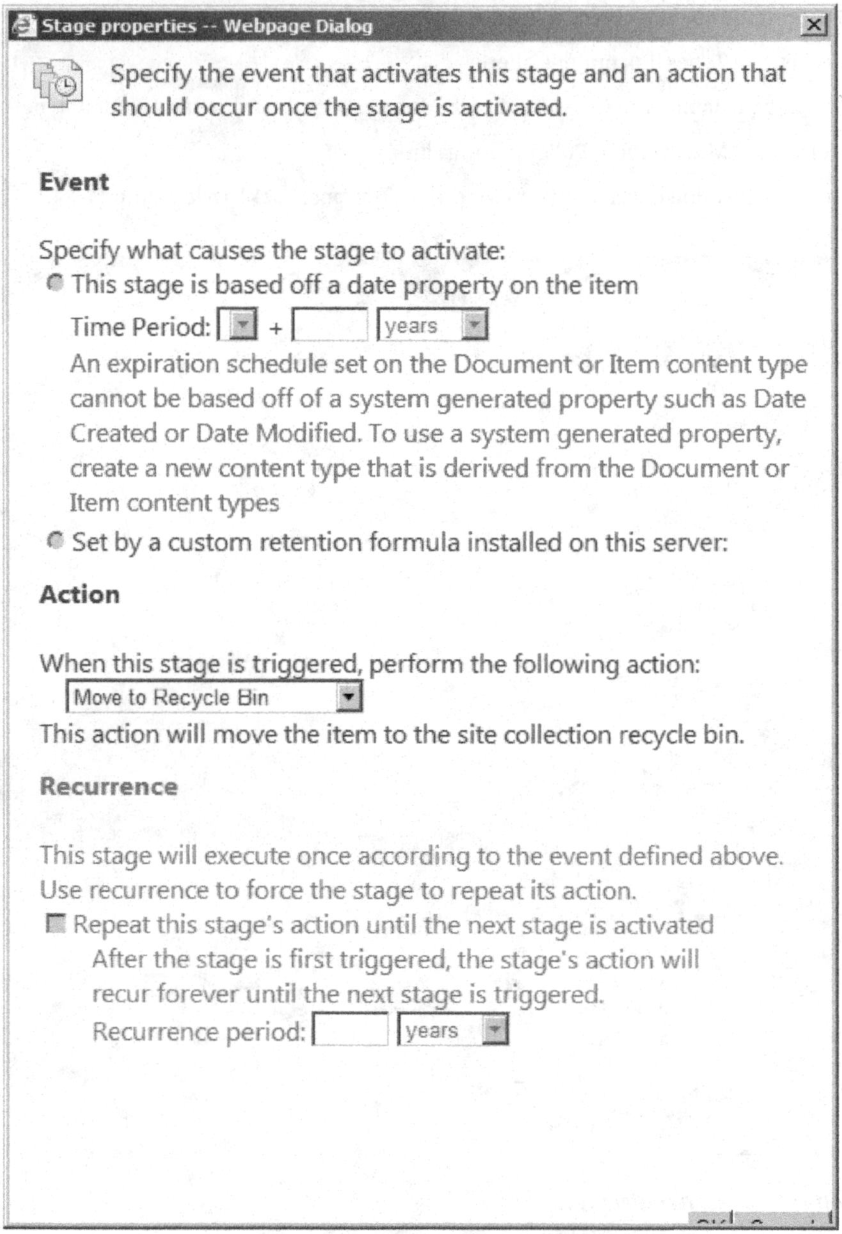

Figure 11-35. *Add a retention stage for a system content type*

10. SharePoint has indicated that you should use a derived content type for stage based on date time, so do that.

11. I created a new content type, called Statement of Work, which derives from the Document content type.

12. Following the previous steps to add retention policy to the new Statement of Work content type, I now see the dialog in Figure 11-35, without the warning.

13. Choose a time after the non-record is created, to execute the policy.

14. Choose an action, as shown in Figure 11-36.

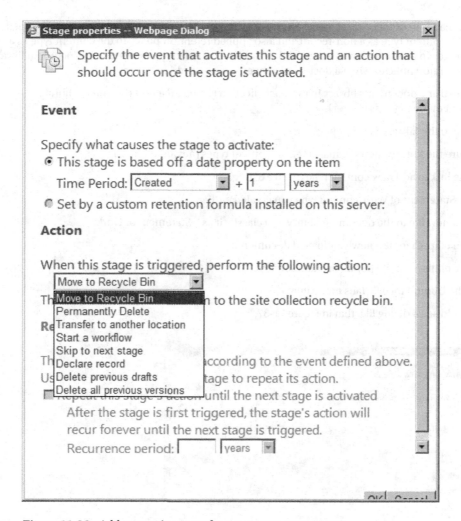

Figure 11-36. Add a retention stage for non-system content type

15. Click the OK button to save the retention stage.

■ **Note** You may only set a custom retention formula from custom code.

---

16. You should be back at the Information Policy Settings page (Figure 11-34).

17. Choose the radio button to define a different retention stage for a record.

18. Repeat the earlier steps, listed previously, to create a new retention stage, only this time for records.

19. Click OK.

I think a quick recap is in order. . . You created a new content type, derived from a document and applied retention policy to the content type as a non-record and also applied retention policy to the content type as a record. Now, let us see the policy in action. Follow the next steps to add the content type to an existing document library and to see the different retention policies when a document converts to a record.

1. Navigate to any documents library in the site collection (I created a new documents library in the root of the Records Center).

2. Navigate to the Library Settings page.

3. Make sure the library allows management of content types (advanced settings).

4. Click the link to add new content types from existing.

5. Add the Statement of Work content type you created earlier.

6. Upload a new file to the document library and classify it as a Statement of Work.

7. Click the ellipses for the newly uploaded document.

8. Click the ellipses on the popup list item settings.

9. Select the Compliance Details menu item.

10. You should see a dialog like that in Figure 11-37.

Figure 11-37. *Compliance details for a document*

11. Notice the policy details at the top of the dialog.

12. Next convert the document to a record.

13. Close the dialog, shown in Figure 11-37.

14. Navigate to the Document Library Settings page.

15. Click the link for records declaration settings.

16. By default, my Records Center does not allow manual declaration of records, so I set this option for the document library.

17. Navigate back to the All Documents view of the library.

18. Select the earlier uploaded document.

19. Click the Files tab on the ribbon.

20. Click the icon to declare the document as a record.

21. Accept the warning message.

22. Follow the earlier steps to view the compliance details of what is now a record.

List Item Retention Policies

List retention policies follow closely those of content type retention policies. Because list retention policies bind to a specific list instance, they are not portable, like content type policies. However, list policies can override content type policies, which you may desire in cases where the overarching policy defined by a site collection is not what you intend for a given list.

The following steps detail how to apply retention policies to items within a list. I will not provide too many steps, as many of the steps are similar to those taken when creating content type retention policies.

1. Navigate to any document library or list in the site (I chose a document library for this example).

2. Navigate to the List/Library Settings page.

3. Click the link for information management policy settings.

4. Click the link to change the source from adhering to content type policy.

5. Add retention stages for all items in the list (see the steps in the section "Content Type Retention Policy").

In-Place Records Management

SharePoint includes the ability to define documents as records in regular document libraries. Prior to SharePoint 2010, you had to move documents to a Records Center with a records library to use records retention and policies (different from those defined for documents). SharePoint now allows for "in-place records management" for document libraries and lists, with configuration starting at the site collection level.

1. Navigate to the root of any site collection.

2. Click the gear icon and select the Site Settings menu item.

3. Click the Site Collection Features link, under the Site Collection Administration heading.

4. Ensure that the In-Place Records Management feature is activated.

5. Navigate back to the Site Settings page.

6. Click the Record Declaration Settings link, under the Site Collection Administration heading.

7. SharePoint presents a page to configure in-place records management (Figure 11-38).

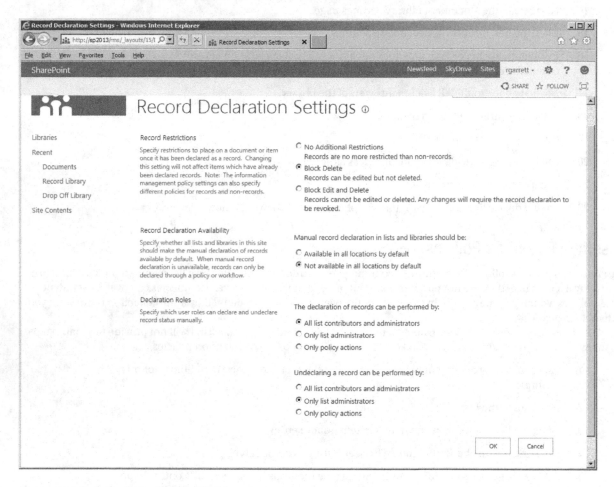

Figure 11-38. *Records Declarations Settings*

8. The page, shown in Figure 11-38, defines settings for the edit/delete restrictions once a document becomes a record, whether in-place records management is available globally in the site collection, and which user roles may turn a document into a record and back again.

9. Navigate to any document library in the site collection.

10. Navigate to the Library Settings page.

11. Click the Record Declaration Settings link.

12. In the next page, you may override the setting at that site collection level to enable/disable in-place records management. You may also check the setting so that all documents added to the library become records.

13. Enable manual declaration of records for the document library.

14. Navigate to the default view page of the document library.

15. Select one or many documents in the view, and then click the Files tab on the ribbon.

16. Check out the document, and then click the Declare Record icon on the ribbon.

Auditing

SharePoint provides basic auditing for events in a list or document library. Similar to the way you configured barcodes in a document library, a list owner may configure auditing at the content type level, as follows:

1. Navigate to the root of the site collection.

2. Click the gear icon, and select the Site Settings menu.

3. Select the link for site content types, under Web Designer Galleries.

4. Choose a non-system content type (Document, Item, etc.).

5. Click the Information Management Policy Settings link.

6. Scroll to the auditing section.

7. Check the check box to allow auditing.

8. Select your choice from the available events to audit.

9. Click OK to save the audit settings.

10. To view audit reports, navigate to the site collection Site Settings page.

11. Click the Audit Log Reports link.

12. In addition to auditing at the content type level (or list), you can track auditing events across the site collection.

13. From the Site Collection Settings page, click the link for site collection audit settings.

Summary

In this chapter, I described the various features for document management within SharePoint. I demonstrated how some of these features allow your users to organize their document content better—often the lifeblood of any organization that processes information.

Among the interesting areas of records management I covered were information management policy, the Records Center, holds and e-Discovery, and auditing. Records management is all about maintaining the life cycle of documents and data in SharePoint in adherence with organization or business policies.

New to SharePoint 2013 is the e-Discovery Center site template and features for better management of holds and discovery, allowing legal teams to place holds on content for review. Also new to SharePoint 2013 are site retention policies, which you spent some time exploring.

In Chapter 12, I shall introduce business intelligence features within SharePoint 2013—stay tuned.

CHAPTER 12

■ ■ ■

Business Intelligence

Business intelligence (BI) is big news for business. Thanks to information storage systems, like SharePoint, information storage and sharing is ubiquitous across many business verticals. What use is this data if we cannot make sense of it in meaningful and useful ways to grow business?

Business intelligence is all about allowing organizations to make intelligent business decisions based on collected data. The subject of business intelligence is vast, and you probably will not be surprised to hear that whole books exist on it. SharePoint contains many new business intelligence offerings, including integrated PerformancePoint Services, which used to exist as a stand-alone Microsoft product (until SharePoint 2010). Although you will not find much information about the implementation of business intelligence concepts or the use of OLAP cubes and data warehouses in this book, you can expect to read about configuration of SharePoint 2013 to support implementation of business intelligence practice. Microsoft introduced a number of great business intelligence features in SharePoint 2010, and SharePoint 2013 improves on the business intelligence feature set with new capabilities, which I will describe in this chapter.

In this chapter, you will take a journey of discovery, installing PerformancePoint Services, Visio Services, and Excel Services. I will also touch on Business Connectivity Services (the successor to the Business Data Catalog in SharePoint 2007), which I cover in detail in Chapter 13.

Before diving in to business intelligence, I want to point out that most if not all the business intelligence features in SharePoint 2013 require an Enterprise license, although in some cases, you can get away with Standard. If you are using a Foundation version of SharePoint 2013, many of the steps and examples in this chapter will not work.

Business Intelligence Features in SharePoint

A large part of business intelligence is about rendering dashboards from existing data. Data may exist in SharePoint, or not; it really should not matter to the end business users. Microsoft has ensured that the business intelligence features of SharePoint are salable, modular—in that you can choose which features to use—and able to integrate with other features of the platform, such as search.

At the core, SharePoint includes the following business intelligence features, each of which I shall review in detail in this chapter.

- **PerformancePoint Services and the Dashboard Designer**: PerformancePoint Services is about providing data analysts and business experts with dashboards of real-time data, hosted within pages of SharePoint. With PerformancePoint Services and Business Connectivity Services, users can hook up their Online Analytical Processing (OLAP) cube and Online Transaction Processing (OLTP) table data to dashboards that allow users to drill down into data and explore axes. The Dashboard Designer is a stand-alone application that installs into Windows and provides the mechanism of implementing rich dashboard technology, which SharePoint can then host for data reviewers.

- **Business Connectivity Services**: Business Connectivity Services replaces the Business Data Catalog of SharePoint Server 2007 and provides sophisticated integration of external data. Business Data Catalog integrated external data via Web Parts, which provided limited control of the view of the data. By contrast, Business Connectivity Services integrates external data via external content types and presents external data to users just as if they were looking at regular list data. Business Connectivity Services provides bidirectional data exchange and can update the external source data as well as aggregate. This is a large improvement over Business Data Catalog, which did not provide updating and could only aggregate external data.

- **Visio Services**: Visio diagrams need no longer remain static and can show real-time data *live*. The power of Visio Services provides this capability, and the best part is you do not need to install Visio on client machines for your users to take advantage of the rich diagrams Visio may provide.

- **Excel Services**: SharePoint provides hosted Excel data, complete with graphing capabilities, without requiring users to deploy the Excel Office application. SharePoint includes PowerPivot, so you may take advantage of the Excel web application in SharePoint to render multiple-axis data contained in OLAP cubes.

- **Reporting Services**: SharePoint makes the inclusion of SQL Server Reporting Services in the platform simpler. Reporting Web Parts allow users to surface report data on SharePoint pages, and the Report Builder facilitates creation of complex reports with data stored in SQL Server.

- **Secure Store Services**: Although Secure Store Services is not directly about business intelligence, the replacement of the Single-Sign-On Service (SSO) in SharePoint 2007 allows integration of multiple channels of data, handling multiple authentication methods. The Secure Store Service is claims authentication–aware. It is a critical element of the business intelligence offering in SharePoint and is required in most cases.

New to SharePoint 2013

As with many other areas in SharePoint, Microsoft did not leave out business intelligence when applying enhancement to the platform.

Excel Services

Microsoft introduced Excel Services to SharePoint 2007 and gave site owners the capability to host Excel data within their SharePoint sites, without users needing Excel installed. SharePoint 2010 enhanced Excel Services with the introduction of PowerPivot and the ability to create engaging views of data in Excel that ported to Excel Services in SharePoint. SharePoint 2013 includes the following Excel Services enhancements:

- Better data analysis with PowerPivot and SQL Analysis; drill down navigation enhancements

- Use of timeline controls, similar to Excel Client

- Ability to designate SQL Analysis Servers for analytics in Excel Services

- Streamlined look to the Business Intelligence Center

- Support for calculated measures and members

PerformancePoint Services

PerformancePoint Services is the heart of business intelligence in SharePoint. PerformancePoint Services provides interactive dashboard and Key Performance Indicator presentation from live data. Prior to SharePoint 2010, PerformancePoint existed as a separate server product. SharePoint 2013 now includes the following enhancements:

- Dashboards have a level A portability—administrators can copy whole dashboards to other users, sites, or site collections. Administrators may also copy dashboards using PowerShell scripts.

- PerformancePoint Services UI is cleaner and allows easier searching of data filters; the BI Center is cleaner and crisper, making the process of dashboard creation easier.

- No need for complicated Kerberos delegation between PerformancePoint Services and SQL Server Analysis services with the support of Analysis Services Effective User.

- PerformancePoint Services now renders on iPad and Safari browsers.

Visio Services

Also introduced in SharePoint 2010, Visio Services provides the ability to view live Visio data in the browser, and users no longer require Visio installed to view diagrams. Visio Services integrates with Workflow to provide a graphical view of workflow design. SharePoint 2013 introduces the following enhancements to Visio Services:

- Administrators can now change the maximum cache size in Central Administration.

- The Health Analyzer reflects usage and adherence to the maximum cache size.

- Provides updated PowerShell Cmdlets.

- Users can annotate hosted Visio diagrams with comments.

In reviewing the preceding enhancements to business intelligence components in SharePoint 2013, you can see that the improvements are less significant than those Microsoft introduced with SharePoint 2010. Therefore, this chapter will provide details about business intelligence that are common to both SharePoint 2010 and SharePoint 2013. However, all of my examples are those tested under SharePoint 2013.

The Secure Store Service

The Secure Store Service is not specifically a business intelligence component but is integral to the operation of other BI services in the SharePoint farm. The Secure Store retains credentials of external systems, such that other services can call out to these external systems for data. Since business intelligence is all about the aggregation and analysis of data, it makes sense that you need the Secure Store Service to maintain credentials to these services.

The Secure Store Service replaces the Single-Sign-On Service from SharePoint 2007 and, of course, includes many enhancements since the early SSO offering. The Secure Store is not just about providing Single-Sign-On, as intended by the previous service, which suggests the name change to Secure Store. All data in the Secure Store is, well, secure and maintained by an encryption key. In the series of steps that follow, I shall demonstrate how to create a new instance of the Secure Store Service in SharePoint 2013, and how to configure it, before I cover the first of the business intelligence components—PerformancePoint Services.

1. Open Central Administration.

2. Click the link to manage service applications, under the Application Management heading.

3. Check to see if the Secure Store Service is already installed.

4. Click the New button on the ribbon and select the Secure Store Service from the menu.

5. SharePoint displays a dialog, like that in Figure 12-1.

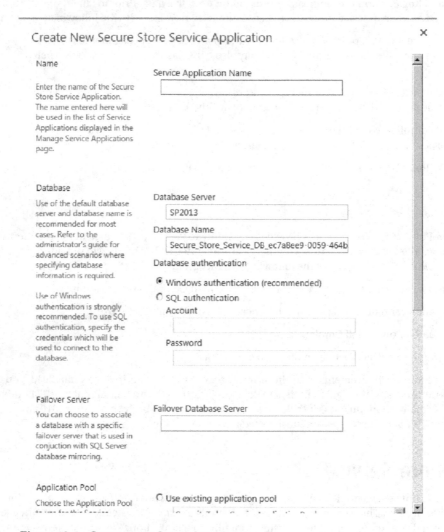

Figure 12-1. *Create a new Secure Store Service*

6. Give the service a name, such as *Secure Store Service*.

7. I like to give the database a more meaningful name.

8. Create a new application pool for the service application.

9. Decide if you want audit enabled (recommended) and the duration for each purge cycle.

10. Click the OK button.

11. Wait a few minutes for SharePoint to provision a new Secure Store Service Application.

Now that you have created a new Secure Store Service, it is time to configure it. SharePoint should have returned you to the list of service applications, and the Secure Store Service should now be in the list. If not, navigate to this page and find the Secure Store Service.

1. Click the Secure Store Service and then click the Manage button on the ribbon.

2. You should see a message about creating a new key before creating a Secure Store Target Application.

3. Click the icon on the ribbon to generate a new key.

4. Provide a passphrase and verification—keep this passphrase safe.

5. Click the OK button to generate the key.

■ **Note**   Keep a record of the Secure Store Service passphrase in a secure place, as you may need it later to reconfigure the service.

This is the only configuration of the Secure Store Service you need for the moment. In the next section of this chapter, I will review the configuration of PerformancePoint Services, which will create a new target application in the Secure Store. Target applications are references in the Secure Store that allow said applications to use credentials in the Secure Store.

PerformancePoint Services

PerformancePoint Services replaces PerformancePoint Server, which used to exist as a stand-alone server application. PerformancePoint Services integrates within SharePoint as a shared service application. PerformancePoint Services works with the Dashboard Designer (more on this later) to execute business intelligence dashboards within SharePoint sites. Before getting into the specific uses of PerformancePoint Services, I shall demonstrate installation in the following steps:

1. Open Central Administration.

2. Click the link to manage service applications.

3. Scroll down the list and make sure that you do not already have PerformancePoint Services installed.

4. Make sure the Secure Store Service is configured and operational (see previous section).

5. Click the New icon from the ribbon.

6. Select PerformancePoint Service Application.

7. Give the new service application a name, such as *PerformancePoint Services*, and choose whether to include the proxy in the farm default list (meaning the PerformancePoint Services application is available to all new web applications).

8. I like to give the database a meaningful name.

9. Create an new application pool for the PerformancePoint Services application.

10. Click the OK button and wait for SharePoint to create the application.

Assuming you ran into no issues with creating a new PerformancePoint Services application, you will now configure the service application to work with the Secure Store Service.

11. Select the PerformancePoint Services application in the list of managed service applications.

12. Click the Manage icon on the ribbon to enter configuration.

13. SharePoint displays a page like that in Figure 12-2.

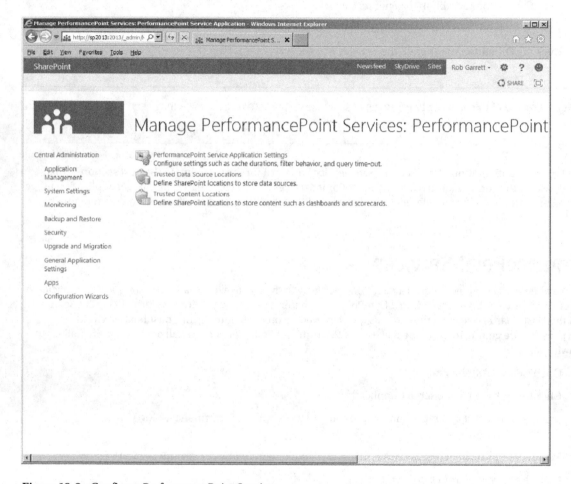

Figure 12-2. *Configure PerformancePoint Services*

14. Click the link for PerformancePoint Services application settings.

15. Provide the credentials of the Unattended Service Account—PerformancePoint Services will use this account when collecting data from external services.

16. The settings page has a number of configuration options for PerformancePoint Services; for now, leave them all as default.

17. Click the OK button.

18. Navigate back to the managed service applications list.

19. Select the Secure Store Service application, followed by a click of the Manage button.

20. You should see a new target application ID for the PerformancePoint Services application.

Creating a New Business Intelligence Center

So far, we have installed and configured a new Secure Store Service and PerformancePoint Service application. Similar to the other enterprise features of SharePoint, SharePoint 2013 includes a dedicated Business Intelligence Center site collection template. This template includes all of the necessary features for business intelligence work. There is nothing stopping you from enabling the business intelligence features in other site collection types, but the Business Intelligence Center provides a one-stop shop for all business intelligence work in a single site collection.

The following steps demonstrate how to create a new business intelligence site collection, using Central Administration:

1. Open Central Administration.

2. Click the link to create a new site collection, under the Application Management heading.

3. Select the web application to host the new site collection (see Chapter 2 for creating new web applications).

4. Give the new site collection a name (such as Business Intelligence Center), a description, and a URL.

5. I chose to host my Business Intelligence Center under an explicit managed path.

6. In the template section, click the Enterprise tab and select the Business Intelligence Center.

■ **Note** If you do not see the Enterprise tab, ensure that you have the Enterprise license version of SharePoint 2013.

---

7. Provide usernames for the primary and secondary administrators.

8. Select the desired quota, then click the OK button.

9. After SharePoint thinks for a moment, you should see a page with a link to the new Business Intelligence Center.

10. Click the link to see the new Business Intelligence Center, which looks something like that in Figure 12-3.

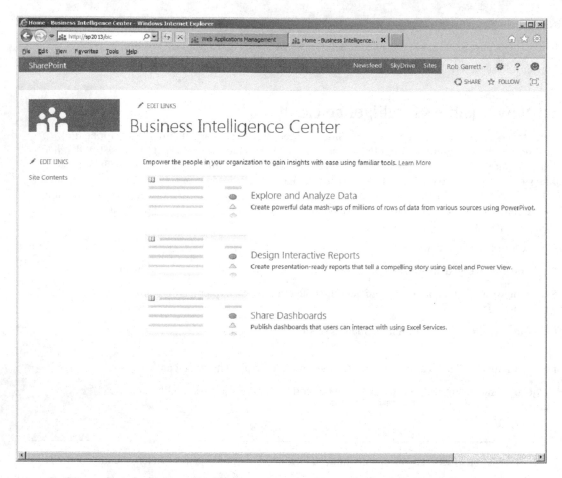

Figure 12-3. *Business Intelligence Center*

The new Business Intelligence Center in SharePoint 2013 has a cleaner look to it. The home page has very little going for it, except for brief information about exploratory analysis of data, designing of interactive reports, and sharing dashboards, but the site is the central hub for hosting PerformancePoint dashboards, Key Performance Indicator lists, maintaining data connectors, etc. To get a hint about what the Business Intelligence Center is all about, click the gear icon and select the menu option to view all site content.

Installing the Dashboard Designer

The Dashboard Designer is a Windows application that enables users to create sophisticated dashboards, which they may then deploy to SharePoint. The Dashboard Designer and PerformancePoint Services work together to provide real-time user interaction with data via the SharePoint web interface. Users who view dashboards, reports, scorecards, and so on do not need the Dashboard Designer, just PerformancePoint Services installed to render first-class objects (FCOs)(more on these shortly) in SharePoint. Only authors of these first-class objects need the Dashboard Designer.

The Dashboard Designer is a click-once application, meaning you can click an icon in SharePoint to download, install, and launch the application. The icon for launching the Dashboard Designer exists anywhere within SharePoint 2013 where a list includes the Web Part Page content type. This is an improvement over SharePoint 2010 in that you can now launch the designer to add dashboard content in more than one location of a site collection, depending on the use of the content type. The following steps demonstrate launching the Dashboard Designer for the Dashboards list in the Business Intelligence Center:

1. Navigate to the Business Intelligence Center.

2. Click the gear icon, and then click the menu item to view site contents.

3. Click the new Dashboards library.

4. Click the PerformancePoint tab on the ribbon.

5. Your page should resemble something like Figure 12-4.

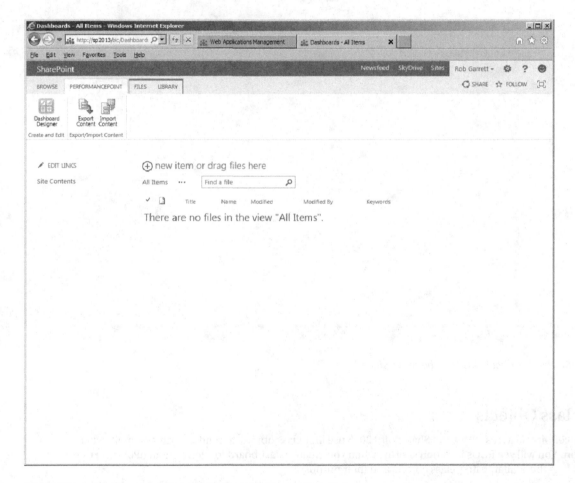

Figure 12-4. *Dashboards library with the PerformancePoint tab*

6. Click the Dashboard Designer icon to launch.

■ **Note**   If you have issues launching the Dashboard Designer, you can launch from the following URL:
http://site-collection/_layouts/PPSWebParts/DesignerRedirect.aspx

Once the Dashboard Designer installs and launches, you should see the application as in Figure 12-5. Now that the Dashboard Designer is installed, I shall walk you through some real examples for creating dashboards and hosting them in the Business Intelligence Center.

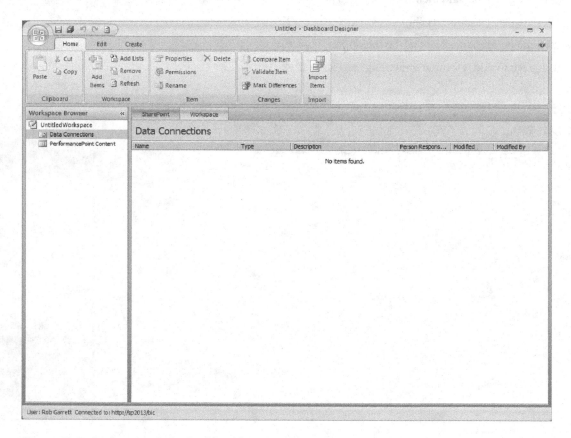

Figure 12-5. PerformancePoint Dashboard Designer

First-Class Objects

PerformancePoint Services (PPS) and SharePoint 2013 use first-class objects to render business intelligence information. You will see FCOs in action shortly, when you create a dashboard for PerformancePoint Services. Table 12-1 lists the available first-class objects and their purpose.

Table 12-1. *First-Class Objects*

FCO	Description
Reports	PerformancePoint Services provides various charts to summarize data visually. These are known as reports and include Excel Services, SQL Server Reporting Reports, Analytic Chart and Grid, and Strategy Map, among others.
KPI	Key Performance Indicator: Provides a status against a known metric and typically displays value based on certain thresholds. Red/Amber/Green indicators are one example of the visual representation of a KPI.
Scorecard	Collection of KPIs on a dashboard, used for tracking status and comparing multiple performance indicators.
Filter	Provides a limited view of a dashboard, as the display is filtered, similar to the way you filter data in Excel by column filters.
Indicator	The visual representation of a KPI, such as the Red/Amber/Green light—the indicator is what displays based on the value of the KPI.
Dashboard	The actual display of reports, scorecards, and KPIs in SharePoint to provide a business intelligence view of data.
Data Source	The source that PPS uses to pull in data for dashboards, reports, KPIs. Examples of data sources include SharePoint lists, Excel Services, SQL Server tables, and OLAP cubes.

Creating a SSAS Database

The business intelligence examples in the following sections of this chapter use a sample OLAP database, hosted by SQL Server Analysis Services (SSAS). I use the Adventure Works sample data warehouse on Codeplex to create my OLAP cubes. To proceed through this section, ensure that you have both SQL Server Analysis Services installed for your version of SQL Server (2008R2 or 2012) and Visual Studio Business Intelligence Studio.

■ **Note** Download the Adventure Works DW database for your version of SQL Server at the following location: http://msftdbprodsamples.codeplex.com/.

---

1. Attach the Adventure Works DW database, using SQL Server Management Studio.

2. Download the Adventure Works sample SSAS project from http://msftdbprodsamples.codeplex.com/releases/view/88252.

3. Open the sample SSAS project in Visual Studio Business Intelligence Studio.

4. From the solution explorer, double-click the Adventure Works DS and point the data source to the data warehouse (DW) database you attached to your SQL Server.

5. Edit the project settings and change the SQL Server and SSAS database under deployment—this is the new SSAS database created when you build and deploy the project.

6. Build the project and deploy it.

7. In the solution explorer, right-click one of the cubes and select the menu item to browse the cube.

8. An example of cube browsing is shown in Figure 12-6.

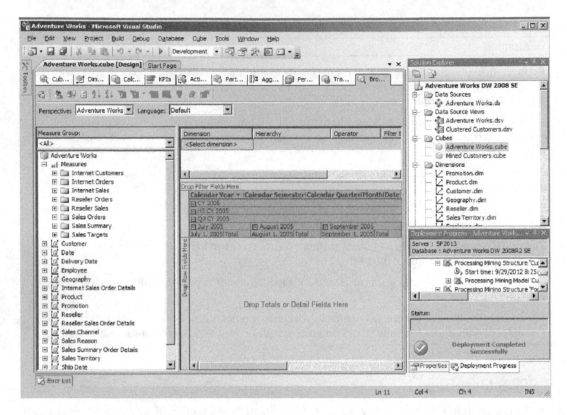

Figure 12-6. *Browse OLAP Cube in VS BI Studio*

Creating a Simple Business Intelligence Dashboard

Although the primary focus of this book is administration, I would be doing you a disservice if I did not demonstrate how easy it is to create a simple dashboard in SharePoint, using PerformancePoint Services and the Dashboard Designer. Dashboards can often get quite complicated, and since there is no end to the shapes and forms that data may take, the same applies to that of data reporting and dashboards.

I should clarify that my goal in this section and those following is not to turn you into a professional data analyst by diving deep into the topic of OLAP and OLTP but simply to show you the power of SharePoint and PerformancePoint Services. The details that follow will show you how to demonstrate dashboard capabilities to business users in your organization and how to manage the administration of PerformancePoint Services.

Creating the Data Source

PerformancePoint Services maintains data connections to data used for dashboards. You can see a list of these data connections in the data connections library in the Business Intelligence Center. Begin by creating a new data connection to the Adventure Works OLAP database you created previously.

1. Open the Dashboard Designer, following the steps in the previous section.

2. Right-click the Data Connections node in the left pane.

3. Select the menu option to create a new data connection.

4. The Dashboard Designer shows a dialog of data connection types (Figure 12-7).

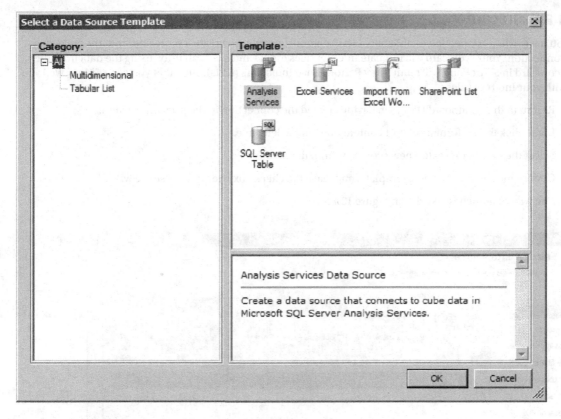

Figure 12-7. *New data source in the Dashboard Designer*

5. My example uses Analysis Services, so select this in the template section.

6. Click the OK button.

7. Give the new connection a name.

8. Provide the name of your SQL Server Analysis Service (typically the same as your SQL Database Server).

9. Select the new OLAP database in the drop-down.

10. Select the cube; I chose the Adventure Works cube.

■ **Note**   If you do not see your OLAP database in the drop-down, the unattended service account for PerformancePoint has no access, or you have not created a SSAS database correctly.

---

11. Click the Test Data Source button to make sure the connection is good.

12. Now is a good time to save the designer workspace project. Click the Save icon from the top bar to save the workspace to disk.

Creating a Scorecard

Now that you have a data connection established, I shall demonstrate how to create a scorecard from the cube data, using this connection. Your scorecard will indicate Internet sales orders and sales quantity, using the data from the cube. The scorecard in SharePoint will render Key Performance Indicators (KPIs), such that you can see how well you are doing with your Internet sales.

1. Return to the Dashboard Designer, having created the connection in the previous section.

2. Right-click the PerformancePoint content node in the left pane.

3. Select the option to create a new scorecard from the menus.

4. Choose the Analysis Services template, and leave the check box checked to use the wizard.

5. The wizard launches, like that in Figure 12-8.

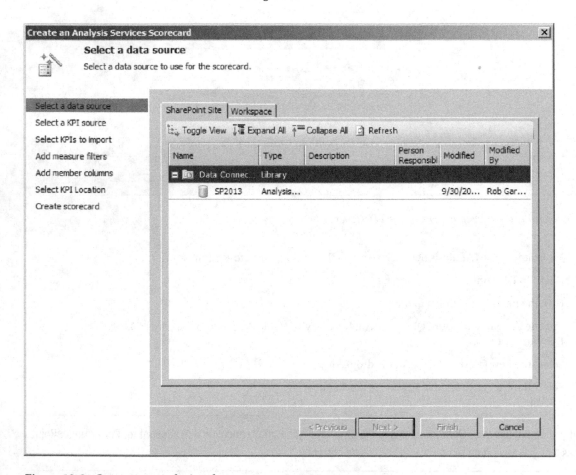

Figure 12-8. Create scorecard wizard

6. Select the relevant data source from those listed in the SharePoint tab, and click the Next button.

7. Leave the radio button selection to create KPIs from SSAS measures, and click Next.

8. You are now ready to choose your KPI measures; click the button to add a KPI.

9. Add the *Internet Sales Amount* with the band method as *Increasing Is Better*.

10. Repeat adding KPI for *Internet Order Quantity*.

11. Click the Next button.

12. Skip the filters page, unless you wish to filter some values, by clicking Next.

13. Skip adding column members (did I say this was a simple example?) by clicking Next.

14. Leave the drop-down option to create KPIs in PerformancePoint content, then click the Finish button.

15. The wizard completes, and you should now see the scoreboard created in the Dashboard Designer.

My scorecard is a little boring! Rather than display the Internet sales for the company as a whole, it would be great to see a breakdown by country offices. This is where dimensions come in . . .

16. Expand the Dimensions node in the details pane of the Dashboard Designer.

17. Expand Sales Territories and then select Countries.

18. Hold the Shift key (this is important), and then left-click-drag the Country dimension to the scorecard so that all the KPI names in the far left column highlight; then let go of the mouse and Shift key.

19. Choose all sales territories and click OK.

20. Your Dashboard Designer should look like Figure 12-9.

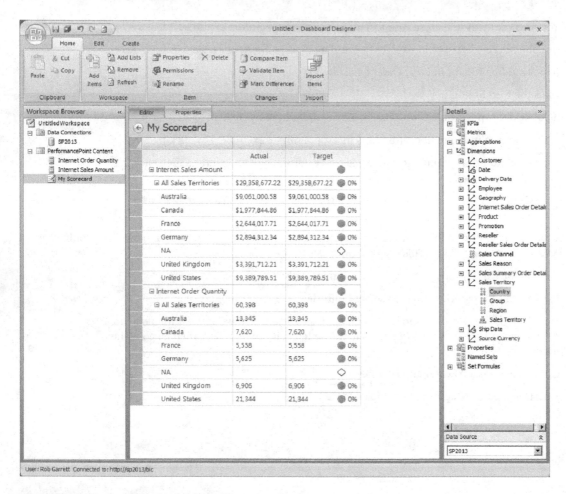

Figure 12-9. *Scorecard with territories dimensions*

You now have a scorecard within your dashboard. Business users might want a nice pie chart to show the percentage of Internet sales per country. Therefore, in the next section I will show you how to create a report.

Creating a Report

In the previous sections, you created a data connection to an OLAP cube, hosted by SQL Server Analysis Services, and used this data connection to create a scorecard of Key Performance Indicators so you could see company Internet sales by country. Your next task is to create a report, so you can visualize the same data in a pie chart report. This is the essence of business intelligence: providing multiple views of the same data to promote business intelligent decisions.

1. Return to the Dashboard Designer.

2. Right-click the PerformancePoint Content node.

3. Select a new report, and choose the Analysis Chart template.

4. Choose the relevant data connection in the wizard.

5. Click the Finish button to generate a default report.

6. From the details pane, drag the Average Sales Amount metric to the Bottom Axis.

7. Drag the Sales Territory Country dimension to the Series Axis.

8. Right-click the chart and change the report type to a pie chart.

9. Your Dashboard Designer view should now look like that in Figure 12-10.

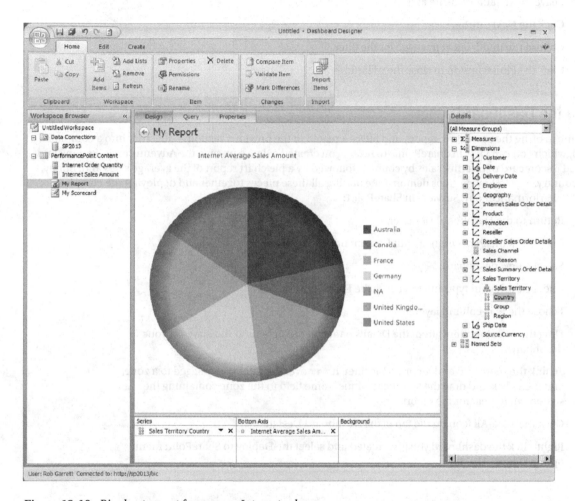

Figure 12-10. *Pie chart report for average Internet sales*

Creating a Filter

No fancy business intelligence dashboard is complete without a way for users to filter their data. Filters enable users to manipulate reports and scorecards and see the results in real time. Filters provide users with a "what if?" mechanism to play with data and home in on the parts of their data that matter most for business decisions.

1. Return to the Dashboard Designer.

2. Right-click the PerformancePoint Content node in the left pane.

3. Select a new members selection filter from the available filter templates.

4. In the wizard, select the appropriate data source connection and click the Next button.

5. Click the Dimensions button and select a dimension for the filter; I chose the Country Territory.

6. Click the Members button and choose some countries for the filter.

7. Leave the default measure as is.

8. Click the Next button.

9. Choose the multi-select tree type for the filter.

10. Click the Finish button to close the wizard.

Creating the Dashboard

It is now time to bring the scorecard, report, and filter—created in the previous sections—together into a completed dashboard, which you can view in SharePoint. To recap, you created a data source to the Adventure Works cube and then created a scorecard of Internet sales by country, followed by a pie chart report of the average sales and, finally, a filter by country. The following steps demonstrate pulling all these pieces together and deploying the complete dashboard to PerformancePoint Services in SharePoint:

1. Return to the Dashboard Designer.

2. Right-click the PerformancePoint Content node in the left panel.

3. Select a new dashboard.

4. Choose the layout type and then click the Finish button.

5. I chose the two-column layout.

6. Drag the BI components from the Details panel on the right onto the Zones of your dashboard.

7. To link the scorecard and report to the filter, hover over the filter you dragged to a zone, and then click and drag the Member Unique Name field to the zone containing the scorecard. Repeat for the report.

8. Click the Save-All icon on the top of the Dashboard Designer.

9. Right-click the dashboard you just created and select the Deploy to SharePoint menu option (Figure 12-11).

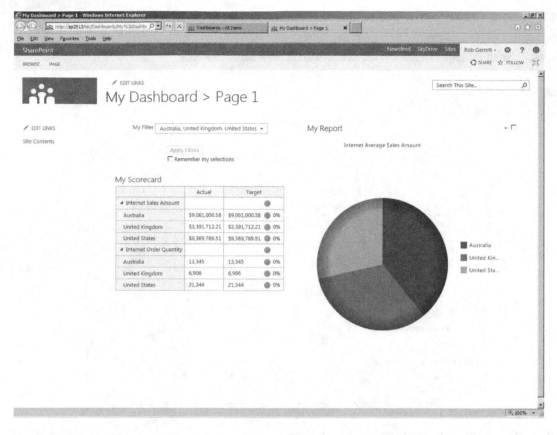

Figure 12-11. *Dashboard in SharePoint*

What is cool about the preceding demo is that you have managed to create an impressive-looking dashboard, containing a filter and two reports, without writing a single line of code. Using PerformancePoint Services and the Dashboard Designer, business intelligence experts can construct some really neat and exciting reports—the best part is that these dashboards run off live data in the OLAP cube. Before leaving the demo, I want to demonstrate all the PerformancePoint content stored in the SharePoint Business Intelligence Center site collection.

1. Open the Business Intelligence Center in SharePoint.

2. Click the gear icon and then view site content menu item.

3. Click to view the PerformancePoint Content library.

4. Figure 12-12 shows the various components you created in the Dashboard Designer, now in the PerformancePoint library.

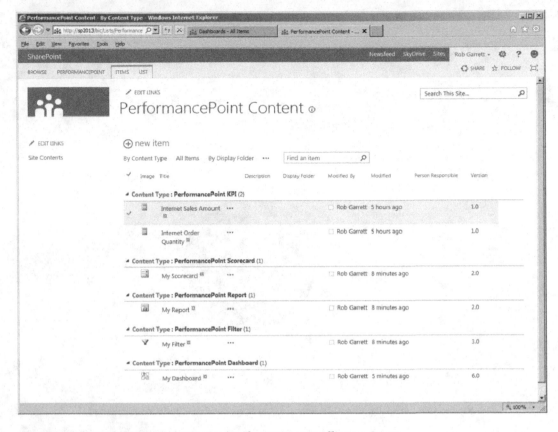

Figure 12-12. PerformancePoint Content in the Business Intelligence Center

5. Each business intelligence component has a different content type.

Security Permissions for PerformancePoint Services

PerformancePoint ties in with the security and permissions system of SharePoint 2013. Some users in your organization will have permissions to create business intelligence dashboards, and others only permission to view dashboards, created by others. For example, data collection experts might collect data in SharePoint, SQL Server, or some other store, and then create data sources to these stores; a business intelligence expert might create the dashboards; and managers consume the data within dashboards to make business decisions.

Certain tasks of PerformancePoint Services map to permission sets within SharePoint, as shown in Table 12-2.

Table 12-2. Permissions for PerformancePoint Services

PerformancePoint Task	Permission Set
View dashboards	Read
Create dashboard items and save them in SharePoint	Contribute
Publish new dashboards from the Dashboard Designer	Design
Manage user permissions	Full Control

PerformancePoint Dashboards in Production

In previous sections of this chapter, I demonstrated how to create PerformancePoint first-class objects and arrange them in dashboards within SharePoint. This process is fine for development, but what happens if you wish to package dashboards and FCOs and deploy to a production environment?

One obvious approach to deploying business intelligence dashboards is to leverage site collection backup and restore, because this approach collects everything in the Business Intelligence Center. However, this approach is less desirable when deploying updates to just dashboard components in an integrated SharePoint site composed of other content, such as an intranet. Fortunately, the Dashboard Designer has a solution for packaging business intelligence dashboards and FCOs.

Before reviewing the steps for a production deployment, I should point out a few caveats for a production deployment to work.

- Both source and destination SharePoint 2013 farms must have *exactly* the same version number; if one farm differs from the other, the import will likely have issues with compatibility.

- Make sure you deploy all dependencies with the FCOs (such as Data Connections); failure to do so will result in your dashboards failing in the destination environment.

- If the Dashboard Designer encounters an FCO or Data Connection in the destination farm with the same name as that of the source, prior to import, the import process will overwrite the version in the destination. This is sometimes desirable for updating an older version of FCOs, but not always the case if the destination contains a completely different FCO of the same name.

Now that you understand the preceding messages, I shall demonstrate the steps for packaging business intelligence dashboards and first-class objects for production deployment.

1. Open the Dashboard Designer (see earlier section of this chapter) in your production environment.

2. From the Home tab, click the Import Items icon.

3. Navigate to the Dashboard Designer project (DDWX file) that you created in your development environment containing your dashboards and first-class objects.

4. The file contains references to the development Business Intelligence Center site collection, so the Dashboard Designer will know how to import the items.

5. When the wizard opens, configure the mapping of importing items to destination locations in the production farm.

6. Decide if you wish to import data sources that already exist in the destination, in which case the Dashboard Designer will replace them, and decide on importing dependencies (usually a good idea).

7. Click the Next button and SharePoint will provide an import summary once the import completes.

8. Check the check box if you want the imported items added to the current open workspace in the Dashboard Designer; otherwise, they just import to the new SharePoint environment only, once you click the Finish button.

9. Click the Finish button to complete the import process.

You should now have the same working business intelligence dashboard and first-class objects in production as you have in development. The preceding steps are not perfect—the person deploying the BI components to production must have knowledge of the Dashboard Designer and complete the preceding series of steps. At the time of writing, there are no SharePoint deployment package options for deploying SharePoint business intelligence dashboards. BI dashboards fall into the category of content, and like most other content in SharePoint, the choices available for deployment to production consist of backup/restore, manual push of content (essentially the preceding steps), or content deployment.

■ **Note**　Content deployment caters to publishing content, so I am unsure that this mechanism will work for business intelligence dashboards and FCOs.

Visio Services

Visio Services is a wonderful addition to the suite of business intelligence tools in SharePoint. Visio Services brings visual design to workflows and provides real-time views of Visio diagrams. Prior to this change, users could upload Visio diagrams to document libraries, but other users required Visio or a Visio viewer application installed on their computer to view these documents. Visio Services now allows users to view and interact with Visio diagrams without needing to install Visio on their computer.

Microsoft introduced Visio Services in SharePoint 2010. The core of Visio Services has not changed greatly in SharePoint 2013, except for added cache support and ability to annotate Visio drawings with comments. All the same, Visio Services is a large part of the business intelligence offerings in SharePoint 2013, so I shall discuss it at length in this part of the chapter.

Like the other BI components, Visio Services exists as a service application in SharePoint, and you provision a new instance via Managed Service Applications in Central Administration, via the farm configuration wizard (see Chapter 2). I shall now demonstrate the steps to install Visio Services from Central Administration.

1. Open Central Administration.

2. Click the link to manage services on server.

3. Ensure that the Visio Graphics Services is started on your application server.

4. Navigate back to the home page of Central Administration.

5. Click the link to manage service applications, under the Application Management heading.

6. Scroll down and look for a Visio Services Application; if not already installed, continue the steps.

7. Click the New icon from the ribbon.

8. Select the Visio Graphics Service from the menu.

9. Give the service a name and configure the application pool to use your application pool managed account (see Chapter 2 for more details on managed accounts).

10. Include the proxy in the farm default group.

11. Click the OK button to provision the Visio Service application.

Save from Visio to SharePoint

If you followed the steps in the previous section, or you ran the farm wizard and checked Visio Services, then you should have a working Visio Service application in your farm. In this section, I shall demonstrate saving a Visio diagram from within Visio (Visio 2013 in my case) directly to SharePoint.

You may save a Visio diagram to SharePoint using the latest version of Visio (Visio 2013) or Visio 2010 Professional or Premium.

■ **Note**   Office 2010 included an option to save to SharePoint from the Save & Send tab in the back office section. Office 2013 appears to support Office 365 but does not include a "Save to SharePoint" option. However, you can provide a URL to your document library in the Save As dialog.

---

1. Open Visio with a diagram you wish to publish to SharePoint (Figure 12-13).

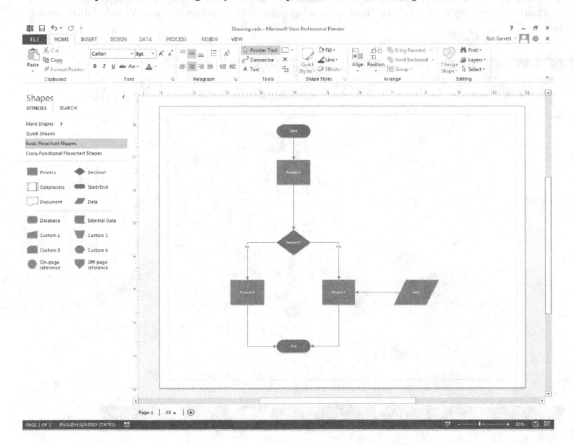

Figure 12-13. *Diagram in Visio*

2. Click the File tab.

3. Click the Save As tab.

4. If you opened a file, or saved a file to SharePoint recently, click the Other Web Locations option, followed by a click of the Browse button.

5. If Other Web Locations is not shown, click Computer and then the Browse button to display the Save As dialog.

6. Paste the URL of your SharePoint document library into the file name field.

7. Press Enter.

8. Provide the file name to save, and then click the Save button to save the file to SharePoint.

A new feature in SharePoint 2013, worth mentioning, is the ability to drag and drop files onto your document library, via the browser. Open the document library in IE, Firefox, or Chrome, and then drag the file from Windows Explorer to the browser.

Now that you have the Visio file in SharePoint, click the file name in the document library from within SharePoint. Assuming you have Visio Services configured (see earlier section of this chapter), SharePoint should render your Visio diagram in the browser without having to launch the Visio application on your desktop (Figure 12-14). Test out this last part by accessing the same Visio file from another computer that does not have Visio installed on the client machine.

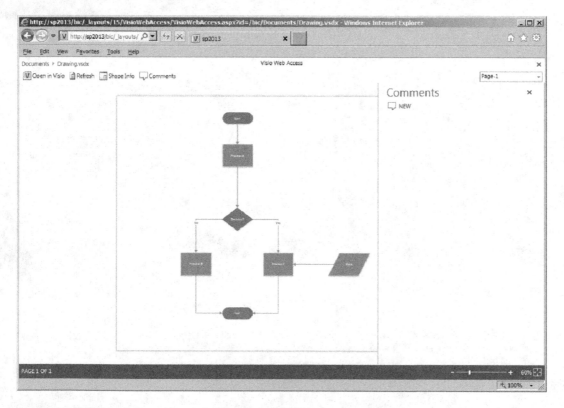

Figure 12-14. *Visio diagram shown in SharePoint via Visio Services*

Figure 12-14 depicts another new feature of SharePoint 2013: the ability to add comments to your Visio diagram. Clicking the Comments button at the top of the page shows the comments pane on the right, where you can add comments.

Create Workflows from Visio

Anyone who has developed his or her own workflow, in Visual Studio or SharePoint Designer, will likely tell you that it can be a difficult process. Microsoft provides a very extensive workflow engine, and this engine operates within the SharePoint platform to provide business-automated process around list items, documents, and sites. However, creation of custom workflows still requires some talent to get working right—usually in the hands of SharePoint developers.

Extensibility of workflows has spawned a number of Consumer Off-The-Shelf (COTS) products—Nintex and K2, to name a couple. These products enhance the out-of-the-box workflow functionality with visual designers and activities that are more sophisticated. Of course, these products typically come with a hefty price tag, on top of the cost for SharePoint and Windows licenses.

Using Visio 2013, SharePoint Designer 2013, and SharePoint 2013, business owners and analysts can now create workflow to automate their business processes with the same visual capabilities offered by third-party products. In this section, I shall demonstrate creating a new workflow inside Visio 2013 and then importing this workflow into SharePoint. You will start by creating a simple workflow in Visio.

1. Open Visio 2013 Professional or Premium.

2. Within the featured categories, create a new Microsoft SharePoint 2013 Workflow.

3. Choose your metrics (US is fine) and click the Create button.

4. Visio now shows an empty workflow, ready to add activities (Figure 12-15).

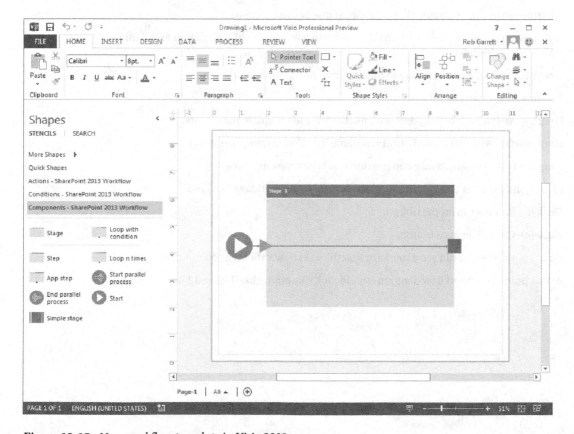

Figure 12-15. *New workflow template in Visio 2013*

5. On the left are the shape stencils for dragging into your workflow.

6. Each stencil represents an activity for your workflow process.

You are now ready to begin construction of your workflow. To make life simpler, I have chosen an easy-to-implement workflow, which fires with the addition of list items in a list. The list is a list of new employees of the company to onboard. Each onboarding employee in the list is represented as a list item and assigned a status. As members of various departments complete successive onboarding tasks, the status of the employee changes, until the employee completes the onboarding process.

■ **Note**   Because of the underlying differences between the Microsoft SharePoint 2010 Workflow template and the SharePoint 2013 Preview Workflow template, you cannot use shapes from one template within a diagram created by the other. You can only use shapes from the SharePoint 2013 Preview Workflow Actions, SharePoint 2013 Preview Workflow Conditions, and SharePoint 2013 Preview Workflow Terminators stencils to build a SharePoint 2013 Preview Workflow.

---

1. Make sure you have Visio 2013 open, as shown in Figure 12-15.

2. From within the SharePoint 2013 Workflow Actions category, drag the Set Field in Current Item activity to the workflow timeline.

3. Rename the activity (double-click it) as Set Status to Onboarding.

4. Notice that you do not have to bind this activity to a list item field—SharePoint Designer takes care of this later.

5. Drag the Send an E-mail activity to the timeline.

6. Rename this activity as Inform HR.

7. Drag the Assign Task activity and rename it as User to complete paperwork.

8. Drag another Assign Task activity and rename it as Create computer accounts.

9. Drag the Send E-mail activity and rename it as Welcome employee.

10. Finally, drag the Set Field in Current Item activity to the workflow timeline.

11. Click the Process tab on the ribbon.

12. Click the Check Diagram button.

13. If all is good, you should see a message that the workflow validation completed.

14. At this point, your workflow diagram should look something like Figure 12-16.

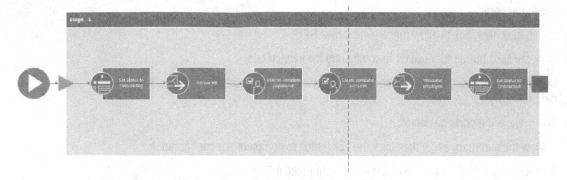

Figure 12-16. *Workflow diagram in Visio 2013*

15.   Save the workflow as a Visio VSDX file.

INSTALLING WINDOWS AZURE WORKFLOW

SharePoint 2013 now abstracts workflow processing to the cloud—using Windows Azure Workflow (WAW). SharePoint still maintains the legacy workflow engine, as part of the .NET Framework 3.5.1, to enable execution of SharePoint 2010 workflows. However, SharePoint 2013 does not install WAW by default. The following steps detail additional configuration:

1.   Ensure that you are not installing on a domain controller—WAW integration does not work with SharePoint 2013 running on a single server domain controller.

2.   Create an account in your domain for WAW.

3.   Add this account to the local administrators group on the SharePoint server and grant log on locally permissions.

4.   Ensure that the SQL Server accepts connections via TCP/IP—use the SQL Server Configuration Manager tool.

5.   Provide the WAW account access to SQL Server and include create database permissions (or you could grant administrative permissions if you are brave).

6.   Log on to the SharePoint server as that account.

7.   Install Workflow Beta 1.0 (http://technet.microsoft.com/en-us/library/jj193478), using the Web Platform Installer.

8.   After installation, you should see the WAW Configuration Wizard.

9.   Click to create a new farm, using Custom settings.

10.   Configure databases and click the Test Connection button for each.

11.   Make sure the WAW service account is correct—use the fully qualified domain name (FQDN); by default it prepopulates the text box with a non-FQDN.

12.   Provide certificate generation keys.

13. Leave the ports as default.

14. Check the check box to allow management over HTTP.

15. Click the Next button to move on to configuring the service bus.

16. Complete similar steps for database, service account, and certificates settings as you did previously.

17. Again, leave the ports as default.

18. Review the summary page, then click the tick button to complete the configuration.

19. Wait for the configuration to complete—this might take a little time.

20. After WAW configuration completes, run the following PowerShell command:

    ```
    Register-SPWorkflowService -SPSite "http://{sitecollectionurl}"
    -WorkflowHostUri "http://{workflowserve}:12291" -AllowOAuthHttp
    ```

21. Assuming no errors, you have now configured WAW in SharePoint 2013 for your site collection.

More information on installing and configuring WAW is available at the following URL: http://technet.microsoft.com/en-us/library/jj658588%28v=office.15%29.

With the visual aspects of your workflow complete, now it is time to import the Visio file into SharePoint, using SharePoint Designer 2013.

Before starting this part of the process, create a custom list in your SharePoint site, with string fields for employee name and onboarding status.

■ **Note**   Do not use the export function in Visio to create a WSP file; SharePoint Designer 2013 reads the VSDX file directly.

1. Open SharePoint Designer 2013.

2. Click the Open Site button.

3. Provide the URL to your SharePoint site.

4. Click Workflows, in the left navigation pane.

5. Click the down arrow on the icon on the ribbon to import from Visio.

6. You should see the option to import from Visio 2013; if not, ensure that Windows Azure Workflow is installed.

7. SharePoint Designer displays a dialog for creating a new workflow from the imported Visio diagram (Figure 12-17).

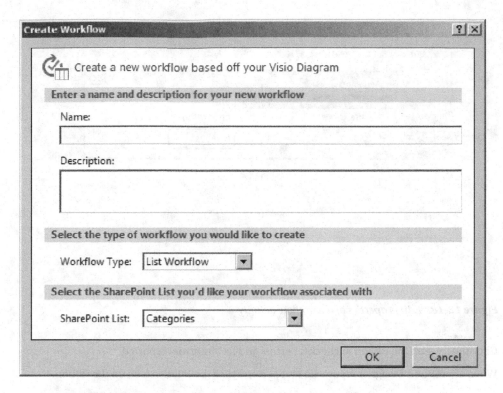

Figure 12-17. *Create a new workflow from a Visio Diagram*

8. Provide a name and description, and type of workflow.

9. I created a List Workflow and so bound the workflow to an existing New Employees list.

10. SharePoint Designer shows the imported Visio Workflow diagram, similar to the look in Visio.

11. For each workflow activity, hover in the bottom left corner and then click on the Properties icon that appears.

12. Set the properties for each activity with fields in the list (Figure 12-18).

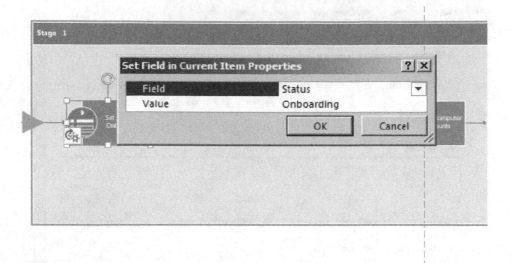

Figure 12-18. *Edit properties of a workflow activity*

13. Click the icon on the ribbon to check for errors and fix any errors reported.

14. When SharePoint Designer reports no more errors, click the Publish icon on the ribbon.

15. You can now open your list in your SharePoint 2013 site and test out the workflow you created.

The Visio Web Part

SharePoint includes a Visio Access Web Part. This Web Part will render a Visio diagram within SharePoint and display any live data in the diagram in real time. Earlier in this chapter, I demonstrated Visio Services rendering a hosted diagram and a screenshot in Figure 12-14. The Visio Access Web Part is essentially the same functionality within a Web Part, so content owners can place Visio-rendered diagrams within their pages.

1. Upload a Visio diagram file to a document library in your site.

2. Edit a Wiki or publishing page (if a publishing site).

3. Insert a Web Part from the ribbon.

4. Choose the Visio Access Web Part from the Business Data folder.

5. Click the link to open the Web Part settings tool pane.

6. Change the Visio Web Drawing URL to the location of your Visio drawing in the document library.

7. Save the Web Part settings and the page.

8. You should now see your Visio diagram on the page (Figure 12-19).

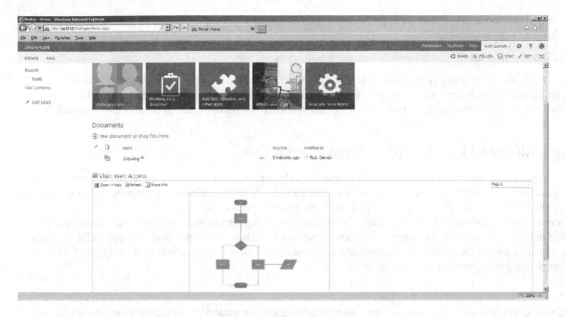

Figure 12-19. *Visio diagram on a page using the Visio Access Web Part*

Excel Services

Excel Services is an enterprise application that allows you to load, calculate, and display Excel workbooks within SharePoint. Microsoft introduced Excel Services in SharePoint 2007, enhanced it in SharePoint 2010, and further enhanced this service in SharePoint 2013.

In the initial version, Excel Services offered considerably less functionality than that of the full Excel application, but when SharePoint 2010 released to market it supported a lot more in the way of data manipulation with pivot tables, better graphs, and ability to connect to external data via Business Connectivity Services. I mentioned some of the new features in Excel Services for SharePoint 2013 at the beginning of this chapter. Like most services in SharePoint, SharePoint 2013 implements Excel Services as a service application. By now, you are probably very knowledgeable at creating new service applications, or perhaps you ran the farm wizard to configure Excel Services. Either way, for the benefit of those readers who may have jumped to this section of the chapter, the following is a series of steps to configure Excel Services in your SharePoint farm:

1. Open Central Administration.

2. Click the link to manage services on server.

3. Ensure that the Excel Calculation Service has started.

4. From the home page in Central Administration, click the link for managing service applications.

5. Scroll down the list and check to see if an Excel Services Application already exists.

6. If not, click the New icon from the ribbon.

7. Select Excel Services Application from the menu.

8. In the page that appears, give the service a name.

9. Configure the application pool using your application pool managed account (see Chapter 2).

10. You may choose to include the Excel Services Application proxy in the default farm group for new web applications.

11. Click the OK button to provision the service application.

With Excel Services configured in the farm, it is now time to demonstrate creating a simple Excel Services dashboard. Of course, when it comes to dashboards, PerformancePoint Services provides a greater level of sophistication, but if you are looking for simple hosting of Excel sheets and pivot tables, Excel Services may suffice.

Creating a Simple Dashboard in Excel Services

The following steps detail creating a simple dashboard, hosted in SharePoint 2013, originating from data stored in an Excel sheet. Excel Services, like Visio Services, allows users to host sheets and workbooks in SharePoint 2013, without requiring the client to have the full-blown Excel application on his or her desktop.

Excel Services is much more than a lightweight Excel sheet-rendering application. Administrators can couple Excel Services to external data, using Business Connectivity Services and the Secure Store Service to render live data. I shall demonstrate a simple dashboard by creating an Excel sheet in the Office application, importing live data from SQL Server, and then promoting it to SharePoint 2013.

■ **Note**   The following demonstration requires the Adventure Works sample databases, available for download at http://msftdbprodsamples.codeplex.com/.

---

1. Open Excel 2013.

2. Click the Data tab, and then click the From Other Sources icon on the ribbon to import data into Excel.

3. I chose to import SQL Server data from the Employee View in my Adventure Works Data Warehouse database.

4. Follow the instructions in the wizard—most of the steps are straightforward. Other than providing the name of my SQL Server, database choice, and table name, I left all options default.

5. When finished, ask the wizard to import the data into an empty Excel sheet as a table at position A1 (Figure 12-20).

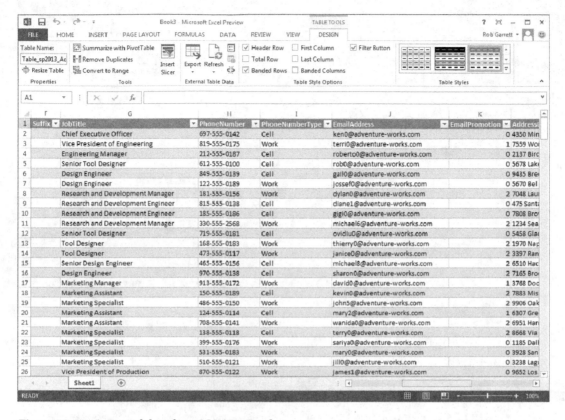

Figure 12-20. *Imported data from SQL into Excel*

6.   Open another sheet in the Excel workbook.

7.   Within the Data tab, click the icon on the ribbon to get external data, and use the existing connection you created a moment ago.

8.   Insert a pivot chart, which also creates you a pivot table.

9.   Your Excel page should look something like that in Figure 12-21.

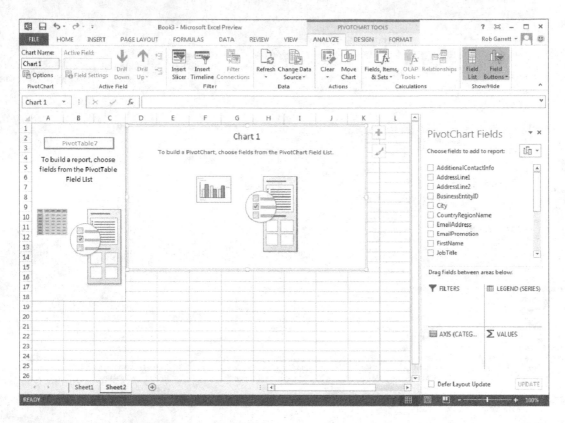

Figure 12-21. *Insertion of a pivot chart and table*

10. Drag the CountryRegionName field to the Report Filter section, and the City to the Row Axis (Categories) and Sum Values.

11. Change the filter value to United States.

12. Right-click the pivot chart and change the chart type to a line graph.

13. Your pivot chart and table should look something like that in Figure 12-22.

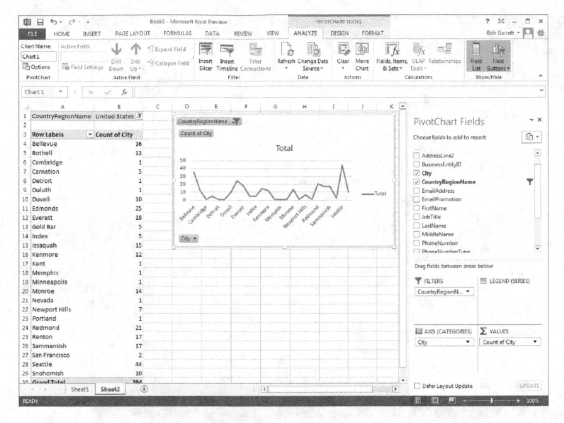

Figure 12-22. *Pivot chart and table after defining axis and totals*

14. Save the workbook to a SharePoint document library (provide the document library URL in the Save As dialog).

15. Open the Excel workbook inside SharePoint by clicking on the file in the document library.

16. Assuming you have Excel Services configured and running, you should see your workbook open in the browser.

17. Close the pivot data fields, and your page should look like that in Figure 12-23.

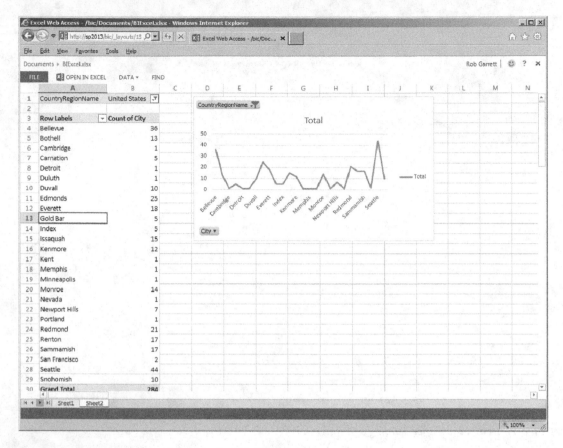

Figure 12-23. *Excel workbook running in Excel Services*

Summary

In this chapter, I covered a variety of business intelligence topics. Understanding the importance of business intelligence in any modern data-centric organization, and the vast capabilities of business intelligence that SharePoint 2013 provides, I aimed to cover the major topics at a high level.

PerformancePoint Services and the Dashboard Designer are still relatively new topics in SharePoint, even though Microsoft introduced them in SharePoint 2010. I demonstrated how to couple PerformancePoint Services to an OLAP cube in SQL Server Analysis to create an appealing data dashboard in SharePoint, with no code whatsoever.

In the latter part of this chapter, you visited Visio Services and Excel Services to render interactive data (dynamic, not static) in Visio diagrams and Excel workbooks. I tried to ensure that you grasped a strong hold on the major components of business intelligence in SharePoint 2013, and the administration that SharePoint requires to install and configure these components.

In the next chapter, Chapter 13, I shall introduce you to Business Connectivity Services and aggregation line-of-business data from third-party data sources.

■ ■ ■

Business Connectivity Services

SharePoint 2013 is a great productivity hub for storing data and creating collaborative solutions so users in your organization can share files and information. However, organizations infrequently store all their data in one platform or application. Despite the wonderful functionality available in SharePoint 2013, other applications might suit an organization's needs better for a specific task, such as an accounting system. Fortunately, the collaborative features and search capabilities of SharePoint are not lost to you because you have data in other systems. Business Connectivity Services (BCS) is a set of components within the SharePoint platform that enables SharePoint to extend its reach to other line of business systems.

Using Business Connectivity Services, you can aggregate data stored in another application, database, web service, or third-party accessible system, using standard protocols. SharePoint exposes external data within SharePoint using the same content type and list model as native SharePoint data. Business solutions within SharePoint may interact with external data, via Business Connectivity Services, just as they would native list content in SharePoint. In Chapter 12, I discussed business intelligence, which provides reports and dashboards from analytical and tabular data. When pairing business intelligence with Business Connectivity Services, business owners can produce some appealing dashboards and reports that include data from external systems. Imagine a dashboard in your organization's team site that marries accounting data from purchasing with project data hosted in SharePoint, and infused with customer information from your association management system (AMS) or customer management system (CMS).

In this chapter, I will describe installing and configuring Business Connectivity Services as part of SharePoint 2013 and integrating some third-party data from web services and SQL sources.

Overview of Business Connectivity Services

Business Connectivity Services replaces the legacy Business Data Catalog (BDC) from SharePoint 2007. Business Connectivity Services allows administrators to configure external data sources or line of business data connectors from almost any source outside SharePoint 2010/2013. Business Connectivity Services then allows users of SharePoint to interact with external data via external content types and lists, which for all intents and purposes, look and behave just like their internal counterparts.

Business Connectivity Services components package with SharePoint 2013 Foundation and allow administrators to configure *external content types* (ECTs) when referencing external data types. These external content types then shape the data exposed to users via external data lists. Administrators and developers define external content types via SharePoint Designer or Visual Studio 2010/2012. By writing them in code, developers have almost limitless capability in exposing external data in SharePoint as long as they can query the external data source via some form of code API.

Business Connectivity Services exists as a service application in your SharePoint 2013 farm. However, the core functionality of Business Connectivity Services consists of a number of services and components. Figure 13-1 shows a visual of the various components. It is worth mentioning that while Business Connectivity Services is available to Foundation users, certain components, such as user profile extensions, Business Data Web Parts, and search integration, are still available only to Enterprise license users. The majority of Business Connectivity Services components, however, reside in the core offering—available to all SharePoint license types—and include connectors to standard data sources via OData, WCF, SQL, and .NET code.

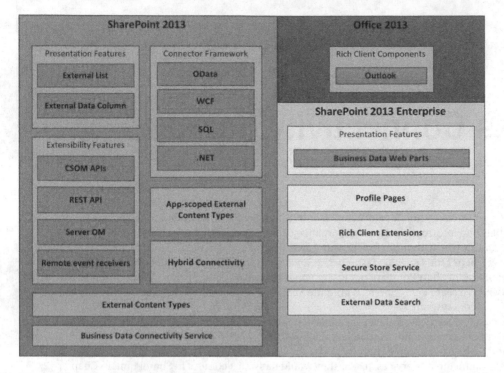

Figure 13-1. *Components of Business Connectivity Services*

Figure 13-1 shows that Business Connectivity Services consists of a number of component areas. Probably the most interesting to administrators are the connector framework components, which control connectivity to external data sources. Developers will most likely take an interest in the extensibility components, which consist of several APIs to develop custom entities and connectors for nonstandard data sources.

You may recognize some of the components in the SharePoint 2013 Enterprise group, which includes Web Parts to surface external data, extensions, search, and use of the Secure Store Service to facilitate management of third-party service credentials.

The grouping of Outlook 2013 components illustrates those components that enable the reuse of Business Connectivity Services components in Outlook. Outlook works closely with SharePoint to provide user access to lists, libraries, and feeds. Now, Outlook 2013 can aggregate certain third-party external data.

Because this section is an overview of Business Connectivity Services, I shall mention some of the following benefits that Business Connectivity Services provides:

- *True integration:* Users view all external data like SharePoint data. SharePoint abstracts the end user from the external data.

- *Read/Write:* Whereas legacy BDC (SharePoint 2007) only allowed read-only view of data, Business Connectivity Services allows write-back. Users can make changes to data in external data lists, and Business Connectivity Services will update the external data source.

- *Office application integration:* Since external data surfaces via SharePoint external lists, any Office application that understands SharePoint list technology may query the external data. Developers may access external data via the same API they would use to open any standard list in SharePoint.

- *Support for BLOBs:* Business Connectivity Services supports source content in the form of Binary Objects (BLOBs).

- *Extensive security control:* Business Connectivity Services provides greater security over data aggregated into SharePoint, as well as the various authentication methods required to access external data sources.

- *Search Integration:* Business Connectivity Services integrates in with SharePoint search, meaning users can search across external data stores, like any source internal to SharePoint.

- *Support for OData:* Business Connectivity Services now supports Open Data protocols (HTTP, JSON, and Atom).

What Is New in SharePoint 2013?

Microsoft introduced Business Connectivity Services in SharePoint 2010, which replaced the Business Data Catalog functionality in SharePoint 2007. Business Connectivity Services also opened up external data integration to Foundation users because Business Connectivity Services is no longer solely an Enterprise license feature (some parts still require an Enterprise license). Now, SharePoint 2013 brings additional enhancements to Business Connectivity Services, as described in Table 13-1.

Table 13-1. *New Business Connectivity Services Functionality in SharePoint 2013*

New Feature	Description
SharePoint can now connect to OData sources	OData is a protocol that uses either HTTP, Atom, or JSON and provides a single URL to access a data source. OData protocols are a growing standard, and their use in Business Connectivity Services allows SharePoint to access a wealth of external data. Business Connectivity Services supports connection to any OData producer to aggregate data. Some examples of OData producers are: • SharePoint 2010 • SQL Azure • Microsoft Dynamics CRM • Windows Live
SharePoint can receive events from external systems	SharePoint handles events via event receivers, attached to lists and sites. An event receiver is a piece of code that traps a particular event and then performs an action based on this event, for example, an action performed when a user updates a list item. Business Connectivity Services previously lacked the ability to integrate event receivers with external lists and content types. New to SharePoint 2013 is the ability to respond to events in external sources, just as you do with internal lists. Thus, if a user updates content in an external data source, you can execute tasks and kick off workflow tasks in response to the event.

(continued)

Table 13-1. (*continued*)

New Feature	Description
You can now scope external types to apps	SharePoint 2010 allowed you to create external content types for a farm. SharePoint 2013 introduces the app model, where an app is an isolated piece of functionality that can execute outside the context of the SharePoint farm. Business Connectivity Services supports apps, such that the apps may use external content via external content types.
Enhancements to the REST Client Object Model	The Client Object Model is an API set that uses the REST protocol to provide SharePoint object model capabilities client-side (within the browser). SharePoint 2013 adds enhancement to the API classes and methods for Business Connectivity Services.

Configuring Business Connectivity Services

Like most architecture components in SharePoint, Business Connectivity Services operates as a service application. In the full server version of SharePoint 2013, Business Connectivity Services makes use of the Secure Store Service. I explained how to install this service application in Chapter 12. The following steps demonstrate how to create a new Business Connectivity Services application:

1. Open Central Administration.

2. Click the link to manage services on the server.

3. Ensure the Business Data Connectivity Service is started.

4. Navigate back to the home page in Central Administration.

5. Click the link to manage service applications, under the Application Management heading.

6. Scroll down the list and see if a Business Connectivity Services application already exists; if not, continue with these steps.

7. Click the New icon on the ribbon.

8. Choose the Business Data Connectivity application in the menu.

9. SharePoint displays a dialog for Business Connectivity Services configuration options.

10. Provide a name and description for the service application.

11. Provide the SQL Server name and database name for Business Connectivity Services.

12. Create a new application pool using your application pool managed account (see Chapter 2 for details on Managed Accounts).

13. Click the OK button to create the Business Connectivity Services application.

14. Once SharePoint finishes provisioning the service application, return to the list and click the newly created Business Connectivity Services application.

15. You should see a page like that in Figure 13-2.

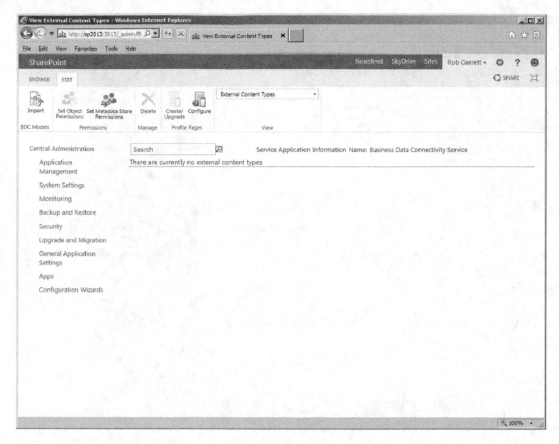

Figure 13-2. *Business Connectivity Services Application page*

Once you have completed the preceding steps, Business Connectivity Services is ready to start hosting external content types. Additionally, you can host profile pages, which provide details about external systems and content types. Click the Configure icon on the ribbon and then provide the URL to the site collection to store external content type profiles on the page shown (Figure 13-3).

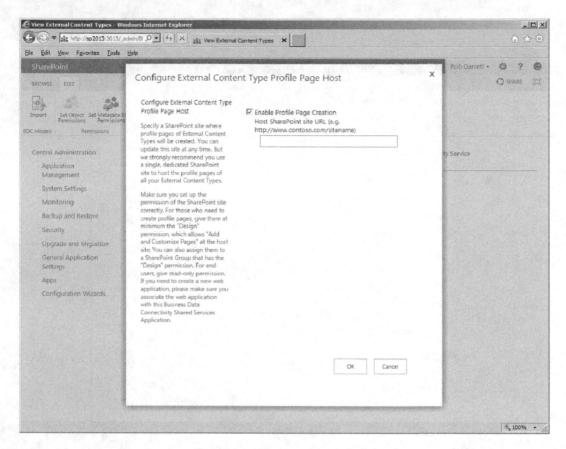

Figure 13-3. *Configure external content type profile host*

■ **Note**   To provide users with the ability to create external content type profile pages, they should have design permissions, or belong to a group that has design permissions. The web application hosting the External Content Type Profile Host site must also associate with this instance of the Business Connectivity Service application.

Configure the Secure Store

Most external data systems require credentials for accessing the contained data. This can pose a problem when you try to access these systems from Business Connectivity Services. Fortunately, Business Connectivity Services can leverage the Secure Store Service to maintain and access account information for external systems. The Secure Store Service ensures that you do not leave credentials for these important line of business systems lying around in configuration files or database rows.

I covered installation of the Secure Store Service in Chapter 12, as part of the PerformancePoint configuration, so I shall not burden you with the installation process here. However, I will cover the steps involved to create a new target application ID, which you can later use for data source connections when creating new external content types.

1. Open Central Administration.

2. Click the link to manage service applications, under the Application Management heading.

3. Scroll down to the Secure Store Service (read the section on configuring the Secure Store Service in Chapter 12 if you do not have an instance already established).

4. Select the Secure Store Service and then click the Manage icon on the ribbon.

5. Click the New icon on the ribbon to create a new target application ID—this is a unique identifier, which your external content types will use.

6. Provide the target application ID—this can be any text value, as long as it is unique across the Secure Store.

7. Provide a display name and contact e-mail for the target application.

8. Change the application type to *Group* because you use one account for all users to access your SQL Server database.

■ **Note**   There are several types of target applications. They fall into two broad categories: individual target applications and group target applications. The type of target applications corresponds to the type of account used to map user credentials. If each user has an account in the target application, choose the individual type. If the target application uses one account for all users, choose the group type. The remaining target application types are based on these two main types.

---

9. Click the Next button.

10. On the next page (Figure 13-4), leave the field name and type in the Windows User Name and Windows Password because you are using Windows account types to authenticate with SQL Server.

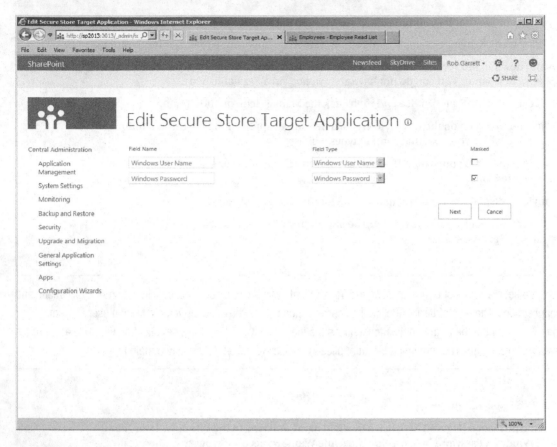

Figure 13-4. *Fields for credentials in the Secure Store Service*

11. Click the Next button.

12. Provide the target application administrators.

13. Specify the users and groups that map to the credentials in the store. I recommend that you create a designated group in your domain, or a specific user in your domain, that all credentials map and you can use in external systems (for simplicity, I used the Authenticated Users group).

14. Click the OK button to return to the Secure Store landing page.

15. Check the check box of the target application you just created.

16. Click the Set icon in the Credentials section of the ribbon.

17. On the next page, provide the Windows username (DOMAIN\username) and password—this is the account that has access to your SQL store.

18. Click OK to set the credential.

You have created a target application ID and specified a domain account that has access to your SQL Server database; you then mapped that account to a group of users (all authenticated users in my case) that can use this credential to access the database. Now, you are ready to create your external content type.

External Content Types

External content types (ECTs) are the linchpin for bridging connectivity between external data sources and SharePoint. Similar to regular content types in SharePoint (see Chapter 9), external content types represent an entity or classification of an object in your solution. An external content type contains fields, which are the attributes of the entity. If you have a background in software development, you may consider external content types analogous to code classes—classes describe objects, which are the concrete instances of a class.

Most content in SharePoint centralizes in content types because they represent a discrete portable entity in the SharePoint farm, which content owners may apply in different situations. Publishing, records management, document management, business intelligence, collaboration lists and libraries—they all leverage content types at the core to describe data schema in SharePoint. External content types integrate and operate in a similar fashion to that of internal content types, except that they describe entities of external data. For example, if you are aggregating personnel records from an external HR system, you might define an external content type that represents an employee, with fields for names, office location, and any other attribute of the employee.

The Business Connectivity Services Application page, shown in Figure 13-2, will display external content types after you define them. To define a new external content type, you must use SharePoint Designer. The following steps demonstrate creation of an external content type, which represents an employee from an Adventure Works SQL database:

■ **Note**   Download the Adventure Works DW database for your version of SQL Server at the following location: http://msftdbprodsamples.codeplex.com/.

---

1. Open SharePoint Designer 2013 (SharePoint Designer 2013 is a free download: http://www.microsoft.com/en-us/download/details.aspx?id=30346).

2. Open your SharePoint 2013 site. I used a simple business intelligence site collection from Chapter 12, but any SharePoint 2013 site collection will do.

3. From the left navigation, click the External Content Types link, under the Site Objects left pane (see Figure 13-5).

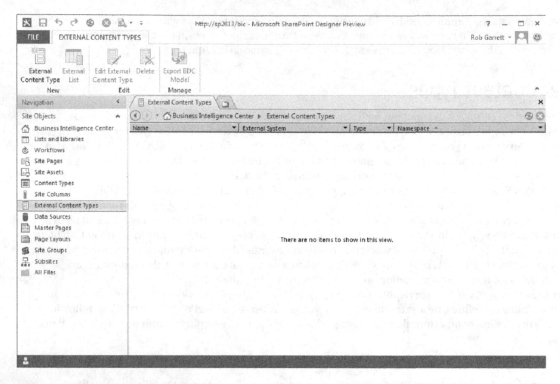

Figure 13-5. *External Content Types in SharePoint Designer 2013*

4. SharePoint Designer will show you any external content types you have in the site collection. In my case, I have none because I have not yet defined any.

5. Click the button for external content type in the new group within the ribbon.

6. On the new External Content Type page, give it a name and display name; I called mine Employee.

7. Set the Office Item type to the List type within SharePoint. I went with a generic list.

8. Decide if you want offline sync, meaning that SharePoint will allow you to read and update external data via cache when the external system is offline.

9. Click the link for the external system to discover your external system connection.

10. You should see a page like that in Figure 13-6.

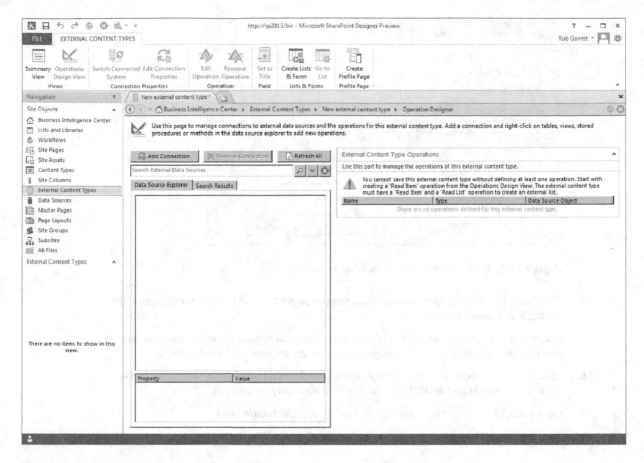

Figure 13-6. *Connect to an external system*

11. Click the Add Connection button.

12. Select the connection type. I chose SQL Server because I am demonstrating connection to the Adventure Works database.

13. Provide the connection details in the dialog box, as shown in Figure 13-7.

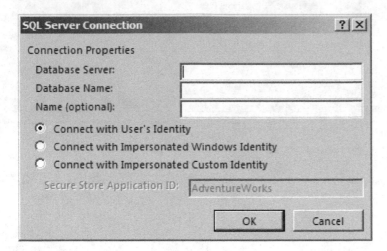

Figure 13-7. *SQL Server connection dialog for ECT creation*

14. The dialog box for SQL Server database is not too helpful in that it will not enumerate the available databases for you.

15. Choose the security method for the connection—here you can use a Secure Store connection (see Chapter 12), or identity of the logged in user, or the impersonated user identity.

16. Choose Connect with Impersonated Windows Identity and provide the application ID from the Secure Store (default is to use the User's Identity, as shown).

17. Click OK and provide the credentials you entered in the Secure Store.

18. You should see the connection to the data source created (Figure 13-8).

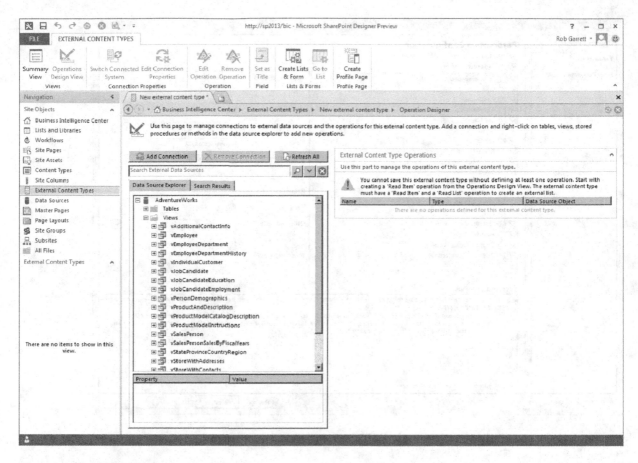

Figure 13-8. *SQL Server data source created*

19. Expand the views node and right-click on the view for Employee.

20. You should see a list of operations to create—these are the Create, Read, Update, and Delete (CRUD) operations, used by SharePoint to access your data entity via the external content type—I chose all operations, to make life simple.

21. SharePoint Designer shows a wizard to configure the operations.

22. Click the Next button to configure the parameters for the entity (Figure 13-9). Here you get to choose the columns from the view and how they map to the external content type entity.

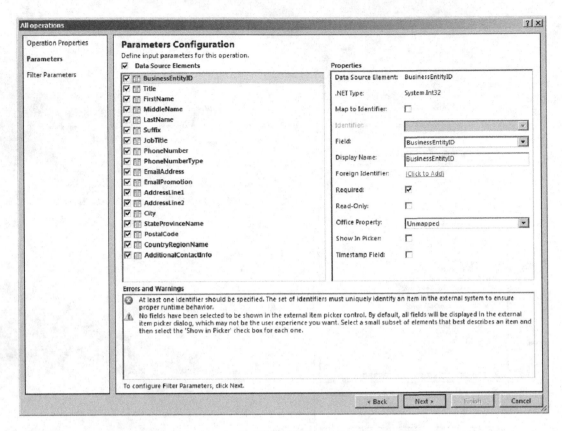

Figure 13-9. Parameters Configuration in the ECT SQL Server Data Source Wizard

23. Click the E-mail Address column and then check the check box to map this field as an identifier.

24. Check the check box to show this column in the picker; this allows you to show values of this column in picker dialogs for choosing a specific entity.

25. Check the check box to show the value in picker dialogs for job title, last name, and first name columns.

26. The last page of the wizard shows the filter options that SharePoint Designer recommends for the data source (Figure 13-10).

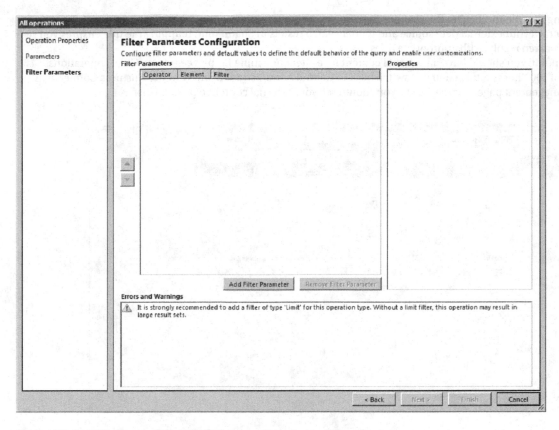

Figure 13-10. Filter page of the ECT SQL Server Data Source Wizard

27. Click the button to add a new filter.

28. Change the Data Source Element to the E-mail Address column.

29. Click the link to add the filter.

30. In the filter dialog, change the type to Limit and then click the OK button.

31. Enter the value 1000 in the Default Value.

32. Click the Finish button.

■ **Note** The wizard shows verbose warning and error messages for correct configuration of your external content type—SharePoint Designer disables the Finish button until you remedy all errors.

---

33. On the External Content Type details page, click the E-mail Address column in the Fields box.

34. Click the Set as Title icon on the ribbon.

Mapping the title to a field in the external content type is important for search. Later in this chapter, I shall show you how to crawl your external data source and render search results in SharePoint; mapping the title ensures you see a nice set of search results with appropriate titles.

At this point, you should have an external content type—I named mine Employee—some CRUD operations, and a limit of 1000 items returned. If you switch back to Central Administration and view the Business Connectivity Services Management page (Figure 13-11), you should see your external content type in the list.

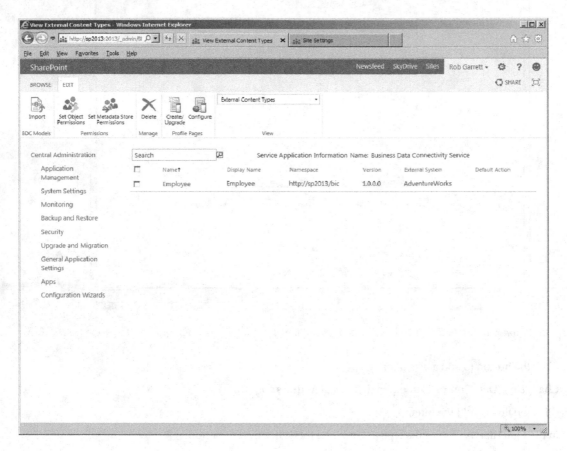

Figure 13-11. *External Content Type listed in the BCS Management page*

External Content Type Profile Pages

In the previous section of this chapter, you created a new external content type, called Employee, which references the Employee view in the Adventure Works SQL database. Before you create an external list and interact with your external data via SharePoint, I would like to demonstrate creating a profile page for your external content type. External content type profile pages display the data for an item of an external content type, and they play an important role when showing details in search results for matches against external lists.

1. Open Central Administration.

2. Click the link to manage service applications.

3. Select the Business Connectivity Services application in the list.

4. Click the Manage icon on the ribbon.

5. Check the check box next to the Employee External Content Type, then click the Configure icon on the ribbon.

6. Provide a site to host external content type profile pages (Figure 13-12). I chose the root site collection, but I recommend you create a site specifically for the purpose.

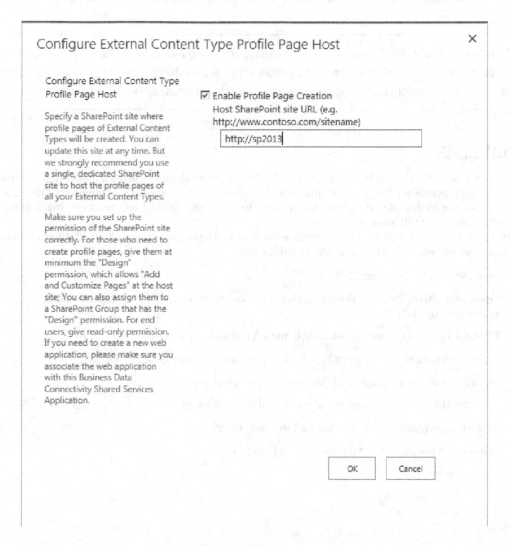

Figure 13-12. Configure location of ECT profile pages

7. Now you will create the profile page for your external content type, using SharePoint Designer.

8. Open SharePoint Designer 2013.

9. Click the External Content Types node in the left navigation pane.

10. Double-click the Employee External Content Type in the list to open.

11. In the External Content Type Detail page, click the Create Profile Page icon on the ribbon.

■ **Note**　An External Content Type Profile page is simply a page containing a Web Part to display the contents of some BCS entity data. You can see the link to this page as a custom action in the external content type within SharePoint Designer. You can create a custom profile page by creating a new default custom action, if you feel inclined.

External Lists

An external list is a list in SharePoint that connects to a third-party external system, using a predefined external content type. In the previous section of this chapter, I demonstrated creating an external content type with a SQL Server database source. In this section, I shall show you how to create an external list from an external content type and how the list operates within your SharePoint site.

Assuming you followed the steps in the previous section, or you have a working predefined external content type, creating an external list within SharePoint Designer 2013 is easy.

1. Open SharePoint Designer 2013.

2. Open your SharePoint 2013 site containing your external content type and where you will create the external list.

3. Click the External Content Types node in the left navigation pane.

4. Right-click the External Content Type in the right pane; I chose my Employee ECT.

5. SharePoint shows a dialog; enter the list name and description.

6. Click the OK button to complete the creation of the external list.

7. In the left navigation, click the node for Lists and Libraries.

8. Scroll down the page to see the external list (Figure 13-13).

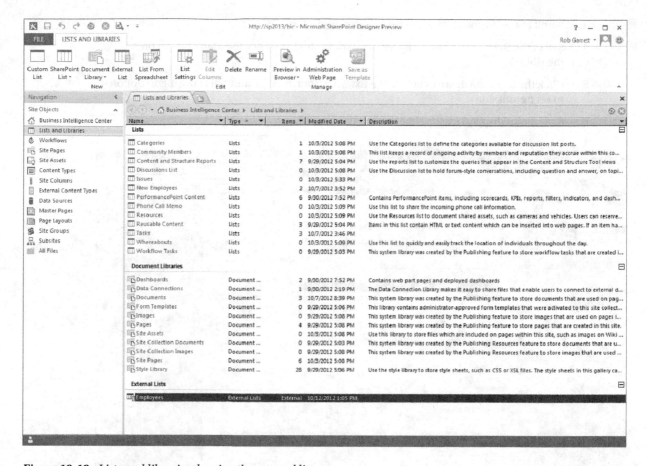

Figure 13-13. *Lists and libraries showing the external list*

This is all there is to do to create an external list in SharePoint Designer. If you click the External List instance in Designer, you will see a page that has all the details about the list (just like regular internal lists). From this page, you can edit the list permissions, create views, create custom actions, etc. Now, view this list in your SharePoint site.

1. Open the SharePoint 2013 site, to which you deployed the external list.

2. Click the gear icon and then select the menu item to view site contents.

3. Scroll down the page until you find the external list—notice how it does not look much different from the regular list, except for the tile icon.

4. Click the tile to open the external list.

If you are lucky, after clicking the tile to view your external list you might see data. The majority of readers (myself included) might see an access denied error. This is because the current logged in user does not have access rights to use the external content type entity to access the external data. I shall demonstrate how to remedy this issue as follows:

1. Open Central Administration.

2. Click the link to manage service applications, under the Application Management heading.

481

3. Scroll to the Business Connectivity Services application.

4. Select the Business Connectivity Services application and click the Manage icon on the ribbon.

5. Click the drop-down arrow next to the External Content Type and select the menu option to set permissions.

6. SharePoint displays a dialog like that in Figure 13-14.

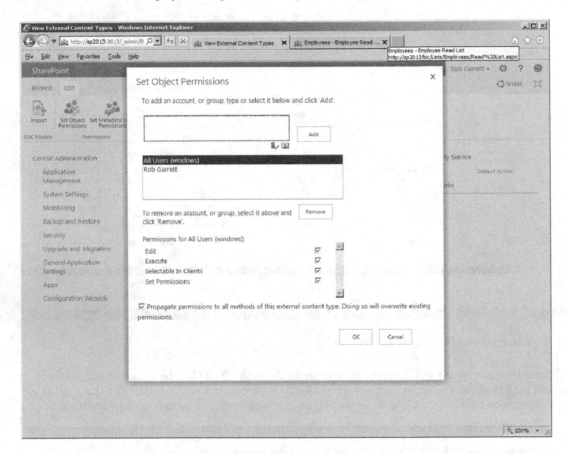

Figure 13-14. *Set permissions for an external content type*

7. Add user to the top-most box and then click the Add button (or you could assign access to the group Authenticated User to allow everyone access to the ECT).

8. For each added user or group, assign permission from those listed (Figure 13-14).

9. Click the OK button to save.

10. Return to the external list in your SharePoint site.

11. Refresh the page and you should see data (Figure 13-15).

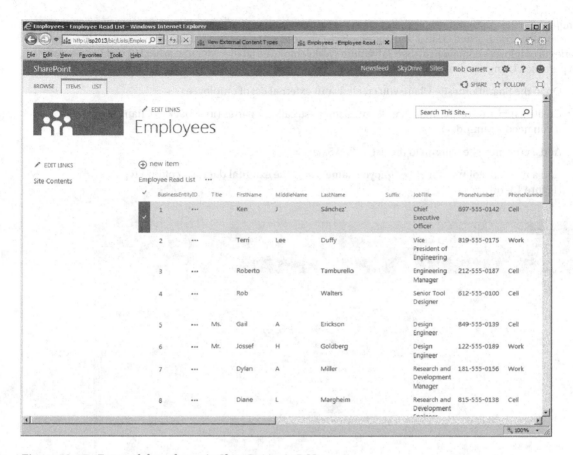

Figure 13-15. *External data shown in SharePoint via BCS*

In the example demonstrated in the preceding steps, you created a new Employee external content type. This ECT connected to the Employees view in an Adventure Works database, within SQL Server. You configured the external content type to implement all CRUD operations, allowing Create, Read, Update, and Delete on the data. From the external content type, you created an external list.

Try viewing the external list in your SharePoint site and then editing one of the rows of data. After saving your changes in SharePoint, switch over to your SQL Server and execute a select of the Employees view—notice how the data reflects the change you made in SharePoint.

External Data Columns

If you have been playing along at home, you should now have an external content type defined for employees in the Adventure Works SQL database, and an external list that uses the Employee external content type to provide user access to the employees via SharePoint.

SharePoint allows content owners to define their data in SharePoint by using an array of site column types and list templates. Since the introduction of Business Connectivity Services in SharePoint 2010, content owners can now include site columns that link to external sources, just as they would use lookup columns to access columns of another internal list.

Continuing with the example, imagine that Human Resources wishes to store a list of employee salaries in SharePoint. A plain list of employee names and salaries with the employee name as string column is a little dull; besides, HR would like to map salaries to employees contained in their Adventure Works employee table—your makeshift HR database, for all intents and purposes. Using external data columns, you can provide exactly what I just described. Here's how.

1. Open the SharePoint site where you created your external list of employees.

2. Create a new run-of-the-mill SharePoint custom list, called Salaries (look back to Chapter 9 if you need a reminder).

3. Add a currency site column to the list, called Salary.

4. Add a new site column for the employee name, using the external data site column type (Figure 13-16).

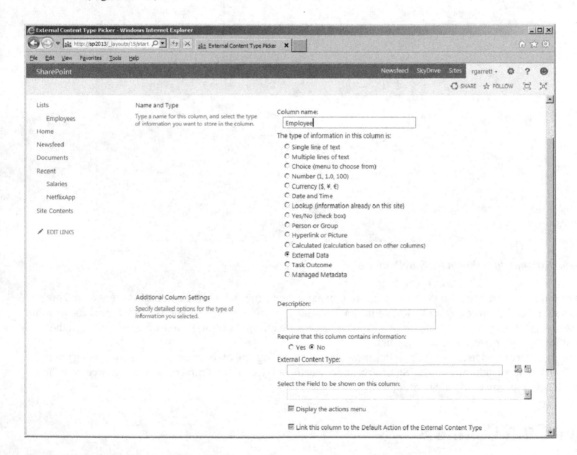

Figure 13-16. *Add an external data column*

5. Click the farthest right icon next to the external content type field.

6. SharePoint displays the External Content Type Picker (Figure 13-17).

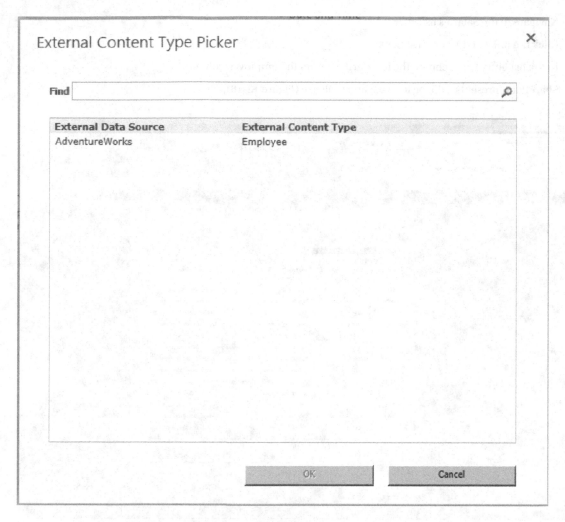

Figure 13-17. External Content Type Picker

7. Select the external content type containing the column to map your external data column.

8. After SharePoint refreshes the page, you should see a drop-down list of the fields to choose for the external data column.

9. Select the column to map. I chose last name.

10. Check the check boxes for any additional columns you would like to create additional linked external data columns.

11. Click OK at the bottom of the page to finish creating the column.

In the previous steps, you configured a new list for employee salaries, added a salary column, and created an external data column, which maps to the employee last name column in the previous defined Employee external content type. Now, you get to see the new list with external data column in action.

1. Navigate to the Salaries list.

2. Click the link to add a new list item.

3. In the list entry form, choose the icon farthest from the Employee column.

4. SharePoint presents a dialog to select an employee (Figure 13-18).

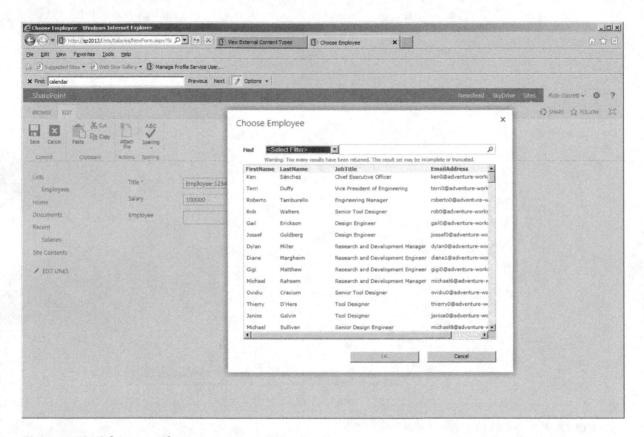

Figure 13-18. *Select an employee*

Hold on a second! Why is the dialog in Figure 13-18 showing e-mail addresses? Cast back a few sections to when you created the external content type for the employee—you selected the e-mail address column to appear in picker dialogs. You essentially told SharePoint that you want to identify users via the e-mail address when selecting from a choice of employees.

5. Select one of the employees in the list.

6. Click the OK button.

7. Since you chose Last Name as your mapped external data column, the last name of the selected employee shows in the Employee column in the form.

8. Add a salary and a title, then click the Save button to save the list item.

Connecting to an OData Source

OData, short for Open Data protocol, is a web protocol to consume Create, Read, Update, and Delete operations using standard web protocols, such as HTTP, Atom, and JSON. OData is a new emerging standard that allows producers to expose their data via a Uniform Resource Locator (URL) and allows consumers to access this data over the web using the aforementioned protocol standards.

Business Connectivity Services in SharePoint 2013 can consume OData feeds. SharePoint 2010 required middleware code to integrate OData, whereas users can now create a simple app connector for SharePoint 2013 and integrate external data.

In this section, I shall provide a short demonstration to integrate a Netflix OData feed into SharePoint. Of course, Netflix is not about to let me make changes to the company' video catalog data, so the feed is read-only, but this service suffices to demonstrate OData integration with SharePoint.

My example makes use of Visual Studio 2012. Although this book is an administrative book, I want to show you how simple OData integration is with a simple connector, built-in Visual Studio.

■ **Note**   Prerequisites for the steps in this section include *Visual Studio 2012* and *Microsoft Office Developer Tools for Visual Studio 2012*: http://msdn.microsoft.com/en-us/office/apps/fp123627.aspx.

---

1. Launch Visual Studio 2012.

2. Start a new project.

3. Select the template App for SharePoint 2013 (Figure 13-19).

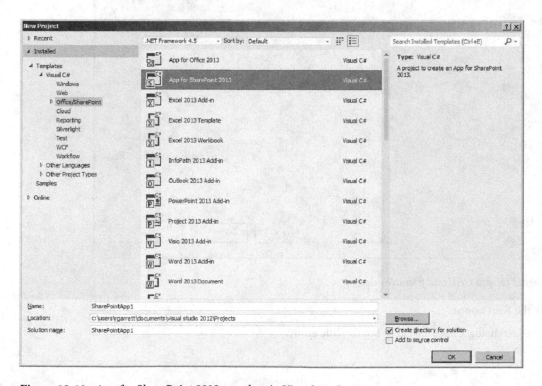

Figure 13-19. *App for SharePoint 2013 template in Visual Studio 2012*

4. Give the app a name and location to store the project on disk.

5. Click the OK button.

6. In the next dialog, confirm the name and URL of the SharePoint site.

7. Change the drop-down option to host the app in SharePoint.

8. Click the Finish button.

9. Right-click the project name in the Solution Explorer.

10. Choose the Add menu item and then select the Content Types for External Data Source sub-menu item.

11. Provide the OData service URL for Netflix and a friendly name—see Figure 13-20.

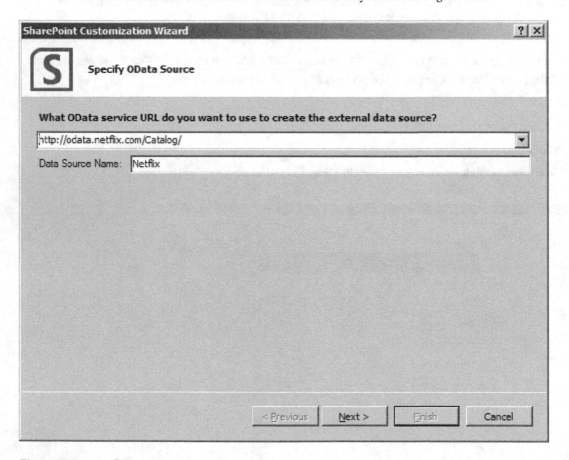

Figure 13-20. Netflix OData URL and friendly name

12. Click the Next button.

13. On the last dialog, check the check box for Title entity.

14. Leave the check box for *Create list instances for the selected data entries (except Service Operations)* to create list instances.

15. Click the Finish button.

Visual Studio has created a new external content type for the OData Netflix Title entity, and created an external list instance for the new external content type. Open the elements.xml file for the Titles list, and you should see the XML for the list definition (Figure 13-21). Be sure to make a note of the list URL.

```xml
<?xml version="1.0" encoding="utf-8"?>
<Elements xmlns="http://schemas.microsoft.com/sharepoint/">
  <ListInstance Url="Lists/Title" Description="Title" OnQuickLaunch="TRUE" Title="Title">
    <DataSource>
      <Property Name="LobSystemInstance" Value="Netflix" />
      <Property Name="EntityNamespace" Value="NetflixCatalogv2" />
      <Property Name="Entity" Value="Title" />
      <Property Name="SpecificFinder" Value="ReadSpecificTitle" />
      <Property Name="MetadataCatalogFileName" Value="BDCMetadata.bdcm" />
    </DataSource>
  </ListInstance>
</Elements>
```

Figure 13-21. *List instance XML for the OData external feed*

16. Right-click the AppManifest.xml file and view the code.

17. Change the start page of the app to load the list you created, using the URL you noted earlier—in my case: ~appWebUrl/Lists/Title.

Deploy the project app to SharePoint (right-click the project name in the solution explorer and then select the deploy menu option).

■ **Note**   The deploy steps assume that you have a working on-premise app domain configured; see http://msdn.microsoft.com/en-us/library/office/apps/fp179923(v=office.15).

---

18. Open your SharePoint site, where you just deployed the app.

19. Click the gear icon.

20. Select the menu item to view site contents.

21. Scroll and find the Netflix Titles list.

22. Click on the tile to open the external list.

23. You should see Netflix aggregated data in SharePoint (Figure 13-22).

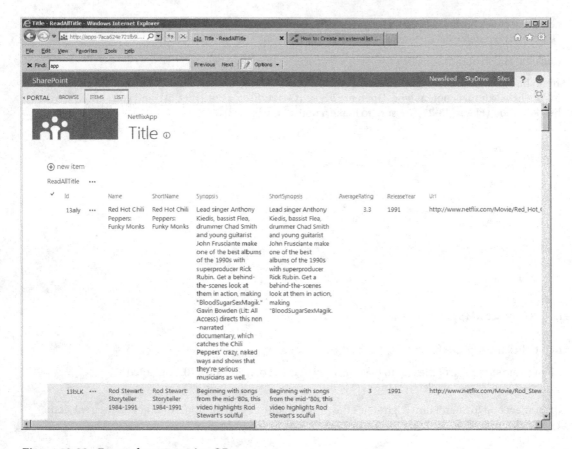

Figure 13-22. *External content using OData*

User Profile Properties

Earlier in this chapter, I demonstrated how to include external data columns in your lists to surface Business Connectivity Services data along with natural SharePoint list data. In Chapter 6, you read about user profiles and how the User Profile Service Application provides synchronization with external directory sources to populate user profile properties. Leveraging Business Connectivity Services, you can integrate line of business data in with user profile data, imported from AD or LDAP.

When it comes to user profiles in SharePoint, I frequently hear the same request: "I'd like to include fields from my HR database in user profiles." In this section, I shall demonstrate how to set up this process. The steps that follow make the following assumptions:

- You have a working User Profile Service Application.

- You have a working User Profile Synchronization with AD or LDAP.

- You have My Sites configured.

- You have created an external content type for Employees in the Adventure Works database, as shown earlier in this chapter.

With the prerequisite assumptions out of the way, it's time to get started with configuring user profile fields that link to Business Connectivity Service sources. For the scenario to work, you need a common attribute that links user profiles in SharePoint and records in your external line of business system. I have chosen the e-mail address attribute, since the e-mail address is present in Active Directory and my Employee external content type.

For simplicity, you will create a new managed user property that links the e-mail address in Active Directory with that in your external line of business system.

1. Open Central Administration.

2. Click the link to manage service applications, under the Application Management heading.

3. Scroll and select the User Profile Service application.

4. Click the Manage icon on the ribbon.

5. Click the link to manage user properties.

6. Click the link to create a new property.

7. Give the property a unique name and display name.

8. Leave the property type as String.

9. Scroll to the Mappings section.

10. Map the AD "mail" attribute using an import mapping.

■ **Note**   If the Source Data Connection drop-down control is empty, then you must configure a sync connection with Active Directory—see Chapter 6 for User Profile Synchronization with Active Directory.

---

11. My mapping looks like that in Figure 13-23.

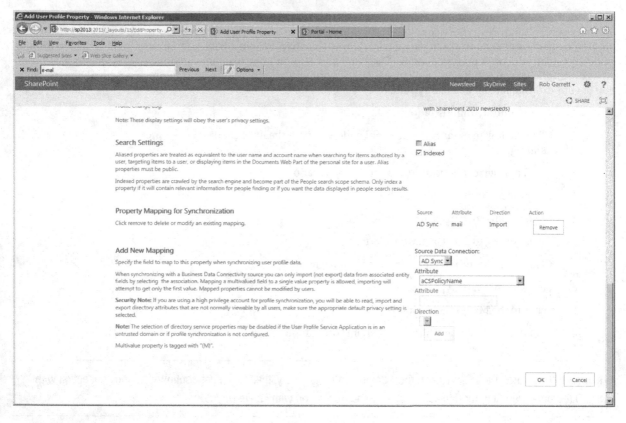

Figure 13-23. *User property mapping to AD attribute*

12. Set the policy for the property as optional and visible to everyone—this is not a requirement, but it makes life easier for dealing with users who do not have the e-mail address populated in AD.

13. Click the OK button to save the property.

14. Return to the main User Profile Service Application home page.

15. Click the link to start a profile synchronization.

16. Start a *full* synchronization.

17. Wait for the synchronization to complete.

18. Click the link to manage user profiles.

19. Search for a user who is present both in SharePoint and AD.

20. Check to see if the e-mail address populated into the custom-created profile property (assuming you populated the e-mail address in AD!).

You now have a custom user profile property, mapped to an attribute in Active Directory; you have completed a full import and confirmed that user profiles contain this field with populated data. Next, you will configure a synchronization connection in the User Profile Service (UPS) Application that maps records in the Adventure Works ECT with user profiles.

21. Return to the main User Profile Service Application home page.

22. Click the link to create a new synchronization connection.

23. On the next page, click the link to create new connection.

24. Change the type to Business Data Connectivity and wait for the page to refresh (Figure 13-24).

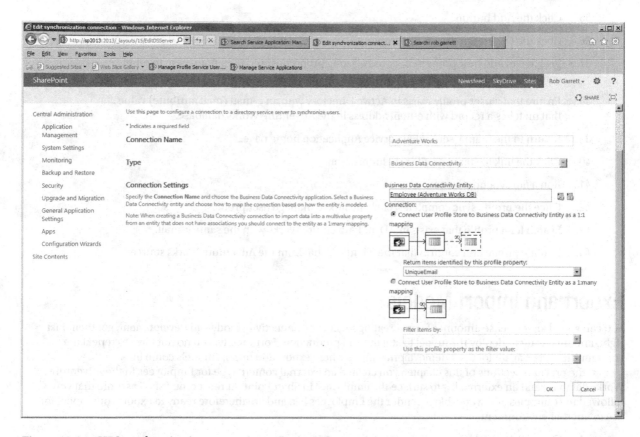

Figure 13-24. *UPS synchronization connection to Business Connectivity Services*

25. Give the connection a name.

26. Choose the external content type using the entity picker.

27. Choose the 1:1 mapping and select the Unique Email property you created earlier for the e-mail mapped to the AD user profile.

28. Click the OK button.

The last set of steps in this demonstration involves surfacing columns from the external content type within user profiles. Profiles in Active Directory map to records in the external Adventure Works database using the e-mail address property you configured earlier.

29. Return to the main User Profile Service Application home page.

30. Click the link to manage user properties.

31. Click the Job Title property and then select Edit in the drop-down control.

32. The Job Title property currently maps to an attribute in AD; scroll to the Mappings section and click the Remove button.

33. Change the Source Data Connection to the external data connection for the Adventure Works database.

34. Select the Job Title column in the attribute drop-down control.

35. Click the Add button.

36. Click the OK button to save the property.

37. Feel free to add new properties, or use existing properties, and then map them to other columns in the Adventure Works Employee external content type.

38. Ensure that a user profile exists in Active Directory with an e-mail (mail attribute) value that matches a record with e-mail address in the Adventure Works database.

39. Return to the main User Profile Service Application home page.

40. Click the link to start a profile synchronization.

41. Run a *full* synchronization.

42. Once the profile sync completes, click the link to manage user profiles.

43. Search for a profile that exists in AD and Adventure Works with the same e-mail.

44. Edit the profile and confirm that the job title is that from the Adventure Works source.

Export and Import Models

You can spend an immense amount of time creating Business Connectivity models in development, get them just right, and then want to deploy the model to staging and production. Fortunately, you do not have to repeat the configuration steps again for each deployment—this is where export and import models come in.

In the previous sections of this chapter, you created an external content type for Employees in the Adventure Works database and an external list to surface the employees in SharePoint. At this point, I shall assume that you followed my examples and were able to render the Employees list, and are therefore ready to export your model for use in another environment.

1. Open Central Administration.

2. Click the link to manage service applications.

3. Select the Business Connectivity Services application in the list.

4. Click the Manage icon on the ribbon.

5. In the view section of the ribbon, change the drop-down control to show BDC models (Figure 13-25).

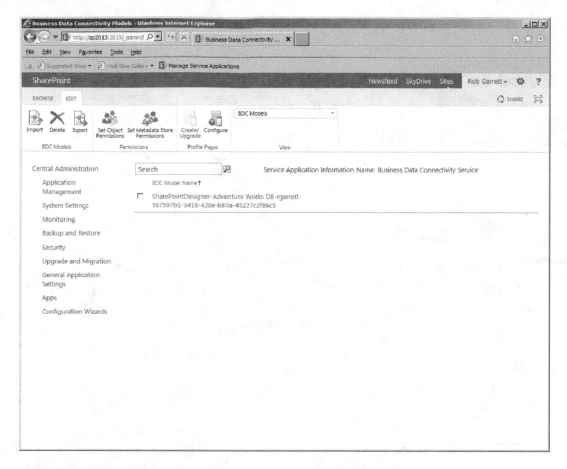

Figure 13-25. *BDC models*

A BDC model is an XML file that contains all of the Business Connectivity Services information for a given data source. In Figure 13-25, see that SharePoint created a model when you created a new data source to the Adventure Works SQL database from SharePoint Designer. You can save this file to disk and open it in a text editor to see the XML. BDC model files are inherent from the legacy Business Data Catalog in SharePoint 2007. Back in those days, you had to create the XML file yourself, or use a third-party tool, such as BDC Meta-man. Although Business Connectivity Services still uses the BDC model file, the capabilities of the service greatly enhance that of BDC.

6. Check the check box next to the BDC model.

7. Click the Export icon on the ribbon.

8. Choose the file type to export and the various advanced attributes to include or exclude from the export (Figure 13-26).

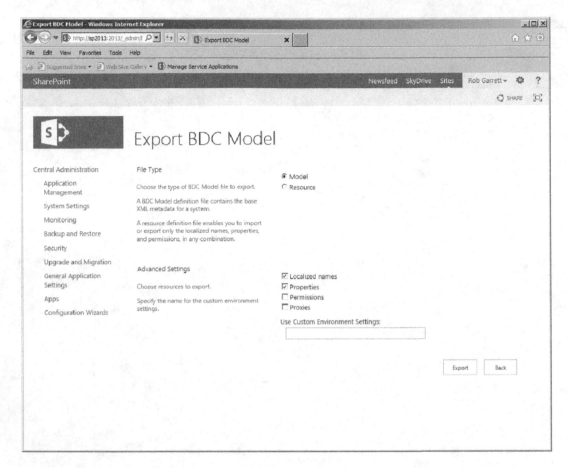

Figure 13-26. *Export BDC Model*

9. Click the Export button to save the file locally to disk.

With a BDC model exported to disk, you can now import the model into another environment, using the Import icon in the Business Connectivity Services application.

***

■ **Note**   After importing a BDC model, you may need to re-create external lists from the imported external content types.

***

Search

One of the powerful features of Business Connectivity Services is the ability to integrate it with search. Microsoft designed the service to expose external line of business data sources inside SharePoint as external lists, which operate identically to internal native SharePoint lists. Ensuring that users can search for data in external sources, just as they would for internal data, completes the integration experience.

Business Connectivity Services data sources surface in search as a specific content source type, similar to the SharePoint, Web Site, and File Share content sources. In this section, I shall briefly cover the configuration steps. These steps assume that you followed the previous steps in this chapter and have a working external employees list, sourced from the Adventure Works SQL database. I shall also assume that you have a working Search Service Application.

■ **Note** I cover provisioning of the Search Service Application in Chapter 15. For now you can create a new SSA using the farm wizard (unless you have one configured already).

1. Open Central Administration.

2. Click the link to manage service application, under the Application Management heading.

3. Scroll down the list of service applications and select your Search Service Application.

4. Click the Manage icon on the ribbon.

5. You should see the Search Administration page, like that in Figure 13-27.

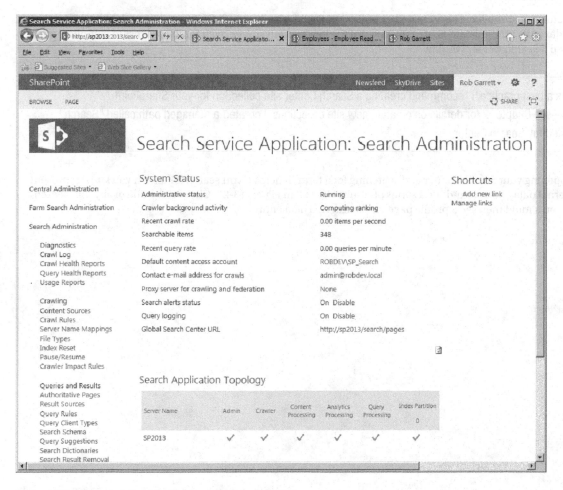

Figure 13-27. *Search Service Application Administration*

6. Click the link for content sources, under the Crawling heading in the left navigation.

7. Click the link to add a new content source.

8. On the next page, give the content source a name.

9. Change the Content Source Type to Line of Business Data.

10. Wait for the page to refresh, then select the Business Connectivity Services Application—I have only the one.

11. You have the option to crawl all data sources associated with the application or particular sources. I have found that it is best to select the desired data sources.

12. Configure crawl schedules and priorities.

13. Click OK.

Congratulations! You have now created a content source for your Business Connectivity Services data source and can now index your external data. Start a full crawl of the new content source, wait for the process to complete, and then open up a Search Center window.

■ **Note**   As a best practice, I recommend creating a Search Center site collection for your SharePoint application—see Chapter 2 for details on creating new site collections. I created a managed path called "Search" where I hosted my Search Center.

After opening your Search Center and searching for a term (it helps if you search for a term you know is present in your external data), you should see a series of results like that in Figure 13-28. Click on the title of any one-search result, and you should then see a profile page for the external data entity.

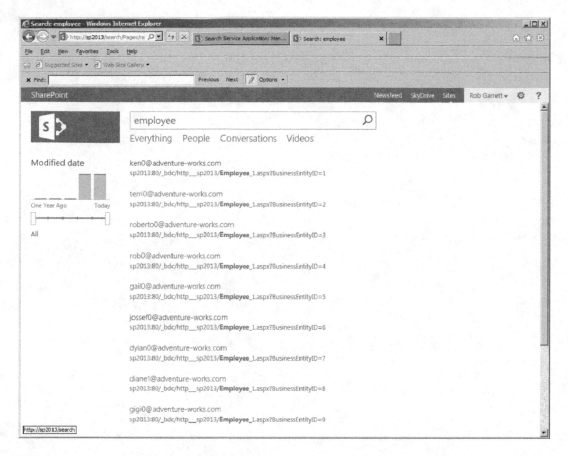

Figure 13-28. *Search results for external data*

Do you remember how to create the External Content Type Profile page? Not to worry if not, just skip back to the section called External Content Type Profile Pages. Profile pages enable users to view external data surfaced in search results.

Summary

In this chapter, you explored all the major aspects of external data aggregation in SharePoint via Business Connectivity Services. I kicked off this chapter with some details about the enhancements to BCS in SharePoint 2013. You then jumped in with configuration of the Secure Store Service and Business Connectivity Services application.

I walked you through the process of creating a new external content type, which represents each employee from the Adventure Works SQL database, a sample SQL Server database. Having created your external content type, you learned how to create an external list, so that you could interact with the external data via the SharePoint user interface.

You got a glimpse of Visual Studio 2012 when you created an external connector to an OData source. Toward the end of this chapter, you read how to integrate Business Connectivity Services in with user profiles and search, in order to provide an experience of complete external data integration within SharePoint 2013.

In Chapter 14, I will continue the theme of integration, this time integrating SharePoint 2013 with Microsoft Office applications.

■ ■ ■

Microsoft Office Integration and Office Web Applications

SharePoint 2013 is a sophisticated web-based information platform that stands tall alongside many of Microsoft's accomplishments. The SharePoint platform succeeds in being the central storage hub for enterprise and organization data, engages users in collaboration, and integrates external data to facilitate business intelligence in a modern-day organization. However, SharePoint is not an island, and Microsoft designed the platform to work alongside and integrate with Microsoft Office—one of the most widely used pieces of software installed on office computers today.

In this chapter I will take the reader on a tour of the main Microsoft Office applications and show how they integrate with SharePoint 2013. As with previous versions of SharePoint, Microsoft designed many of the new integration features to work with the latest version of Office—in this case Office 2013. This is not to say that users of Office 2003, 2010, and even Office XP cannot integrate with SharePoint 2013, but the feature set and end-user experience are better when working with Office 2010 or 2013.

Office 2013 and an Overview of Integration

Pay a visit to any typical corporate or government office today and you are certain to see a number of people in front of computers. Statistically, most of these computers will be running Microsoft Windows, and I would bet you they also have a copy of Microsoft Office installed.

With the exception of software developers, most organization workers use Office applications several times a day. Take Outlook, as an example; despite several rather appealing alternatives, Microsoft Outlook is one of the most popular business applications in use in organizations each day. As another example, Word is the most widely used word processing application and is the application I chose to write this book.

What are all those users doing with the files that they create from Microsoft Office applications? Sadly, many documents, spreadsheets, presentation decks, diagrams, etc. end up on shared drives (on the network) or embedded in e-mail messages. A typical Microsoft Word document ranges in size from a few kilobytes to megabytes. Now imagine a large Word document floating around the e-mail system—several copies in every recipient's e-mail box, different versions in multiple e-mail messages. Aside from the confusion in ascertaining the most recent version, the IT department has a hard time dealing with Exchange e-mail boxes that continue to grow over the life of an employee at an organization.

In Chapter 11, I wrote about the document management features of SharePoint. I demonstrated how SharePoint provides a central location for all documents, to meet the needs of users. This is all good, but how tedious is it if a user working on a masterpiece in Microsoft Word has to exit the application and then remember to upload the document to SharePoint, and what about the nice metadata and categorization of documents in SharePoint? Users would love to access this same metadata in the Office application. Fortunately, Microsoft designed SharePoint and Office applications to communicate with each other.

Users can access SharePoint features from the comfort of their Office application, and may access their Office application from the web interface of SharePoint. Earlier versions of SharePoint (2003/2007) and Office (2003/2007) made similar claims but, honestly, the integration was somewhat half-baked. Since SharePoint 2010, SharePoint and Office have gone a step further and truly provide seamless integration.

By now, I assume you are familiar with the Windows 8 look and feel of SharePoint 2013. Users of Office 2013 also experience a similar look and feel as part of the user interface. Figure 14-1 shows a screenshot from PowerPoint 2013, which has a clean crisp look to it, similar to that of SharePoint 2013.

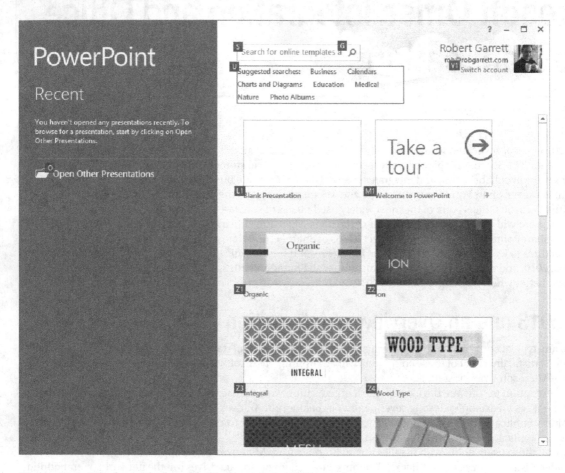

Figure 14-1. *Windows 8 look and feel in PowerPoint 2013*

The Backstage Area

All Office 2010 and 2013 applications have a File tab in the main menu of their main screen; clicking this tab navigates you to the backstage area. Clicking the File tab in Microsoft Word shows a page like that in Figure 14-2.

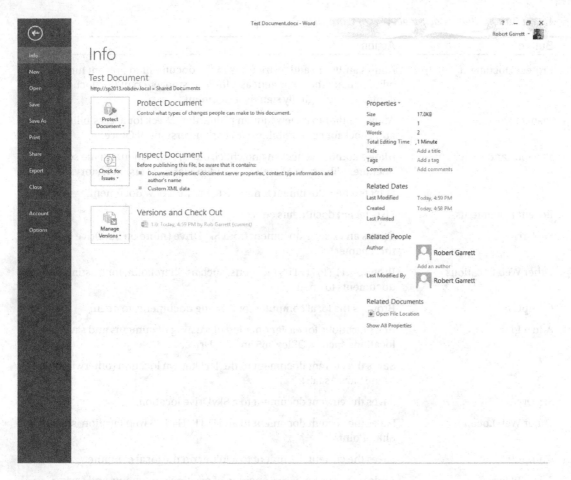

Figure 14-2. *The backstage area in Microsoft Word 2013*

On the left of the page shown in Figure 14-2, you can see the familiar Save, Save As, Open, and Close options—similar to what you came to expect of the File menu in pre-2010 versions of Office applications.

The middle area of the Backstage page typically displays operation and action buttons and links for the tab selected on the left. To give you a sense of capabilities of the backstage area, Table 14-1 lists the various actions available in Word 2013, depending on the tab selected in the left navigation. Table 14-1 is not exhaustive, and the actions available will likely differ between the Office applications in the suite. The far right panel, shown in Figure 14-2, also changes depending on the selected left tab; it currently shows properties of the document, since I have the Info tab selected.

Table 14-1. *Action Buttons in the Backstage Area of Word 2013*

Tab	Button	Action
Info	Protect Document	Allows author to add restrictions to the document to prevent further editing, mark the document as a final version, encrypt the document contents, and digitally sign the document.
Info	Inspect Document	Allows author to review hidden properties, check for accessibility issues, and check for compatibility with earlier versions of Office.
Info	Versions and Check Out	Allows author to check in and check out the document via the source document library in SharePoint, and to manage version history.
New	-	Selects a new document template to create a new document.
Open	Recent Documents	Lists recent documents edited.
Open	SkyDrive	Opens an existing document from SkyDrive (more on SkyDrive later in this chapter).
Open	Other Web Locations	Browses HTTP/HTTPS locations, such as SharePoint, for existing documents to open.
Open	Computer	Browses the local computer for existing documents to open.
Open	Add a Place	Adds locations for easier opening of existing documents and saving, locations such as Office 365 and SkyDrive.
Save	-	Saves the current document to the last known location (otherwise same as the Save As tab).
Save As	SkyDrive	Saves the current document to a SkyDrive location.
Save As	Other Web Locations	Saves the current document to an HTTP/HTTPS web location, such as SharePoint.
Save As	Computer	Saves the current document to a folder on the local computer.
Save As	Add a Place	Adds locations for easier opening of existing documents and saving, locations such as Office 365 and SkyDrive.
Print	-	Allows author to choose a printer associated with the local computer, change print options, and print the current document.
Share	Invite People	Changes permissions of the current document in the SharePoint document library, such that other users can read or edit the document from SharePoint.
Share	E-mail	Allows author to convert the current document to different formats (such as PDF) and add as an attachment to e-mail, using the default e-mail application.
Share	Present Online	Uploads document to a temporary cloud location on Live.com and provides author a unique URL—author can then send link to other users for presentation purposes. After closing the presentation, Live.com deletes the document from the cloud.
Share	Post to Blog	Allows the author to post a blog, hosted on SharePoint, Wordpress.com, Blogger, etc.

(continued)

Table 14-1. (*continued*)

Tab	Button	Action
Export	Create PDF/XPS Document	Creates a PDF or XPS document version of the current document.
Export	Change File Type	Allows the author to change the file type of the current open document, such as DOC to DOCX format.
Close	-	Closes the current document; the Office application will ask you if you wish to save any unsaved changes.
Account	-	Accesses connected account information, such as Facebook, Flickr, SkyDrive, Twitter, etc.
Options	-	Accesses preferences of the Office application.

■ **Note** If you have opened an Office document from SharePoint, the details in the Info tab change to those when opening a document from disk.

Opening and Saving to SharePoint

Office and SharePoint are like husband and wife, especially in enterprise environments (although perhaps not for the real husband and wife relationship in the workplace). After opening an Office document on your local PC, you surely want to upload it to SharePoint for version management and collaboration.

As a general practice, I upload any document in process to SharePoint immediately, because this gives me peace of mind that my document is in a safe place and available, should my local PC crash. You will see later that uploading unfinished documents to SharePoint also allows for co-authoring and editing, which is possible only when your document resides in a shared location.

I assume that by now you are familiar with SharePoint document libraries and how you upload documents to these libraries via your web browser. However, there must be a better way—can you open and save documents from and to SharePoint directly from the Office application?

Saving to SharePoint

I shall start with a scenario in which you might have opened a new instance of PowerPoint—or any other Office application—have made some edits to a new document, and now wish to save the document to SharePoint. As described earlier, you start from the backstage area by clicking the File tab on the ribbon.

1. Click the File tab in the Office application (my example uses PowerPoint 2013).

2. Click the Save As left navigation tab.

3. You should see some saving options, like those in Figure 14-3.

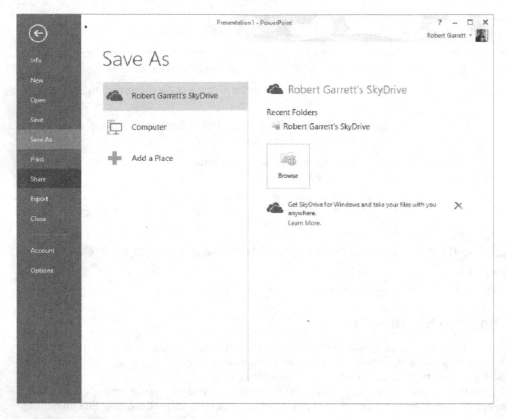

Figure 14-3. *Save As tab in PowerPoint 2013*

Looking at the Save As tab in Figure 14-3, you can see three options: save to SkyDrive, save to the local computer, or add another place. I shall cover saving to SkyDrive further on in this chapter. Saving to the computer is self-explanatory: clicking this option and the Browse button on the right will bring up a familiar Save As dialog with locations on disk to save the open document.

Saving to SharePoint from Office 2013 is different from that of Office 2010. Forget looking for the Send to SharePoint operation under the Save and Send heading—Microsoft has changed the save operations to: Saving to the cloud via SkyDrive and Office 365, Saving to on-premise SharePoint via SkyDrive Pro, and publishing for a specific purpose, such as publishing to a blog from Word, or publishing to a slide library from PowerPoint.

Personally, I miss the very explicit option to save to SharePoint within Office 2010 but can understand Microsoft's need to reduce confusion, now that SharePoint exists both as an on-premise service and in the cloud. I shall leave the theorizing on this topic to the books on business and strategy.

Fortunately, Office 2013 and SharePoint still support saving to a URL (via WebDAV). The following steps continue to demonstrate how to save an open document to SharePoint by providing the URL of the destination document library:

4. Select the option to save to the computer.

5. Click the Browse icon.

6. In the dialog that appears, enter the on-premise SharePoint document library URL in the location field (at the top of the dialog).

7. Give the file a name.

8. Click the Save button.

Opening from SharePoint

Opening an existing Office document from SharePoint is less confusing than Save As, but just as easy. In this scenario and my example, a document resides in a document library in a SharePoint 2013 team site.

Figure 14-4 shows a screenshot of my example document library in my SharePoint 2013 team site. Depending on whether you have installed Office Web Applications (OWA), clicking on the document name (link) will either open the document on the Office application on the local computer (assuming you installed Office) or within OWA. The following steps demonstrate how to open the document in the local Office application:

1. Click the ellipsis to the right of the document name in the document library.

2. A pop-up should appear.

3. Click the Edit link.

4. Accept the warning about opening files from the web (assuming you trust the document).

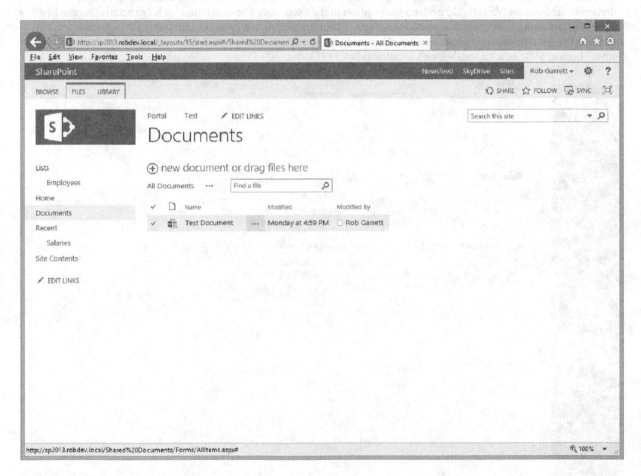

Figure 14-4. *Document in SharePoint 2013 document library*

Now that you have opened a document from SharePoint (or successfully saved a new document to SharePoint, I would like to point out a few user interface changes in the Office application. Figure 14-5 shows the quick save icon at the top left of the application, with synchronization symbol. This indicates that the document resides in a location that supports collaboration (such as SharePoint); clicking this icon will save any local changes and retrieve any changes from the server.

Figure 14-5. *New quick save icon*

From within your Office application, click the File tab and then the Save As tab in the left navigation, as I demonstrated earlier. You should notice a new option in the list of save options: Other Web Locations (Figure 14-6). Office is smart enough to know that you opened/saved your document to a location accessible via web browser. This option in the Save As tab now provides a list of recent locations that you have saved documents to and the familiar Browse button to browse to another web location (via WebDAV).

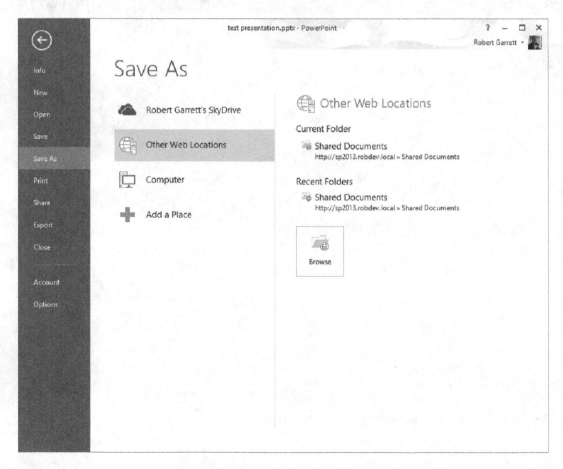

Figure 14-6. *Save to Other Web Locations*

You can also open a document from SharePoint via the Office application user interface, as follows:

1. Click the File tab in the Office application.

2. Click the Open tab in the left navigation tabs.

3. If you saved the document to a SharePoint location earlier, you may see the same location in Recent Folders under the Other Web Locations.

4. You can browse the location of a SharePoint document library, similarly to how you browsed to a save location. Either use the Browse button under Other Web Locations or under Computer and paste a URL of a SharePoint site.

SkyDrive and Office 365

Thanks to a large proliferation of online storage services and hosted solutions, consumers and organizations are now taking advantage of the "cloud." As the days of saving sensitive and important data on local computers and servers become outdated, so does the complexity that typically associates with maintaining recent and relevant backups.

As with most new inventions, the home market was the first to embrace the cloud with services to sync and host working files, such that home users could save files to a working folder on their computer and software would ensure that these files replicated on a cloud service, somewhere on the Internet. The commercial and government markets soon followed the home market when organizations began to realize the cost savings and benefits of hosting important data on secure replicated cloud services.

Microsoft has long been a player in the race to provide cloud-computing services, competing with such organizations as Google and Amazon. You may have heard of Microsoft Windows Azure Services—a cloud solution for hosting scalable server infrastructure and services like SQL Server, Exchange, and now SharePoint.

After the release of SharePoint 2010, Microsoft launched Office 365, an online-hosted Office solution for small, medium, and large businesses to take advantage of Microsoft Office Enterprise software solutions for a monthly fee. Office 365 has gained a lot of interest over the last few years because organizations no longer need to purchase and own costly network infrastructure and pay licenses for Windows Server, Exchange, SQL Server, SharePoint, and Office on workstations. As a result, Microsoft has increased marketing for Office 365 and targeted this platform as the way forward for all business organizations to embrace SharePoint in the cloud.

In the previous sections of this chapter, I mentioned Office 365 and SkyDrive. Microsoft is pushing integration of these online services in Office 2013, and you saw brief examples of this integration in the screenshots I provided earlier. Although specific discussion about Office 365 is outside the scope of this book, I shall cover the integration points with Office 2013 applications, before discussing SkyDrive and SkyDrive Pro.

Office 365

As I mentioned in the previous section, Office 365 (O365) is Microsoft's hosted Office solution, which includes SharePoint. For the purposes of this discussion, I shall focus only on the SharePoint aspects of O365 and leave discussion of the Enterprise services to another book.

The great thing about Office 365 is that organizations can host SharePoint solutions, be it an intranet, extranet, or publishing site, via Microsoft's O365 platform and make the service available to their audience of choice seamlessly. The end user has no idea that the SharePoint solution is in the cloud, rather than on-premise (hosted by the organization). Office 365 will federate with an organization's Active Directory and can host on any purchased domain name; thus, SharePoint in O365 looks and feels like an on-premise hosted version of SharePoint, accessible via a common organization-specified URL.

Because Office 365 is a large topic and beyond the scope of this book, I shall cover only the integration with Office 2013. For the following text, assume that you have a hosted version of a SharePoint team site in O365, complete with a document library for saving Office documents.

■ **Note**   At the time of writing, Office 365 provides both SharePoint 2010 for older customers and 2013 for new customers. Microsoft is in the process of migrating customers from 2010 to 2013.

In the following set of steps, I shall demonstrate saving a new Word document to a team site that I have hosted in Office 365 Preview (SharePoint 2013).

1. Open Word 2013 and create a new blank document.

2. Add some content/text.

3. Click the File tab.

4. Click the Save As tab in the left navigation tabs.

5. Click the Add a Place option and then select Office 365 SharePoint (Figure 14-7).

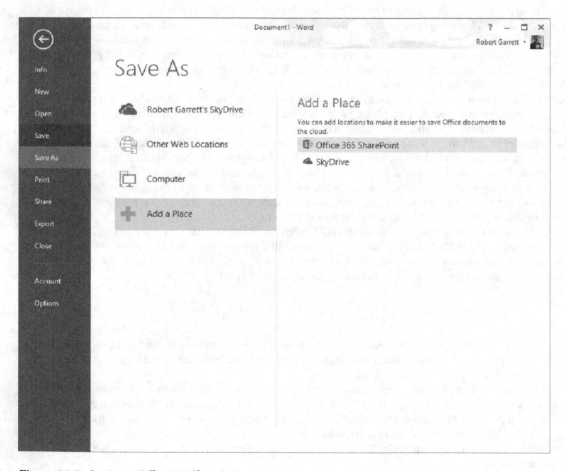

Figure 14-7. *Saving to Office 365 SharePoint*

6. Sign in to your O365 SharePoint—unless your organization has federated authentication, your username will likely be something like user @company.onmicrosoft.com.

7. After signing in, click the Browse button.

8. Similar to how we saved a document to an on-premise SharePoint site, Word displays a Save As dialog with browse capability in the O365 SharePoint site (Figure 14-8).

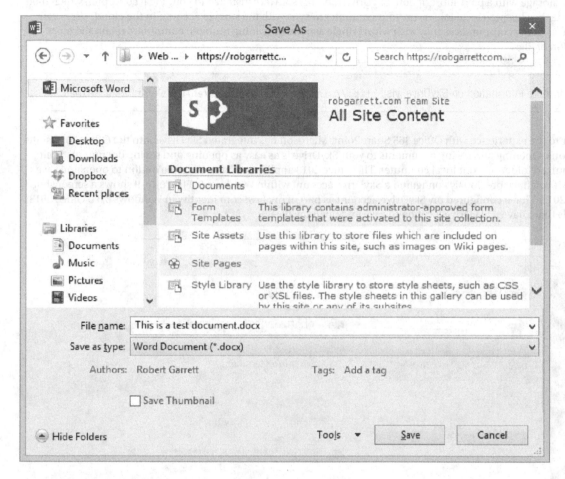

Figure 14-8. *Save As Dialog to save to SharePoint*

9. Navigate to the Documents document library.

10. Provide a file name for the new document.

11. Click the Save button.

As you can see, saving to Office 365 SharePoint is almost identical to saving to a SharePoint on-premise instance. This is exactly the point—Microsoft has achieved the same user experience with Office 365 as users would experience with an on-premise hosted version of SharePoint 2013.

Opening a file from Office 365 SharePoint is as easy as opening a document from on-premise SharePoint. You can navigate to the document via the SharePoint web interface and edit the document or open the document from within the Office application, as I demonstrated in the section "Opening from SharePoint."

SkyDrive and SkyDrive Pro

SkyDrive is Microsoft's answer to synchronized files in the cloud, and part of the Live.com suite of services. SkyDrive is a free service with a limited amount of disk space (7GB at the time of writing), but it offers users the ability to increase the storage with a paid subscription. SkyDrive requires software installed to your local computer, which then handles the task of keeping local folders on your computer in sync with the storage account in the cloud. Users can synchronize as many computers as they wish with a single account, meaning multiple computers retain the most recent version of files.

■ **Note** For more information on SkyDrive, visit `http://windows.microsoft.com/en-US/skydrive/download`.

Similar to the experience with Office 365 SharePoint, Microsoft has integrated SkyDrive into the Office 2013 suite of applications. Opening and saving documents to your SkyDrive is as easy as opening and saving documents from the synchronized folder on your local computer. The Office 2013 applications also have the option to open and save to SkyDrive if you have previously configured a SkyDrive account within Windows 8. Figure 14-9 shows a screenshot from Excel 2013. I have configured my SkyDrive account as part of my Live.com identity in Windows 8, so Office 2013 understands that I have a SkyDrive location to save and open my files.

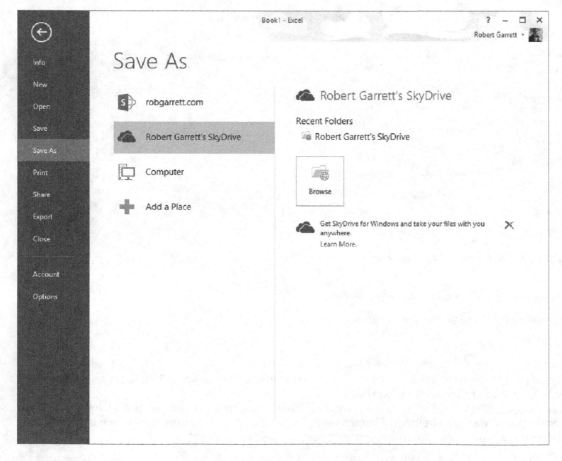

Figure 14-9. *Save to SkyDrive*

There appears to be some confusion in the marketplace regarding the existence of SkyDrive Pro with on-premise and O365 SharePoint. SkyDrive Pro is a version of SkyDrive that ships with Office 2013 and allows synchronization of files with on-premise and O365 SharePoint. SkyDrive Pro caters to business and enterprise users.

For many of those who are not developers or prerelease software advocates, Office 2013 is out of mind until it releases to the general populous, whereas SkyDrive and Live.com are very much mainstream, which may have contributed to confusion on the role played by SkyDrive Pro. Some thought that SkyDrive Pro was the paid subscription service of SkyDrive. SkyDrive Pro is very different from SkyDrive on Live.com, but both offer similar functionality for management and synchronization of Office files in the cloud and enterprise. For the remainder of this section, I shall concentrate on how SkyDrive Pro relates to SharePoint.

Figure 14-10 shows the SkyDrive and SkyDrive Pro tiles that I have installed in my Windows 8. I included this figure to illustrate that SkyDrive and SkyDrive Pro are very different applications. For the following examples, I assume that you have SkyDrive Pro installed on your Windows 7 or Windows 8 computer.

Figure 14-10. *SkyDrive Pro and SkyDrive tiles in Windows 8*

1. Click the tile to launch SkyDrive Pro on your local computer (Figure 14-10).

2. When launching SkyDrive Pro for the first time, you should see a dialog like that in Figure 14-11.

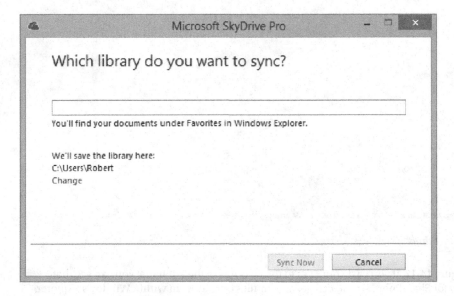

Figure 14-11. *SkyDrive Pro opening dialog*

3. Provide the URL of a SharePoint (on-premise or O365) document library in the text box.

4. Optionally, change the local sync folder location on disk (click the Change link).

5. Click the Sync Now button when ready.

If you followed all the previous steps, you should now have a synchronized folder on your computer, which synchronizes with the document library in SharePoint. You can open, edit, and save documents on the local computer and SkyDrive Pro will synchronize the changes to SharePoint. Similarly, you (or someone else on your team) can open, edit, and save documents via SharePoint, and SkyDrive Pro ensures that all changes synchronize with those on the local disk. By default (unless you changed the location), SkyDrive creates sync locations in the profile folder for the current user (`c:\users\username\SharePoint`).

SkyDrive Pro is smart enough to handle multiple SharePoint locations. I created a sync location for a document library in my O365 SharePoint team site, and a sync location for a document library in my on-premise SharePoint. Looking in the `c:\user\username\SharePoint` folder on my disk, I see the two locations, as in Figure 14-12.

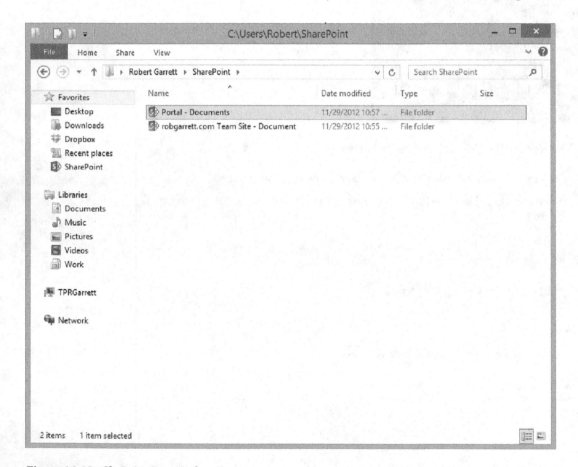

Figure 14-12. *SkyDrive Pro sync locations*

Look at the screenshot in Figure 14-12; if you cast your eyes to the favorites in the left pane, you can see that SkyDrive Pro has created an entry for SharePoint, so you can get at your files quickly from within Windows Explorer.

There is a more convenient method for adding sync locations via the SharePoint web interface.

1. Open your SharePoint 2013 site.

2. Navigate to any document library to which you have permissions.

3. Click the Sync link in the top left of the page (Figure 14-13).

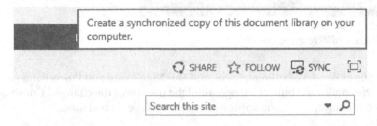

Figure 14-13. *Sync link from within SharePoint 2013*

What do you think happens if you open a file from SharePoint, via SkyDrive Pro, and another user on your team performs the same action? The good news is that SharePoint and SkyDrive Pro understand live co-authoring, which is the topic in the next section. Both users can edit the same document and save whenever they wish, and SharePoint will manage live editing and keeping changes to the same file in sync. SharePoint 2010 and Office 2010 included the capability to live co-author, but third-party disk sync tools did/do not support it.

Live Co-Authoring

Prior to Office 2010, any user wanting to edit a document checked out by another user in SharePoint had to wait until the other user checked the document back in. This situation did not present a big issue in small groups, but when many users collaborated and worked on a large document, checkout on a central document prevented efficient progress.

With the integration of SharePoint, users of Microsoft Word, PowerPoint, and OneNote may now co-author a document in real time. The following steps demonstrate live co-authoring in action, using Office 2013:

1. Have User 1 open a PowerPoint 2013 document from a SharePoint document library, and ensure that this user opens the document in Edit mode.

2. Have User 2 open the same document from SharePoint, also in Edit mode (on a different computer).

3. Look to the bottom bar of PowerPoint 2013 and you should see a notification, like that in Figure 14-14, that multiple users are editing the document. You may click this notification to see the users editing the document.

Figure 14-14. *Multiple users editing a document*

Office 2013 supports co-authoring in Word, PowerPoint, Excel, and OneNote. Word and PowerPoint support formal co-authoring, meaning that the application buffers changes until the user saves the changes. Conversely, Excel and OneNote support semiformal co-authoring, meaning anyone can make changes in real time.

■ **Note** Co-authoring requires at least Office 2010 or Office Web Applications. Previous versions of Office do not support co-authoring. For more information on co-authoring, see `http://office.microsoft.com/en-us/ sharepoint-server-help/document-collaboration-and-co-authoring-HA101812148.aspx`.

Document Information Panel

In Chapter 9, I demonstrated metadata in SharePoint. Metadata is data associated with a document in a SharePoint document library. Metadata exists as site columns (fields) in content types and lists. For example, metadata about a proposal document might consist of the client name and proposal unique identifier.

Microsoft Word, Excel, and PowerPoint 2013 display metadata of documents sourced from SharePoint via the Document Information Panel. To view the Document Information Panel in Word 2013, complete the following steps:

1.   Click the File tab to enter the backstage area.

2.   Ensure that the Info tab in the left navigation tabs is selected.

3.   Click the Properties drop-down on the far right of the page (Figure 14-15).

Figure 14-15. *How to show the Document Panel in Word 2013*

4. Word will show the Document Information Panel (Figure 14-16).

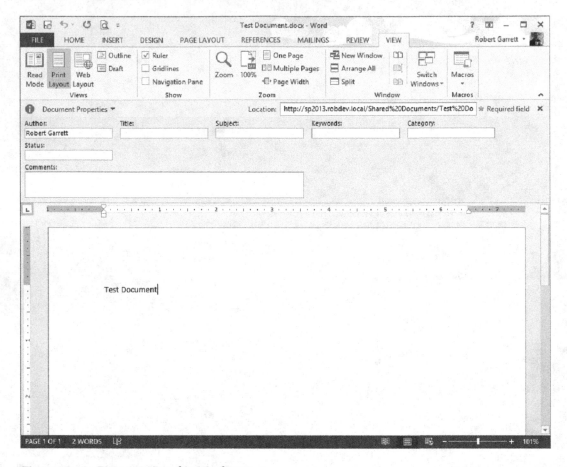

Figure 14-16. *Document Panel in Word 2013*

SharePoint maintains default settings, per document library, for the Document Information Panel for documents of given content types contained in the document library. The following steps demonstrate accessing these settings and changes administrators may apply:

1. Open the document library to the default view.

2. Click the Library tab from the ribbon.

3. Click the Library Settings icon from the ribbon.

4. Click the Advanced Settings link.

5. Ensure that the library allows management of content types.

6. Navigate back to the Settings page for the library.

7. Click the name of the content type that classifies documents where you wish to make Document Information Panel Settings changes.

8. Click the Document Information Panel Settings link.

9. SharePoint shows a page like that in Figure 14-17.

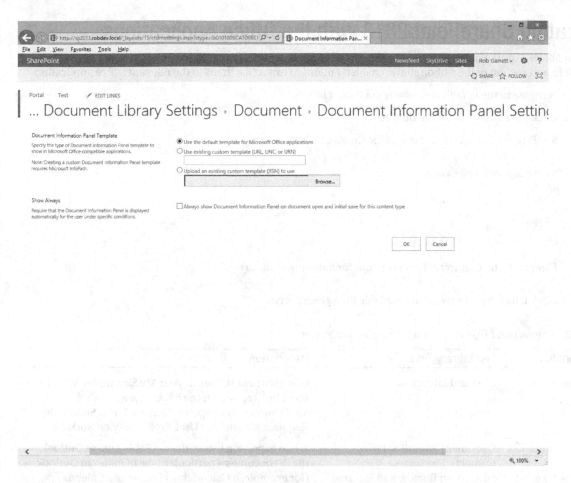

Figure 14-17. *Document Information Panel Settings for a document content type*

10. The Template section allows you to provide a default document template to use; for example, you may have a proposal document template from which you start all new proposals.

11. Check the check box in the Show Always section to ensure that the Document Information Panel displays whenever a user opens a document of this content type in the Office application.

■ **Note** Perform the same steps for content types in the site Content Types Gallery if you want to enable Document Information Panel Settings globally to documents of the content type at the site level.

519

Integrating SharePoint 2013 with the Office Applications

SharePoint allows export of most lists and libraries to Office applications. Depending on the list/library type, the Connect & Export section of the ribbon shows enabled options to export list items to the relevant Office application.

1. Navigate to the default view of any document library.

2. Click the Library tab on the ribbon.

3. See Figure 14-18 as an example of the Connect & Export section.

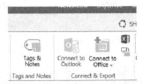

Figure 14-18. *Connect & Export options for a document library*

Table 14-2 details the various options available for a given list type.

Table 14-2. *Connect and Export Options for Lists and Libraries*

Export Function	List/Library Type	Description
Connect to Office	Lists and Libraries	Creates a favorite link in your My Site, under My Links; these links appear in the backstage area of Office applications when opening and saving to SharePoint. Requires My Site and User Profile Service working.
Connect to Outlook	Document Libraries, Tasks, Contacts, Calendars, Discussion Boards, and External Content Lists	When exporting lists of the available type to Outlook, the list becomes a particular type of folder in Outlook (for example, a Calendar list becomes a Calendar folder in Outlook). Users may read and edit the list items from Outlook.
Export to Excel	Lists and Libraries	Exports all metadata of a list or library to columns and row data in an Excel sheet.
Open with Project	Tasks	Opens the tasks from the task list in Microsoft Project as a new series of project tasks.
Open with Access	Lists and Libraries	Opens Microsoft Access and shows the list or library metadata in an Access table. Editing the data in Access updates the list data in real time.

The great thing about interacting with SharePoint lists and libraries from Office applications is that most of the export capabilities work with external lists (Business Connectivity Services; see Chapter 13). For example, you can use Excel to open and edit a list in SharePoint that connects to a table in SQL Server via BCS.

Thus far, you have seen common and general Office application integration with SharePoint, both from the backstage area of Office and as export from SharePoint 2010. The following sections of this chapter address the specific areas of Office application integration for each application.

Microsoft Word

In addition to the aforementioned integration features, Microsoft Word works with SharePoint to allow users to write blog posts, compare document versions, and add Quick Parts. The following sections discuss these features.

Writing Blog Posts

Microsoft Word includes a template to author blog posts. Microsoft Word works with many blogging engines, not just SharePoint, but because this book is about SharePoint 2013 administration, I will focus on creating blog posts for the SharePoint platform.

1. Open Microsoft Word.

2. Click the File tab and then the left tab item, named New.

3. Search for the Blog Post template.

4. Click the Create button (Figure 14-19).

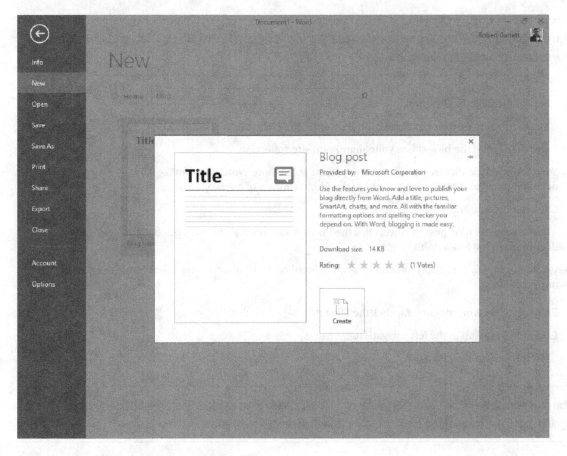

Figure 14-19. *Blog post template in Word 2013*

If you have not registered a blogging service (such as SharePoint), Word will give you the option to do so, with a dialog, as shown in Figure 14-20.

Figure 14-20. *Notice to register a blog account*

■ **Note**   You may register new blogging service accounts at any time by clicking the Manage Accounts icon in the Blog section of the ribbon. Then click the New button.

---

1. Click the Register Now button.

2. Change the blog provider to SharePoint Blog and then click the Next button.

3. Enter the URL of the blog site in your SharePoint site collection.

4. You may click the Picture Options button to configure where Word saves images; by default, SharePoint stores the pictures in the Photos library of the blog site.

5. Click the OK button.

6. After editing the blog post in Word, click the Publish icon on the ribbon to publish the document to the SharePoint blog.

You may wish to publish a regular Word document to SharePoint without creating a new blog post document and using copy-and-paste.

1. From an open Word document, click the File tab.

2. Click the Share tab in the left navigation.

3. Click the Post to Blog Post link.

■ **Note**   You may launch Word with a fresh instance of a blog template from within a SharePoint blog site by clicking the Launch Blogging App link from the Blog tools callout on the left of the blog site pages.

Compare Document Versions

Microsoft permits users to manipulate versions of a document opened from a SharePoint document library with versioning enabled. The following steps demonstrate how to enable version settings for a document library, and how to compare versions of a document from Microsoft Word:

1. Navigate to the default view of a document library in SharePoint.

2. Click the Library tab on the ribbon and then click the Library Settings icon.

3. Click the Versioning Settings link.

4. Under the section Document Versioning History, enable the desired version scheme.

   Create Major Versions: Every document version represents a major version, therefore published for each save or check-in.

   Create Major and Minor Versions: Every check-in or save creates a minor version, meaning that the document is in draft mode; users must publish a major version to make the document changes available to other users, which may involve approval workflow.

5. Click the OK button.

6. Navigate back to the default view of the document library.

7. Select the name of a Word document in the document library (click the Upload icon on the ribbon and upload a Word document if none exists).

8. Click the ellipsis and then click the Edit option.

9. Provide credentials for SharePoint, if asked.

10. Wait for Microsoft Word to open.

11. Make some changes to the document.

12. Save the document (which saves it back to SharePoint).

13. Click the Review tab on the ribbon in Microsoft Word.

14. Click the Compare icon in the Compare section of the ribbon.

15. See Figure 14-21 for the options available.

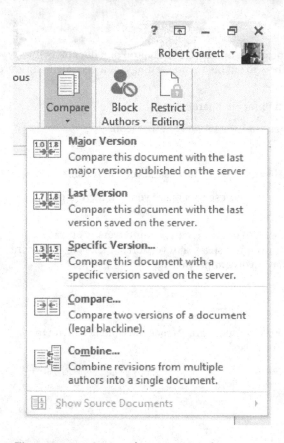

Figure 14-21. Options for comparing document versions in Microsoft Word

Most of the options available in Figure 14-21 are self-explanatory. Users may compare the current open document with a major version, the latest version, or another specific version, and they may combine document versions.

Quick Parts

Microsoft Word documents allow authors to enter Quick Parts, which, when you open a document from SharePoint, allow inclusion of field values from metadata attached to the document library. The following steps demonstrate adding a Quick Part to your open Word document:

1. Navigate to the default view of the document library.

2. Select the name of a Word document in the document library (click the Upload icon on the ribbon and upload a Word document if none exists).

3. Click the ellipsis, and then click the Edit option.

4. Provide credentials for SharePoint, if asked.

5. Wait for Microsoft Word to open.

6. Click the Insert tab on the ribbon in Word.

7. In the Text section of the ribbon, click the Quick Parts icon.

8. Select the Document Property menu item and then select the metadata field from the sub-menu.

9. Figure 14-22 shows an example where I added the author Quick Part—whenever the author of the document changes in SharePoint, Word will update this value, because the author property is part of the document metadata.

Figure 14-22. *Quick Part property added to a Word document*

Microsoft Excel

Microsoft Excel does a phenomenal job of managing columns and rows in a sheet. Users can import Excel spreadsheets as custom lists into SharePoint with the same columns and row data as list items. Users may also reverse the process, exporting existing lists as new Excel sheets. SharePoint also includes Excel Services, a business intelligence service to host Excel spreadsheets within SharePoint for BI data manipulation, sourced from Excel. I covered business intelligence and Excel Services in Chapter 12, so I will not cover BI in this section. However, I shall demonstrate the simple aspects of importing and exporting Excel data into SharePoint 2013.

The following steps demonstrate how to import an existing Excel spreadsheet into SharePoint as a new custom list. Before starting, ensure that your Excel sheet contains the correct formatting. The first row of the sheet defines the columns (fields) of the new custom list, so make sure to use nice neat short column names. Start data from row two in the sheet. The first column of the sheet maps to the mandatory Title column in the list, so ensure that this contains text data. I created my columns as described in Table 14-3.

Table 14-3. *Columns Created in Excel*

Column Number	Column Name
Column 1	Name
Column 2	Address 1
Column 3	Address 2
Column 4	City
Column 5	State
Column 6	ZIP

After adding the first row for the column headings, add some data in the successive rows. Complete the following steps to import your Excel sheet as a new list in SharePoint:

■ **Note** If you have trouble with import and export of Excel data, ensure that your SharePoint site is in the IE browser Trusted Sites Zone or Local Intranet Zone.

1. Open the SharePoint site to import the Excel sheet as a new list.

2. Click the gear icon in the top right.

3. Select the menu option for Site Contents.

4. Click the tile to add an app.

5. Page through the available apps until you find the tile for Importing from a Spreadsheet; click this tile.

6. Provide the name and description of the custom list and then click the Browse button to browse your local disk for the Excel Spreadsheet file (Figure 14-23).

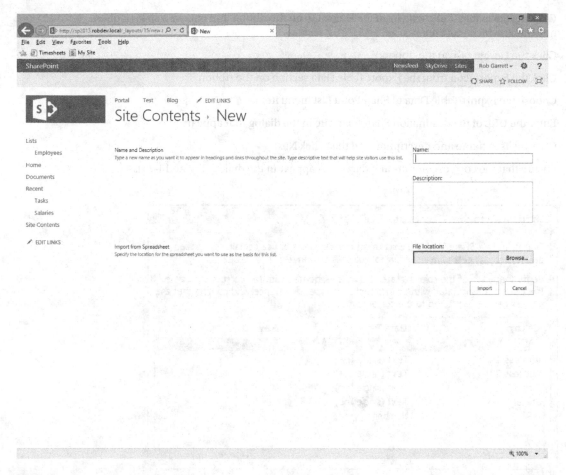

Figure 14-23. *Import spreadsheet as a new custom list*

7. Click the Import button.

8. Excel opens with a dialog asking what data to import—Table Range, Range of Cells, or Named Range. I went with Range of Cells and then highlighted the cells in the sheet.

9. Click the Import button on the dialog. After a brief pause, SharePoint will load the page with the default view of the new column.

■ **Note** SharePoint makes an educated guess about the types of columns to create in SharePoint, based on column formatting and data in the Excel column. For example, ZIP codes may come over as numeric fields unless formatted correctly as text in Excel.

An alternative way to import data into SharePoint from Excel is as follows:

1. Open Excel and the file to import into SharePoint.

2. Select the cells to import.

3. Click the Format as Table icon from the Home tab on the ribbon and choose a style (it does not matter which you choose).

4. Click the Design tab on the ribbon.

5. Click the Export icon from the Export Table Data section on the ribbon.

6. Choose the Export Table Data to SharePoint List menu item.

7. Enter the URL of the destination SharePoint site in the dialog that appears.

8. Give the list a name and description and then click Next.

9. Ensure that the correct columns and data types appear in the dialog (Figure 14-24).

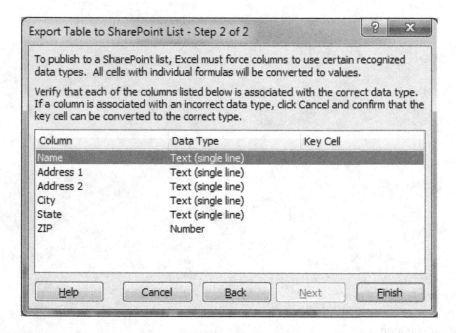

Figure 14-24. Export table to SharePoint dialog

10. Click the Finish button.

11. Excel shows a final dialog with export result (hopefully successful) and a link to the new list in SharePoint. Click the link to see the Datasheet view of the new list in your browser.

The following steps demonstrate the reverse of the above—exporting data from an existing SharePoint list to Excel:

1. Navigate to a Datasheet view of a list, to export to Excel, from within SharePoint.

2. Click the List tab on the ribbon, and then the Datasheet View icon (Figure 14-25).

Figure 14-25. Datasheet view of SharePoint list

3. Click the Export to Excel icon on the ribbon.

■ **Note** If this button is disabled, check the settings for the list to make sure Datasheet is permitted; also check if the site is in either the Trusted Sites Zone or Local Intranet Zone in your browser.

Excel Services

Since SharePoint 2007, SharePoint has included Excel Services. Excel Services allows the hosting of Excel sheets and Excel data within SharePoint pages, without the need for Excel installed on the SharePoint Server, nor installed on the client. I covered Excel Services as part of business intelligence in Chapter 12.

Microsoft PowerPoint

Office 2013 includes functionality to present documents to others. PowerPoint 2010 included this functionality with SharePoint 2010. Now with the cloud taking an active presence in the workplace, you can share your Office documents with others via Office in the cloud. The following steps demonstrate how to broadcast PowerPoint slides:

1. From an open PowerPoint deck, click the File tab to enter the backstage area of the application.

2. Click the Share tab in the left navigation tabs.

3. Click the option to present online.

4. If you Lync installed, change the drop-down option to Office Presentation Service.

5. Click the Present Online button.

6. Click the Broadcast Slide Show item and then click the Broadcast Slide Show button.

7. PowerPoint provides a link to give to viewers of the broadcast (Figure 14-26).

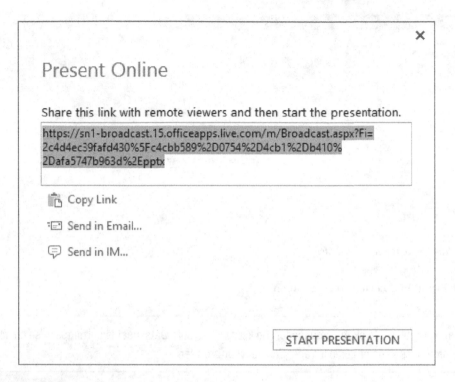

Figure 14-26. *Present Online dialog*

8. Click the Start Presentation button to begin.

Slide Libraries

Since SharePoint 2007, SharePoint has included a Slide Library list type (available only with SharePoint Standard edition and above). Slide libraries consist of collections of slides, taken from one or many PowerPoint decks. The idea is to collect a repository of popular and commonly used slides for new presentations.

As of SharePoint 2013, the slide library template is no longer available in the list of app/list templates accessed from the site contents area. Microsoft might depreciate slide libraries completely in later versions of SharePoint, but for now you can still access the Create page for slide libraries by typing the following link into your browser:

```
http://your-site-collection/_layouts/15/slnew.aspx?FeatureId={0be49fe9-9bc9-409d-abf9-
702753bd878d}&ListTemplate=2100
```

1. Give the library a name and description.

2. Click the Create button.

3. Open PowerPoint and a slide deck with a selection of slides.

4. Click the File tab to enter the backstage area.

5. Click the Share tab in the list of left navigation tabs.

6. Click the option to publish slides and then the Publish Slides button.

7. PowerPoint then displays a dialog asking you which slides to publish (Figure 14-27).

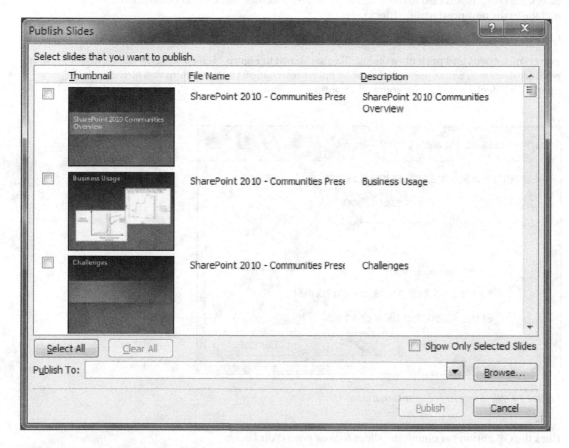

Figure 14-27. Select slides to publish to SharePoint

8. Check the check boxes (or click the Select All button for all) for publishing.

9. Enter the URL of the slide library location in the Publish To box (note that you do not need the filename.aspx in the URL, such as AllItems.aspx).

10. Click the Publish button.

■ **Note** You may need to authenticate with your username and password.

Head over to your slide library in SharePoint, and you should start seeing the slides appearing (hit Refresh a few times). You may not see all the slides immediately, as SharePoint processes and creates thumbnails for each slide before showing the slide in the library.

Now that you have a set of slides in your slide library, I can demonstrate creating a new PowerPoint deck from a selected number of slides from the new slide library, as follows:

1. Navigate to your slide library.

2. Check the check boxes next to the slides in the SharePoint slide library that you wish to include in the new presentation (deck).

3. Click the Copy Slide to Presentation link at the top of the list, just below the ribbon.

4. PowerPoint opens and presents a dialog, like that shown in Figure 14-28, asking the user whether to copy to a new presentation or an open presentation (if PowerPoint was already open with a deck loaded), with some other options, as shown.

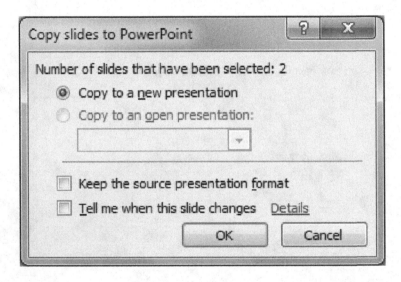

Figure 14-28. Copy to presentation dialog

5. Click the OK button to commit the slides to your PowerPoint deck.

Microsoft OneNote

Microsoft OneNote is a powerful note-taking application, allowing textual notes, images, media, and handwriting note-authoring capabilities. With the integration with SharePoint, OneNote goes beyond a personal note-taking tool and becomes a collaborative tool, much like the rest of the Office suite applications. Similar to Microsoft Word and Microsoft PowerPoint, Microsoft OneNote works with live co-authoring—discussed earlier in this chapter. OneNote also works with SkyDrive; thus, you can store all of your important notes in the cloud.

There is not a whole lot to demonstrate with OneNote's integration with SharePoint, except the following steps to save a new OneNote notebook to a SharePoint document library from the backstage area of the application:

1. Click the File tab to enter the backstage area.

2. Click the New tab from the left navigation tabs.

3. Choose the option to store on your computer (for the moment).

4. Provide a new name for your notebook.

5. Click the link to create the note in a different folder; a dialog appears.

6. Enter the SharePoint site URL in the notebook name box.

7. Navigate to a document library to save the notebook.

8. Provide the notebook file name in the document library.

9. Click the Create button.

10. OneNote asks if you wish to share your notebook with others (Figure 14-29).

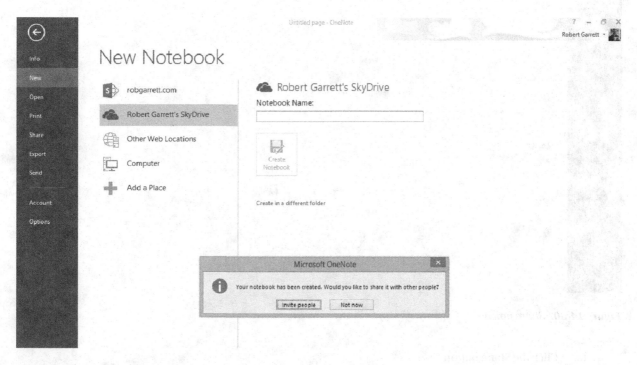

Figure 14-29. *Invite others to share your notebook*

11. Click the Invite People button.

12. Enter names or e-mails of people to invite (Figure 14-30).

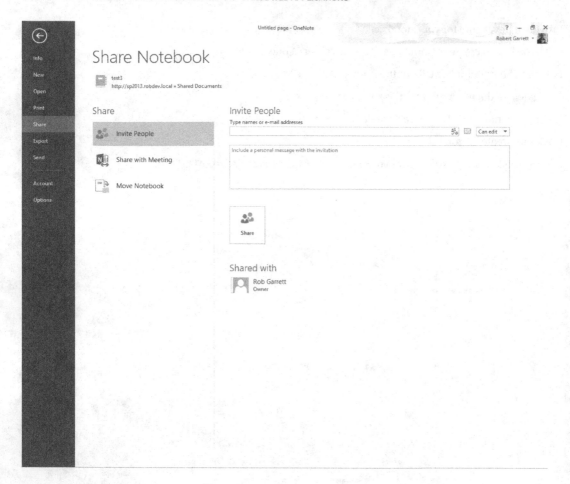

Figure 14-30. Share notebook

13. Click the Share button.

14. Users with collaboration permissions may now co-author content in the new OneNote notebook.

Microsoft Access

Microsoft Access is a small file-based Relational Database Management System (RDBMS). Microsoft Access is less powerful than, and does not scale for performance and enterprise use like, SQL Server, but it is portable and ideal for manipulation of small chunks of data in relational form.

Similar to SQL Server and other RDBMS applications, Access uses terminology to define certain features and functionality, as described in Table 14-4.

Table 14-4. *Microsoft Access Terminology*

Terminology	Description
Table	Stores all data, just like SQL Server and SharePoint lists. A table consists of columns and rows, where the columns define the data fields and the rows define the data itself (the records).
Queries	Think of queries like saved T-SQL queries in SQL Server. Queries produce result data by querying one or many tables, using T-SQL syntax.
Forms	Forms allow users to interact with data in tables. Defining a form allows a user to enter data into text boxes, check boxes, radio buttons, drop-down list controls, and the like.
Reports	Reports in Access, as in any other data reporting system, display data queried from Access in a readable format for end users.

With the terminology out of the way, I shall demonstrate how to export data in a SharePoint list to Access from SharePoint, and how to import lists in SharePoint to Access.

1. Open a SharePoint list at the default view.

2. Click the Library tab on the ribbon.

3. In the Connect & Export section of the ribbon, click the Open with Access icon.

4. Microsoft Access opens and displays a dialog, asking if you wish to link the list or export the data as a copy (Figure 14-31).

Figure 14-31. *Open in Microsoft Access dialog*

■ **Note**   SharePoint disables the Open with Access button if you do not have Access installed. This icon does not exist at all for document libraries.

Link Tables in Access allow users to work with data, as they would any other Access table, except that the data does not reside in Access—in this case, it is within a SharePoint list. With Microsoft Access, SharePoint, and Link Tables, you could create a lightweight Access application that provides a business intelligent interface for entering data into SharePoint.

Connecting to SharePoint from Microsoft Access, and importing data, is just as painless as exporting from SharePoint.

1. Open Access.

2. Choose to create a blank desktop database from the list of templates (Figure 14-32).

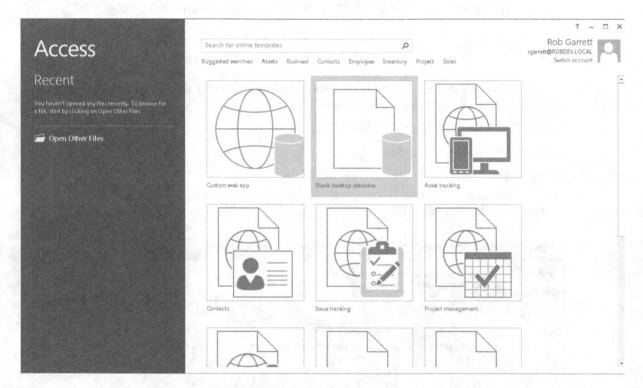

Figure 14-32. *Access—create a blank desktop database*

3. Give the new database a name and location on disk.

4. Click the Create button.

5. Define a table that you will import into SharePoint.

6. Add some data; my table looks like that in Figure 14-33.

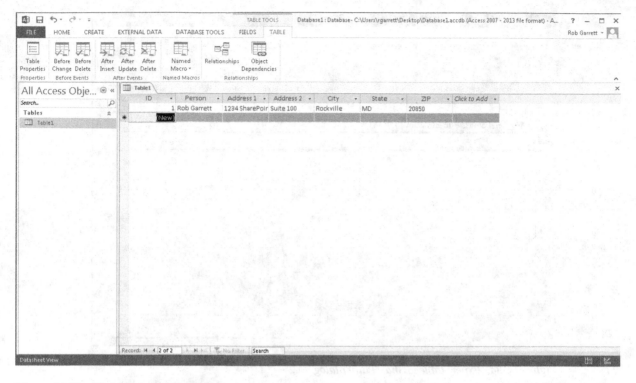

Figure 14-33. *My table in Access 2013*

7. Save the file.

8. Click the Database Tools tab on the ribbon.

9. Click the SharePoint icon on the ribbon.

10. Access opens a dialog, asking where to export data into SharePoint (Figure 14-34).

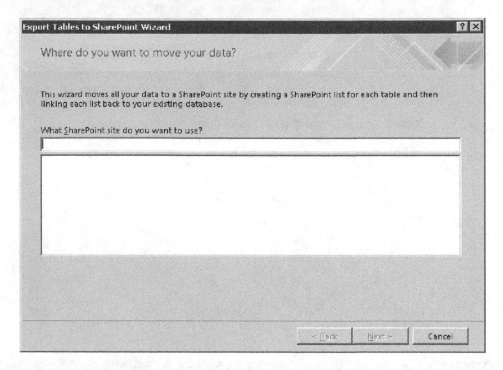

Figure 14-34. *Export table to SharePoint dialog*

11. Provide the URL to your SharePoint site.

12. Click the Next button.

13. Authenticate with SharePoint, if asked.

14. Access makes the necessary connection to SharePoint. If all goes well then Access shows a confirmation of completion dialog.

You now have a table in your Access database that connects directly with SharePoint. Your table data is no longer contained in the Access database, but in SharePoint, which is why Access created a backup database of your original database file.

Access Services

SharePoint includes a managed service application for Access—Access Services. With Access Services, users can do much more than just host an Access file in a document library, or link lists with Access tables. Access Services integrates the complete Access functionality into SharePoint, so legacy Access users need not rely on the Office Access application to host forms, run queries, and provide reports.

Access Services provides several benefits to collaborative users of data retained in an Access file using SharePoint.

- Access Services locks objects and not the entire file when users make changes (unlike the full Access application).

- Access Services secures data in an Access database using the same SharePoint permissions model.

- Access Service is a middle-tier service and web service application, so users can share access to their Access data across the farm and other connecting SharePoint farms.

- Everything runs in the world of the browser; users do not need the Access Office application on their computer.

The following steps demonstrate how to set up Access Services, via Central Admin, and how to leverage the capabilities of Access Services:

1. Open Central Administration.

2. Click the Manage Services on Server link, under the System Settings heading.

3. Make sure the Access Database Service is in a started state.

4. Click the Manage Service Applications link, under the Application Management heading, from the Central Admin home page.

5. Scroll down the list and see if an Access Services application already exists. If not, continue.

6. Click the New icon on the ribbon and select Access Services from the menu.

7. In the dialog, give the service a name and create an application pool.

8. Click the OK button and wait while SharePoint creates the new service application.

9. You may configure the settings for Access Services by selecting the service application; then click the Manage icon on the ribbon.

■ **Note** Access Services is different from Access Services 2010, the latter being the service to support Access applications created in SharePoint 2010.

Now that you have Access Services configured, I shall demonstrate how to create an Access web application. This is an Access database application residing in SharePoint. Much like Excel Services, Access Services allows you to host Access databases in SharePoint and manipulate them without the requirement of Access installed on client computers.

1. Navigate to your SharePoint site, to host your Access web app.

2. Click the gear icon in the top right.

3. Select the menu item to add an app.

4. Page through the available templates until you find the Access app.

5. Click the tile and then the button to add it.

6. SharePoint will prompt you for a name for your app (Figure 14-35).

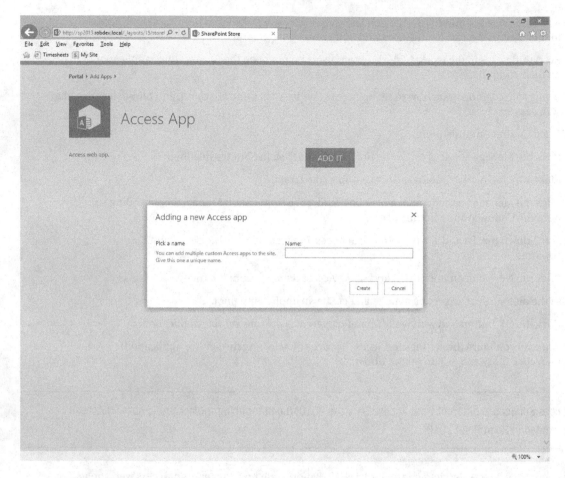

Figure 14-35. *Add an Access app to SharePoint 2013*

7. Provide a name and click the Create button.

8. Wait a moment while SharePoint creates the Access app.

If you prefer to start your Office applications from the Office application, you can also create a new Access application using Access 2013, as follows:

1. Open Access 2013.

2. Choose the Custom Web App template.

3. Give the application a name.

4. Provide the location of the app as your SharePoint site.

5. Click the Create button.

6. You may need to authenticate, as necessary.

Microsoft InfoPath

Microsoft introduced InfoPath in Office 2003 as an application to visually create forms and deploy them to an audience to fill out. As a stand-alone Office application, InfoPath provides good form design capabilities, and the author of a form has various deployment options.

In 2007, Microsoft Office SharePoint Server (MOSS) 2007 included InfoPath Server as an Enterprise license feature. The purpose of InfoPath Server was to render forms, designed in InfoPath, within the SharePoint environment, to users with a web browser. InfoPath 2007 included the new SharePoint InfoPath Server deployment path.

The problem with InfoPath Server in MOSS 2007 was that the expectation from Microsoft that InfoPath Server would provide site designers the overarching solution for integrating custom forms into the SharePoint platform missed the mark. InfoPath Server came to SharePoint as an additional feature and did not fully integrate into the platform, and so InfoPath-hosted forms in MOSS 2007 looked more like an afterthought.

Since SharePoint 2010, InfoPath and SharePoint now fully integrate. For example, SharePoint 2013 allows administrators to customize any list-based form, via SharePoint Designer 2013, which consists of converting the form to an InfoPath form. Most of the annoying branding that informed the user that InfoPath Server was powering the form rendering is gone, and forms render within the same SharePoint site chrome.

The InfoPath 2013 Office application itself is in two parts: Designer and Filler. You use the Designer part of the application for designing and deploying new forms, and the Filler for users to complete forms. Form designers may deploy both browser-based forms and those that are not browser based to SharePoint. Forms that are browser based and sourced from a form library with setting to render InfoPath forms in the browser will do so. Forms that are not browser based or those sourced from a forms library that does not permit browser rendering will open InfoPath Filler on the client desktop.

SharePoint supports three deployment options for browser-based InfoPath forms, as follows:

- *Form Library:* A SharePoint Form Library is a special type of document library that contains XSN files—the XML definition of an InfoPath form. Form Libraries work well when deploying forms to a single location at the current site level and when the form creator has no expectation of hosting the form in other sites or libraries.

- *Site Content Type:* Forms may now deploy as content types in SharePoint to the site or site collection Content Type Gallery. This method supports reuse of the form across sites and libraries in the hierarchy.

- *Administrator-approved Form Template:* This type of form deployment involves deploying the form to the InfoPath Forms Services application in the farm (via Central Admin). Administrator-approved forms are reusable across the farm as templates wherever the farm has access to the InfoPath Forms Services.

Before you dive into the various deployments of InfoPath forms and see InfoPath Forms Services in action, you must first configure InfoPath Forms Services, via Central Admin.

1. Open Central Administration.

2. Click the General Application Settings heading.

3. Click the Configure InfoPath Forms Services link, under the InfoPath Forms Services heading.

4. SharePoint shows a page like that in Figure 14-36.

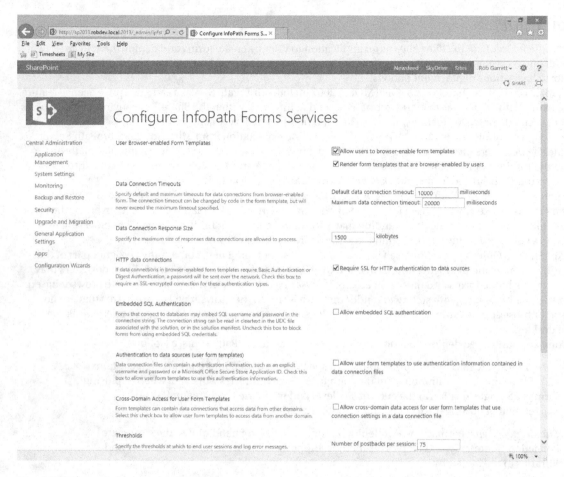

Figure 14-36. *Configure InfoPath Forms Services*

Most of the settings on this page are self-explanatory. The User Browser-enabled Form Templates are specifically of interest because unchecking these options prevents browser-based forms from rendering in the browser.

1. Go back to the General Application Settings page and review the various links under the InfoPath Forms Services heading:

- *Manage form templates:* Navigates the administrator to the master form templates list. By default, this list contains forms for use in various workflows across the farm.

- *Configure InfoPath Forms Services:* As described previously, this link takes the administrator to a page to configure the general settings for InfoPath Forms Services.

- *Upload form template:* Provides a page where the administrator can upload an administrator-approved form to the master list.

- *Manage data connection files:* InfoPath forms typically use data connection files to define how to integrate data into the form (such as for drop-down list values) and where to submit posted data. This link provides the administrator with a place to upload and manage data connection files.

- *Configure InfoPath Forms Services Web Service Proxy:* Allows the administrator to enable a web service proxy for forms.

Deploying a Form Via Central Administration

Forms deployed to Central Admin by administrators are available for use by other users in designated site collections. The following steps detail how to upload an InfoPath template (XSN file) to Central Administration:

1. Open Central Administration.

2. Click the General Application Settings heading.

3. Under the InfoPath Forms Services heading, click the Upload Form Template link.

4. Browse to the location of the XSN on disk.

5. You may click the Verify button to confirm that the form has no errors (I recommend doing this).

6. Click the Upload button and then look to the Status page, which should read success.

7. From the Manage Form Templates page, hover over the name of the form template you just uploaded.

8. Click the Activate to a Site Collection link.

9. Choose a site collection to activate the form; after completing this step, SharePoint makes the form available as a content type in the Content Type Gallery, for users to add to new and existing lists/libraries.

Rendering a Form Using the InfoPath Form Web Part

SharePoint 2007 used to render forms in a new browser window executed by SharePoint, or site designers could host InfoPath forms in a Forms Server User Control. Neither option was particularly compelling. SharePoint now provides an InfoPath Web Part.

The InfoPath Web Part allows any page contributor to host an existing InfoPath form on pages that support Web Parts, such as wiki pages and pages with Web Part zones. After inserting the Web Part on the page, you should see something like Figure 14-37. Click the link to show the tool pane and follow these steps to configure the Web Part to an existing InfoPath form:

1. The list or library drop-down control contains all lists and libraries using InfoPath form content types. Select the desired list to render the form.

2. Select the appropriate InfoPath form content type in the next drop-down control.

3. The check box Show InfoPath Ribbon or Toolbar instructs the Web Part to display the InfoPath ribbon in the Web Part rendering. Unchecking this option will cause the Web Part to render only the form (which is often desirable for end users).

4. The check box Send Data to Connected Web Parts When Page Loads instructs the Web Part to activate any Web Part connections during page load.

5. The remaining controls pertain to rendering, such as the default view to render and what happens to the form after submission.

6. Click the OK button at the bottom of the tool pane to save your changes.

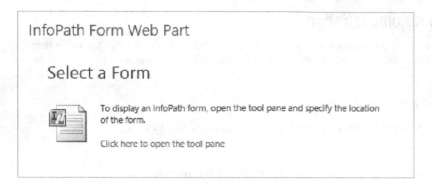

Figure 14-37. *The InfoPath Web Part*

Customizing the Document Information Panel and List Forms

Earlier in this chapter, I introduced the Document Information Panel, which displays the metadata of a document from within the Office application. The Document Information Panel associates with a particular SharePoint content type for the open document. Using InfoPath and SharePoint, administrators may customize the look of the Document Information Panel, following these steps:

1. Open InfoPath Designer 2013.

2. In the list of available templates shown, click the Document Information Panel template.

3. Click the Design Form button on the right.

4. A wizard dialog appears (see Figure 14-38). Enter the URL of the SharePoint document library and then click the Next button.

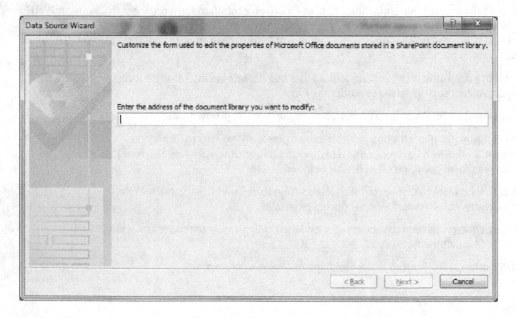

Figure 14-38. *Data Source Wizard for editing the Document Information Panel from InfoPath Designer 2013*

5. Select the content type to edit the Document Information Panel and click the Next button.

6. The wizard displays a message about publishing the content type for the InfoPath form to work; click the Finish button.

7. InfoPath Designer 2013 now shows you a form to edit, complete with the Document Information Panel fields (see Figure 14-39).

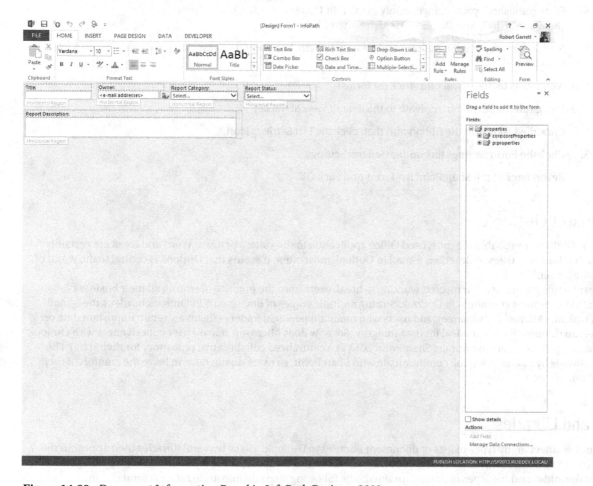

Figure 14-39. *Document Information Panel in InfoPath Designer 2013*

8. Experiment with editing the form; for example, change some colors, fonts, and so on.

9. To publish your changes to SharePoint, click the File tab and then the Quick Publish button.

InfoPath Designer also allows administrators to edit List Form pages, such as the Edit form, or the New Item form. The following steps demonstrate this:

1. Navigate to the SharePoint list or library.

2. Click the List tab on the ribbon and then click the Customize Form icon on the ribbon.

3. InfoPath Designer opens, showing the Edit form with the active fields.

4. Customize the form. You may change the presentation any way you like, even adding or removing fields.

5. To publish your changes to SharePoint, click the File tab and then the Quick Publish button.

6. Once published, your changes apply to the Edit (`EditForm.aspx`), New Item (`NewForm.aspx`), and Display (`DispForm.aspx`) forms.

7. Navigate to the list in SharePoint and add a new item. You should see the new InfoPath form loaded.

How do you revert to the SharePoint stock list forms?

1. Using Internet Explorer, navigate to the default view of the list.

2. Click the List tab on the ribbon and then click the List Settings icon.

3. Click the Form Settings link under General Settings.

4. Revert back to the SharePoint list forms and click OK.

Microsoft Outlook

Microsoft Outlook is probably the most used Office application in the suite. Microsoft Word and Excel are certainly popular, but business users look at their e-mail in Outlook most often. It seems that Outlook is central to the world of the business user.

Despite this popularity, Microsoft is working to break users from the practice of storing all their business information in e-mails contained in Outlook. Storing multiple copies of documents in Outlook burdens the e-mail server (typically Microsoft Exchange), and users who maintain personal folders effectively retain important data on their personal computers—not ideal for data integrity. So, how does Microsoft release user cohesiveness with Outlook and encourage these users to leverage SharePoint 2013 as a centralized collaborative repository for their data? The short answer is by making Outlook communicate with SharePoint, so users do not have to leave the comfort of their favorite e-mail client.

Lists and Libraries

Users may connect many types of lists or document libraries to Outlook. These lists and libraries then appear in the hierarchy of folders with which users of Outlook are familiar. Furthermore, the list type determines how Outlook displays the folder and the types of items contained. The following steps demonstrate how to connect a shared calendar in SharePoint with Outlook:

1. Open SharePoint and navigate to a shared calendar, default view.

2. Click the Calendar tab on the ribbon and then click the Connect to Outlook icon in the Connect & Export section of the ribbon (Figure 14-40).

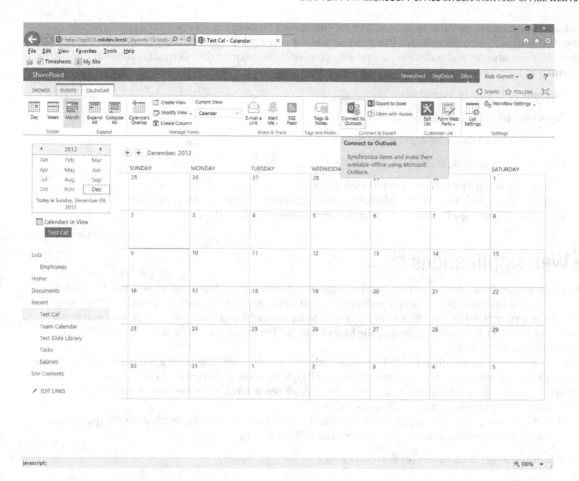

Figure 14-40. *Connect to Outlook from SharePoint 2013*

3. Outlook launches and displays a dialog asking you to confirm connecting the list to Outlook.

4. You may click the Advanced button to see additional options, such as to edit the name of the folder in Outlook.

5. Click the Yes button; Outlook displays the new calendar in the calendar area of the folder hierarchy.

6. If you have events in your SharePoint calendar, you should see them in Outlook (after the next Send & Receive); you can also make direct changes to the calendar in Outlook and see the changes reflected in SharePoint.

Outlook allows users to connect the following lists to Outlook in a similar process to the preceding steps: Document Libraries, Calendars, Tasks, Contacts, Picture Libraries, Document Sets (Individual Owned), Discussion Boards, and Project Tasks.

Outlook stores all connected list data in an offline PST file, called `SharePoint Lists.pst`. Readers should note that SharePoint downloads *all* content to this PST file, so if you have a large document library connected to Outlook, the combination of documents and metadata may take up considerable space on the client machine (not the e-mail server). Fortunately, administrators and list owners may prevent download of list content with the following steps:

1. Navigate to the list in SharePoint.

2. Click the List or Library tab on the ribbon.

3. Click the List or Library Settings on the ribbon.

4. Click the Advanced Settings link.

5. Change the setting for Offline Client Availability to No. SharePoint then disables the Connect to Outlook icon on the ribbon. Users with previous downloaded content still retain the offline copy in Outlook but can no longer sync with SharePoint.

Office Web Applications

Office Web Applications (Office Web Apps) are web browser–based applications that enable users to edit Word, Excel, PowerPoint, and OneNote files without needing Microsoft Office applications installed on client machines. The Windows Live service provides an Office Web Apps service for personal users and consumers, and enterprise organizations may install Office Web Apps within the SharePoint 2013 infrastructure, which is what I shall discuss in this section of this chapter.

SharePoint Office Web Applications (OWA) no longer exists as a service application in a SharePoint farm. Instead, OWA 2013 installs a separate server farm. You must now install Office Web Apps Server on a different server from SharePoint 2013. This has the advantage that you can maintain patches to OWA separate from SharePoint and can maintain both farms differently from a user load perspective.

Unlike SharePoint, the Office Web Applications installer does not include a prerequisites installer application. Make sure you install the following prerequisites before installing OWA 2013:

- Windows Server 2008 R2 SP1 (or Windows 2012)

- .NET Framework 4.5

- Windows PowerShell 3.0

- KB2592525 (http://www.microsoft.com/en-us/download/details.aspx?displaylang=en&id=27929)

After completing installation of the prerequisites, open a new PowerShell window on the server and execute the following Cmdlets—for Windows 2008 R2:

```
Import-Module ServerManager

Add-WindowsFeature Web-Server,Web-WebServer,Web-Common-Http,Web-Static-Content,Web-App-Dev,Web-Asp-Net,Web-Net-Ext,Web-ISAPI-Ext,Web-ISAPI-Filter,Web-Includes,Web-Security,Web-Windows-Auth,Web-Filtering,Web-Stat-Compression,Web-Dyn-Compression,Web-Mgmt-Console,Ink-Handwriting,IH-Ink-Support
```

Restart the server if/when prompted. If you are running Windows Server 2012, execute the following PowerShell Cmdlets instead of those preceding:

```
Add-WindowsFeature Web-Server,Web-Mgmt-Tools,Web-Mgmt-Console,Web-WebServer,Web-Common-Http,Web-
Default-Doc,Web-Static-Content,Web-Performance,Web-Stat-Compression,Web-Dyn-Compression,Web-
Security,Web-Filtering,Web-Windows-Auth,Web-App-Dev,Web-Net-Ext45,Web-Asp-Net45,Web-ISAPI-Ext,Web-
ISAPI-Filter,Web-Includes,InkandHandwritingServices
```

Now, you are ready to install the OWA 2013 binaries. Run the setup.exe file in the OWA installation media. If you have a single IMG or ISO file, you may need to burn this to a DVD, or extract the package using a tool, such as WINISO or WINRAR.

I recommend that you install the OWA language packs if you plan to display multi-language documents from your OWA Server. Installation of the language packs is straightforward and requires you to run the installer.

Configuring OWA for SharePoint 2013

I hope that you have installed the Office Web Apps prerequisites and binaries without error. If so, now you are ready to configure OWA for SharePoint 2013. Simply installing OWA is not enough, SharePoint requires configuration to communicate with the OWA Server, now that it is not an included service application with SharePoint.

1. Create an OWA farm—execute the following PowerShell on the OWA Server:

    ```
    New-OfficeWebAppsFarm -InternalURL "http://servername" -AllowHttp -EditingEnabled
    ```

■ **Note**   If you receive 500 server errors when executing OWA Cmdlets, try the following command, followed by an IISRESET: %systemroot%\Microsoft.NET\Framework64\v4.0.30319\aspnet_regiis.exe -iru.

---

2. Verify the OWA Server is serving data via HTTP by navigating to http://servername/hosting/discovery.

3. You should see some XML returned, which is the WOPI (Web app Open Platform Interface) discovery file.

4. Ensure that your SharePoint web applications use Claims-Based-Authentication.

5. Open the SharePoint 2013 Management Shell (PowerShell) as ELEVATED.

6. Execute the following Cmdlet to bind SharePoint to the OWA Server; if you forget the parameter to allow HTTP, the Cmdlet will assume HTTPS:

    ```
    New-SPWOPIBinding -ServerName <WacServerName> -AllowHTTP
    ```

7. Run the following Cmdlet to determine the zone that SharePoint uses to connect to OWA:

    ```
    Get-SPWOPIZone
    ```

8. If the preceding Cmdlet returns the zone as internal-https, then change the zone to internal-http with the following Cmdlet:

    ```
    Set-SPWOPIZone -zone "internal-http"
    ```

9. Ensure that you can use OAUTH to communicate with the OWA Server with the following Cmdlets:

```
$config = (Get-SPSecurityTokenServiceConfig)
$config.AllowOAuthOverHttp = $true
$config.Update()
```

10. Test that you can open Office documents from SharePoint 2013 via OWA.

Of course, the previous steps should work fine for a non-production environment, but for production deployment, I recommend using HTTPS between SharePoint and your OWA Server. In this case, drop the `-AllowHTTP` parameter in step 6, and use "external-https" in step 8.

Summary

In this chapter, I covered most of the default applications part of the Microsoft Office 2013 suite. I showed you how these applications integrate with SharePoint 2013. You learned the basics of exporting and importing data, the commonalities in the backstage area, live co-authoring, and the Document Information Panel.

As you progressed through the chapter, you looked at each application in turn, and I demonstrated some of the specific integration features with SharePoint 2013.

You took a quick tour of InfoPath 2013—the Filler and Designer applications. You saw how to customize SharePoint 2013 list forms and the Document Information Panel.

At the end of this chapter, you tackled the installation and configuration of Office Web Applications, so your users can view and edit Office documents without the Office applications installed on client machines.

In the next chapter, I shall tackle the mammoth topic of SharePoint search.

■ ■ ■

CHAPTER 15

SharePoint Search

What use is a system if users cannot find the information contained within it? It seems like the days of hunting and browsing for content in an information system have passed and users want to type keywords into a text box and retrieve information rapidly. Google revolutionized e-mail by offering its users the ability to store all their e-mail and search it quickly, using Google's search engine technology. Unlike earlier e-mail systems, users no longer need to store e-mail in folders and sub-folders to find their most important information quickly. Another great example of how search has revolutionized the way we do business is in the phase out of large network drives in favor of document management systems, like SharePoint. We have replaced large laborious network drives with SharePoint document libraries, tagging, metadata, and advanced search capabilities.

In this chapter, you will learn about the SharePoint search platform (ESP—Enterprise Search Platform). I shall start with an overview of the search platform and the components involved and then move on to configuration of search to meet the needs of your organization. I shall spend some time showing you how to get the best out of search and how to structure your data such that search is most effective at retrieving it. Toward the end of this chapter I shall discuss the reporting functionality that SharePoint search provides, which is often overlooked by administrators, in understanding what users search for and the health of the search platform.

New Architecture

Microsoft has redesigned the architecture of SharePoint 2013 search. Unlike previous versions of SharePoint, the search platform is the same across all version types of SharePoint 2013: Foundation, Standard, and Enterprise. SharePoint 2013 search uses a combination of components to create the search platform, and provides pervasive search functionality throughout the product.

SharePoint 2010 provided an Enterprise version of search, to suit the needs of most. In addition, organizations could purchase the FAST version of search, which existed as a true Enterprise Search Platform and came at a premium cost. SharePoint 2013 now includes the major components of FAST in the search offering, and installs them by default as part of SharePoint Enterprise Search, after executing the Farm Configuration Wizard.

SharePoint 2013 brings many new advantages, including but not limited to the following:

- Search-driven navigation

- Better people and expertise search

- Compliance via eDiscovery

- Easier management for administrators

- Catalog-based search and recommendations for business users

- New improved user interface and experience (Figure 15-1)

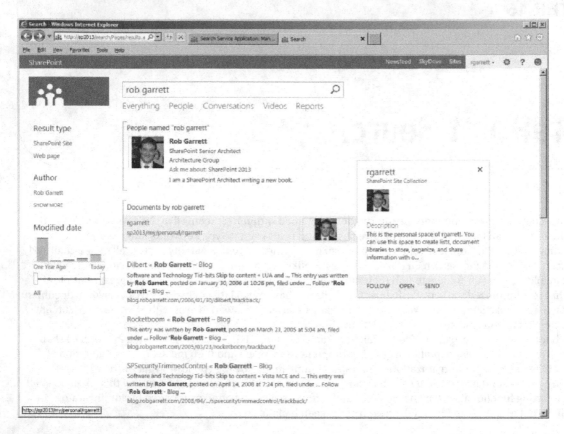

Figure 15-1. *Example search results*

The new architecture addresses the need for a search platform that caters to configuration and greater redundancy. The architecture consists of several databases and search processing components. Search processing components reside on SharePoint application servers and search databases reside within SQL Server. Both work together cohesively to provide the overall search functionality. In the next few sections, I will review the major components and the part they each play in the overall search platform architecture. Figure 15-2 shows the components within the SharePoint 2013 Logical Architecture.

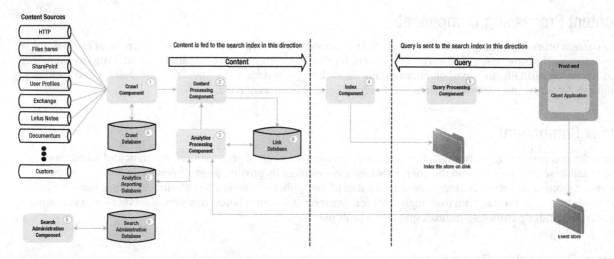

Figure 15-2. *SharePoint Search 2013 Logical Architecture*

Components

SharePoint 2013 search consists of several components in the overarching search architecture. The search components associate with each Search Service Application (SSA) in the farm, and administrators may scale the components to multiple application servers to distribute load and provide redundancy. The following sections cover each of the search components at a high level.

Crawl Component

The crawl component is responsible for crawling over multiple content sources, which might vary in type. The following lists most of the content source types available, and you may create multiple content sources of any type to crawl data for SharePoint search results:

- SharePoint content
- SharePoint user profiles
- Web pages via HTTP
- File shares
- Exchange
- Lotus Notes
- Custom sources

Later in this chapter, I shall demonstrate setting up content sources for SharePoint and web pages over HTTP. In Chapter 13, you read about Business Connectivity Services (BCS) and I demonstrated how to integrate third-party data into SharePoint. Using BCS, SharePoint can crawl over third-party data and expose this data within SharePoint search results.

Content Processing Component

The content processing component is responsible for processing items crawled by the crawl component and passing these items to the index component. This component is responsible for parsing document content, property mapping, and leveraging IFILTERs to parse content from Office and third-party document types. This component also handles language detection and entity extraction, which were originally features of FAST.

Index Component

The index component serves two purposes: to take items from the content processing component and index them and to satisfy search queries from the query processing component by providing search results. In both cases, the index component utilizes index files, stored on the disk of the application server. Just like in FAST, the structure of indexes is in tabular format, with rows representing index replicas—redundancy in groups of servers—and columns representing index partitions—indexes split across multiple servers.

Query Processing Component

The query processing component handles search query linguistics. Functions of this component include processing of words, stemming, spell check, thesaurus, etc. This component understands Keyword Query Language (KQL) and FAST Query Language (FQL) syntax for complex structured queries. The query processing component feeds processed queries to the index component to produce a set of search results.

■ **Note**   The following URL provides a reference for Keyword Query Language and FAST Query Language:
http://msdn.microsoft.com/en-us/library/sharepoint/jj163973%28v=office.15%29.

Analytics Component

The analytics component monitors search queries, the results produced, and usage of search results. This component effectively learns what the users search and how the search infrastructure provides the results required by users to meet their needs. Organizations often overlook the analytics component, once search is up and running. However, this component provides some valuable insights into how users are searching and leveraging results from searches.

Search Administration Component

The search administration component provides the user interface for configuring and managing search settings, of the various components. This component consists of a service application, running within SharePoint, and accessed via Managed Application Settings.

Topology

Figure 15-3 shows an example search topology within a SharePoint 2013 farm. The topology assumes multiple application servers, web-front-end (WFE) servers, and databases. In this example, the hosts are physical servers and servers within each host exist as virtual machines.

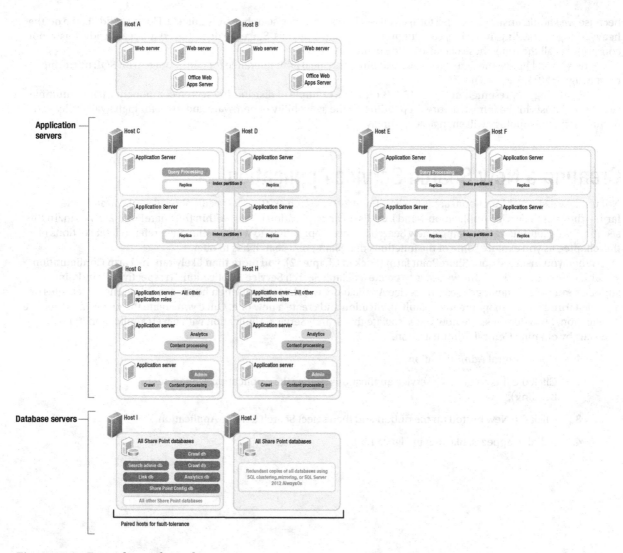

Figure 15-3. *Example search topology*

Notice how none of the WFE servers host search components—this is advantageous and recommended in highly scalable and highly redundant scenarios, consisting of multiple SharePoint servers. Typically, you want to ensure that your WFE servers do what they do best, which is to server pages to users.

The application servers in Figure 15-3 are where all the search components reside. In this example, hosts C through F maintain replicated indexes, each index replica is a mirror image of another, and there are four replicas. Partitions consist of splitting the index across two web application servers. The replicas ensure redundancy—should one set of servers (host) fail, then the index resides on three other hosts. Partitioning the index replicas across two virtual servers ensures division of load when crawling and querying the index. In Figure 15-3 two query processing components exist (on hosts C and E) to split the job of responding to user search queries. In this case, hosts D and F provide redundancy for partition pairs. We could add additional query processing components on these hosts also, but providing two query processing components is enough coverage in the event that one physical host server fails.

Hosts G and H contain the remaining search components, including a crawl component on one virtual application server of each host. In this example, we have separated query from the rest of the search components because we should ensure query performs well, such that users see search results quickly. Hosts G and H take on the heavy lifting of crawling, indexing, content processing, and analytics. Since we do not need the search administration components all the time, these can also reside on hosts G and H.

Hosts I and J house the SQL databases and provide typical fault tolerance for data storage with SQL mirroring, clustering, or 2012 Always-On.

The topology represented in Figure 15-3 is only one example of distributing search components across multiple servers and hosts in the infrastructure. Depending on the availability of hardware and need for high availability and redundancy, the topology will change accordingly.

Creating a New Search Service Application

Not unlike most other functional areas in SharePoint 2013, search exists as a specific service application in the farm—the Search Service Application—and installs on an application server, within the SharePoint 2013 farm. In this section, I will demonstrate creating a new Search Service Application, to which I shall then refer in later sections of this chapter, as you explore some of the functions that SharePoint search has to offer.

When you installed your SharePoint farm (back in Chapter 2), you more than likely ran the Farm Configuration Wizard. One of the tasks of this wizard is to create a default Search Service Application. Irrespective, SharePoint supports multiple instances of Search Service Application, which is typical when hosting multiple client web sites on a single farm, so you can ignore the default application and create a new one. Once you create the new Search Service Application, I will demonstrate how you associate this Search Service Application with a web application in the farm. You start by opening Central Administration.

1. Open Central Administration.

2. Click the link to manage service applications (under the Application Management heading).

3. Click the New button on the ribbon and then select Search Service Application.

4. A dialog appears, like that in Figure 15-4.

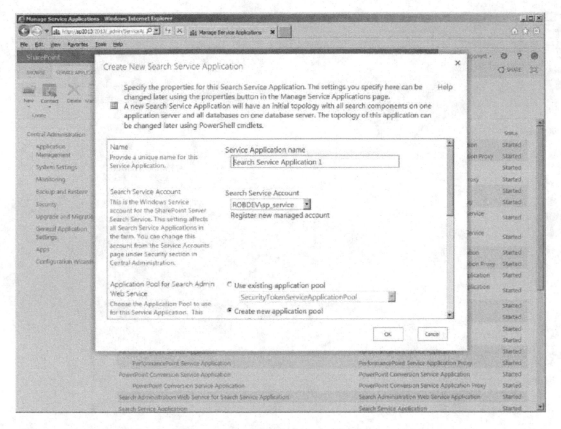

Figure 15-4. *Create a new Search Service Application (topology)*

5. Give the Search Service Application a name.

6. Select the managed service account—you should have a service account defined already from the install process in Chapter 2.

7. Create a new application pool for the administration component, using a managed account for the application pool identity.

8. Create a new application pool for the Search Query and Settings web service, using your application pool identity managed account.

9. Click the OK button, and then wait while SharePoint creates the new Search Service Application topology.

10. Once complete, you should see a dialog like that in Figure 15-5.

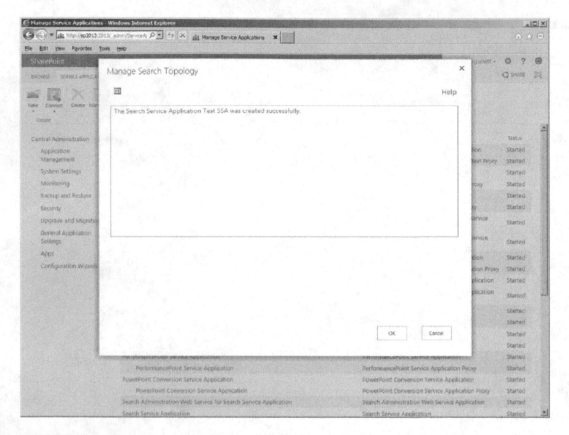

Figure 15-5. *New Search Service Application (topology) created*

11. Click the OK button the exit the dialog.

12. Scroll down the list of managed service applications until you find the Search Service Application you just created.

13. Click the application name and then press the Manage button on the ribbon to access the new Search Service Application settings.

Splitting Search Service Application Components Across Multiple Servers

Earlier in the chapter, I listed the various components of a Search Service Application and discussed the possibility of scaling these components to different servers. In the "Topology" section, I provided a sample scenario and diagram of the Search Service Application components spread across several hosts and virtual machines. Central Administration does not appear to offer users the capability to distribute Search Service Application components across different servers, so to achieve Search Service Application redundancy and load distribution of these components, use PowerShell.

The UI in Central Administration caters to typical topology situations. The scenario I described earlier in this chapter provides redundancy and load distribution for a large enterprise search solution. On the other hand, what you typically see in the majority of SharePoint deployments are SharePoint farms with dedicated servers for the entirety of a Search Service Application. It is likely for this reason, and to reduce complexity in the UI, that Central Administration provides the simplest creation of a complete Search Service Application.

Of course, you are reading this book so that you may understand how to distribute Search Service Application components for maximum benefit in your SharePoint farm deployments. Therefore, I will demonstrate the various PowerShell commands required to achieve Search Service Application component distribution. I shall assume you are familiar with PowerShell; if not, just flip back to Chapter 3 in this book.

Figure 15-6 shows a screen capture from my SharePoint development farm Search Service Application main administration page. The grid shows the status of the various Search Service Application components and server placement. Unfortunately, my development farm does not have enough capacity to host multiple SharePoint servers, but if it did, they would be listed in the grid. Nonetheless, I shall now cover the steps required to deploy the various Search Service Application components across different servers, using PowerShell. For the purposes of the following steps assume that I have two search servers: SEARCH1 and SEARCH2.

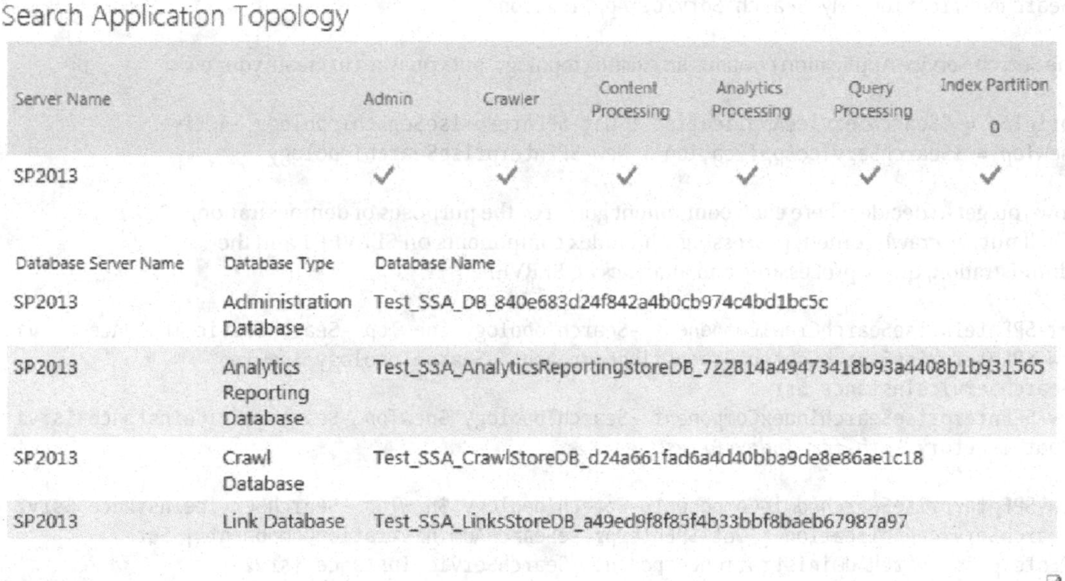

Search Application Topology

Server Name	Admin	Crawler	Content Processing	Analytics Processing	Query Processing	Index Partition 0
SP2013	✓	✓	✓	✓	✓	✓

Database Server Name	Database Type	Database Name
SP2013	Administration Database	Test_SSA_DB_840e683d24f842a4b0cb974c4bd1bc5c
SP2013	Analytics Reporting Database	Test_SSA_AnalyticsReportingStoreDB_722814a49473418b93a4408b1b931565
SP2013	Crawl Database	Test_SSA_CrawlStoreDB_d24a661fad6a4d40bba9de8e86ae1c18
SP2013	Link Database	Test_SSA_LinksStoreDB_a49ed9f8f85f4b33bbf8baeb67987a97

Figure 15-6. *Search Service Application Topology*

1. Open SharePoint 2013 Management Shell (it is usually a good idea to run this elevated) on the application server in your farm.

2. If you have already created a Search Service Application, skip to step #7.

3. Create a new application pool for the Search Service Application and the administration.

    ```
    $SearchServiceApplicationPool = New-SPServiceApplicationPool -name "My Search Service
    Application App Pool" -account Account-Name
    $adminPool = New-SPServiceApplicationPool -name "My Search Service Application Admin App
    Pool" -account Account-Name
    ```

4. Start the search service instances on each server.

    ```
    Start-SPEnterpriseSearchServiceInstance –identity "SERVER1"
    Start-SPEnterpriseSearchServiceInstance –identity "SERVER2"
    $srv1 = Get-SPEnterpriseSearchServiceInstance –identity "SERVER1"
    $srv2 = Get-SPEnterpriseSearchServiceInstance –identity "SERVER2"
    ```

5. Create a new Search Service Application.

```
$SearchServiceApplication = New-SPEnterpriseSearchServiceApplication
-Name "My Search Service Application"
-ApplicationPool $SearchServiceApplicationPool
-DatabaseServer  "SERVERNAME"
-DatabaseName  "DATABASE NAME"
```

6. Create a new Search Service Application proxy.

```
New-SPEnterpriseSearchServiceApplicationProxy -Name "My Search Service Application Proxy"
-SearchApplication "My Search Service Application"
```

7. The Search Service Application contains an existing topology, but you want to create your own.

```
$origTop = $SearchServiceApplication | Get-SPEnterpriseSearchTopology –Active
$newTop = $SearchServiceApplication | New-SPEnterpriseSearchTopology
```

8. Now you get to decide where each component goes. For the purposes of demonstration, I shall put the crawl, content processing, and index components on SERVER1 and the administration, query processing, and analytics on SERVER2.

```
New-SPEnterpriseSearchCrawlComponent -SearchTopology $newTop -SearchServiceInstance $srv1
New-SPEnterpriseSearchContentProcessingComponent -SearchTopology $newTop
-SearchServiceInstance $srv1
New-SPEnterpriseSearchIndexComponent -SearchTopology $newTop -SearchServiceInstance $srv1
–RootDirectory Path-for-Index-Files

New-SPEnterpriseSearchAdminComponent -SearchTopology $newTop -SearchServiceInstance $srv2
$SearchServiceApplication | Get-SPEnterpriseSearchAdministrationComponent | Set-
SPEnterpriseSearchAdministrationComponent -SearchServiceInstance $srv2
$SearchServiceApplication | Get-SPEnterpriseSearchAdministrationComponent

New-SPEnterpriseSearchQueryProcessingComponent -SearchTopology $newTop
-SearchServiceInstance $srv2
New-SPEnterpriseSearchAnalyticsProcessingComponent -SearchTopology $newTop
-SearchServiceInstance $srv2
```

9. Now replace the existing Search Service Application topology with the new.

```
$newTop | Set-SPEnterpriseSearchTopology
```

10. Finally, clean up the old topology.

```
$SearchServiceApplication | Get-SPEnterpriseSearchTopology | Where {$_.State -eq "Inactive" }|
Remove-SPEnterpriseSearchTopology -Confirm:$false
```

11. After completing these steps, open the Search Service Application Administration page on SERVER2, and confirm the components are associated with the correct server.

Crawling

I am assuming, at this point, that you have created yourself a new Search Service Application (via the Farm Wizard, manually via Central Administration, or through PowerShell). Your Search Service Application needs to start doing some work of crawling content before you can begin to see search results. Remember from earlier in the chapter that the crawl component takes on the heavy lifting of crawling over content, and the content processing component parses found content from the crawler and passes raw content to the indexing component.

Content SharePoint Sources

The Crawl Component will crawl over a number of content sources, available out of the box. The following is a list of the available content sources that SharePoint provides:

- SharePoint content
- SharePoint user profiles
- Web pages via HTTP
- File shares
- Exchange
- Lotus Notes

Of the previous content sources, the easiest to comprehend is SharePoint content. This content source is also the most popular; after all, you surely want the capability to search content stored in SharePoint, as well as other sources. The following set of steps demonstrates how to set up a new content source to crawl over SharePoint content. For this demonstration, I shall assume a default site collection on my server http://sp2013.

1. Open Central Administration.
2. Click the General Application Settings header.
3. Click the Farm Search Administration link (under the Search heading).
4. Click the relevant Search Service Application from the list.
5. From herein, I shall generalize the preceding four steps as "Open the Search Service Application Administration page."
6. Figure 15-7 shows a view of my Search Service Application Administration page.

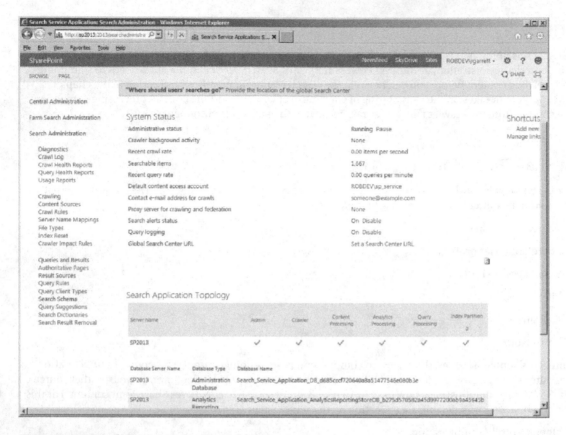

Figure 15-7. *Search Service Application Administration page*

■ **Note** You might want multiple Search Service Applications in a multi-tenant farm, where each web application associates with a different Search Service Application.

The administration page, shown in Figure 15-7, contains a number of interesting regions. On the left is the search administration navigation—most of the configuration options live here. The grid in the bottom half of the page is that which I discussed a few sections ago; it shows the status of the search components belonging to this Search Service Application and hosting server. The middle-top region of the page displays the system status of the Search Service Application, which includes the status of the crawler, crawler performance, default service account (more on this later), proxy server for federation, alert/log options, and the URL of the default Search Center.

■ **Note** In solutions consisting of multiple site collections, it is good practice to create a Search Center to centralize all search results (especially if branding the UI).

The steps now resume to configure a content source for SharePoint content.

7. Click the Content Sources link (under Crawling in the left navigation).

8. You should see a page like that in Figure 15-8.

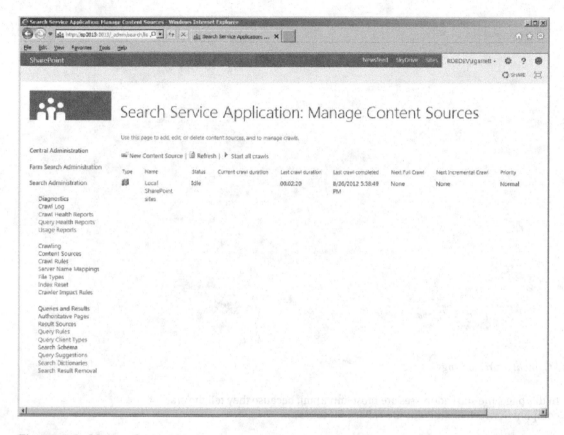

Figure 15-8. *Manage Content Sources*

9. Notice that your Search Service Application has a default content source already. The "Local SharePoint sites" is an all-encompassing content source for all site collections in the farm (at least at the time the Search Service Application was created).

10. However the content source name, and then click the Edit option in the pop-up menu.

11. Figure 15-9 shows the page for the content source settings.

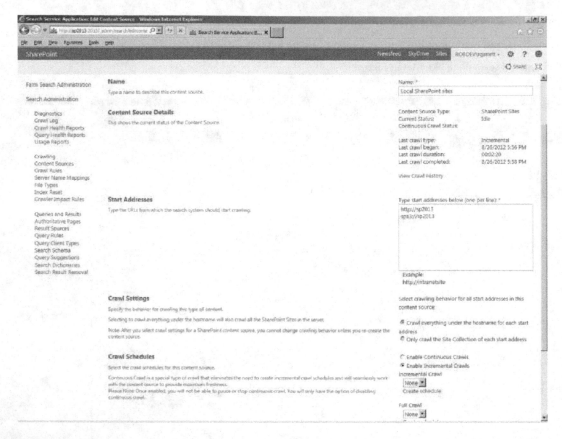

Figure 15-9. Content source settings

12. In this page, the start addresses are most important, because they tell the crawler component which SharePoint site collections to crawl.

■ **Note** You cannot include the same start address in multiple SharePoint content sources of the same Search Service Application.

---

13. The SPS3://sp2013 is a special start address that references the people profiles in the farm. This address instructs the crawler component to crawl the user profiles and surface people in a People search.

14. The default content source works fine for most purposes, but for demonstration purposes you will create a new SharePoint content source.

15. Since you cannot crawl the same starting address twice within the same Search Service Application with multiple content sources, remove the main HTTP site collection (http://sp2013 in my case).

16. Scroll to the bottom of the page and click the OK button.

17. You should see the list of content sources again (Figure 15-8).

18. Click the New Content Source link.

19. You should see a page like that in Figure 15-9, but empty of settings.

20. Provide a name for the content source.

21. Leave the content source type as SharePoint.

22. In the start addresses, add the URL you deleted in the previous default content source. If you forgot to remove it or have included the same URL in another content source, SharePoint will give you an error message when you try to save the content source.

23. Under the crawl settings, decide if you want the crawl component to crawl over everything under the start host address, or remain inside the site collection. In my case, I have one site collection at the root of the domain and nothing else. If I had multiple site collections under the host name, the option to crawl everything would include these site collections also.

24. New to SharePoint 2013 is the option to crawl continuously. Continuous crawls instruct SharePoint to crawl new content as it becomes available, such as in newsfeeds and blogs. This option avoids the issue of new content not showing up in search results until the incremental schedule kicks in.

25. Finally, you have a crawling schedule and priority (if not using continuous crawling).

26. Click the OK button to save the new content source.

27. Microsoft dropped the option to start a full crawl in the Content Source Settings page, so to start a full crawl, click the new content source, then select the option to "Start a Full Crawl" from the pop-up menu.

Crawling External Web Sites

The steps in the preceding section are essentially all there is to setting up a content source, although different content source types provide different options. To demonstrate I shall now walk you through the steps to crawl a third-party web site.

1. Open the Search Service Application Administration page.

2. Click the Content Sources link in the left navigation.

3. Click the link to create a new content source.

4. Give the content source a name.

5. Change the type to Web Sites.

6. Provide the home page URL of the web site you intend to crawl.

■ **Note** Sites that restrict crawling with a `robots.txt` will not allow SharePoint to crawl their content.

---

7. Set the crawl settings to crawl the start page—the crawl component will ignore links to other pages, stay within the server of the start address, or configure maximum server hops and page depth from the source.

8. Set up the schedule and priority.

9. Notice, there is no option to crawl continuously, because this is a feature of SharePoint content sources.

10. Click OK, then start a full crawl of the new content source.

11. If you have a Search Center configured for the web application associated with the Search Service Application, you can try searching for results against the web site you just crawled.

Other Content Sources

You might be wondering about the other content sources. Table 15-1 lists the details on all the out-of-the-box content source types (including those we already discussed) provided by SharePoint 2013.

Table 15-1. *Content Source Types*

Content Source Type	Details
SharePoint Sites	Crawls SharePoint site content, including People data from user profiles; you can configure continuous crawling or schedule crawls and designate crawling of a number of SharePoint or single site collections
Web Sites	Crawls external web sites; configured with server hops and depth; this content source crawls on a designated schedule
File Shares	Crawls file content at one or many UNC path or file:// locations; this content source crawls on a designated schedule; the content processing component uses IFILTERs to extract content from files for known file types
Exchange Public Folders	Crawls one or many Exchange public folder locations, using HTTP; this content source crawls on a designated schedule
Line of Business Data	Crawls external line of business (external) data, accessible via Business Connectivity Services; this content source crawls on a designated schedule; this content source assumes correct configuration of BCS entities and sources
Custom Repository	Crawls custom locations based on registered connectors; custom search connector development is outside the scope of this book; this content source crawls on a designated schedule

Crawl Rules

Crawl rules define a set of rules such that the crawl processor can determine whether to process a piece of content for indexing. For example, earlier in the chapter I set up a content source to crawl over my blog site. If I want to exclude some pages or subsites of my blog, I can create crawl rules to restrict what the crawler considers content to index.

There is more to crawl rules than just inclusion or exclusion of entities in the search index. Crawl rules also allow users to instruct the crawler what authentication to apply to given content. By default, the crawler uses a Search Service account (defined when you installed SharePoint 2013) to access content. In the case of external content, you may need to apply alternate authentication methods to crawl the content.

From the Search Service Application Administration page, click the link for Crawl Rules to access a page where you can administer existing crawl rules and new rules. Figure 15-10 shows an example of the Crawl Rules page in my environment. Notice that I already have a crawl rule for the crawling of my blog—it is typically a good idea to create at least one crawl rule for any content source that crawls over external web site content.

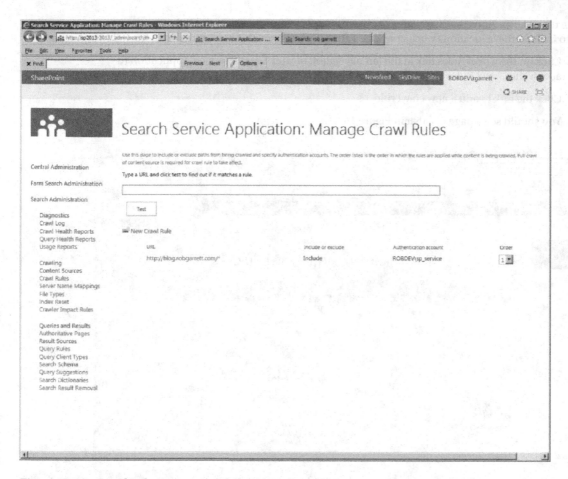

Figure 15-10. *Crawl Rules page*

■ **Note**   When crawling over external web site content it is a good idea to create a crawl rule to include all content at the given entry URL.

At the top of the Crawl Rules page (Figure 15-10), SharePoint provides a test text box and button. This enables you to quickly check if a given URL of a content source matches any of the listed rules. For example, a user complains to you that some of the pages of a web site do not show up in search results. You confirmed that you created a content source for the web site and no errors or warnings surface in the log for the missing results. Entering the URL into the test box of the Crawl Rules page will immediately tell you if any rule exists prohibiting the crawl of the specified page.

The crawler is good at crawling over SharePoint, but when it comes to other sources, the crawler is only as good as the structure of the content. Web sites provide a good example: crawlers and spiders rely on HREF links to pages within web sites to discover new content. In some cases, a web site might contain a number of orphaned pages. Orphaned pages are those where no other parent page in the hierarchy or page within sibling sub trees points to the orphaned page. This can often happen when creating non-navigable subsites or pages in a site, which users access by knowing the direct URL. Since the SharePoint crawler has no way of getting to orphaned pages, the crawler must be instructed to include these locations when crawling. I shall demonstrate this configuration in the following steps:

1. Click on the Crawl Rules link in the left navigation of your Search Service Application to access the Crawl Rules page.

2. Click the link to add a new crawl rule.

3. You should see a page like that in Figure 15-11.

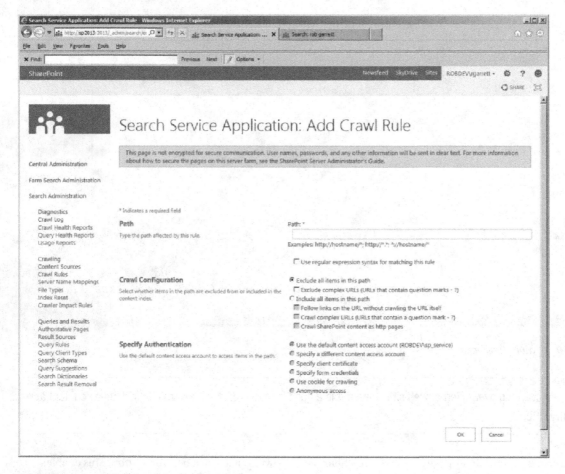

Figure 15-11. *Adding a crawl rule*

4. SharePoint might indicate at the top of the page that the page is unencrypted and to be careful passing credentials—you might see many warnings like this in your dealings with SharePoint 2013 when not using SSL.

5. Provide the path to content for your crawl rule. You can use regular expressions by checking the check box. The path allows wildcard characters.

6. The Crawl Configuration allows you to specify whether the crawler includes or excludes content matching the rule.

7. Depending on whether you choose inclusion or exclusion, you have additional options to crawl complex URLs.

8. Finally, the crawl rule allows you to specify the authentication. This part is slightly different from that in SharePoint 2010 in that there are additional options to authenticate via cookies, certificates, etc.

9. Click the OK button to save the rule.

10. You can test the rule using the text box and test button.

Server Name Mappings

Sometimes content sources are set up for crawling content on an internal domain name. A good example of this is in crawling over line of business (LOB) content, using BCS. The LOB system might reside on a local URI and the content configured as such. An issue arises when the search results, seen by end users, include the internal name locations instead of an addressable URI by the end users. Use server name mappings to solve this issue.

1. Click the Server Name Mappings link in the Search Service Application left navigation.

2. Click the link to add a new mapping (Figure 15-12).

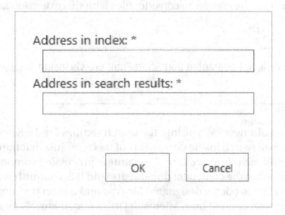

Figure 15-12. Mapping server names

3. Provide the server name in use by the crawler (without a protocol prefix—HTTP/HTTPS).

4. Provide the domain name for search results.

5. Click the OK button to save the rule.

■ **Note** Server name mapping rules map only server domain names and will not allow you to convert complete URLs.

File Types

By default, SharePoint 2013 search will crawl and index only files of known type. Out of the box, SharePoint supports all the Office-type documents, e-mail files, ZIP files, and PDF documents.

■ **Note**   SharePoint 2007 and 2010 did not natively support PDF documents, and required additional configuration to crawl and index PDF files.

Using the File Types page, you can add new files types for SharePoint to crawl. Simply click the link for File Types in the Search Service Application Administration page and then add a new extension. Adding an icon for your new extension requires some tinkering in the hive.

1. Navigate to the folder on each SharePoint server, as follows:

   `C:\Program Files\Common Files\Microsoft Shared\Web Server Extensions\15\TEMPLATE\IMAGES`

2. Add a new icon GIF file to this folder.

3. Navigate to the following XML folder on each SharePoint server:

   `C:\Program Files\Common Files\Microsoft Shared\Web Server Extensions\14\TEMPLATE\XML`

4. Open the `DOCICON.XML` file and add a new mapping node for the extension and GIF file.

Adding a new file extension and image file will instruct the crawler to consider files with this extension and to display the designated icon in the search results.

■ **Note**   Adding a new file extension and icon mapping will not guarantee that SharePoint crawls inside documents of unknown type.

I must point out that adding the extension and icon of a new file type into the search settings for the Search Service Application will not guarantee that the crawler will search inside documents of this type, just that the crawler will not ignore the files to start and that search results will include a nice icon. The content processing component in your Search Service Application is responsible for processing the content of documents, and it accomplishes this with IFILTERs. An IFILTER is a compiled DLL that contains logic to open a designated file type and extract the content as text. Microsoft provides IFILTERs with SharePoint, to extract content from Microsoft Office documents. Prior to this version of SharePoint, the Adobe PDF IFILTER had to be installed to index inside PDF files (as well as adding a file extension and icon mapping). SharePoint 2013 includes support for PDF documents and ships with IFILTER to extract content inside PDF files.

Crawler Impact Rules

When crawling over content outside of SharePoint—especially web sites—you must observe the impact of searching these sources. Web site administrators are all too familiar with their web sites crashing because of too many concurrent user requests or high activity on their web servers. Search crawlers and spiders are often the culprits in causing slow web site performance. Most crawlers run multiple concurrent requests and queue up page requests until the crawler has covered all pages in a given web site. Typically, crawlers do not pose an issue for large-scale web sites, designed to handle high load, but this is not the case for all web sites. SharePoint incorporates throttling of the search crawler, using impact rules.

1. Click the link for Crawler Impact Rules in the left navigation of Search Service Application Administration.

2. Click the link to add a rule. You should see a page like that in Figure 15-13.

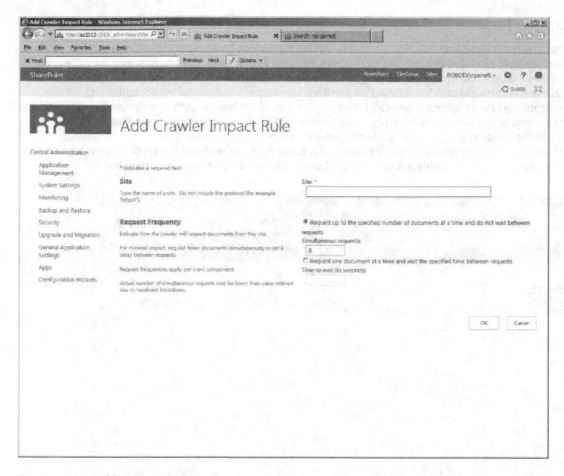

Figure 15-13. *Adding a crawler impact rule*

3. Provide the domain name of the site, without the protocol (HTTP/HTTPS).

4. Tweak the number of simultaneous requests or time between single requests.

In the case of a fragile web site, you should lower the number of concurrent requests or choose the option to request pages/documents one at a time with duration in between requests. Lessening the impact of crawling over a web site will cause SharePoint to take longer to crawl over the site, but ensure that the site does not fall over from too much traffic.

Queries and Results

In this section of the chapter, I discuss search queries and search results. SharePoint 2013 handles search query processing via the query processing control (within each Search Service Application) and renders results from query of search indexes. The query processor provides many options, configurable via Search Service Application Administration, which I cover in the following subsections.

Authoritative Pages

SharePoint 2013 includes some sophisticated relevance-ranking algorithms, to determine order of search results, based on search criteria, provided by users. In certain cases, you may wish to help SharePoint search by influencing search results based on your own criteria of ranking, which is where Authoritative Pages come in.

Authoritative Pages are pages in SharePoint that you designate as requiring special mention in search results. Within the Authoritative Pages section of Search Service Application Administration, you can designate any number of pages as first-, second-, or third-level authority. SharePoint considers the level of these pages when rendering search results. Pages designated as top-most authority present soonest in search results.

Figure 15-14 shows an example Authoritative Pages configuration page in Search Service Application Administration. Configuring certain pages as authoritative is a simple case of adding them to the first, second, or third box.

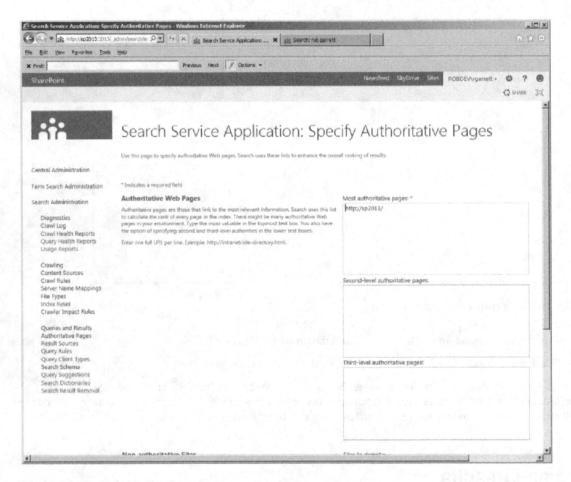

Figure 15-14. *Authoritative Pages*

Scrolling down the page (not shown in Figure 15-14), you should see a box to enter pages to demote. Demoted pages are those that you feel are unimportant, and those that you do not wish to see high in the list of search results. Sometimes the query processor decides a page is highly relevant because it contains many instances of a keyword, or matches many query rules, but your content owners may feel differently. Having the ability to demote a page ensures that the content owners remain happy.

Result Sources

SharePoint 2013 has done away with search scopes and replaced them with result sources. Search scopes used to allow users to refine search results returned from an index, so that you could scope the results for a particular scenario. For example, a search scope might restrict search results of a particular subsite and below in a site collection, so that users who use this scope in their search see only results for a narrow set of content. Result sources provide a similar function to search scopes, but with greater control over the filtering.

■ **Note**   Result sources effectively combine search scopes and federated locations, which existed in SharePoint 2010.

Clicking on the Result Sources link in the left navigation shows a page like that in Figure 15-15. SharePoint provides a number of result sources, based on what users typically search. Among those on the list are Pages, Documents, Pictures, and Local People Results. To understand how a result source works, you will now explore one of them by clicking the name and selecting the view option in the pop-up menu. I chose the Local People Results entry, which provides a page like that in Figure 15-16.

Figure 15-15. *Result Sources in SharePoint 2013 Search Service Application*

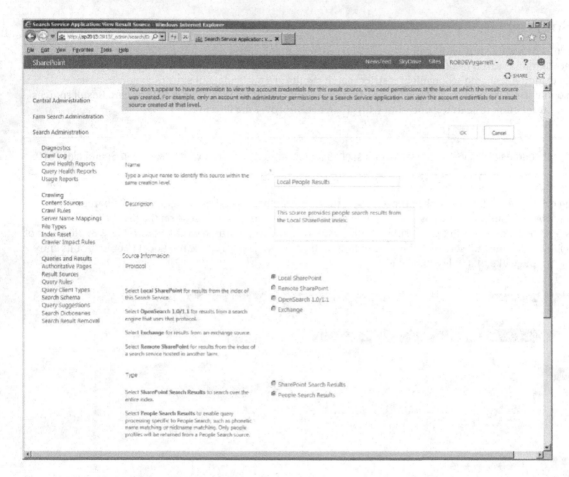

Figure 15-16. *Result Source for Local People Results*

SharePoint provides a large warning message at the top of the page, indicating that you do not have permissions to modify this result source. This is a little misleading, in this case, because you do not have rights to edit any out-of-the-box result source. I am a farm administrator and administrator of my Search Service Application, so this clearly is not a permissions issue. In a moment, I shall demonstrate creating a new result source, where you do not see this warning.

Every result source has a name and description, and applies to Local SharePoint content, Remote SharePoint content, Open Search 1.0/1.1 content, or Exchange. Open Search is interesting in that you can request result sources from other search engines that support the 1.0/1.1 protocol. For brevity, I shall concentrate on result sources that apply to Local SharePoint content in this book.

The result source type applies to either SharePoint Search Results or People Search Results—SharePoint treats these types of search as distinctly different and applies different result sources to each accordingly.

Scroll to the Query Transform section of the Result Source page and you get into something more interesting. Before moving onto this sub-topic, I shall finish my summary of this result source with a brief mention about the authentication options at the bottom of the page. You have the choice to configure the result source using the common search account identity, or by providing a specific account—this comes in handy if you want results sets that a specific account has read rights to view.

To demonstrate query transform for result sources, I shall back out of the page (Figure 15-16) and return to the list of the Result Sources page (Figure 15-15). To create a new result source, execute the following steps:

1. Click the New Result Source link.

2. Provide a name and description—I created a result source that shows blog posts from my blog in the last month, so created a name and description as appropriate.

3. Choose the Local SharePoint to scope results from SharePoint content in the Search Service Application local index.

4. Leave all options default.

5. Click the Launch Query Builder button to configure the Query Transform.

6. You should see a dialog like that in Figure 15-17.

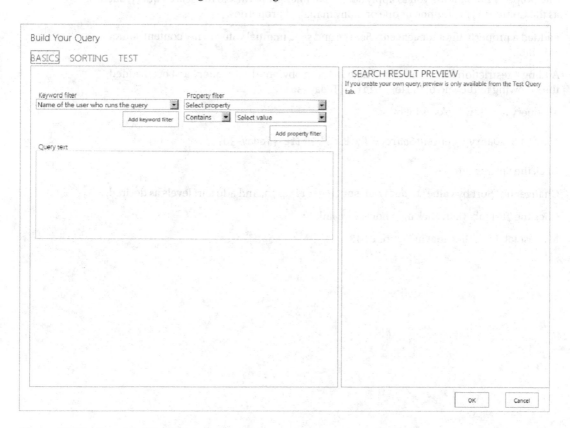

Figure 15-17. Query builder for result source

The query builder understands both Keyword Query Language (KQL) and FAST Query Language (FQL), which are used to define result source criteria. KQL and FQL provide superior query syntax to that of CAML (Collaborative Application Markup Language), used in earlier versions of SharePoint. SharePoint 2013 inherits FQL from that of the FAST ESP, which Microsoft included in the SharePoint 2013 platform. The syntax available for KQL and FQL is vast, so I shall provide you a reference at the following location: `http://msdn.microsoft.com/en-us/library/sharepoint/jj163973%28v=office.15%29`.

7. The keyword filter provides filter capabilities of the entered keywords of a given search. For example, you can easily create a result source that lists recent documents edited by the user performing the search, or include a parameter from the query string in the search criteria. For my example, I only need the query from the search box.

8. Choose your keyword filter and then click the button to add the keyword filter.

9. The property filter allows you to apply additional filter properties to the search query, such as the Content Type, Author, or one or many managed properties.

10. I added a property filter for `Content Source` and set a manual value to my content source: "My Blog."

11. Adding a restriction for last modified date is not so obvious. In the query text box I added the following to the end of the text: `Write>{Today-30}`

12. My query text now looks as follows:

    `{SearchBoxQuery} ContentSource="My Blog" Write>{Today-30}`

13. Click the Sorting tab.

14. Change the "Sort by value" to `desired sorting criteria`, and add sort levels as desired.

15. Click the Test tab; then click the Show More link.

16. My Test tab looks like that in Figure 15-18.

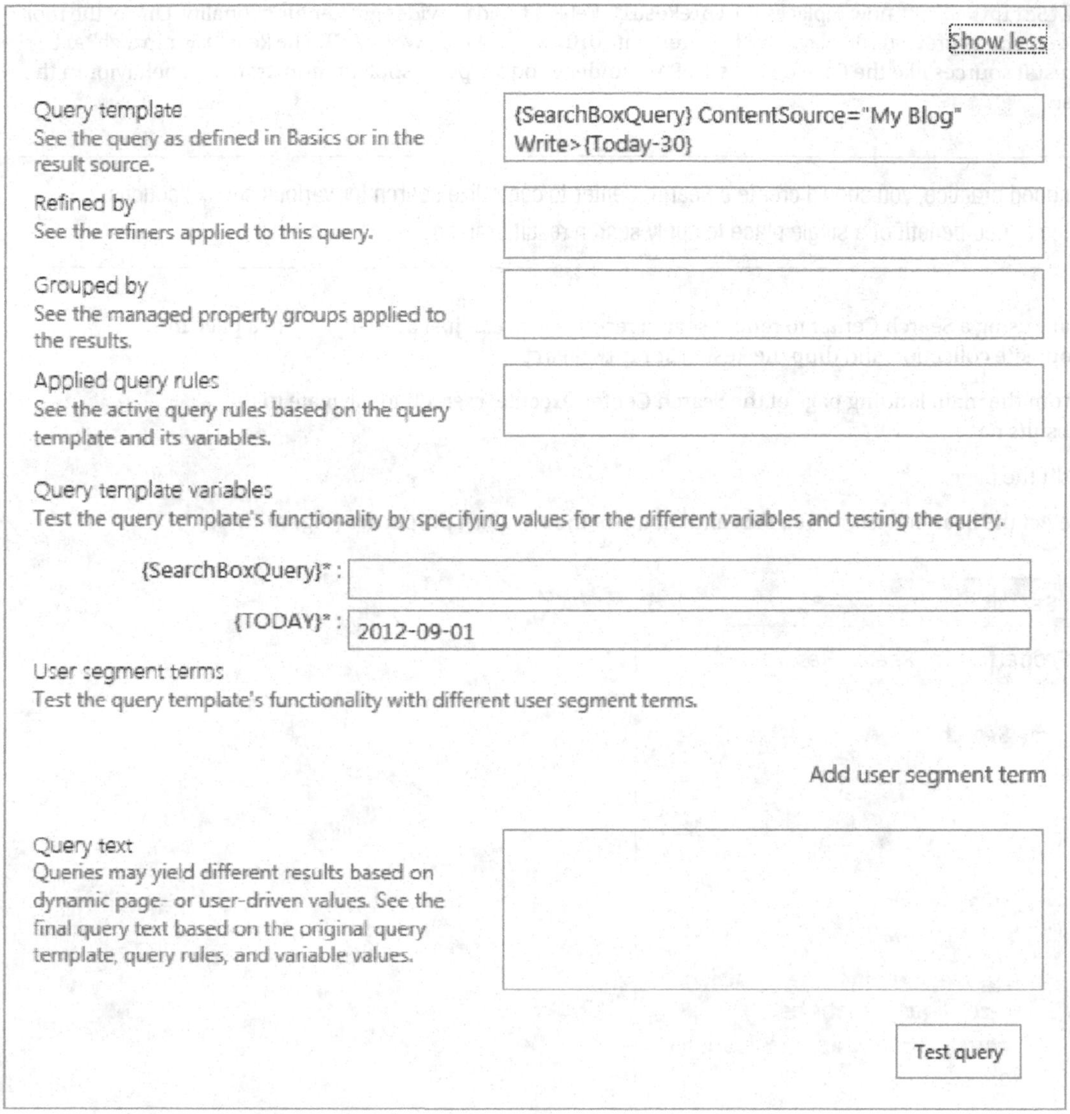

Show less

Query template
See the query as defined in Basics or in the result source.

{SearchBoxQuery} ContentSource="My Blog"
Write>{Today-30}

Refined by
See the refiners applied to this query.

Grouped by
See the managed property groups applied to the results.

Applied query rules
See the active query rules based on the query template and its variables.

Query template variables
Test the query template's functionality by specifying values for the different variables and testing the query.

{SearchBoxQuery}* :

{TODAY}* : 2012-09-01

User segment terms
Test the query template's functionality with different user segment terms.

Add user segment term

Query text
Queries may yield different results based on dynamic page- or user-driven values. See the final query text based on the original query template, query rules, and variable values.

Test query

Figure 15-18. Test tab in the query builder

17.   Provide a search query value to test.

18.   Click the Test query button to see the results in the right pane.

19.   Click the OK button to return to the Result Source page.

20.   Click OK again to save the result source.

At this stage, you might be wondering how to use the result source in your search results. Similar to how SharePoint 2010 allowed you to use scopes in search result Web Parts, SharePoint also allows you to apply result sources to search result Web Parts.

The ResultScriptWebPart now replaces the CoreResultsWebPart and provides greater functionality. One of the more obvious improvements is previous display, which SharePoint 2010 only provided with FAST. The ResultScriptWebPart understands result sources like the CoreResultsWebPart understood scopes. I shall demonstrate this behavior in the following steps:

■ **Note**   As a good practice, you should create a Search Center to centralize search for various site collections. This provides the added benefit of a single place to apply search result branding.

---

1. I am using a Search Center to render search results—you can just as easily create a page in your site collection and drop the ResultScriptWebPart.

2. From the main landing page of the Search Center, execute a search to navigate to the Results page.

3. Edit the page.

4. Select the Search Results Web Part and then edit the Web Part properties (Figure 15-19).

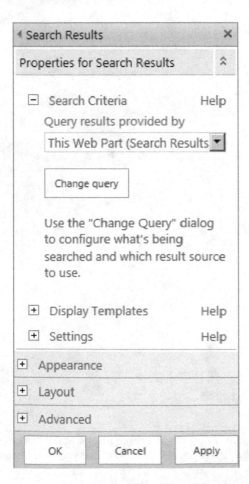

Figure 15-19. *Properties for the Search Results Web Part*

5. Click the Change query button.

6. You should see a query builder dialog appear (similar to that when creating a result source)—see Figure 15-20.

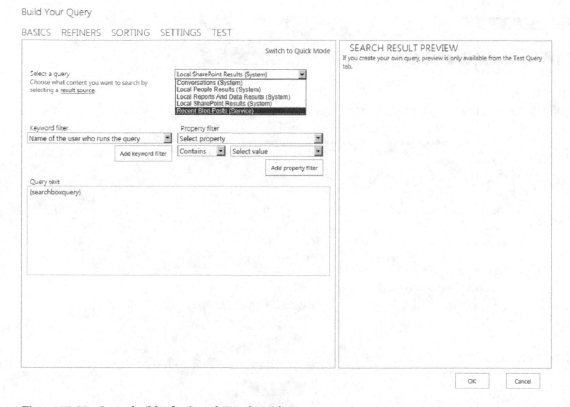

Figure 15-20. *Query builder for Search Results Web Part*

7. Since you have a query builder in front of you, you can create some on-the-fly query filtering. In your case you just need to select the Result Source from the drop-down menu.

8. Click the OK button.

9. Click OK on the Web Part properties box and then save the page.

10. Execute a search via the Search Center, and the results returned will be those filtered by your result source.

Query Rules

Query rules are a new feature of SharePoint 2013 that allows users to tailor search results in a flexible manner. Query rules consist of conditions and actions that SharePoint applies when a search query meets a condition. Think of query rules as a replacement for Best Bets, only smarter.

We are all familiar with Bing and Google, and you have probably seen promoted results when searching for a comment term. You can accomplish the same behavior using query rules in SharePoint 2013.

1. Click the Query Rules link in the left navigation of your Search Service Application.

2. Change the source drop-down to Local SharePoint Results.

3. You should see a page like that in Figure 15-21.

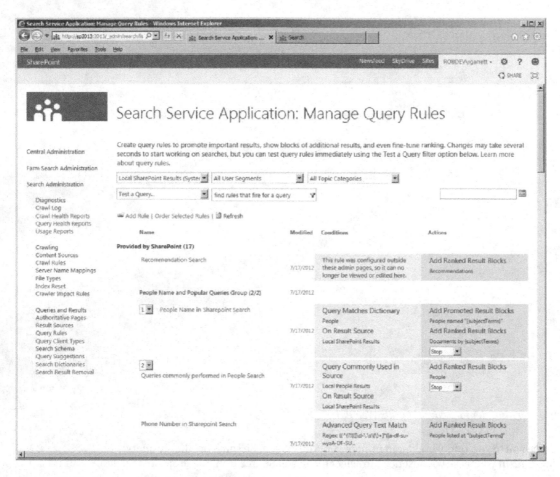

Figure 15-21. *Query rules for the Local SharePoint Results source*

Figure 15-21 shows a page of query rules for the result source: Local SharePoint Results. The query rules consist of several conditions and matching actions. Take the "People Name in SharePoint Search" as an example. This query rule consists of a condition that matches the search terms with the People dictionary to determine if any of the terms match a person's name. If the search terms satisfy the condition, the action promotes the search result at the top of all other search results, and additionally executes another sub-search for the last two recent documents modified by the person. When searching for my name in my Search Center, I see the result in Figure 15-22.

Figure 15-22. *Promoted search results with query builder*

To demonstrate creation of custom query rules, I shall provide some steps to include a promoted block at the top of the search results when a user searches for the term "SharePoint." I previously created a content source to crawl my blog, and am using the "Local SharePoint Results" results source in my demonstration.

1. Click on Query Rules from the left navigation of the Search Service Application.

2. Change the source to Local SharePoint Results (System).

3. Click the Add Rule button.

4. On the next page, provide a name for the rule.

5. Choose the option to match a keyword exactly.

6. Provide the keyword: SharePoint.

7. Scroll down the page and click the Add Promoted Result link.

8. In the dialog that appears, give the promotion a title, URL, and description—I used my blog.

9. Click the Save button on the promotion result dialog.

10. Click the Save button on the Query Result page.

11. Open the Search Center and execute a search, using the keyword "SharePoint" (make sure to type the casing correctly).

12. My results look like that in Figure 15-23.

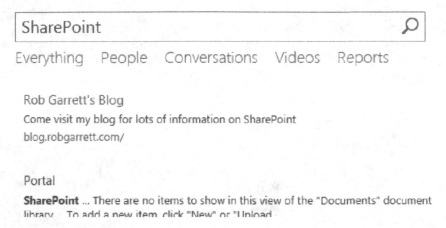

Figure 15-23. *Promoted result in search results*

Of course, my example was a trivial one. Feel free to add multiple query rules and order them according to your desired rank. You can also arrange certain query rules to fire in certain date ranges, so you can promote content for different times.

Query Client Types

There really is not a whole lot to say about query client types—they are a series of labels, used by different applications. Each application that requires the use of SharePoint 2013 search should provide a client type. SharePoint then throttles performance of search result generation based on three tiers: top, middle, or bottom. For example, applications using the client type as "Alerts" get a top tier search classification, whereas applications using the client type "Monitoring" receive a bottom tier classification.

■ **Note** SharePoint provides search results at regular performance until exceeding resource limits, and then assumes throttle mode, which attends top tier searches first, then middle, then bottom.

Query client types come in handy when monitoring search query reports. Figure 15-24 shows the query latency report, filtered by query client type. Filtering by client type allows you to see what applications are consuming most resources for search.

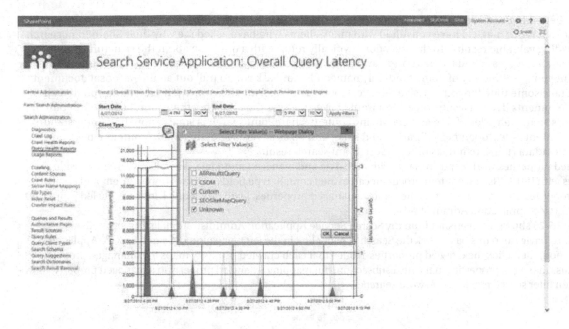

Figure 15-24. *Query Latency*

Search Schema

Search schema is the new name for managed properties and crawled properties. Managed properties and crawled properties are metadata properties that drive search results and map back to content. SharePoint 2010 introduced refiners, which are essentially facets and allow filtering of search results by different fields, such as Author, Language, etc. Managed and crawled properties facilitate refiners. I shall tackle each of these properties' types separately.

Crawled Properties

Crawled properties consist of automatically extracted crawled content, grouped by category based on the protocol handler or IFILTER used by the content processor. In layperson's terms, the SharePoint crawler crawls content from a content source and extracts metadata—such as that defined by content owners. When the crawler extracts the content for a piece of metadata it creates a new crawled property and assigns it the value of the extracted content. For example, a document might contain title metadata, which defines the title of the document within a content type or document library. When the crawler stumbles upon a document with the title metadata, it will create a new crawled property for the title field.

Why are crawled properties important? They essentially define discrete pieces of information within content and allow users to search by keywords. Without crawled properties, the search index has no real value, because SharePoint indexes consist of many crawled properties that map content to potential searchable keywords.

■ **Note** Search is not magic! It requires some assistance with good content organization and classification with metadata (content types) and managed metadata (tags).

In the beginning of this chapter, I mentioned good structuring of content for search. Contrary to mistaken opinion, search is not magic! I have consulted with many clients who have asked me why their SharePoint search is not providing valuable results. To this question I typically retort with a question about the structure of their content. Search is only as good as the content available and some form of organization. Look at it this way—if I was to point you at a directory of many randomly named files and ask you to pull out all the proposal documents, this might take some time for you to visit every file, laboriously checking the content. If I then told you that all proposal documents lived in a sub-folder, you would have an easier time locating them. Similarly, SharePoint search needs some help identifying and classifying content. SharePoint search is smart enough to understand context of content (sites, document libraries, and lists), and takes advantage of metadata (content types), and managed metadata (tags), to index content for relevant search results.

Crawled properties work hand-in-hand with metadata and managed metadata. As well as searching inside documents with IFILTERs, the content processor can extract content type fields and tags from content and create crawled properties. Before I move on to the topic of managed properties, I will take a quick look at crawled properties in Search Service Application Administration.

Figure 15-25 shows a screenshot from my Search Service Application Administration, listing crawled properties. To navigate to this page, click the Search Schema link in the left navigation of Search Service Application Administration, then click the crawled properties. Notice that each crawled property maps to a managed property. I shall discuss managed properties in the next subsection, but mapping a crawled property to a managed property allows users to then filter search results in keyword searches.

Property Name	Mapped To Property
_dlc_DocIdItemGuid	
0xf	
Basic:10	
Basic:10	Title, Filename
Internal:107	FallbackLanguage
Basic:11	
Basic:11	Path, OriginalPath
Basic:12	
Basic:12	Size
Office:12	Created

Figure 15-25. *Crawled properties*

You will not find a link or button to create a new crawled property—remember that the crawler has the responsibility of creating crawled properties, based on discovered content. Looking down the list of available crawled properties (Figure 15-25), you should notice that they do not all have names conducive to their purpose. However, you do not need to concern yourself with the name of crawled properties because you map them to zero or many managed properties, which have friendly names.

Clicking on any of the listed crawled properties shows a page about the crawled property (Figure 15-26). Each crawled property has a Name, Category, Property Set ID, and mappings to managed properties (not all crawled properties map to a managed property, in which case the check box to include the property in the full-text index determines whether values of a given crawled property show up in search results).

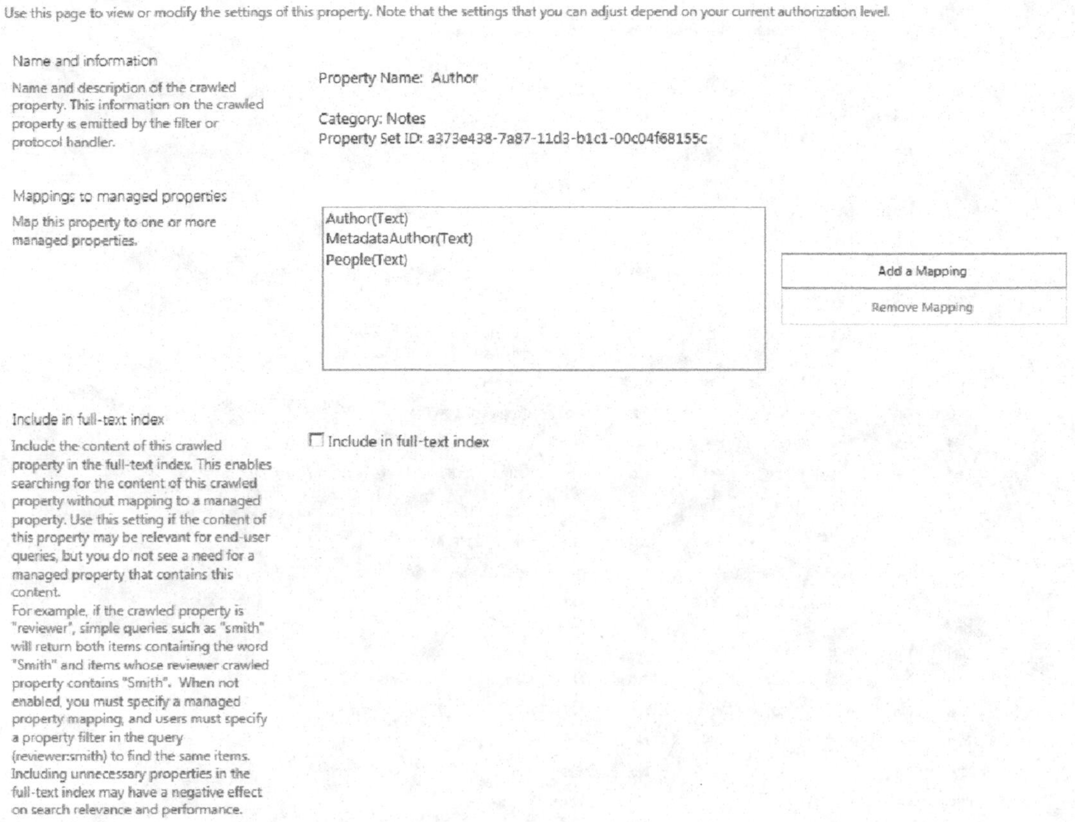

Use this page to view or modify the settings of this property. Note that the settings that you can adjust depend on your current authorization level.

Name and information

Name and description of the crawled property. This information on the crawled property is emitted by the filter or protocol handler.

Property Name: Author

Category: Notes
Property Set ID: a373e438-7a87-11d3-b1c1-00c04f68155c

Mappings to managed properties

Map this property to one or more managed properties.

```
Author(Text)
MetadataAuthor(Text)
People(Text)
```

Add a Mapping

Remove Mapping

Include in full-text index

Include the content of this crawled property in the full-text index. This enables searching for the content of this crawled property without mapping to a managed property. Use this setting if the content of this property may be relevant for end-user queries, but you do not see a need for a managed property that contains this content.

For example, if the crawled property is "reviewer", simple queries such as "smith" will return both items containing the word "Smith" and items whose reviewer crawled property contains "Smith". When not enabled, you must specify a managed property mapping, and users must specify a property filter in the query (reviewer:smith) to find the same items. Including unnecessary properties in the full-text index may have a negative effect on search relevance and performance.

☐ Include in full-text index

Figure 15-26. *Crawled Property Settings page*

Managed Properties

Microsoft must like the word "Managed," because SharePoint contains the term in various places: Managed Metadata, Managed Service Applications, Managed Properties, etc. However, in this section I shall focus on managed properties as they belong to search.

Figure 15-27 shows a screenshot from my Managed Properties page in my Search Service Application Administration. To navigate to this page, click the Search Schema link in the left navigation of Search Service Application Administration, then click the Managed Properties. Notice how "Managed Properties" is a nicer name than "Crawled Properties"; this is how managed properties are exposed to end users in search refiners and search filters. Each managed property has a number of settings, as described in Table 15-2.

Property Name	Type	Multi	Query	Search	Retrieve	Refine	Sort	Mapped Crawled Properties	Aliases
AboutMe	Text	No	Yes	No	Yes	No	No	People:AboutMe, ows_Notes	
Account	Text	No	Yes	No	Yes	No	No	ows_Name	
AccountName	Text	No	Yes	Yes	Yes	No	No	People:AccountName	
acronym	Text	No	No	No	Yes	No	No		
acronymaggre	Text	No	Yes	Yes	Yes	No	No		
acronymexpansion	Text	No	No	No	Yes	No	No		
acronymexpansionaggre	Text	No	No	No	Yes	No	No		
AnchorText	Text	No	No	Yes	No	No	No	Basic:28	
anchortextcomplete	Text	No	Yes	No	No	No	No		
AssignedTo	Text	No	Yes	No	Yes	No	No	ows_AssignedTo, ows_Assigned_x0020_To	
AttachmentDescription	Text	No	No	No	Yes	No	No	ows_MediaLinkDescription	
AttachmentType	Integer	No	Yes	No	Yes	Yes	No	ows_MediaLinkType	
AttachmentURI	Text	No	No	No	Yes	No	No	ows_MediaLinkURI	
Author	Text	Yes	Yes	Yes	Yes	No	Yes	Author, MailFrom, Mail:6	urn:schemas-microsoft-com:office:office#Author, DocAuthor
AuthorOWSUSER	Text	No	Yes	No	Yes	No	No	ows_q_USER_Author	
BaseOfficeLocation	Text	No	Yes	No	Yes	Yes	No	People:SPS-Location	
BasicScope	Binary Data	No	No	No	Yes	No	No		
body	Text	No	No	Yes	No	No	No		
CategoryNavigationUrl	Text	No	Yes	No	No	No	No	Basic:CategoryUrlNavigation	
CCAMetadata	Text	No	No	No	Yes	No	No		
charset	Text	No	Yes	No	Yes	No	No		
clickdistance	Integer	No	No	No	No	No	Yes		
CollapsingStatus	Integer	No	No	No	Yes	No	No		

Figure 15-27. *Managed properties*

Table 15-2. *Managed Property Settings*

Setting	Description
Property Name	Name of the managed metadata property, name contains no spaces or special characters.
Description	Description of the managed property.
Type	The type describes the type of data associated with this managed property. Types available are: Text, Integer, Decimal, Date and Time, Yes/No, Double precision float, and Binary.
Searchable	SharePoint includes values of this managed property into the full-text index; e.g., if the managed property is "Author" and a user searches for "Smith," then the search results include all results where the managed property contains an author with the value Smith.
Queryable	Allows the search terms to contain the managed property, e.g., Author:Smith, which provides results where the Author property is Smith. This is subtly different from the Searchable settings.
Retrievable	SharePoint returns contents of this managed property in search results—this allows you to display managed property values in the search result template.

(continued)

Table 15-2. (*continued*)

Setting	Description
Allow Multiple Values	Allow multiple values of the same type; e.g., if the managed property is Author, and a document has authors Garrett and Kaplan, then searching `Author:Garrett` or `Author:Kaplan` will produce the same document result.
Refinable	Allows the managed property to appear as a refiner in the search results. Has three values: Yes, No, and Yes Latent. Yes creates a refiner for the property but requires a full crawl; latent does not create a refiner now, but allows flipping from latent to yes, later, without the need of a full crawl. No indicates that this managed property is not a refiner.
Sortable	Allows sorting of search results by this managed property, after search execution, such as in cases when the search results are too large to allow search result retrieval and sort at the same time. Has three values: Yes, No, and Yes Latent. Yes allows sorting for the property but requires a full crawl; latent does not allow sorting now, but allows flipping from latent to yes, later, without the need of a full crawl. No indicates that this managed property does not allow sorting.
Alias	An alias is another name for a managed property. Use the original managed property name to map to a crawl property and an alias if you would like to use a different name in search results and queries. If you possess insufficient permissions to create managed properties, you may create aliases for existing managed properties.
Token Normalization	When checked, the managed properties will return results from the content regardless of case or diacritics (special characters).
Complete Matching	When checked, SharePoint will only match results when the value of the managed property matches exactly that of what the user provided; e.g., ID:12345 will only match ID:12345 and not ID:12345678 or ID:12 345
Mappings to Crawled Properties	Maps the managed property to one or many crawled properties. Generally managed properties have at least one crawled property, otherwise they are of little use, whereas crawled properties need no managed property to provide search results. Managed properties can map values to all specified crawled properties, or the first non-empty Crawled Property listed.
Company Name Extraction	Enables the system to extract company name entities from the managed property when crawling new or updated items. There is a pre-populated dictionary for company name extraction. The system saves the original managed property content unchanged in the index and, in addition, copies the extracted entities to the managed property "companies."
Custom Entity Extraction	Allows association of custom entity extractor such that content values in this Managed Property appear within custom refiners.

Query Suggestions

Query Suggestions show search suggestions as users' type text into search boxes. SharePoint maintains a list of search terms and a list of terms not to show. You may import and export both lists via text files, as shown in Figure 15-28. The file format calls for one term per line (each term may include spaces).

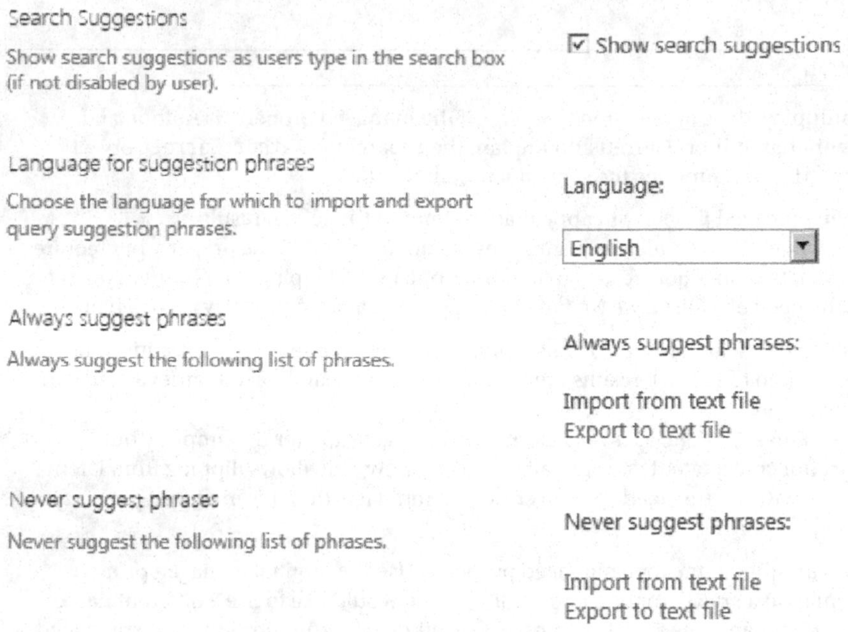

Search Suggestions

Show search suggestions as users type in the search box (if not disabled by user).

☑ Show search suggestions

Language for suggestion phrases

Choose the language for which to import and export query suggestion phrases.

Language:

English ▼

Always suggest phrases

Always suggest the following list of phrases.

Always suggest phrases:

Import from text file
Export to text file

Never suggest phrases

Never suggest the following list of phrases.

Never suggest phrases:

Import from text file
Export to text file

Figure 15-28. *Query Suggestions Configuration*

Search Dictionaries

Search Dictionaries use the Managed Metadata Term Store to contain dictionaries for storage of company names, people, and spelling. A dictionary – just like a real world dictionary – contains a series of words for classification, only in the case of SharePoint, the dictionaries do not provide English meaning to words, but instead enhance search queries.

Anyone familiar with the Managed Metadata Term Store in SharePoint 2010/2013 will recognize the interface (shown in Figure 15-29) for search dictionaries.

1. Open Search Service Application Administration

2. Click the link for Search Dictionaries

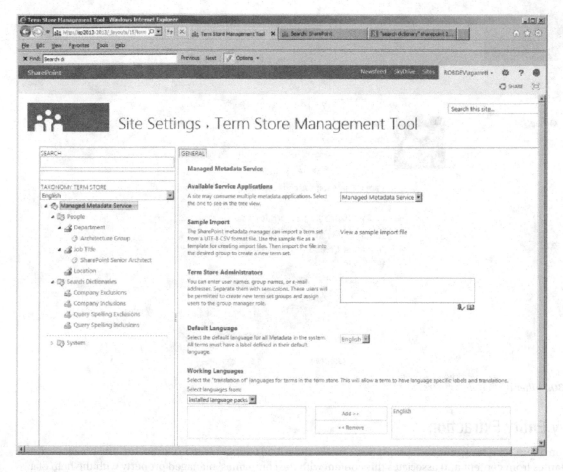

Figure 15-29. *Search Dictionaries*

People

The People Dictionary contains a structure for people, consisting of Department, Job Title, and Location. When the Crawler crawls over the people profile store it extracts these field values and populates the values of these fields in the term store under the People node. The terms values provide distinct values for searching people – for example, we can search or filter all people by a specific location and job title, using specific values in the term store.

Figure 15-30 shows an example of searching the People Result Source. The results provide include refiners (on the left) corresponding to the Department, Job Title, and Location (my profile does not happen to include a location). This example is a little thin because I have only one user in my farm, but if I had multiple users then the refiners would contain a selection of locations, departments, and job title values from which to choose.

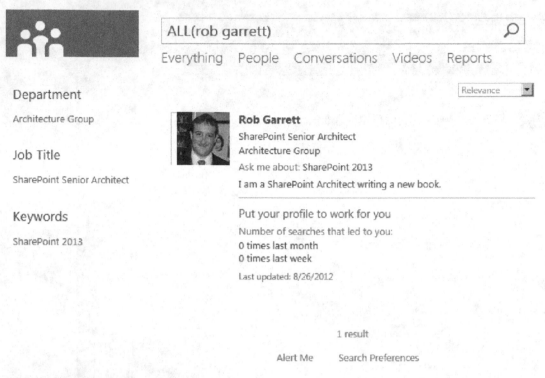

Figure 15-30. *Filter by People refiners*

Company Entity Extraction

In the section about searching managed properties, I briefly described company name extraction. The crawler extracts company names from content and associates this content with the companies' managed property with the help of a Company dictionary.

Figure 15-31 shows the default search dictionaries provided by SharePoint. The Company Name dictionary consists of Enterprise keyword term sets for inclusions and exclusions. When crawling over content, if the crawler encounters words in the inclusion term set, it then adds the values to the company name managed property. If the crawler encounters words in the exclusion term set, SharePoint ensures no entry for the value in the company's managed property. The following steps demonstrate adding a new company name to the inclusion and exclusion term sets:

1. Open Search Service Application Administration.

2. Click Search Dictionaries.

3. Click the Managed Metadata Service node.

4. Ensure the username of the current user is listed in the Term Store Administrators (if not, add name and click the Save button).

5. Click the node Company Inclusions (under the Search Dictionaries group).

6. Click the down arrow and add a new term.

7. Repeat the last two steps for Company Exclusions.

8. Ensure that one of your managed properties (see earlier section) has the check box checked for Company Name extraction.

9. Run a full crawl.

10. Issue a search, and you should start seeing company name refiners.

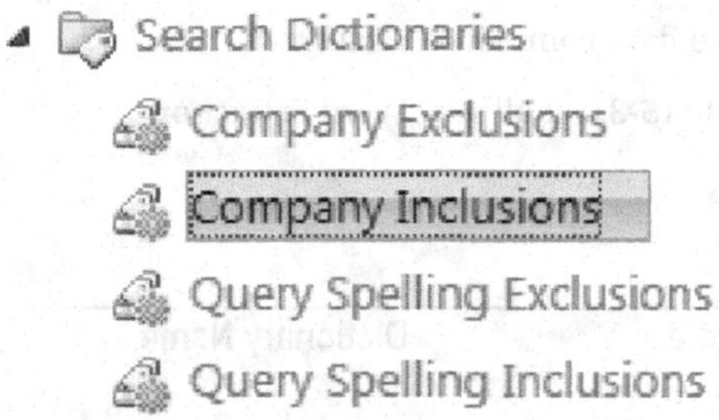

▲ 🗀 Search Dictionaries

  🔊 Company Exclusions

  🔊 Company Inclusions

  🔊 Query Spelling Exclusions

  🔊 Query Spelling Inclusions

Figure 15-31. *Search dictionaries*

Query Spell Check

Similar to the Company Name dictionary, SharePoint provides a Query Spelling dictionary. This dictionary consists of a term set for inclusions and exclusive terms to match spelling. When users enter incorrectly spelled names in the search query box, SharePoint uses the terms in the Query Spelling Inclusion and Query Spelling Exclusion term sets to provide a "Did you mean?" message. I shall provide you an example in the following steps:

1. Open Search Service Application Administration.

2. Click Search Dictionaries.

3. Click the Managed Metadata Service node.

4. Ensure that the username of the current user is listed in the Term Store Administrators (if not, add name and click the Save button).

5. Click the node Query Spelling Inclusions.

6. Click the down arrow and type in the term "SharePoint."

7. Wait 10–15 minutes.

8. Run a search for SHAREPINT (intentionally misspelled) in the Search Center.

Custom Entity Extraction

In the last few subsections, you read how search dictionaries provide search query enhancement with people refiners, company name extraction, and query spelling. You probably thought that it sure would be wonderful if you could create your own custom dictionaries and extractors to match content and provide your own refiners. It turns out that SharePoint 2013 *does* provide this functionality, and I will show you how, in this section of this chapter.

  Before getting into the specifics of custom entities and refiners, I'd like to recap the process by which SharePoint uses the out-of-the-box dictionaries to create refiners.

1. SharePoint provides a dictionary, consisting of inclusion and exclusion term sets.

2. The search crawler finds a word or term as part of the crawl process.

3. The crawler matches the word/term against the inclusion term set.

4. If the crawler matches the word/term with a term in the exclusion term set, the word/term is ignored.

5. If not, the crawler applies to the word/term a crawl property and mapped managed property.

The process of custom term extraction is similar to the preceding process. The following steps demonstrate how to create a custom extractor for "product names" and how to create a refiner for search results:

1. Ensure that you have a content source defined and have completed a full crawl.

2. Decide on the type of entity extraction, using Table 15-3. I shall use "Word Extraction" in my example.

Table 15-3. Entity Extraction Types

Custom entity extractor / custom entity extractor dictionary	Description	Example	Dictionary Name
Word Extraction	Case-insensitive, dictionary entries matching tokenized content, maximum 5 dictionaries	The entry "anchor" matches "anchor" and "Anchor," but not "anchorage"	Microsoft.UserDictionaries. EntityExtraction.Custom.Word.n [where n = 1,2,3,4 or 5]
Word Part Extraction	Case-insensitive, dictionary entries matching un-tokenized content, maximum 5 dictionaries	The entry "anchor" matches "anchor," "Anchor," and "anchorage"	Microsoft.UserDictionaries. EntityExtraction.Custom. ExactWord.1
Word Exact Extraction	Case-sensitive, dictionary entries matching tokenized content, maximum 1 dictionary	The entry "anchor" matches "anchor" but not "Anchor" or "Anchorage"	Microsoft.UserDictionaries. EntityExtraction.Custom.Wordpart.n [where n = 1,2,3,4 or 5]
Word Part Exact Extraction	Case-sensitive, dictionary entries matching un-tokenized content, maximum 1 dictionary	The entry "anchor" matches "anchor" and "anchorage" but not "Anchor"	Microsoft.UserDictionaries. EntityExtraction.Custom. ExactWordpart.1

3. Open PowerShell and execute the following script:

```
$searchApp = Get-SPEnterpriseSearchServiceApplication
Import-SPEnterpriseSearchCustomExtractionDictionary –SearchApplication
$searchApp –Filename <Path> -DictionaryName <Dictionary name>
```

4. Provide the CSV file in the file path.

5. The dictionary name corresponds to the last column in Table 15-3.

6. Create a CSV file with two columns: Key and Display Form.

7. Provide rows of keys to match terms and optional display form (display name) for the refiner—if not then the refiner value is the same as the key name.

8. Return to Search Service Application Administration.

9. Click the Search Schema link.

10. Click the Managed Properties link.

11. Search for the Managed Property to apply the custom extractor.

12. Click the name of the Managed Property to edit the settings.

13. Check the custom entity extractor to use (under Custom Entity Extraction), based on Table 15-3.

14. Run a full crawl.

15. Next, add a custom refiner Web Part to your Search Results page (or use an existing refiner Web Part if already on the page).

16. Edit the refiner Web Part settings and add the custom refiner, for example: WordCustomRefiner1.

17. Execute a search, and you should see your refiner values showing up.

Search Result Removal

Picture this scenario: SharePoint has crawled some content and this content is appearing in search results, only someone in the organization is unhappy about it. Someone has asked you to remove a search result from the SharePoint index. How do you go about it?

Lucky for you, SharePoint provides a mechanism for you to remove individual search results, without having to reset the index and re-crawling over all content, after adding exclusion crawl rules.

1. Open Search Service Application Administration.

2. Click the Search Removal Result link.

3. In the page that appears, paste the offending URLs in the "URLs to Remove" box.

4. Click the Remove Now link.

5. That is all there is to it.

Diagnostics

SharePoint 2013 provides a number of diagnostic tools to assist with performance tuning and error diagnosis. In this section of the chapter, you will explore the tools available as part of the Search Service Application.

Crawl Log

Crawling over data does not always go as planned, especially when crawling over data that is outside the SharePoint farm. Perhaps a line of business system is not operational, perhaps an external web site has a too restrictive robots.txt file, maybe SharePoint does not have permission to crawl all folders in a file share . . . the possibilities for failure are endless. Fortunately, SharePoint provides sophisticated crawl logging.

The crawl log is separate to that of the ULS log. The ULS log will certainly contain search-related events, but these tend to be infrastructure related, whereas the crawl log contains events relating to crawling of content sources.

Figure 15-32 shows a screenshot from the Search Service Application in my environment. I have two content sources: the default Local SharePoint sites and a content source to crawl the content of my external blog. Look a little closer at the log details on this page.

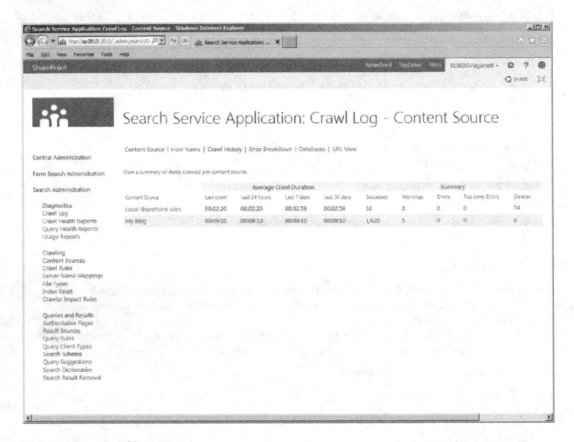

Figure 15-32. *Crawl Log page*

The summary grid (Figure 15-33) provides crawl durations and a summary count of successes, warnings, errors, and deletes.

Content Source	Average Crawl Duration				Summary				
	Last crawl	Last 24 hours	Last 7 days	Last 30 days	Successes	Warnings	Errors	Top Level Errors	Deletes
Local SharePoint sites	00:02:20	00:02:20	00:02:59	00:02:59	16	0	0	0	74
My Blog	00:09:10	00:09:10	00:09:10	00:09:10	1,620	5	0	0	0

Figure 15-33. *Crawl log summary*

The Average Crawl Duration summary (blue) speaks for itself. It is here you can see the average crawl times over the last 24 hours, 7 days, and 30 days and the duration of the current crawl. A crawl that takes longer than the average duration might suggest an issue with performance and ability to crawl the source. Of course, it could also mean a recent addition of a lot of content at source, and now the crawl takes longer.

The main summary (green) provides a cumulative count of successes, warnings, errors, top-level errors, and deletes. You might be wondering why the crawl processor keeps track of deletions. This is important because as content disappears from the source—perhaps because users delete it or move it elsewhere—you should understand why your search results do not contain the same results now compared to an earlier time. A high number of deletes might suggest that the crawler is unable to crawl parts of the content, and has therefore instructed the indexer to remove entries from the index. Table 15-4 lists the different log classification types and their meaning.

Table 15-4. *Crawl Log Classification*

Classification	Meaning
Success	The crawler successfully crawled an item, the indexer created an entry in the index, or the index entry was already present.
Warning	The crawler found an issue with content, which the crawler crawled, partially crawled, or failed to crawl. In some cases the crawler might crawl some content but the content processor cannot extract content from the item to index the content, which would result in an error.
Error	The crawler encountered an error crawling content. These errors include top-level as well as items deeper in the source hierarchy, such as second-level pages in a web site.
Top-Level Error	The crawler encountered an issue crawling some content at the entry point of a content source. These errors suggest access issues to the content source, such as not having access to a web site, or a site collection is offline. Top-level errors are a subset of errors.
Delete	Deletions are items removed from the index because the content entry is no longer available, perhaps because a user deleted content or a crawl rule excludes the content entry from the index.

■ **Note** The crawl log summary contains cumulative values across multiple content source crawls.

Looking at Figure 15-32, we see the crawler encountered five warnings when crawling my blog, found no errors (which is good!), and successfully crawled 1,620 entries, which the indexer added to the index. I shall click the value for the warning classification so we may view the warnings. After clicking the value, we see a page like that in Figure 15-34.

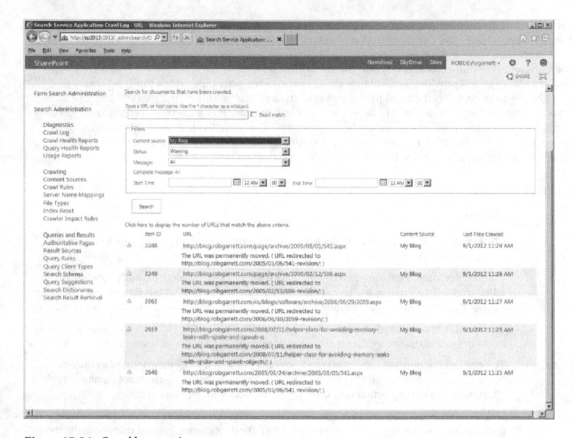

Figure 15-34. *Crawl log warnings*

The page shown in Figure 15-34 is the same as that for the other classifications. Had I clicked the 1,620 value in the previous page, I would have seen a similar page to that in Figure 15-34, only showing the successes instead of the warnings. The value links in the crawl summary (Figure 15-33) link to the same page with the status filter present. Try changing the status in the filter to another classification, followed by a click of the Search button, to see a different set of log results.

Back to my five warnings—here see that the crawler attempted to crawl some pages in my blog and encountered an HTTP 301, indicating that the content permanently moved to a new location. We see this a lot with public web sites—web site administrators preserve links to old content so that users with bookmarks may still access content at the new location with an HTTP 301 or 302 redirect. In this case, the crawler reported an error to help users understand that the content is available and indexed, but in a different location from that which might be expected.

As I previously mentioned, the crawl log can grow beyond a page with each scheduled crawl attempt. Finding warnings, errors, and successes requires use of the filter controls at the top of the Log page (Figure 15-34). The filter allows you to filter the log based on content source, classification (status), date/time range, and even message type (such as, "the content was permanently moved"). If you know the URL of the content, and are interested, you can provide it in the search box. This feature is especially useful when a user reports, "I searched for *x* and it did not show up in the search results."

Returning to the Crawl Log Summary page (Figure 15-32), the Search Service Application provides other details about previous content crawls. See the following links at the top of the page:

- Content Source—shows logs by content source

- Host Name—shows logs by host domain name

- Crawl History—shows statistics on previous crawl attempts (Figure 15-35)

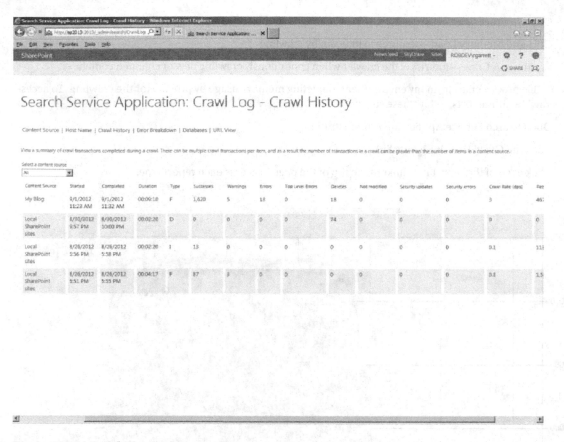

Figure 15-35. *Crawl History*

- Error Breakdown—provides a breakdown of errors in the crawl log
- Databases—shows the state of databases used by the Search Service Application
- URL View—shows the crawl log filtered by a specific URL

Crawl Health Reports

SharePoint provides information on the health of the crawling and content processes via crawl health reports. These reports offer a pictorial view of how search crawling affects system resources. Each of the reports provides the ability to filter by date/time range, and some of the reports provide filtering by content source, search component, and server.

SharePoint 2013 includes the following crawl health reports:

- Crawl Rate—rate of crawl based on item status types
- Crawl Latency—time spent in SQL, adding to repositories, crawl, etc.
- Crawl Queue—shows the historical chart of items in the queue for crawling
- Crawl Freshness—percentage of content that is new versus n days or weeks old

- Content Processing Activity—activity load managed by the content processor

- CPU and Memory Load—resource load taken by crawling

- Continuous Crawl—metrics of the crawler when continuously crawling new or changed content

Figure 15-36 shows a chart from my environment, depicting memory usage by process for the crawling. To access the various crawl health reports, follow these steps:

1. Open Search Service Application Administration.

2. Click the Crawl Health Reports link.

3. Click each of the report type links at the top of the page to access each report type.

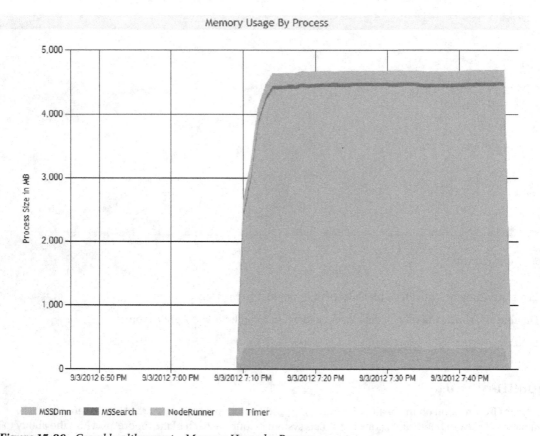

Figure 15-36. *Crawl health report—Memory Usage by Process*

Query Health Reports

The query health reports are to query what the crawl health reports are to crawling. SharePoint 2013 closely monitors active searches and results provided to users to provide you with reports on performance of the query components.

SharePoint 2013 includes the following query health reports:

- Trend—query latency over time for different percentile searches

- Overall—query latency over time for server rendering, object model, and back-end processes

- Main Flow—query latency over time based on flow through query processes

- Federation—query latency over time for various federated sources

- SharePoint Search Provider—query latency over time for SharePoint search processes

- People Search Provider—query latency over time for People search processes

- Index Engine—query latency over time for calls to the index

All query health reports provide filtering by date, and some provide filters for client type, server, etc. Figure 15-37 shows a screenshot of the index engine health report in my environment. To access the various query health reports, follow these steps:

1. Open Search Service Application Administration.

2. Click the Query Health Reports link.

3. Click each of the report type links at the top of the page to access each report type.

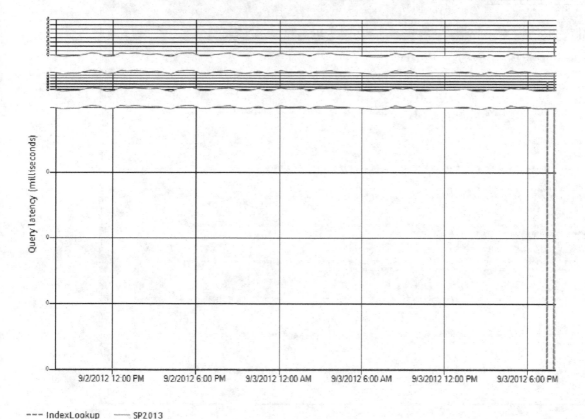

Figure 15-37. Query health report—Index Engine

Usage Reports

Usage reports provide a series of Excel documents that detail historical data about how users are using SharePoint 2013 search. Examples include top queries by day and month and no result queries. You may download these reports and distribute them to content owners and marketing individuals in your organization, so they can gain an understanding of what users search and the results they look to obtain. The query analysis component is mainly responsible for the generation of data in these reports.

To access the various usage reports, follow these steps:

1. Open Search Service Application Administration.

2. Click the Usage Reports link.

3. Click each of the report type links at the top of the page to access each report type. Figure 15-38 shows a screenshot of the various available usage reports.

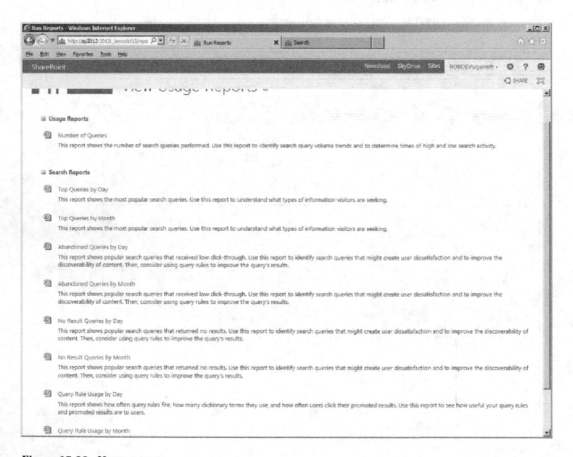

Figure 15-38. *Usage reports*

Summary

Search is a large SharePoint topic, and is very important to allow your users the ability to find content in your SharePoint farm. In this chapter, my aim was to break down the various parts of search—much of which we have inherited from FAST ESP.

To start with, I introduced the new SharePoint 2013 Search Architecture and how the various components come together to provide crawl, content processing, indexing, and query capabilities. I demonstrated how to create a new Search Service Application and access its configuration via the Search Service Application Administration pages. Using PowerShell, I demonstrated how to provide redundancy and load distribution of search components across various SharePoint servers as part of search topology design.

I dissected the crawling and querying aspects of a typical Search Service Application and introduced a number of new features and features brought over from SharePoint 2010.

Finally, I completed this chapter with an overview of the various reporting and diagnostic tools to triage issues with performance or search component errors.

I hope that this chapter gave you enough information to understand the major components of SharePoint 2013 search. In approximately 60 pages, I attempted to impart knowledge on all areas of the search platform, a subject about which others have written complete books.

In my next chapter, Chapter 16, you will read about SharePoint designer and branding.

■ ■ ■

SharePoint Designer and Branding

I was hesitant to include a chapter on SharePoint Designer and branding in this administration book. However, SharePoint 2013 includes a wonderful new user interface. I would be doing you, the reader, a disservice if I did not cover branding SharePoint's user interface at least a high level. Microsoft coined the name "Metro" to describe its new brand of recent applications and operating systems. The plan for Metro is to provide a clean and simple brand design that works on a number of applications, platforms, and devices. Pick up a new Windows 8 phone and you will see the common user interface paradigms present in Windows 8 on desktop computers and on the Xbox 360. Alas, due to legal issues in using the name "Metro," Microsoft now calls the brand "Windows 8 Theme," although the design and user interface is the same.

Since SharePoint 2007, Microsoft has provided a Windows application called SharePoint Designer to allow designers to modify the look of SharePoint. When discussing SharePoint branding, I have to discuss SharePoint Designer. With the release to manufacturing of SharePoint 2013, Microsoft released SharePoint Designer 2013 shortly thereafter.

In this chapter, you will visit the Windows 8 branding in SharePoint 2013. You will read about the Design Manager—a new feature of SharePoint 2013 that supports simple branding of SharePoint—before getting into advanced branding with SharePoint Designer. I will not insult the authors of the many books on the subject of SharePoint branding and SharePoint Designer by trying to cover everything within the topic here. Nonetheless, I hope that you shall leave, having read this last chapter of my book, with some basic understanding of SharePoint branding and knowledge to support the designers in your organization as their SharePoint administrator.

SharePoint 2013 User Interface

I shall assume at this point that you are familiar with SharePoint 2013's user interface (at least a little), or that you have flipped through the pages of this book and seen some of the screenshots of SharePoint 2013 in action. Of course, you might be standing in a book store (or online) and have decided to turn directly to this chapter to get a keen sense of the user interface design changes in SharePoint 2013, so I have provided you with a screenshot of Central Administration in Figure 16-1.

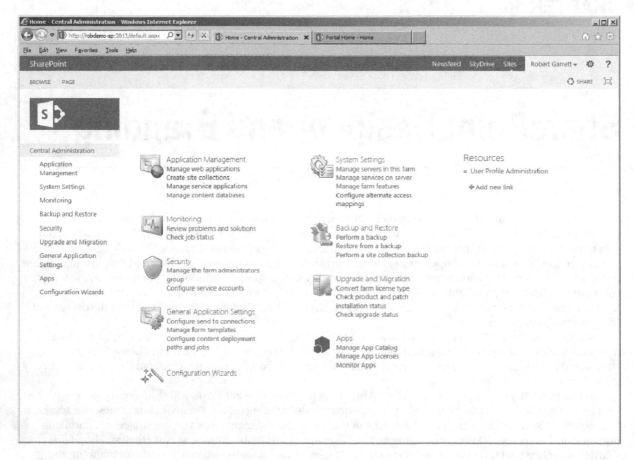

Figure 16-1. *New look in Central Administration*

I mentioned that Microsoft has adopted a new "Metro" design for its applications and operating systems, and SharePoint 2013 joins the fold with this new look to the user interface. Because the code name "Metro" is no longer used (due to legal conflict), we now refer to the new design branding, or theme, as "Windows 8." However, before moving on from this history lesson, I shall mention that the code name had significance. The metro branding emulates the look and feel of signage in typical metropolitan transport facilities, with greater emphasis on text than graphics, to provide clear and concise instruction to users. Those familiar with Windows 8, Xbox 360, and the new Windows Phone can appreciate the simplicity of the new Windows 8 design.

Because the new Windows 8 branding is less graphic intensive and geared more to simplicity with text, the coding behind the design is less complex. Designers can easily integrate the design of custom functionality with minimal use of Cascading Style Sheet (CSS) elements and HTML. This is not to say that the user interface loses capability. Much of SharePoint 2013 continues to use AJAX and JQuery to achieve direct user feedback without multiple page refresh cycles that plagued users of SharePoint 2007 and earlier. Spend some time in SharePoint 2013 and you will get used to the "Working" message appearing in the top right of the page, indicating that SharePoint is processing a request without page post-back and that the user interface will reflect update shortly.

■ **Note**   SharePoint 2013 continues to use AJAX and JQuery rather than page post-back cycles to update the user interface. Look for the "Working" message that appears in the top right corner when SharePoint is busy processing the page.

SharePoint 2010 introduced the ribbon interface, also present in the other Office applications, which provided greater navigation around the vast functions available in SharePoint. The ribbon provides functional context by showing icons for only those functions pertinent to the current user context. For example, if editing the settings for web applications, the ribbon displays icons for those functions relevant to web application settings. SharePoint 2013 does not disappoint—the new branding includes updates to the ribbon, so the icons fit in with the Windows 8 style and provide users with snappy navigation. Figure 16-2 shows a view of the new SharePoint 2013 ribbon.

Figure 16-2. *Ribbon in SharePoint 2013*

The ribbon is not the only area that has a fresh new face. The Site Contents area (shown in Figure 16-3) now displays lists and libraries with tiles. SharePoint 2013 refers to lists and libraries as "apps," hence the main icon to "add an app" rather than a link to create a new list or library. No need to fear: lists and libraries work the same as they always have (for the most part). Microsoft now considers everything an app in SharePoint to fit in with the App Development Model, which is the new way of developing portable applications that work in SharePoint and other Office applications. Office and SharePoint App Development is outside the scope of this book, but I recommend that you take the time to read more on the subject.

Figure 16-3. *Tiles in the Site Contents page*

Notice how the tiles, shown in Figure 16-3, provide a very simple graphic and monotone coloring. This is provides a crisp look to icons and tiles in the user interface without confusing the user—exactly like the signs displayed in the Washington, DC, Metro Transit System, most major airports, and the subway system in New York City. I wonder where Microsoft got its inspiration!

You might be wondering what happened to the Site Actions menu (or not if you have read other chapters in this book). SharePoint 2013 did away with the Site Actions menu and replaced it with the gear icon in the top right. Figure 16-4 shows a cluster of icons in the top right of every SharePoint site (except custom branded sites and publishing sites in anonymous user mode). Clicking the gear icon is akin to clicking the Site Actions menu in SharePoint 2010—it is here that you can get access to the site settings, site contents view, and some owner and administrative functions.

Figure 16-4. *New icon cluster, including the site settings gear*

The Newsfeed, SkyDrive, and Sites links navigate you to these areas within SharePoint. If you have My Sites and user profiles enabled, these links are your access to personal content. Typically, users like to access their personal content most, which is why these links reside in this cluster as pervasive links with the site. In similar fashion, you can access details about your profile by clicking your name, which shows a drop-down to access your user profile, customize the page, or sign out of SharePoint. You can read more about user profiles and My Sites in Chapter 6.

The Share icon is the new approach to granting permissions to the site. If you have permissions to grant others access to the site, the Share icon displays a dialog box (Figure 16-5) to invite other users to the site. Sharing versus granting permissions aligns with what you see in social networking sites. You do not grant users access to your Facebook page, but you do share information on the page with others.

Share 'Portal Home'   ✕

88 Shared with ☐ ROBDEMO\SP_Admin

Invite people to 'Approve'

```
Enter names, email addresses, or 'Everyone'.


```

SHOW OPTIONS

Share   Cancel

Figure 16-5. *Invite others with sharing*

The box icon on the far right bottom of the cluster (Figure 16-4) is an interesting feature of the design. Clicking this icon tells SharePoint to focus the page on content by hiding the site icon and header information. After clicking this icon, notice in Figure 16-6 that the ribbon and pervasive links remain intact, because you still need this information on the page to navigate and access important personal content.

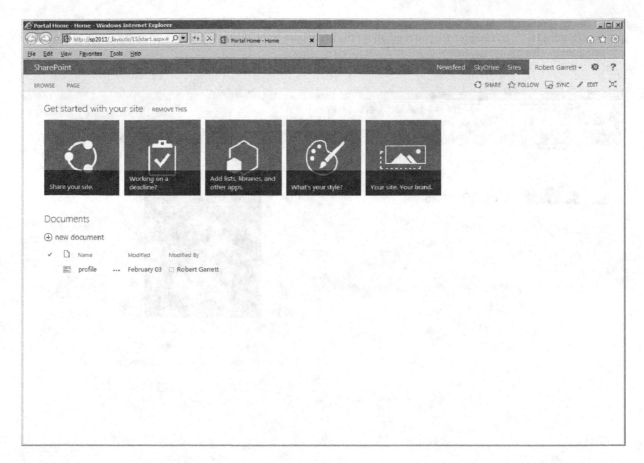

Figure 16-6. *Focus on content view*

Aesthetics are not the only changes in the new SharePoint 2013 user interface. The design brings some functional enhancements too. One of the more significant changes is the ability to drag and drop files into document libraries. Open your browser, navigate to the document library, and then try dragging a file from your disk to the browser. You should see a drag area appear where you can drop the file, which the browser then uploads to SharePoint. Wait... I can hear the Safari, Firefox, and Chrome users screaming from here, "I bet it's only supported in Internet Explorer." The good news is that drag and drop to document libraries works on the latest version of Safari, Firefox, Chrome, and Internet Explorer. Curiously, Internet Explorer 8 and 9 also support drag and drop, but only if you install Office 2013.

■ **Note**   Drag and drop to document libraries works in the latest version of Safari, Firefox, Chrome, and IE (IE 8 and 9 work also, with Office 2013 installed).

The new SharePoint 2013 branding brings many, many, new enhancements—far too many to cover in one chapter of this book. If you are interested in a SharePoint 2013 deep dive, I recommend reading *Pro SharePoint 2013 Branding and Responsive Web Development*, by Eric Overfield, Rita Zhang, Oscar Medina, and Kanwal Khipple (Apress, 2013). Before moving on to discussing branding SharePoint 2013 with the new Design Manager, I shall quickly demonstrate the new preview capabilities in the SharePoint document libraries. If SharePoint recognizes an image file type uploaded to a document library, hovering over the document library entry in the browser shows a brief preview (Figure 16-7). In Chapter 15, you read about the new SharePoint 2013 search features. Search results now include preview for many document types, not just images.

Figure 16-7. *Preview in document libraries*

Branding with the Design Manager

Branding SharePoint has never been a trivial task. I know a number of talented SharePoint UI designers who have devoted their careers to doing just that. Designing a good user interface brand for any web site requires experience and knowledge of web rendering principles. A good web designer knows the intricacies of a good design that promotes usability. Designs are very much at home with technologies like Cascading Style Sheets (CSS), HTML, JQuery, JavaScript, Silverlight, Flash, and many others geared for styling rendered content on the web. Add SharePoint into the mix and the game changes, because SharePoint brings about its own constraints and complexity in what it will and will not allow in the user interface. It is no wonder that SharePoint UI designers are not hurting for work. The good news is that Microsoft has gone a long way in simplifying branding of SharePoint, as you will see in this section.

One of the new design features of SharePoint 2013 is the Design Manager. The Design Manager makes life a little easier for those without a career in user interface and user experience design to apply some branding to SharePoint publishing sites.

■ **Note**   Either create a SharePoint Publishing Site Collection or enable the publishing infrastructure feature to use the Design Manager.

To demonstrate the Design Manager and to simplify my demonstrations, I created a new site collection in Central Administration. If you need a refresher on how to accomplish this, flip back to Chapter 2, where I discuss installing web applications and new site collections as part of setting up SharePoint 2013. It is also worth your time to read Chapter 10, where I discuss the publishing infrastructure and publishing features of SharePoint 2013.

Figure 16-8 shows a screenshot of my publishing site that I created in my SharePoint 2013 development farm. Similar to other out-of-the-box SharePoint 2013 site templates, and Central Administration, the publishing site starts out with the Windows 8 branding. Typically, organizations use the publishing template in SharePoint for hosting public-facing web sites and extranets, because this template allows the greatest flexibility in custom branding, along with content management features. Publishing separates branding from content, with master pages, page layouts, and content management features, so content owners may concentrate on the content and web designers may concentrate on the look and feel, separately.

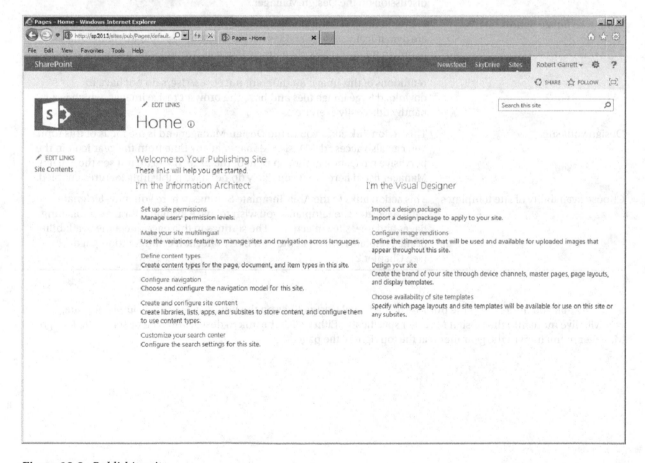

Figure 16-8. *Publishing site*

Of course, there is nothing preventing you from enabling the publishing infrastructure site collection feature for an existing team site, or any other site that is not a publishing site. This enables all the benefits of a publishing site within a site created earlier for a different purpose.

In this chapter, I shall concentrate on the Design Manager and branding aspects of publishing. If you wish to learn more about the overall publishing features of SharePoint 2013, flip back and read Chapter 10. Without further delay, you will now take a closer look at the Design Manager.

As you see from Figure 16-8, SharePoint makes life easy by listing the actions available to you if you are an information architect or a visual designer. Because this chapter focuses on SharePoint branding, I will concentrate on the links on the right side of the page. Table 16-1 lists the available actions for a visual designer and a summary of each operation.

Table 16-1. *Visual Designer Actions*

Action	Summary
Import a design package	Allows importing of an existing design package, for use by site collection administrators. I shall demonstrate creating a design package as part of my discussion on the Design Manager.
Configure Image Renditions	I covered Image Renditions in Chapter 10. Essentially, Image Renditions are dynamically scaled versions of one single image upload. Rather than maintain multiple sizes of an image (such as a thumbnail, a low-res version, and a hi-res version), you can maintain a single hi-res version and multiple renditions of this image for different purposes. Users do not have to download large image files and have the browser resize images, which is a bandwidth-costly exercise.
Design your site	This action link takes you to the Design Manager and is the focus of this topic. You can also access the Design Manager at any time from the gear icon in the pervasive navigation at the top right of the page. If you do not see the Design Manager listed here, then you likely do not have publishing features enabled.
Choose availability of site templates	This action links to the Area Template Settings, where you may designate what page and site templates you wish to make available for new publishing pages and new site collections. The settings in this page affect the availability of site templates shown in the new Site Collection Configuration page (see Chapter 2).

Now that you understand the purpose of the Visual Design links on the home page of your publishing site, you will dive more into the Design Manager specifically. Either click the link to design your site or select the Design Manager menu item in the gear menu at the top right of the page.

Figure 16-9 shows a screenshot of the Design Manager Welcome page. The Design Manager includes a series of high-level steps to undertake to complete the redesign of your publishing site brand. Before you visit each of these steps, notice the link to install a predefined look. Clicking this link takes you to the page to select a site composition. A composition is essentially a color scheme that applies to a brand—the physical layout of information in a brand remains consistent, but the composition changes the colors and possibly some of the graphics to provide an overall theme change of the existing brand. Figure 16-10 illustrates this point by showing a number of views of the same page; notice how each image looks similar in layout and content, but the colors differ—this is the whole point of compositions.

Figure 16-9. *Design Manager Welcome page*

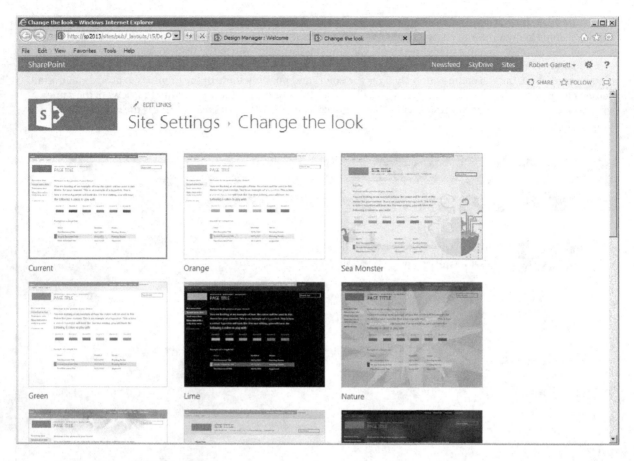

Figure 16-10. *Change the Look page*

SharePoint 2013 themes work differently from how they did in the previous versions of SharePoint. Themes are now a component part of compositions. Compositions live in a special gallery, called Composed Looks (Figure 16-11), which you can access from the Web Designer Galleries section under the site collection settings for a publishing site. Each composition consists of a master page, color palette, fonts, thumbnail image, name, and display order (for the gallery). Compositions provide greater flexibility than the older themes structure because designers can mix and match color palettes and font schemes with different master pages to create unique compositions. The color palette and the font scheme *are* the theme files. Color palettes consist of XML markup files (.SPCOLOR) that describe different colors, whereas font schemes describe fonts, also in XML (.SPFONT).

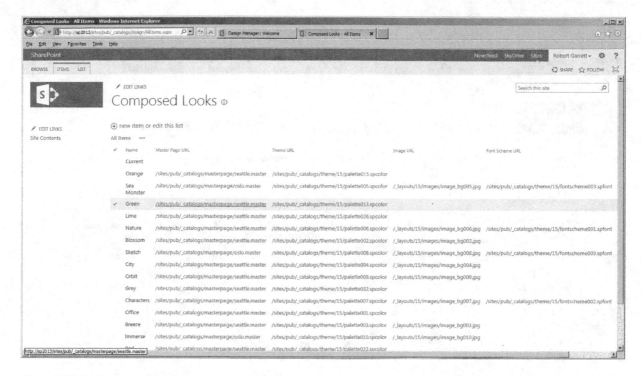

***Figure 16-11.** Composed Looks*

Theme files reside in their own gallery, called Themes, also accessed via the site collection settings. The best way to understand Theme files and Composition files is to navigate to the aforementioned galleries in a publishing site collection and open the files to see the markup contained. Because the files reside in SharePoint galleries and consist of standard XML markup, you can easily create new or modify existing compositions by editing these files and uploading them via the site user interface. As you continue looking at the various capabilities of the Design Manager, you shall see that Microsoft is trying to lessen the reliance on SharePoint Designer and the need for sophisticated expertise in branding SharePoint. As more and more users adopt SharePoint in the cloud, via Office 365, it is important that users can brand their sites with minimal complication.

Getting back to the Design Manager, now that you have reviewed the Welcome page, you will click the link in the left navigation to manage device channels. Device channels allow targeting of specific content to certain device types. For example, you might want to restrict display of heavy UI controls, such as Flash and Silverlight, on devices that do not render this type of content. Device channels work off the user agent string—sent with every page request—and allow SharePoint to determine what type of page markup to return.

By default, SharePoint displays the same content to all device types until you define additional device channels. Figure 16-12 shows a screenshot of my SharePoint site in the Device Channels page. I only have the default channel defined, which SharePoint created with my publishing site.

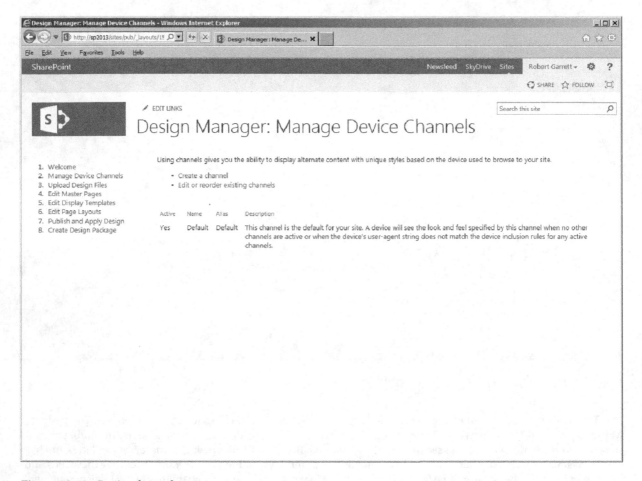

Figure 16-12. *Device channels*

1. Click the link to create a new channel.

2. In the dialog, provide a name for the new channel.

3. Provide an alias, which you use in code to indicate that markup is destined for a particular channel.

4. Provide a description.

5. Provide some device inclusion rules—these are substrings that appear in the user agent string and define the device type.

6. Check the check box to make the device channel active.

7. Click the Save button to save the new rule.

If you were playing along at home, you now have a new device channel. If you specified a real user agent substring, then you can try accessing SharePoint from a device that sends this user agent string to see the device channel in action. However, you have only defined a new device channel; you have yet to change the markup in rendered pages such that it renders differently for your new device channel.

1. Navigate to the Site Settings page (via the gear icon).

2. Click the link to change the master page, under the Look and Feel section.

3. You should see the option to select a site and system master page for each device channel listed (Figure 16-13).

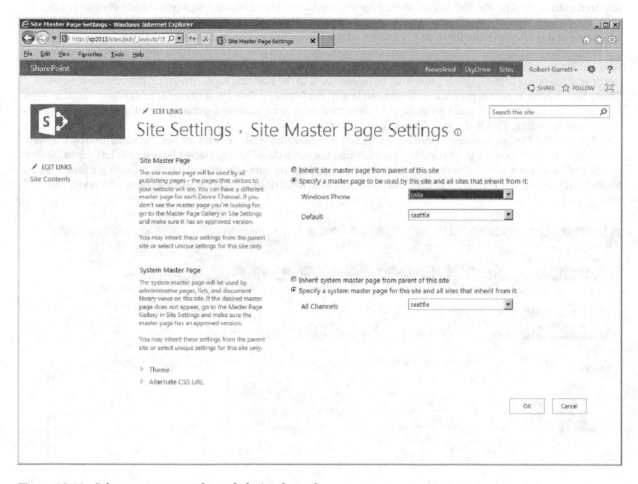

Figure 16-13. *Select a master page for each device channel*

Selecting a different master page for each device type is a good practice. However, you might want granular control of content on the page for different devices. For example, perhaps your SharePoint pages render fine on an Apple iPad, but you really want to disable the Flash control, embedded on your home page, for these device types. Rather than define a separate master page just for iPads, you can use the Device Channel Panel (a nice ring to that name, you think?). The Device Channel Panel control only renders content within the panel when the current channel alias matches that specified for the panel. You may specify that the Device Channel Panel render the content for multiple channel types by providing comma-separated alias names in the IncludedChannels attribute/property of the control.

Creating a Brand

You are now getting to the fun part of Design Manager: the capability to design a SharePoint brand from raw HTML, CSS, and JavaScript files.

In previous versions of SharePoint, Microsoft advised users that it is a best practice to apply all custom branding to an existing SharePoint master page (e.g., v5.master). This ensures that the finished master page contains the required markup and JavaScript so SharePoint pages do not break. Those adventurous types could start with a clean slate and create a new master page with the required elements (remember those talented designers I spoke of in the beginning of this chapter), but for most of us, using an out-of-the-box master page is the way to go.

Sometimes, organizations hire a different group of people to design a site brand from the SharePoint developers who implement it. This is common in business scenarios in which organizations hire large design firms to handle the overall branding of the organization, from business cards, to the building logo, and yes … the company web site. These design firms typically produce web site branding in the form of Adobe Photoshop files, high-resolution images, and (if you are lucky) HTML and CSS markup. Seldom do design firms provide a working SharePoint master page with the custom branding. This is the job of the development team.

Step 3 of the Design Manager addresses uploading designer files to SharePoint, as possibly delivered by a design firm. Figure 16-14 shows the page resulting from clicking the action link Upload Design Files on the left menu. Notice that SharePoint is not asking you to upload master pages, or page layouts—these are SharePoint-specific files; instead, SharePoint is asking for your HTML, CSS, and JavaScript files. Most designs include some images, which you can also upload.

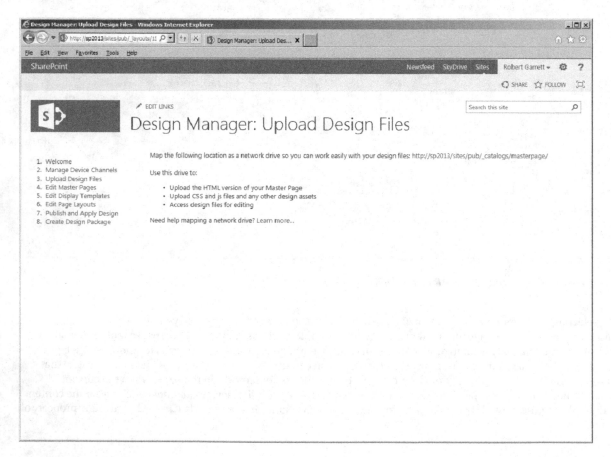

Figure 16-14. *Uploading design files*

The page shown in Figure 16-14 provides an HTTP location of the Master Page Gallery. SharePoint 2013 supports the WebDAV protocol, which allows users to access the Master Page Gallery from a Windows Explorer window. If you have a typical installation of Windows and SharePoint 2013, you can add a network location from Windows Explorer to the Master Page Gallery, at the URL provided, and then upload files via this network path. If, for some reason, WebDAV is not working for you (perhaps your organization does not allow it on your network), you can access the Master Page Gallery from the Site Collection Settings page. Uploading multiple files might be painful, but it gets the job done.

■ **Note**   If you are familiar with SharePoint Designer, you can upload files directly to the site Master Page Gallery. However, the whole point of the Design Manager is to avoid you needing this tool.

To demonstrate creating a new brand for SharePoint 2013, I have a simple HTML file that I shall later convert to a site master page file, using the Design Manager. You can follow along at home with an HTML file that you create from scratch or grab from the Internet.

As you can probably imagine, converting an HTML file to a SharePoint master page automatically has some caveats. The following list includes some best practices to adopt with your HTML file, before uploading it to SharePoint:

- Consider the SharePoint page model—SharePoint renders pages from page list content applied to page layouts, which themselves use a master page. If you have an HTML page that includes sophisticated layout and lots of content, it may not convert to a good master page. HTML files will convert to master pages, but not page layouts, so choose an HTML file that has the basic essentials of what will be the master page brand in use across the site.

- Ensure that your HTML is XHTML compliant (which overrides some HTML 5 standards). SharePoint uses a DOM model to convert HTML to a master page and can only work with XHTML-compliant pages.

- Remove any FORM tags from HTML.

- Convert any embedded CSS styles (in the head section of your HTML) to their own CSS files and link the file to your HTML. SharePoint will strip any embedded CSS styles from the page head before converting.

- The conversion process creates a master page file with the same name as the HTML file, but without the suffix. Therefore, `Index.html` and `Index.htm` both convert to `Index.master`.

- Make sure that any embedded JavaScript inside SCRIPT tags resides on a separate line from the opening SCRIPT tag element.

Having uploaded your design files and observing the best practices, you will now begin the conversion process to create a new master page.

1. Return to the Design Manager.

2. Click the Edit Master Pages link (option 4 in the left navigation).

3. Click the link to convert an HTML file to a SharePoint master page.

4. Select the HTML file you uploaded earlier.

5. Click the Insert button on the File Selection dialog.

6. SharePoint converts your HTML file to a new master page file with the same name.

7. View the status column of the new master page in the Master Page Gallery.

    a. "Warnings and Errors" means that the conversion encountered some issues.

    b. "Conversion Successful" indicates a complete conversion with no issues.

8. Click the status value in the column to see a preview of the new master page.

9. You can see my demonstration result in Figure 16-15.

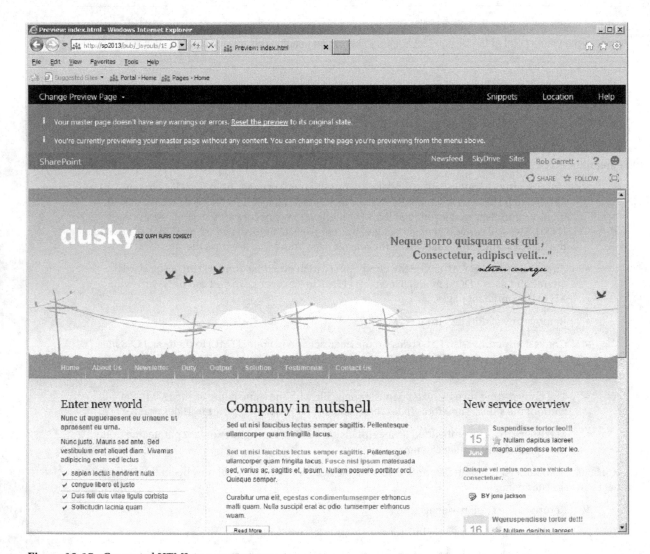

Figure 16-15. *Converted HTML to a master page*

You need not worry if you have errors in your converted master page. You can review the errors and then make changes to the original HTML. It is important to edit the HTML errors in the version of the file that resides in the Master Page Gallery. SharePoint has linked the uploaded HTML file with the new master page file, such that any changes you make to the uploaded HTML file translate to the master page file.

■ **Note**   Edit the HTML file that resides in SharePoint, not the version on disk.

With your HTML converted to a SharePoint master page, it is time to take advantages of Snippets. Snippets are small pieces of HTML markup that replace HTML in your converted master page to provide SharePoint functionality. For example, you removed all FORM tags (per the earlier best practices) and have no SharePoint search box at the top of your page. Even if the conversion process could configure a SharePoint search box from the form on the page (it cannot!), there is no guarantee that this is what you want. Now that you have this sophisticated HTML to master page converter, it seems a shame to have to call in the expert designers to add SharePoint functionality to your master page—this is where Snippets help you. There exists a Snippet for the SharePoint search box, which you can pluck out of the Snippets Gallery as follows:

1.   Open the Design Manager.

2.   Click the Edit Master Pages action link.

3.   Choose the master page or page layout to edit (you can use Snippets in page layouts!).

4.   Preview the master page or page layout.

5.   Click the Snippets link at the top right of the page to open the Snippets Gallery.

6.   Figure 16-16 shows a screenshot of the Snippets Gallery on my server.

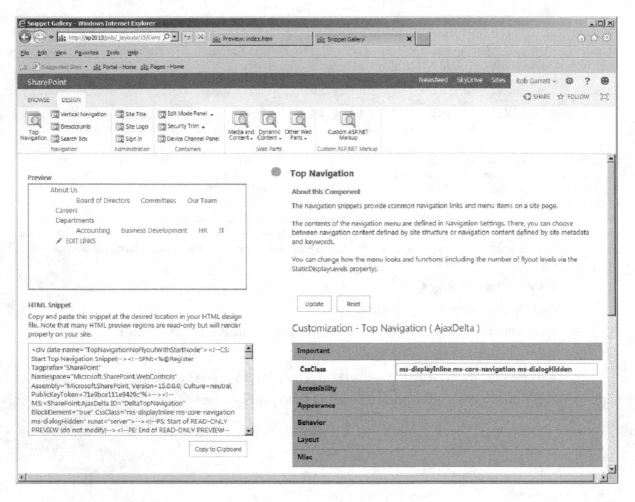

Figure 16-16. *Snippets Gallery*

7. From the Design tab, choose the Snippet you wish to add to your page.

8. Configure any properties of the Snippet in the right pane.

9. After changing Snippet properties, click the Update button to reflect the change in the preview pane.

10. When happy with the Snippet configuration, click the button to copy it to the clipboard.

11. Paste the markup into the HTML for the master page in the Master Page Gallery.

12. You may also paste Snippets into converted master pages and page layouts.

■ **Note**   The properties most important for the core purpose of the Snippet appear in the top section named "Important."

Before you publish and apply your new design to the site, look at steps 5 and 6 in the Design Manager. I covered both these areas in Chapter 10 but shall mention them here for completeness (because you are reading about the Design Manager as a whole).

In Chapter 15, I covered the new SharePoint 2013 search platform, which now includes the FAST elements (an additional expense in SharePoint 2010). SharePoint 2013 boasts a number of neat features, including search result preview and different displays for different result types. For example, if I search SharePoint 2013 for the term "Garrett," I see search results for any documents I have uploaded as well as People search results for my profile. Document search results and People search results display differently on the page, as shown in Figure 16-17. SharePoint 2013 achieves mixed display result rendering using display templates. In previous versions of SharePoint, all search results rendered the same and the only way to change the rendered results was to edit complicated XSL files. In the spirit of making life easier and performing design operations via the SharePoint UI, you can now edit design templates and upload them via the Design Manager to change the look and feel of search results.

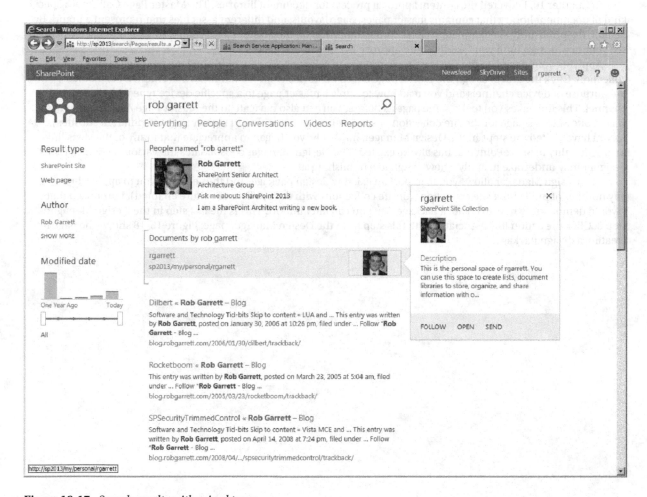

Figure 16-17. *Search results with mixed types*

Step 6 focuses on page layout creation. In a publishing site, page layouts define the content regions on a page and map page content to HTML markup. Think of a page layout as a blueprint of a page, or template of sorts. The page layout does not contain any real content but contains placeholders for content instead, with HTML markup surrounding the placeholders to apply styling to what will be the finished page. Page instances then invoke page layouts to render specific content in a page layout presentation. In a typical publishing site, you might design a handful of page templates for different page styles: articles, press releases, landing pages, etc. Page layouts differ from master pages in that publishing sites typically employ one or two (at most) master pages to provide the common branding of *all* pages in the site, whereas page layouts define *flavors* of page types in the site. If you are interested in learning more about page layouts and master pages, flip back and read Chapter 10.

With your site design essentially complete, it is now time to package and apply this design to the publishing site (up to now you have seen your design in preview). Return to the Design Manager and click the action link for step 7: Publish and Apply Design. On the resulting page, what you see might surprise you. Publishing and applying a design is a simple process of publishing any uploaded files in the Master Page Gallery and applying a new master page to the site.

In Chapter 10, I covered the content approval process for document libraries. The Master Page Gallery is a special kind of document library that contains master pages, page layouts, and different asset files that represent a brand. By default, the publishing site template enables content approval on the Master Page Gallery, so your audience will not see your new design until you "publish" and approve the files in this gallery.

Applying your design to the site is a simple process of selecting the new published master page for the site collection. Click the link to assign the master page based on device channel. Earlier in this chapter, I explained the purpose of device channels and you read how to apply a master page to a specific device type with designated channel. This link takes you to the same page as before. You can also navigate to the Master Page Assignment page via the Site Settings page for the site collection or site (you can assign different master pages to different subsites). As you have visited the steps in the Design Manager, hopefully, you began to appreciate that many of the steps link to functionality in SharePoint that has always existed. The Design Manager consolidates the various actions a visual designer may undertake to apply a new design to a publishing site.

The Design Manager allows you to import an existing design package, and thus enables you to apply a brand to any number of publishing site collections (or site collections with the publishing feature enabled). I promised that I would demonstrate how to create a package that you can later import. This is the last step in the Design Manager: step 8. Click the action link associated with this step from the Design Manager page. Figure 16-18 shows the page for creating a design package.

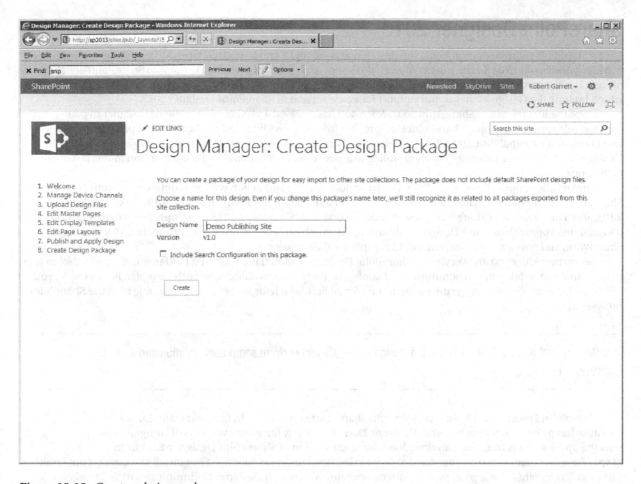

Figure 16-18. Create a design package

On the page, shown in Figure 16-18, SharePoint has prepopulated the package design name, using the name of the site collection. Feel free to change this name to describe the package. Remember, the idea of design packages is to reuse them on other site collections, so choose a name that reflects your design, rather than a name that describes the site where the design applies.

The Design Manager is smart enough to include only design elements that you created as part of your brand. You need not worry that the package contains a copy of the out-of-the-box design files.

Earlier I touched on design templates for search results. The check box on the Export page allows you to decide whether to include these templates with your design. If your design does not include any design templates for search results, you can leave this check box unchecked.

Click the Create button when you are ready to create a design package. SharePoint displays a nice message indicating that it is working before displaying a page indicating successful creation of the design package (or error if something went wrong). Do not be alarmed if the creation process takes a little while; SharePoint has to package up several files and ensure that no out-of-the-box files make their way into the package. When complete, SharePoint will provide a link to allow you to download the package as a WSP file.

WSP files are SharePoint solution files, which SharePoint uses for both farm and user solution packages. It makes sense that Microsoft chose this same package model to package design files. After downloading the WSP file, you may import the design into another site collection from the Design Manager of the other site.

SharePoint Designer 2013

In this SharePoint administration book, site design is a fringe topic, and I am stretching the boundaries by including it. Many good books exist on the subject of web site design, and plenty of these books tailor to SharePoint-specific design. It was not my goal to compete with such publications, but to cover the core enhancements in SharePoint 2013, which include the Design Manager and support for a new version of SharePoint Designer 2013.

Since the first release of SharePoint 2007, Microsoft has released a version of SharePoint Designer to pair with the release of SharePoint. SharePoint Designer is a free Windows installed application that provides design and configuration capabilities for advanced users. Authors have written whole books on the subject of SharePoint Designer also, but since Designer is a close sibling to SharePoint, I felt I should include a mention in this last chapter of my book.

Unlike Office applications, SharePoint Designer does not mix and match well with different versions of SharePoint. SharePoint Designer 2007 works with SharePoint 2007, SharePoint Designer 2010 works with SharePoint 2010, and a new release of SharePoint Designer 2013 works with SharePoint 2013. I can only guess that Microsoft adopted this approach because Designer contains many capabilities that rely on specific functionality present in SharePoint, and cross-version support would complicate the product.

Before providing you an overview of SharePoint Designer, I should mention that Designer is not just a design tool (as its name suggests). You can administer and configure many areas of SharePoint with Designer. For example, you can open list settings and change the configuration for all lists, which for some is more desirable than the SharePoint browser interface.

■ **Note**   SharePoint Designer is not just a design tool—you can perform some configuration and administration functions with it also.

SharePoint Designer 2013 does not ship with SharePoint Server 2013. In fact, some administrators are quite happy never needing to install Designer. Users had to pay for earlier versions of Designer, but now the application is free. You can download the latest version of SharePoint Designer 2013 from http://www.microsoft.com/en-us/download/details.aspx?id=30346. You need not install Designer on the same server as SharePoint—it is a good practice not to—because SharePoint Designer communicates with SharePoint using the SharePoint Server web services.

Like most Microsoft applications, Designer ships as both 32-bit and 64-bit. It is important to know which version you want to install before downloading it. If you have any other Office applications installed you must ensure that you download and install the same architecture version of Designer. SharePoint Designer 64-bit will not install on a server that has Office 32-bit, and vice versa.

■ **Note**   You can download the latest version of SharePoint Designer from http://www.microsoft.com/en-us/download/details.aspx?id=30346.

Figure 16-19 shows a screenshot of my installation of SharePoint Designer 2013 after I opened my publishing site collection. SharePoint Designer 2013 looks and feels much like its Office 2013 siblings with the Windows 8 brand. From a usability standpoint, Designer has a similar layout to the previous version, with the left pane containing site objects and the right side panes showing open object in context. Similar to the previous version, SharePoint Designer 2013 also includes a ribbon.

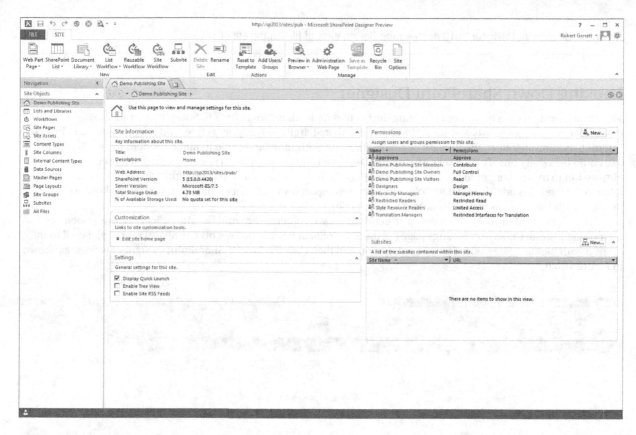

Figure 16-19. *SharePoint Designer 2013*

New Features

SharePoint 2013 includes all of the existing capabilities of the previous version with some new features and enhancements.

In Chapter 12, I briefly touched on workflow changes in SharePoint 2013, as part of my demonstration on business intelligence. SharePoint 2013 includes the same .NET 3.5 workflow capabilities you had in SharePoint 2010, but .NET 4.0 now hosts workflow in the cloud with Windows Azure. To take advantage of the new workflow features in SharePoint Designer, you must configure Windows Azure Workflow (as described in Chapter 12). SharePoint Designer 2013 now allows you to create state machine based workflows; previously you needed Visual Studio to create state machine workflows because Designer only supported creation of serial workflows. SharePoint Designer 2013 includes several enhancements to the visual workflow designer, supports loops, integrates with REST services, and allows you to package workflows.

Probably one of the biggest changes in SharePoint Designer 2013 is no Design View. The Design View used to show a visual view of a file while editing. You could switch between Design View and Code View and configure SharePoint Design into split view (showing both). SharePoint Designer 2013 now supports only Code View for editing files. I can only speculate on why Microsoft chose to depreciate this functionality—word is that Designer's editor is not in line with recent versions of Internet Explorer, which supports HTML 5. The change does have some repercussions on how some users use Designer from a WYSIWYG perspective. Editing Data View Web Parts is one significant loss without the Design View, since you can no longer see a view of the Data View Web Part populated with data in the editor.

■ **Note**   SharePoint Designer 2013 dropped the Design View of files in the editor.

Locking Down SharePoint Designer

SharePoint Designer is a great tool for editing design files, uploading files in bulk to SharePoint, and making configuration changes to lists and sites. However, now that SharePoint Designer is free, and easy to download from the Internet, as administrators, the thought of anyone in the organization being able to make changes to our SharePoint site could be a scary one. Fortunately, SharePoint Designer respects SharePoint security—thus, if a user has no permission to make changes to files in the Master Page Gallery, then that user has no rights via SharePoint Designer. SharePoint itself has additional SharePoint Designer settings to restrict further what operations you allow users to perform with Designer, as you will discover in this section.

SharePoint 2013 provides Designer restrictions at the web applications and the site collection level. Open up the publishing Site Collection Settings page (or the Site Collection Settings page on any SharePoint site). Scroll to the section with heading Site Collection Administration and then click the link for SharePoint Designer Settings, as shown in Figure 16-20.

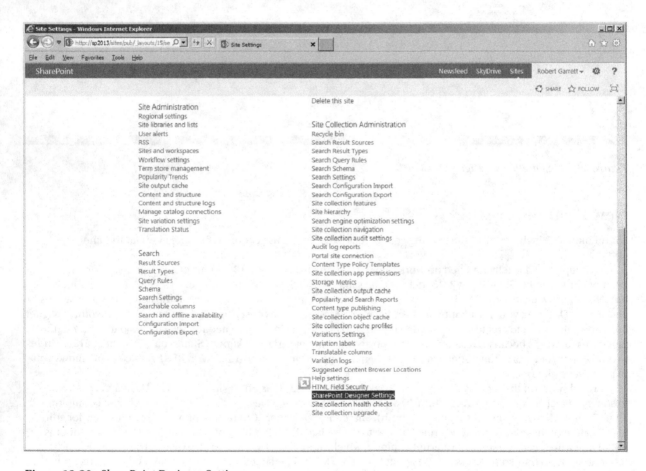

Figure 16-20. *SharePoint Designer Settings*

Clicking the link for SharePoint Designer Settings takes you to a page like that in Figure 16-21. From here you have control over whether designers can customize master pages and page layouts, deviate from the site definition (detach page), and alter the structure of the site. This page also includes an overarching setting to disable SharePoint Designer access completely.

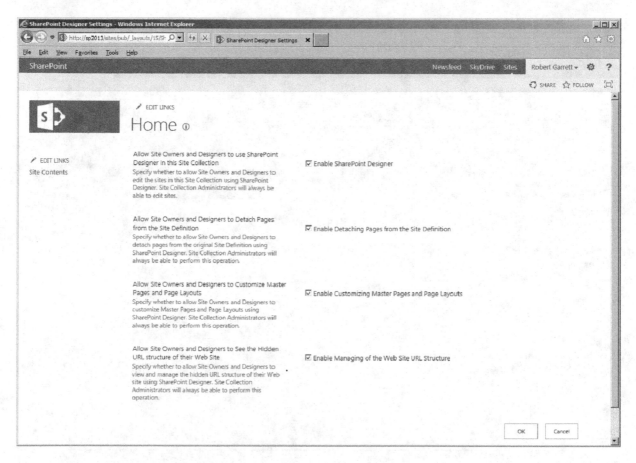

Figure 16-21. *Site collection SharePoint Designer settings*

Of course, you can manage permissions granted to users in the site collection to prevent many actions via SharePoint Designer. However, depending on the design of your security model, this might get quite complicated. In some circumstances, you might want to simply turn off SharePoint Designer access (perhaps when your site goes live) and not have to worry about tweaking permissions.

If the decision to restrict change, via SharePoint Designer, sits in the hands of those higher up the food chain than site collection administrators, you can affect the same settings for the web application. Changing SharePoint Designer settings for a web application requires access to Central Administration, which ensures a higher level of access.

1. Open Central Administration.

2. Click the heading for Application Management.

3. Click the link to manage web applications.

4. Select one of the web applications in the list.

5. Click the drop-down arrow on the General Settings icon on the ribbon.

6. Select the SharePoint Designer menu item (Figure 16-22).

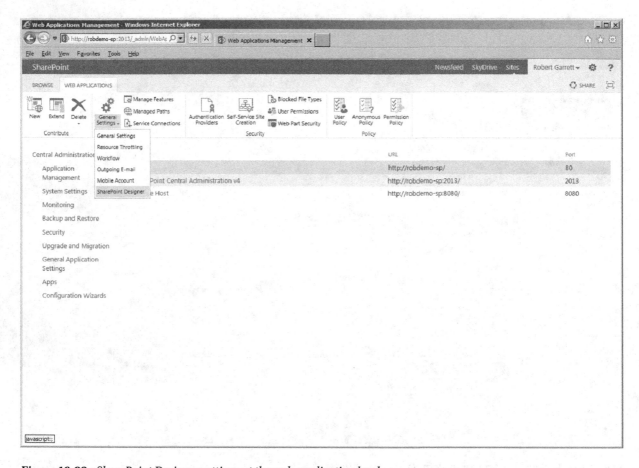

Figure 16-22. *SharePoint Designer settings at the web application level*

The SharePoint Designer settings at the web application level emulate those at the site collection level, but the settings at the web application level trump those at the site collection level. For example, if you disable SharePoint Designer access at the web application level, site collection administrators cannot enable the settings at the site collection level.

Summary

The end of this chapter concludes this book. In this chapter, I provided a brief overview of the new Windows 8 branding in SharePoint 2013 and how this brand aligns with other Microsoft applications and operating systems by providing a metro-like feel to the imagery in the site.

You read about how the Design Manager encapsulates both existing and new designer functionality into workable action steps for visual designers. Furthermore, I demonstrated that you do not require extensive experience in SharePoint design and knowledge of SharePoint Designer to upload an HTML file for your site design, which you can then convert to a SharePoint master page.

In the last part of this chapter, I touched on SharePoint Designer. To keep this chapter light, I mentioned only some of the changes that SharePoint Designer 2013 brings and how, as an administrator, you can lock down Designer to prevent users in your organization from misusing the tool and making changes to your SharePoint sites.

I hope that you have enjoyed the journey with me as we have explored SharePoint 2013 administration in this book. In its more than 600 pages, I have tried to cover the major topics from a setup, configuration, and administration perspective. I am sure there are areas I could dive into deeper, so if I piqued your interest in a certain topic, feel free to explore further, using the wealth of free information on the Internet and in other books and magazines.

If you were new to SharePoint when you started this book, I hope to have provided you with some insight and knowledge to get you started in SharePoint 2013 administration. If you are a seasoned SharePoint professional, then I hope you gleaned some new useful knowledge to complement what you already know in the field of SharePoint administration. With this, I shall leave you with one last thought: SharePoint is a vast platform; just when you think you have mastered all there is to know, there is still more to learn. Happy SharePoint learning.

Index

■ N

■ O